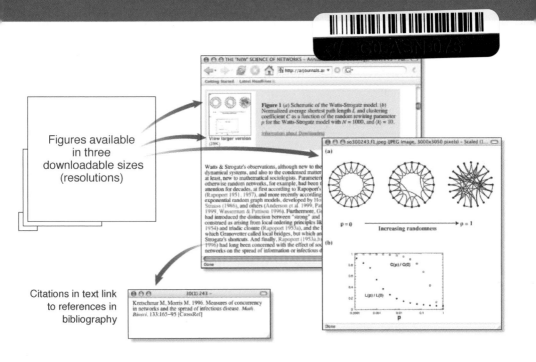

Figures available in three downloadable sizes (resolutions)

Citations in text link to references in bibliography

Figure 1 (a) Schematic of the Watts-Strogatz model. (b) Normalized average shortest path length L and clustering coefficient C as a function of the random rewiring parameter p for the Watts-Strogatz model with $N = 1000$, and $\langle k \rangle = 10$.

$p = 0$ — Increasing randomness → $p = 1$

Kretschmar M, Morris M. 1996. Measures of concurrency in networks and the spread of infectious disease. *Math. Biosci.* 133:165–95 [CrossRef]

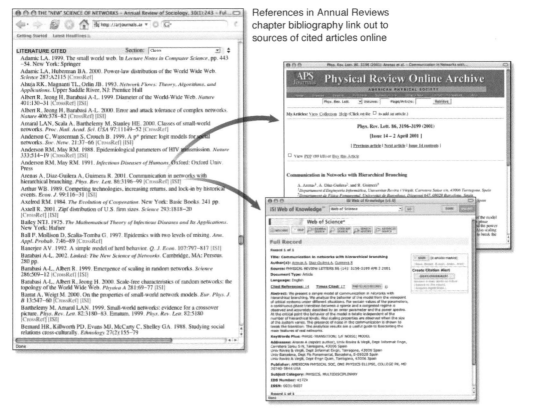

References in Annual Reviews chapter bibliography link out to sources of cited articles online

LITERATURE CITED

Adamic LA. 1999. The small world web. In *Lecture Notes in Computer Science*, pp. 443–54. New York: Springer

Adamic LA, Huberman BA. 2000. Power-law distribution of the World Wide Web. *Science* 287:A2115 [CrossRef]

Ahuja RK, Magnanti TL, Orlin JB. 1993. *Network Flows: Theory, Algorithms, and Applications*. Upper Saddle River, NJ: Prentice Hall

Albert R, Jeong H, Barabási A-L. 1999. Diameter of the World-Wide Web. *Nature* 401:130–31 [CrossRef] [ISI]

Albert R, Jeong H, Barabási A-L. 2000. Error and attack tolerance of complex networks. *Nature* 406:378–82 [CrossRef] [ISI]

Amaral LAN, Scala A, Barthelemy M, Stanley HE. 2000. Classes of small-world networks. *Proc. Natl. Acad. Sci. USA* 97:11149–52 [CrossRef]

Anderson C, Wasserman S, Crouch B. 1999. A p* primer: logit models for social networks. *Soc. Netw.* 21:37–66 [CrossRef] [ISI]

Anderson RM, May RM. 1988. Epidemiological parameters of HIV transmission. *Nature* 333:514–19 [CrossRef] [ISI]

Anderson RM, May RM. 1991. *Infectious Diseases of Humans*. Oxford: Oxford Univ. Press

Arenas A, Díaz-Guilera A, Guimera R. 2001. Communication in networks with hierarchical branching. *Phys. Rev. Lett.* 86:3196–99 [CrossRef] [ISI]

Arthur WB. 1989. Competing technologies, increasing returns, and lock-in by historical events. *Econ. J.* 99:116–31 [ISI]

Axelrod RM. 1984. *The Evolution of Cooperation*. New York: Basic Books. 241 pp.

Axtell R. 2001. Zipf distribution of U.S. firm sizes. *Science* 293:1818–20 [CrossRef] [ISI]

Bailey NTJ. 1975. *The Mathematical Theory of Infectious Diseases and Its Applications*. New York: Hafner

Ball F, Mollison D, Scalia-Tomba G. 1997. Epidemics with two levels of mixing. *Ann. Appl. Probab.* 7:46–89 [CrossRef]

Banerjee AV. 1992. A simple model of herd behavior. *Q. J. Econ.* 107:797–817 [ISI]

Barabási A-L. 2002. *Linked: The New Science of Networks*. Cambridge, MA: Perseus. 280 pp.

Barabási A-L, Albert R. 1999. Emergence of scaling in random networks. *Science* 286:509–12 [CrossRef] [ISI]

Barabási A-L, Albert R, Jeong H. 2000. Scale-free characteristics of random networks: the topology of the World Wide Web. *Physica A* 281:69–77 [ISI]

Barrat A, Weigt M. 2000. On the properties of small-world network models. *Eur. Phys. J. B* 13:547–60 [CrossRef] [ISI]

Barthelemy M, Amaral LAN. 1999. Small-world networks: evidence for a crossover picture. *Phys. Rev. Lett.* 82:3180–83. Erratum. 1999. *Phys. Rev. Lett.* 82:5180 [CrossRef] [ISI]

Bernard HR, Killworth PD, Evans MJ, McCarty C, Shelley GA. 1988. Studying social relations cross-culturally. *Ethnology* 27(2):155–79

APS Journals — **Physical Review Online Archive**
AMERICAN PHYSICAL SOCIETY

Phys. Rev. Lett. ▾ Volume: Page/Article: Retrieve

MyArticles: View Collection Help (Click on the ☐ to add an article.)

Phys. Rev. Lett. 86, 3196–3199 (2001)

[Issue 14 – 2 April 2001]

[Previous article | Next article | Issue 14 contents]

☐ View PDF (89 kB) or Buy this Article

Communication in Networks with Hierarchical Branching

A. Arenas, A. Díaz-Guilera and R. Guimerà

ISI Web of Knowledge — Web of Science

Web of Science®

Full Record

Record 1 of 1

Title: Communication in networks with hierarchical branching
Author(s): Arenas A, Diaz-Guilera A, Guimera R
Source: PHYSICAL REVIEW LETTERS 86 (14): 3196-3199 APR 2 2001
Document Type: Article
Language: English
Cited References: 14 Times Cited: 17

Abstract: We present a simple model of communication in networks with hierarchical branching. We analyze the behavior of the model from the viewpoint of critical systems under different situations. For certain values of the parameters, a continuous phase transition between a regime and a congested regime is observed and accurately described to an order parameter and the power spectra. At the critical point the behavior of the model is totally independent of the number of hierarchical levels. Real scaling properties are observed when the size of the system varies. The presence of noise in the communication is shown to break the transition. The analytical results are a useful guide to forecasting the main features of real networks.

KeyWords Plus: PHASE-TRANSITION; 1/F NOISE; MODEL

Addresses: Arenas A (reprint author), Univ Rovira & Virgili, Dept Informat Engn, Carretera Salou S-N, Tarragona, 43006 Spain
Univ Rovira & Virgili, Dept Informat Engn, Tarragona, 43006 Spain
Univ Barcelona, Dept Fis Fonamental, Barcelona, E-08028 Spain
Univ Rovira & Virgili, Dept Engn Quim, Tarragona, 43006 Spain

Publisher: AMERICAN PHYSICAL SOC, ONE PHYSICS ELLIPSE, COLLEGE PK, MD 20740-3844 USA

Subject Category: PHYSICS, MULTIDISCIPLINARY
IDS Number: 417ZX
ISSN: 0031-9007

Record 1 of 1

Copyright © 2005 Annual Reviews, Nonprofit Publisher of the *Annual Reviews* Series

ANNUAL REVIEW OF SOCIOLOGY

EDITORIAL COMMITTEE (2005)

MARY C. BRINTON, Harvard University
BRUCE G. CARRUTHERS, Northwestern University
KAREN S. COOK, Stanford University
PETER HEDSTRÖM, Nuffield College
MICHAEL HOUT, University of California, Berkeley
ARNE L. KALLEBERG, University of North Carolina, Chapel Hill
DOUGLAS S. MASSEY, Princeton University
LYNN SMITH-LOVIN, Duke University

RESPONSIBLE FOR THE ORGANIZATION OF VOLUME 31
(EDITORIAL COMMITTEE, 2003)

MARY C. BRINTON
KAREN S. COOK
JOHN HAGAN
PETER HEDSTRÖM
ARNE L. KALLEBERG
DOUGLAS S. MASSEY
LYNN SMITH-LOVIN
CAROL HEIMER (GUEST)

Production Editor: ERIN WAIT
Bibliographic Quality Control: MARY A. GLASS
Electronic Content Coordinator: SUZANNE K. MOSES
Subject Indexer: BRUCE TRACY

ANNUAL REVIEW
OF SOCIOLOGY

VOLUME 31, 2005

KAREN S. COOK, *Co-Editor*
Stanford University

DOUGLAS S. MASSEY, *Co-Editor*
Princeton University

www.annualreviews.org   science@annualreviews.org   650-493-4400

ANNUAL REVIEWS
4139 El Camino Way • P.O. Box 10139 • Palo Alto, California 94303-0139

ANNUAL REVIEWS
Palo Alto, California, USA

COPYRIGHT © 2005 BY ANNUAL REVIEWS, PALO ALTO, CALIFORNIA, USA. ALL RIGHTS RESERVED. The appearance of the code at the bottom of the first page of an article in this serial indicates the copyright owner's consent that copies of the article may be made for personal or internal use, or for the personal or internal use of specific clients. This consent is given on the condition that the copier pay the stated per-copy fee of $20.00 per article through the Copyright Clearance Center, Inc. (222 Rosewood Drive, Danvers, MA 01923) for copying beyond that permitted by Section 107 or 108 of the U.S. Copyright Law. The per-copy fee of $20.00 per article also applies to the copying, under the stated conditions, of articles published in any *Annual Review* serial before January 1, 1978. Individual readers, and nonprofit libraries acting for them, are permitted to make a single copy of an article without charge for use in research or teaching. This consent does not extend to other kinds of copying, such as copying for general distribution, for advertising or promotional purposes, for creating new collective works, or for resale. For such uses, written permission is required. Write to Permissions Dept., Annual Reviews, 4139 El Camino Way, P.O. Box 10139, Palo Alto, CA 94303-0139 USA.

International Standard Serial Number: 0360-0572
International Standard Book Number: 0-8243-2231-2
Library of Congress Catalog Card Number: 75-648500

All Annual Reviews and publication titles are registered trademarks of Annual Reviews.

⊗ The paper used in this publication meets the minimum requirements of American National Standards for Information Sciences—Permanence of Paper for Printed Library Materials, ANSI Z39.48-1992.

Annual Reviews and the Editors of its publications assume no responsibility for the statements expressed by the contributors to this *Annual Review*.

TYPESET BY TECHBOOKS, FAIRFAX, VA
PRINTED AND BOUND BY MALLOY INCORPORATED, ANN ARBOR, MI

Annual Review of Sociology
Volume 31, 2005

CONTENTS

Frontispiece—*James S. Coleman*   xii

PREFATORY CHAPTER

The Sociology of James S. Coleman, *Peter V. Marsden*   1

SOCIAL PROCESSES

Doing Justice to the Group: Examining the Roles of the Group in Justice Research, *Karen A. Hegtvedt*   25

Identity Politics, *Mary Bernstein*   47

The Social Psychology of Health Disparities, *Jason Schnittker and Jane D. McLeod*   75

Assessing Immigrant Assimilation: New Empirical and Theoretical Challenges, *Mary C. Waters and Tomás R. Jiménez*   105

INSTITUTIONS AND CULTURE

Reading and the Reading Class in the Twenty-First Century, *Wendy Griswold, Terry McDonnell, and Nathan Wright*   127

FORMAL ORGANIZATIONS

New Directions in Corporate Governance, *Gerald F. Davis*   143

POLITICAL AND ECONOMIC SOCIOLOGY

Emerging Inequalities in Central and Eastern Europe, *Barbara Heyns*   163

The Social Consequences of Structural Adjustment: Recent Evidence and Current Debates, *Sarah Babb*   199

DIFFERENTIATION AND STRATIFICATION

Inequality of Opportunity in Comparative Perspective: Recent Research on Educational Attainment and Social Mobility, *Richard Breen and Jan O. Jonsson*   223

White Racial and Ethnic Identity in the United States, *Monica McDermott and Frank L. Samson*   245

INDIVIDUAL AND SOCIETY

Agency Theory, *Susan P. Shapiro*   263

DEMOGRAPHY

Multiethnic Cities in North America, *Eric Fong and Kumiko Shibuya*   285

URBAN AND RURAL COMMUNITY SOCIOLOGY

Black Middle-Class Neighborhoods, *Mary Pattillo*   305

Macrostructural Analyses of Race, Ethnicity, and Violent Crime: Recent
Lessons and New Directions for Research, *Ruth D. Peterson
and Lauren J. Krivo*   331

POLICY

Affirmative Action at School and on the Job, *Shannon Harper
and Barbara Reskin*   357

Emerging Theories of Care Work, *Paula England*   381

INDEXES

Subject Index   401
Cumulative Index of Contributing Authors, Volumes 22–31   423
Cumulative Index of Chapter Titles, Volumes 22–31   427

ERRATA

An online log of corrections to *Annual Review of Sociology* chapters
may be found at http://soc.annualreviews.org/errata.shtml

Related Articles

From the *Annual Review of Anthropology*, Volume 33 (2004)

Talk and Interaction Among Children and the Co-Construction of Peer Groups and Peer Culture, Amy Kyratzis

Christianity in Africa: From African Independent to Pentecostal-Charismatic Churches, Birgit Meyer

The Globalization of Pentecostal and Charismatic Christianity, Joel Robbins

The Body Beautiful: Symbolism and Agency in the Social World, Erica Reischer and Kathryn S. Koo

Inscribing the Body, Enid Schildkrout

Culture, Globalization, Mediation, William Mazzarella

The World in Dress: Anthropological Perspectives on Clothing, Fashion, and Culture, Karen Tranberg Hansen

From the *Annual Review of Clinical Psychology*, Volume 1 (2005)

State of the Science on Psychosocial Interventions for Ethnic Minorities, Jeanne Miranda, Guillermo Bernal, Anna Lau, Laura Kohn, Wei-Chin Hwang, and Teresa La Fromboise

Cultural Differences in Access to Care, Lonnie R. Snowden and Ann-Marie Yamada

Decision Making in Medicine and Health Care, Robert M. Kaplan and Dominick L. Frosch

From the *Annual Review of Political Science*, Volume 8 (2005)

Immigration and Politics, Wayne A. Cornelius and Marc R. Rosenblum

The Political Evolution of Principal-Agent Models, Gary J. Miller

Unpacking "Transnational Citizenship", Jonathan Fox

Making Sense of Religion in Political Life, Kenneth D. Wald, Adam L. Silverman, and Kevin S. Fridy

The Development of Interest Group Politics in America: Beyond the Conceits of Modern Times, Daniel J. Tichenor and Richard A. Harris

The Globalization Rorschach Test: International Economic Integration, Inequality, and the Role of Government, Nancy Brune and Geoffrey Garrett

Does Deliberative Democracy Work?, David M. Ryfe

Citizenship and Civic Engagement, Elizabeth Theiss-Morse
and John R. Hibbing

From the ***Annual Review of Psychology***, Volume 56 (2005)

*Behavioral Inhibition: Linking Biology and Behavior Within a Developmental
Framework*, Nathan A. Fox, Heather A. Henderson, Peter J. Marshall,
Kate E. Nichols, and Melissa A. Ghera

Prosocial Behavior: Multilevel Perspectives, Louis A. Penner,
John F. Dovidio, Jane A. Piliavin, and David A. Schroeder

The Social Psychology of Stigma, Brenda Major and Laurie T. O'Brien

*Work Motivation Theory and Research at the Dawn of the Twenty-First
Century*, Gary P. Latham and Craig C. Pinder

*Teams in Organizations: From Input-Process-Output Models
to IMOI Models*, Daniel R. Ilgen, John R. Hollenbeck,
Michael Johnson, and Dustin Jundt

Presidential Leadership, George R. Goethals

Personnel Psychology: Performance Evaluation and Pay For Performance,
Sara L. Rynes, Barry Gerhart, and Laura Parks

From the ***Annual Review of Public Health***, Volume 26 (2005)

Social Marketing in Public Health, Sonya Grier and Carol A. Bryant

Urban Health: Evidence, Challenges, and Directions, Sandro Galea
and David Vlahov

*Acculturation and Latino Health in the United States: A Review of the
Literature and its Sociopolitical Context*, Marielena Lara, Cristina Gamboa,
M. Iya Kahramanian, Leo S. Morales, and David E. Hayes Bautista

*Adolescent Resilience: A Framework for Understanding Healthy
Development in the Face of Risk*, Stevenson Fergus
and Marc A. Zimmerman

Psychosocial Factors and Cardiovascular Diseases, Susan A. Everson-Rose
and Tené T. Lewis

Abortion in the United States, Cynthia C. Harper, Jillian T. Henderson,
and Philip D. Darney

Patient Perceptions of the Quality of Health Services, Shoshanna Sofaer
and Kirsten Firminger

ANNUAL REVIEWS is a nonprofit scientific publisher established to promote the advancement of the sciences. Beginning in 1932 with the *Annual Review of Biochemistry*, the Company has pursued as its principal function the publication of high-quality, reasonably priced *Annual Review* volumes. The volumes are organized by Editors and Editorial Committees who invite qualified authors to contribute critical articles reviewing significant developments within each major discipline. The Editor-in-Chief invites those interested in serving as future Editorial Committee members to communicate directly with him. Annual Reviews is administered by a Board of Directors, whose members serve without compensation.

2005 Board of Directors, Annual Reviews

Richard N. Zare, *Chairman of Annual Reviews*
   Marguerite Blake Wilbur Professor of Chemistry, Stanford University
John I. Brauman, *J.G. Jackson–C.J. Wood Professor of Chemistry, Stanford University*
Peter F. Carpenter, *Founder, Mission and Values Institute, Atherton, California*
Sandra M. Faber, *Professor of Astronomy and Astronomer at Lick Observatory,*
   University of California at Santa Cruz
Susan T. Fiske, *Professor of Psychology, Princeton University*
Eugene Garfield, *Publisher*, The Scientist
Samuel Gubins, *President and Editor-in-Chief, Annual Reviews*
Steven E. Hyman, *Provost, Harvard University*
Daniel E. Koshland Jr., *Professor of Biochemistry, University of California at Berkeley*
Joshua Lederberg, *University Professor, The Rockefeller University*
Sharon R. Long, *Professor of Biological Sciences, Stanford University*
J. Boyce Nute, *Palo Alto, California*
Michael E. Peskin, *Professor of Theoretical Physics, Stanford Linear Accelerator Center*
Harriet A. Zuckerman, *Vice President, The Andrew W. Mellon Foundation*

Management of Annual Reviews

Samuel Gubins, President and Editor-in-Chief
Richard L. Burke, Director for Production
Paul J. Calvi Jr., Director of Information Technology
Steven J. Castro, Chief Financial Officer and Director of Marketing & Sales

Annual Reviews of

Anthropology	Fluid Mechanics	Physical Chemistry
Astronomy and Astrophysics	Genetics	Physiology
Biochemistry	Genomics and Human Genetics	Phytopathology
Biomedical Engineering	Immunology	Plant Biology
Biophysics and Biomolecular	Law and Social Science	Political Science
Structure	Materials Research	Psychology
Cell and Developmental	Medicine	Public Health
Biology	Microbiology	Sociology
Clinical Psychology	Neuroscience	
Earth and Planetary Sciences	Nuclear and Particle Science	
Ecology, Evolution,	Nutrition	SPECIAL PUBLICATIONS
and Systematics	Pathology: Mechanisms	Excitement and Fascination of
Entomology	of Disease	Science, Vols. 1, 2, 3, and 4
Environment and Resources	Pharmacology and Toxicology	

James S. Coleman

Annu. Rev. Sociol. 2005. 31:1–24
doi: 10.1146/annurev.soc.31.041304.122209
Copyright © 2005 by Annual Reviews. All rights reserved
First published online as a Review in Advance on January 24, 2005

THE SOCIOLOGY OF JAMES S. COLEMAN[1]

Peter V. Marsden

Department of Sociology, Harvard University, Cambridge, Massachusetts 02138;
email: pvm@wjh.harvard.edu

Key Words   education, mathematical sociology, rational choice theory, social capital, social networks

■ **Abstract**   This chapter surveys the career and scholarship of James S. Coleman. It tracks scholarly usage of his work, with attention to references after 1995 and the subject areas in which its use is concentrated. At base a scholar of problems in social organization, Coleman made influential contributions that range across the sociology of education, policy research, mathematical sociology, network/structural analysis, and sociological theory. Works from several phases of Coleman's career are cited widely by scholars in sociology, education, economics, business/management, and other social science fields; during the past decade his conceptual work on social capital has been most influential. Coleman's widely debated *Foundations of Social Theory* is receiving increasing attention and has helped to establish a stable if limited niche for rational choice analysis within sociology.

INTRODUCTION

For 40 years—between receiving his PhD at Columbia University in 1955 and his death in 1995—James S. Coleman was a prominent, prolific, and contro-versial figure in American sociology. The amount and breadth of his academic work make it difficult to classify Coleman into a conventional sociologist's role (Sørensen & Spilerman 1993, Clark 1996, Fararo 1997, Lindenberg 2000). His work encompassed theory, substantive research, modeling, methodology, and pol-icy research—often two or more of these simultaneously.

---

[1] Since 1986, the *Annual Review of Sociology* has featured invited chapters by distinguished senior sociologists. James S. Coleman's death came before he could accept the *Review*'s invitation to author one, though his late-career (1994a) essay "A Vision for Sociology" forthrightly sets out his views about the desirable course for the discipline. I was pleased to be asked to recount Coleman's major contributions to social science and assay their contemporary influence. In keeping with the mission of the *Review*, I have attempted to highlight Coleman's many important writings, to track their influence (emphasizing the past decade), and to offer selected illustrations of scholarship that has drawn on or advanced his work.

At base, however, Coleman was a student and scholar of problems in social organization. Throughout his career, he saw understanding the functioning of social systems as the central problem for sociology. It was his conviction that social science and social theory should contribute to the development of improved social organization, with a system's responsiveness to the interests of persons as his normative standard of performance.

After a biographical sketch, this chapter surveys Coleman's work, beginning with the primarily substantive studies of social organization that he conducted as a graduate student and shortly afterwards. It then turns to his extensive research on education. Next I cover Coleman's writing on mathematical sociology and methodology. The final section is about the theoretical work that he regarded as his most important, on purposive action, rational choice, and corporate actors. I use the *Social Sciences Citation Index* (*SSCI*; Institute for Scientific Information 2004) to track the usage of Coleman's scholarship, with special attention to references after 1995 and the subject areas in which use of his work is concentrated.[2] I selectively call attention to recent studies that draw on Coleman's writings.

BIOGRAPHICAL SKETCH

Coleman's only published autobiographical statement (1990a) focuses on his graduate student life at Columbia between 1951 and 1955. Other information appears in reflections on his educational research (Coleman 1991), an interview conducted by Swedberg (1990), and correspondence with Clark (1996). Merton (1996) offers the perspective of one of Coleman's graduate teachers.

Born in 1926, Coleman was raised in the southern and midwestern United States, receiving his high school diploma from Dupont Manual High School in Louisville, Kentucky. He attended three undergraduate institutions, earning a degree in chemical engineering from Purdue University in 1949. Subsequently, Coleman took some evening courses in social psychology while he worked as a chemist. Unsatisfied with his work and intrigued by the social sciences, he enrolled in the Columbia graduate program in sociology.

At Columbia, Coleman studied primarily with Paul Lazarsfeld, Robert Merton, and Seymour Martin Lipset. He credited Merton for conveying theoretical inspiration and a vision of sociology as a calling, Lazarsfeld for orienting him toward mathematical sociology, and Lipset for teaching him about the integration of macrosocial questions and quantitative methods (Coleman 1990a, pp. 92–95).

---

[2] I conducted cited reference searches during early November 2004 on many of Coleman's major works, allowing for variants and typographical errors in titles and one-year errors in dates. Counts are based on citations to both "JS Coleman" and "J Coleman." I used the "Analyze" feature of the cited reference search to tabulate time trends and subject field distributions for the citations located. Subject field distributions are based on field codes assigned by the *SSCI*.

As part of a student group known as the "Young Turks," Coleman was actively involved in projects at the Bureau of Applied Social Research. He reported having difficulty with his oral qualifying examination and that he received no job offers the year he completed his PhD.

Coleman spent a postdoctoral year at the Center for Advanced Study in the Behavioral Sciences before beginning an assistant professorship at the University of Chicago in 1956. He was recruited to help establish a Department of Social Relations at Johns Hopkins University in 1959. He remained there until 1973, returning to Chicago for the remainder of his career. Among his many honors were membership in the U.S. National Academy of Sciences, the presidency of the American Sociological Association (ASA) in 1991–1992, and at least ten honorary degrees.

EARLY CAREER SUBSTANTIVE STUDIES

Coleman's early career was an unusually productive period during which he developed several major substantive studies as well as his first wave of work on mathematical sociology. About a decade after his doctorate, he wrote (1964c, p. 184) that he was principally interested in the relationship of individual to society, and in how social order and individual freedom could be balanced. This is in keeping with his self-description as a Durkheimian during this period (1990a, p. 93).

Pluralism in Organizations and Communities

For Coleman, the existence of multiple centers of power and avenues of status attainment were central ingredients in maintaining the freedom-order balance. Coleman's interest in such questions is reflected in his 1955 dissertation ("Political Cleavage within the International Typographical Union"), which is part of *Union Democracy (UD)* (Lipset et al. 1956). *UD* attributes democracy in the union to a confluence of historical and social structural factors, including local autonomy, the existence of independent power bases such as secret societies, and the occupational community among printers. Legitimate competition is an important condition that helps to keep the organization attentive to member concerns.

Pluralism is also a significant theme of Coleman's short monograph *Community Conflict* (1957), which reviews case studies of disputes over such questions as fluoridation, civil liberties, and school desegregation, abstracting patterns in their initiation and development. Among social structural conditions he linked to the course of conflict are the existence of a stable two-party system, cross-cutting social ties of participants across issues and factions, and organizational density.

Coleman's interest in pluralistic arrangements and his concern that power concentration compromises the performance of a social system are seen in many of his subsequent writings. They are evident, for example, in his advocacy of pluralism in educational systems (Coleman 1992a, Moynihan 1993), research design (Coleman et al. 1982, p. 222), and policy research in general (Coleman 1980).

Medical Innovation

Medical Innovation, A Diffusion Study (*MI*) (Coleman et al. 1966b) was published in the mid-1960s, but many findings appeared earlier in articles (e.g., Coleman et al. 1959). Primarily concerned with factors influencing the timing of a physician's decision to adopt a new drug, *MI* is known for its attention to multiple sources of information—both formal media and interpersonal contacts. It found that drug adoption processes differed between physicians well integrated into local social networks and those in peripheral or isolated positions.

A recent review calls *MI* a "classic example" of a diffusion analysis involving media exposure and network interactions (Wejnert 2002, p. 317). Several studies use contemporary network models in secondary analyses of the *MI* data, beginning with Burt's (1987) assertion that a process of role taking rather than socialization of proximate others governs interpersonal similarities in adoption. A recent reanalysis (Van den Bulte & Lilien 2001) contends that apparent contagion patterns proxy marketing efforts by drug companies.

MI has attracted steady attention from scholars, as much today as it did immediately after its publication. The *SSCI* records more citations to *MI* since 1995 (147) than between 1966 and 1976 (139). This likely reflects rising interest in the study of diffusion in such fields as globalization, organizational analysis, and network analysis (Wejnert 2002). Subject fields that give extensive attention to *MI* include sociology, health and public health, and business/management.

EDUCATION AND SOCIAL POLICY

Coleman's empirical research after Columbia concentrated on education.[3] Many of his key writings on it are collected in Coleman (1990b). Ravitch (1993) chronicles the three "Coleman Reports" that profoundly influenced U.S. debates surrounding educational policy; Heckman & Neal (1996) offer an overview and commentary on this work.

Coleman's (1991) account of how he became involved in educational research contains an element of serendipity. A late graduate school dinner conversation contrasting high school experiences evidently stimulated him toward research for *The Adolescent Society* (*AS*) (Coleman 1961b). He opted to study schools less out of intrinsic interest than because they were relatively closed social systems in which he might pursue his interest in the sources of status pluralism (1964c, p. 187).

The introduction to *AS* nonetheless discloses that Coleman had a long-standing concern with improving the functioning of high schools (Coleman 1961b, p. vii). That he thought there was room for improvement is also evident in his

---

[3]The main exception is an early 1970s line of work on mobility and labor force entry (e.g., Coleman et al. 1972).

autobiographical comments, in which Coleman observes that an assignment from Lazarsfeld early in graduate school was "the first time ever in the educational system [he] felt that someone had given [him] a responsible task to do" (1990a, p. 85) and that he "came to Columbia resolving to give the educational system one last chance" (p. 97).

The Adolescent Society

AS (1961b), Coleman's first educational study, examines structures and status systems in the student bodies of ten midwestern U.S. high schools. He writes (1964c, p. 202) that *AS* departed from his plan to study status pluralism. He judged that the study's more important findings bore on the character, sources, and consequences of adolescent cultures and social structures. *AS* focuses on the value climates, role systems, and sociometric structures of the schools, giving special attention to the elites or "leading crowds" of students. These varied somewhat across schools, but in general social and athletic success were more valued than academic pursuits. Coleman concluded that "the adolescent subcultures in these schools exert a rather strong deterrent to academic achievement" (1961b, p. 265).

AS gives much attention to macro-micro problems, assessing the psychological and scholastic effects of adolescent status systems on students. Toward its end, however, Coleman asks about the sources of adolescent value systems, settling responsibility on the adults in charge of educational organization and policy. Coleman sounds themes that recur often in his later work: that social relations increasingly involve interactions with institutions rather than with other persons (1961b, p. 328); that schools must engage adolescents actively and collectively rather than passively and individually (pp. 315–19); and that restructuring would strengthen secondary education (p. 329).

Heckman & Neal (1996) discern roots of Coleman's later rational choice orientation in *AS*, which devotes much attention to how students respond to formal and informal incentive systems. Coleman (1959) draws parallels between the student culture's discouragement of academic effort and output-restriction norms in work groups, asserting that "the response of the group is purely rational" (p. 345).

Coleman followed up on the concerns in *AS* with youth development in a continuing strand of work on socialization and the transition to adulthood (e.g., Coleman et al. 1974). Husén (1996, p. 23) terms *AS* "a seminal work on youth culture" and observes that Coleman's sociological analysis of adolescence—stressing the changing organization of family and work, as well as shifts in responsibility for socialization to extra-familial institutions—complements psychological perspectives. Kandel (1996) contends that *AS* overemphasized school and peer influences on socialization, and that Coleman later grew more attentive to family factors.

Kandel (1996, p. 36) highlights the long-standing influence of *AS* on scholarship, presenting citation trends through 1993. This influence continues since Kandel wrote. The *SSCI* records about 25 citations per year to *AS* since 1993. It is used primarily in sociology, education, and developmental psychology. Recent studies of resistance to learning (McFarland 2001), oppositional cultures in education (Ainsworth-Darnell & Downey 1998, Farkas et al. 2002), the role of cultural capital in educational success (Dumais 2002, Kaufman & Gabler 2004), and adolescent relationships (Giordano 2003) reference *AS*.

Equality of Educational Opportunity

Coleman entered public policy debates abruptly with *Equality of Educational Opportunity* (*EEO*) (Coleman et al. 1966a). Mandated by the U.S. Civil Rights Act of 1964, the *EEO* project spanned only 16 months from initiation to publication. Although it is widely known as "The Coleman Report," Coleman often reminded others of its multiple authorship.

At the time, educational opportunity was typically assessed by measuring "inputs" such as facilities, textbooks and other equipment, or teacher salaries and qualifications. *EEO* examined rural/urban, regional, and race/ethnic differences in inputs, finding differences in resources to be generally fewer and smaller than anticipated, and greater by region than by race/ethnicity. Importantly, *EEO* also focused attention on outcomes of education (assessed primarily via test scores) and on the relationship between inputs and outputs, drawing on a massive national survey of thousands of schools and over 600,000 students. Sharp race/ethnic differences in achievement were evident. Analyses pointed to family background as the principal source of achievement differences, followed by characteristics of a student's peers and teacher characteristics. School characteristics, including per capita expenditures, appeared weakly related to achievement. These findings stimulated controversy, debate, and much reanalysis. Coleman (1969) observed that the peer characteristics finding implied that school integration would raise achievement among blacks, and *EEO* was widely invoked in support of integration (Ravitch 1993).

Heckman & Neal (1996, p. 84) describe *EEO* as a "watershed in social science research" by virtue of its scale and policy impact. Nearly four decades after publication, *EEO* is still cited roughly 50 times per year, mostly in education, sociology, and economics. Blau (1996, p. 4) describes *EEO* as "an influential study that spawned a voluminous literature," observing that three decades of research have generally supported its conclusions. Heckman & Neal (1996) concur in this assessment, notably excepting the peer effects finding. Moynihan (1993, p. 124) credits *EEO*'s stress on educational outputs for establishing a new standard of accountability. One recent manifestation of this emphasis is state-level performance testing (Muller & Schiller 2000).

For his part, Coleman (1991) referred to *EEO* as a "detour," presumably because it gave comparatively little attention to the internal functioning of schools as social systems. Be that as it may, it is hard to overstate *EEO*'s influence on the subsequent social science research agenda on education. Vigorous debates continue over the extent to which school resources influence both test scores and post-educational outcomes (Hanushek 1996, Card & Krueger 1999) and over the presence of peer effects (e.g., Cheng & Starks 2002, Hanushek et al. 2003). *EEO* remains a central reference point for studies of black-white differences in educational attainment (Gamoran 2001, Hallinan 2001).

Games and Experiential Learning

Toward the end of the *AS* research, Coleman developed an interest in simulation games, for two distinct reasons. First, he saw games as educational innovations that could better engage the attention of students and permit separation of the "instructor" and "judge" aspects of a teacher's role (Boocock & Coleman 1966). He wrote about differences between "information assimilation" and "experiential" approaches to learning, contending that the experiential mode makes a more immediate linkage between information and action (Coleman 1976). Second, Coleman regarded games as tools similar to experiments for studying social systems. Constructing rules amounted to developing a theory of a given system's operations; observing the play of the game offered some evidence as to the plausibility of the theory (Coleman 1989).

Boocock (1996) reflects on the Hopkins Games Project, noting that "it would be hard to argue that simulation gaming is in the mainstream, educationally or sociologically" (p. 143). Although sociologists occasionally use such devices (Podolny 1990, Feld 1997b), this strand of Coleman's work has only a slight influence on contemporary scholarship. Coleman, however, saw the games project as pivotal in his intellectual development (Clark 1996, pp. 5, 7; Heckman & Neal 1996, p. 99), serving to crystallize his interest in rational choice theory.

School Desegregation and "White Flight"

Perhaps Coleman's most controversial work on education found that mandatory school desegregation plans tended to accelerate residential moves by whites away from central cities, thereby contributing to resegregation. Presented in Coleman et al. (1976), it found that increases in between-district segregation due to residential movements countered within-district declines in segregation due to government policy. The research concluded that court-ordered desegregation was not an effective instrument of social policy; Ravitch (1993) reviews the often-heated disputes that ensued.

By comparison with *EEO* and Coleman's later work on public and private schools, this work received modest attention from subsequent scholars, concentrated largely in the decade after its publication. However, as noted by Heckman & Neal (1996, pp. 91, 98), it displays a well-developed rational choice orientation on Coleman's part. Reflecting on this research, Coleman (1981b, p. 189) coined what he termed "Schultze's Law" about unintended consequences of social policies: "If a social policy does not actively employ the interests of those on whom it has an impact, it will find those interests actively employed in directions that defeat its goals."

Public and Private Schools, Families, and Educational Outcomes

The 1966 *EEO* report was widely regarded as demonstrating that schools have few effects on academic achievement, although many regard this as a misreading (e.g., Alexander 1997). In any case, as noted by Ravitch (1993) and Sørensen (1996), both *AS* and Coleman's late-career project on public and private schools conclude that features of social structure within and around schools do shape educational outcomes. Coleman et al. (1982) and Coleman & Hoffer (1987) present major findings from the public-private project, the earlier work using cross-sectional data, and the later one drawing on panel data. Both books assess differences between public, Catholic, and other private schools in academic achievement and sociodemographic composition of several kinds. Coleman & Hoffer (1987) examine a wider range of outcomes extending beyond high school and probe more deeply into the sources of differences between educational sectors.

This work concludes that sectoral segregation by race and income was less than anticipated, and that academic achievement in several subjects was higher in private than in public schools. Hoffer et al. (1985) report greater growth in verbal and mathematics achievement in Catholic than in public schools, especially among students from less advantaged backgrounds. Catholic schools had especially low dropout rates. These differences were attributed to varying academic demands (homework and academic coursework) and different disciplinary climates. Also implicated were differences in school environments. The authors point to the existence of "functional communities" around Catholic schools, involving intergenerational closure and social density among parents. These were said to supply sanctions and monitoring in support of proachievement norms. Coleman first used the concept of "social capital" in this context (Coleman & Hoffer 1987).

Hoffer et al. (1985, p. 96) suggested that "a little competition might not be harmful for American public schools," an inference that was widely contested and debated; again, see Ravitch (1993) or Heckman & Neal (1996). Especially controversial was Coleman's support for policies to expand school choice via such means as vouchers or tuition tax credits. Many critiques focused on selectivity—both in parental/student decisions to enroll in private schools and in the discretion of private schools to exclude students—as an explanation for sectoral differences, observing that distinct policy implications follow from these varying accounts for sectoral differences in achievement.

Issues raised by Coleman's public-private schools work remain active. The *SSCI* records about 20 references per year to each of its two reports since 1995, primarily within the fields of education, sociology, and economics. Highly germane to debates over school choice, they are acknowledged in such recent articles as Neal's (2002) discussion of educational voucher plans and Arum's (1996) argument that private school competition heightens achievement among public school students by increasing public school resources rather than efficiency. Other relevant research includes Neal's (1997) finding that the benefits of Catholic schools are especially large for urban minorities, and Lee et al.'s (1998) report indicating that Catholic school students take more advanced mathematics courses and that ability-related differences in such course-taking are smaller in Catholic schools. Morgan (2001) examines sectoral differences in achievement using propensity-score matching methods, suggesting that the Catholic school effect may be greatest among the students least apt to attend such schools.

Several investigations have examined the claim that functional communities promote better educational outcomes, with special attention to intergenerational closure. Morgan & Sørensen (1999) find that mathematics achievement gains rise with closure among students, but fall with closure among parents. Their data suggest, however, that parental closure may raise achievement in Catholic schools. They highlight potential drawbacks of parental closure, and they conjecture that these liabilities outweigh the benefits except in the presence of strong norms. Carbonaro (1998) reports that parental closure is associated with greater mathematics achievement but that the association vanishes after prior achievement level is controlled. He also finds an inverse relation between parental closure and dropout rates. Dijkstra et al. (2004) examine deviant behavior as well as academic achievement using several indicators of closure; they find strong student-teacher relationships to be most beneficial, but characterize their results as "disappointing" for the functional community hypothesis.

Kandel (1996) observes that Coleman's theorizing about functional communities as sources of social capital led him to emphasize the role of families in youth development in his later work, linking it to a major finding of *EEO*. Coleman wrote extensively (e.g., Coleman 1994b) about structural transformations that alter families and change the nature of familial interests in children; he argued for innovations that would increase the resources of families or other actors interested in children. He contended that resources shaping the attitudes, effort, and self-conception of children were in especially short supply (Coleman 1987). His interest in school choice as one parental option for influencing a child's education also continued. Schneider et al. (1996) note that sufficiently resourceful parents already choose schools via residential mobility or school sector, and examine parental propensities toward choice within public school systems, finding that when available, choice among public schools is most often exercised by disadvantaged minorities.

Discussion

Several authors comment on linkages between Coleman's educational research and other branches of his scholarship. Sørensen (1996) focuses on Coleman's mathematical sociology, observing that Coleman did not specify explicit process models in his educational studies. Heckman & Neal (1996, p. 100) likewise note "his fairly casual use of empirical evidence and his failure to use formal social science frameworks." Characterizing Coleman as a "true empiricist," they account for this by observing that, when he conducted the research, strong a priori models were lacking, that he wished to reach a broad audience, and that he accorded priority—as in his work on *UD* with Lipset—to substantive explanations over formal techniques. Mayer (1997), too, concludes that empirical findings drove

Coleman's development of theory here. Heckman & Neal (1996) also consider the links between the "education" and "rational choice" Colemans, perceiving a rational choice orientation from *AS* forward, but conveying Coleman's view that "no simple account of his evolution as a social scientist can be told" (p. 96).

Social Policy Research

The policy debates and controversies surrounding his educational studies led Coleman to reflect on the development of policy research as a new genre of social science (see, e.g., Coleman 1978). He argued that contemporary social theory ought to provide an account for the role of social science in influencing society as part of a "rational reconstruction of society" (Coleman 1993b). Characterizing policy research as social science providing information about current or prospective policy initiatives, he contrasted it with exposés of social problems and basic disciplinary research. A vitally important consideration for him was that sponsors interested in its outcomes, rather than investigators, set agendas for policy research.

Coleman was highly concerned that sponsors of policy research would exercise undue control over research questions, research design, or the dissemination of findings, especially because research results often serve to empower opponents of a policy initiative by providing a factual basis for opposition. He advocated (e.g., Coleman 1980) a model of "pluralistic policy research" that engages a broad range of interested parties in the formulation of projects and review of research. Observing that specialist research organizations are better able than universities to manage the scale and schedule required of policy research, he nonetheless saw the autonomy of university-based researchers as an important assurance against the suppression of results by sponsors (Coleman 1982a).

Bulmer (1996) and Kilgore (1996) cover Coleman's writings about policy research in greater depth; Kilgore gives special attention to Coleman's pluralistic model. Focusing on sociological practice in Belgium, Van Hove (1993) observes that policy makers often call on consultant companies rather than university-based researchers for information. Van Hove also gives examples of centers and thematic research programs that incorporate pluralistic elements.

MATHEMATICAL SOCIOLOGY AND METHODS

Coleman brought substantial mathematical knowledge to sociology from his studies in chemistry and physics. He was drawn to mathematical applications for studying process rather than developing statistical indexes/methods or representing social structures. His very first published work (Coleman 1954) was an expository analysis of some mathematical social process theories. Among Coleman's major books on mathematical sociology are *Introduction to Mathematical Sociology* (*IMS*; 1964b) and *The Mathematics of Collective Action* (*MCA*; 1973). Fararo (1997) and Feld (1997a) identify Coleman as a highly central figure in mathematical sociology.

IMS is widely credited as a foundational work. Fararo (1997, p. 80) states that it "made mathematical sociology an identifiable part of modern sociology," while Edling (2002, p. 198) refers to it as "*the* classic."

Stochastic Process Models

IMS emphasizes the use of mathematics for representing social processes. Of its 18 chapters, 11 develop continuous-time, discrete-space stochastic process models for studying transitions. Coleman used such models in theorizing about phenomena including attitude change, diffusion, voting behavior, and group contagion. He developed the implications of these models for both cross-sectional and two-wave panel data, emphasizing the equilibrium assumptions entailed by cross-sectional applications. Coleman (1981a) later revisited such models using more sophisticated methods of estimation.

IMS continues to attract attention; the *SSCI* records nearly total 100 citations since the mid-1990s. This indicator likely understates the influence of this work vastly, however. *IMS*'s focus on a regime of transition rates underlying the distribution of units into states is of enduring importance. This way of thinking is now widespread, most evident in the use of event-history models for longitudinal data. Tuma & Hannan (1984, p. 26) credit Coleman for introducing it into sociology.

Structural Research Methods

Notwithstanding his interest in process, Coleman conducted a great deal of "structural" research during his early career, including sociometric analyses in *AS*, analyses of friendship ties as an element of occupational community in *UD*, and diffusion analyses (which join structural and process concerns) in *MI*. Highly committed to quantitative research methods, Coleman sought methods for studying social organization without neglecting social structure. An early article (Coleman 1958) covers both analytic techniques and data collection methods used in his empirical studies. Some later chapters of *IMS* are devoted to structural measures, and during the early 1960s he authored articles on identifying network subgroups (Coleman & MacRae 1960) and simulation methods for studying reference group and other network-related phenomena (Coleman 1961a).

Freeman's (2004) history of network analysis points to Coleman as an influential bridge between a cluster of sociologists and an "eclectic hodgepodge" of scholars in other disciplines (pp. 130–31). Beyond this work on methods and models, social networks are a vital element in Coleman's theoretical work, e.g., on the development of trust and norms (1990c) and social capital (1988).

Exchange/Purposive Action Models

As his rational choice orientation developed, Coleman's modeling work shifted toward social exchange models. Founded on assumptions of purposive action, they appealed to him as formal devices for the micro-macro transition. *MCA* (1973) reports his first wave of work on such models. The closing section of *Foundations of Social Theory* (1990c) includes further developments, including extensions beyond exchange to unreciprocated transfers of control.

Hernes (1993) observes that the basic structure of Coleman's exchange model parallels that of an open market (see also Coleman 1992b). Coleman used it in studying exchange in the labor market (e.g., Coleman & Hao 1989) as well as collective decisions (in *MCA*), the latter application requiring specification of a decision rule as part of the environment for exchange. He pointed to the simultaneous determination of the value of resources (or events) and the distribution of power among actors as an example of the micro-macro transition.

Scholars interested in social networks and exchange theory have extended Coleman's exchange framework in several directions. Among recent contributions are Yamaguchi's (1996) power measure for systems of constrained exchanges, and Braun's (1997) effort to develop a rational choice foundation for network centrality measures by modeling network relations as interindividual investments.

PURPOSIVE ACTION AND RATIONAL CHOICE THEORY

Over his last 30 years of writing, Coleman became an enthusiastic practitioner of, and vigorous advocate for, rational choice theory in sociology. When Swedberg (1990) asked about the genesis of this interest, Coleman pointed to Homans's (1958) exchange theory, a commentary on Parsons's paper on influence as a generalized medium of exchange (Coleman 1963), and his own 1960s work on simulation games. One of his late-career publications (1992b) described his rational choice work as "The Economic Approach to Sociology," albeit applied to phenomena that initially do not appear amenable to economic analysis. In this body of work, Coleman first concentrated on problems of collective choice and the exchange model; articles originally published between 1964 and 1978 are collected in Coleman (1986a).

Foundations of Social Theory (*FST*; 1990c) was Coleman's principal theoretical project and the work that he regarded as his most significant (Clark 1996, pp. 2–3). It aspires toward a transdisciplinary theory of the functioning of social systems that allows social science to aid in designing improved forms of social organization. *FST* developed over many years; its basic concept appears to have been in place by the mid-1970s (Coleman 1975). Proceeding under methodological individualism, Coleman assumed simple microfoundations: interrelated purposive actors using resources to pursue interests. From such assumptions, *FST* worked toward accounts for such social phenomena as authority systems, structures of trust, social norms, collective behavior, corporate actors, and revolutions.

Coleman begins *FST* by highlighting the micro-macro transition as the foremost theoretical problem for social science, arguing that explanations of system behavior in terms of lower-level constituent elements are apt to be more general and more useful for interventions than those that do not probe beneath the system level.

He was compelled by the capacity of economic approaches for such "synthetic" analyses. Mayntz (2004) refers to Coleman's strategy as one of "causal regression" in the explanation of macro phenomena. This position is congenial to advocates of a "mechanism" approach to social theory. Hedström & Swedberg (1998) discuss "situational," "action-formation," and "transformational" mechanisms corresponding to what Coleman (1986c) terms type 1 (macro-micro), 2 (micro-micro), and 3 (micro-macro) transitions. Stinchcombe (1993) discusses conditions under which mechanism-based theorizing is more and less useful, stressing the pragmatic criterion of adding insight at the macro level.

Elementary units in Coleman's framework are actors and resources (sometimes termed events) linked by interest and control relations. Interests, the motive governing actions, reflect a resource's impact on an actor's well-being. Control refers to rights to direct the use of resources; the concept of rights grew increasingly central for Coleman as *FST* developed (see Coleman 1992c, 1993c).

FST assumes the tractable model of the rational actor in economics partly on pragmatic grounds, so that analysis focuses on features of social organization rather than nuances of the micro model. Coleman is careful, however, to disavow assumptions that actions are independent, faulting many economic models for their neglect of social structure (Coleman 1984) and contending that such deficiencies are more crucial than micro-level inadequacies (Coleman 1986b). Social structure—interdependencies, networks, authority structures, norms, organizations, and other features—is present throughout *FST*. Noting this, Udehn (2002) labels Coleman's methodological approach as "structural individualism."

From this beginning, the remainder of the first part of *FST* fashions explanations for authority and trust relations. Part II covers meso-level structures—exchange, authority, and trust systems, as well as norms. These involve transfers of control among actors, compensated when they have distinct interests, but sometimes unilateral if interests are shared. Part III proceeds to theories of the constitution, construction/design, and destruction of corporate actors. Coleman regards the prominence of corporate actors as distinctive to contemporary society, and Part IV examines problems related to corporate actors, setting out Coleman's case for "a new social science" to aid the "purposive reconstruction of society" (Coleman 1990c, p. 652). An extended formalization of many of *FST*'s earlier qualitative arguments appears in Part V.

At nearly 1000 pages, *FST* has been read at many levels. In the following sections, I focus on several specific segments of the book that drew subsequent attention, on trust, norms, social capital, and corporate actors.

Trust

FST models an actor's choice of whether to trust another as a decision under risk, asserting that trust will be extended when prospective benefits are sufficiently large. Assessing a trustee's likely reliability is seen as especially problematic owing to incomplete information and lack of assurance about future performance. Coleman argues that social structures, including dense networks, norms, and third-party intermediaries (advisors, guarantors, and entrepreneurs), facilitate the extension of trust as a form of social credit, thereby expanding a system's action capacity.

Hardin (2001) views Coleman's analysis of trust as one variant of an "encapsulated interest" account, stressing that few trust relations are unilateral and that reciprocal trust relations are mutually reinforcing. Ensminger (2001) contrasts such rationalist theories of trust with a general trust that rests on belief in a partner's goodwill, suggesting that knowledge-based rationalist views are applicable to situations in which risks can be assessed, whereas general trust arises in situations involving a less calculable social uncertainty.

Many recent contributions to the social science literature examine structural sources of trust, drawing on Coleman's analyses among other sources. Examples include Raub & Weesie's (1990) demonstration that social density heightens trustworthy behavior by circulating information about reputations, and Buskens & Weesie's (2000) argument that network embeddedness increases trust through learning and increased control potential. Burt & Knez (1995) contend that strong connections to third parties amplify trust, while weak ones may raise distrust. Buskens's (1998) analyses suggest that not only network density but also network centralization may increase the placement of trust.

Norms

Coleman's concern with norms was long-standing, dating from his earliest writing (1964a) about collective decisions and rational choice. Persuaded that norms are significant features of social systems, he insisted that they should be explained rather than assumed. *FST* (p. 243) conceptualizes a norm as a rights allocation under which control over a target action is held by actors other than the one who might take the action. Coleman's theory of effective norms stresses three conditions: that beneficiary actors demand control over the target action owing to its external effects on them; that they cannot attain such control via exchanges; and that social organization can supply a sanctioning system sufficient to enforce conformity. The theory contends that network closure can be an important support for sanctioning.

Opp (2001) terms Coleman's perspective an "instrumentality" approach to understanding the emergence of norms, observing that several other accounts use a similar logic. Coleman's approach has very clear affinities with Hechter's theory of group solidarity, stressing interdependence and control capacity (e.g., Hechter & Kanazawa 1993). An active literature has developed around accounts of this kind. Among recent contributions acknowledging *FST* are Bendor & Swistak's (2001) use of evolutionary game theory to work from rational choice assumptions to norms and Horne's (2004) experimental research demonstrating that norms tend to be enforced when actors can anticipate benefits from doing so. Nyborg & Rege's (2003) study of norms about smoking behavior observes that compliance can bring benefits to targets as well as beneficiaries, and that formal regulations about smoking in some settings can affect norms in unregulated areas. Elster (2003) is very critical of Coleman's analysis of norms. He contends that some norms do not benefit anyone and argues that conformity with norms is driven more by a wish to avoid shame and contempt than by the anticipation of gain.

Social Capital

As noted, Coleman's interest in social capital grew out of his empirical studies of education. It has garnered the most subsequent attention of any of his theoretical work. As of late 2004, his article "Social Capital in the Creation of Human Capital" (1988) has been cited more than 1300 times. Among *FST* citations designating a specific chapter or page, many more refer to the chapter on social capital than to any other part. That this work has received such attention is somewhat ironic, for Coleman (1990c, pp. 304–5) noted that "social capital" serves to group together other processes he discusses in *FST*, rather than to introduce fundamentally different ones.

For Coleman (1988, p. S98), social capital refers to features of social structure that facilitate action. Among these are systems of trust and obligations, networks disseminating information, norms accompanied by sanctioning systems, centralized authority structures arising through transfers of control, and "appropriable social organization" that may be used for purposes distinct from those that led to establishing it. This variety in forms of social capital makes it clear that Coleman regarded it more as a covering term for "useful social organization" than as an identifiable "variable." He noted that benefits of social capital often accrue to actors other than those who produce it, concluding that it may be undersupplied owing to public-goods problems.

Virtually all recent discussions of social capital give substantial attention to Coleman's conceptualization (e.g., Portes 1998, Burt 2000, Lin 2001, Sobel 2002, Kadushin 2004). Its functional definition has been widely critiqued: Whether a given feature of social structure represents social capital cannot be ascertained without knowing its consequences. Portes (1998), among others, stresses the potential negative consequences of social capital.

It is clear that many, if not all, of Coleman's examples of social capital involve social network phenomena: networks of dependency creating obligations, networks of consultation offering access to information, social density supporting sanctioning systems for norms. Several commentators contend that a more useful definition would restrict the concept to network-related phenomena; Lin (2001, p. 25) prefers "resources embedded in social networks accessed and used by actors" and Kadushin (2004, p. 88) suggests "networked resources."

Many discussions remark on the network forms that give rise to social capital. Coleman's work on education stressed network closure, while others, notably Burt (1992), emphasize open network configurations that offer opportunities for autonomous action. These images can likely be reconciled. Coleman was concerned with a situation in which agents of control (parents and teachers) seek to create human capital by constraining students to remain in school and take actions that further academic achievement, and social density arguably facilitates this. Other circumstances, such as career competition among managers, may place priority on the access to opportunities and information that open networks grant. Because social capital is less liquid or fungible than other forms of capital (Coleman 1988, p. S98), different social structures generating social capital are apt to be useful for different goals (Sobel 2002).

Organizations and Corporate Actors

Coleman accords "new corporate actors" or "constructed social organization" a very central place in *FST*; indeed, his (1993b) ASA presidential address was on this subject. He regarded role-based social organization as "probably the most fundamental social invention until now in the history of society" (1970, p. 163). Coleman had previously published two books about corporate actors (*Power and the Structure of Society* [*PSS*; 1974] and *The Asymmetric Society* [1982b]). He was most struck by the pervasiveness of corporate actors in modern society.

FST's view of authority relations is Barnardian: Rights to exercise authority are granted (and may be withdrawn) by subordinates in anticipation of benefit. Systems of authority expand the potentially viable forms of social organization, allowing forms in which not all dyadic transactions must be mutually profitable. Reflecting *UD*'s concerns with Michelsian goal displacement, Coleman stressed the agency problems that may plague authority systems when subordinates pursue their ends rather than a principal's, as well as usurpation of authority by superiors who extend their reach beyond the bounds specified by a subordinate's grant.

On a larger scale, the latter sort of drift in power is especially significant for Coleman. Favell (1993) observes that a major value premise of *FST* is that "corporate actors merit existence only insofar as they further the ends of natural persons" (Coleman 1990c, p. 351). Concerned about their capacity to concentrate power and about the welfare of those (notably children) not strongly affiliated with corporate actors, Coleman placed especially high priority on the social control of corporate actors. Among suggested tactics for restitution were both manipulation of external environments (via, e.g., tax laws, maintenance of pluralistic competition, creation of countervailing corporate actors, external audits) and interventions in the internal structure of corporate actors (e.g., adding representatives of workers or other stakeholders to governance structures, increasing the power of outside directors, altering reward structures for agents, creating shorter "backward policing" feedback loops). He made proposals (e.g., Coleman 1993a) to redesign schools, the organizations he knew best.

Swedberg (1996, 2003) views this work as a significant contribution to economic sociology, writing favorably of Coleman's account of the origin of corporate actors and his approach to their redesign. Scott (2004, p. 9) remarks that *PSS* "eloquently reframed" concerns about organizations as systems of power by stressing the division of power between organizations per se and individual persons rather than among individuals alone.

At present, though, the influence of this body of Coleman's scholarship appears more modest than he might have hoped. Stern & Barley (1996, p. 147) describe *PSS* as a "classic treatise," but also opine that Coleman and other scholars concerned with the impact of organizations on society are "increasingly marginal to mainstream organization theory" (p. 149). Taken together, Coleman's two books on corporate actors (1974, 1982b) have been cited only about six times per year since 1995 in sources indexed by *SSCI*, and few references to *FST* point specifically to parts focused on corporate actors. Stern & Barley (1996) offer several conjectures about why current organizational research rarely assumes a "social systems perspective," including career incentives and the professional-school locus in which much organizational research is now pursued. Lindenberg (2003), however, argues that Coleman's theoretical system is insufficiently complex for the task of institutional design, contending that this requires a broader "social rationality" that takes socialization and preexisting social organization into account.

Discussion

FST was reviewed very widely after its publication in 1990. At least four review symposia—in *Contemporary Sociology* (November 1990), *Acta Sociologica* (June 1991), *Theory and Society* (April 1992), and *Analyse & Kritik* (Spring 1993)—were devoted to it. Although the tone and content of reviews varied and most acknowledged *FST* as a major theoretical work, on balance they tended to be critical. Many commentators were dubious of the rational micro model and skeptical that sociology can be constructed on individualist postulates, observing, among other things, that choice takes place within existing institutional complexes. Coleman (1992c) offered a relatively concise statement of the points in *FST* that he regarded as most central. The book continues to receive scrutiny: Ten essays (most in French) about it appear in the April–June 2003 *Revue française de sociologie*.

In some subsequent overall discussions of *FST*, Fararo (1996) compares its rational-individualist approach to other foundational efforts in theoretical sociology. Among his critical points is that while Coleman often takes account of social relations, he does not account for them. Lindenberg (1996) is sympathetic to a rational choice approach but calls for a broader "relationalist" version involving a more elaborate micro-level model; elsewhere (2000) he calls attention to the importance of macro-micro as well as micro-macro transitions. Favell (1993) discusses Coleman's effort to link positive social theory and moral philosophy, concluding that *FST* compares favorably with other attempts to develop a normative sociology, but that much remains to be accomplished before rational choice approaches can establish persuasive connections.

Some broader discussions of rational choice theory in sociology highlight *FST*. Hechter & Kanazawa (1997, p. 195) term it the most important theoretical development in this field. Collins (1996) considers the prospects for rational choice as a unified approach to social science, observing that it is most useful at meso-levels of analysis, arguing that more attention to emotions at the micro level is needed and suggesting several institutional features of sociology that may inhibit such unification. Smelser (1992) argues that the "individualistic positivism" in *FST* and other rational choice theories is a historically specific epistemological preference. He also cautions that efforts to cleanse rational choice models by relaxing restrictive assumptions run the risk of degeneration toward theoretical indeterminacy. Abell (2003, p. 258) is generally sympathetic to a reasoned/rational action approach as a "least bad" starting point for theoretical sociology, but he argues for a somewhat broader narrative action theory within a methodological individualist framework. Abell's narrative action theory assumes consistency and optimization of self-interest on the part of actors, but it allows beliefs and preferences to rest on past experience as well as on anticipated consequences.

Figure 1 displays annual citation counts to *FST* since its publication, as recorded by the *SSCI*. As of late 2004, more than 1850 indexed works have referenced it, the trend generally increasing over time. About 36% of *FST* citations are from within sociology; 13% come from economics, and 11% from the combination of business and management. The remainder are spread across the social sciences. The work receives a great deal of attention from European scholars. More than 20 articles in each of the following journals cite *FST*: the *Kölner Zeitschrift für Soziologie und Sozialpsychologie* (31), the *Zeitschrift für Soziologie* (23), *Acta Sociologica* (22),

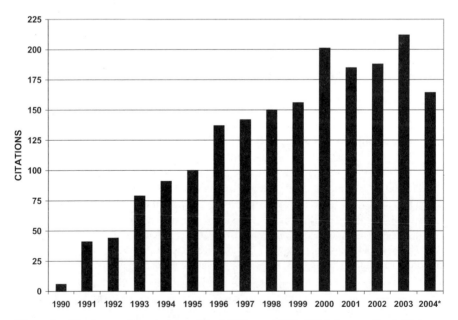

Figure 1   Citations to *Foundations of Social Theory*, 1990–2004. Source: *Social Science Citation Index*. *Annualized based on count through October 2004.

and the *Zeitschrift für die gesamte Staatswissenschaft* (22).[4] At a minimum, *FST* has occasioned very animated consideration of an approach to sociology founded on rational action.

CONCLUSION

Lindenberg (2000, p. 541) wrote that "Coleman's place among sociologists of the second half of the twentieth century is likely to remain unequalled." This is high praise, and although there are doubtless many who would contest such a broad claim, Coleman's accomplishments and continuing influence on contemporary social science are of extraordinary magnitude indeed. His education studies leave a massive legacy for social science research and public policy alike. He arguably defined the field of mathematical sociology, and made widely recognized contributions to network theory and methods. *FST*'s ambitious program statement inspired widespread debate over the character and direction of sociological theory and helped to establish a stable if limited niche for rational choice theory in sociology. Coleman's education and rational choice work are linked at several points, most visibly in currently vibrant scholarship on social capital.

Beyond his voluminous writing, Coleman influenced the training of legions of educational and rational choice sociologists, many of them cited in the preceding sections. He also made enduring institutional contributions as the founding editor of *Rationality & Society* and a prime mover behind the establishment of the ASA Section on Rational Choice.

ACKNOWLEDGMENTS

For helpful comments on previous drafts, I am grateful to Editor Karen Cook, Peter M.E. Hedström, and Chris Winship. The photograph of James S. Coleman is courtesy of the University of Chicago News Office.

The *Annual Review of Sociology* is online at http://soc.annualreviews.org

LITERATURE CITED

Abell P. 2003. The role of rational choice and narrative action theories in sociological theory: the legacy of Coleman's *Foundations*. *Rev. Fr. Sociol.* 44:255–74

Ainsworth-Darnell JW, Downey DB. 1998. Assessing the oppositional culture explanation for racial/ethnic differences in school performance. *Am. Sociol. Rev.* 63:536–53

Alexander KL. 1997. Public schools and the public good. *Soc. Forces* 6:1–30

---

[4]Across all indexed journals, *Rationality and Society* contains the highest number of citations to *FST* (61), followed by the *American Journal of Sociology* (41), *Social Forces* (36), and the *American Sociological Review* (35).

Arum R. 1996. Do private schools force public schools to compete? *Am. Sociol. Rev.* 61:29–46

Bendor J, Swistak P. 2001. The evolution of norms. *Am. J. Sociol.* 106:1493–545

Blau FD. 1996. Symposium on primary and secondary education. *J. Econ. Perspect.* 10:3–8

Boocock SS. 1996. Games with simulated environments: educational innovation and applied sociological research. See Clark 1996, pp. 133–46

Boocock SS, Coleman JS. 1966. Games with simulated environments in learning. *Sociol. Educ.* 39:215–36

Braun N. 1997. A rational choice model of network status. *Soc. Netw.* 19:129–42

Bulmer M. 1996. The sociological contribution to social policy research. See Clark 1996, pp. 103–18

Burt RS. 1987. Social contagion and innovation: cohesion versus structural equivalence. *Am. J. Sociol.* 92:1287–335

Burt RS. 1992. *Structural Holes: The Social Structure of Competition.* Cambridge, MA: Harvard Univ. Press

Burt RS. 2000. The network structure of social capital. *Res. Organ. Behav.* 22:345–423

Burt RS, Knez M. 1995. Kinds of third-party effects on trust. *Ration. Soc.* 7:255–92

Buskens V. 1998. The social structure of trust. *Soc. Netw.* 20:265–89

Buskens V, Weesie J. 2000. An experiment on the effects of embeddedness in trust situations: buying a used car. *Ration. Soc.* 12:227–53

Carbonaro WJ. 1998. A little help from my friend's parents: intergenerational closure and educational outcomes. *Sociol. Educ.* 71:295–313

Card D, Krueger AB. 1998. School resources and student outcomes. *Ann. Am. Acad. Polit. Soc. Sci.* 559:39–53

Cheng S, Starks B. 2002. Racial differences in the effects of significant others on students' educational expectations. *Sociol. Educ.* 75:306–27

Clark J, ed. 1996. *James S. Coleman.* London: Falmer

Coleman JS. 1954. An expository analysis of some of Rashevsky's social behavior models. In *Mathematical Thinking in the Social Sciences,* ed. PF Lazarsfeld, pp. 105–65. Glencoe, IL: Free Press

Coleman JS. 1957. *Community Conflict.* New York: Free Press

Coleman JS. 1958. Relational analysis: the study of social organizations with survey methods. *Hum. Organ.* 17:28–36

Coleman JS. 1959. Academic achievement and the structure of competition. *Harv. Educ. Rev.* 29:330–51

Coleman JS. 1961a. Analysis of social structures and simulation of social processes with electronic computers. *Educ. Psychol. Meas.* 21:203–18

Coleman JS. 1961b. *The Adolescent Society: The Social Life of the Teenager and Its Impact on Education.* New York: Free Press

Coleman JS. 1963. Comment on "On the concept of influence." *Public Opin. Q.* 27:63–82

Coleman JS. 1964a. Collective decisions. *Sociol. Inq.* 34:166–81

Coleman JS. 1964b. *Introduction to Mathematical Sociology.* New York: Free Press

Coleman JS. 1964c. Research chronicle: *The Adolescent Society.* In *Sociologists at Work: Essays on the Craft of Social Research,* ed. PE Hammond, pp. 184–211. New York: Basic Books

Coleman JS. 1969. A brief summary of the Coleman Report. In *Equal Educational Opportunity,* ed. Editor. Board Harv. Educ. Rev., pp. 253–61. Cambridge, MA: Harvard Univ. Press

Coleman JS. 1970. Social inventions. *Soc. Forces* 49:163–73

Coleman JS. 1973. *The Mathematics of Collective Action.* Chicago: Aldine

Coleman JS. 1974. *Power and the Structure of Society.* New York: Norton

Coleman JS. 1975. Social structure and a theory of action. In *Approaches to the Study of Social Structure,* ed. PM Blau, pp. 76–93. New York: Free Press

Coleman JS. 1976. Differences between experiential and classroom learning. In *Experiential Learning*, ed. MT Keeton, pp. 49-61. San Francisco: Jossey-Bass

Coleman JS. 1978. Sociological analysis and social policy. In *A History of Sociological Analysis*, ed. T Bottomore, R Nisbet, pp. 677–703. New York: Basic Books

Coleman JS. 1980. The structure of society and the nature of social research. *Knowl.: Creat. Diffus. Util.* 1:333–50

Coleman JS. 1981a. *Longitudinal Data Analysis*. New York: Basic Books

Coleman JS. 1981b. The role of incentives in school desegregation. In *Race and Schooling in the City*, ed. A Yarmolinsky, L Liebman, CS Schelling, pp. 182–93. Cambridge, MA: Harvard Univ. Press

Coleman JS. 1982a. Policy, research, and political theory. In *The Social Sciences: Their Nature and Uses*, ed. WH Kruskal, pp. 95–99. Chicago: Univ. Chicago Press

Coleman JS. 1982b. *The Asymmetric Society*. Syracuse, NY: Syracuse Univ. Press

Coleman JS. 1984. Introducing social structure into economic analysis. *Am. Econ. Rev.* 74:84–88

Coleman JS. 1986a. *Individual Interests and Collective Action: Selected Essays*. New York: Cambridge Univ. Press

Coleman JS. 1986b. Psychological structure and social structure in economic models. *J. Bus.* 59:S365–69

Coleman JS. 1986c. Social theory, social research, and a theory of action. *Am. J. Sociol.* 91:1309–35

Coleman JS. 1987. Families and schools. *Educ. Res.* 16:32–38

Coleman JS. 1988. Social capital in the creation of human capital. *Am. J. Sociol.* 95:S95–120

Coleman JS. 1989. Simulation games and the development of social theory. *Simul. Games* 20:144–64

Coleman JS. 1990a. Columbia in the 1950s. In *Authors of Their Own Lives: Intellectual Autobiographies by Twenty American Sociologists*, ed. BM Berger, pp. 75–103. Berkeley: Univ. Calif. Press

Coleman JS. 1990b. *Equality and Achievement in Education*. Boulder, CO: Westview

Coleman JS. 1990c. *Foundations of Social Theory*. Cambridge, MA: Harvard Univ. Press

Coleman JS. 1991. Reflections on schools and adolescents. In *Reflections*, ed. DL Burleson, pp. 62–70. Bloomington, IN: Phi Delta Kappa Educ. Found.

Coleman JS. 1992a. Some points on choice in education. *Sociol. Educ.* 65:260–66

Coleman JS. 1992b. The economic approach to sociology. In *Universal Economics: Assessing the Achievements of the Economic Approach*, ed. G Radnitzky, pp. 133–48. New York: Paragon House

Coleman JS. 1992c. The vision of *Foundations of Social Theory*. *Anal. Krit.* 14:117–28

Coleman JS. 1993a. The design of organizations and the right to act. *Sociol. Forum* 8:527–46

Coleman JS. 1993b. The rational reconstruction of society: 1992 presidential address. *Am. Sociol. Rev.* 58:1–15

Coleman JS. 1993c. The role of rights in a theory of social action. *J. Inst. Theor. Econ.* 149:213–32

Coleman JS. 1994a. A vision for sociology. *Society* 32:29–34

Coleman JS. 1994b. Social capital, human capital, and investment in youth. In *Youth Unemployment and Society*, ed. AC Petersen, JT Mortimer, pp. 34–50. New York: Cambridge Univ. Press

Coleman JS, Blum ZD, Sørensen AB, Rossi PH. 1972. White and black careers during the first decade of labor force experience. Part I: Occupational status. *Soc. Sci. Res.* 1:243–70

Coleman JS, Bremner RH, Clark BH, Davis JB, Eichorn DH, et al. 1974. *Youth: Transition to Adulthood*. Chicago: Univ. Chicago Press

Coleman JS, Campbell EQ, Hobson CJ, McPartland J, Mood AM, et al. 1966a. *Equality of Educational Opportunity*. Washington, DC: US Gov. Print. Off.

Coleman JS, Hao L. 1989. Linear systems analysis: macrolevel analysis with microlevel data. *Sociol. Methodol.* 19:395–422

Coleman JS, Hoffer T. 1987. *Private and Public Schools: The Impact of Communities.* New York: Basic Books

Coleman JS, Hoffer T, Kilgore S. 1982. *High School Achievement: Public, Catholic, and Private Schools Compared.* New York: Basic Books

Coleman JS, Katz E, Menzel H. 1966b. *Medical Innovation: A Diffusion Study.* Indianapolis, IN: Bobbs-Merrill

Coleman JS, Kelly SD, Moore JA. 1976. *Trends in School Desegregation, 1968–73.* Washington, DC: The Urban Inst.

Coleman JS, MacRae D. 1960. Electronic processing of sociometric data for groups up to 1,000 in size. *Am. Sociol. Rev.* 25:722–27

Coleman JS, Menzel H, Katz E. 1959. Social processes in physicians' adoption of a new drug. *J. Chronic Dis.* 9:1–19

Collins R. 1996. Can rational action theory unify future social science? See Clark 1996, pp. 329–42

Cook KS, ed. 2001. *Trust in Society.* New York: Russell Sage Found.

Dijkstra AB, Veenstra R, Peschar J. 2004. Social capital in education: functional communities around high schools in the Netherlands. In *Creation and Returns of Social Capital: A New Research Program*, ed. H Flap, B Völker, pp. 119–44. London: Routledge

Dumais S. 2002. Cultural capital, gender, and school success: the role of habitus. *Sociol. Educ.* 75:44–68

Edling CR. 2002. Mathematics in sociology. *Annu. Rev. Sociol.* 28:197–220

Elster J. 2003. Coleman on social norms. *Rev. Fr. Sociol.* 44:297–304

Ensminger J. 2001. Reputations, trust and the principal agent problem. See Cook 2001, pp. 185–201

Fararo TJ. 1996. Foundational problems in theoretical sociology. See Clark 1996, pp. 263–84

Fararo TJ. 1997. Reflections on mathematical sociology. *Sociol. Forum* 12:73–101

Farkas G, Lleras C, Maczuga S. 2002. Does oppositional culture exist in minority and poverty peer groups? *Am. Sociol. Rev.* 67:148–55

Favell A. 1993. James Coleman: social theorist and moral philosopher? *Am. J. Sociol.* 99:590–613

Feld SL. 1997a. Mathematics in thinking about sociology. *Sociol. Forum* 12:3–9

Feld SL. 1997b. Simulation games in theory development. *Sociol. Forum* 12:103–15

Freeman LC. 2004. *The Development of Social Network Analysis: A Study in the Sociology of Science.* Vancouver, BC: Empirical Press

Gamoran A. 2001. American schooling and educational inequality: a forecast for the 21st century. *Sociol. Educ.* Extra Issue:135–53

Giordano PC. 2003. Relationships in adolescence. *Annu. Rev. Sociol.* 29:257–81

Hallinan MT. 2001. Black-white inequalities in American schooling. *Sociol. Educ.* Extra Issue:50–70

Hanushek EA. 1996. Measuring investment in education. *J. Econ. Perspect.* 10:9–39

Hanushek EA, Kain JF, Markman JM, Rivkin SG. 2003. Does peer ability affect student achievement? *J. Appl. Econom.* 18:527–44

Hardin R. 2001. Conceptions and explanations of trust. See Cook 2001, pp. 3–39

Hechter M, Kanazawa S. 1993. The production of social order with special reference to contemporary Japan. See Sørensen & Spilerman 1993, pp. 187–207

Hechter M, Kanazawa S. 1997. Sociological rational choice theory. *Annu. Rev. Sociol.* 23:191–214

Heckman JJ, Neal D. 1996. Coleman's contributions to education: theory, research styles, and empirical research. See Clark 1996, pp. 81–102

Hedström P, Swedberg R. 1998. Social mechanisms: an introductory essay. In *Social Mechanisms: An Analytical Approach to Social Theory*, ed. P Hedström, R Swedberg, pp. 1–31. New York: Cambridge Univ. Press

Hernes G. 1993. Hobbes and Coleman. See Sørensen & Spilerman 1993, pp. 93–104

Hoffer T, Greeley AM, Coleman JS. 1985. Achievement growth in public and Catholic schools. *Sociol. Educ.* 58:74–97

Homans GC. 1958. Social behavior as exchange. *Am. J. Sociol.* 63:597–606

Horne C. 2004. Collective benefits, exchange interests, and norm enforcement. *Soc. Forces* 82:1037–62

Husén T. 1996. Youth and adolescence: a historical and cultural perspective. See Clark 1996, pp. 23–31

Inst. Sci. Inf. 2004. *Social Sciences Citation Index* (online ed.). Philadelphia, PA: ISI

Kadushin C. 2004. Too much investment in social capital? *Soc. Netw.* 26:75–90

Kandel DB. 1996. Coleman's contributions to understanding youth and adolescents. See Clark 1996, pp. 33–45

Kaufman J, Gabler J. 2004. Cultural capital and the extracurricular activities of girls and boys in the college attainment process. *Poetics* 32:145–68

Kilgore S. 1996. The political context of social policy research. See Clark 1996, pp. 119–31

Lee VE, Chow-Hoy TK, Burkham DT, Geverdt D, Smerdon BA. 1998. Sector differences in high school course taking: a private school or Catholic school effect? *Sociol. Educ.* 71:314–35

Lin N. 2001. *Social Capital: A Theory of Social Structure and Action.* New York: Cambridge Univ. Press

Lindenberg S. 1996. Constitutionalism versus relationism: two versions of rational choice sociology. See Clark 1996, pp. 299–311

Lindenberg S. 2000. James Coleman. In *The Blackwell Companion to Major Social Theorists*, ed. G Ritzer, pp. 513–44. Malden, MA: Blackwell

Lindenberg S. 2003. *Institutional design and its discontents: Coleman's neglect of social rationality.* Work. Pap., Cent. Study Econ. Soc., Cornell Univ.

Lipset SM, Trow M, Coleman JS. 1956. *Union Democracy: The Inside Politics of the International Typographical Union.* New York: Free Press

Mayer KU. 1997. James Coleman's studies of the American education system and how they relate to his theory of action and society. *Berl. J. Soziol.* 7:347–56 (In German)

Mayntz R. 2004. Mechanisms in the analysis of social macro-phenomena. *Philos. Soc. Sci.* 34:237–59

McFarland DD. 2001. Student resistance: how the formal and informal organization of classrooms facilitate everyday forms of student defiance. *Am. J. Sociol.* 107:612–78

Merton RK. 1996. Teaching James Coleman. See Clark 1996, pp. 351–56

Morgan SL. 2001. Counterfactuals, causal effect heterogeneity, and the Catholic school effect on learning. *Sociol. Educ.* 74:341–74

Morgan SL, Sørensen AB. 1999. Parental networks, social closure and mathematics learning: a test of Coleman's social capital explanation of school effects. *Am. Sociol. Rev.* 64:661–81

Moynihan DP. 1993. Educational goals and political plans. See Sørensen & Spilerman 1993, pp. 107–27

Muller C, Schiller KS. 2000. Leveling the playing field? Students' educational attainment and states' performance testing. *Sociol. Educ.* 73:196–218

Neal D. 1997. The effects of Catholic secondary schooling on educational achievement. *J. Labor Econ.* 15:98–123

Neal D. 2002. How vouchers could change the market for education. *J. Econ. Perspect.* 16:25–44

Nyborg K, Rege M. 2003. On social norms: the evolution of considerate smoking behavior. *J. Econ. Behav. Organ.* 52:323–40

Opp K-D. 2001. Social networks and the emergence of protest norms. In *Social Norms*, ed. M Hechter, K-D Opp, pp. 234–73. New York: Russell Sage Found.

Podolny J. 1990. On the formation of exchange relations in political systems. *Ration. Soc.* 2:359–78

Portes A. 1998. Social capital: its origins and applications in modern sociology. *Annu. Rev. Sociol.* 24:1–24

Raub W, Weesie J. 1990. Reputation and efficiency in social interactions: an example of network effects. *Am. J. Sociol.* 96:626–54

Ravitch D. 1993. The Coleman Reports and American education. See Sørensen & Spilerman 1993, pp. 129–41

Schneider B, Schiller KS, Coleman JS. 1996. Public school choice: some evidence from the National Education Longitudinal Study of 1988. *Educ. Eval. Policy Anal.* 18:19–29

Scott WR. 2004. Reflections on a half-century of organizational sociology. *Annu. Rev. Sociol.* 30:1–21

Smelser NJ. 1992. The rational choice perspective: a theoretical assessment. *Ration. Soc.* 4:381–410

Sobel J. 2002. Can we trust social capital? *J. Econ. Lit.* 40:139–54

Sørensen AB. 1996. Educational opportunities and school effects. See Clark 1996, pp. 207–25

Sørensen AB, Spilerman S, eds. 1993. *Social Theory and Social Policy: Essays in Honor of James S. Coleman.* Westport, CT: Praeger

Stern RN, Barley SR. 1996. Organizations and social systems: organization theory's neglected mandate. *Admin. Sci. Q.* 41:146–62

Stinchcombe AL. 1993. The conditions of fruitfulness of theorizing about mechanisms in social science. See Sørensen & Spilerman 1993, pp. 23–41

Swedberg R. 1990. *Economics and Sociology.*

Redefining Their Boundaries: Conversations with Economists and Sociologists. Princeton, NJ: Princeton Univ. Press

Swedberg R. 1996. Analyzing the economy: on the contribution of James S. Coleman. See Clark 1996, pp. 313–28

Swedberg R. 2003. *Principles of Economic Sociology.* Princeton, NJ: Princeton Univ. Press

Tuma NB, Hannan MT. 1984. *Social Dynamics: Models and Methods.* Orlando, FL: Academic

Udehn L. 2002. The changing face of methodological individualism. *Annu. Rev. Sociol.* 28:479–507

Van den Bulte C, Lilien GL. 2001. Medical innovation revisited: social contagion versus marketing effort. *Am. J. Sociol.* 106:1409–35

Van Hove E. 1993. The practice of sociology in public affairs. See Sørensen & Spilerman 1993, pp. 233–40

Wejnert B. 2002. Integrating models of diffusion of innovations: a conceptual framework. *Annu. Rev. Sociol.* 28:297–326

Yamaguchi K. 1996. Power in networks of substitutable and complementary exchange relations: a rational-choice model and an analysis of power centralization. *Am. Sociol. Rev.* 61:308–32

Annu. Rev. Sociol. 2005. 31:25–45
doi: 10.1146/annurev.soc.31.041304.122213
Copyright © 2005 by Annual Reviews. All rights reserved
First published online as a Review in Advance on April 7, 2005

DOING JUSTICE TO THE GROUP: Examining the Roles of the Group in Justice Research

Karen A. Hegtvedt

Department of Sociology, Emory University, Atlanta, Georgia 30322;
email: khegtv@emory.edu

Key Words   distributive justice, procedural justice, group processes

■ **Abstract**   Although the abstract notion of justice implies attention to fairness not simply for one individual but for many, emphasis on how individuals perceive and react to injustice obscures the role of the group in justice research. Justice, as distinct from individual deserving, holds promise for the well-being of the group. Indeed, the group plays multiple roles in justice research, as a collective standard, a structure in which evaluations occur, a source of identity, and a context of interaction. Analyses of these roles help to explain underlying orientations of group members, delimiting the scope of justice in groups and the implications of justice in conflict situations. This review concludes with directions for future research that more explicitly draw attention to the rightful role of the group in understanding justice in society.

INTRODUCTION

In the week following the September 11 terrorist attack, the U.S. government labeled its coordinated response to the tragic event "Operation Infinite Justice." As a justice scholar, my immediate response to that label was, "Justice for whom?" I anticipated that some groups around the world might consider the operation more aptly titled "Infinite Injustice." Indeed, Muslim Americans took offense at the government's label and pointed out that only Allah could determine justice. Out of respect for the opinions of this minority group, the government rechristened the response "Operation Enduring Freedom." These contrasting views epitomize the overarching theme of this paper: Justice is not simply in the eyes of an individual beholder, but it is in the eyes of a community, however defined.

Given the age-old concern with the just society, few would dispute that, in theory, justice is a phenomenon that extends beyond the individual. Yet, typically what resonates for people is their concern with injustice regarding their own treatment. Children cope with feelings of injustice resulting, for example, from being left out of a ball game, ignored at the lunchroom table, or ridiculed for how they dress. Adults question the fairness of pay distributions, the household division of labor, health care insurers' willingness to cover certain treatments, etc. These and other concrete situations illustrate social psychological scholars' concerns

0360-0572/05/0811-0025$20.00

with abstract questions of justice: What distribution rule is just? How do people perceive injustice? How do people respond to injustice? Although researchers use a variety of methodologies to examine these questions, they focus mostly on the individual's position or characteristics, perceptions, and responses. Yet implicitly, and recently explicitly, some formulations recognize that group context and group processes matter in determining not only individual-level assessments but also group consequences as well. As Tyler et al. (1997) stress, "Justice standards. . .are the 'grease' that allows groups to interact productively without conflict and social disintegration" (p. 6).

Here, I first examine two issues inherent in expanding the purview of justice research to encompass the group more explicitly: (*a*) the distinction between individual deserving and justice, and (*b*) the conceptualization of the group. Then I review how the group plays multifaceted, yet unheralded, roles in a wide range of justice research. Specifically, I focus on the group as a collective standard, a structure, a source of identity, and a dynamic process. The review crosscuts the domains of distributive and procedural justice, highlighting the importance of the group context. What grows apparent is that the real, implied, or even imagined influence of the group affects justice assessments and reactions—at the individual level as well as at the group level. Realization of the relevance of the collective element of justice becomes clearly evident under the condition of social conflict. Before concluding, I note how disputes vividly demonstrate the fundamental role of the group in understanding justice processes and consequences. I end with some suggestions for how researchers might extend current research paradigms to rightfully return justice concerns to the community.

JUSTICE, INDIVIDUAL DESERVING, AND THE GROUP

Although many scholars in the social sciences and humanities define and study justice processes, social psychologists commonly assert that "justice exists when there is congruence between expectations for outcomes based on [a] normative rule and actual outcomes" (Hegtvedt & Markovsky 1995, p. 259). That definition, however, begs the question of what constitutes a normative rule. In addition, it may confound what individuals expect as just for themselves and what they deem as just for a larger collectivity. As Jasso (1983) points out, what is fair at the individual level may not always be fair at the aggregate level. To discuss the role of the group in assessing justice and responding to injustice, I distinguish between notions of individual deserving and justice per se, and conceptualize the range of meanings inherent in the term group.

Research on distributive justice primarily focuses on individuals' preferences for certain types of distributions, their perceptions of the fairness of those distributions, and their reactions to perceived injustice. In much of that research, individuals are the recipients of the distributed outcomes. As a consequence, the level of their own outcomes are highly salient. In making assessments, it may be difficult to discern what individuals believe they deserve and what is just. Indeed, some theorists (e.g., Feather 1999, Wagstaff 1994) equate the two concepts.

Cohen (1979) analyzes the important distinction between individual deserving and distributive justice. Lerner et al. (1976) define deserving as "the relation between a person and his [sic] outcomes. A person deserves an outcome if he [sic] has met the appropriate 'preconditions' for obtaining it" (p. 134). The preconditions may include rules regarding the distribution of outcomes, including the comparison to others' outcomes. Classic social psychological perspectives on distributive justice (e.g., Adams 1965, Homans 1974, Walster et al. 1978) focus on individuals' assessments and reactions to their outcomes in comparison with others' outcomes. Cohen argues that what is missing in such analyses is the assessment of allotments *across* individuals. In an allocation situation, it may be impossible to ensure that there are sufficient resources to go around if each person receives what he or she deserves. Thus, a comparison across individuals is key to the normative evaluation of a distribution of goods across recipients that is central to the notion of distributive justice.

Complementing Cohen's argument, Hareli (1999) notes that "while justice forces one to consider the situation of others, deservingness does not" (p. 189), and "[i]f justice is the issue, rules and conventions as well as arguments about similar others may dominate the struggle, whereas if deservingness is the issue, personal merits may be stressed" (p. 191). Stressing personal merits highlights the individual's own responsibility for outcomes (Feather 1994). In contrast, concerns with justice may raise the question of people's and an institution's responsibility toward others. For example, in a school district including both affluent and poor neighborhoods, students at schools in the affluent areas may rationalize their resources and amenities in terms of their higher performance on national standardized tests, thus emphasizing deserving. Yet, responsibility lies with the district to ensure adequate resources to all schools, thereby creating a just distribution.

Cohen and Hareli's distinctions between justice and individual deserving emphasize that justice extends beyond individual welfare to that of the group. Other social psychologists (Deutsch 1975, Reis 1986) similarly argue that justice should foster social cooperation and promote mutually agreeable exchanges. Tyler & Blader (2000) cement the link between justice and cooperation. Focusing on procedural justice, they argue that the fairness of group processes and procedures affects how people relate to each other in groups and thus represents a key antecedent to group-oriented cooperative behavior. In addition, philosophers (Barry 1989, Rawls 1971) and social psychologists (Frohlich & Oppenheimer 1992, Leventhal et al. 1980) draw attention to the importance of impartiality for discerning just distributions. When decision makers are neutral and unbiased in their allocations, concerns with their own individual deserving are secondary. As a consequence, what is fair for one person is likely to suffice as fair for another. Recipients within a group are more likely to agree on distributions that do not reflect the bias of the distributor and that facilitate group cooperation. Consensus on such distributions provides the basis for creating a normative principle—at least within that particular group.

Application of a principle of justice requires designation of the group to which it will apply. For example, the American Declaration of Independence claims that "all men are created equal," and thus guaranteed equal rights. Yet, despite that proclamation, for many years only white males were allowed to vote, leaving women and people of color outside of the group to which the rights applied. In some instances, circumscribing the group is fairly clear cut, and in other instances it is more ambiguous. Whether the boundaries of the group are clear depends on several factors, including the abstract definition of a group, characteristics of the distribution itself, and the motivations of those involved as allocators or recipients.

Classic social psychological definitions of a group emphasize common interests, sense of identity, interaction, shared norms, and structure (e.g., positions, roles). In contrast, social identity perspectives (e.g., Hogg & Abrams 1988, 2001; Tajfel & Turner 1979) discuss groups more broadly—according to social categories (i.e., collections of people who share socially relevant characteristics, but who do not necessarily interact or share norms). Sex, race/ethnicity, age, religious beliefs, region, etc., constitute categories. Many social policies (e.g., affirmative action, Medicare) involving the distribution of benefits apply to social categories, not to groups per se. Within an organization, however, it may be appropriate to distribute a bonus to the members of a specific work group responsible for higher profits. Regardless of definitions, the boundaries of the collectivity to which a distribution applies are paramount.

Deutsch (1985) and Cohen (1991) stress that justice principles apply to a moral community—those who share beliefs about right and wrong. Optow (1990) argues that these beliefs circumscribe fairness considerations to those in the group, leading to the sharing of community resources as well as to the making of sacrifices for others' welfare. Moral communities vary across cultures and shift over time. Relationship changes, stimulated by conflict or differentiation, resulting in a feeling of unconnectedness, signal the beginning of the moral exclusion process, which identifies people perceived to be outside the boundaries to which the perceiver's moral values and rules apply. Individuals then develop rationalizations and justifications to support the moral exclusion, deeming outsiders as undeserving or even as nonentities, which in turn provides the grounds for harm that may come their way. Such reasoning, for example, underlies the seething hatred of Americans by Muslim extremists.

Tyler et al. (1997) use these boundaries to define the scope of justice. They further argue that the perceived boundaries depend on the nature of an individual's orientation. Generally, the instrumental orientation is akin to self-interest, whereas the relational orientation harkens to concerns for others, perhaps even other-advantage. Individuals with an instrumental orientation exclude others from their scope of justice based on self- or group interests. In contrast, those with a relational orientation use normative and social concerns as a basis for exclusion, thereby excluding others who are distinct from themselves, behave differently, do not share their cultural and social values, and, essentially, threaten social identities. Such identities function to ensure differentiation of justice from individual deserving and may provide the basis for distinguishing how people substantively define a circle of recipients.

To the extent that individuals have multiple social identities, however, defining the moral community grows more difficult. Tyler & Lind (1990) argue that exclusionary practices are stronger in groups that value hierarchical or subgroup distinctions. In addition, contextual circumstances may make one identity or subgroup membership more salient than another or reinforce overlapping identities. Clay-Warner (2001) suggests that an individual's subgroup memberships affect perceptions of justice. Individuals are likely to identify most closely with those with whom they share the greatest number of status identities. In addition, she argues that characteristics of the subgroups themselves (i.e., the permeability of their boundaries, their stability, and their legitimacy) in conjunction with perceptual processes that draw attention to more powerful people influence identification with a particular group. Other aspects of the social context, such as consideration of which benefit, burden, or procedure is at stake, may also increase the salience of some identities over others. Wenzel (2003) examines the impact of different levels of identification (e.g., with a subgroup, with a superordinate group) on perceptions of injustice. Such work highlights how identity salience may define the scope of justice.

By moving beyond the individual and his or her level of deserving in justice considerations, the role of the group increases in several ways. First, at the group level, assessments of justice require a comparison across individuals. Second, performing such comparisons involves specification of the scope of justice. And, third, specifying the scope of justice demands that individuals be aware of their social identities and those of others, which may result in the realization of divergent perceptions of justice. For example, secretaries within one company may assess whether they are equitably paid by comparing the ratio of their pay to their skill and experience levels across all similarly categorized workers within their company, thereby ensuring the comparison across individuals and specifying the scope of justice. Yet heightened awareness of particular social identities may lead to divergent perceptions of justice, such as when managers want to compensate line workers by skill alone, whereas the laborers believe experience or years on the job also count. Despite the relevance of the group to the nature of justice itself, the explicit role of the group in social psychological justice research has been largely overlooked.

THE ROLES OF THE GROUP IN JUSTICE RESEARCH

Existing justice research reveals a number of implicit roles that the group has played. As indicated in Table 1, four roles may be categorized according to whether each is inherent in the process of making justice evaluations (e.g., comparison standard and source of identity) or focuses on aspects of the group itself (e.g., its structure and dynamics). Also noted in the table and described below, some roles have been explored more extensively in distributive justice research, whereas others pertain more to the realm of procedural justice investigations.

TABLE 1   Categorization of the roles of the group in justice research

| | **Relevant categories** | | | |
Role	**Aspect of justice process**	**Aspect of groups**	**Characteristic of distributive justice research**	**Characteristic of procedural justice research**
Group Standard	*		*	
Group Structure		*	**	*
Group Identity	*		*	**
Group Processes		*	**	*

* Indicates that the role fits into a particular category.

** Indicates that the role is more predominant in a particular type of justice research.

Use of a Group Standard to Determine Justice

Characteristic of distributive justice research, the group exists as a standard of comparison to determine whether an individual or a group's rewards are just. Comparisons to personal rewards in the past or to a single other actor generally emphasize individual deserving. In contrast, comparisons to a referential structure, representing the general reward level of others like themselves (Berger et al. 1972) or to another group (Markovsky 1985) accentuate consideration of the group, however delimited, in justice analysis.

Berger et al. (1972) introduce the referential standard as key to their status value theory of distributive justice. Presumably, what individuals bring to a situation (their inputs) and what they gain from it (their outcomes) carry status value or prestige, on the basis of a group's cultural beliefs about worthiness. People develop stereotyped conceptions of the links between socially valued characteristics and rewards. The referential comparison captures the consistency between characteristics and rewards for generalized others. This conceptualization incorporates the group through both status value and through aggregating inputs and outcomes of similar others.

Berger et al. (1972) expect that it is necessary to compare the local situation (i.e., one's input/outcome ratio to that of another individual) to the referential situation to determine justice. Fairness obtains "when you and I get what people like us in general receive" (Hegtvedt & Markovsky 1995, p. 269). In other words, the group context of the individual-level comparisons provides the basis for justice evaluations. In the absence of information about the referential standard, individuals may infer only that one gets less (or more) than the other, which may raise issues of individual deserving but not distributive justice per se. Törnblom (1977) combines the various types of comparisons (internal, local, referential) to determine the severity of injustice.

More formally, Jasso (1980) introduces the justice evaluation (JE) formula to measure degrees of perceived injustice: JE $=$ ln (actual share/just share). Her notion of just share, defined as what the evaluator considers to be just, implicitly takes into account group influences. Calculating the just share incorporates the referential standard. A later representation, which includes population values, expands the purview of the just evaluation beyond the seemingly individual deserving focus of the original formula (see Jasso 2002). The mathematical formulation of injustice allows identification of patterns of justice evaluations across group members. Such collective assessments of justice, Jasso argues, have a variety of consequences for the group, including the potential for revolution and criminal activities.

Markovsky (1985) draws from relative deprivation theory (see Hegtvedt & Markovsky 1995) to promote the group itself as a standard for comparison. His multilevel theory of justice also includes local and referential comparisons. By including the group as a comparison standard, he moves theoretical reasoning beyond an emphasis on individual deserving. Markovsky's (1985) results show that increasing group identification leads individuals to respond more frequently on behalf of their groups than on their own behalf.

Although Markovsky's work specifies one condition under which a particular type of comparison will be invoked, most justice work constrains comparisons to either a local level or a referential standard, and thus little is known about factors affecting the choice of a comparison standard. An individual's orientation— instrumental or relational—may affect the choice. A relational orientation is more likely to draw attention to referential and group-level comparisons, whereas an instrumental orientation may lead to the selection of the comparison that serves to justify higher outcomes. If a situation stimulates multiple social identities, the question of which referential or group-level comparison is raised and the answer may depend on both the social context and type of evaluation at issue (Wenzel 2003). Ultimately, the selection of a comparison standard may denote whether an individual is concerned about his or her own deserving or about justice per se. Characteristics of the group structure are relevant to these concerns.

The Effects of Group Structure on Determining Justice

As a key aspect of groups themselves, group structure refers to the patterning of relationships among group members. The patterns may stem from power or status differences, role differentiation, performance levels, or sentiments. The structure of the group, however, may interact with other contextual factors to affect what people perceive as fair. Concerns with group structure crosscut research in distributive and procedural justice.

Even though status and power are fundamental concepts in social psychology, their effects on perceptions of justice (or, more accurately, individual deserving) have received little attention. Although a number of studies have examined the effect of sex (see Major & Deaux 1982) on preferences for different distribution rules, only one investigation conceptualizes sex as a status characteristic representing different levels of prestige. Wagner (1995) shows that group members differentiated by status (e.g., a male and a female) prefer equitable allocations, whereas status equals desire an equal distribution, regardless of task contributions. And, as discussed further below, power dynamics play an important role in justice assessments.

Attention to role differentiation is typically implicit in terms of the interdependence of the group members. Researchers have presented typologies of relationships according to the interdependence of actors and associated principles of justice. Interdependence assumes a necessary reliance on another, which is likely to affect (positively or negatively) one's own outcomes. Although interdependence is neither a classic criterion for defining a group nor a particular issue in defining a moral community, it suffices as a way to join people together.

Greenberg & Cohen (1982) combine the dimensions of interdependence (control over another's resources) and intimacy (closeness of the bond between individuals) in a model to conceptualize the effects of the nature of the relationship on preferences for distribution rules [see reviews by Cook & Hegtvedt (1983), Leventhal et al. (1980), and Törnblom (1992)]. Importantly, their model recognizes the potential conflict between concern for one's own interests in a distribution (i.e., individual deserving) and concern for other's interests (more akin to justice). They describe four types of relationships and predicted justice principles: married, needs; friends, equality; bargainers, self-interested justice; strangers, own desires. Subsequent models (e.g., Clark 1984, Kayser et al. 1984) produce variations on the combinations of relational dimensions, taking into consideration other factors (e.g., class of resources, direction of the transaction). Generally, emphasis on others or on the community promotes the use of equality rules, whereas emphasis on self, agency, or rankings correlates with equity principles.

These recipient-preferred justice patterns dovetail with research on observers' assessments of the fairness of certain distribution principles for specified group goals. Studies consistently show that people rate equity as fair for promoting group productivity, equality for achieving group harmony, and needs for ensuring social welfare (see Leventhal et al. 1980).

The contrast between the preferences or evaluations of recipients and observers provides an indirect assessment of orientations. When an individual serves as both allocator and recipient in an impersonal group, the situation is more likely to elicit a self-serving orientation. Indeed, distribution rule preferences under such conditions demonstrate that high performers prefer an equitable distribution and low performers prefer an equal distribution—a pattern of preferences that maximizes the outcomes to the allocator (see Hegtvedt 1992). Similarly, when judging an actual distribution, individuals who fare well in the distribution are more likely to assess it as fair than those who are disadvantaged by it (Cook & Hegtvedt 1986, Messick & Sentis 1979). In contrast, impartial allocators who are not also recipients are likely to allocate rewards in a manner that benefits all group members (e.g., Frohlich et al. 1987, Frohlich & Oppenheimer 1992).

Clearly, in making and judging distributions, nonrecipients may be more objective and less self-serving in their evaluations. But even allocators who also receive outcomes may display "other-serving" orientations by emphasizing a partner's or the relationship's welfare when there is an affective attachment among group members, the distribution is public, face-to-face discussion about distributions occurs, and rewards are insufficient to meet expectations of all group members (see Hegtvedt & Markovsky 1995).

In summary, in analyzing the impact of group structure, researchers have theorized about orientations associated with the relationships within the group, which in turn determine which types of distributions constitute justice. Little research actually operationalizes these orientations. Instead, researchers emphasize situational conditions that create deviations from self-interested or instrumental patterns of allocation. To the extent that situational conditions draw attention to the interdependence among group members and highlight the allocator's responsibility for the welfare of others, individuals are less likely to make self-interested distributions. In the studies noted above, the experimental situation circumscribes attention to the immediate group as the scope of justice. But more complex situations, involving multiple groups, raise concerns over the primacy of group identity.

The Influence of Group Identity on Justice Assessments and Reactions

When individuals invoke group standards to assess justice, they recognize themselves as embedded in a network of relationships defined by the specific groups to which they belong. Thus, group identity is a key aspect of the justice process. Identification with groups is the result of a multifaceted process, described by social identity theory (Tajfel & Turner 1979, 1986), involving self-categorization, in which individuals develop a sense of their similarity to others, thereby creating an in-group identity. "When a social identity is engaged, a shared understanding of group attributes, norms, and goals. . .is sufficient to produce uniformity of behavior and purpose among those who share that social identity" (Brewer & Silver 2000, p. 154). Although the development of a group identity has consequences for what is perceived as distributively just across groups, it has been studied most extensively with regard to procedural justice within groups.

Some of the earliest work on social identity theory focuses on the effects of defining groups according to trivial criteria—so-called minimal groups—on allocation preferences and the fairness of existing distributions (see Tajfel & Turner 1979). Results typically indicate that individuals allocate more to their own groups and evaluate their own group more positively. Such in-group favoritism characterizes allocations of positive resources but does not extend to the distribution of negative resources (Otten & Mummendey 1999). Within groups, greater identification with the group decreases individuals' preferences for self-interested allocations (Wenzel 2002). Thus, the minimal group paradigm shows results consistent with an instrumental or self-interested view of fairness when contrasts are between groups, but the paradigm also shows that group identity instills more of a relational orientation (i.e., other-advantage) toward justice processes within groups.

In addition to the focus on the fairness of distributions, group identity is also relevant to reactions to perceived injustice. As noted above, Markovsky (1985) finds that the increased salience of group identity produces more group-level comparisons and protests based on group injustice. In addition, studies show that revolutionary coalitions consisting of two subordinate members develop when they recognize their shared plight and respond to a leader who has treated them unfairly (see Hegtvedt & Markovsky 1995). Lalonde & Silverman (1994) demonstrate specifically that the salience of disadvantaged group membership is particularly critical to collective reactions when group boundaries are impermeable.

The group-value model of procedural justice (Lind & Tyler 1988) provides the most integrated framework, emphasizing the role of group identity in justice processes. Lind and Tyler use social identity theory to argue that people desire to belong to positively valued groups and that such membership has positive consequences for the individual's self-worth. Individuals who join positively evaluated groups develop pride in their group, distinguishing it from less favorable groups by accentuating its positive aspects and derogating characteristics of other groups. Moreover, once associated with a positively valued group, individuals want to know they are valued group members. People examine the procedures in the group as well as their treatment to measure their value to the group. To the extent that authorities treat them in an unbiased fashion (neutrality), show them respect (standing), and presume them trustworthy (trust), they are likely to perceive themselves as fairly treated and valued group members (Tyler & Lind 1992).

Lind & Tyler (1988) show that procedural justice has an effect on outcomes, net of outcome levels, thereby providing evidence for the group-value model. In addition, recent research indicates that procedural justice exerts stronger effects than distributive justice on evaluations of group authorities, institutions, and rules in legal, managerial, and political settings (see Tyler et al. 1997). But like issues of the collective standard and group structure, individuals may identify with multiple groups. Tyler & Smith (1999) note that if actors identify with a subgroup, they may be less concerned about identity-relevant information provided by overall group authorities, thereby implying concerns over the scope of justice.

Support for the group-value model of procedural justice generally confirms the importance of group identity for understanding justice issues. In doing so, it reveals the impact of a relational orientation and thus moves justice concerns beyond the dyad. The emphasis on treatment within a group constitutes an aspect of group processes critical to justice evaluations and reactions.

The Role of Group Interaction Processes on Justice Assessments and Reactions

The scholarly area of group processes includes a variety of topics: social exchange, power, group decision making, bargaining, legitimacy, etc. Classic approaches to reactions to injustice stem from a framework of social exchange. As a consequence, the study of the role of group processes has a longer history in distributive justice than in procedural justice. Despite the number of empirical studies on the reactions to injustice (see Cook & Hegtvedt 1983, Hegtvedt & Markovsky 1995), the role of group dynamics is downplayed, and individual deserving rather than justice per se may be the actual emphasis in this body of literature. This section focuses on studies that explicitly involve group dynamics and their impact on justice evaluations.

Typically, social exchange researchers examine how the power structure of the network affects the dynamics of the actors and, ultimately, the exchange rate, which defines the final distribution of resources (see Molm & Cook 1995). Although power-disadvantaged actors typically perceive the final distribution of outcomes to be less fair than do power-advantaged actors (Cook & Hegtvedt 1986, Stolte 1983), when negotiators grow aware of accumulated unequal outcomes, they somewhat constrain their use of power, decreasing overall outcome inequality in the network (Cook & Emerson 1978). The constraining effect, however, does not emerge in networks involving non-negotiated, reciprocal exchange. In such situations, justice concerns legitimize the inequality on the basis of power differences (Molm et al. 1994).

Other studies have examined the extent to which power dynamics affect network members' perceptions of fairness. Molm et al. (1993) show that actors in a power-balanced network judge reward- and punishment-based strategies as more unfair than reciprocal strategies. In addition, individuals are more likely to judge their partner's behavior as fair under conditions of reciprocal exchange than under conditions of negotiated exchange (Molm et al. 2003). Although negotiation ostensibly involves many of the characteristics of procedural justice (e.g., communication, means to control outcomes), these elements also seem to highlight the potential for conflict. In contrast, reciprocal exchange requires an element of trust that enhances the perceived fairness of the partner's behavior.

Group decision making involves exchanging information and ideas, rather than resources. Only a few studies, noted above, examine the establishment of a justice principle through group discussion. Kahn et al. (1982) show that group members typically agree on distributions offered by the individual who does not suggest a principle promoting self-interest. Frohlich & Oppenheimer (1992) demonstrate that group members who are unaware of their particular interests act impartially and readily reach consensus on a fairness principle. Lind et al. (1998) reveal more explicitly the influence processes operating in these studies by establishing the polarizing effects of group discussion on procedural assessments. Compared to individual judgments, group ratings of the fairness of a group supervisor were consistently lower.

Although few studies examine the impact of group interaction on justice evaluations, dynamic influence processes are at the core of bargaining. Typically, negotiation studies (see Lawler & Ford 1995) focus on how people resolve their differences through concessions and communication to come to a mutually agreed upon resource distribution. Communication in negotiation sessions represents a form of persuasive debate (Lamm 1986) and may activate norms that generate conformity pressures to enhance trust, create feelings of cohesion, and thus increase the goodness or fairness of collective outcomes (see Hegtvedt 1992).

Tjosvold (1977) demonstrates that in bargaining situations when high-status negotiators make justice appeals, more agreements result. Likewise, when bargainers recognize the claims of others in their assessment of what would be a fair decision rather than express an egocentric fair division, disputes settle quickly (Thompson & Lowenstein 1992). In effect, the dynamics of communication and the meaning of what is offered in bargaining situations reveal how much one negotiator supports the motives of another. Hegtvedt et al. (1995) show that individuals are more likely to invoke fairness claims to support self-interested distributions in three-person groups than to support allocations that reflect others' interests.

More generally, legitimacy focuses on the impact of collective support for a variety of things, including a rule, a distribution, or an authority (Walker & Zelditch 1993, Zelditch & Walker 1984). In a series of studies, Zelditch and colleagues have demonstrated that even in the absence of personal approval, individuals are likely to clamor for a change to an unjust structure when they perceive that others fail to support it. Johnson & Ford (1996) examine the effects of two collective sources of legitimacy on a worker's reaction to an unfair pay situation: authorization (the support of authorities) and endorsement (the support of subordinates). Both forms of legitimacy tend to reduce individual reactions to their unjust pay situation.

Although legitimacy researchers set up an unfair situation in their studies, little of their original theorizing integrates legitimacy with distributive or procedural justice.[1] Hegtvedt & Johnson (2000) build upon prior legitimacy work to link endorsement and authorization to processes underlying justice assessments and potential responses to disadvantageous injustice, effectively identifying how the evaluations of others affect those of a focal actor. Presumably, collective sources of legitimacy for an unfair distribution attenuate the severity of the perceived injustice, negative emotional expressions about the injustice, and behavioral reactions to it. In addition, they note that identification with peers or authorities determines the relative impact of endorsement or authorization, respectively. Hegtvedt et al. (2003) analyze the effects of the legitimacy of an allocator, and his or her use of fair procedures, on disadvantaged actors' reactions to an unfair distribution. The theoretical argument combines elements of group value with those of the group's influence to predict reactions to injustice more specifically.

Lind et al.'s (1998) focus on the shared experience of injustice is akin to work on legitimacy. When a group's supervisor distributes unfair treatment across all group members, those individuals are likely to perceive the supervisor as more unfair than when he or she repeatedly treats only one member unfairly. The distributed injustice seems to undermine endorsement for the supervisor. Ultimately, when researchers include legitimacy processes in distributive justice analysis, they ensure examination of the promise of justice beyond the individual.

Likewise, the group-value model of procedural justice (Lind & Tyler 1988) moves beyond the individual. The dual emphases of procedural justice—decision making and the treatment of others (Tyler & Blader 2000)—solidify the group

---

[1] In a retrospective on his work, Zelditch (2001) draws more attention to justice processes. Jost & Major (2001) also offer psychological analyses of justice and legitimacy.

by regulating process and structure, largely in terms of authority relations. With regard to decision making, the procedural justice rules focus on the suppression of bias, accuracy of information, representativeness of participants to the decision, consistency across individuals, and mechanisms to correct bad decisions (Leventhal et al. 1980). The extension of representativeness to include the "voice" of individuals in expressing opinions prior to an actual decision implies a dynamic process (see Tyler et al. 1997). Voice provides individuals with a sense of control and increases feelings of inclusion in the group. And, as noted above, to the extent that individuals are treated with neutrality, respect, and trust, they perceive themselves as valued members of the group, which enhances perceptions of procedural justice (Tyler 1994) and may increase self-esteem. Procedural justice, in turn, mediates the effects of relational factors on an individual's willingness to remain in the group and to comply with group rules or an authority (see Tyler et al. 1997). Indeed, De Cremer (2002) shows that when group members act respectfully toward each other, they communicate important relational information that contributes to the group's welfare and in the long run enhances cooperation.

Tyler connects relational factors and justice to notions of the legitimacy of authorities. Within his framework, legitimacy refers to "the feeling of obligation to follow the decisions of group authorities and group rules" (Tyler et al. 1997, p. 176–77), thereby recognizing the feelings of obligation that are also inherent in Walker & Zelditch's (1993) framework. Tyler implicitly addresses collective sources of support when he argues that fair decision-making procedures "act as a cushion of support allowing authorities to deliver unpopular decisions without losing support in the eyes of the public" (Tyler et al. 1997, p. 177).

The distributive and procedural justice traditions tend to highlight different aspects of situations involving questions of fairness. The distributive justice approach reveals concerns with power and negotiations, whereas the procedural justice approach highlights authority relationships and legitimacy, albeit not in the collective sense discussed by Walker & Zelditch (1993). Thus, the role of group processes in justice research has made various inroads, but few roads merge.

Summary: Group Context Matters

Although essentially discrete roles, how relationships are structured, what individuals believe about their groups, and how individuals interact within the groups define the group context in which people invoke different standards to assess fairness and to shape the nature of their reactions to injustice. No single theoretical tradition spells out all the implications of these group elements. Most empirical research either ignores group elements or constrains the situations to allow researchers to examine only one or two of these roles.

The group-value model of procedural justice and the research it has generated comes closest to highlighting the importance of the group in justice analysis. This framework stresses issues of group identity, structure (in the form of authority relationships), and processes (in the form of the treatment of group members). Procedural rules such as representativeness may imply a collective standard. Indeed, procedural justice theorists (Lind & Tyler 1988, Tyler et al. 1997) stress that procedural justice appears more important than distributive justice, and, moreover, support for procedural justice indicates support for a relational orientation. But such support is hardly surprising when an element of procedural justice is treatment of individuals. And although people may use information on the fairness of procedures heuristically to evaluate outcome justice (van den Bos et al. 2001), when information on the distribution of outcomes (and inputs) across all group members is available, concerns with distributive justice may remain equally important. Thus, it may be that no one perspective can exist as the standard bearer of all justice research.

In addition, both distributive and procedural justice researchers tend to beg the question of the scope of justice by severely constraining it in their investigations. What is generally missing is the meaning of the group to the evaluator, especially in contrast to other groups [see Tyler & Blader (2000) as an exception]. Circumscribing the moral community underlying justice evaluations has at least two consequences. First, it highlights the need to specify the conditions that activate a self-interested or relational orientation and other conditions that specify the outcomes of those orientations. Examination of such conditions may also reveal when procedural justice or distributive justice is more important. Only one study shows how structural conditions shape the impact of various types of justice for individuals' behavior in organizations (Clay-Warner et al. 2005).

Second, as a great deal of justice-related research illustrates, people's perceptions of what is just varies depending on a number of factors, including their own standards and implicit beliefs about their moral communities. Rarely, however, do investigators examine a fundamental consequence of different perceptions of justice: conflict.

SOCIAL CONFLICT: HIGHLIGHTING THE IMPACT OF THE GROUP ON JUSTICE ASSESSMENTS AND REACTIONS

"Conflict occurs when two or more interdependent actors have incompatible preferences and perceive or anticipate resistance from each other" (Lawler & Ford 1995, p. 236). Although many disputes over preferences stem unabashedly from individuals' own interests, feelings of injustice may also stimulate conflict. Conflict is potentially inherent in any situation involving the distribution of (scarce) resources. If different individuals or groups advocate divergent norms about the appropriate ways to distribute outcomes and the shape of the resulting distribution, the situation may be transformed from one focused on self-interests to one dealing with social injustice. Key to understanding that transformation is recognizing the social categories and groups to which the disputing parties belong (see Tyler et al. 1997). Despite the potential for conflict whenever individuals or groups disagree over processes or distributions, and despite the plethora of actual conflicts epitomized by policy debates, environmental battles, territory disputes, etc., until recently justice researchers had hardly studied conflict.[2]

Omission of conflict from distributive justice research stems from the theoretical assumption embedded in classic equity formulations of consensus on a particular distribution rule and from the empirical difficulty in discerning conflict stemming from self-interested disputes and conflict stemming from justice disputes. Although concern with conflict resolution fueled initial procedural justice research, the advent of the group-value model shifted emphasis to other issues (see Tyler & Lind 1988). Two attempts to analyze conditions stimulating conflict between competing distributive justice claims (Hegtvedt 1992, Lamm 1986) focus on the role of bargaining, yet justice concerns are often overlooked in negotiation research (Albin 1993).

More recently, Deutsch (2000) and Mikula & Wenzel (2000) have expanded upon the role of justice in conflict situations. Their perspectives overlap in the recognition that (*a*) perceptions of justice may be a source of conflict, (*b*) justice arguments may lead to conflict over what is just (thereby inflaming a dispute), and (*c*) securing a just resolution to the conflict may be necessary to ensure stability. Underlying these roles of justice in conflict situations are the dual assumptions that sometimes people pursue their own interests, such as when they use justice rhetoric to support their own position or to invoke it as a negotiation tactic, and that sometimes people recognize the need for justice that transcends personal or group interests.

Insofar as social conflicts are supported by normative arguments, both types of orientation likely drive the dispute. To understand the conflict, then, one must examine the beliefs and values of the interdependent actors—individuals or groups. Conflict itself is likely to highlight the group issues discussed above. At the most elementary level, the process of social categorization provides cues to individuals and groups of their own identities in relationship with others. By highlighting similarities (especially within a group) and differences (especially across groups), social categorization reveals the interests embedded in those categories and the normative principles potentially associated with those groups. In doing so, categorization begins to define moral communities that constitute the scope of justice, which in turn set the stage for injustices (Tyler et al. 1997). For example, Sunshine & Tyler (2003) show that people are more likely to cooperate with the police (and,

---

[2]In a democracy, concerns regarding exploitation and immiseration raise questions of social justice (Feagin 2001). The notion of "intergroup dialogue" may be a force to contend with such injustices (Schoem 2003). For example, issues of social justice underlie discussions of race and ethnic relations (e.g., Hare 2002), gender (e.g., Twine & Blee 2002) and economic (e.g., Kluegel & Smith 1986) inequality, international policy debates (e.g., Bystydzienski & Schacht 2002), war and strife (e.g., Long & Brecke 2003), and the impetus behind social movements (e.g., Kelly 2003). Abstract theorizing and related empirical work regarding distributive and procedural justice processes are typically not brought explicitly to bear on the discussions.

conversely, less likely to be in conflict with them) when they define the police as prototypical representations of their group's moral values. In a related vein, fair treatment by authorities may be a means to bridge differences between groups that are fueled by diversity within an organization (Huo & Tyler 2001). In such cases, authorities bring people together by creating a superordinate identity (Huo 2003).

The activation of a moral community is likely to solidify a group identity and, as a consequence, determine the comparative standard invoked to assess justice. Emphasis on differences between groups may fuel conflict, however (Tajfel & Turner 1986). The success of the group in rectifying injustice may depend on the structure and dynamics within a group (as well as processes of resource mobilization, organizational dynamics, etc.). For the group to remain cohesive requires that individuals feel as if they are valued members of the group. Moreover, procedurally just treatment and decision making ensure that individuals are more likely to comply with the requests of group leaders. Sousa & Vala (2002) show that members of an organization are more likely to accept changes, which had originally stimulated conflict, if they experience respect within the group and pride in the group. And Rahim et al. (2000) find that more fair treatment by authorities corresponds to more cooperative styles of conflict resolution.

Two examples illustrate the role of group elements in understanding conflict and justice. The affirmative action debate encourages the formation of interest groups based on race or gender (Beaton & Tougas 2001). It is no surprise that minority group members and women will advocate the principle because it ensures them greater access to jobs. Yet, some research indicates that white men do not perceive affirmative action as detrimental for their career opportunities or more generally unjust (Parker et al. 1997). Such views demonstrate impartiality that ensures justice beyond individual interests.

Environmental justice disputes (e.g., Bullard & Wright 1992, Hartley 1995, Perrolle 1993) draw lines between individuals who are disadvantaged by the location of toxic dumps or incinerators, workplace risks, global warming, etc., and those in the business community who benefit from them. Some environmentalists also see themselves as invested in protecting natural resources from developers who seek their own gains under the auspices of increasing economic production. Each side represents different viewpoints, which affect what they perceive as the scope of justice. Yet the conflicts are rarely simple. Pellow et al. (2001) argue that environmental inequality involves actors with cross-cutting allegiances. Such work highlights the implications of multiple identities for understanding justice evaluations, as well as the impact of changes over time in perceptions of and responses to injustice.

CONCLUSION: BRINGING THE GROUP BACK IN

By avoiding the investigation of conflict situations, justice researchers readily confine their focus to the individual. After all, the individual is the processor of information, the evaluator of a situation as just or unjust, and ultimately an actor (although, perhaps, in conjunction with other actors). With conflict situations, however, it is necessary to analyze the perceptions, evaluations, and actions of at least two actors. Such a dyad is an embryonic group. Certainly one direct way to bring the group back into justice analysis is to theorize about and empirically examine conflict situations. Yet because of the inherent importance of the group to justice per se, future research must go beyond the bounds of current paradigms.

First, given the conceptual ambiguity between individual deserving and justice per se, researchers might contrast beliefs about justice for self with beliefs about justice for others. In doing so, studies may also examine the impact of different orientations and situational conditions on the salience of different types of justice, perceptions of justice, and types of reactions to injustice.

Second, related to justice standards, group structure, and group identity is the concern for the scope of justice. Understanding how people perceive the boundaries of groups that are the recipients of benefits or burdens facilitates prediction of when conflict may emerge and, potentially, how individuals will respond to differences in what is perceived as just.

And, third, researchers may pursue several avenues of study on the specific roles of the group in justice research. The process by which individuals select their comparisons and combine multiple comparisons remains to be developed further, both theoretically and empirically. Researchers who have focused on group structure define relationships in terms of sentiment, yet the impact of classical structural elements like power and status is hardly known beyond the work in procedural justice on authority relationships. With regard to group identity, the issue of multiple identities requires systematic examination, especially in terms of the effect on defining the scope of justice and resolving conflict. Finally, despite origins of distributive justice research in the social exchange tradition, more work on the impact of the dynamics of group processes is needed. By allowing groups to realize that individual members have different perceptions of justice, discussion of those differences may provide a basis for understanding how groups develop justice principles, the legitimacy of those principles, and how conflict over justice is resolved.

By examining "social justice in a diverse society," Tyler et al. (1997) elevate justice research to concerns beyond the individual. Their book and this review accentuate the roles of the group in justice analysis. By doing so, individuals may come to recognize interests beyond their own in order to ensure a more just society.

ACKNOWLEDGMENTS

I thank Karen Cook, Marty Kaplan, and two anonymous reviewers for their helpful comments on earlier versions of this paper and Ashby Walker for her research assistance.

The *Annual Review of Sociology* is online at http://soc.annualreviews.org

LITERATURE CITED

Adams JS. 1965. Inequity in social exchange. *Adv. Exp. Soc. Psychol.* 2:267–99

Albin C. 1993. The role of fairness in negotiation. *Negot. J.* 9:223–44

Barry B. 1989. *Theories of Justice.* Berkeley: Univ. Calif. Press

Beaton AM, Tougas F. 2001. Reactions to affirmative action: group membership and social justice. *Soc. Justice Res.* 14:61–78

Berger J, Zelditch M Jr, Anderson B, Cohen BP. 1972. Structural aspects of distributive justice: a status value formation. In *Sociological Theories in Progress*, ed. J Berger, M Zelditch Jr, B Anderson, pp. 119–46. Boston: Houghton Mifflin

Bierhoff H, Cohen RL, Greenberg J, eds. 1986. *Justice in Social Relations.* New York: Plenum

Brewer MB, Silver MD. 2000. Group distinctiveness, social identification, and collective mobilization. In *Self, Identity, and Social Movements*, ed. S Stryker, T Owens, RW White, pp. 153–71. Minneapolis: Univ. Minnesota Press

Bullard RD, Wright BH. 1992. The quest for environmental equity: mobilizing the African-American community for social change. In *American Environmentalism*, ed. RE Dunlap, AG Mertig, pp. 39–50. Philadelphia, PA: Taylor & Francis

Bystydzienski JM, Schacht SP, eds. 2002. *Forging Radical Alliances Across Difference: Coalition Politics for the New Millennium.* Lanham, MD: Rowman & Littlefield

Clark MS. 1984. Record keeping in two types of relationships. *J. Pers. Soc. Psychol.* 47:549–57

Clay-Warner J. 2001. Perceiving procedural injustice: the effects of group membership and status. *Soc. Psychol. Q.* 64:224–38

Clay-Warner J, Hegtvedt KA, Roman P. 2005. Procedural justice, distributive justice: how experiences with downsizing condition their impact on organizational commitment. *Soc. Psychol. Q.* 68:89–102

Cohen RL. 1979. On the distinction between individual deserving and distributive justice. *J. Theory Soc. Behav.* 9:167–85

Cohen RL. 1991. Membership, intergroup relations, and justice. In *Social Justice in Human Relations:* Volume 1: *Societal and Psychological Origins of Justice*, ed. R Vermunt, H Steensma, pp. 239–58. New York: Plenum

Cook KS, Emerson RM. 1978. Power, equity, and commitment in exchange networks. *Am. Sociol. Rev.* 43:721–39

Cook KS, Fine GA, House JS, eds. 1995. *Sociological Perspectives on Social Psychology.* Boston: Allyn Bacon

Cook KS, Hegtvedt KA. 1983. Distributive justice, equity, and equality. *Annu. Rev. Sociol.* 9:217–41

Cook KS, Hegtvedt KA. 1986. Justice and power. See Bierhoff et al. 1986, pp. 19–41

De Cremer D. 2002. Respect and cooperation in social dilemmas: the importance of feeling included. *Pers. Soc. Psychol. Bull.* 28:1335–41

Deutsch M. 1975. Equity, equality, and need: What determines which value will be used as the basis for distributive justice? *J. Soc. Issues* 31:137–49

Deutsch M. 1985. *Distributive Justice: A Social Psychological Perspective.* New Haven, CT: Yale Univ. Press

Deutsch M. 2000. Justice and conflict. In *The Handbook of Conflict Resolution: Theory and Practice*, ed. M Deutsch, PT Coleman, pp. 141–64. San Francisco: Jossey-Bass

Feagin JR. 2001. Social justice and sociology: agendas for the twenty-first century. *Am. Sociol. Rev.* 66:1–20

Feather NT. 1994. Human values and their relation to justice. *J. Soc. Issues* 50:129–51

Feather NT. 1999. *Values, Achievement, and Justice: Studies in the Psychology of Deserving*. New York: Kluwer Academic/Plenum

Frohlich N, Oppenheimer JA. 1992. *Choosing Justice: An Experimental Approach to Ethical Theory*. Berkeley: Univ. Calif. Press

Frohlich N, Oppenheimer JA, Eavey CL. 1987. Choices of principles of distributive justice in experimental groups. *Am. J. Pol. Sci.* 31:606–36

Greenberg J, Cohen RL. 1982. Why justice? Normative and instrumental interpretations. In *Equity and Justice in Social Behavior*, ed. J Greenberg, RL Cohen, pp. 437–69. New York: Academic

Hare BR, ed. 2001. *Race Odyssey: African Americans and Sociology*. New York: Syracuse Univ. Press

Hareli S. 1999. Justice and deservingness judgments—refuting the interchangeability assumption. *New Ideas Psychol.* 17:183–93

Hartley TW. 1995. Environmental justice: an environmental civil rights value acceptable to all world views. *Environ. Ethics* 17:277–89

Hegtvedt KA. 1992. Bargaining for justice: a means to resolve competing justice claims. *Soc. Justice Res.* 5:155–72

Hegtvedt KA, Brezina T, Funk S. 1995. *When cries of 'it's not fair' are not fair: factors affecting the negotiated resolution of justice conflict*. Presented at Annu. Meet. Am. Sociol. Assoc., Washington, DC

Hegtvedt KA, Clay-Warner J, Johnson C. 2003. The social context of responses to injustice: considering the indirect and direct effects of group-level factors. *Soc. Justice Res.* 16:343–66

Hegtvedt KA, Johnson C. 2000. Justice beyond the individual: a future with legitimation. *Soc. Psychol. Q.* 63:298–311

Hegtvedt KA, Markovsky B. 1995. Justice and injustice. See Cook et al. 1995, pp. 257–80

Hogg MA, Abrams D. 1988. *Social Identifications*. London: Routledge

Hogg MA, Abrams D, eds. 2001. *Intergroup Relations: Essential Readings*. Philadelphia, PA: Psychology Press

Homans GC. 1974. *Social Behavior: Its Elementary Forms*. New York: Harcourt, Brace and World

Huo YJ. 2003. Procedural justice and social regulation across group boundaries: Does subgroup identity undermine relationship-based governance? *Pers. Soc. Psychol. Bull.* 29:336–48

Huo YJ, Tyler TR. 2001. Ethnic diversity and the viability of organizations: the role of procedural justice in bridging differences. In *Advances in Organizational Justice*, ed. J Greenberg, R Cropanzano, pp. 213–44. Stanford, CA: Stanford Univ. Press

Jasso G. 1980. A new theory of distributive justice. *Am. Sociol. Rev.* 45:3–32

Jasso G. 1983. Fairness of individual rewards and fairness of the reward distribution: specifying the inconsistency between micro and macro principles of justice. *Soc. Psychol. Q.* 46:185–99

Jasso G. 2002. Formal theory. In *Handbook of Sociological Theory*, ed. JH Turner, pp. 37–68. New York: Kluwer Academic/Plenum

Johnson CJ, Ford R. 1996. Dependence power, legitimacy, and tactical choice. *Soc. Psychol. Q.* 59:126–39

Jost JT, Major B, eds. 2001. *The Psychology of Legitimacy: Emerging Perspectives on Ideology, Justice, and Intergroup Relations*. Cambridge, UK: Cambridge Univ. Press

Kahn A, Nelson RE, Gaeddert WP, Hearn JL. 1982. The justice process: deciding upon equity or equality. *Soc. Psychol. Q.* 45:3–8

Kayser E, Schwinger T, Cohen RL. 1984. Lay persons' conceptions of social relationships: a test of contract theory. *J. Soc. Pers. Rel.* 1:433–58

Kelly CA. 2003. *Tangled Up in Red, White, and Blue: New Social Movements in America*. Lanham, MD: Rowman & Littlefield

Kluegel JR, Smith ER. 1986. *Beliefs About Inequality*. New York: Aldine

Lalonde RN, Silverman RA. 1994. Behavioral preferences in response to social injustice: the effects of group permeability and social identity salience. *J. Pers. Soc. Psychol.* 66:78–85

Lamm H. 1986. Justice consideration in interpersonal conflict. See Bierhoff et al. 1986, pp. 43–63

Lawler EJ, Ford R. 1995. Bargaining. See Cook et al. 1995, pp. 236–56

Lerner MJ, Miller DT, Holmes JG. 1976. Deserving and the emergence of forms of justice. *Adv. Exp. Soc. Psychol.* 9:133–62

Leventhal GS, Karuza J Jr, Fry WR. 1980. Beyond fairness: a theory of allocation preferences. In *Justice and Social Interaction*, ed. G Mikula, pp. 167–218. New York: Springer-Verlag

Lind EA, Kray L, Thompson L. 1998. The social construction of injustice: fairness judgments in response to own and others' unfair treatment by authorities. *Org. Behav. Hum. Decis. Process* 75:1–22

Lind EA, Tyler TR. 1988. *The Social Psychology of Procedural Justice.* New York: Plenum

Long WJ, Brecke P. 2003. *War and Reconciliation: Reason and Emotion in Conflict Resolution.* Cambridge, MA: MIT Press

Major B, Deaux K. 1982. Individual differences in justice behavior. In *Equity and Justice in Social Behavior*, ed. J Greenberg, RL Cohen, pp. 43–76. New York: Plenum

Markovsky B. 1985. Toward a multilevel distributive justice theory. *Am. Sociol. Rev.* 50: 822–39

Messick DM, Sentis KP. 1979. Fairness and preference. *J. Exp. Soc. Psychol.* 15:416–34

Mikula G, Wenzel M. 2000. Justice and social conflict. *Internat. J. Psychol.* 35:126–35

Molm LD, Cook KS. 1995. Social exchange and exchange networks. See Cook et al. 1995, pp. 209–35

Molm LD, Peterson G, Takahashi N. 2003. In the eye of the beholder: procedural justice in social exchange. *Am. Sociol. Rev.* 68:128–52

Molm LD, Quist TM, Wiseley PA. 1993. Reciprocal justice and strategies of exchange. *Soc. Forces* 72:19–44

Molm LD, Quist TM, Wiseley PA. 1994. Imbalanced structures, unfair strategies: power

and justice in social exchange. *Am. Sociol. Rev.* 59:98–121

Optow S. 1990. Moral exclusion and injustice: an introduction. *J. Soc. Issues* 46:1–20

Otten S, Mummendey A. 1999. To our benefit or at your expense? Justice considerations in intergroup allocations of positive and negative resources. *Soc. Justice Res.* 12:19–38

Parker CP, Baltes BB, Christiansen ND. 1997. Support for affirmative action, justice perceptions, and work attitudes: a study of gender and racial-ethnic group differences. *J. Appl. Psychol.* 82:376–89

Pellow DN, Weinberg A, Schnaiberg A. 2001. The environmental justice movement: equitable allocation of the costs and benefits of environmental management outcomes. *Soc. Justice Res.* 14:423–39

Perrolle JA. 1993. The emerging dialogue on environmental justice. *Soc. Probl.* 40:1–4

Rahim MA, Magner NR, Shapiro DL. 2000. Do justice perceptions influence styles of handling conflict with supervisor? What justice perceptions, precisely? *Int. J. Conflict Manag.* 11:9–31

Rawls J. 1971. *A Theory of Justice.* Boston: Harvard Univ. Press

Reis HT. 1986. Levels of interest in the study of interpersonal justice. See Bierhoff et al. 1986, pp. 187–209

Schoem D. 2003. Intergroup dialogue for a just and diverse democracy. *Sociol. Inq.* 73:212–27

Sousa F, Vala J. 2002. Relational justice in organizations: the group-value model and support for change. *Soc. Justice Res.* 15:99–121

Stolte JF. 1983. The legitimation of structural inequality: reformulation and test of the self-evaluation argument. *Am. Sociol. Rev.* 48: 331–42

Sunshine J, Tyler TR. 2003. Moral solidarity, identification with the community, and the importance of procedural justice: the police as prototypical representatives of a group's moral values. *Soc. Psychol. Q.* 66:153–65

Tajfel H, Turner J. 1979. An integrative theory

of intergroup conflict. In *Psychology of Intergroup Relations*, ed. WG Austin, S Worchel, pp. 33–47. Monterey, CA: Brooks/Cole

Tajfel H, Turner J. 1986. The social identity theory of intergroup behavior. In *Psychology of Intergroup Relations*, ed. S Worchel, WG Austin, pp. 7–24. Chicago: Nelson Hall. Rev. ed.

Thompson L, Loewenstein G. 1992. Egocentric interpretations of fairness and interpersonal conflict. *Org. Behav. Hum. Decis. Process* 51:176–97

Tjosvold D. 1977. Commitment to justice in conflict between unequal status persons. *J. Appl. Soc. Psychol.* 7:149–62

Törnblom KY. 1977. Distributive justice: typology and propositions. *Hum. Rel.* 31:1–24

Törnblom KY. 1992. The social psychology of distributive justice. In *Justice: Interdisciplinary Perspectives*, ed. K Scherer, pp. 177–236. Cambridge, UK: Cambridge Univ. Press

Twine FW, Blee KM, eds. 2002. *Feminism and Anti-Racism: International Struggles for Justice*. New York: NY Univ. Press

Tyler TR. 1994. Psychological models of the justice motive: antecedents of distributive and procedural justice. *J. Pers. Soc. Psychol.* 67:850–63

Tyler TR, Blader SL. 2000. *Cooperation in Groups: Procedural Justice, Social Identity, and Behavioral Engagement*. Philadelphia, PA: Psychology Press/Taylor & Francis

Tyler TR, Boeckmann RJ, Smith HJ, Huo YJ. 1997. *Social Justice in a Diverse Society*. Boulder, CO: Westview

Tyler TR, Lind EA. 1990. Intrinsic versus community-based justice models: When does group membership matter? *J. Soc. Issues* 46:83–94

Tyler TR, Lind EA. 1992. A relational model of authority in groups. *Adv. Exp. Soc. Psychol.* 25:115–91

Tyler TR, Smith HJ. 1999. Justice, social identity, and group processes. In *The Psychology of the Social Self: Applied Social Research*, ed. TR Tyler, RM Kramer, pp. 223–64. Mahwah, NJ: Lawrence Erlbaum

van den Bos KE, Lind EA, Wilke HAM. 2001. The psychology of procedural and distributive justice viewed from the perspective of fairness heuristic theory. In *Justice in the Workplace*, ed. R Cropanzano, pp. 49–66. Mahwah, NJ: Lawrence Erlbaum

Wagner D. 1995. Gender differences in reward preference: a status-based account. *Small Group Res.* 26:353–71

Wagstaff GF. 1994. Equity, equality, and need: three principles of justice or one? An analysis of 'equity as desert.' *Current Psychol.* 13:138–52

Walker HA, Zelditch Jr. M 1993. Power, legitimacy, and the stability of authority: a theoretical research program. In *Theoretical Research Programs*, ed. J Berger, M Zelditch Jr, pp. 364–81. Stanford, CA: Stanford Univ. Press

Walster E, Walster GW, Berscheid E. 1978. *Equity: Theory and Research*. Boston: Allyn and Bacon

Wenzel M. 2002. What is social about justice? Inclusive identity and group values as the basis of the justice motive. *J. Exp. Soc. Psychol.* 38:205–18

Wenzel M. 2003. Social identification as a determinant of concerns about individual-, group-, and inclusive-level justice. *Soc. Psychol. Q.* 67:70–87

Zelditch M, Jr. 2001. Processes of legitimation: recent developments and new directions. *Soc. Psychol. Q.* 64:4–17

Zelditch M, Jr, Walker HA. 1984. Legitimacy and the stability of authority. *Adv. Group Process.* 1:1–25

Annu. Rev. Sociol. 2005. 31:47–74
doi: 10.1146/annurev.soc.29.010202.100054
Copyright © 2005 by Annual Reviews. All rights reserved
First published online as a Review in Advance on February 11, 2005

IDENTITY POLITICS

Mary Bernstein

*Department of Sociology, University of Connecticut, Storrs, Connecticut 06269-2068;
email: Mary.Bernstein@uconn.edu*

Key Words   social movements, collective identity, protest, culture and politics,
activism

■ **Abstract**   This review presents an overview of research on identity politics. First,
I distinguish between various approaches to defining identity politics and the challenges presented by each approach. In the process, I show that these approaches reflect
competing theoretical understandings of the relationship between experience, culture,
identity, politics, and power. These debates raise theoretical issues that I address in the
second section, including (*a*) how to understand the relationship between personal experience and political stance, (*b*) why status identities are understood and/or portrayed
as essentialist or socially constructed, (*c*) the strategic dilemmas activists face when
the identities around which a movement is organized are also the basis for oppression,
(*d*) when to attribute certain movement outcomes to status identities, and (*e*) how to link
collective action to specific notions of power to help explain the cultural and political
goals at which identity politics is aimed. I conclude by recommending some promising
avenues for future research.

INTRODUCTION

The term identity politics is widely used throughout the social sciences and the humanities to describe phenomena as diverse as multiculturalism, the women's movement, civil rights, lesbian and gay movements, separatist movements in Canada
and Spain, and violent ethnic and nationalist conflict in postcolonial Africa and
Asia, as well as in the formerly communist countries of Eastern Europe. The seeds
of these partially overlapping conversations are apparent from the very first uses
of the term identity politics in the scholarly journals. In 1979, Anspach first used
the term identity politics to refer to activism by people with disabilities to transform both self- and societal conceptions of people with disabilities. Over the next
decade, only three scholarly journal articles employed the term identity politics in
their abstracts, to describe (*a*) ethnicity as a contemporary form of politics (Ross
1982); (*b*) a form of critical pedagogy that links social structure with the insights
of poststructuralism regarding the nature of subjectivity, while incorporating a
Marxist commitment to politics (Bromley 1989); and (*c*) general efforts by status-
based movements to foster and explore the cultural identity of members (Connolly

1990). By the mid-1990s, references to identity politics as violent ethnic conflict (Meznaric 1993), and nationalism more generally (Alund 1995), emerged.

In addition to using the term identity politics to describe any mobilization related to politics, culture, and identity, scholarly analyses have often elided normative political evaluations of identity politics as a political practice with sociological analyses of the relationship between identity and politics. Brubaker & Cooper (2000) argue that the literature on identity politics has too many protagonists and not enough analysts. Lichterman (1999) calls identity politics "a slippery term" (p. 136), while Bickford (1997) claims that the concept has developed more as a critique of certain political practices than as a coherent area of study. Fraser (1997, p. 113) concludes that "the expression 'identity politics' is increasingly used as a derogatory synonym for feminism, anti-racism, and anti-heterosexism."

This review shows that beneath the normative political claims about identity politics lie competing theoretical ways to understand the relationship between experience, culture, identity, politics, and power. Although I occasionally reference multiculturalism and ethnic/nationalist movements and suggest some benefits to research that crosses these divides, I focus this review on research that views identity politics as the activism engaged in by status-based social movements and do not address those movements based on ethnic/nationalist status.[1]

In the first section, I examine approaches to defining identity politics as a distinct political practice, including neo-Marxist and more general works that distinguish identity politics from class politics; new social movement approaches that differentiate class-based movements from other movements; and postmodern/poststructuralist analyses that view identity politics as political activism rather than cultural activism. This discussion illustrates that substantial disagreement exists over what constitutes identity politics, but it also raises a focused set of research questions that are addressed in the second section. While acknowledging the role identity plays in all social movements, I emphasize research that examines the specific processes that arise when a movement's identity is, to some extent, externally imposed and forms part of the basis for grievances. These studies examine how to understand the relationship between personal experience and political stance, why status identities are understood and/or portrayed as essentialist or socially constructed, the strategic dilemmas movement organizers face when the identities around which a movement is organized are also the basis for oppression, when to attribute certain movement outcomes to status identities, and how to link collective action to specific notions of power to help explain the cultural and political goals at which identity politics is aimed. Similar processes may operate when other movement identities become the basis for external categorization

---

[1]Owing to space limitations, I cannot do justice to the wealth of literature on ethnic/ nationalist movements, although in the conclusion, I suggest the benefits of comparing ethnic/nationalist movements with movements organized around other social statuses. For recent reviews of nationalism and nationalist movements, see Calhoun (1993a), Brubaker & Laitin (1998), and Olzak (2004).

and are thus relevant for anyone concerned with explaining efforts to alleviate inequality or with understanding the relationships between identity and politics. Although the term identity politics itself may not be salvageable as an analytic concept, the questions raised in this literature deserve more concerted sociological attention. I conclude by recommending some promising avenues for future research.

APPROACHES TO DEFINING IDENTITY POLITICS

Neo-Marxist Approaches to Identity Politics

The approaches to identity politics that I group together in this section are concerned with the macro-level issues regarding what constitutes power and what are the forces of oppression. Although many of the works discussed here are not explicitly Marxist or neo-Marxist, and many of the authors themselves would eschew this label, these works evoke at least one of two key theoretical assumptions associated with Marxist and neo-Marxist theory. First, these views rest on a (sometimes implicit) theory of power that views class inequality as the only real source of exploitation and oppression. Second, many of these works view activists who want to alleviate economic inequality and to challenge the class structure as the primary agents of social change. Because of these theoretical assumptions, identity politics is not seen as a political practice that challenges important relations of power, but is understood in symbolic, cultural, or psychological terms. As a result, this literature sometimes makes normative political claims that dismiss the value of identity politics. Theoretically, these analyses separate culture from institutions, politics, and the economy, rather than view culture as constitutive, structuring, and constraining of institutions (Polletta 2002, Swidler 1995, Williams 2004). As Sewell (1992, p. 3) more generally observes, structure is "thought of as 'hard' or 'material' and therefore as primary and determining, whereas culture is regarded as 'soft' or 'mental' and therefore as secondary or derived." As a result, these accounts do not see class as an identity that has a dynamic cultural or psychological aspect; hence, identity politics is viewed as a distinct political practice in contradistinction to class politics. Similarly, identities based on social rather than economic status are not seen as having institutional or economic aspects, and the intersections between class and status identities are ignored.

IDENTITY POLITICS AS CULTURAL POLITICS   In contrast to the logic of Marxist and neo-Marxist theory, social movements that emerged in the 1960s and 1970s, such as the civil rights and women's movements, seemed to be more concerned with culture and identity than with challenging the class structure. With these movements in mind, Kauffman (1990, p. 67) defined identity politics in cultural terms as expressing "the belief that identity itself—its elaboration, expression, or affirmation—is and should be a fundamental focus of political work;" identity politics politicized areas of life not previously defined as political, including "sexuality, interpersonal relations, lifestyle and culture." Kauffman is one of the few in this group who distinguishes between cultural claims related to institutions and structures and efforts geared toward personal expression and self-transformation. While seeing some merit to the former, Kauffman (1990) dismisses the latter as irrelevant and self-indulgent cultural activism. Most others who view class inequality as the primary source of exploitation and oppression do not distinguish among different types of cultural activism. Instead, all claims related to social identities are considered to be "cultural politics" and are equated with and dismissed as identity politics (Gitlin 1994, 1995).

Identity politics is assumed to be cultural not only because identity is putatively unrelated to institutional structures and the political economy, but also because these scholars see identity groups as advocating for recognition of and respect for their cultural differences, which derive from their distinct group identities. They assume that activists organized around status identities understand these identities with their associated cultures in essentialist rather than socially constructed terms. Therefore, these scholars are critical of what they view as activists' equating identity groups with a culture, and they question what forms the basis for that culture. For example, Brown (1995) argues that marginalization forms the basis for the culture of identity groups. She contends that advocating for rights based on marginalized cultural identities will only lead to the increased social regulation of those groups by dominant groups that control the state. Employing language that suggests a normative evaluation, Gitlin (1995) claims that "identity politics" on college campuses is "the recognition of a collective hurt, followed by the mistaking of group position for a 'culture,' followed by the mistaking of a 'culture' for a politics" (pp. 147–48). Feher (1996) suggests that drawing from identity politics, the political right has also adopted a language of victimhood. Macedo (1995) and Spragens (1999) contend that equating identity groups with a culture is patently false and potentially dangerous because it could lead to the recognition and validation of, for example, white racist groups who portray themselves as defending a denigrated culture.

However, such views rest on untested assumptions about how activists understand their identities, ignoring relationships among identity, institutions, and the political economy. Bickford (1997) argues that this danger of a "subjectivity" rooted in ressentiment does not characterize most of the political uses of identity, and it ignores feminist theory on identity politics. Philosophers Taylor (1989), Young (1990), and Kymlicka (1995) illustrate that admitting the socially constructed nature of group differences does not preclude organizing around the identities that mark those groups. They acknowledge that cultural differences among groups are socially constructed, resulting from shared histories of oppression. Nonetheless, they contend that these differences create distinct social groups, which justifies demands for group-differentiated citizenship rights and challenges to negative representations. Because these identity groups share a history of oppression, granting them official recognition does not entail also giving such recognition to antidemocratic groups.

Epstein (1995) argues that identity politics' concern with language and representation as well as its challenge to the notion that any one social actor will spark a historical transformation accounts for its association with postmodernism in the academy (e.g., Wrong 2003, Bell 2001, Gitlin 1995). Scholarly and nonscholarly journals as well as the popular press equate identity politics with multiculturalism and "political correctness" on college campuses (e.g., Hollander 1996, Spragens 1999). Epstein suggests that the term political correctness is used primarily as a way to attack racial inclusion efforts and curricular reform on campuses, while at the same time promote a specific set of conservative values. Nonetheless, she contends that identity politics' concern with language and representation tends toward moralizing, which opens it to derision by critics. Smelser & Alexander (1999) see this as a debate between "radical multiculturalists," who identify diversity rather than common values as the highest moral good, and their "traditional values" opponents, who view society as fragmented into multiple identity groups that have undermined the common cultural fabric of American society. Smelser & Alexander (1999) argue that this "discourse of discontent," which indicates widespread crisis and polarization, obscures the integrative processes of institutionalizing diversity that take place in a variety of institutions and are reflected through daily social practices. The essays in their collection (Smelser & Alexander 1999) document how diversity is institutionalized and practiced.

CONSEQUENCES OF IDENTITY POLITICS   Analysts associate a number of problems with identity politics. They contend that the essentialism of identity politics precludes the articulation of a universal vision for social change, such as the New Left had done, instead making particularistic claims for group-based benefits and leading to the decline of the left. They claim that because identity groups tend to splinter into ever more narrow categories, they cannot agree on or sustain anything but opposition to a common enemy. For example, by targeting white heterosexual men, identity politics leaves them no space to participate politically, which results in an unproductive defensiveness. Such politics leads to an inability to form coalitions that can agitate for progressive or revolutionary social change (Kauffman 1990; Gitlin 1994, 1995; Harvey 1996; Hobsbawm 1996; Piore 1995).

However, these studies generally do not consider other possible explanations for these outcomes. Thus, many of the deleterious outcomes associated with identity politics come from studies that ignore cases in which claiming essentialist differences is a strategic maneuver made by activists rather than an ontological position. These studies also ignore cases in which groups may adopt essentialist perspectives but may nonetheless create a universal vision for social change, form coalitions, and work with white heterosexual men. Furthermore, these studies often generalize from a specific case to make claims about all cases of identity politics.

Bickford (1997) argues that achieving commonality does not depend on a tradeoff between commitment to one's group and a commitment to the broader social good, "but rather on acting together in ways that could *create* a democratic commons—one that is plural, egalitarian, and communicative" (p. 124). Ryan

(1997) argues that the crisis over identity politics in the women's movement is overstated because multicultural organizing efforts often recognize the value of separate organizing by groups that face racism, sexism, homophobia, classism, and heterosexism. In short, research on identity politics must consider alternative causal explanations for a variety of outcomes and must not take the public claims of activists at face value.

CLASS POLITICS VERSUS IDENTITY POLITICS   Although he agrees that identity politics is psychological in nature, Wrong (2003) sees the contemporary rise of identity politics as a product of economic well-being and the lack of viable alternatives to capitalism, whereas Langman (1994) sees it as a misplaced response to rapid social change resulting from economic dislocation. Both Wrong (2003) and Bell (2001) suggest that an economic downturn could provoke renewed attention to class-based politics, which implies that identity politics would decline in the face of "real" issues related to the political economy. For Wrong (2003), the emphasis on diversity and cultural identities is a new incarnation of a pervasive American search for community, particularly in the face of popular culture and consumerism. Piore (1995), by contrast, views identity politics as responding to stigmatization, but, more importantly, "these new groups have also been fostered by governmental and business policies designed [to] escape the constraints of existing social structures, particularly unions" (p. 19). Thus, the claims of identity politics have replaced collective bargaining and have undermined the trade union movement. Because, according to Piore (1995), these identity groups are unrelated to economic structures, they fail to see how the economy constrains the country's ability to meet the group's demands, such as daycare. Once again, claims about the relationship between identity politics and organizing around social class are simply asserted, rather than tested empirically. Furthermore, Piore's (1995) examples of issues targeted by identity groups [daycare and health care (p. 27), for example] imply that some relationship exists between identity groups and the political economy, in contrast to his own assertions.

Some critics argue that the cultural left (a term often used interchangeably with identity politics) has decreased the "sadism" (Rorty 1998, p. 83) of sexism, racism, and homophobia in America. But this view also holds that identity politics has forsaken issues related to exploitation, class, poverty, and globalization that exacerbate economic inequality (Bourne 1987, Gitlin 1995, Rorty 1998, Walzer 1996). For example, Wolfe & Klausen (1997) argue that identity politics' symbolic concerns regarding language and representation lead activists to advocate more open immigration policies to increase the population of a particular ethnic/racial identity group, which undermines the capacity of the welfare state to provide for its members. Furthermore, they claim that affirmative action and racial redistricting inhibit the development of national citizenship by fostering a commitment to the solidarity of subgroups and are thus antithetical to the health of the welfare state.

Neo-Marxist analyses of identity politics have also been challenged on both historical and theoretical grounds. These critics reverse the causal arrow and attribute the emergence of identity politics to failures of the New Left, arguing that the language of and appeals to commonality by the left are in practice exclusionary. The left has been unable (or unwilling) to adequately address the inequality associated with gender, race, and sexual orientation (Bickford 1997, Lott 1999, Roper 1994, Ryan 2001). For example, Rossinow (1998) examines how conceptions of whiteness and masculinity animated the New Left, and precluded an analysis of inequality that included race and gender. He also argues that state policies led to the New Left's decline. In this view, identity politics is not responsible for fragmenting and hardening the boundaries between groups. Rather, as Rossinow (1998) argues, there are continuities between the quest for authenticity by the New Left and the search for self in identity politics (see also Boggs 1995).

Neo-Marxist approaches to identity politics can also be criticized for challenging the separation of culture from class and the political economy. For example, signifiers of class have an interactional reality that may be just as constructed as status identities and that class manifests in cultural expression (Bourdieu 1984, Calhoun 1993b, Aronowitz 1992). Similarly, sex, race, and other status identities not only have cultural dimensions and meanings but also are linked to concrete material and structural locations (Fraser 1997, Naples 2003). Feminist philosopher Fraser (1997) maintains that the division between a cultural politics of recognition and a social politics of justice and equality, on which discussions of identity politics rest, ignores the interrelatedness of socioeconomic injustice rooted in society's political-economic structure and cultural or symbolic injustice rooted in social patterns of representation, interpretation, and communication. She argues that both race and gender constitute "bivalent" collectivities—that is, groups affected by both the political economy and the cultural-valuational structure of society. For example, race structures the division of labor between low-paid menial labor and domestic work on the one hand and professional-managerial jobs disproportionately held by whites on the other. Thus, capitalist exploitation takes place in gender- and race-specific ways. Yet, Eurocentrism also devalues people of color, and racist stereotypes persist independently of the political economy, although the two types of injustice reinforce each other dialectically. She suggests that redistributive remedies generally necessitate some sort of recognition of groups whom the redistribution will affect and that maintaining nonexclusionary identities would require shifts in the political economy.

These debates raise a number of important theoretical issues, including: How should oppression that is not related to social class be conceptualized? What is the causal role of identity in determining a variety of movement outcomes, such as the ability to form coalitions or the decline of the New Left? In what ways is identity a part of all social movements?

The New Social Movement Approach to Identity Politics

New social movement (NSM) theory moves beyond the parameters of Marxist frameworks to understand the variety of social movements that emerged in the

1960s and 1970s that were not ostensibly organized around social class. Although NSM theory does not employ the language of identity politics [even if some NSM theorists refer to it as an "identity-oriented" paradigm (e.g., Touraine 1981)], it represents the first concerted theoretical effort to understand the role of identity in social movements, and it ultimately provoked the more rationalist strands of social movement theory, resource mobilization, and political process theory, to attend to issues of identity and culture. Like social movement theory more generally, NSM theory attempted to explain mobilization—that is, why and when people act. By taking this approach, NSM theory displaced the assumption that activism based on anything other than class was epiphenomena or psychologically rooted, raising the possibility of alternative causal explanations for identity politics. NSM theory both challenges and affirms the idea that identity politics is a distinct political practice.

Whereas Marxist and neo-Marxist frameworks distinguish class politics and oppression from other possible sources of politics and oppression, NSM theory distinguishes class-based movements, especially past labor and socialist movements, from contemporary movements organized on the basis of ideology and values, such as the peace, environmental, youth, and antinuclear movements, as well as movements organized around status (Melucci 1985, 1989; see review in Johnston et al. 1994). NSM theory views these movements as historically new forms of collective action resulting from the macrostructural changes of modernization (Melucci 1989) and a shift to a postindustrial society (Touraine 1981). These macrostructural changes produced postmaterial values concerned with achieving democracy rather than with economic survival (Inglehart 1981, 1990). Thus, new social movements were viewed as efforts to regain control over decisions and areas of life increasingly subject to state control, to resist the colonization of the lifeworld, and to transform civil society (Habermas 1985, Cohen 1985, Melucci 1989). NSM theory views these movements as efforts to "fight to expand freedom, not to achieve it; they mobilize for choice rather than emancipation," and focus primarily on expressing identity (Cerulo 1997, p. 393) to seek "recognition for new identities and lifestyles" (Polletta & Jasper 2001, p. 286). NSMs are said to advocate direct democracy, employ disruptive tactics, and enact the democratic organizational forms they seek to achieve (Pichardo 1997). According to Melucci (1996), NSMs challenge dominant normative and cultural codes, and identity politics in particular evokes the question of how difference is dealt with in a given society. Thus, NSM theory identifies a broader purpose for identity politics and does not dismiss it for being "merely" cultural, symbolic, or psychological.

However, NSM theory continues to separate identity and culture from the political economy. For example, Duyvendak & Giugni (1995) and Duyvendak (1995) argue that movements such as the lesbian and gay movement are internally oriented and follow an "identity" logic of action, so that their goals are realized in their expressive actions, which are aimed simply at reproducing the identity on which the movement is based.

NSM theory has been criticized for ignoring conservative social movements that could also be considered NSMs (Pichardo 1997) because of these movements' concern with identity, culture, and values. Thus, NSM theory edges into normative political evaluations of identity politics. For example, Touraine (1998) makes an ontological distinction between identity politics and NSMs. He does not regard movements such as the women's and lesbian movements as identity politics because they have radical and inclusive tendencies and have themselves criticized identity politics. In contrast, he does consider conservative social movements as identity politics because they respond to economic globalization and the decline of a national culture (Touraine 1998, p. 131) by forming movements based in ethnicity, religion, or nationalism, such as political Islamism or Serbian nationalism. In these cases, the new movement is divorced from both social and economic practices, so cultural values become resources that strengthen communities and "harden communalist policies" (Touraine 1998, p. 136). Thus, for Touraine, identity politics involves movements that have exclusive tendencies, rather than movements that are organized around a variety of status identities that may alternate between exclusivity and inclusivity. In this way, Touraine does not account for why some status-based movements are exclusive and others inclusive and how these orientations may change over time, but rather defines identity politics once again in a normative political fashion.

The validity of the two primary historical and comparative claims on which NSM theory rests—that such movements are a product of postindustrial society and that they differ in fundamental ways from past labor and socialist movements—has been called into question (Calhoun 1993b, Pichardo 1997, Polletta & Jasper 2001, Young 2002). NSM theorists are left the task of finding alternative causal explanations for the emergence of these movements and of reconsidering the distinction between political and cultural movements (Polletta & Jasper 2001). Despite these limits, by underscoring the similarity between movements organized on the basis of status identities and those organized around values and ideology, NSM theory challenges the view that identity politics is a distinct political practice and provides a broader conceptualization of identity politics.

Darnovsky et al. (1995b, p. xiv–xv) argue that the most important questions regarding identity politics are not addressed by NSM theory: "Why has culture become a major focus of movement concern since the 1960s? What is the relationship between culture and politics in the new movements?" Furthermore, NSM theory does not adequately address other key questions raised in the literature on identity politics regarding the relationship between identity, culture, and the political economy; whether and why status identities are understood and deployed in essentialist or constructionist ways; and what is the causal relationship between organizing based on status identities and a variety of movement consequences. To answer these questions, sociologists have drawn on social constructionism, postmodernism, and queer theory.

Social Constructionist, Postmodernist, and Poststructuralist Approaches to Identity Politics

Postmodernist analyses of identity politics conceptualize power in terms that are starkly different from neo-Marxist and NSM perspectives. In these views, the existence of status categories constitutes a form of regulation. Therefore, any activism in the name of those categories will not alleviate inequality but will reify those categories, which will increase the use of those categories to regulate and dominate subordinate status groups. Thus, identity politics hardens rather than redefines differences in status identities that are the basis for inequality. These approaches view organizing on the basis of those identities as ultimately essentialist. Instead of viewing power in terms of economic inequality, which renders organizing on the basis of status identities as primarily symbolic and cultural activism, understood through postmodern views of power, identity politics appears to be narrow, political, state-centered activism that fails to adequately address the cultural bases of power. Rather than being too cultural, identity politics is not cultural enough (Vaid 1995).

This view of identity politics is both a response to the emergence of "queer politics" in the late 1980s and a function of postmodernist and poststructuralist theories. Embodied in the short-lived group Queer Nation, queer politics was identified by scholars as the antithesis of identity politics: a theory and a politics with which to transcend group categories and to bring diverse groups of marginalized people together under one umbrella (Gamson 1995, Epstein 1998, Valocchi 1999, Warner 2000). Queer politics emerged in response to the lesbian and gay movement's dominance by middle-class gay white men and single-issue, gay-only politics. These new organizations reframed the discourse around sexual orientation as they employed novel tactics and set out to challenge the very categories of identity that had previously motivated activism. Reappropriating the word "queer" and redefining it to mean anything that contradicts dominant cultural norms, queer activists attempted to form a multiracial, multigendered movement of people with diverse sexualities (Seidman 1993, Epstein 1998).

Observers of queer politics looked to postmodernism, poststructuralism, and Foucauldian understandings of sexuality and identity (e.g., Foucault 1978) to explain these new forms of organizing. Seidman (1993, 1997) suggests that queer politics was an attempt to deconstruct the "hetero/homo" binary. Concerned with the politics of gender, Butler's (1990, 1993) theory of identity argues that gender identity is realized through the performative acts that constitute gender but do not actually reflect an inner core, in contrast to identity politics, which makes claims in the name of a subject and thus assumes that identity itself has a core. Thus, political activism in the name of a subject obscures and reifies the processes that create woman as subject and sets the conditions of subordination. If the category woman is externally imposed, then the goal of politics should be to challenge, not affirm, such identities with their associated notions of difference. Therefore, Butler (1990) theorizes a politics of performativity as a way to resist the quotidian enactment of gender. Queer politics is often understood in performative terms as challenging power and deconstructing categories and is a privileged strategy within poststructuralism (Adam 1998, Collins 1998). Within these theoretical frameworks, what seems to be purely expressive action from the purview of neo-Marxist and NSM theories is understood as a fundamental challenge to power.

In contrast to queer politics, advocating in the name of a lesbian/gay subject appears always to result in a hierarchical ordering that marks the homosexual subject as different from and less than the heterosexual subject and will not challenge heteronormativity or systemic prejudices (Dennis 1997, Bower 1997, Halley 1994). Some analysts argue that the movement for same-sex marriage constitutes a move toward normalizing monogamous lesbian and gay couples at the expense of other constellations of intimate relationships (Warner 2000, Walters 2001). In this way, the threat of diverse sexualities can be contained within conventional forms of monogamous commitment. Chasin (2000) contends that in its efforts to normalize homosexuality, lesbian and gay identity politics mistakes niche marketing to white middle-class gays as a sign of social tolerance and acceptance. By redrawing the lines of normalcy, the market exercises power (Alexander 1999) that renders lesbians and gay men of color invisible within the market and substitutes for "transformative" cultural change (Chasin 2000).

Rimmerman (2002, p. 3) assesses whether the lesbian and gay movement "will merely pursue a reformist strategy embracing a narrow form of identity politics" and divides the lesbian and gay movement into two mutually exclusive groups: the assimilationists, who "typically embrace a rights-based perspective and work within the broader framework of liberal, pluralist democracy, fighting for a seat at the table," and the liberationists, who favor "more radical, cultural change, change that is transformational in nature and that often arises from outside the political mainstream" (Rimmerman 2002, p. 2). Viewed through postmodern understandings of power, identity politics constitutes narrow legal/political activism that fails to address cultural sources of oppression.

In addition to failing to challenge "real" relations of power, observers argue that identity politics does not challenge the social construction of status categories, ignores the intersection of identities, forces those with multiple identities to privilege some aspects of identity over others, fails to recognize diversity within groups, imposes a uniform identity on groups that are diverse, and essentializes a group's identity (Ryan 1997, Humphrey 1999, Phelan 1989, Alexander 1999). Others suggest that identity politics' essentialist claims can backfire. For example, Solomos (1998) argues that although appeals to authenticity and difference can be used to justify challenging dominant representations, such claims lead "to a strange convergence in the language of the racist right and of the black or ethnic nationalists, as both infuse categories such as 'race' or 'ethnicity' with essentialist, and supposedly naturally inherited, characteristics" (Solomos 1998, p. 52). Kimmel (1993) suggests that essentialist arguments support conservative claims by antifeminists who root their activism in an understanding of gender differences as biologically based and ignore the ways that gender organizes homosexuality.

These studies evaluate the consequences of identity politics on the basis of the studies' own theoretical assumptions about how power functions. They tend toward making normative political evaluations about identity politics because they do not explicitly identify the causal mechanisms that link identity politics to these purported outcomes, they ignore the possibility that claims to essentialism may be strategic, and they overlook the difficulties in eliminating social categories as a political strategy. For example, Anzaldua (1987) challenges the idea that identity as an organizing tool is antithetical to fostering a politics of commonality. Her concept of "borderlands" acknowledges the multiplicity of individual identities and shows their connection to fostering broad-based political organizing, thus pointing toward the need to find alternative explanations for movement fragmentation. Garza (1995) challenges the assumption that activists and theorists understand their identities as ontologically prior to their activism and suggests that a performative politics or a politics of deconstruction and decentering will not work for groups whose difference is marked on the body (Garza 1995, Collins 1998).

INTEGRATIVE APPROACHES: CONTESTING
THE TERMS OF THE DEBATE

At minimum, the challenges to neo-Marxist, NSM, and postmodern approaches to identity politics suggest what has become commonplace in social movement theory: that identity plays a role in all social movements (Friedman & McAdam 1992, Hunt et al. 1994, Robnett 1997, Rupp & Taylor 1990, Whittier 1995). In their recent review article, Polletta & Jasper (2001) explore the relationship between a variety of dynamics operative in all social movements and collective identity, defined as "an individual's cognitive, moral, and emotional connection with a broader community, category, practice or institution" (p. 285). In contrast, I emphasize research that examines movements organized on the basis of status identities that are, to varying extents, externally defined, where the identity itself forms a part of the basis for grievances. For example, although environmentalists may share a collective identity as environmentalists, that identity is not generally externally imposed or used as an official basis for categorization. Jasper (1997) differentiates "citizenship" movements that seek inclusion in societal institutions from "postcitizenship" movements whose members are already integrated into society. He also distinguishes collective identity, including status identities, from movement identities such as environmentalist, that can be more easily adopted or discarded. Thus, citizenship movements are linked to collectivities that are defined independently of the movements, although when their goals are more cultural, they can take the form of postcitizenship movements.

I am not arguing that scholars return to the task of distinguishing between movements organized on the basis of status and movements organized on some other basis. However, in attempting to define identity politics as a distinct political practice, scholars have raised important theoretical questions that are only beginning to be addressed systematically by the social movement literature as it develops analytic strategies for understanding collective struggle over longstanding cultural and discursive assessments regarding who deserves honor (Alexander 2003). These questions include the following: How do we understand the relationship between personal experience and political stance? Why are status identities understood and/or portrayed as essentialist or socially constructed? What are the strategic dilemmas faced when the identities around which a movement is organized are also the basis for oppression? When do we attribute certain movement outcomes to status identities? How do we link collective action to specific notions of power that help to explain the types of cultural and political goals at which identity politics is aimed? Social movements will differ depending on how and to what extent identities are externally imposed. The consequences of that imposition will vary across movements, identities, time, and place.

Experience, Identity, and Strategy

Bernstein (1997) argues that the concept of "identity" as it relates to social movements has at least three distinct analytic levels: First, a shared collective identity is necessary for mobilization of any social movement (Morris 1992), including the classic labor movement (Calhoun 1993b). Second, expressions of identity can be deployed at the collective level as a political strategy, which can be aimed at what are traditionally thought of as cultural and/or political goals. Third, identity can be a goal of social movement activism, either gaining acceptance for a hitherto stigmatized identity (Calhoun 1994a) or deconstructing categories of identities such as "man," "woman," "gay," "straight" (Gamson 1995), "black," or "white." I discuss these dimensions in turn.

Many studies show that to act politically, all social movements need identity for empowerment (Bernstein 1997) or an oppositional consciousness (Mansbridge & Morris 2001) to create and mobilize a constituency (Calhoun 1994a). Snow & Benford (1988) argue that when movements diagnose problems that need to be addressed, they attribute identities to the social movement, to those responsible for the problems, and to those who should be charged with alleviating them (see Hunt et al. 1994). Klandermans (1992) adds that movements that fail to create an identity from which to mobilize will not be able to produce political claims at all. Taylor & Whittier (1992) argue that social movements develop and maintain a collective identity that is characterized by maintaining boundaries between group members and nonmembers, developing a political consciousness that defines and analyzes interests, and negotiating everyday symbols and actions as strategies of personalized resistance (see Hunt & Benford 2004 for a recent review of this research). Whether the movement in question is organized on the basis of a lesbian/gay identity, a concern for animal rights, or a class identity, the collective identity approach suggests that the processes of maintaining those identities are similar (Polletta & Jasper 2001).

Polletta & Jasper (2001) also argue that activists choose strategies that relate to who they are as activists and that movement identities can become associated with particular tactical styles (Polletta 2002, Ferber 2004, Taylor & Van Dyke 2004). For example, peace organizations would generally eschew violent strategies. Although this research clearly identifies an important link between collective identity and strategic choices, it does not address how status groups negotiate their designation as a minority based on a particular social status.

Why, given the insights of social constructionism and postmodernism, are identities invoked and/or felt as if they were essentialist (Epstein 1987, Calhoun 1994a, Benhabib 1999)? Calhoun argues that mobilizing essentialized identities is related to the political context and how particular identity categories have been "repressed, delegitimated or devalued in dominant discourse" (1994, p. 18). Valocchi (1999) shows that in addition to being internally defined, lesbian and gay identities have been externally imposed by the normative and coercive institutions of psychiatry and law enforcement. Ray's (1999) concept "political field" explains how the distribution of power and prevailing interaction routines influence whether women's movements pursue pragmatic economistic or explicitly feminist goals. Political opportunities (Meyer et al. 2002) and recourse to the law (Katzenstein 1998) also influence the development of collective identity and how much movements emphasize political and cultural goals.

Although often ignored in the social movement literature, the feminist literature on standpoint theory, intersectionality, and materialist feminism draws on Marxist historical materialism (Naples 2003) to conceptualize identity politics as a way to produce knowledge that derives from the material conditions, lived experience, and social location of participants. Activists thus formulate political strategies (Hartsock 1983; Collins 1990, 1998; Mohanty 1992a, 1992b; Haraway 1988) that depend on how power or "the relations of ruling" (Smith 1987) are expressed in everyday life. Although standpoint theory is sometimes portrayed as essentialist (e.g., Benhabib 1999), Naples (2003) argues that people do not translate personal experience into political action in an unreflective, essentialist way. Instead, political analyses are arrived at through collective interpretation and analysis (see Nicholson 1990 and Naples 2003 for the evolution of these debates). In this view, self-definition and the creation of knowledge through the development of a standpoint (Collins 1998) is part and parcel of political activism and does not rely on falsely universal understandings of categories such as race, gender, or class. Through standpoint analysis, the intersection of class and status identity is made clear. Feminist standpoint theory parallels the literature on multiculturalism and critical pedagogy that is premised on the idea that personal subjectivity derived from experiences of oppression can be empowering and provide the impetus for social change (Bromley 1989).

According to Anspach (1979), personal experience with stigma led physically disabled people and former mental patients to engage in identity politics with the goal of altering the self-conceptions of the participants and the negative social representations of the group. Anspach suggests that identity politics challenges deviance theory, which views the labeling process as unidirectional, imposed on the stigmatized, rather than negotiated or contested. Britt & Heise (2000) define identity politics as a form of emotion work needed to translate isolation, fear, and shame into anger, solidarity, pride, and action, in order to mobilize stigmatized groups. Epstein (1987) views gay, lesbian, and bisexual identities and movements as "reverse affirmations" (Foucault 1978) of social labels that have been used to categorize, control, and stigmatize. Epstein (1987) suggests that, despite the insights of social constructionism, lesbian and gay identities are experienced in ways similar to contemporary ethnicity, and he argues that claiming a minority status is a strategic way to gain access to the American polity.

Pérez (1993) and Sandoval (1991) also see organizing around identity as strategic rather than unchanging and essentialist. Sandoval (1991) argues that U.S. Third World feminists operate under a "differential" consciousness, alternating between viewing their differences "for which they have been assigned inferior status" (p. 12) as invented and false or as real and valid. Phelan (1993) argues that lesbians and gay men know that engaging in the essentialist/social constructionist debate is strategic, but acknowledging the strategic nature of essentialism would undermine any claims based on essentialist arguments.

Accounts of bitter division over group membership are common in feminist and gay/lesbian movements (Echols 1989, Ryan 1992, Taylor & Rupp 1993, Phelan 1989, Bernstein 1997). Scholars of Third World women's movements and postcolonial movements argue that by organizing on the basis of the category "women," these movements have ignored differences among women that are based on class, race, and sexual orientation. Thus, these movements have been dominated by the concerns of Western women (Alexander & Mohanty 1997, Narayan 1997, Grewal & Kaplan 1994, Ryan 1997). Similar charges have been leveled at black essentialism for ignoring differences within the category black, which is politically and culturally constructed (Solomos 1998).

Gamson (1997) argues that debates over inclusion and exclusion to decide "who we are" and "who we are not" are fundamentally gendered and shaped by the communicative environment and the audience to be addressed. Movements must not only identify antagonists but also struggle over contested membership. Blee (2002) shows that the concept of "race traitor" helps racist activists set a symbolic boundary to distinguish themselves from whites not in the movement. Examining black gay identities and AIDS, Cohen (1999) argues that the outcomes of these struggles have concrete material effects on how resources, legitimacy, and services are allocated within communities and, according to Gamson (1997), depend on who raises the issue of boundaries and for what political purposes. Such processes may be prevalent in all social movements as activists publicly refute opponents' claims about their identities and motivations (Einwohner 2002, Bernstein & Jasper 1996), even when they privately affirm opponents' assessments (Einwohner 2002).

Bernstein (1997) developed the concept of identity deployment to capture the strategic processes that explain how activists deploy their identities for political change. Her formal model argues that activists alternately emphasize similarities to or differences from the norm because of the interactions among social movement organizations, state actors, and opposing movements, and the model suggests that all social movements go through similar processes. She argues that identities are deployed strategically as a form of collective action to change institutions; to transform mainstream culture, its categories, and values, and perhaps by extension its policies and structures; to transform participants; or simply to educate legislators or the public. As a political strategy, identity deployment means expressing identity such that the terrain of conflict becomes the individual person so that the values, categories, and practices of individuals become subject to debate. For example, in contrast to viewing political action as the result of community identity, Gotham (1999) argues that, in the case of a challenge to the building of a major highway, community identity was a cultural resource strategically deployed. Movements may engage in both identity and nonidentity strategies. The lesbian and gay movement, for example, often couches its claims in terms of universal appeals to social justice and avoids making the content of gay and lesbian identities subject to debate. The political implications of essentialist and constructionist arguments shift over time, altering their strategic value (Bernstein 2002a,b). Armstrong (2002) similarly argues that identity politics, which she defines as a "political logic" whose purpose is to overcome alienation through creating, expressing, and affirming collective identities, is simply one type of politics in which movements may engage. She contrasts an identity political logic with both an interest group political logic that seeks changes in laws and policies and with a redistributive political logic that attempts to transform society's economic and political structures.

Another strategic dilemma occurs when the identity around which the movement is organized is also the basis for grievances. Gamson (1995) contends that deconstructive strategies that loosen categories of identity are better suited to contesting cultural sources of oppression than institutional sources of oppression, whose logic requires the tightening of categories. Whichever way activists decide to go, they face a paradox: Seeking to erase boundaries requires recognizing them, which ultimately confirms them or, in the process of confirming boundaries, underscores that they are, in fact, socially constructed (Lorber 1999). Furthermore, Gamson (1995) questions whether movements aimed at deconstructing social categories will ultimately undermine their own existence. Gamson identifies this as the "queer dilemma," although Lorber (1999) suggests that, with the increased number of people who identify as multiracial, racially based social movements face similar conundrums. Turner's (1999) study of the intersex movement illustrates empirically the difficulties in organizing politically around a social identity while simultaneously acknowledging the social forces that construct the self. By presenting themselves as "hermaphrodites with attitude," intersexed activists adopt a medicalized identity and risk reinforcing the hetero/homo binary. According to Turner (1999), intersexuals organize for recognition of an essential intersexed body, prior to medical intervention, and, by invoking a unique history of oppression, they create themselves as an identity group. However, by choosing a body that is neither male nor female, they refuse the hetero/homo binary and challenge the immutability of heterosexuality itself.

Over time, the content and meaning of identities and the goals associated with movements organized around identities change. Hall (1989) suggests that politics based on ethnicity undergoes two distinct phases. First, groups rediscover their histories and are thus preoccupied with identity. Second, this preoccupation with identity gives way to more complex analyses that make connections across types of discrimination. Stein's (1992, 1997) analysis of lesbian feminism supports Hall's notion of a two-step model, whereas Broad (2002) finds that transgender organizing does not follow the step model, as activists simultaneously build identity and work to deconstruct it.

Attributing Causality to Identity

Several works find and test alternative mechanisms to account for the relationship between organizing around certain identities and particular movement outcomes. For example, Turner (1999) assumes that essentialist identities inhibit the formation of coalitions, and she claims that focusing on choice of identity enables the intersexed movement (in this case the choice to forego surgery and hormonal treatment for ambiguous genitals) to form coalitions with transsexual activists and with groups opposed to male circumcision and female genital mutilation. However, Bernstein's (2002a) historical analysis of the lesbian and gay movement finds that structural and contextual factors as well as strategic decisions, rather than an essentialist view of identity, account for a movement's emphasis on cultural and political change and the ability to form coalitions (see also Bernstein 2003). Armstrong (2002) argues that it is not the identities of gay white men that produced exclusions of race, gender, and class in the lesbian and gay movement, but rather the reduced viability of multi-issue politics owing to a shifting political environment. Lichterman (1999) suggests that fostering solidarity across identities depends on the ability to freely discuss the identities that activists claim. This "identity talk" in the public sphere is culturally constructed through interactional routines and can exacerbate or mitigate tensions between identity claims. Van Dyke (2003) suggests that external threats provide the impetus for cross-movement alliances and that organizational ideology may have a greater impact than movement identities in forming coalitions.

Bytstydzienski & Schacht's (2001) and Anner's (1996) collections of essays on identity politics show that organizations based on status identities sometimes socialize individuals into activism and make them available to mobilize for a variety of political purposes not directly related to status identities, including class-based organizing. Yet the essays also show that status identities can inhibit the creation of radical coalitions. One approach to understanding the relationship between movement identities and the formation of coalitions across identities and issues is to examine how activists use their identity to legitimate participation in a social movement in which they are not directly implicated. So, for example, women involved in coal mining strikes who are not miners can justify participation on the basis of their relationship to miners, such as mother or wife. The choice of identity affects future activism (Beckwith 1996).

Several studies assume that organizing around status identities leads to the commodification of protest (Kauffman 1990, Lehr 1999) so that consumption itself "becomes a form of political participation, perhaps supplanting other more direct models of participation" (Chasin 2000, p. 24). Rather than attributing the commodification of protest to identity politics, Collins (1998) argues that the state transforms identity politics so that "the *person* is distilled to his or her *image* and becomes a commodity exchanged in the marketplace of ideas" (p. 54) and thus "authentic, essential difference" associated with status characteristics is commodified without any substantive structural change. In this way, books by African American authors such as Maya Angelou or Zora Neale Hurston can be included in college curricula without African Americans having equal access to those college campuses as either faculty or students. The distribution of images is altered, while the structural factors that make race a major determinant of individual life chances are ignored (see also Young 1990). In short, identity politics has been coopted by the state through the commodification of diversity itself. Furthermore, Collins (1998) argues that despite its critiques of commodification, postmodernism's strategies of deconstruction and decentering also assume that individuals can choose and construct "the different facets of one's subjectivity," ignoring structural power (p. 149).

Identity Politics and Institutionalized Power

Examining how groups are represented in language and images may help explain how beliefs about those groups are constructed (Howard 2000, Monroe et al. 2000, Stryker et al. 2000). In a media-driven culture, such analyses become especially important. In a review article, political scientists Monroe et al. (2000) raise many of the same questions asked by sociologists, such as which categories coalesce into groups and what contexts determine the identifications that will become most salient. They argue that social identity theory can help explain the cognitive and cultural processes involved in fostering group identities and how those translate into prejudice, conflict, and even violence. They suggest that all explanations for group behavior and conflict reflect some underlying psychological assumptions about how much social identity is passively or actively constructed, which in turn influences accounts of intergroup behavior and social change.

Other scholars challenge assumptions that identity politics represents a retreat into culture that does not engage with institutionalized structures of power, and they theorize that inequality based on status is relational rather than categorical (Connell 1987). Young (1990) suggests that identity movements of the left, such as feminism and black liberation, do not organize to obtain recognition of their group's suffering, but rather seek the ability to participate in social life. She conceptualizes these movements as engaged in collective action, whose goal is not to remedy how material goods are distributed, but to alter how decisions are made, how worth is evaluated, and how labor is divided. For example, Polletta (1994) asserts that "[s]tudent-organizers of the Student Nonviolent Coordinating Committee

(SNCC) saw their task as to mobilize and secure recognition for a new collective identity—poor, 'unqualified' southern blacks—in a way that would transform national and local politics by refashioning criteria of political leadership" (p. 85). Identity deployment (Bernstein 1997) in the workplace by lesbian and gay employees is aimed both at cultural goals—challenging and reducing stigma—and at changing concrete organizational workplace policies and practices (Taylor & Raeburn 1995, Creed & Scully 2000). Armstrong (2002) and Staggenborg et al. (1993/1994) find that a movement's cultural expressions and events provide the backbone for more conventionally political activities and, as in the case of drag performances (Rupp & Taylor 2003), constitute strategic collective action. Thus, demands for recognition are intertwined with material concerns and alter social relations that are institutionally based.

Several studies contest the separation of the political economy from the realms of culture and identity that bifurcate movements into expressive, cultural, and identity-oriented movements on the one hand, and political, instrumental, and strategic movements on the other. For example, Elbaz's (1997) and Stockdill's (2001) studies of AIDS activism illustrate that because of the economic position of communities of people of color, many AIDS activists of color prioritized gaining access to the health care system, whereas white AIDS activists were more interested in issues related to treatment. Divisions between women and men centered around what to do about the exclusion of women from clinical drug trials. Women advocated noncooperation with medical authorities, while men opposed such a strategy. Elbaz (1997) claims that such "differences can be traced back both to people's positioning relative to the economic, cultural and research power structures as well as their individual choices" (p. 149).

Castells (1997) links the identities of social movements to structural changes related to globalization and the development of a network society. In the network society, Castells argues, "the new power lies in the codes of information and in the images of representation around which societies organize their institutions, and people build their lives, and decide their behavior. The sites of this power are people's minds" (p. 359). Stychin's (2003) examination of liberal law reform efforts regarding same-sex sexualities in the context of European integration and globalization provides important links between economic inequality and policies regarding sexualities. For example, he illustrates that the economic disparity between Europe's east and west provides the context for Romania's desire for European Union accession. But to gain entry into the European Union, Romania first had to decriminalize homosexuality. Globalization also facilitates the emergence of movements organized around status identities as global communication and networks (Keck & Sikkink 1998) enable movements in some countries to emulate the identities deployed and tactics used in other countries. In the case of the lesbian and gay movement, this often means adopting "western" gay identities at the expense of local ways of organizing same-sex erotic behavior (Adam et al. 1998). Identity politics also emerges on the global political stage with demands by indigenous groups for political sovereignty (e.g., Wilmer 1993). The relationship between globalization, identity, and social movements will become an increasingly important area for future research.

Cultural interpretations of structural political changes are constructed through emotions and discourse on race, gender, sexuality, and nation, and they provide a basis for mobilization (Dobratz & Shanks-Meile 1997, Ferber 2004, Stein 2001, Gallagher 1997). Gallaher (2003) notes that in the case of the patriot movement, the discourse on patriotism deflects class analysis, supports notions of racial superiority, and produces policies that are economically counterproductive to movement members. Blee (2002) suggests that, at least for female racists, the link between the political economy and racist activism is less clear cut. Instead, she shows that cultural expressions of white racists, such as shaved heads, invite social responses that in turn reinforce a racist identity. Thus, the relationship between identity and the political economy varies across movements and possibly across groups within the same movement.

CONCLUSION: CAUTIONS AND FUTURE RESEARCH DIRECTIONS

Identity politics is not a theory of social movements analogous to resource mobilization or political process theories because it does not set out to explain the emergence of social movements (in this case, movements organized on the basis of status identities) or other aspects of their development. The first part of this review shows that designating movements organized on the basis of status identities as identity politics emerged primarily through scholars' efforts to identify a particular political practice that is cultural, symbolic, or psychological in nature, distinct from class politics and class movements. Working from different theoretical assumptions, postmodernism reached the opposite conclusion and defined identity politics as reformist political activism rather than transformative cultural activism. Thus, the purpose of the term identity politics is primarily descriptive rather than explanatory. Because of the divergent notions of power derived from competing theoretical traditions, analyses of identity politics are often mixed with normative political evaluations about what constitutes worthwhile collective efforts geared toward social change, rather than toward explaining mobilization, activist strategies, and movement outcomes. Analysts of identity politics make axiomatic predictions about the types of outcomes that will ensue as a result of organizing around status identities (such as movement fragmentation). However, the interpretive understandings and assumptions about causality are taken for granted rather than realized through rigorous empirical analysis. As a result, the term identity politics obscures more than clarifies and, if the term is used at all, its meaning should be clearly defined.

Nonetheless, these efforts to identify a particular political practice called identity politics raise a series of important theoretical questions that I addressed in the second part of this review. This literature moves beyond efforts to decide what identity politics "really is" to look at the collective identity approach to social movements that examines the role of identity in all social movements in terms of mobilization, strategies, and goals. I then looked more specifically at research that underscores how movements strategically deploy identities that are, to some extent, externally imposed. This section examined how experiences of identity are translated into political action, the strategic dilemmas that movements face when the identity that serves as the source of political organizing is also the basis for oppression, and whether status identities can account for a variety of movement outcomes. This section also looked at the relationship between status identities and institutionalized relations of power, and how identities are deployed to challenge those institutional relations. Yet researchers must avoid several pitfalls when studying the relationship between identity and politics.

First, analysts of identity politics must not take the public claims made by movements organized around status identities at face value. When movements appear to rest on essentialist assumptions, theorists must determine whether that essentialism is strategic, influenced by social, political, and cultural factors, and how activists themselves understand the sources of their identities. The master narratives of both status- and non-status-based movements can be explored through in-depth case study approaches.

Second, careful attention must be paid to developing and testing alternative causal models to explain the relationship between organizing based on status identities and particular movement outcomes. Simply because a certain outcome is correlated with organizing based on status identities is not sufficient evidence of a causal relationship. Careful cross-sectional and historical comparisons of organizing based on the same status identity as well as comparisons across movements based on different status identities will help to clarify causal relationships.

Research on nationalism invokes the language of identity politics and raises similar questions regarding how culture is related to the political economy, how identities are strategically deployed as essentialist, and how outcomes are related to organizing based on status identities. Therefore, I recommend research that compares movements based on nationalist identities with movements based on other status identities (see also Calhoun 1993b). Such systematic and comparative studies of how identities become political might distinguish between identities based on how much such identities are a part of routine social interaction. Tilly (2002) refers to identities not experienced on a daily basis as "detached" identities and calls those identities that are invoked in everyday practices as "embedded" identities. These studies might compare the implications of organizing based on identities that are experienced in daily life, often based on gender, shared language, ethnicity, religion, and culture, from "corporate identity forms," which are officially recognized by the state and its institutions and confer special rights and privileges. Comparative examinations of the political and social reasons why essentialist identities are invoked and/or felt will also yield more complex analyses.

To facilitate such comparisons, researchers must pay more attention to what can be called the rules of engagement (Bernstein & Armstrong 2003), which build on

Tilly's (2002) argument that the historical, political, and cultural contexts provide the basis for recognizing certain classes of identities as valid political actors. Countries may differ in how much they recognize ethnic minorities as specific groups, for example, through the granting of social welfare benefits, which will influence the categories around which groups mobilize (Soysal 1994). Becoming an environmentalist or a member of a labor movement entails adopting a different kind of identity, depending on whether such movement organizations are banned in a given regime. Over time, as new actors are admitted and old classes of identities lose their salience, the rules of engagement shift. These variations over time suggest the need for social movement theorists to "think bigger." That is, they must take seriously concerns related to fragmentation and to the shifting sets of movement actors that are mobilized, but without falling into normative analyses of these changes or returning to the overgeneralizations of new social movement theory.

Finally, the relationship between identity and social movements in the context of globalization is an increasingly important area of research. For example, how do transnational social movements develop an empowering identity from which to mobilize? How are identities deployed politically to challenge global governance institutions? How does globalization alter efforts to deconstruct status categories or efforts to gain rights based on those status categories? How do status identities spread across nation states? If, in the context of globalization, the nation state declines in political importance, as some argue, will status identities become even more important bases for political organizing? How are changing social policies related to status identities linked to the development of global governance structures?

Research on identity politics raises many important questions that sociologists are only beginning to explore. Sociologists can contribute a great deal to the analysis of the relationship between experience, culture, identity, politics, and power. By taking seriously how conceptions of power inform collective action, sociologists are well positioned to show how activist concerns with representation and recognition are related to both institutional structures and the political economy.

ACKNOWLEDGMENTS

I thank Elizabeth Armstrong, Kathleen Blee, Myra Marx Ferree, David Greenberg, Judith Howard, James Jasper, Nancy Naples, Charles Tilly, and Steve Valocchi for their insightful comments on earlier drafts of this review.

The *Annual Review of Sociology* is online at http://soc.annualreviews.org

LITERATURE CITED

Adam BD. 1998. Theorizing homophobia. *Sexualities* 1(4):387–404

Adam BD, Duyvendak DW, Krouwel A, eds. 1998. *The Global Emergence of Gay and Lesbian Politics: National Imprints of a Worldwide Movement.* Philadelphia, PA: Temple Univ. Press

Alexander J. 1999. Beyond identity: queer

values and community. *J. Gay Lesbian Bisex. Identity* 4(4):293–314

Alexander JC. 2003. *Rethinking strangeness: from structures in space to discourses in civil society.* Presented at Annu. Meet. Am. Sociol. Assoc., Atlanta

Alexander MJ, Mohanty CT, eds. 1997. *Feminist Genealogies, Colonial Legacies, Democratic Futures.* New York: Routledge

Alund A. 1995. Alterity in modernity. *Acta Sociol.* 38(4):311–22

Aminzade R. 2000. The politics of race and nation: citizenship and Africanization in Tanzania. *Polit. Power Soc. Theory* 14:53–90

Anner J, ed. 1996. *Beyond Identity Politics: Emerging Social Justice Movements in Communities of Color.* Boston, MA: South End Press

Anspach RR. 1979. From stigma to identity politics: political activism among the physically disabled and former mental patients. *Soc. Sci. Med.* 13A:765–73

Anzaldua G. 1987. *Borderlands/La Frontera.* San Francisco: Spinsters/Aunt Lute Found.

Armstrong EA. 2002. *Forging Gay Identities: Organizing Sexuality in San Francisco, 1950–1994.* Chicago: Univ. Chicago Press

Aronowitz S. 1992. *The Politics of Identity: Class, Culture, Social Movements.* New York: Routledge

Beckwith K. 1996. Lancashire women against pit closures: women's standing in a men's movement. *Signs* 21(4):1034–68

Bell D. 2001. Election 2000 and future prospects. *Society* 38(4):78–82

Benhabib S. 1999. Civil society and the politics of identity and difference in a global context. See Smelser & Alexander 1999, pp. 293–312

Bernstein M. 1997. Celebration and suppression: the strategic uses of identity by the lesbian and gay movement. *Am. J. Sociol.* 103(3):531–65

Bernstein M. 2002a. Identities and politics: toward a historical understanding of the lesbian and gay movement. *Soc. Sci. Hist.* 26(3):531–81

Bernstein M. 2002b. The contradictions of gay ethnicity: forging identity in Vermont. See Meyer et al. 2002, pp. 85–104

Bernstein M. 2003. Nothing ventured, nothing gained? Conceptualizing social movement 'success' in the lesbian and gay movement. *Sociol. Perspect.* 46(3):353–79

Bernstein M, Armstrong E. 2003. *Moving beyond movements: how the study of LGBT politics illuminates the limitations of social movement-centric scholarship.* Presented at Annu. Meet. East. Sociol. Assoc., Philadelphia

Bernstein M, Jasper JM. 1996. Interests and credibility: whistleblowers in technological conflict. *Soc. Sci. Inf.* 35(3):565–89

Bickford S. 1997. Anti-anti-identity politics: feminism, democracy, and the complexities of citizenship. *Hypatia* 12(4):111–31

Blee KM. 2002. *Inside Organized Racism: Women in the Hate Movement.* Berkeley: Univ. Calif. Press

Boggs C. 1995. *The Socialist Tradition: From Crisis to Decline.* New York: Routledge

Bourdieu P. 1984. *Distinction: A Social Critique of the Judgement of Taste.* Cambridge, MA: Harvard Univ. Press

Bourne J. 1987. Homelands of the mind: Jewish feminism and identity politics. *Race Class* 29(1):1–24

Bower L. 1997. Queer problems/straight solutions: the limits of 'official recognition.' In *Playing With Fire: Queer Politics, Queer Theories*, ed. S Phelan, pp. 267–91. New York: Routledge

Britt L, Heise D. 2000. From shame to pride in identity politics. See Stryker et al. 2000, pp. 252–68

Broad KL. 2002. GLB + T?: gender/sexuality movements and transgender collective identity (de)constructions. *Int. J. Sex. Gender Stud.* 7(4):241–64

Bromley H. 1989. Identity politics and critical pedagogy. *Educ. Theory* 39(3):207–23

Brown W. 1995. *States of Injury: Power and Freedom in Late Modernity.* Princeton, NJ: Princeton Univ. Press

Brubaker R, Cooper F. 2000. Beyond 'identity.' *Theory Soc.* 29:1–47

Brubaker R, Laitin DD. 1998. Ethnic and nationalist violence. *Annu. Rev. Sociol.* 24:423–52

Butler J. 1990. *Gender Trouble: Feminism and the Subversion of Identity*. New York: Routledge

Butler J. 1993. *Bodies That Matter*. New York: Routledge

Bytstydzienski JM, Schacht SP. 2001. *Forging Radical Alliances Across Difference: Coalition Politics for the New Millennium*. London: Rowman & Littlefield

Calhoun C. 1993a. Nationalism and ethnicity. *Annu. Rev. Sociol.* 12:211–39

Calhoun C. 1993b. 'New social movements' of the early 19th century. *Soc. Sci. Hist.* 17(3):385–427

Calhoun C. 1994a. Social theory and the politics of identity. See Calhoun 1994b, pp. 9–36

Calhoun C, ed. 1994b. *Social Theory and the Politics of Identity*. Cambridge, MA: Blackwell

Castells M. 1997. *The Information Age: Economy, Society and Culture: The Power of Identity*. Oxford: Blackwell

Cerulo KA. 1997. Identity construction: new issues, new directions. *Annu. Rev. Sociol.* 23:385–409

Chasin A. 2000. *Selling Out: The Gay and Lesbian Movement Goes to Market*. New York: Palgrave

Cohen CJ. 1999. *The Boundaries of Blackness: AIDS and the Breakdown of Black Politics*. Chicago: Univ. Chicago Press

Cohen J. 1985. Strategy or identity: new theoretical paradigms and contemporary social movements. *Soc. Res.* 52:663–716

Collins PH. 1990. *Black Feminist Thought: Knowledge, Consciousness, and the Politics of Empowerment*. New York: Routledge

Collins PH. 1998. *Fighting Words: Black Women and the Search for Justice*. Minneapolis: Univ. Minn. Press

Connell RW. 1987. *Gender and Power: Society, the Person and Sexual Politics*. Stanford, CA: Stanford Univ. Press

Connolly C. 1990. Splintered sisterhood: antiracism in a young women's project. *Fem. Rev.* 36(Autumn):52–64

Creed WED, Scully MA. 2000. Songs of ourselves: employees' deployment of social identity in workplace encounters. *J. Manag. Inq.* 9(4):391–412

Darnovsky M, Epstein B, Flaks R, eds. 1995a. *Cultural Politics and Social Movements*. Philadelphia, PA: Temple Univ. Press

Darnovsky M, Epstein B, Flaks R. 1995b. Introduction. See Darnovsky et al. 1995a, pp. vii–xxiii

Dennis D. 1997. AIDS and the new medical gaze: bio-politics, AIDS, and homosexuality. *J. Homosex.* 32(3–4):169–84

Dobratz BA, Shanks-Meile SL. 1997. *White Power, White Pride: The White Separatist Movement in the United States*. New York: Twayne

Duyvendak JW. 1995. Gay subcultures between movement and market. See Kriesi et al. 1995, pp. 165–80

Duyvendak JW, Giugni MG. 1995. Social movement types and policy domains. See Kriesi et al. 1995, pp. 82–110

Echols A. 1989. *Daring to Be Bad: Radical Feminism in America 1967–1975*. Minneapolis: Univ. Minn. Press

Einwohner RL. 2002. Bringing outsiders in: opponents' claims and the construction of animal rights activists' identity. *Mobilization* 7(3):253–68

Elbaz G. 1997. AIDS activism, communities and disagreements. *Free Inq. Creat. Sociol.* 25(2):145–54

Epstein B. 1995 [1991]. 'Political correctness' and collective powerlessness. See Darnovsky et al. 1995a, pp. 3–19

Epstein S. 1987. Gay politics, ethnic identity: the limits of social constructionism. *Social. Rev.* 93/94:9–56

Epstein S. 1998. Gay and lesbian movements in the United States: dilemmas of identity, diversity, and political strategy. See Adam et al. 1998, pp. 30–90

Feher M. 1996. Empowerment hazards: affirmative action, recovery psychology, and identity politics. *Representations* 55:84–91

Ferber AL, ed. 2004. *Home-Grown Hate: Gender and Organized Racism.* New York: Routledge

Foucault M. 1978. *The History of Sexuality: An Introduction.* Vol. I. New York: Vintage

Fraser N. 1997. *Justice Interruptus: Critical Reflections on the 'Postsocialist' Condition.* New York: Routledge

Fraser N. 2000. Why overcoming prejudice is not enough: a rejoinder to Richard Rorty. *Crit. Horiz.* 1(1):21–28

Friedman D, McAdam D. 1992. Collective identity and activism: networks, choices, and the life of a social movement. See Morris & Mueller 1992, pp. 156–73

Gallagher CA. 1997. Redefining racial privilege in the United States. *Transformations* 8(1):28–39

Gallaher C. 2003. *On the Fault Line: Race, Class, and the American Patriot Movement.* Lanham, MD: Rowman & Littlefield

Gamson J. 1995. Must identity movements self-destruct? A queer dilemma. *Soc. Probl.* 42(3):390–407

Gamson J. 1997. Messages of exclusion: gender, movement, and symbolic boundaries. *Gen. Soc.* 11(2):178–99

Garza CM. 1995. Chicana lesbian identity and strategic essentialism: signifying self(ves). *Hum. Soc.* 19(2):25–36

Gitlin T. 1994. From universality to difference: notes on the fragmentation of the idea of the left. See Calhoun 1994b, pp. 150–74

Gitlin T. 1995. *The Twilight of Common Dreams: Why America Is Wracked by Culture Wars.* New York: Metropolitan

Gotham KF. 1999. Political opportunity, community identity, and the emergence of a local anti-expressway movement. *Soc. Probl.* 46(3):332–54

Grewal I, Kaplan C, eds. 1994. *Scattered Hegemonies: Postmodernity and Transnational Feminist Practices.* Minneapolis: Univ. Minn. Press

Habermas J. 1985. *The Theory of Communicative Action.* Vol. 1: *Reason and the Rationalization of Society.* Boston, MA: Beacon

Hall S. 1989. Cultural identity and cinematic representation. *Framework* 36:68–82

Halley JE. 1994. Reasoning about sodomy: act and identity in and after *Bowers v. Hardwick. Va. Law Rev.* 79:1721–80

Haraway D. 1988. Situated knowledges: the science question in feminism and the privilege of partial perspective. *Fem. Stud.* 14(3):575–99

Hartsock N. 1983. *Money, Sex and Power: Toward a Feminist Historical Materialism.* New York: Longman

Harvey D. 1996. *Justice, Nature and the Geography of Difference.* Oxford: Blackwell

Hekman S. 2000. Beyond identity: feminism, identity and identity politics. *Fem. Theory* 1(3):289–308

Hobsbawm E. 1996. Identity politics and the Left. *New Left Rev.* 217:38–47

Hollander P. 1996. Reassessing the adversary culture. *Acad. Quest.* 9(2):37–48

Howard JA. 2000. Social psychology of identities. *Annu. Rev. Sociol.* 26:367–93

Humphrey JC. 1999. Disabled people and the politics of difference. *Disabil. Soc.* 14(2):173–88

Hunt SA, Benford RD. 2004. Collective identity, solidarity, and commitment. See Snow et al. 2004, pp. 433–57

Hunt SA, Benford RD, Snow DA. 1994. Identity fields: framing processes and the social construction of movement identities. See Laraña et al. 1994, pp. 185–208

Inglehart R. 1981. Post-materialism in an environment of insecurity. *Am. Polit. Sci. Rev.* 75(4):880–900

Inglehard R. 1990. *Culture Shift in Advanced Industrial Society.* Princeton, NJ: Princeton Univ. Press

Jasper JM. 1997. *The Art of Moral Protest: Culture, Biography, and Creativity in Social Movements.* Chicago: Univ. Chicago Press

Johnston H, Laraña E, Gusfield JR. 1994. Identities, grievances, and new social movements. See Laraña et al. 1994, pp. 3–35

Katzenstein MF. 1998. *Faithful and Fearless: Moving Feminist Protest Inside the Church and Military*. Princeton, NJ: Princeton Univ. Press

Kauffman LA. 1990. The anti-politics of identity. *Social. Rev.* 90(1):67–80

Keck ME, Sikkink K. 1998. *Activists Beyond Borders: Advocacy Networks in International Politics*. Ithaca, NY: Cornell Univ. Press

Kimmel MS. 1993. Sexual balkanization: gender and sexuality and the new ethnicities. *Soc. Res.* 60(3):571–87

Klandermans B. 1992. The social construction of protest and multiorganizational fields. See Morris & Mueller 1992, pp. 77–103

Kriesi H, Koopmans R, Duyvendak JW, Giugni MG, eds. 1995. *New Social Movements in Western Europe: A Comparative Analysis*. Minneapolis: Univ. Minn. Press

Kymlicka W. 1995. *Multicultural Citizenship*. Oxford: Clarendon

Langman L. 1994. From capitalist tragedy to postmodern farce: the eighteenth broomstick of H. Ross Perot. *Rethink. Marx.* 7(4):115–37

Laraña L, Johnston H, Gusfield JR, eds. 1994. *New Social Movements: From Ideology to Identity*. Philadelphia, PA: Temple Univ. Press

Lehr V. 1999. *Queer Family Values: Debunking the Myth of the Nuclear Family*. Philadelphia, PA: Temple Univ. Press

Lichterman P. 1999. Talking identity in the public sphere: broad visions and small spaces in identity politics. *Theory Soc.* 28(1):101–41

Lorber J. 1999. Crossing borders and erasing boundaries: paradoxes of identity politics. *Sociol. Focus* 32(4):355–70

Lott E. 1999. Boomer liberalism: When the New Left was old. *Transition* 8(2):24–44

Macedo S. 1995. Liberal civic education and religious fundamentalism: the case of God v. John Rawls? *Ethics* 105(April):468–96

Mansbridge J, Morris A. 2001. *Oppositional Consciousness: The Subjective Roots of Social Protest*. Chicago: Univ. Chicago Press

Melucci A. 1985. The symbolic challenge of contemporary movements. *Soc. Res.* 52:789–816

Melucci A. 1989. *Nomads of the Present*. London: Hutchinson Radius

Melucci A. 1996. *Challenging Codes: Collective Action in the Information Age*. Cambridge, UK: Cambridge Univ. Press

Meyer DS, Whittier N, Robnett B, eds. 2002. *Social Movements: Identity, Culture, and the State*. New York: Oxford Univ. Press

Meznaric S. 1993. The rapists' progress: ethnicity, gender and violence. *Rev. Sociol.* 24(3–4):119–29

Mohanty CT. 1992a. Cartographies of struggle: third world women and the politics of feminism. See Mohanty et al. 1992, pp. 1–50

Mohanty CT. 1992b. Under Western eyes: feminist scholarship and colonial discourses. See Mohanty et al. 1992, pp. 51–80

Mohanty CT, Russo A, Torres L, eds. 1992. *Third World Women and the Politics of Feminism*. Bloomington/Indianapolis: Indiana Univ. Press

Monroe KR, Hanin J, Van Vechten RB. 2000. The psychological foundations of identity politics. *Annu. Rev. Polit. Sci.* 3:419–47

Morris AD. 1992. Political consciousness and collective action. See Morris & Mueller 1992, pp. 351–73

Morris AD, Mueller CM, eds. 1992. *Frontiers in Social Movement Theory*. New Haven, CT: Yale Univ. Press

Naples NA. 2003. *Feminism and Method: Ethnography, Discourse Analysis, and Activist Research*. New York: Routledge

Narayan U. 1997. *Dislocating Cultures: Identities, Traditions and Third World Feminism*. New York: Routledge

Nicholson LJ, ed. 1990. *Feminism/Postmodernism*. New York: Routledge

Olzak S. 2004. Ethnic and nationalist social movements. See Snow et al. 2004, pp. 666–93

Pérez E. 1993. Sexuality and discourse: notes from a Chicana survivor. In *Chicana Critical Issues*, ed. N Alarcón, pp. 159–84. Berkeley, CA: Third Woman Press

Phelan S. 1989. *Identity Politics: Lesbian Feminism and the Limits of Community*. Philadelphia, PA: Temple Univ. Press

Phelan S. 1993. (Be)coming out: lesbian identity and politics. *Signs* 18(4):765–90

Pichardo NA. 1997. New social movements: a critical review. *Annu. Rev. Sociol.* 23:411–30

Piore MJ. 1995. *Beyond Individualism: How Social Demands of the New Identity Groups Challenge American Political and Economic Life*. Cambridge, MA: Harvard Univ. Press

Polletta F. 1994. Strategy and identity in 1960s black protest. *Res. Soc. Mov. Confl. Change* 17:85–114

Polletta F. 2002. *Freedom Is an Endless Meeting: Democracy in American Social Movements*. Chicago: Univ. Chicago Press

Polletta F, Jasper JM. 2001. Collective identity and social movements. *Annu. Rev. Sociol.* 27:283–305

Ray R. 1999. *Fields of Protest: Women's Movements in India*. Minneapolis: Univ. Minn. Press

Rimmerman C. 2002. *From Identity to Politics*. Philadelphia, PA: Temple Univ. Press

Robnett B. 1997. *How Long? How Long? African American Women in the Struggle for Civil Rights*. New York: Oxford Univ. Press

Roper DC. 1994. Whither the left? A reply to Todd Gitlin. *Contention* 3(2):201–4

Rorty R. 1998. *Achieving Our Country: Leftist Thought in Twentieth Century America*. Cambridge, MA: Harvard Univ. Press

Ross JA. 1982. Urban development and the politics of ethnicity: a conceptual approach. *Ethn. Racial Stud.* 5(4):440–56

Rossinow D. 1998. *The Politics of Authenticity: Liberalism, Christianity, and the New Left in America*. New York: Columbia Univ. Press

Rupp LJ, Taylor V. 1990. *Survival in the Doldrums: The American Women's Rights Movement, 1945 to the 1960s*. Columbus: Ohio State Univ. Press

Rupp LJ, Taylor V. 2003. *Drag Queens at the 801 Cabaret*. Chicago: Univ. Chicago Press

Ryan B. 1992. *Feminism and the Women's Movement: Dynamics of Change in Social Movement Ideology and Activism*. New York: Routledge

Ryan B. 1997. How much can I divide thee, let me count the ways: identity politics in the women's movement. *Humanit. Soc.* 21(1):67–83

Ryan B. 2001. *Identity Politics in the Women's Movement*. New York: New York Univ. Press

Sandoval C. 1991. U.S. Third World feminism: the theory and method of oppositional consciousness in the postmodern world. *Genders* 10:1–24

Seidman S. 1993. Identity and politics in a 'postmodern' gay culture: some historical and conceptual notes. In *Fear of a Queer Planet: Queer Politics and Social Theory*, ed. M Warner, pp. 105–42. Minneapolis: Univ. Minn. Press

Seidman S. 1997. *Difference Troubles: Queering Social Theory and Sexual Politics*. Cambridge, UK: Cambridge Univ. Press

Sewell WH Jr. 1992. A theory of structure: duality, agency, and transformation. *Am. J. Soc.* 99:1–29

Smelser NJ, Alexander JC, eds. 1999. *Diversity and Its Discontents: Cultural Conflict and Common Ground in Contemporary American Society*. Princeton, NJ: Princeton Univ. Press

Smith D. 1987. *The Everyday World as Problematic*. Boston, MA: Northeast. Univ. Press

Snow DA, Benford RD. 1988. Ideology, frame resonance, and participant mobilization. In *International Social Movements Research*. Vol. 1: *From Structure to Action*, ed. B Klandermans, H Kriesi, S Tarrow, pp. 197–217. Greenwich, CT: JAI Press

Snow DA, Soule SA, Kriesi H, eds. 2004. *The Blackwell Companion to Social Movements*. Malden, MA: Blackwell

Solomos J. 1998. Beyond racism and multiculturalism. *Patterns Prejud.* 32(4):45–62

Soysal YN. 1994. *Limits of Citizenship: Migrants and Postnational Membership in Europe*. Chicago: Univ. Chicago Press

Spragens T Jr. 1999. Identity politics and the liberalism of difference: missing the big picture. *Responsive Community* 9(3):12–25

Staggenborg S, Eder D, Sudderth L. 1993/1994. Women's culture and social change: evidence from the national women's music festival. *Berkeley J. Sociol.* 38:31–56

Stein A. 1992. Sisters and queers: the decentering of lesbian feminism. *Social. Rev.* 22(1): 33–55

Stein A. 1997. *Sex and Sensibility: Stories of a Lesbian Generation*. Berkeley: Univ. Calif. Press

Stein A. 2001. *The Stranger Next Door: The Story of a Small Community's Battle over Sex, Faith, and Civil Rights*. Boston, MA: Beacon

Stockdill BC. 2001. Forging a multidimensional oppositional consciousness: lessons from community-based AIDS activism. See Mansbridge & Morris 2001, pp. 204–37

Stryker S, Owens TJ, White RW, eds. 2000. *Self, Identity, and Social Movements*. Minneapolis: Univ. Minn. Press

Stychin CF. 2003. *Governing Sexuality: The Changing Politics of Citizenship and Law Reform*. Oxford: Hart

Swidler A. 1995. Cultural power and social movements. In *Social Movements and Culture*, ed. H Johnston, B Klandermans, pp. 25–40. Minneapolis: Univ. Minn. Press

Taylor C. 1989. *Sources of the Self: The Making of the Modern Identity*. Cambridge, MA: Harvard Univ. Press

Taylor V, Raeburn NC. 1995. Identity politics as high-risk activism: career consequences for lesbian, gay, and bisexual sociologists. *Soc. Probl.* 42(2):252–73

Taylor V, Rupp LJ. 1993. Women's culture and lesbian feminist activism: a reconsideration of cultural feminism. *Signs: J. Women Cult. Soc.* 19:33–61

Taylor V, Van Dyke N. 2004. 'Get up, stand up': tactical repertoires of social movements. See Snow et al. 2004, pp. 262–93

Taylor V, Whittier NE. 1992. Collective identity in social movement communities: lesbian feminist mobilization. See Morris & Mueller 1992, pp. 104–29

Tilly C. 2002. *Stories, Identities, and Political Change*. Lanham, MD: Rowman & Littlefield

Touraine A. 1981. *The Voice and the Eye: An Analysis of Social Movements*. Cambridge, UK: Cambridge Univ. Press

Touraine A. 1998. Sociology without society. *Curr. Sociol.* 46(2):119–43

Turner SS. 1999. Intersex identities: locating new intersections of sex and gender. *Gen. Soc.* 13(4):457–79

Vaid U. 1995. *Virtual Equality: The Mainstreaming of Gay and Lesbian Liberation*. New York: Anchor

Valocchi S. 1999. The class-inflected nature of gay identity. *Soc. Probl.* 46(2):207–24

Van Dyke N. 2003. Crossing movement boundaries: factors that facilitate coalition protest by American college students, 1930–1990. *Soc. Probl.* 50(2):226–50

Walters SD. 2001. *All the Rage: The Story of Gay Visibility in America*. Chicago: Univ. Chicago Press

Warner M. 2000. *The Trouble with Normal: Sex, Politics and the Ethics of Queer Life*. Cambridge, MA: Harvard Univ. Press

Williams RH. 2004. The cultural contexts of collective action: constraints, opportunities, and the symbolic life of social movements. See Snow et al. 2004, pp. 91–115

Wilmer F. 1993. *The Indigenous Voice in World Politics*. Newbury Park, CA: Sage

Wolfe A, Klausen J. 1997. Identity politics and the welfare state. *Soc. Philos. Policy* 14(2):231–55

Wrong DH. 2003. *Reflections on a Politically Skeptical Era*. New Brunswick, NJ: Transaction Books

Young IM. 1990. *Justice and the Politics of Difference*. Princeton, NJ: Princeton Univ. Press

Young MP. 2002. Confessional protest: the rebellious birth of U.S. national social movements. *Am. Sociol. Rev.* 67:660–68

Walzer M. 1996. Minority rites. *Dissent* 43(3): 53–55

Whittier N. 1995. *Feminist Generations: The Persistence of the Radical Women's Movement*. Philadelphia, PA: Temple Univ. Press

Annu. Rev. Sociol. 2005. 31:75–103
doi: 10.1146/annurev.soc.30.012703.110622
Copyright © 2005 by Annual Reviews. All rights reserved
First published online as a Review in Advance on April 13, 2005

THE SOCIAL PSYCHOLOGY OF HEALTH DISPARITIES

Jason Schnittker[1] and Jane D. McLeod[2]

[1]*Department of Sociology, University of Pennsylvania, Philadelphia, Pennsylvania
19104-6299; email: jschnitt@ssc.upenn.edu*
[2]*Department of Sociology, Indiana University, Bloomington, Indiana 47405;
email: jmcleod@indiana.edu*

Key Words   health, inequality, social status, discrimination

■ **Abstract**   In recent years, scholars from a variety of disciplines have turned to the potential psychosocial determinants of health in pursuit of an explanation for socioeconomic and racial/ethnic disparities. This review discusses the literature on psychosocial factors and mental and physical health, focusing on the roles of subjective status, self/identity, and perceived discrimination. We argue that current research may have obscured important social psychological considerations and that it is an opportune time to reconsider the social psychology of disparities. A social psychology of disparities could provide a bridge between those who encourage research on health's "upstream" causes and those who encourage research on "downstream" mechanisms precisely because social psychology is concerned with the vast "meso" level of analysis that many allude to but few explicitly traverse. We point to the importance of person-environment interactions, contingencies, reciprocality, and meaning. Although psychosocial factors might not explain disparities in the manner much psychosocial research would seem to suggest, psychosocial factors are important causes in their own right and, when considered in a more sophisticated social psychological light, may help to refine disparities theory and research.

INTRODUCTION

We review the realized and potential contributions of social psychology to research on health disparities. Health disparities refer to differences in health profiles across major subgroups of the population, including a broad spectrum of physical and mental health outcomes, from self-rated health to mortality, from psychological well-being to major mental disorders.[1] We emphasize disparities based on

---

[1]Our definition of disparities pertains only to differences. Other definitions, especially concerning health care, seek to eliminate from consideration as disparities those differences that result from clinically appropriate treatment or patient preferences (Smedley et al. 2003, p. 4). We do not consider these definitions here because our focus is simply on the contribution of social psychology to patterned differences in health.

race/ethnicity and socioeconomic position (SEP) in Western industrialized countries because these have received the most attention from health scholars.[2] Research on racial/ethnic and socioeconomic differences in health also resonates strongly with a core mission of sociology, "[d]ocumenting the importance of social class in human life" (House 1981, p. 548).

This is an opportune moment to consider the contributions of social psychology to health research. Although scholars have long recognized that advantaged social groups enjoy longer and healthier lives than disadvantaged groups (Kitagawa & Hauser 1973), research on the topic accelerated dramatically in the 1990s and continues to be important today. This acceleration was inspired in large part by the persistence of racial/ethnic and socioeconomic disparities during the late twentieth century, a time when many scholars presumed that disparities would be reduced dramatically, if not eliminated entirely, by improvements in access to care or public health initiatives (Berkman & Kawachi 2000a, Black et al. 1988, Kadushin 1964, Marmot 1997, Marmot & McDowall 1986, Marmot et al. 1997, North et al. 1993, Rosen 1963, Williams & Collins 1995). The persistence of health disparities raises important questions about the origins of these disparities in the structural, cultural, and personal conditions of life.

Current research on health disparities is dominated by two seemingly contradictory approaches. In the first, health psychologists, often in collaboration with sociologists, have directed their attention to "downstream" mechanisms through which social experiences "get under the skin" and create disparities in physical and mental health (Taylor et al. 1997).[3] Studies within this approach emphasize the role of psychosocial factors in health disparities, particularly stress, coping, health behaviors, and their physiological correlates. Although many of these studies acknowledge the origins of psychosocial factors in broad social structures, the psychosocial factors themselves are the focus of analysis, with little attention given to their structural origins or to the possibility that social structures may modify their effects on health. In the second approach, public health and sociological scholars urge recognition that health disparities are attributable to basic social processes that are not reducible to any particular proximal risk factor. Calling for attention to "upstream" explanations (McKinlay 1975), to the "fundamental social causes of disease" (House et al. 1990, Link & Phelan 1995), and the social processes that distribute the determinants of health unequally (Graham 2004), these scholars aim to redirect attention from psychosocial risk factors to the

---

[2]There is a long tradition of research concerned with the determinants of health in developing countries, and with disparities in health between the developed and developing world. This tradition emphasizes basic material deprivations and typically does not invoke social psychological theories.

[3]The distinction between downstream and upstream mechanisms derives from McKinlay's (1975) influential article in which he relates a story told by Irving Zola. In the story, a physician describes his job as standing downstream in a river, pulling out people as they drown, never having time to figure out who is upstream pushing them in.

distribution of knowledge, power, and resources as they are implicated in health disparities.

By highlighting the paradigmatic concerns of psychology and sociology, respectively, these approaches neglect important social psychological processes that shape health disparities. Social psychological processes bridge the gap between individual and society by identifying mesolevel structures and interactions through which macrosocial conditions shape the experiences of, and come to have meaning for, individuals. They remind us that knowledge, power, and resources influence health not only through their direct effects on the material conditions of life, but also as they derive symbolic importance in social interaction, and as they define the contexts for individual responses to those conditions. Concerning the symbolic aspects of life conditions, we emphasize two social psychological processes with origins in symbolic interactionist writings: social comparisons and self/identity. With respect to the definition of social contexts, we draw on insights from social structure and personality research regarding the implications of incongruence between structural constraints and individual propensities.[4] Despite their very different orientations, both theoretical traditions emphasize the interface between socially structured arrangements and intraindividual processes, an interface that remains the defining concern of social psychology.

PATTERNS OF HEALTH DISPARITIES

The basic contours of socioeconomic and racial/ethnic disparities in health are well known (see Robert & House 2000 for a review, Williams & Collins 1995).[5] Socioeconomic status is inversely associated with virtually all major indicators of health status, including functional impairments, self-rated health, disease-specific morbidity, and mortality. These associations are often dramatic. For example, persons near the top of the income distribution enjoy mortality risks approximately half of those near the bottom (Rogot 1992, Sorlie et al. 1995); life expectancy differs by up to seven years between different income groups (House & Williams 2000). Similarly dramatic health disparities exist for other indicators of SEP, including educational attainment (Ross & Wu 1995) and occupational prestige (Marmot et al. 1984, 1991). Although the possibility of reciprocal effects between SEP

---

[4]By necessity, we cannot discuss all social psychological work that is relevant to research on health disparities. In particular, we omit any extensive discussion of expectations states theory (see Correll & Ridgeway 2004 for a review) and ethnomethodology, despite their obvious relevance to understanding clinical encounters. We also omit discussion of role theory as it has been applied to the study of group-specific stress. George (2001) provides a useful review of the latter line of research.

[5]Most of the research we review concerns the United States and the United Kingdom because most relevant research has been conducted in those countries. We cite selectively because of space limitations. Interested readers can find more information about specific studies on health disparities in the review articles that we highlight.

and health remains a lingering concern (Smith 1999), most research supports the conclusion that SEP influences health as much or more as the reverse (Blane et al. 1993, House & Williams 2000, Link & Phelan 1995, Menchik 1993, Pritchett & Summers 1996). Indeed, health scholars agree that SEP is one of the most powerful social risk factors for disease (House & Williams 2000).

Research on racial/ethnic disparities in health has a shorter history but is no less compelling in its conclusions (see Williams & Collins 1995 for a review). African Americans today live shorter and less healthy lives than do whites (Elo & Preston 1997), much as they did over a century ago (see Rao 1973 for trends). Black infant mortality rates are now almost twice those of whites (Wise 2003). Racial differences in adult morbidity and mortality are also substantial (Anderson 1989, Manton & Stallard 1997), with black mortality rates over twice those of whites among middle-aged adults (Elo & Preston 1994, 1997). Blacks rate their health as worse than whites (e.g., Ferraro & Farmer 1996) and they are at greater risk of specific disease conditions, including hypertension, diabetes, asthma, AIDS, and certain forms of cancer (Natl. Cent. Health Stat. 2004, US Dep. Health Hum. Serv. 2002). While some multivariate analyses find that controls for SEP eliminate racial/ethnic differences in health (Hayward et al. 2000, Rogers 1992), most studies find that race/ethnicity has independent effects (Sorlie et al. 1992, Williams 1997, Wise 1993).

Racial/ethnic differences in health become more complicated when we consider other groups. Latinos maintain better health on some dimensions than non-Hispanic whites, but far worse health on others. For example, Latinos have lower or similar rates of cardiovascular disease and lower death rates from heart disease and cancer than non-Hispanic whites, but higher rates of infectious disease and of deaths from tuberculosis, diabetes, and homicide (Sorlie et al. 1993, Vega & Amaro 1994, Williams & Collins 1995). Moreover, considerably different patterns exist within the heterogeneous category of Hispanic, with Puerto Ricans and Mexicans generally having worse health profiles than Cubans. Infant mortality rates are higher for American Indians than for whites, but lower for most Asian Pacific Islanders (APIA; Natl. Cent. Health Stat. 2004). In addition, despite relatively favorable overall health in the APIA population, Native Hawaiians have high mortality rates for heart disease and Japanese Americans have high rates of stomach cancer (Lin-Fu 1993).

The evidence is even more mixed for mental health. Some studies find that racial/ethnic minorities report more symptoms of psychological distress than do whites, but other studies do not find this difference (see Brown et al. 1999 for a review, Vega & Rumbaut 1991).[6] The results for major mental disorders further

---

[6]Psychological distress refers to nonspecific symptoms, generally of lesser severity, that may be experienced by people with a range of mental health problems, such as having trouble sleeping or feeling worried. In contrast, major mental disorders refers to specific constellations of symptoms (e.g., major depression, social phobia) that have been classified as discrete disorders by the American Psychiatric Association and that involve functional impairment.

complicate the picture. African Americans have a lower prevalence of most disorders than whites, whereas Hispanics have a higher prevalence of mood disorders and comorbid disorders but not of substance use disorders (Williams & Harris-Reid 1999). Inconsistencies in results between different racial/ethnic groups and between different indicators of physical and mental health are not well understood but point to the importance of considering the diverse meanings of race/ethnicity as they are relevant to health.

SOCIAL STRUCTURE AND PERSONALITY AS AN ORIENTING FRAMEWORK

Current research on health disparities draws on multilevel explanatory models that implicate macrosocial structures and processes (e.g., the economy, racism), mesolevel environments (e.g., work settings, neighborhoods, the health care system), and individual behaviors, perceptions, dispositions, and physiology (e.g., Anderson 1989, Berkman & Kawachi 2000b, Krieger 1994, McKinlay & Marceau 2000, Singer & Ryff 2001, Smedley et al. 2003, Susser & Susser 1996a,b; see Graham 2004 for a review). Although their specific emphases differ, these models share the common goal of expanding the scope and imagination of epidemiology beyond conventional risk factors (e.g., smoking, exercise, stress, coping) to consider their origins in macro- and mesosocial conditions and, thereby, the relevance of those conditions for health.[7]

Multilevel models of health owe an intellectual debt to the social structure and personality (SSP) framework in sociological social psychology (House 1981, Kohn 1989, McLeod & Lively 2004). This framework is concerned with the relationship between macrosocial systems or processes and individual feelings, attitudes, and behaviors. SSP researchers trace the processes through which components of the social system influence individuals and through which individuals affect social systems through analysis of the implications of macrosocial systems for proximate life experiences (e.g., in the workplace, families, and neighborhoods) and the implications of those experiences for individual outcomes. The framework has been applied specifically to the study of health by several scholars, both inside and outside of sociology (Ryff 1987, Seeman & Crimmins 2001, Williams 1990).

Multilevel models of health orient scholars to the full range of social, psychological, and biological factors that determine the health of individuals. However,

---

[7]Interest in multilevel models of health disparities extends beyond the academy into government and policy organizations. To offer two examples, in the year 2000, the National Institutes of Health launched a major research and education initiative concerned with health disparities that targets the contributions of macro-, meso-, and microlevel risk factors. In that same year, the Office of Behavioral and Social Sciences Research held an influential conference on the contributions of the social sciences to understanding health, "Towards Higher Levels of Analysis: Progress and Promise in Research on Social and Cultural Dimensions of Health."

as is true for the SSP framework more generally, by emphasizing discrete levels of analysis, these models also divert attention from the processes that traverse levels, particularly those through which macrostructural conditions shape the symbolic and material realities of people's lives and through which those realities shape responses to health risks (McLeod & Lively 2004). While some macrosocial conditions transcend perception, others influence health only to the extent that they come to have meaning for individuals (Fine 1991). In addition, although material and symbolic realities mediate the effects of macrosocial conditions on health, they also modify those effects by defining the constraints and opportunities within which individuals negotiate their physical and social environments. These considerations implicate the field of social psychology and lie at the heart of our review.

SOCIOECONOMIC POSITION AND HEALTH: UNCOVERING AND SPECIFYING THE SUBJECTIVE

SEP is a broad term intended to encompass both resource-based and prestige-based indicators of social class position (Krieger et al. 1997). Health scholars actively debate the strengths and weaknesses of different socioeconomic indicators, particularly educational attainment, income, and occupational prestige, centering on their relative abilities to capture stability and change in socioeconomic experience, their relevance for understanding individual, household, and neighborhood components of SEP, and the strength of their empirical associations with health (Kessler 1982, Krieger et al. 1997, Lynch & Kaplan 2000, Miech & Hauser 2001). For example, some researchers argue that educational attainment is the key indicator of SEP because it is easy to measure, more plausibly antecedent to health than is income, and often has effects on health independent of other socioeconomic indicators. However, education fails to capture the most important socioeconomic dynamics of adulthood, has a more restricted range than income and occupational prestige, and is less predictive of capital assets. In contrast, income fluctuates considerably over the adult life course, permitting an analysis of socioeconomic dynamics as they relate to health, but it is difficult to measure comprehensively and accurately.

Regardless of the specific indicators they choose, most researchers of health disparities apply a material conceptualization of SEP. This conceptualization posits that higher socioeconomic positions confer material advantages that improve the health of their occupants. This conceptualization is evident in early economic models of health that emphasized the effects of absolute deprivation (Preston & Taubman 1994), as well as in more recent models that assert variations in resources across the income continuum (Lynch et al. 2000). Research on occupation and health, likewise, focuses on the physical and psychological hazards of different occupational environments, including toxic exposures, physical demands, psychological demands, decision latitude, and routine (Karasek & Theorell 1990, Marmot et al. 1991, Reynolds 1997, Uselding 1976). Research on education emphasizes the knowledge and mastery that education provides, as they are relevant to lifestyle and health behaviors. More generally, decades of risk-factor epidemiology demonstrate that SEP is linked to health through a variety of objective pathways, including access to care, environmental exposures, and life stressors (Rothman 1986, Susser et al. 1985).

Status-based conceptualizations of SEP complement the materialist conceptualization by highlighting the subjective components of status. Socioeconomic positions provide more than material resources; they serve as reference points for social comparison and as personal and social identities that influence perceptions, desires, and social affiliations. These nonmaterial components of social status underlie some of the more interesting current research agendas in health disparities research.

Subjective Components of Socioeconomic Position

Research on socioeconomic differences in health provides both direct and indirect evidence for the effects of subjective status on health. Direct evidence derives from research that incorporates measures of subjective status; indirect evidence derives from research that explores the relationship between income inequality and health. Both lines of research draw on social psychological theories of social evaluation processes.

INCOME INEQUALITY   Richard Wilkinson's research is widely credited with bringing scholarly attention to the association between income inequality and health (Wilkinson 1992, 1994, 1997). In a small sample of OECD countries, Wilkinson documented a correlation between income inequality and life expectancy that appeared to be independent of absolute levels of aggregate income and, indeed, somewhat larger in magnitude (Wilkinson 1992). Scholars have since extended these basic findings to U.S. states and to metropolitan areas, as well as to a wide variety of additional health indicators, including self-rated health (Kaplan et al. 1996; Kawachi et al. 1999; Kennedy et al. 1996, 1998).

Wilkinson explained his findings using social psychological concepts. Specifically, he argued that income inequality is linked to health because it leads to distressing social comparisons (Easterlin 1995; Wilkinson 1996, 1997, 1999).[8] People who live in areas with high rather than low income inequality are more concerned about how they compare to others (status anxiety) and feel deprived, marginalized, and angry as a result (relative deprivation). In turn, status anxiety and relative deprivation are linked to health both directly, through emotions and their physiological counterparts, and indirectly, through smoking and related health behaviors (Wilkinson 1997, 1999).

---

[8]The psychosocial interpretation is not the only interpretation of the link from income inequality to health. Kaplan and colleagues (1996) attribute the association to diminished human capital investment in inequitable societies. Kawachi and colleagues (1997) emphasize the effects of income inequality on declines in social capital.

Although Wilkinson's simple social psychological account appears reasonable on the face, research provides very little evidence that social comparisons are as automatic as he assumes. Rather, most social psychological research suggests that individuals are flexible, motivated, and even biased in their choices of comparative standards (Festinger 1954, Kruglanski & Mayseless 1990). Comparisons typically involve others with whom one shares some degree of similarity, even if those persons are equal to or somewhat better than the self (Wood 1989). Moreover, even when potentially distressing upward comparisons are made, individuals tend to cope in ways that severely attenuate the link from feelings of relative deprivation to feelings of distress (Diener & Fujita 1997). Consistent with these observations, in their review of studies exploring the income inequality thesis, Lynch and colleagues (2004) found less evidence for the thesis in studies that use smaller units of aggregation—the units within which social comparisons are most likely to occur. Thus, to the extent that there is an income inequality effect on health, it does not appear to result from status anxiety or relative deprivation. Worthy of note, recent studies that incorporate comprehensive controls and apply fixed-effects regression models find no evidence for effects of income inequality on population health, calling even the basic empirical finding into question (Beckfield 2004, McLeod et al. 2004).

Nevertheless, studies that incorporate more sophisticated measures of relative deprivation suggest that the concept is still promising for the study of health disparities. To give just one example, Eibner & Evans (2005) developed indicators of relative income deprivation that incorporate differing assumptions regarding comparative reference groups (within the state and/or within age, race, and educational groups). They report significant associations between those indicators and mortality, self-rated health, and poor health habits, particularly when the indicators incorporate within-state group-based comparisons. Their research does not go beyond documenting these significant associations to consider how other reference group comparisons arise or the conditions that might modify the effects of those comparisons on health. Future research that further specifies how comparisons are made and with which specific persons or groups would inform our understanding of social comparison processes related to income, and also provide a more precise description of income-based health disparities. It will also be useful to consider the centrality of SEP to the self when estimating the effects of relative deprivation. Social psychological theories of the self predict that low SEP will be less strongly associated with feelings of relative deprivation and with health among persons who do not value status or for whom achieved status is not a central component of the self (Rosenberg 1979). There is little reason to expect that income is equally salient for all persons, even in a status-oriented culture.

SUBJECTIVE STATUS   A second line of research tests the effects of subjective status on health directly. The MacArthur Scale of Subjective Social Status is the most widely used instrument (see Goodman et al. 2001 for a discussion regarding one version). The instrument features a ladder. Respondents are asked to think of the ladder in the following way:

> At the top of the ladder are people who are the best off—those who have the most money, the most education, and the most respected job. At the bottom are the people who are the worst off—who have the least money, least education, and the least respected jobs or no job. The higher up you are on this ladder, the closer you are to the people at the very top; the lower you are, the closer you are to the people at the very bottom (Adler et al. 1999).

After being read the description, respondents are asked to place themselves on one of the ladder's rungs, and their position serves as their subjective status score.

Using the ladder, scholars have explored the relationship between subjective status and health, independent of objective status. The emerging evidence suggests a generally robust association between ladder scores and health. Subjective status has been associated with obesity, depression, and susceptibility to respiratory infection (Goodman et al. 2001). In Adler and colleagues' (2000) research, subjective status was more strongly related to a variety of psychological outcomes than was objective status. In contrast, Singh-Manoux and colleagues (2003) explored five health outcomes (angina, diabetes, respiratory illness, perceived health, and depression) and found that all were associated with subjective status, although not all these associations remained when objective status was controlled. Subjective status is an especially strong predictor of health outcomes when respondents' comparisons are anchored in local environments (e.g., compare your status to that of others within your school) rather than in society at large (Goodman et al. 2001, 2003).[9]

Although these effects may reflect relative deprivation processes, social psychological research concerned with discontinuities between subjective and objective status suggests two other possibilities that have not been considered in health research (Bell & Robinson 1980, Goyder 1975, Jackman 1979, Jackman & Jackman 1983). First, research demonstrates that subjective class identification is affected by one's objective status, one's current status relative to past statuses (including status from one's family of origin), and the status of one's spouse. These components of subjective status parallel objective status characteristics that have been found to influence health in prospective studies of health over the life course, suggesting that subjective status may influence health because it serves as a proxy for features of objective status not captured by traditional indicators. For example, low socioeconomic status during childhood was significantly associated with risk

---

[9]Enthusiasm for these findings must be tempered by their preliminary nature. Two artifactual explanations have been proposed but not yet tested: that health status factors into individual ratings of subjective status because health perceptions influence judgments of whether one is "better off" or "worse off" than others, and that subjective status and health status are both functions of self-worth or other personal attributes (Ostrove et al. 2000).

factors for and the prevalence of adult disease in several studies (Davey Smith et al. 1997, Lynch et al. 1997, Power & Matthews 1997). In addition, subjective class identification changes over time with changes in culture, opportunity, and the macroeconomy. Husbands, for example, increasingly factor their wives' employment characteristics into their personal evaluations of status, whereas wives now consider their own status in addition to their husbands' (Davis & Robinson 1988, 1998). These changes are rooted as much in the changing collective fortunes of women as they are rooted in changes in specific women's status experiences. Scholars interested in the association between subjective status and health rarely consider these contributions to reports of subjective status. Because an individual's construal of her status is a potential source of anxiety, subjective status may indeed affect health in substantial ways. But researchers cannot fully understand the mechanisms behind these effects without adequately understanding from where individuals derive their senses of status. Researchers may incorrectly infer a health effect of subjective status when, in actuality, the effect reflects objective features of work or family, features that tend to go unobserved in conventional analyses.

Explaining the Association of SEP with Health

Social psychological theories and concepts are also relevant to understanding the diverse pathways through which SEP influences health. Although researchers have considered a variety of material conditions of life as they are relevant to health differentials (e.g., environmental exposures, neighborhood environments, access to medical care; Lynch et al. 2000), in recent years researchers have shifted attention to psychosocial factors. Psychosocial factors refer broadly to social and psychological factors that have the potential to influence health and well-being. They include life stressors, the structure and content of interpersonal relationships, self and identity, personality traits, and emotions and affect. Many psychosocial factors have been associated with health both cross-sectionally and prospectively. Major life events and chronic stressors produce identifiable damage in physiological systems, which, in turn, increases the risk of disease (see Seeman et al. 1997 for an example). The absence of social support increases the risk of morbidity and mortality, on par with smoking and a Type A behavior pattern (House et al. 1988). Personality traits such as mastery, optimism, and lack of hostility increase life expectancy, impede disease progression, and decrease the risk of a variety of disease conditions such as myocardial infarction (Rodin 1986, Scheier & Carver 1985, Scheier et al. 1989). Affective states such as depression and anxiety increase the risk for coronary heart disease and/or worsen its course (Esler et al. 1982, Glassman & Shapiro 1998, Januzzi et al. 2000, Kawachi et al. 1994, Kubzansky et al. 1997). All these factors are distributed unequally across socioeconomic groups, making them plausible mediators of the SEP-health association.

Empirical evidence for the role of psychosocial factors in health disparities is mixed, despite emerging consensus about their importance (Robert & House 2000). Studies of mortality find that psychosocial factors explain some, but not all, of the association between SEP and health. For example, Fiscella & Franks (1997) explore the relationship between baseline depression, life dissatisfaction, and hopelessness and mortality as assessed through follow-up interviews over the course of approximately ten years. All three psychosocial factors predicted mortality, but they explained only a small fraction of the link between SEP and health. Using a similar design, Lynch and colleagues (1996) found that psychosocial factors explained a large fraction of the association between income and cardiovascular mortality (the relative hazard for the lowest income quintile decreases from 2.66 to 1.71 with simultaneous controls for depression, hopelessness, marital status, participation in organizations, and social support), but explained little of the association between income and fatal or nonfatal myocardial infarction (from 4.34 to 4.25).

The most comprehensive test of the mediational power of psychosocial factors was conducted by Marmot and colleagues using cross-sectional data from the United States (Marmot et al. 1998). They explored the associations among educational attainment, nine types of psychosocial factors (neighborhood poverty, childhood socioeconomic environment, smoking, social relationships, social support, relationship strain, perceived inequalities, the psychosocial work environment, and perceived control), and three health outcomes (self-reported physical health, waist:hip ratio, and psychological well-being). Although each factor accounted for only a small fraction of the effects of SEP on health, controlling for all psychosocial factors simultaneously explained substantial proportions of those effects. For example, with all explanatory variables controlled, the odds ratio for fair/poor health in the lowest educational group was reduced from 5.96 to 3.25 for men and from 8.00 to 3.21 for women. Importantly, however, several of these psychosocial factors, including neighborhood poverty, childhood socioeconomic environment, and perceived inequalities, might reasonably be considered alternative indicators of SEP rather than psychosocial explanatory variables per se.

The mixed findings regarding the mediational effects of psychosocial factors may reflect interactions among SEP and psychosocial factors when predicting health. Substantial evidence for such interactions exists, although the general principles that govern them have not yet been identified. One possibility is that SEP modifies the effects of psychosocial factors on health through its associations with material, interpersonal, and psychological resources. For example, negative life events affect physical and mental health more strongly among persons in lower socioeconomic positions, presumably because those persons have fewer resources with which to respond (Berkman & Syme 1979, McLeod & Kessler 1990). At the same time, psychological resources such as perceived control or high self-esteem may substitute for a lack of socioeconomic resources because they are less common in low SEP groups (Mirowsky et al. 2000). Consistent with that possibility, Lachman & Weaver (1998) found that perceived control had a stronger relationship with physical and mental health among those with fewer economic resources. Similarly, although in a different context, Krupat and colleagues (1999) reported that lower SEP breast cancer patients gained more treatment benefits from assertive behavior than did higher SEP patients; their assertiveness led to more careful diagnostic testing. Finally, through its association with environmental demands, SEP also appears to modify the physiological pathways through which psychosocial factors influence health (Seeman et al. 2001). For example, men with high cardiovascular reactivity combined with high workplace demands showed much more pronounced progression in atherosclerosis over a four-year period than did men with high cardiovascular reactivity but low workplace demands (Everson et al. 1997; see also Lynch et al. 1998).

From these studies, we conclude that SEP influences health by shaping individual responses to proximal life conditions as well as by affecting the conditions themselves. Our conclusion resonates with the basic social psychological insight that the degree of fit between individual predispositions and the opportunities and constraints of the social structure importantly determines individual well-being (House 1981). It also opens up new research opportunities concerning the diverse social psychological pathways through which SEP affects health—as a determinant of resources and environmental demands, as an identity, and also as an ascriptive characteristic that shapes interpersonal (including clinical) encounters.

RACE, DISCRIMINATION, AND HEALTH

In research on health disparities, race/ethnicity is usually treated as a proxy for the real determinant of health, which is racism. Racism is explicitly conceptualized as a multilevel phenomenon, incorporating institutional discrimination, personal experiences of discrimination, and internalized racism (Cain & Kington 2003, Williams & Williams-Morris 2000). Racism affects health through multiple pathways, categorized by Krieger (2003) as: (*a*) economic and social deprivation, (*b*) toxic exposures and other hazardous conditions, (*c*) targeted marketing of commodities that harm health, (*d*) inadequate medical care, (*e*) personal experiences of racially motivated discrimination or violence, and (*f*) health-damaging self-perceptions. These pathways implicate both material (institutional and personal discrimination) and subjective (racial/ethnic identity and internalized racism) components of race/ethnicity. Yet, as with research on subjective status, research on the subjective components of race/ethnicity has not adequately considered the complexity and dynamics of racial/ethnic identity or adequately linked these complex identities to experiences of discrimination.

Racial/Ethnic Identity

Racial/ethnic identity has been evaluated for its direct and indirect effects on health in race-specific samples. With respect to a direct effect, some scholars hypothesize a positive effect of group identification on health on the basis of the assumption that people who identify strongly with their racial/ethnic group benefit from feelings of common origin, culture, and activities (Azibo 1992, Crocker & Major 1989, Cross 1991, Tajfel & Turner 1986). Other scholars hypothesize that group identification increases vulnerability to stigma and, thereby, harms health (Fordham & Ogbu 1986, Penn et al. 1993). The limited empirical research that exists has not resolved the issue. Although some studies occasionally find a positive relationship between strong in-group identification and mental health (Mossakowski 2003, Sellers et al. 2003), other studies do not, or find effects of a relatively weak magnitude (Williams et al. 1999).[10]

These empirical inconsistencies suggest the need for more sophisticated models of racial/ethnic identity in health research that draw on social psychological theory. Within social psychology, the term identity is used to refer to "categories people use to specify who they are, to locate themselves relative to other people" (Michener & Delamater 1990, p. 91). Identities can be personal (e.g., traits, characteristics), social (group- or role-based), and collective (an identity that is interactive and shared). They shape individual behavior as well as the expectations of others (Stryker 1980). Social psychological theories of identity emphasize the multiple dimensions of identity, the heterogeneity of racial/ethnic identity within racial/ethnic groups, and the environmental factors that shape identity, all important considerations when gauging the relevance of identities for health (Stryker 1980). However, although health scholars regularly call for more multidimensional measures, the development of more sophisticated measures has been slow (Phinney 1990, 1996), and very few studies have explored linkages between the most sophisticated measures of identity and health.

Currently, the most well-developed conceptualization is the Multidimensional Model of Racial Identity (MMRI) (Sellers et al. 1998). Sellers and colleagues divide racial/ethnic identity into four dimensions: the salience of the identity (the situational relevance of an identity), the centrality of the identity (the importance of an identity to the self), regard for the group (personal and public evaluations of the group), and the ideology of the group (beliefs about how a member of the group should act). They found that these four dimensions have different associations with psychological distress. Specifically, using data from a sample of African American adolescents, they found that youth who reported more central racial/ethnic identities were less distressed than other youth, whereas distress did not vary based on perceived public regard for the group (e.g., "other groups view blacks in a positive manner").

We identify three potentially interesting lines of future investigation that bring further social psychological insight to these efforts. First, racial/ethnic identity has yet to be understood within the hierarchy of identities held by individuals. Although many researchers agree in principle to the multiplicity of identity (Sellers et al. 1997, Turner et al. 1994, White & Burke 1987), most research on racial/ethnic

---

[10]Most research on racial/ethnic identity has evaluated its association with health among African Americans. Williams et al. (1999) also estimated the effects of whites' racial identity (how close they felt to the group of whites) and whites' racial self-concept (how much their racial group was an important part of their self-image). Neither component of identity was associated with health alone or in interaction with race-related stressors.

identity on health has operationalized identity with reference to a single in-group versus out-group distinction (whites versus African Americans). Social psychological research demonstrates that individuals construe the complexity of their multiple in-groups in heterogeneous ways, from recognizing a single identity at the intersection of social identities (African American woman), to compartmentalizing as the situation allows (asserting an identity as African American in some situations and an identity as a woman in others), adopting a dominant and prevailing identity (consistently identifying as black, rather than as a black woman), or merging and embracing multiple identities (where all identities are equally salient across situations) (Roccas & Brewer 2002). Variations in how people understand their racial/ethnic identities vis-à-vis other potential identities may be associated with health. Identity theory would lead us to expect, for example, that people whose racial/ethnic identities are more salient would experience more physical and mental health problems in response to race-specific stressors (Thoits 1999).

Social psychological research also points to the dynamics of identity and the associations between these dynamics and stress (Stryker & Burke 2000). Persons may shift their social identities across situations in the face of potentially threatening upward comparisons with other group members (Mussweiler et al. 2000). More generally, people continually adjust their behaviors to maintain congruence between their identities and the responses of others (Burke 1991). Research has not yet considered how the situational relevance of racial/ethnic identities would affect their associations with health. Coping research suggests that people whose racial/ethnic identities are flexible may be better able to negotiate stressful situations (Pearlin & Schooler 1978, Mattlin et al. 1990).

Second, and related to this, research on racial/ethnic identity and health has yet to incorporate multiracial identities, despite their importance. Census data from 2000 reveal that approximately 2.3% of the U.S. population identifies as multiracial, a percentage that probably underestimates the multiracial population (Harris & Sim 2002). Reports of multiracial identity vary across social contexts, suggesting that identities are fluid and amenable to individual manipulation (Harris & Sim 2002). What remains unclear is how these identities shape health-relevant life conditions and the extent to which health promotion efforts reflect both ascribed statuses and personal identities. For example, racial/ethnic minorities who are able to pass for white in certain settings may avoid discrimination while still taking advantage of the health-promoting resources associated with their minority communities.

Finally, the concept of racial/ethnic identity may also give researchers some leverage when evaluating the relevance of health behaviors for racial/ethnic disparities. Group-specific health practices, such as eating certain kinds of food or avoiding alcohol, are often attributed to culture. Although culture is clearly relevant to health, conceptualizing these health practices as expressions of racial/ethnic identity may be equally useful. This conceptualization adds precision to the concept of culture, while also permitting analysis of within-group heterogeneity in the adoption of these practices.

Discrimination and Health

Most empirical research on racial/ethnic disparities in health focuses on personal experiences of discrimination, encompassing event-based discriminatory acts and chronic experiences of discrimination, or "everyday racism" (see Williams et al. 2003). Although institutional forms of discrimination clearly influence health, their effects are inferred from population-level patterns of health, rather than evaluated directly, because they are often invisible to the individual and, therefore, not amenable to self-reporting (Krieger 2003).

Evidence for the effects of perceived discrimination on health comes from both experiments and surveys. Experimental evidence shows that racist stimuli provoke more change in blood pressure than do neutral stimuli among blacks (Armstead et al. 1989). Race-related stressors also provoke changes in blood pressure among whites, although these changes are accompanied by less anger among whites than when experienced by blacks (Fang & Myers 2001).[11] Even relatively mild forms of mistreatment can yield powerful cardiovascular responses: In a sample of African American and white women, Guyll et al. (2001) find that subtle discrimination (measured using a six-item scale containing items such as "you are treated with less courtesy than other people") increases cardiovascular reactivity among African Americans, but less so for whites.

Survey evidence supports and expands these results (see Williams et al. 2003 for a review). Typical survey measures inquire about racial discrimination directly, or ask respondents to report instances of discrimination or "unfair treatment" along with the reason (e.g., race, age, gender, sexual orientation). Measures of discrimination vary in the time frame that they cover and in their coverage of major, event-based (e.g., fired from a job) and chronic, daily (e.g., threatened or harassed) forms of discrimination. On the basis of these types of measures, research finds that racial and ethnic minorities report both more major discrimination and day-to-day discrimination than do non-Hispanic whites (Kessler et al. 1999, Krieger 1999). Furthermore, self-reported discrimination is significantly associated with physical and mental health. In a national sample of adult Americans, persons who reported a high level of day-to-day discrimination had over twice the odds for major depression and over three times the odds for generalized anxiety disorders as people who did not, regardless of race (Kessler et al. 1999). Perceived discrimination has also been associated with self-rated health, chronic conditions, disability, and blood pressure and other cardiovascular risk factors, although the results for the latter are

---

[11]The race-related stressors differed slightly between groups, although both involved instances of explicit racism culled from popular films. For whites, the race-related stressor was a clip taken from the film *Higher Learning* depicting a white fraternity member being beaten by several black men. For blacks, the race-related stressor was a clip taken from *Do the Right Thing* showing a white man using racial slurs toward two black men, eventually resulting in a physical confrontation. For both stressors, subjects were instructed to identify with the same-race character(s).

complex (Williams et al. 2003). Longitudinal survey data support a causal effect of perceived discrimination on health: Baseline discrimination reduces subsequent physical health (Pavalko et al. 2003), and baseline psychological distress does not appear to affect subsequent reports of discrimination (Brown et al. 2000).

Anxiety about potential discrimination may affect health even in the absence of overtly discriminatory acts. Williams & Neighbors (2001) introduced the concept of "heightened vigilance," which refers to the psychological vigil and chronic physiological arousal resulting from the threat of exposure to violence and discrimination (see also Williams et al. 1994). They contend that heightened vigilance is a stressor that has effects on health irrespective of the immediate hostility of the environment, especially with essential hypertension and other cardiovascular problems. Heightened vigilance affects health in a variety of ways, including the depletion of physical and mental energy through impression management and the psychological costs associated with persistently monitoring out-group members' actions (Frable et al. 1990, Saenz 1994). In combination with reported discriminatory events, the concept of heightened vigilance suggests that the sum psychological toll of a discriminatory environment and culture may be substantial.

Nevertheless, self-reported discrimination does not fully explain racial/ethnic disparities in health in mediational models. Although some studies find that controls for racial discrimination eliminate black-white disparities (Williams et al. 1997), most studies report reduced, but still significant, differences (Kessler et al. 1999, Krieger & Sidney 1996, Ren et al. 1999). Although few would deny the effects of discrimination on the health of racial and ethnic minorities, the mediational power of discriminatory experiences may be attenuated by the weak power of many measures to capture the full extent of discrimination or, perhaps more importantly, group-based, individual, and situational differences in the propensity to perceive and report discrimination, and in group and individual coping responses. Social psychological research offers insight into both.

Perceiving and Reporting Discrimination

There is no objective standard against which to judge an action as discriminatory (Meyer 2003). Discrimination is, by its very nature, a subjective experience. By implication, reports of discrimination are subjective as well and depend on a complex process involving the perception, recall, and reporting of past life experiences. Contemporary forms of discrimination may be difficult for their targets to detect, concealed as benevolence, and delivered automatically by the discriminator (Fiske 1998, Jackman 1994). The complex nature of discrimination argues for using survey measures that sample a wide variety of life events and circumstances and that ask very specific questions about the nature of the experience (Blank et al. 2004).

In general, research suggests that standard survey measures underestimate experiences of discrimination among racial/ethnic minorities because most surveys sample from a small window of potential discriminatory experiences. The interview context may also produce under-reporting of discrimination by racial/ethnic minority groups if the interviewer is white because members of those groups are less forthcoming about experiences with and emotions surrounding discrimination in the presence of white interviewers (Cose 1993, Krysan & Couper 2003). At a more basic level, some research suggests that perceived discrimination may be more psychologically painful for lower-status groups to acknowledge, and therefore to report, because it cues feelings regarding more pervasive and uncontrollable discrimination and devaluation (see Schmitt et al. 2002 regarding gender). Among other things, such results suggest that responses to survey questions about discrimination may not be comparable across groups. Future research on minority-majority differences in health should evaluate the implications of differential reporting on estimates of the mediating effects of discrimination.

Beyond reporting differences, there may be dispositional differences in perceptions of discrimination according to Allport's (1954) early research on vigilance, mistrust, and suspicion among minority groups. Hypervigilance, defined as the chronic expectation of discrimination, increases the likelihood of reporting discriminatory intent in ambiguous events (Inman & Baron 1996).[12] Perceptions of discrimination also increase with the strength of racial/ethnic identity for African Americans (Operario & Fiske 2001, Sellers & Shelton 2003, Shelton & Sellers 2000). In contrast, internalized racism (the acceptance of the larger society's negative characterizations of one's group as characteristic of the self; see Cross 1991 and Kardiner & Ovesey 1951) may suppress reports of discrimination because respondents perceive the unfair treatment as deserved. To the degree that hypervigilance, identity, and internalized racism affect health directly, studies that fail to control for them will generate biased estimates of the effects of discrimination on health. Social psychological research demonstrates that internalized stereotypes can be activated in such a way as to increase anxiety and impair social and psychological functioning among members of disadvantaged groups (e.g., Steele 1997). Internalized racism, specifically, increases the risk of obesity (Tull et al. 1999), alcohol consumption (Taylor & Jackson 1990), and depression (Tomes et al. 1990), and diminishes self-esteem (Brown et al. 2002).

While these studies identify important individual differences in perceptions of discrimination, it may be equally important to consider situational determinants of these perceptions. Social psychological research demonstrates that members of stigmatized groups are sensitive to environmental cues that make discrimination a more or less plausible explanation for an outcome. When contextual cues

---

[12]The concept of hypervigilance is different from that of heightened vigilance and, indeed, points to limitations in frameworks that seek only to uncover chronic stress. As noted above, heightened vigilance is usually cast as a unique form of chronic stress that elevates blood pressure, irrespective of experiencing any discriminatory events. Hypervigilance, by contrast, is generally cast in a more cognitive framework, as a chronic predisposition to perceive discrimination in particular events. The distinction points to the ambiguity in interpreting the health consequences of concepts that target a heightened sense of threat, but do not explicitly consider the actual environment. Indeed, Allport (1954) contends that the vigilance often found among minorities may be adaptive in hostile environments, even though such vigilance might also increase perceived discrimination (Inman & Baron 1996).

signal a "legitimate" social order (i.e., that social mobility is possible), perceptions of discrimination by otherwise vigilant disadvantaged groups decline (Major et al. 2002, Major & Schmader 2001). Perceptions of discrimination also decline when perceivers believe that the people with whom they are interacting are not prejudiced or when they believe that others are not aware of their social identities (see Crocker & Quinn 2000 for a review). These findings support the claim that perceptions of discrimination are a social product, arising from the interaction between individual propensities and the situation as it is defined and understood by participants. Although these types of situational considerations have received extensive attention in social psychological studies of the effects of discrimination on self-esteem (Crocker & Quinn 2000), they have not yet been incorporated into studies of health.

Contingencies in the Effects of Discrimination on Health

The same dispositional and situational factors that influence perceptions of discrimination also modify their effects on health. Strong racial/ethnic identity, for example, appears to buffer the effects of discrimination (Mossakowski 2003, Sellers et al. 2003). Furthermore, discrimination has stronger effects on physical health among persons with self-blaming rather than system-blaming attributional styles (LaVeist et al. 2001) and, relatedly, among those who accept discrimination rather than challenge it (Krieger & Sidney 1996). In fact, some studies report that the active suppression of discriminatory experiences (inferred from self-reports of having experienced no discrimination) may be more harmful to health than acknowledging discrimination and talking to others, particularly when the discrimination is relatively minor (Clark et al. 1999, Krieger 1990), a result consistent with other research on thought suppression and psychological adjustment (Major & Gramzow 1999).

The effects of discrimination also vary with individual coping efforts. Most studies find that active coping styles (e.g., talking to others, taking action) are associated with better health in the presence of discrimination (Krieger 1990, Noh & Kaspar 2003, Williams et al. 1997). The health benefits of active coping depend on other environmental contingencies, however. In contrast to most studies, Noh et al. (1999) reported that forbearance, a passive coping strategy, was associated with lower depression among recent Southeast Asian refugees to Canada. They attribute their unusual finding to the lack of effective problem-solving opportunities for members of that group (Noh & Kaspar 2003). Unfamiliar with the language, behavioral norms, and legal rights, Southeast Asian refugees rely heavily on cultural norms of conflict avoidance. In contrast, Korean immigrants to Canada, who had lived there for an average of 20 years, were better able to enact active problem-solving strategies. Consistent with what we observed for SEP, then, the fit between individual efforts and environmental contingencies influences the effects of discrimination on health.

All this research suggests that the associations among racial/ethnic identity, discrimination, and health are far more complex than research on health disparities has assumed. Health disparities research has developed quite apart from the relevant social psychological theories, with little attention to the situational contingencies that shape the meaning of race/ethnicity and discrimination. Social psychological theories offer powerful means by which to conceptualize and operationalize identity and discrimination as they are reciprocally related, as they are negotiated in specific interactional contexts, and as they influence health. Indeed, without a consideration of social psychological theories, health researchers may inadequately capture the relevance of discrimination and identity for health, in some cases overstating the importance of discrimination and identity and understating it in others.

CONCLUSION

This review has highlighted realized and potential contributions of social psychology to research on health disparities. From the organizing framework of social structure and personality, to symbolic interactionist theories of identity, social psychology bridges the gap between the two dominant approaches in the field: those who encourage the exploration of health's upstream causes and those who explore the many downstream mechanisms behind disparities. This bridging of perspectives is important because current sociological emphasis on fundamental causes—while an important corrective to research focused on proximate mechanisms—leaves sociology with little to contribute beyond the basic description of contemporary and historical patterns of health disparities. Social psychological theories redirect our attention not only to fundamental social causes but also to the fundamental interactional processes through which disparities are created and sustained. These interactional processes bridge levels of analysis by highlighting the vast mesolevel environment that lies between features of the macrosocial order (e.g., regional levels of income inequality) and the biological underpinnings of health.

Our review demonstrates that the material and psychosocial factors that motivate much health disparities research take us only part of the way toward explaining those disparities. To be sure, they do contribute to the statistical explanation of the associations between SEP, race/ethnicity, and health, especially if measured and modeled appropriately. However, a narrow focus on their mediational potential misses equally important contingencies in health-related processes, contingencies that derive from the interaction between persons and environments. Social psychological processes, including construal, social comparison, and identity, involve knowledge, power, and resources, but they are also distinct. More generally, SEP and race/ethnicity are constituted within mesolevel environments that give them salience and meaning. By implication, the processes through which they have effects on health will vary across cultural, geographic, and historical contexts and cannot be neatly separated from them.

Our review suggests several new directions for research on the social psychology of health disparities, from further studies of social comparison processes, to the role of social environments in modifying SEP's effects on health, to more nuanced analyses of the health-damaging and health-promoting effects of racial/ethnic identity and discrimination. Most research on health disparities presents broad-based comparisons across socioeconomic or racial/ethnic groups. Some of our suggestions can be implemented in studies of that type with improved measures and interaction analyses. However, our emphasis on meaning and the interactional basis of health disparities highlights the utility of studies that analyze the social psychology of disparities in specific disease conditions. As illustration, Lutfey & Freese (2004) take this more focused approach in their study of SEP differences in diabetes treatment regimens. Using ethnographic data, they observed that lower SEP patients received less demanding (and therefore less effective) treatment regimens, in part because doctors perceived them to be less motivated and to have lower cognitive ability. The doctors' perceptions are consistent with the predictions of expectations states theory, which concerns the emergence and implications of status hierarchies in task-oriented interactions (Correll & Ridgeway 2004). Comparable studies of SEP differences in other disease conditions or in specific treatment processes would inform our understanding of how the ascriptive components of SEP influence health.

We also find value in studies that focus on health-related processes within specific population subgroups. The promise of a within-group approach can be seen in research on African American health, which has yielded important insights regarding the health implications of different dimensions of racial/ethnic identity. By extending this research to other racial/ethnic groups, it will be possible to determine whether these same dimensions have the same relationship with physical and mental health in those groups (Phinney 1990) or whether the relevance of racial/ethnic identity varies across situational contexts (see our earlier discussion of Noh & Kasper 2003). Although within-group studies do not directly address between-group disparities when taken individually, when viewed as complementary case studies, their results can be used to specify the person-environment interactions responsible for population-level disease profiles. Such "particularism" (see also Kunitz 1990) may be inconsistent with efforts to generate general theories of disparities that apply across diverse between-group comparisons, but nevertheless it can yield important insight about the complex social processes underlying disparities.

Similarly, future research on health disparities would benefit from considering exceptional patterns in disparities, rather than their usual manifestation. Exceptional patterns have brought important insights to light in the past. The observation that African Americans have lower rates of major mental disorders than do whites, for example, has led to a consideration of the role of religious coping in the African American community (Williams & Harris-Reid 1999). The unexpectedly positive health profiles of other racial/ethnic groups raise equally important questions about the processes through which the subjective and material components of status positions combine to influence health (McLeod & Nonnemaker 1999).

Although we have emphasized the contributions of social psychology to the study of health disparities, we note that health research may also inform developments in social psychology. Unusual patterns in the link between perceived discrimination and health (e.g., nonlinear relationships) occasioned much of the current speculation on the meaning of self-reported discrimination. Studies of the diverse mechanisms through which SEP influences health have the potential to enhance our understanding of the nonmaterial components of SEP, particularly in relation to theories of the self and of social comparison processes.

In sum, we believe that health researchers must move beyond models that emphasize either the material conditions of life or psychosocial risk factors toward models that place their interaction at the center of inquiry. These interactions lie at the heart of social psychology, a field devoted to analysis of the society-individual interface. By taking social psychology seriously, and by using its most sophisticated and recent insights, health research can lay a foundation for new theoretical insights about basic social psychological processes even as it illuminates the role of social psychological mechanisms in producing group differences in health.

ACKNOWLEDGMENTS

The authors thank Sheida Tabaie for research assistance and David Takeuchi and Matt Hunt for helpful comments. This research was supported by grant 1 R03 AG021762-01 to Jason Schnittker.

The *Annual Review of Sociology* is online at http://soc.annualreviews.org

LITERATURE CITED

Adler N, Cohen S, Matthews K, Schwartz J, Seeman T, Williams D. 1999. The MacArthur scale of subjective social status. *Psychosocial Notebook*, Res. Netw. Socioecon. Status Health, MacArthur Found., Chicago, IL. http://www.macses.ucsf.edu/Research/Psychosocial/notebook/usladder.html. Accessed March 2005

Adler NE, Epel ES, Castellazzo G, Ickovics JR. 2000. Relationship of subjective and objective social status with psychological and physiological functioning: preliminary data in healthy white women. *Health Psychol.* 19:586–92

Allport G. 1954. *The Nature of Prejudice*. New York: Doubleday Anchor

Anderson NB. 1989. Racial differences in stress-induced cardiovascular reactivity and hypertension: current status and substantive issues. *Psychol. Bull.* 105:89–105

Aneshensel CS, Phelan JC. 1999. *Handbook of the Sociology of Mental Health*. New York: Kluwer/Plenum

Armstead CA, Lawler KA, Gorden G, Cross J, Gibbons J. 1989. Relationship of racial stressors to blood pressure responses and anger expression in black college students. *Health Psychol.* 8:541–56

Azibo D. 1992. *Liberation Psychology*. Trenton, NJ: African World

Beckfield J. 2004. Does income inequality harm health? New cross-national evidence. *J. Health Soc. Behav.* 45:231–48

Bell W, Robinson RV. 1980. Cognitive maps of class and racial inequalities. *Am. J. Sociol.* 86:320–49

Berkman LF, Kawachi I. 2000a. A historical framework for social epidemiology. See Berkman & Kawachi 2000b, pp. 3–12

Berkman LF, Kawachi I. 2000b. *Social Epidemiology.* New York: Oxford Univ. Press

Berkman LF, Syme SL. 1979. Social networks, host resistance, and mortality: a nine year follow-up study of Alameda County residents. *Am. J. Epidemiol.* 109:186–204

Black D, Morris JN, Smith C, Townsend P, Whitehead M. 1988. *Inequalities in Health: The Black Report: The Health Divide.* London: Penguin

Blane D, Smith GD, Bartley M. 1993. Social selection: what does it contribute to social class differences in health? *Soc. Health Ill.* 15:1–15

Blank RM, Dabady M, Citro CF. 2004. *Measuring Racial Discrimination.* Washington, DC: Natl. Acad. Press

Brown TN, Sellers SL, Brown KT, Jackson JS. 1999. Race, ethnicity, and culture in the sociology of mental health. See Aneshensel & Phelan 1999, pp. 167–82

Brown TN, Sellers SL, Gomez JP. 2002. The relationship between internalization and self-esteem among black adults. *Soc. Focus* 35:55–71

Brown TN, Williams DR, Jackson JS, Neighbors H, Torres M, et al. 2000. "Being black and feeling blue": the mental health consequences of racial discrimination. *Race Soc.* 2:117–31

Burke PJ. 1991. Identity processes and social stress. *Am. Sociol. Rev.* 56:836–49

Cain VS, Kington RS. 2003. Investigating the role of racial/ethnic bias in health outcomes. *Am. J. Public Health* 93:191–92

Clark R, Anderson NB, Clark VR, Williams DR. 1999. Racism as a stressor for African Americans. *Am. Psychol.* 54:805–16

Correll SJ, Ridgeway CL. 2004. Expectation states theory. In *Handbook of Social Psychology,* ed. J Delamater, pp. 29–51. New York: Kluwer/Plenum

Cose E. 1993. *The Rage of a Privileged Class.* New York: Harper Collins

Crocker J, Major B. 1989. Social stigma and self-esteem: the self-protective properties of stigma. *Psychol. Rev.* 96:608–30

Crocker J, Major B, Steele C. 1998. Social stigma. In *Handbook of Social Psychology,* ed. D Gilbert, ST Fiske, G Lindzey, pp. 504–53. Boston: McGraw-Hill

Crocker J, Quinn DM. 2000. Social stigma and the self: meanings, situations, and self-esteem. In *The Social Psychology of Stigma,* ed. TF Heatherton, RE Kleck, MR Hebl, JG Hull, pp. 153–83. New York: Guilford

Cross WE. 1991. *Shades of Black: Diversity in African-American Identity.* Philadelphia, PA: Temple Univ. Press

Davey Smith G, Hard C, Blane D, Gillis D, Hawthorne V. 1997. Lifetime socioeconomic position and mortality: prospective observational study. *Brit. Med. J.* 314:547–52

Davis NJ, Robinson RV. 1988. Class identification of men and women in the 1970s and 1980s. *Am. Sociol. Rev.* 53:103–12

Davis NJ, Robinson RV. 1998. Do wives matter? Class identities of wives and husbands in the United States, 1974–1994. *Soc. Forces* 76:1063–86

Diener E, Fujita F. 1997. Social comparisons and subjective well-being. In *Health, Coping, and Well-Being: Perspectives from Social Comparison Theory,* ed. BP Buunk, FX Gibbons, pp. 329–57. Mahwah, NJ: Erlbaum

Easterlin RA. 1995. Will raising the incomes of all increase the happiness of all? *J. Econ. Behav. Org.* 27:35–47

Eibner C, Evans WN. 2005. Relative deprivation, poor health habits, and mortality. *J. Hum. Res.* In press

Elo IT, Preston SH. 1994. Estimating African American mortality from inaccurate data. *Demography* 31:427–58

Elo IT, Preston SH. 1997. Racial and ethnic differences in mortality at older ages. In *Racial and Ethnic Differences in the Health of Older*

Americans, ed. LG Martin, BJ Soldo, pp. 10–42. Washington, DC: Natl. Acad. Press

Esler M, Turbott J, Schwarz R, Leonard P, Bobik A, et al. 1982. The peripheral kinetics of norepinephrine in depressive illness. *Arch. Gen. Psychiatry* 39:295–300

Everson SA, Lynch JW, Chesney MA, Kaplan GA, Goldberg DE, et al. 1997. Interaction of workplace demands and cardiovascular reactivity in progression of carotid atherosclerosis: population based study. *Brit. Med. J.* 314:553–58

Fang CY, Myers HF. 2001. The effects of racial stressors and hostility on cardiovascular reactivity in African American and Caucasian men. *Health Psychol.* 20:64–70

Ferraro KJ, Farmer MM. 1996. Double jeopardy to health hypothesis for African Americans: analysis and critique. *J. Health Soc. Behav.* 37:27–43

Festinger L. 1954. A theory of social comparison processes. *Hum. Rel.* 7:117–40

Fine GA. 1991. On the microfoundations of macrosociology: constraints and the exterior reality of structure. *Sociol. Q.* 32:161–77

Fiscella K, Franks P. 1997. Does psychological distress contribute to racial and socioeconomic disparities in mortality? *Soc. Sci. Med.* 45:1805–9

Fiske ST. 1998. Stereotyping, prejudice, and discrimination. In *The Handbook of Social Psychology*, ed. DT Gilbert, ST Fiske, G Lindzey, pp. 357–411. Boston: McGraw-Hill

Fordham S, Ogbu JU. 1986. Black students' school success: coping with the burden of 'acting white'. *Urban Rev.* 18:176–206

Frable DE, Blackstone T, Scherbaum C. 1990. Marginal and mindful: deviants in social interactions. *J. Pers. Soc. Psychol.* 59:140–49

George LK. 2001. The social psychology of health. In *Handbook of Aging and the Social Sciences*, ed. R Binstock, LK George, pp. 217–37. San Diego, CA: Academic

Glassman AH, Shapiro PA. 1998. Depression and the course of coronary artery disease. *Am. J. Psychiatry* 155:4–11

Goodman E, Adler NE, Daniels SR, Morrison JA, Slap GB, Dolan LM. 2003. Impact of obesity and subjective social status on obesity in a biracial cohort of adolescents. *Obes. Res.* 11:1018–26

Goodman E, Adler NE, Kawachi I, Frazier AL, Huang B, Colditz GA. 2001. Adolescents' perceptions of social status: development and evaluation of a new indicator. *Pediatrics* 108:1–8

Goyder JC. 1975. A note on the declining relation between subjective and objective class measures. *Brit. J. Sociol.* 26:102–9

Graham H. 2004. Social determinants and their unequal distribution: clarifying policy understandings. *Milbank Q.* 82:101–24

Guyll M, Matthews KA, Bromberger JT. 2001. Discrimination and unfair treatment: relationship to cardiovascular reactivity among African American and European American women. *Health Psychol.* 20:315–25

Harris DR, Sim JJ. 2002. Who is multiracial? Assessing the complexity of lived race. *Am. Sociol. Rev.* 67:614–27

Hayward MD, Crimmins EM, Miles TP, Yang Y. 2000. The significance of socioeconomic status in explaining the racial gap in chronic health conditions. *Am. Sociol. Rev.* 65:910–30

House JS. 1981. Social structure and personality. In *Social Psychology: Sociological Perspectives*, ed. M Rosenberg, RH Turner, pp. 525–61. New York: Basic

House JS, Kessler RC, Herzog AR, Mero RP, Kinney AM, Breslow MJ. 1990. Age, socioeconomic status, and health. *Milbank Q.* 68:383–411

House JS, Landis KR, Umberson D. 1988. Social relationships and health. *Science* 241:540–45

House JS, Williams DR. 2000. Understanding and reducing socioeconomic and racial/ethnic disparities in health. In *Promoting Health: Intervention Strategies from Social and Behavior Research*, ed. BD Smedley, SL Syme, pp. 81–124. Washington, DC: Natl. Acad. Press

Inman ML, Baron RS. 1996. Influence of prototypes on perceptions of prejudice. *J. Pers. Soc. Psychol.* 70:727–39

Jackman MR. 1979. The subjective meaning of social class identification in the United States. *Public Opin. Q.* 43:443–62

Jackman MR. 1994. *The Velvet Glove: Paternalism and Conflict in Gender, Class, and Race Relations.* Berkeley: Univ. Calif. Press

Jackman MR, Jackman RW. 1983. *Class Awareness in the United States.* Berkeley: Univ. Calif. Press

Januzzi JL Jr, Stern TA, Pasternak RC, DeSanctis RW. 2000. The influence of anxiety and depression on outcomes of patients with coronary artery disease. *Arch. Int. Med.* 160:1913–21

Kadushin C. 1964. Social class and the experience of ill health. *Soc. Inq.* 35:67–80

Kaplan GA, Pamuk ER, Lynch JW, Cohen RD, Balfour JL. 1996. Inequality in income and mortality in the United States: analysis of mortality and potential pathways. *Brit. Med. J.* 312:999–1003

Karasek RA, Theorell T. 1990. *Healthy Work.* New York: Basic

Kardiner A, Ovesey L. 1951. *The Mark of Oppression.* New York: Norton

Kawachi I, Kennedy B, Glass R. 1999. Social capital and self-rated health: a contextual analysis. *Am. J. Public Health* 89:1187–93

Kawachi I, Kennedy BP, Lochner K, Prothrow-Stith D. 1997. Social capital, income inequality, and mortality. *Am. J. Public Health* 87:1491–98

Kawachi I, Sparrow D, Vokonas P, Weiss S. 1994. Symptoms of anxiety and risk of coronary heart disease: the normative aging study. *Circulation* 90:2225–29

Kennedy BP, Kawachi I, Prothrow-Stith D. 1996. Income distribution and mortality: cross-sectional ecological study of the Robin Hood index in the United States. *Brit. Med. J.* 312:1004–7

Kennedy BP, Kawachi I, Prothrow-Stith D, Lochner K, Gupta V. 1998. Social capital, income inequality, and firearm violent crime. *Soc. Sci. Med.* 47:7–17

Kessler RC. 1982. A disaggregation of the relationship between socioeconomic status and psychological distress. *Am. Sociol. Rev.* 47:752–64

Kessler RC, Mickelson KD, Williams DR. 1999. The prevalence, distribution, and mental health correlates of perceived discrimination in the United States. *J. Health Soc. Behav.* 40:208–30

Kitagawa EM, Hauser PM. 1973. *Differential Mortality in the United States: A Study of Socioeconomic Epidemiology.* Cambridge, MA: Harvard Univ. Press

Kohn M. 1989. Social structure and personality: a quintessentially sociological approach to social psychology. *Soc. Forces* 1:26–33

Krieger N. 1990. Racial and gender discrimination: risk factor for high blood pressure. *Soc. Sci. Med.* 30:1273–81

Krieger N. 1994. Epidemiology and the web of causation: Has anyone seen the spider? *Soc. Sci. Med.* 39:887–903

Krieger N. 1999. Embodying inequality: a review of concepts, measures, and methods for studying health consequences of discrimination. *Int. J. Health Serv.* 29:295–352

Krieger N. 2003. Does racism harm health? Did child abuse exist before 1962? On explicit questions, critical science, and current controversies: an ecosocial perspective. *Am. J. Public Health* 93:194–99

Krieger N, Sidney S. 1996. Racial discrimination and blood pressure: the CARDIA study of young black and white adults. *Am. J. Public Health* 86:1370–78

Krieger N, Williams DR, Moss NE. 1997. Measuring social class in US public health research: concepts, methodologies, and guidelines. *Annu. Rev. Public Health* 18:341–78

Kruglanski AW, Mayseless O. 1990. Classic and current social comparison research: expanding the perspective. *Psychol. Bull.* 108:195–208

Krupat E, Irish JT, Kasten LE, Freund KM, Burns RB, et al. 1999. Patient assertiveness and physician decision-making among older breast cancer patients. *Soc. Sci. Med.* 49:449–57

Krysan M, Couper MP. 2003. Race in the live and the virtual interview: racial deference, social desirability, and activation effects in attitude surveys. *Soc. Psychol. Q.* 66:364–83

Kubzansky LD, Kawachi I, Spiro A, Weiss ST, Vokonas PS, Sparrow D. 1997. Is worrying bad for your heart? A prospective study of worry and coronary heart disease in the normative aging study. *Circulation* 95:818–25

Kunitz SJ. 1990. The value of particularism in the study of the cultural, social, and behavioral determinants of mortality. In *What We Know About Health Transition: The Cultural, Social, and Behavioral Determinants of Health*, ed. J Caldwell, S Findley, P Caldwell, G Santow, W Cosford, J Braid, D Broers-Freeman, pp. 92–109. Canberra: Aust. Natl. Univ. Print. Serv.

Lachman ME, Weaver SL. 1998. The sense of control as a moderator of social class differences in health and well-being. *J. Pers. Soc. Psychol.* 74:763–73

LaVeist TA, Sellers R, Neighbors HW. 2001. Perceived racism and self and system blame attribution: consequences for longevity. *Ethn. Dis.* 11:711–21

Lin-Fu JS. 1993. Asian and Pacific Islander Americans: an overview of demographic characteristics and health care issues. *Asian Pac. Isl. J. Health* 1:20–36

Link BG, Phelan JC. 1995. Social conditions as fundamental causes of disease. *J. Health Soc. Behav.* extra issue:80–94

Lutfey K, Freese J. 2004. *Toward some fundamentals of fundamental causality: socioeconomic status and health in the routine clinic visit for diabetes*. Work. Pap., Dep. Soc., Univ. Minn.

Lynch J, Davey Smith G, Harper S, Hillemeier M, Ross N, et al. 2004. Is income inequality a determinant of population health? Part 1. A systematic review. *Milbank Q.* 82:5–99

Lynch J, Kaplan G. 2000. Socioeconomic position. See Berkman & Kawachi 2000b, pp. 13–35

Lynch JW, Everson SA, Kaplan GA, Salonen R, Salonen JT. 1998. Does low socioeconomic status potentiate the effects of heightened cardiovascular responses to stress on the progression of carotid atherosclerosis? *Am. J. Public Health* 88:389–94

Lynch JW, Kaplan GA, Cohen RD, Tuomilehto J, Salonen JT. 1996. Do cardiovascular risk factors explain the relation between socioeconomic status, risk of all-cause mortality, cardiovascular mortality, and acute myocardial infarction? *Am. J. Epidemiol.* 144:934–42

Lynch JW, Kaplan GA, Salonen JT. 1997. Why do poor people behave poorly? Variation in adult health behaviors and psychosocial characteristics by stages of the socioeconomic life course. *Soc. Sci. Med.* 44:809–19

Lynch JW, Smith GD, Kaplan GA, House JS. 2000. Income inequality and mortality: importance to health of individual income, psychosocial environment, or material conditions. *Brit. Med. J.* 320:1200–4

Major B, Gramzow RH. 1999. Abortion as stigma: cognitive and emotional implications of concealment. *J. Pers. Soc. Psychol.* 77:735–45

Major B, Gramzow RH, McCoy SK, Levin S, Schmader T, Sidanius J. 2002. Perceiving personal discrimination: the role of group status and legitimizing ideology. *J. Pers. Soc. Psychol.* 82:269–82

Major B, Schmader T. 2001. Legitimacy and the construal of social disadvantage. In *The Psychology of Legitimacy: Emering Perspectives on Ideology, Justice, and Intergroup Relationships*, ed. JT Jost, B Major, pp. 176–204. New York: Cambridge Univ. Press

Manton KG, Stallard E. 1997. Health and disability differences among racial and ethnic groups. In *Racial and Ethnic Differences in the Health of Older Americans*, ed. LG Martin, B Soldo, pp. 43–105. Washington, DC: Natl. Acad. Press

Marmot M. 1997. Inequality, deprivation and alcohol use. *Addiction* 92:S13–20

Marmot M, Davey Smith G, Stansfeld S, Patel C, North F, et al. 1991. Health inequalities among British civil servants: the Whitehall II study. *Lancet* 337:1387–93

Marmot MG, Fuhrer R, Ettner SL, Marks NF, Bumpass LL, Ryff CD. 1998. Contribution of psychosocial factors to socioeconomic differences in health. *Milbank Q.* 76:403–48

Marmot MG, McDowall ME. 1986. Mortality decline and widening social inequalities. *Lancet* 339:275–76

Marmot MG, Ryff CD, Bumpass LL, Shipley M, Marks NF. 1997. Social inequalities in health: next questions and converging evidence. *Soc. Sci. Med.* 44:901–10

Marmot MG, Shipley MJ, Rose G. 1984. Inequalities in death—specific explanations of a general pattern? *Lancet* 1:1003–6

Mattlin JA, Wethington E, Kessler RC. 1990. Situational determinants of coping and coping effectiveness. *J. Health Soc. Behav.* 31:103–22

McKinlay JB. 1975. A case for refocusing upstream—the political economy of sickness. In *Behavioral Aspects of Prevention*, ed. A. Enelow, pp. 9–25. Dallas, TX: Am. Heart Assoc.

McKinlay JB, Marceau LD. 2000. To boldly go. *Am. J. Public Health* 90:25–33

McLeod JD, Kessler RC. 1990. Socioeconomic status differences in vulnerability to undesirable life events. *J. Health Soc. Behav.* 31:162–72

McLeod JD, Lively KJ. 2004. Social structure and personality. In *Handbook of Social Psychology*, ed. JD Delamater, pp. 77–102. New York: Kluwer/Plenum

McLeod JD, Nonnemaker JM. 1999. Social stratification and inequality. See Aneshensel & Phelan 1999, pp. 321–44

McLeod JD, Nonnemaker JM, Call KT. 2004. Income inequality, race, and child well-being: an aggregate analysis in the 50 United States. *J. Health Soc. Behav.* 45:249–64

Menchik P. 1993. Economic status as a determinant of mortality among nonwhite and white older males: or, does poverty kill? *Popul. Stud.* 47:427–36

Meyer IH. 2003. Prejudice as stress: conceptual and measurement problems. *Am. J. Public Health* 93:262–65

Michener HA, DeLamater JD, Schwartz SH. 1990. *Social Psychology*. San Diego: Harcourt Brace Jovanovich. 2nd ed.

Miech R, Hauser RM. 2001. Socioeconomic status and health at midlife: a comparison of educational attainment with occupational-based indicators. *Ann. Epidemol.* 11:75–84

Mirowsky J, Ross CE, Reynolds J. 2000. Links between social status and health status. In *Handbook of Medical Sociology*, ed. CE Bird, P Conrad, A Fremont, pp. 47–67. Upper Saddle River, NJ: Prentice Hall

Mossakowski KN. 2003. Coping with perceived discrimination: Does ethnic identity protect mental health? *J. Health Soc. Behav.* 44:318–31

Mussweiler T, Gabriel S, Bodenhausen GV. 2000. Shifting social identities as a strategy for deflecting threatening social comparisons. *J. Pers. Soc. Psychol.* 79:398–409

Natl. Cent. Health Stat. 2004. *Health, United States*. Hyattsville, MD: Natl. Cent. Health Stat.

Noh S, Beiser M, Kaspar V, Hou F, Rummens J. 1999. Perceived racial discrimination, depression, and coping: a study of Southeast Asian refugees in Canada. *J. Health Soc. Behav.* 40:193–207

Noh S, Kaspar V. 2003. Perceived discrimination and depression: moderating effects of coping, acculturation, and ethnic support. *Am. J. Public Health* 93:232–38

North F, Syme SL, Feeney A, Head J, Shipley MJ, Marmot MG. 1993. Explaining socioeconomic differences in sickness absence: the Whitehall II study. *Brit. Med. J.* 306:361–66

Operario D, Fiske ST. 2001. Ethnic identity moderates perceptions of prejudice: judgments of personal versus group discrimination and subtle versus blatant bias. *Pers. Soc. Psychol. Bull.* 27:550–61

Ostrove JM, Adler NE, Kuppermann M, Washington AE. 2000. Objective and subjective assessments of socioeconomic status and their relationship to self-rated health in an ethnically diverse sample of pregnant women. *Health Psychol.* 19:613–18

Pavalko E, Mossakowski KN, Hamilton VJ. 2003. Does perceived discrimination affect heath? Longitudinal relationships between work discrimination and women's physical and emotional health. *J. Health Soc. Behav.* 44:18–33

Pearlin LI, Schooler C. 1978. The structure of coping. *J. Health Soc. Behav.* 19:2–21

Penn ML, Gaines SO, Phillips L. 1993. On the desirability of own group preferences. *J. Black Psychol.* 19:303–21

Phinney JS. 1990. Ethnic identity in adolescents and adults: review of research. *Psychol. Bull.* 108:499–514

Phinney JS. 1996. When we talk about American ethnic groups, what do we mean? *Am. Psychol.* 51:918–27

Power C, Matthews S. 1997. Origins of health inequalities in a national population. *Lancet* 350:1584–89

Preston SH, Taubman P. 1994. Socioeconomic differences in adult mortality and health status. In *Demography of Aging*, ed. LG Martin, SH Preston, pp. 279–318. Washington, DC: Natl. Acad. Press

Pritchett L, Summers LH. 1996. Wealthier is healthier. *J. Hum. Res.* 31:841–68

Rao SLN. 1973. On long-term mortality trends in the United States, 1850–1968. *Demography* 10:405–19

Ren XS, Amick BC, Williams DR. 1999. Racial/ethnic disparities in health: the interplay between discrimination and socioeconomic status. *Ethn. Dis.* 9:151–65

Reynolds JR. 1997. The effects of industrial employment conditions on job-related distress. *J. Health Soc. Behav.* 38:105–16

Robert SA, House JS. 2000. Socioeconomic inequalities in health: an enduring sociological problem. In *Handbook of Medical Sociology*, ed. CE Bird, P Conrad, AM Fremont, pp. 79–97. Upper Saddle River, NJ: Prentice Hall

Roccas S, Brewer MB. 2002. Social identity complexity. *Pers. Soc. Psychol. Rev.* 6:88–106

Rodin J. 1986. Aging and health: effects of the sense of control. *Science* 233:1271–76

Rogers RG. 1992. Living and dying in the U.S.A.: sociodemographic determinants of death among blacks and whites. *Demography* 29:287–303

Rogot E. 1992. *A Mortality Study of 1.3 Million Persons by Demographic, Social, and Economic Factors: 1979–1985 Follow-Up*. Bethesda, MD: Natl. Inst. Health, Natl. Heart, Lung, Blood Inst.

Rosen G. 1963. The evolution of social medicine. In *Handbook of Medical Sociology*, ed. HE Freeman, S Levine, LG Reeder, pp. 1–61. Englewood Cliffs, NJ: Prentice Hall

Rosenberg M. 1979. *Conceiving the Self*. New York: Basic

Ross CE, Wu C. 1995. The links between education and health. *Am. Sociol. Rev.* 60:719–45

Rothman K. 1986. *Modern Epidemiology*. Boston, MA: Little, Brown

Ryff CD. 1987. The place of personality and social structure research in social psychology. *J. Pers. Soc. Psychol.* 53:1192–202

Saenz DS. 1994. Token status and problem-solving deficits: detrimental effects of distinctiveness and performance monitoring. *Soc. Cogn.* 12:61–74

Scheier MF, Carver CS. 1985. Optimism, coping, and health: assessment and implications of generalized outcome expectancies. *Health Psychol.* 4:219–47

Scheier MF, Matthews KA, Owens JF, Magovern GJ Sr, Lefebvre RC, et al. 1989. Dispositional optimism and recovery from coronary artery bypass surgery: the beneficial effects on physical and psychological well-being. *J. Pers. Soc. Psychol.* 57:1024–40

Schmitt MT, Branscombe NR, Kobrynowicz D, Owen S. 2002. Perceiving discrimination against one's gender group has different implications for well-being in women and men. *Pers. Soc. Psychol. Bull.* 28:197–210

Seeman TE, Crimmins E. 2001. Social environment effects on health and aging: integrating epidemiologic and demographic approaches and perspectives. *Ann. N.Y. Acad. Sci.* 954:88–117

Seeman TE, McEwan BS, Rowe JW, Singer BH. 2001. Allostatic load as a marker of cumulative biological risk: MacArthur studies of successful aging. *Proc. Nat. Acad. Sci. USA* 98:4770–75

Seeman TE, Singer BH, Rowe JW, Horwitz RI, McEwen BS. 1997. Price of adaptation–allostatic load and its health consequences. MacArthur studies of successful aging. *Arch. Int. Med.* 157:2259–68

Sellers RM, Caldwell CH, Schmeelk-Cone KH, Zimmerman MA. 2003. Racial identity, racial discrimination, perceived stress, and psychological distress among African American young adults. *J. Health Soc. Behav.* 43:302–17

Sellers RM, Rowley SJ, Chavous TM, Shelton JN, Smith MA. 1997. Multidimensional inventory of black identity: a preliminary investigation of reliability and construct validity. *J. Pers. Soc. Psychol.* 73:805–15

Sellers RM, Shelton JN. 2003. The role of racial identity in perceived racial discrimination. *J. Pers. Soc. Psychol.* 84:1079–92

Sellers RM, Smith M, Shelton JN, Rowley SJ, Chavous TM. 1998. Multidimensional model of racial identity: a reconceptualization of African American racial identity. *Pers. Soc. Psychol. Rev.* 2:18–39

Shelton JN, Sellers RM. 2000. Situational stability and variability in African American racial identity. *J. Black Psychol.* 26:27–50

Singer BH, Ryff CD. 2001. *New Horizons in Health: An Integrative Approach.* Washington, DC: Natl. Acad. Press

Singh-Manoux A, Adler NE, Marmot MG. 2003. Subjective social status: its determinants and its association with measures of ill-health in the Whitehall II study. *Soc. Sci. Med.* 56:1321–33

Smedley BD, Stith AY, Nelson AR, eds. 2003. *Unequal Treatment: Confronting Racial and Ethnic Disparities in Health Care.* Washington, DC: Natl. Acad. Press

Smith JP. 1999. Healthy bodies and thick wallets: the dual relation between health and economic status. *J. Econ. Perspect.* 13:145–67

Sorlie P, Rogot E, Anderson R, Johnson NJ, Backlund E. 1992. Black-white mortality differences by family income. *Lancet* 340:346–50

Sorlie PD, Backlund E, Johnson NJ, Rogot E. 1993. Mortality by Hispanic status in the United States. *JAMA* 270:2464–68

Sorlie PD, Backlund E, Keller J. 1995. U.S. mortality by economic, demographic, and social characteristics: the national longitudinal mortality study. *Am. J. Public Health* 85:949–56

Steele CM. 1997. A threat in the air: how stereotypes shape intellectual identity and performance. *Am. Psychol.* 52:613–29

Stryker S. 1980. *Symbolic Interactionism: A Social Structural View.* Menlo Park, CA: Benjamin-Cummings

Stryker S, Burke PJ. 2000. The past, present, and future of an identity theory. *Soc. Psychol. Q.* 63:284–97

Susser M, Susser E. 1996a. Choosing a future for epidemiology: I. Eras and paradigms. *Am. J. Public Health* 86:668–73

Susser M, Susser E. 1996b. Choosing a future for epidemiology: II. From black box to Chinese boxes and eco-epidemiology. *Am. J. Public Health* 86:674–77

Susser M, Watson W, Hopper K. 1985. *Sociology in Medicine.* New York: Oxford Univ. Press

Tajfel H, Turner JC. 1986. The social identity theory of intergroup behavior. In *The Social Psychology of Intergroup Relations*, ed. WG Austin, S Worchel, pp. 33–48. Chicago: Nelson-Hall

Taylor J, Jackson B. 1990. Factors affecting alcohol consumption in black women, part II. *Int. J. Addict.* 25:1415–27

Taylor SE, Repetti RL, Seeman T. 1997. Health psychology: What is an unhealthy environment and how does it get under the skin? *Annu. Rev. Psychol.* 48:411–47

Thoits PA. 1999. Self, identity, stress, and mental health. See Aneshensel & Phelan 1999, pp. 345–68

Tomes E, Brown A, Semenya K, Simpson J. 1990. Depression in black women of low socioeconomic status: psychological factors and nursing diagnosis. *J. Natl. Black Nurses Assoc.* 4:37–46

Tull ES, Wickramasuriya T, Taylor J, Smith-Burns V, Brown M, et al. 1999. Relationship of internalized racism to abdominal obesity and blood pressure in Afro-Caribbean women. *J. Natl. Med. Assoc.* 9:447–51

Turner J, Oakes P, Haslam SA, McGarty C. 1994. Self and collective: cognition and social context. *Pers. Soc. Psychol. Bull.* 20:454–63

US Dep. Health Hum. Serv. 2002. *HHS disparities initiative fact sheet.* http://www.omhrc.gov/inetpub/wwwroot/rah/indexnew.htm

Uselding P. 1976. In dispraise of muckrakers: United States occupational mortality, 1890–1910. *Res. Econ. Hist.* 1:334–71

Vega WA, Amaro H. 1994. Latino outlook: good health, uncertain prognosis. *Annu. Rev. Public Health* 15:39–67

Vega WA, Rumbaut R. 1991. Ethnic minorities and mental health. *Annu. Rev. Sociol.* 17:351–83

White CL, Burke PJ. 1987. Ethnic role identity among black and white college students: an interactionist approach. *Soc. Perspect.* 30:310–31

Wilkinson RG. 1992. Income distribution and life expectancy. *Brit. Med. J.* 304:165–68

Wilkinson RG. 1994. The epidemiological transition: from material scarcity to social disadvantage? *Daedalus* 123:61–77

Wilkinson RG. 1996. *Unhealthy Societies: The Afflictions of Inequality.* New York: Routledge

Wilkinson RG. 1997. Socioeconomic determinants of health: health inequalities: relative or absolute material standards? *Brit. Med. J.* 314:591–95

Wilkinson RG. 1999. Health, hierarchy, and social anxiety. *Ann. N.Y. Acad. Sci.* 896:48–63

Williams DR. 1990. Socioeconomic differences in health: a review and redirection. *Soc. Psychol. Q.* 53:81–99

Williams DR. 1997. Race and health: basic questions, emerging directions. *Ann. Epidemiol.* 7:322–33

Williams DR, Collins C. 1995. U.S. socioeconomic and racial differences in health: patterns and explanations. *Annu. Rev. Sociol.* 21:349–86

Williams DR, Harris-Reid M. 1999. Race and mental health: emerging patterns and promising approaches. In *A Handbook for the Study of Mental Health: Social Contexts, Theories, and Systems,* ed. AV Horwitz, TL Scheid, pp. 295–314. New York: Cambridge Univ. Press

Williams DR, Lavizzo-Moury R, Warren RC. 1994. The concept of race and health status in America. *Public Health Rep.* 109:26–41

Williams DR, Neighbors H. 2001. Racism, discrimination, and hypertension: evidence and needed research. *Ethn. Dis.* 11:800–16

Williams DR, Neighbors HW, Jackson JS. 2003. Racial/ethnic discrimination and health: findings from community studies. *Am. J. Public Health* 93:200–8

Williams DR, Spencer MS, Jackson JS. 1999. Race, stress, and physical health: the role of group identity. In *Self, Social Identity, and Physical Health,* ed. RJ Contrada, RD Ashmore, pp. 71–100. New York: Oxford Univ. Press

Williams DR, Williams-Morris R. 2000. Racism and mental health: the African American experience. *Ethn. Health* 5:243–68

Williams DR, Yu Y, Jackson JS, Anderson NB. 1997. Racial differences in physical and mental health: socioeconomic status, stress, and discrimination. *J. Health Psychol.* 2:335–51

Wise PH. 1993. Confronting racial disparities in infant mortality: reconciling science and politics. *Am. J. Prev. Med.* 9:7–16

Wise PH. 2003. The anatomy of a disparity in infant mortality. *Annu. Rev. Public Health* 24:341–62

Wood JV. 1989. Theory and research concerning social comparison of personal attributes. *Psychol. Bull.* 106:231–48

Annu. Rev. Sociol. 2005. 31:105–25
doi: 10.1146/annurev.soc.29.010202.100026
Copyright © 2005 by Annual Reviews. All rights reserved
First published online as a Review in Advance on April 7, 2005

ASSESSING IMMIGRANT ASSIMILATION: New Empirical and Theoretical Challenges

Mary C. Waters and Tomás R. Jiménez

*Department of Sociology, Harvard University, Cambridge, Massachusetts 02138;
email: mcw@wjh.harvard.edu, tjimenez@wjh.harvard.edu*

Key Words   immigration, generation, incorporation, immigrant gateways

■ **Abstract**   This review examines research on the assimilation of immigrant groups. We review research on four primary benchmarks of assimilation: socioeconomic status, spatial concentration, language assimilation, and intermarriage. The existing literature shows that today's immigrants are largely assimilating into American society along each of these dimensions. This review also considers directions for future research on the assimilation of immigrant groups in new southern and midwestern gateways and how sociologists measure immigrant assimilation. We document the changing geography of immigrant settlement and review the emerging body of research in this area. We argue that examining immigrant assimilation in these new immigrant gateways is crucial for the development of theories about immigrant assimilation. We also argue that we are likely to see a protracted period of immigrant replenishment that may change the nature of assimilation. Studying this change requires sociologists to use both birth cohort and generation as temporal markers of assimilation.

INTRODUCTION

American sociology owes its birth to the desire to understand the great changes that our society underwent at the beginning of the twentieth century—urbanization, industrialization, and perhaps most importantly, immigration. Between 1880 and 1920, the United States absorbed roughly 24 million immigrants, the great majority of them from southern and eastern Europe. The beginning of the twenty-first century is also marked by an era of massive immigration, and sociologists are once again trying to make sense of the impact of immigration on our society and on the immigrants themselves. By 2002, 23% of the U.S. population, or 34.2 million people, were foreign-born or second generation—the children of the foreign-born. The concept of assimilation, which played such a great role in understanding the experiences of European immigrants, is once again center stage.

The last comprehensive review of sociological research on immigration and assimilation outlined an increase in immigrants from Latin American and Asia and their prospects for assimilation (Massey 1981). This review pointed to significant evidence in sociological research that, on balance, these immigrants were well

0360-0572/05/0811-0105$20.00

on their way to becoming fully integrated into American society. Although there was variation between groups, research on spatial concentration, intermarriage, and socioeconomic advancement from one generation to the next all suggested that these immigrant groups were becoming Americans in much the same way that European immigrant groups did before them. Twenty-four years after this last review, we find continued support for this position.

The core measurable aspects of assimilation formulated to study European immigrants are still the starting points for understanding immigrant assimilation today: How different or similar to other Americans are immigrants and their children in terms of socioeconomic standing, residential segregation, language use, and intermarriage? In this review we very briefly examine the current evidence on these benchmarks of immigrant assimilation. We then highlight two factors that are shaping the present day immigrant assimilation but hitherto have received little research attention—the geographic dispersal of immigrants to nontraditional receiving areas, and the continuing replenishment of immigrants through ongoing immigration. We argue here that these two factors have important implications both for the kinds of empirical research social scientists should undertake and for the theoretical tools and concepts they use to shape their research.

A number of scholars have noted that both popular and scholarly notions of what constitutes success for post-1965 immigrants to the United States are either implicitly or explicitly comparative with the experiences of immigrants who came in the last mass immigration between 1880 and 1920 (Alba & Nee 2003, Foner 2000, Gerstle & Mollenkopf 2001, Reider & Steinlight 2003). Yet we should also recognize that many of the methods and theories we use to assess immigrant assimilation are also derived from the study of these earlier immigrants. The Chicago school of sociology took as one of its main subjects understanding immigrant assimilation in that city. With the publication of *The Polish Peasant in Europe and America* by W.I. Thomas and Florian Znaniecki in 1918, a new agenda for sociology was set, one that, in Martin Bulmer's words, shifted sociology "from abstract theory and library research toward a more intimate acquaintance with the empirical world, studied nevertheless in terms of a theoretical frame" (Bulmer 1984, p. 45). Robert Park, Ernest Burgess, and W.I. Thomas trained a cadre of graduate students to study the experience of immigrants in Chicago, and provided methodological and theoretical tools for making sense of the patterns they found.

The influence of these early sociologists is seen in the research that stressed the role of the city and spatial dynamics in the experience of European immigrants (Lieberson 1963, 1980). In addition, the theories of immigrant assimilation developed during the twentieth century and culminated in Gordon's influential 1964 book, *Assimilation in American Life*, which highlighted generational change as the yardstick to measure changes in immigrant groups. The first generation (the foreign-born) were less assimilated and less exposed to American life than were their American-born children (the second generation), and their grandchildren (the third generation) were in turn more like the core American mainstream than their parents.

The shift in settlement patterns among immigrants to new destinations and the continuing replenishment of new immigrants through ongoing migration streams mean that the emerging literature on immigration will have to take a new empirical and theoretical focus. Empirically, it is time to move away from city-based studies in traditional gateways and look at the transformation of the South, the Midwest, and small cities, towns and rural areas, and suburban areas as sites of first settlement. In the 1990s, appreciable numbers of immigrants settled in the South and rural Midwest—regions that have had little experience with immigration. We describe the effect that region of settlement might have on immigrant assimilation, and we outline a research agenda for sociological study of this new phenomenon. Theoretically, we argue that the concept of "generation" and its centrality to immigration research must be rethought, given the ongoing replenishment of new immigrants likely to characterize immigration flows for the foreseeable future. The social, political, and economic forces that spur and perpetuate migration appear to be well entrenched, and we believe that there will be a resulting replenishment of immigrants that is likely to be a defining characteristic of American immigration for years to come. The experience of European immigrants in the twentieth century was sharply defined by the cutoff in immigration that occurred as a result of the Depression and the restrictive immigration laws of the 1920s. This restriction created conditions that made generation a powerful variable. Not only did one's generation define one's distance from immigrant ancestors, but it also served as a proxy for birth cohort and for distance from all first-generation immigrants. The power of generation as an independent variable predicting degree of assimilation was tied, in ways few social scientists recognized, to the specific history of the flows of immigration from Europe. In this review we examine some of the ways that immigrant assimilation itself is likely to be different under conditions of ongoing immigration, and we specifically argue that generation will become a much weaker predictive variable in studies of that experience.

IMMIGRANT ASSIMILATION: THE CURRENT STATE OF THE FIELD

After nearly 40 years of immigration from around the globe, a number of summary studies of immigrant assimilation paint a rather optimistic picture of their absorption into American society. Alba & Nee (2003) rehabilitate the sometimes controversial term assimilation to describe the experience of these immigrants. Bean & Stevens (2003) also summarize the economic, linguistic, social, and spatial incorporation of the foreign-born, and report in summary that there is great reason to hope for a positive outcome for most of these immigrants.

The standard measures of immigrant assimilation have been employed by social scientists to document this generally optimistic story. These include (*a*) socioeconomic status (SES), defined as educational attainment, occupational specialization, and parity in earnings; (*b*) spatial concentration, defined in terms of dissimilarity in spatial distribution and of suburbanization; (*c*) language assimilation, defined in terms of English language ability and loss of mother tongue; and (*d*) inter-marriage, defined by race or Hispanic origin, and only occasionally by ethnicity and generation. Quantitative studies use statistical data, primarily from the census but also from large sample surveys, to assess the gap between the American mainstream, sometimes defined as native whites of native parentage, sometimes defined as native-born Americans who share the same race or Hispanic origin as the foreign-born, and sometimes defined as all native-born Americans. Progress for immigrants is measured in time since arrival, and progress for groups overall is measured by generation. There is also a rich and ongoing tradition of qualitative research involving ethnographic fieldwork or in-depth interviewing, which also owes its roots to the Chicago school of sociology (some good examples include Hondagneu-Sotelo 1994, Hondagneu-Sotelo 2003, Kasinitz et al. 2004, Kibria 2003, Kurien 2003, Levitt 2001, Mahler 1995, Menjivar 1999, Waters 1999).

Socioeconomic Status

Generalizations about immigrants gloss over huge class, race, ethnic, gender, and legal status differences. Yet when economists debate the socioeconomic outcomes of immigrants, they often commit this error. Economists Barry Chiswick (1978) and George Borjas (1994) represent two different positions on the experience of immigrants in the American labor market. Chiswick, using cross-sectional census data, compared immigrants who had been in the United States a long time with those who had been here less time and concluded that after a period of about 20 years immigrants caught up to native-born people with the same human capital characteristics. Borjas used successive censuses to look at synthetic cohorts of immigrants and argued that more recent immigrants were of lower "quality" and would not catch up to the native-born or see the same kind of earnings growth that Chiswick identified. [The National Institutes of Health has now funded a National Longitudinal Survey of Immigrants, but it will be a number of years before that survey will yield true cohorts of immigrants whose earnings can be followed over time (Jasso et al. 2000).] However, if one compares immigrants in the census data to native-born individuals of the same ethnic group (not all native-born Americans in the labor market), then immigrants do achieve economic parity in earnings. Yet, the low educational levels of Mexicans and other Central Americans remain a cause for concern because even if the immigrants earn as much as natives with such low educational profiles, they are still very much at risk of poverty in the American labor market, especially given the changes in the American economy marked by a rising premium on higher education, rising income inequality, and declining real wages at the bottom of the distribution (Ellwood 2000).

The educational attainment of the second generation has been an increasing object of study. Portes & Rumbaut's (2001) Children of Immigrants Longitudinal Study in Miami and San Diego found that 1.5-generation (those who arrive before age 13) and second-generation children tend to do better than their native-born schoolmates in grades, rates of school retention, and behavioral aspects such as homework. Using census data, Farley & Alba (2002) and Hirschman (2001) find the same outcomes. The New York Second Generation study finds that second-generation West Indians do better than native-born blacks in the city, and Dominicans, Colombians, Ecuadorans, and Peruvians do better than Puerto Ricans. Chinese do better in high school graduation rates and college attendance than all the other groups, including native whites of native parentage (Kasinitz et al. 2004). The one cause for concern once again in this large picture is Mexican Americans. Although the second generation is not doing too badly, especially compared with the very low levels of education of their parents, there is some evidence of third-generation decline among the grandchildren of Mexican immigrants (Bean et al. 1994, Livingston & Kahn 2002, Ortiz 1996, Perlmann & Waldinger 1997).

Residential Patterns

Although we focus below on the experience of immigrants in the areas of new geographic settlement in the South and Midwest, the majority of immigrants still settle in the large gateway cities—Los Angeles, New York, Miami, San Francisco, Chicago, Dallas, and Houston. Sociologists Richard Alba and John Logan have explored patterns of segregation in large cities and their suburbs in the 1980s and 1990s, and sociologist William Frey examined patterns of distribution of the foreign-born and natives by city and region (Alba et al. 1999, 2000; Alba & Logan 1993; Frey 1996; Logan et al. 1996). These studies all find that Asian and Latino immigrants have moderate degrees of segregation from white Anglos—much lower than the segregation that blacks experience from whites. These studies also document a big difference between current immigrants and earlier European immigrants: Large numbers of current new immigrants settle in suburban areas upon initial arrival in the United States. Indeed, Alba & Nee (2003, p. 254) report that among immigrants who arrived in the 1990s, 48% of those living in metropolitan areas resided outside of central cities in suburban areas. Yet, overall these studies of residential concentration of immigrant groups uphold what Massey (1985) calls the spatial assimilation model. This model, based on the theories of Park (1950) and other sociologists in the Chicago school, posits that increasing socioeconomic attainment, longer residence in the United States, and higher generational status lead to decreasing residential concentration for a particular ethnic group.

Linguistic Patterns

Despite the sometimes fevered pitch of public debates about language use by immigrants and their children, and the related debate about bilingual education, the evidence on language assimilation is quite optimistic. Although the absolute number of people who speak a language other than English in their homes is quite high (47 million people), the documented changes over time in language use point to high levels of language assimilation. Bean & Stevens (2003), using data from the 2000 U.S. Census, point out that among immigrants from non-English speaking countries, only 10% did not speak English at all at the time of the census. Bean & Stevens (2003) find a strong positive association between a foreign-born person's time in the United States and his or her ability to speak English well. Using 1990 U.S. Census data, Alba et al. (2002) find that even among Mexicans and Cubans, two thirds to three quarters, respectively, of the third generation do not speak any Spanish. Thus, the three-generation model of language assimilation appears to hold for most of today's immigrants: The immigrant generation makes some progress but remains dominant in their native tongue, the second generation is bilingual, and the third generation speaks English only.

Intermarriage

Intermarriage is often seen as the litmus test of assimilation. Gordon (1964) certainly posited that it would be the ultimate proof of assimilation. Most studies of intermarriage in the United States tend to focus on broad racial groups—Asians, Latinos, African Americans, American Indians, and whites—but not on specific national-origin groups. For instance, Lee & Bean (2004) assess the relationship between rising immigration, high rates of intermarriage, and the increasing number of multiracial individuals. Studies that focus on race find much higher intermarriage rates with whites among Asians and Latinos than among blacks with whites. Gilbertson et al. (1991) differentiates between the native- and foreign-born, and finds that the native-born have higher intermarriage rates than the foreign-born. Yet, there is evidence that there is significant intermarriage among the subgroups that make up the broad racial categories. Rosenfeld (2002) uses 1970–1980 U.S. Census data to show that Mexican Americans experience no significant barriers to intermarriage with non-Hispanic whites. Despite the growth of the Mexican population and the related increase in the number of eligible Mexican marriage partners, Mexican American–non-Hispanic white intermarriage rates suggest that where marriage is concerned, social barriers between Mexican Americans and whites are thin. Perlmann & Waters (2004) compare patterns of intermarriage among Italian Americans between 1920 and 1960 with patterns among Mexican Americans in 1998–2001. They find that Italians in the first half of the twentieth century out-married at about the same rate that Mexicans of the same generation did at the end of the twentieth century, despite the fact that Mexicans are a much larger group and thus have far more chances to in-marry than did the Italians. They conclude that the constraints other than group size that operated against out-marriage were actually greater for Italian women living at that time than for Mexicans now (Perlmann & Waters 2004, p. 271). There is also significant intermarriage among the groups that make up broad racial groups, yielding pan-ethnic unions. Rosenfeld (2001) finds that Hispanics and Asians display strong marital affinity for individuals from the same broad racial category, even if marriage partners are not from the same ethnic group (i.e., Puerto Ricans marrying Mexicans or Chinese marrying Koreans). The high rates of marriage within the broad racial categories suggest that these categories are meaningful in how individuals select their mates.

This brief review of national-level data using standard sociological measures of assimilation, and using generation to track changes over time within groups, tells us much about immigrant assimilation and shows some great continuities between the experiences of earlier European immigrants and current, predominantly non-European immigrants. We turn now to a discussion of two less-documented phenomena, which mark a potentially sharp difference between the two waves of immigration: settlement in nontraditional areas and the ongoing replenishment of immigrants through continuing immigration.

NEW IMMIGRANT GATEWAYS

The 1990s ushered in a new period of American immigration characterized by a change in the destinations of immigrants. Although the overwhelming majority of immigrants still concentrate in traditional gateway states, such as New York, Massachusetts, Florida, Illinois, Texas, and California, the southern and midwestern states have seen unprecedented gains in their foreign-born populations. To be sure, these states were home to a number of immigrant groups during previous periods of American immigration (Pozzetta 1991), but the recent growth is unparalleled by any other period.

To illustrate the changes in the geographic distribution and rates of growth of immigration in the United States, Table 1 shows the number of foreign-born individuals in states where the foreign-born population grew by a factor of two or more between 1990 and 2000. The largest percentage growth in the foreign-born population took place in the midwestern and southern states, with North Carolina experiencing the greatest increase at 273.7%. Of the 19 states in the table, 16 are located either in the Midwest or the South, and the Table includes none of the traditional gateway states. Table 1 also shows the top three sending countries for each state as a percentage of the total 2000 foreign-born population in that state. Mexican immigrants make up the largest share of immigrants in each state, accounting for as much as 49.1% (Colorado) and as little as 10.6% (Minnesota) of the total immigrant population in a state. Whereas Mexicans make up at least a tenth of immigrants in each state, no other country contributes a tenth of all immigrants in any state, except for Laos, which barely contributes 10% of immigrants in Minnesota. Traditional gateway states did not increase at the same rate as new gateway states, partly because new gateways had a much smaller absolute number of immigrants to begin with. Yet, the rate of growth of the immigrant population in new immigrant gateways represents a significant shift in the settlement patterns of immigrants.

The changing geography of this new immigration is especially vivid in select locales within these states, some of which had virtually no immigrant population prior to the 1990s. For example, census data show that the foreign-born population in Dawson County, Nebraska, rose from 138 in 1990 to 3866 in 2000, a 2701.4% increase. Similarly, Whitfield County, Georgia, saw its foreign-born population

TABLE 1   States in which the foreign-born population doubled between 1990 and 2000 and the top three sending regions

State	Foreign-born pop. 1990[a]	Foreign-born pop. 2000[a]	% Growth 1990–2000	Top three sending countries for each state by% of 2000 total[b]		
				1	2	3
North Carolina	115,077	430,000	273.7	Mexico 40.0%	India 3.8%	Germany 3.8%
Georgia	173,126	577,273	233.4	Mexico 33.0%	India 4.8%	Vietnam 4.4%
Nevada	104,828	316,593	202.0	Mexico 48.6%	Philippines 9.9%	El Salvador 3.8%
Arkansas	24,867	73,690	196.3	Mexico 45.7%	El Salvador 6.1%	Germany 4.5%
Utah	58,600	158,664	170.8	Mexico 41.9%	Canada 4.9%	Germany 3.2%
Tennessee	59,114	159,004	169.0	Mexico 28.1%	Germany 5.2%	India 4.8%
Nebraska	28,198	74,638	164.7	Mexico 40.8%	Vietnam 7.2%	Guatemala 4.7%
Colorado	142,434	369,903	159.7	Mexico 49.1%	Germany 4.5%	Canada 3.7%
Arizona	278,205	656,183	135.9	Mexico 66.4%	Canada 4.0%	Germany 2.4%
Kentucky	34,119	80,271	135.3	Mexico 19.3%	Germany 8.3%	India 6.2%
South Carolina	49,964	115,978	132.1	Mexico 27.3%	Germany 6.8%	United Kingdom 5.9%
Minnesota	113,039	260,463	130.4	Mexico 10.6%	Laos 10.0%	Vietnam 6.0%
Idaho	28,905	64,080	121.7	Mexico 55.3%	Canada 7.1%	United Kingdom 3.5%
Kansas	62,840	134,735	114.4	Mexico 47.0%	Vietnam 6.8%	India 3.7%
Iowa	43,316	91,085	110.3	Mexico 27.7%	Vietnam 7.0%	Bosnia & Herzegovina 6.3%
Oregon	139,307	289,702	108.8	Mexico 39.0%	Canada 5.9%	Vietnam 5.7%
Alabama	43,533	87,772	101.6	Mexico 26.5%	Germany 8.4%	India 4.9%
Delaware	22,275	44,898	101.6	Mexico 17.5%	India 8.3%	United Kingdom 5.6%
Oklahoma	65,489	131,747	101.2	Mexico 42.5%	Vietnam 7.6%	Germany 4.7%

[a] Source: 1990 and 2000 United States Census.

[b] Source: Migration Policy Institute.

grow by 652.7%, from 1846 in 1990 to 13,895 in 2000. These demographic changes are especially pronounced in these locales because of their small total population. Whereas the 1990 foreign-born population made up only 0.7% and 2.5% in Dawson County and Whitfield County, respectively, by 2000 the foreign-born populations swelled to 15.9% of Dawson County's and 16.6% of Whitfield County's total populations.

While the impact of immigration is especially pronounced in rural areas, urban centers with very little or no previous history of immigration have seen a recent and dramatic increase in their foreign-born population. As Singer (2004) points out, many of these urban immigrant gateways have virtually no significant history of immigration (Austin, Charlotte, and Raleigh-Durham, for example), while others are re-emerging gateways that have seen a resurgence of immigration after a long hiatus (Denver, San Jose, and Oakland).

A small but growing body of sociological literature examines the immigrant experience in these new gateways. The bulk of this research documents the changing geography of immigrant settlement and explains why there has been a change in immigrant settlement during the 1990s (Camarota & Keeley 2001, Durand et al. 2000, Gouveia & Saenz 2000, Gozdziak & Martin 2005, Johnson et al. 1999, Kandel & Cromartie 2004, Kandel & Parrado 2005a, Massey et al. 2002, Singer 2004). In the following sections, we identify and summarize two main lines of research on the immigrant experience in new gateways. The first explains why there has been a proliferation of immigration to areas that have been historically unpopular destinations for immigrants. The second line of research describes how the influx of immigrants to new gateways transforms the communities to which they migrate. We follow our summary of this research by suggesting how research on immigrants in new gateways can be strengthened and point out areas of research that have yet to be explored.

Accounting for the Changing Geography of American Immigration

Much of the research on immigration and new gateways focuses on why new immigrant gateways have emerged, providing both macro and micro explanations. The few existing explanations focus primarily on Mexican immigration. At the macro level, Massey et al. (2002) used demographic data from the Mexican Migration Project to show how a convergence of factors led to the diversification of U.S. destinations for Mexican immigrants. The 1986 Immigration Reform and Control Act (IRCA), which legalized 2.3 million formerly undocumented Mexican immigrants, freed newly legalized immigrants from fear of apprehension, and many traveled beyond states nearest to the U.S.-Mexican border. Several pieces of legislation militarized popular crossing areas for Mexican immigrants, driving them to cross at more remote points in the border and into new destinations outside of California. Conditions in California, the most popular destination for Mexican immigrants, became less tenable for Mexican immigrants in the 1990s, both socially and economically. The rise of ardent anti-immigrant sentiment, culminating in the passage of Proposition 187, which barred undocumented immigrants from accessing many publicly funded services,[1] made California a more hostile context for Mexican immigrants. An unusually deep recession in California and a more rapid economic recovery elsewhere meant that Mexican immigrants could find better economic opportunities in other regions of the country. These factors—the freedom to become mobile that IRCA allowed, militarization of the Tijuana/San Diego border region, growing anti-immigrant sentiment, and an economic recession in California—led many Mexican immigrants to flee California and settle in regions of the country that had not previously been popular destinations. As Durand et al. (2000) show, mass migration out of California resulted in a decline in the percentage of Mexican immigrants in California from 57.8% to 46.6% between 1990 and 1996 and an increase in the percentage of Mexican immigrants in nongateway states from 10.3% to 21.0% during that same period.

Hernández-León & Zúñiga's (2000) study of Carpet City, Georgia, illustrates how microlevel processes explain the emergence of new gateways. They use ethnographic and survey data to show that the emergence and growth of the Mexican populations in Carpet City is a result of networks established through secondary migrations of male pioneering immigrants legalized by IRCA. Initially, a few Mexican immigrants who received amnesty under IRCA migrated to Carpet City from the western United States. These pioneering migrants established networks with sending regions in Mexico, allowing post-IRCA immigrants (often women and children) to come directly to Carpet City from Mexico.

Yet, the movement of immigrants, especially Latinos, away from traditional gateways is rooted in factors beyond individual and familial decision of migrants who are "pushed" out of traditional gateways. Immigrants are drawn to new gateways by economic opportunities in industries where there is a high demand for low-wage labor. Gouveia & Saenz (2000) cite international, national, and local forces that work to attract Latino immigrants to the Midwest. At the international level, stiffening global competition has spurred firms in agriculture and agroindustry to reduce costs and increase production. To accomplish these goals, firms increase profit margins by speeding up production and using advances in technologies and biotechnologies to increase yields that turn seasonal work into year-round work. According to Gouveia & Saenz, these strategies have created a demand for an abundant low-wage labor force. U.S. immigration policies help create a supply of low-wage labor though IRCA's Seasonal Agricultural Work Proviso, which allows a large number of immigrants to remain in the United States, and through more direct recruitment with H2 visas programs, which provide a year-round supply of workers.

Production strategies in specific industries also play a key role in attracting immigrants to new gateways. Griffith's (1995) research on poultry plants shows that increased line-speeds and other production changes have created an increased

---

[1]Proposition 187 was later found to be unconstitutional in a U.S. District Court.

demand for low-skill labor and a need for firms to control workers. Poultry plants increase their Latino workforce through network recruiting, wherein employees are asked to refer potential new employees, often family and friends, to work in the plants. Griffith finds that 80% to 85% of new workers in Georgia's and North Carolina's plants are recruited through personal networks, and many plants give workers cash bonuses for bringing in new workers as long as the recruits remain on the job for a designated period. Similarly, Johnson-Webb (2003) shows that employers in North Carolina have a strong preference for immigrant labor over all native-born workers (black or white), and these employers invoke a number of methods, both informal and formal, actively and in some cases aggressively, to recruit Latino immigrant workers. Word-of-mouth is the most popular form of recruitment, but employers also use ads in local Spanish-language newspapers, recruitment at job fares, and employment intermediaries, such as the Mexican consulates and temporary agencies. In some cases, employers even attempt to "steal" employees from other firms, partly because of competition for workers in a tight labor market.

As shown in Table 1, immigration from Mexico accounts for much of the immigrant population in new gateway states, but Vietnamese immigration is prominent as well. The presence of Vietnamese immigrants in these gateways is not a matter of choice as much as it is a function of federal settlement policies. Zhou & Bankston's (1998) examination of the Vietnamese second generation notes that the dispersal of Vietnamese refugees to a range of communities was orchestrated by the U.S. Department of Health and Human Services' Office of Refugee Resettlement (ORR), which hoped to help Vietnamese refugees gain economic independence. ORR resettled Vietnamese refugees in places where there was very virtually no recent or significant history of immigration, including New Orleans (the site of Zhou & Bankston's study), Kansas City, Oklahoma City, and Biloxi. Rumbaut's (1995) overview of Vietnamese, Cambodian, and Laotian Americans similarly points out that the dispersal of these refugee groups in new gateways is a function of governmental resettlement programs. Although refugees were initially dispersed across the United States, many refugees have made secondary migrations to join larger communities of coethnics in California. However, many Asian refugee groups remain concentrated in new gateways. For example, Rumbaut (1995) points out that the Hmong remain heavily concentrated in Minnesota and Wisconsin and that Vietnamese make up the largest Asian group in Texas, Louisiana, Mississippi, Arkansas, Kansas, and Oklahoma.

Immigrants in the New Gateways

In addition to documenting the demographic changes in new gateways, research has also focused on the influence that new immigrants have on the communities to which they migrate. This body of literature primarily employs ethnographic methods to explore how immigrants influence the social and economic landscape of communities that are largely unaccustomed to an immigrant presence.

The ethnographic analysis of Garden City, Kansas, by Stull et al. (1992) high-lights how new immigrants influence community relations vis-à-vis beef packing plants. Interaction between the main groups in Garden City—Latinos (almost en-tirely Mexican), Asians (Vietnamese and Cambodians), and whites—is stymied by conditions within the plants and in the larger community. Inside the beef plants, the loud noise and the undivided concentration required to keep up with the high speed of the processing line (or "the chain") limit interaction between groups. In the larger community, Stull et al. (1992) find that the high turnover rate of plant workers, due in part to high injury rates in the beef plants, make the immigrant workforce transient. The transient nature of the immigrant population means that native-born residents have few interactions with immigrants and that schools strain to meet the needs of an immigrant student population that cycles in and out during the school year.

Cravey's (1997) study of the rise of the Latino population in Siler City, North Carolina, highlights tensions surrounding relations in this new, primarily Latino immigrant population and the established community. One such tension is over residential segregation. There are few options for low-income housing, and Latinos have moved into neighborhoods that were once dominated by African Americans. The shortage of low-income housing has sparked competition between Latinos and African Americans.

Immigrant populations in new gateways impact nearly every facet of life. Hackenberg & Kukulka's (1995) ethnographic study of Garden City, Kansas, high-lights the strains new immigrant populations place on primary health care. In this small beef packing town, beef plants have impacted health care by attracting many poor immigrants to work in an industry in which injury rates are very high. The large number of poor immigrants strains primary health care services, especially because most doctors do not accept Medicaid.

Schools also face significant challenges in new, rural immigrant gateways. Kandel & Parrado (2005b) show that growth in the school-aged Hispanic pop-ulation far outpaces the growth of school-aged non-Hispanic whites in both metro and nonmetro areas. The rapid increase of school-aged Hispanics in schools in new gateways leaves some schools scrambling to meet the needs of this large student population. Using case studies from rural Mississippi and urban North Carolina, Kandel & Parrado (2005a) find that these challenges come from the language bar-riers and the transience of some students who leave schools when their parents find work in other locales.

Although much of the research on new gateways examines how immigrants influence the context they encounter, recent research also looks at the dynamics of change in new gateways. Millard & Chapa's (2004) ethnographic and demo-graphic analysis of several rural midwestern villages and towns explores the social, political, economic, and religious dynamics resulting from the influx of Latino immigrants. Millard, Chapa, and several coauthors find that relations between Anglos and Latino immigrants are a mixed bag. Latinos report blatant forms of discrimination in nearly all aspects of life, but the authors also site significant efforts on the part of the communities to improve relations between Anglos and Latino immigrants. They also describe a growing second generation that is often caught between the immigrant experience of their parents and the Anglo experience of their peers. Where religious life is concerned, Latino Protestants form their own congregations, providing both religious services in Spanish and crucial social services. The staff within these congregations connects Latino immigrants to services, including food stamps, Medicaid, emergency food, and clothing. Where Latino congregations aid immigrants, other institutions are often ill-equipped to meet the needs of the growing Latino immigrant population. Bilingual workers are in short supply making accessing necessary services more difficult for Latino immigrants.

The strength of the existing literature on the immigrant experience in new gateways is its ability to account for why immigrants have settled in these new gateways, to describe the work that immigrants do, and, to some extent, to describe how immigrants have influenced the places to which they have migrated. However, most of the existing literature is largely divorced from broader theoretical debates on immigration and assimilation. One notable exception is Hernández-León & Zúñiga's (2005) study of social capital among Mexican immigrants in Dalton, Georgia. Using descriptive statistics and ethnographic data, they find that immigrants who previously lived in established gateways mobilize "funds of knowledge" and social capital gained in established gateways to expedite their settlement and integration in new gateways. Leaders of these new immigrant communities draw on these "funds of knowledge" in establishing soccer leagues, running for local office, and starting community associations. Individual immigrants also benefit from social capital accumulated while living in newly established gateways to start small businesses.

Uniqueness of New Immigrant Gateways

As Hernández-León & Zúñiga (2005) begin to show, there is good reason to believe that immigrant assimilation in these new gateways may differ in fundamental ways from the experiences of immigrants in more established gateways. One potential difference is in intergroup relations. The long history of immigration in more established gateways means that notions about the place of immigrants in the class, racial, and ethnic hierarchies of these established gateways are well-entrenched. In contrast, the lack of immigration history in new gateways means that the place of immigrants in the class, racial, and ethnic hierarchies is less crystallized, and immigrants may thus have more freedom to define their position.

The size of new gateways may also influence immigrant assimilation. Many of the new immigrant gateways are rural towns, where social isolation does not exist as it does in larger urban centers. Unlike larger locales, where immigrants often live in enclaves and children attend schools that have large immigrant and minority populations, immigrants and native-born residents in smaller gateways frequently interact. Although, as Kandel & Cromartie (2004) point out, residential separation between Hispanics and non-Hispanic whites increased in the 1990s, there is reason to believe that this residential separation may not result in complete social isolation. Jiménez's (2005) research in Garden City, Kansas, a town with a total population of about 30,000, shows that the large Latino immigrant population frequently interacts with the native-born population in part because of the small size of the town. There is one high school, one public swimming pool, two large grocery stores, one YMCA, and one junior college. Immigrants and native-born residents alike must share these few resources, impeding social isolation and facilitating intergroup interactions.

An additional difference between new gateways and more established ones is in the institutional arrangements that influence immigrant assimilation. Established gateways have numerous institutions set up to aid immigrants, including legal-aid bureaus, health clinics, social organizations, and bilingual services. Previous waves of immigrants have necessitated the establishment of these institutions, and immigrants who arrive today continue to benefit from them. For instance, ethnographies conducted for the New York Second Generation Project found that West Indian workers stepped in easily to a union founded by Jewish immigrants and recently run by African Americans (Foerster 2004). Ecuadoran, Peruvian, Colombian, and Dominican immigrants and their children took advantage of educational programs originally devised for New York City's Puerto Rican population (Trillo 2004). And the city's large Russian immigrant community benefited greatly from the organizations founded by the Jewish immigrants who arrived in New York a century earlier (Zeltzer-Zubida 2004). Indeed, Kasinitz et al. (2004) argue that the legacy of the Civil Rights Movement, along with the legacy of New York City's history as an immigrant-absorbing community, have significantly positively affected the ability of current immigrants to feel almost immediately included and to consider themselves New Yorkers.

New gateways, in contrast, may lack the institutional arrangements designed to serve the immigrant population precisely because there has been no need for such arrangements until recently. As some of the research cited above shows, many new gateways lack arrangements, such as bilingual services, necessary to accommodate the new immigrant population. Thus, immigrants may not have access to institutions and the services in new gateways that immigrants in more established gateways have. We can only speculate how these differences influence immigrant assimilation, but we believe that comparing new gateways to more established gateways will yield greater theoretical insight into immigrant assimilation. We also believe that comparing the experience of immigrants in these two types of gateways along the dimensions that we highlight here—development of racial and ethnic hierarchies, level of segregation, and types of institutional arrangements—holds great promise for furthering our understanding of immigrant assimilation more generally. To this end, Zúñiga & Hernández-León's (2005) new edited collection of research on Mexican immigrants in new immigrant destinations will further what we know theoretically and empirically, and sociologists will do well to follow this line of research.

IMMIGRANT REPLENISHMENT

A second factor important for the study of assimilation is the extent to which immigration from a particular sending country is replenished. Sociologists only began to study European immigrant assimilation as this wave of immigration was coming to an end. Restrictive laws passed in 1924 and the Great Depression largely ensured the halt of large-scale immigration from Europe to the United States. Thus, major studies examined the experience of immigrants and their descendants as they became Americans in a society absent of any significant immigrant replenishment. Each successive generation and cohort born in the United States had less contact with immigrants, attenuating the salience of ethnicity in their lives (Alba 1990, Waters 1990).

To be sure, immigrant replenishment was part of the Great European Migration. Continuous German and Irish immigration was a feature of American immigration throughout much of the nineteenth century. Yet, the absence of sociological research on immigrant assimilation during this period leaves sociologists with no starting point from which to understand how immigrant replenishment shapes assimilation today. Much like the German and Irish experience in the nineteenth century, today's immigration appears to be continuous, and each wave of immigrants is replenished by another. The forces that initiate immigration (economic integration, growing economic development) and that sustain immigration flows (embeddedness of social capital, social networks) appear to be permanent features of the social, political, and economic global context (see Massey 1995, Massey 1999). As a result, the replenishment of immigrants is likely to define the immigrant experience in the United States well into the foreseeable future. As Massey (1995) points out, "In all likelihood, therefore, the United States has already become a country of perpetual immigration, one characterized by the continuous arrival of large cohorts of immigrants from particular regions" (p. 664). We believe that immigrant replenishment has significant implications for immigrant assimilation itself and for how sociologists study it.

Consider the case of the Mexican origin population in the United States. Unlike any other current immigrant group, Mexican immigration has been a permanent feature of American immigration for well over 100 years. Mexicans are the only immigrant group to span the Great European Migration, the post-1965 era of immigration, and the period in between. Mexican immigration has been particularly heavy in the last two decades, and they make up nearly one third of the total immigrant population.

The implications of Mexican immigrant replenishment are perhaps best seen by focusing on the descendents of the earliest Mexican immigrants. The descendents of these early Mexican immigrants, "Mexican Americans," are generationally distant from their immigrant ancestors, and many of them have assimilated, both socially and structurally, into American society (Alba et al. 2002, Perlmann & Waters 2004, Smith 2003). Yet, this generational distance does not mean that they have no meaningful contact with immigrants. In fact, because of the heavy replenishment of Mexican immigration, even later-generation Mexican Americans interact with their immigrant coethnics (Ochoa 2004).

Jiménez's (2005) research on Mexican Americans in Garden City, Kansas, and Santa Maria, California, illustrates in concrete terms how immigrant replenishment affects one dimension of assimilation, ethnic identity. Using in-depth interviews with 123 Mexican Americans and participant observations, Jiménez (2005) finds that within families, the salience of ethnic identity attenuates from one generation to the next. The passage to subsequent generations of the traits, customs, traditions, and language of the immigrant generation weakens within families. Much of this attenuation of ethnic identity is owed to an ideology of forced Americanization that was prevalent when many second- and third-generation individuals came of age. Yet, the replenishment of Mexican immigrants helps to refresh the ethnic identity of Mexican Americans through both everyday contact with immigrants, in which many Mexican Americans have ample opportunity to speak Spanish, and more meaningful friendships and romantic relationships that develop between immigrants and Mexican Americans. In some cases, Mexican Americans marry Mexican immigrants and second-generation individuals, and their children are a mix of generations—third or fourth on their father's side and second on their mother's, for example. The replenishment of immigrants also gives Mexican Americans access to a supply of ethnic "raw materials" that, without immigrant replenishment, would cease to exist. Mexican festivals, restaurants, ethnic-specific food stores, and Spanish-language media are all now part of a Mexican American's ethnic repertoire that the large immigrant population makes possible. Indeed, Massey's (1995) prediction that immigrant replenishment would mean that "the character of ethnicity will be determined relatively more by immigrants and relatively less by later generations, shifting the balance of ethnic identity toward the language, culture, and ways of life of the sending society" (p. 645) appears to be an empirical reality for the Mexican-origin population and will likely be true for other immigrant groups in the future.

The case of the Mexican-origin population speaks to a need for social scientists to reconceptualize how to gauge immigrant assimilation. Heretofore, students of immigration have privileged "generation" as a temporal gauge of immigrant group assimilation, where "generation" is the ancestral distance from the point of arrival in a society (Alba 1988, p. 213). Theories of assimilation have been structured around the principle that the more generations removed an individual is from the immigrant generation, the more integrated into American society an individual would be. Early theories of assimilation posited a three-generation model, wherein by the third-generation individuals would be well integrated into Americans society both structurally and culturally (Fishman 1965, Gordon 1964, Warner & Srole 1945). Using generation as a temporal gauge makes sense when examining the experiences of groups for which there is no protracted immigrant replenishment, as in research done on the immigrants and descendents of the Great European Migration. Each successive generation born in the United States had less contact with an immigrant generation, both within and outside of the family, precisely because there was no significant replenishment from European countries when those groups were studied.

An additional reason for using generation is that there is a high correlation between the generation from which European-origin individuals come and the birth cohort from which they come. Because many European groups immigrated during a compressed period of time, older individuals tended to be of earlier generation (i.e., first and second), whereas younger people were from later generations (i.e., third and fourth). Thus, each generation of European-origin individuals also experienced American society as a birth cohort, i.e., a group of people who experience fluctuations in life chances and constraints at roughly the same point in their life cycle.

When looking at today's immigrant groups and the fact that each wave of immigration is likely to be succeeded by another, using generation as a temporal gauge does not mean what it used to. Assumptions about generation are invalid when there is immigrant replenishment because at any point in time each generation is a mix of cohorts and each cohort has a mix of generations. Individuals from different generations but of the same birth cohort, then, may experience similar shifts in life chances that society offers (because they are in the same birth cohort), even if they experience a different dynamic internal to the ethnic group (because they are from different generations). As Alba (1988) notes, "[T]he generational perspective tends to deflect attention from the structural basis of ethnicity, the linkage between ethnic group and the economy and the polity of the larger society, and to focus instead on the internal dynamic of change" (p. 214).

We do not argue that generation is an entirely invalid temporal gauge but rather that it must be considered alongside birth cohort. By using birth cohort in conjunction with generation, sociologists will better capture processes of ethnic change internal to the group that generation captures as well as the historical fluctuations in opportunities and constraints external to groups that birth cohort captures.

CONCLUSION

After nearly 40 years of high levels of immigration, primarily from Latin America, the Caribbean, and Asia, most careful sociological research supports the notion that immigrants are being successfully incorporated into American society. This research does not lead to the kinds of alarmist, unsupported claims made by writers such as the political scientist Samuel Huntington (2004, p. 30), who argued that, "Unlike past immigrant groups, Mexicans and other Latinos have not assimilated into mainstream U.S. culture." Quite the contrary, the United States continues to show remarkable progress in absorbing new immigrants. It may be that continual immigrant replenishment makes this assimilation less visible than it was for European immigrants and their descendants, but that makes it all the more important that these findings on immigrant incorporation be prominent in public and scholarly debates on this topic.

At the end of the nineteenth and beginning of the twentieth centuries, the United States saw the influx of massive numbers of immigrants from European nations such as Ireland, Italy, Germany, Russia, Poland, Hungary, and Slovenia. It was during this same time that sociology gained recognition as an academic field, and the settlement of immigrants in urban centers provided opportunities for sociologists to develop theories about group interaction, ethnic inequality, and assimilation.

Understanding the differences between these earlier waves of immigration and today's reveals a need to rethink the theoretical and empirical assumptions used to study these two groups. We have argued that the immigrant experience has changed recently with respect to the range of settlement regions and the persistence of immigrant flows. More than ever immigrants are settling in areas that have received virtually no immigration in recent history. Much like today, an earlier time period saw the settlement of immigrants in rural areas, particularly in the South and Midwest. However, most of what we know about the experiences of immigrants who settled away from the centers comes from historical accounts (Pozzetta 1991), and the immigrant experience in these places passed under the sociological radar. Early students of immigration and assimilation provided a strong foundation for current theories, and today's sociologists have a golden opportunity to build our empirical and theoretical understanding of immigrant assimilation by researching these new gateways.

We have also argued that the United States is likely to see a protracted period of immigration in which the immigrant population is continually replenished. Generation is still a useful temporal measures of immigrant assimilation. However, we argue that sociologists must also consider birth cohort as a temporal gauge of assimilation in order to tease out the effects of protracted immigrant replenishment on assimilation.

The *Annual Review of Sociology* is online at http://soc.annualreviews.org

LITERATURE CITED

Alba R, Logan J, Lutz A, Stults B. 2002. Only English by the third generation? Loss and preservation of the mother tongue among the grandchildren of contemporary immigrants. *Demography* 39:467–84

Alba R, Nee V. 2003. *Remaking the American Mainstream: Assimilation and Contemporary Immigration*. Cambridge, MA: Harvard Univ. Press

Alba RD. 1988. Cohorts and the dynamics of ethnic change. In *Social Structure and Human Lives*, ed. M White Riley, pp. 211–28. Newbury Park, CA: Sage

Alba RD. 1990. *Ethnic Identity: The Transfor-*

mation of White America. New Haven, CT: Yale Univ. Press. 374 pp.

Alba RD, Logan JR. 1993. Minority proximity to whites in suburbs: an individual level analysis of segregation. *Am. Sociol. Rev.* 98: 1388–427

Alba RD, Logan JR, Stults BJ. 2000. The changing neighborhood contexts of the immigrant metropolis. *Soc. Forces* 79:587–621

Alba RD, Logan JR, Stults B, Marzan G, Zhang W. 1999. Immigrant groups and suburbs: a reexamination of suburbanization and spatial assimilation. *Am. Sociol. Rev.* 64:446–60

Bean FD, Chapa J, Berg RR, Sowards KA.

1994. Educational and sociodemographic incorporation among Hispanic immigrants in the United States. In *Immigration and Ethnicity: The Integration of America's Newest Arrivals*, ed. B Edmonston, J Passel, pp. 73–96. Washington, DC: Urban Inst.

Bean FD, Stevens G. 2003. *America's Newcomers and the Dynamics of Diversity*. New York: Russell Sage Found.

Borjas GJ. 1994. The economics of immigration. *J. Econ. Lit.* 32:1667–717

Bulmer M. 1984. *The Chicago School of Sociology: Institutionalization, Diversity, and the Rise of Sociological Research*. Chicago: Univ. Chicago Press

Camarota S, Keeley J. 2001. *The New Ellis Islands: Examining Non-Traditional Areas of Immigrant Settlement in the 1990s*. Washington, DC: Cent. Immigr. Stud.

Chiswick BR. 1978. The effect of Americanization on the earnings of foreign-born men. *J. Polit. Econ.* 86:897–921

Cravey AJ. 1997. Latino labor and poultry production in rural North Carolina. *Southeast. Geog.* 37:295–300

Durand J, Massey DS, Charvet F. 2000. The changing geography of Mexican immigration to the United States: 1910–1996. *Soc. Sci. Q.* 81:1–15

Ellwood DT. 2000. Winners and losers in America: taking the measure of the new economic realities. In *A Working Nation: Workers, Work and Government in the New Economy*, ed. DT Ellwood, pp. 1–41. New York: Russell Sage Found.

Farley R, Alba R. 2002. The new second generation in the United States. *Int. Migr. Rev.* 36:669–701

Fishman JA. 1965. The status and prospects of bilingualism in the United States. *Mod. Lang. J.* 49:143–55

Foerster A. 2004. Isn't anybody here from Alabama? Solidarity and struggle in a mighty, mighty union. See Kasinitz et al. 2004, pp. 197–226

Foner N. 2000. *From Ellis Island to JFK: New York's Two Great Waves of Immigration*. New Haven, CT: Yale Univ. Press

Frey WH. 1996. Immigrant and native migrant magnets. *Am. Demogr.* 18:36–42

Gerstle G, Mollenkopf JH. 2001. *E Pluribus Unum: Contemporary and Historical Perspectives on Immigrant Political Incorporation*. New York: Russell Sage Found.

Gilbertson GA, Fitzpatrick JP, Yang L. 1991. Hispanic intermarriage in New York City: new evidence from 1991. *Int. Migr. Rev.* 30:445–59

Gordon MM. 1964. *Assimilation in American Life: The Role of Race, Religion, and National Origins*. New York, NY: Oxford Univ. Press

Gozdziak E., Martin S. 2005. *Beyond the Gateway: Immigrants in a Changing America*. Lanham, MD: Lexington Books

Gouveia L, Saenz R. 2000. Global forces and Latino population growth in the Midwest: a regional and subregional analysis. *Gr. Plains Res.* 10:305–28

Griffith D. 1995. Hay trabajo: poultry processing, rural industrialization, and the Latinization of low-wage labor. In *Any Way You Cut It: Meat Processing and Small-Town America*, ed. DD Stull, MJ Broadway, D Griffith, pp. 129–51. Lawrence: Univ. Kansas Press

Hackenberg RA, Kukulka G. 1995. Industries, immigrants, and illness in the new Midwest. In *Any Way You Cut It: Meat Processing and Small-Town America*, ed. DD Stull, MJ Broadway, D Griffith, pp. 187–211. Lawrence: Univ. Kansas Press

Hernández-León R, Zúñiga V. 2000. "Making carpet by the mile": the emergence of a Mexican immigrant community in an industrial region of the U.S. historic South. *Soc. Sci. Q.* 81:49–66

Hernández-León R, Zúñiga V. 2005. Mexican immigrant communities in the rural South and social capital: the case of Dalton, Georgia. *South. Rural Sociol.* In press

Hirschman C. 2001. The educational enrollment of immigrant youth: a test of the segmented assimilation hypothesis. *Demography* 38:317–37

Hondagneu-Sotelo P. 1994. *Gendered Transitions: Mexican Experiences of Immigration*. Berkeley: Univ. Calif. Press. 258 pp.

Hondagneu-Sotelo P. 2003. *Domestica: Immigrant Workers Cleaning and Caring in the Shadows of Affluence*. Berkeley: Univ. Calif. Press

Huntington S. 2004. The Hispanic challenge. *Foreign Policy* March/April:30–45

Jasso G, Massey D, Rosenzweig MR, Smith JP. 2000. The New Immigrant Survey Pilot (NIS-P): overview and new findings about U.S. legal immigrants at admission. *Demography* 37:127–38

Jiménez TR. 2005. *Replenished identities: Mexican Americans, Mexican immigrants and ethnic identity*. PhD thesis. Harvard Univ., Cambridge, MA

Johnson JHJ, Johnson-Webb KD, Farrel W Jr. 1999. Newly emerging Hispanic communities in the United States: a spatial analysis of settlement patterns, in-migration fields, and social receptivity. In *Immigration and Opportunity: Race, Ethnicity, and Employment in the United States*, ed. FD Bean, S Bell-Rose, pp. 263–310. New York: Russell Sage Found.

Johnson-Webb KD. 2003. *Recruiting Hispanic Labor: Immigrants in Non-Traditional Areas*. New York: LFB Scholarly Pub.

Kandel W, Cromartie J. 2004. New patterns of Hispanic settlement in rural America. *Rep. 99*. US Dep. Agric./Econ. Res. Serv.

Kandel W, Parrado E. 2005a. Hispanic population growth, age composition shifts, and public policy impacts in nonmetro counties. In *Population Change and Rural Society*, ed. W Kandel, D Brown. Berlin: Springer-Kluwer-Plenum. In press

Kandel W, Parrado E. 2005b. Hispanic population growth, age structure, and public school response in new immigrant destinations. In *The New South: Latinos and the Transformation of Place*, ed. H Smith, O Furuseth. Aldershot, UK: Ashgate. In press

Kasinitz P, Mollenkopf JH, Waters MC, eds. 2004. *Becoming New Yorkers: Ethnographies of the New Second Generation*. New York: Russell Sage Found.

Kibria N. 2003. *Becoming Asian American: Second Generation Chinese and Korean American Identities*. Baltimore, MD: Johns Hopkins Univ. Press

Kurien P. 2003. Gendered ethnicities: creating a Hindu Indian identity in the United States. In *Gender and US Immigration: Contemporary Trends*, ed. P Hondagneu-Sotelo, pp. 151–73. Berkeley: Univ. Calif. Press

Lee J, Bean FD. 2004. America's changing color lines: immigration, race/ethnicity, and multiracial identification. *Annu. Rev. Sociol.* 30:221–42

Levitt P. 2001. *The Transnational Villagers*. Berkeley: Univ. Calif. Press

Lieberson S. 1963. *Ethnic Patterns in American Cities*. New York: Free Press

Lieberson S. 1980. *A Piece of the Pie: Blacks and White Immigrants Since 1880*. Berkeley: Univ. Calif. Press

Livingston G, Kahn JR. 2002. An American dream unfulfilled: the limited mobility of Mexican Americans. *Soc. Sci. Q.* 83:1003–12

Logan J, Alba R, McNulty T, Fisher B. 1996. Making a place in the metropolis: residential assimilation and segregation in city and suburb. *Demography* 33:443–53

Mahler SJ. 1995. *American Dreaming: Immigrant Life on the Margins*. Princeton, NJ: Princeton Univ. Press

Massey D. 1985. Ethnic residential segregation: a theoretical synthesis and empirical review. *Sociol. Soc. Res.* 69:315–50

Massey D. 1995. The new immigration and ethnicity in the United States. *Popul. Dev. Rev.* 21:631–52

Massey DS. 1981. Dimensions of the new immigration to the United States and prospects for assimilation. *Annu. Rev. Sociol.* 7:57–85

Massey DS. 1999. Why does immigration occur? A theoretical synthesis. In *The Handbook of International Migration: The American Experience*, ed. C Hirschman, P Kasinitz, J DeWind, pp. 34–52. New York: Russell Sage Found.

Massey DS, Durand J, Malone NJ. 2002. *Beyond Smoke and Mirrors: Mexican Immigration in an Era of Free Trade*. New York: Russell Sage Found.

Menjivar C. 1999. *Fragmented Ties: Salvadoran Immigrant Networks in America*. Berkeley: Univ. Calif. Press

Millard AV, Chapa J. 2004. *Apple Pie and Enchiladas: Latino Newcomers in the Rural Midwest*. Austin: Univ. Texas Press

Ochoa G. 2004. *Becoming Neighbors in a Mexican American Community: Power, Conflict and Solidarity*. Austin: Univ. Texas Press

Ortiz V. 1996. The Mexican-origin population: permanent working class or emerging middle class? In *Ethnic Los Angeles*, ed. RD Waldinger, M Bozorgmehr, pp. 247–77. New York: Russell Sage Found.

Park R. 1950. *Race and Culture*. Glencoe, IL: Free Press

Perlmann J, Waldinger R. 1997. Second generation decline? Children of immigrants, past and present—a reconsideration. *Int. Migr. Rev.* 31:893–922

Perlmann J, Waters MC. 2004. Intermarriage then and now: race, generation and the changing meaning of marriage. In *Not Just Black and White: Immigration, Race and Ethnicity, Then to Now*, ed. N Foner, G Frederickson, pp. 262–77. New York: Russell Sage Found.

Portes A, Rumbaut R. 2001. *Legacies: The Story of the Immigrant Second Generation*. Berkeley: Univ. Calif. Press

Pozzetta GE. 1991. *Immigrants on the Land: Agriculture, Rural Life, and Small Towns*. New York: Garland

Reider J, Steinlight S. 2003. *The Fractious Nation: Unity and Division in Contemporary American Life*. Berkeley: Univ. Calif. Press

Rosenfeld MJ. 2001. The salience of pannational Hispanic and Asian identities in U.S. marriage markets. *Demography* 38:161–75

Rosenfeld MJ. 2002. Measure of assimilation in the marriage market: Mexican Americans 1970–1990. *J. Marriage Fam.* 64:152–62

Rumbaut RG. 1995. Vietnamese, Laotian, and Cambodian Americans. In *Asian Americans: Contemporary Trends and Issues*, ed. PG Min. Thousand Oaks, CA: Sage

Singer A. 2004. *The Rise of New Immigrant Gateways*. Washington, DC: Brookings Inst.

Smith JP. 2003. Assimilation across the Latino generations. *Am. Econ. Rev.* 93:315–19

Stull DD, Broadway MJ, Erickson EP. 1992. The price of a good steak: beef packing and its consequences for Garden City, Kansas. In *Structuring Diversity: Ethnographic Perspectives on the New Immigration*, ed. L Lamphere, pp. 35–64. Chicago: Univ. Chicago Press

Thomas WI, Znaniecki F. 1918. *The Polish Peasant in Europe and America*. Chicago: Univ. Chicago Press

Trillo A. 2004. Somewhere between Wall Street and El Barrio: community college as a second chance for second-generation Latino students. See Kasinitz et al. 2004, pp. 57–78

Warner WL, Srole L. 1945. *The Social Systems of American Ethnic Groups*. New Haven, CT: Yale Univ. Press

Waters MC. 1990. *Ethnic Options: Choosing Identities in America*. Berkeley: Univ. Calif. Press

Waters MC. 1999. *Black Identities: West Indian Immigrant Dreams and American Realities*. New York/Cambridge, MA: Russell Sage Found., Harvard Univ. Press

Zeltzer-Zubida A. 2004. Affinities and affiliations: the many ways of being a Russian Jewish American. See Kasinitz et al. 2004, pp. 339–60

Zhou M, Bankston CL. 1998. *Growing Up American: How Vietnamese Children Adapt to Life in the United States*. New York: Russell Sage Found.

Zúñiga V, Hernández-León R. 2005. *New Destinations of Mexican Immigration in the United States: Community Formation, Local Responses and Inter-Group Relations*. New York: Russell Sage Found. In press

Annu. Rev. Sociol. 2005. 31:127–41
doi: 10.1146/annurev.soc.31.041304.122312
Copyright © 2005 by Annual Reviews. All rights reserved
First published online as a Review in Advance on March 11, 2005

READING AND THE READING CLASS IN THE TWENTY-FIRST CENTURY

Wendy Griswold, Terry McDonnell, and Nathan Wright

Department of Sociology, Northwestern University, Evanston, Illinois 60208;
email: w-griswold@northwestern.edu, t-mcdonnell@northwestern.edu,
n-wright@northwestern.edu

Key Words   literacy, media use, culture, cultural practice

■ **Abstract**   Sociological research on reading, which formerly focused on literacy, now conceptualizes reading as a social practice. This review examines the current state of knowledge on (*a*) who reads, i.e., the demographic characteristics of readers; (*b*) how they read, i.e., reading as a form of social practice; (*c*) how reading relates to electronic media, especially television and the Internet; and (*d*) the future of reading. We conclude that a reading class is emerging, restricted in size but disproportionate in influence, and that the Internet is facilitating this development.

INTRODUCTION

Researchers once studied reading in terms of literacy, asking who could read, how people learned to read, and what difference literacy made to socioeconomic development. Much of this work was inspired by the assumption that literacy was key to development and to individual social mobility, an assumption that skeptics called the "literacy myth" (Graff 1987). Although literacy raises valid questions, in the 1990s the research focus shifted to reading as a social practice, now asking who reads what, how people read, and how their reading relates to their other activities. This review draws together what sociologists and other scholars know about these questions. Its sections examine the demographic characteristics of readers and reading as a form of social practice. Our emphasis is on reading (especially reading books) as a leisure-time activity; this emphasis is consistent with conventional scholarly usage. We review the research on reading and electronic media (especially television) and then look at the emerging data on the relationship between reading and the Internet. We conclude with our thesis that a reading class is emerging, restricted in size but disproportionate in influence, and that the Internet is facilitating this development.

The sociology of reading is intellectually robust but organizationally dispersed. Much of the research takes place in history departments, where the well-established "history of the book" has given rise to a "history of reading" (Amtower 2000,

0360-0572/05/0811-0127$20.00

Andersen & Sauer 2002, Coleman 1996). The two overlap, but the former emphasizes books as material objects, whereas the latter recognizes books as part of a system involving readers, writers, technologies, publishers, editors, texts, booksellers, reviewers, and schools. This books-in-the-broader-context approach is sociological, whether applied to historical or contemporary materials. A second field of inquiry is that of new literacy studies, which may take place in departments of education or English and which emphasize literacies in the plural (Olson & Torrance 2001). Gender studies are a third academic base, emphasizing a key variable to the understanding of the who, what, and how of reading (Currie 1999, Parush 2004). Area studies and ethnic studies sometimes play a role as well (McHenry 2002, Newell 2002). And card-carrying sociologists, typically those involved in cultural sociology, have focused attention on reading.

We take this broad domain, this dispersed set of subfields, as the actors producing a sociology of reading. We draw upon them in exploring four questions.

WHO READS?

The short answer to who reads is just about everyone. This is the case in the West and Japan, and is increasingly the case in the developing world. Polls show that most Americans and Europeans read during their leisure time. In a "normal day," people report spending an average of over a half hour reading magazines, close to three quarters of an hour reading newspapers, and over an hour reading books; moreover, the overwhelming majority report reading some from all three categories of reading each day. Books involve the heaviest time commitment. Although a quarter of people do not read any books in a typical day, more than half read books for over an hour. In 1998, when the General Social Survey asked if respondents had "read novels, short stories, poems, or plays, other than those required by work or school" during the past twelve months, 70% reported that they had (Gen. Soc. Surv. 1998).

People think they ought to read even more. More than nine out of ten are convinced that reading is "a good use of your time" (Gallup Org. 1990, question 23). And they think they ought to be able to read more, for very few people find reading "too hard to do" (Gallup Org. 1990, question 48b). They expect to read more in the future. When asked, "Do you think you'll find yourself reading more in the months and years ahead, reading less, or is the amount of reading you do probably going to stay the same," 45% said more, 3% less, and 51% the same (Gallup Org. 1990, question 24). People particularly intend to read more materials that are educational or will improve their lives, such as nonfiction books, newspapers, and the Bible. A British survey finds that people actually believe they are reading more. "Despite competition from new media, and increasing pressure on people's leisure time, relatively few people think they are reading books less now than five years ago. Most (80%) claim to be reading about the same or more" (Book Mark. Ltd. 2000, p. 9). Most Britons report that the only thing that would make them read more is having more leisure time.

The demographic characteristics of readers have remained constant: Reading is associated above all with education. This association is the case worldwide. A 20-country survey concludes that "formal educational attainment is the main determinant of literacy proficiency. For 17 of the 20 countries it is both the first and the strongest predictor" (OECD Stat. Can. 2000, p. 58). In addition to education level, reading is associated with affluence (affluent people read more), race (whites read more than African Americans or Hispanics), gender (women read more than men), and place of residence (suburbanites read more than rural or inner city residents) (Book Mark. Ltd. 2000, NEA 2004; see also Cushman et al. 1996 for the universality of the gender difference).

Historically, reading by the populace at large began as a metropolitan phenomenon. Cities that were commercial or administrative centers—Shanghai, Lagos, Moscow—have led the rest of their respective countries in the literacy and print revolutions, although more strictly industrial cities have lagged behind the others (Brooks 1985, Furet & Ozouf 1982, Griswold 2000, Link 1981). Men gain literacy first, but when this difference evens out, women read more.

Another universal pattern is that as soon as a popular reading culture gets established, commentators start worrying about the decline of reading. Headlines from China's *People's Daily* report that "Chinese People Read Less," according to a new survey (People's Daily Online 2004). Educated Africans bemoan that the reading cultures of the late colonial and early independence period are decaying (Griswold 2000). Such worries, regardless of their basis in reality, suggest the value accorded to the practice of reading.

In the United States, the impact of race and ethnicity on reading is striking and troubling. To cite just one of many studies, the 2004 National Endowment of the Arts (NEA) survey found that 26% of Hispanics, 37% of African Americans, and 51% of white Americans read literature. This pattern holds for every educational and income level and every age. Women read more than men in each race/ethnicity category. White women have by far the highest reading rate (61%), followed by white men and African American women (41% and 43%, respectively). Hispanic (18%) and African American (30%) men read the least (NEA 2004, table 9, p. 11). The NEA study confirms earlier work that suggested that African Americans and Hispanics read less regardless of income or education (DiMaggio & Ostrower 1992). The recent growth of African American "chick-lit" suggests that black women's reading may move closer to that of white women (Lee 2004).

Reading starts early. Two thirds of Americans report that they started reading by age seven (Gallup Org. 1990, question 42). Parents read to their children even during their first year of life; most have started this reading by the time their child is three, and often continue (or even begin) during the years when the children can read by themselves (Gallup Org. 1990, questions 44, 48).

A national survey of children's media use conducted by Roberts and the Kaiser Family Foundation looked at the media habits of 1090 young (2–7) children and 2014 older (8–18) children (Roberts & Foehr 2004). They found that children averaged 45 minutes per day in recreational reading, which included being read to for the younger group. Most kids—between 80% and 90%—read at least some every day, and a good percentage (49% for 2- to 7-year-olds and 42% for 8- to 18-year-olds) read more than 30 minutes each day. Recreational reading drops in the late teenage years (ages 15–18) down to 34%. But by ages 15–18, more than half of kids are looking at a newspaper for at least 5 minutes, and a comparison with past research shows that "the proportion of U.S. children and adolescents who do so [read newspapers] has remained fairly constant over the past 50 years" (Roberts & Foehr 2004, p. 99). Overall reading time declines with age, and this decline is entirely due to a drop in reading books.

> As youngsters move from elementary school into middle and high school, they are typically asked to engage in a good deal more school-related reading than was formerly the case, a factor that probably reduces both desire and time to read outside school. In addition, during late adolescence, myriad additional activities vie for young people's time—sports, extracurricular activities, social events, earning a diver's license, part-time jobs, dating. . . . As seems to be the case for noninteractive screen media then, leisure time print exposure is also related to available time, and available time is related to age (Roberts & Foehr 2004, pp. 100–1).

They note that it makes sense that books, which require a relatively large commitment of time, would be affected more than magazines or newspapers (which actually increase).

A strong association exists between parents' education and their children's print exposure. Taking all ages together, Roberts & Foehr (2004) find that "statistically significant differences related to education emerge for each of the three individual print media. Youths whose parents completed no more than high school spend less time with all print, particularly books" (p. 103). Figure 1 (see color insert) shows that the primary difference in print exposure is between children whose parents have a high school education or less and children whose parents have at least some college education.

Roberts & Foehr (2004) conclude that both physical and social environments are related to youth reading, with the social environment being the more powerful. The physical environment includes access (printed materials in home, magazine subscriptions) and income. The social environment includes parents' education (most important) and television orientation (negative relation to print use). "Finally, in spite of claims to the contrary . . . there is little evidence that young people's leisure reading has changed much over the past half-century. . . . If anything, the averages we found are a bit higher than those that seem to have held for some time. Perhaps the increasing number of magazines aimed at children and adolescents and such children's book phenomena as the recent Harry Potter craze may be helping reading gain a bit" (Roberts & Foehr 2004, p. 112).

The same seems to be the case in England. A 1994 survey of 8000 English children ages 10, 12, and 14 found that since 1971, reading for most categories of children had either increased or remained steady (Hall & Coles 1999).

They found that the children's attitude toward reading was positive, and most reported themselves to be good readers. Two thirds of the sample reported doing some reading the previous evening. As in the United States there was a relationship between socioeconomic background and number of books read; more advantaged kids read more.

If they receive the same education (which is often not the case, especially in many African and Muslim countries), girls read more and better than boys. This gender advantage seems to be true universally. Research comparing children's reading in 32 countries shows girls to be consistently ahead of boys in their reading abilities (Wagemaker 1996, table 7, p. 34). A survey of British children shows gender differences appear very early. When the survey asked, "How often do you read story books?" to very young children (ages 4–7), 67.6% of girls but only 55.5% of boys responded "very often" or "often"; by ages 7–11 the responses had gone up for both sexes, with 80.5% girls and 68.6% boys claiming to read often or very often (Children's Lit. Res. Cent. 1996, p. 60). Reading by both sexes declined in the early teenage years, but the decline in boys' reading was sharper as they moved into adolescence. When 11- to 13-year-old children were asked, "How often do you read fiction?" 65.8% of girls and 52.6% of boys reported often or very often; by ages 14–16, the girls had dropped to 56.5% and the boys to 38.6%. Another survey of English children suggests that reading increased significantly for all 10-year-olds and for 12-year-old girls between 1971 and 1994, whereas reading for 14-year-old boys had decreased significantly (Hall & Coles 1999).

Alarming reports suggest, however, that reading may be in decline. Although this has been a concern for decades, a recent study commissioned by the NEA that compared reading in 1982, 1992, and 2002 shows a steady decline in reading, especially the reading of literature and especially among young adults (NEA 2004; for earlier evidence of the small proportion of readers who do "literary reading"— poetry, drama, serious fiction—see Zill & Winglee 1990).

A comparable long-term study in the Netherlands paints a similar picture (Knulst & Kraaykamp 1997, 1998). Survey data in that country over four decades (1955–1995) shows a steady decline in leisure reading, contrary to expectations of those who predicted reading would go up with increased education. While the percentage of Dutch who read books during the week declined, "the people who did read newspapers and books in 1995 . . . spent more time doing so than the larger group of readers two decades earlier. This demonstrates that especially newspaper and book readers who spent relatively little time reading have dropped out" (Knulst & Kraaycamp 1997, p. 137). The same concentration effect is found in the NEA study: Heavy readers read as much or more than ever, but more casual reading has declined.

The Dutch study suggests that heavy readers are aging and not being replaced. Younger cohorts (post–World War II) read less at all ages; moreover, they do not read more as they grow older the way previous cohorts did. Knulst & Kraaycamp (1997, 1998) see television as the major reason (their study ended in 1995, before the Internet had become ubiquitous). All groups, regardless of education, have seen an increase in television viewing and a decrease in reading. There is a generation gap—older, highly educated people hang on to the reading habit, but younger ones do not. Now the group of heavy readers "largely consists of people with an intermediate and higher degree of education from the pre-war cohorts." Educated people still do the most reading, but in younger cohorts the reading of the highly educated has declined much the same as that of their less-educated peers.

HOW DO WE READ?

"How do we read?" can be a cognitive question: How do people learn to de-code written texts? But it has become a sociological question as well: Under what circumstances and on what occasions do people who can read actually do so? Reading research has proceeded along these two paths. The more established tra-dition, rooted in cognitive psychology, assumes reading to be a "universally similar psychological process that exists within the minds of individual people" (Cherland 1994, p. 5). A newer line of work, rooted in anthropology and sociolinguistics, sees reading as "an external, social act, performed by people in interaction and in a particular context" (Cherland 1994, p. 5). Of course, literacy is neither only a set of mental skills nor only a social performance. It is "a concept that embraces the cultural resources of a literate tradition—including the writing system(s) of this tradition—and the ensemble of abilities necessary to exploit these cultural resources. . . . Literacy is a form of cultural organization itself, what we may call 'societal literacy' " (Brockmeier et al. 2002, p. 11; see also Wagner et al. 1999, especially essays by Finnegan and Heath).

A review of the societal literacy research suggests that two answers to the "How do we read?" question have emerged to challenge the customary view that reading is the act of an individual sitting down and reading a book. First is the practice thesis: Reading is a social practice, and people read all the time as an unnoticed part of their everyday pursuits, in addition to their more formal occasions of sitting down and reading. Second is the collective thesis: People read in groups, and even individual reading is the result of collective memberships.

Practice

The emphasis on practice, reading as it is actually done, has largely displaced the old dualisms of literate/illiterate, oral/literate, reading/writing, and reading/ misreading. Contemporary researchers are more apt to envision reading as a net-work of practices, one that is unstable and contingent upon shifting contexts (Fernandez 2001).

The point about contexts is more complicated than it first appears. Contexts first and foremost involve the material and institutional circumstances of read-ing: whether people are literate; whether they have access to print materials, free time, and sufficient light; whether they read for school, work, or leisure; whether their buses are comfortable or packed; whether the electricity is reliable (Griswold

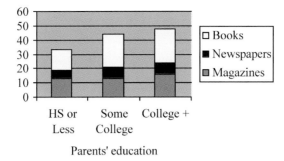

Figure 1   Daily reading by parental education.

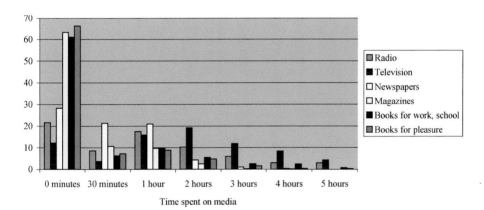

Figure 2   Average daily media use.

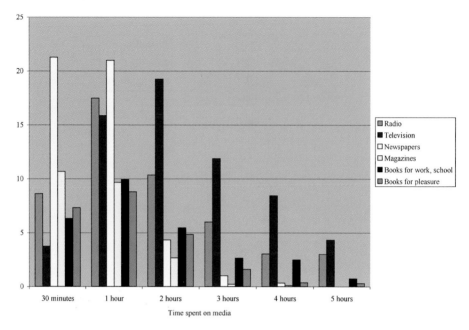

Figure 3   Media use previous day, users only.

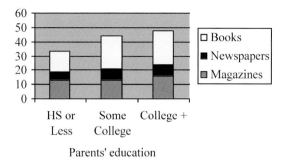

Figure 1   Daily reading by parental education.

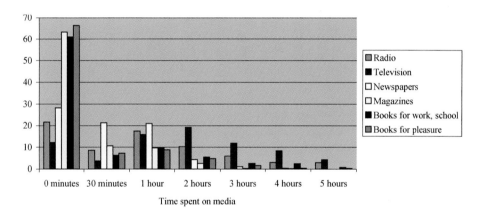

Figure 2   Average daily media use.

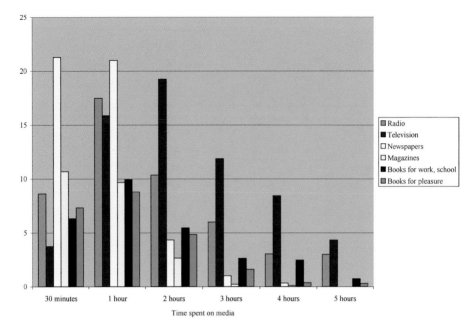

Figure 3 Media use previous day, users only.

2000). The idea of context has expanded beyond such conditions to include the geopolitical context [Anghelescu & Poulain (2001) show the impact of the cold war on reading], the gender context (Barton & Hamilton 1998, chapter 10; Cherland 1994; Currie 1999; Roberts & Foehr 2004; and many others have shown how reading both conforms to and reproduces gender), and even the literacy context itself.

On this last point, Brandt (2001) compared the reading practices of a great-grandmother, Genna (born in 1898), and her great-grandson, Michael (born in 1981):

> In the sparse setting of Genna May's prairie farmhouse, paper, hard to come by, was reserved for her father's church work [she used a slate]. In Michael May's print-clutter suburban ranch home, his parents introduced him to writing and reading amid the background chatter of network television. For members of the community in which Genna May grew up, the ability to write the words of everyday life often marked the end of formal schooling, whereas for Michael May, these same experiences served as a preparation for kindergarten (Brandt 2001, p. 74).

Genna and her great-grandson both acquired literacy but in radically different literacy contexts, so their similar reading skills meant very different things. "If Genna carved out a turn-of-the-century literacy amid a scarcity of print, her great-grandson must carve one out amid a material and ideological surplus" (p. 74). Genna's reading was a ticket to upward social mobility, whereas so far Michael's reading is merely an indication of normal development.

Barton & Hamilton (1998, p. 7) identified six aspects of the practice model:

- Literacy is a set of social practices, which can be inferred from events mediated by written texts.
- Different literacies are associated with different domains of life.
- Social institutions and power relationships pattern literacy practices, with some literacies becoming more dominant, visible, and influential.
- Literacy practices are purposeful and embedded in broader social goals and cultural practices.
- Literacy is historically situated.
- Literacy practices change, and new ones are frequently acquired through informal learning and sense making.

In a rich demonstration of the practice approach, Barton & Hamilton (1998) studied everyday literacy practices—both reading and writing—in Lancaster, England. In addition to general ethnographic observations, they offer a close look at the literacy practices of four individuals. For example, Harry is a retired fireman and veteran who reads a lot, especially newspapers (which he discusses over weekly tea with an old friend) and histories of World War II. Scorning novels, he wants "the real authentic thing," e.g., authentic war accounts. Harry uses literacy to make sense of his own life. Others use literacy for community activism, for household accounts, for writing fan letters. Barton & Hamilton (1998) stress the enormous "diversity of literacies" in people's private lives. Literacy practices include two kinds of reading, one in which reading is the main goal of the activity and the other in which reading is a means to another end, as well as several kinds of writing. Overall, Barton & Hamilton find people use their repertoire of literacy practices to organize their lives, communicate, entertain themselves, document their experiences, make sense of their worlds, and participate in social life beyond the immediate household. Not all of these activities are directly social, but some are. This social dimension of the practice approach is stressed in our second line of research.

Groups

Since the burst of production-of-culture studies in the late 1970s and 1980s, sociologists have successfully established the collective nature of literary and artistic production, as in Howard Becker's oft-cited example of how Trollope's coffee-pouring servant was essential to his vast literary output (Becker 1982). But if the collective nature of authorship has become a commonplace, the collective nature of readership is less obvious. Most people still envision readers like Jo in *Little Women*, sitting alone by the window, munching apples.

Long (2003) points out that the "ideology of the solitary reader" ignores the social infrastructure of reading itself: Books are social products, but reading must also be taught; gatekeepers, such as Oprah Winfrey or the *New York Times Book Review*, steer reading choices; and for many people the reading experience is intrinsically social. The case of Harry regularly discussing his reading with an old crony is very typical. Perhaps the ultimate expression of this form of social literacy is the contemporary book club or reading group; the two terms, used interchangeably, refer to a group of people who meet on regular basis in their leisure time to discuss books (Hartley 2001).

Two recent studies of reading groups show how these rapidly increasing clubs structure reading and its satisfactions. Long (2003) confined her study to women's groups, all in Houston. She focused on four groups in particular; overall she identified 121 groups in the city, of which 64% were all female, 3% were male, and 33% had members of both sexes. The women's groups followed a long tradition stemming from the nineteenth century women's club movement. Long's survey of contemporary groups suggests that book clubs attract highly educated members who tend to be affluent, stable, and traditional in terms of marriage and religion. Most groups grew out of neighborhoods or circles of acquaintances, but prior connections are not always necessary, e.g., some came from bookstore notices. Members claim their reading groups satisfy their needs for intellectual stimulation; housewives with young children were a typical example, and another club was made up of women working in technical, male-dominated fields who wanted to have intelligent conversation with other women.

In the United Kingdom, Hartley (2001) surveyed 350 reading groups. She found a sex ratio comparable to that found by Long: 69% of groups were all female, 4%

all male (including some of the oldest and most formal groups), and the rest were mixed. Although reading in groups is not new, she notes their enormous growth in the late 1990s. (Internet reading groups are both new and legion, but are not included in either Hartley's or Long's studies.) She notes how reading groups do not necessarily compete with but are sometimes facilitated by mass media, such as Oprah's Book Club beginning in 1996 (each month television personality Oprah Winfrey announces her choice of a book, and a month later devotes half her show to discussing it). Face-to-face groups have been organized by public libraries, bookstores, newspapers, a telecommunications company in the United Kingdom, the magazine *Good Housekeeping*, and entire cities, as in Chicago's "One Book, One Chicago" program.

Cities' and celebrities' sponsorship of the public's engagement with books reminds us of the extraordinary value that society attributes to reading. It is hard to imagine another medium being promoted so aggressively. The almost unquestioned assumption seems to be that reading and talking about reading is a social good. Historian Harvey Graff (1987) has worked to debunk the "literacy myth" that links literacy, schooling, modernization, democracy, and individual social mobility, but such critical voices have had little impact on the public or its institutions. Regardless of whether people are actually spending much time reading, they honor and encourage it to a remarkable extent.

READING AND OTHER MEDIA

In their magisterial *History of Reading in the West*, Cavallo & Chartier (1999) argue that authors do not write books; they produce texts—written objects—that readers handle in different ways. This practice-oriented approach to reading has changed the way we think about the relationship between reading and other media use. Instead of dividing time into a pie chart—a fat slice to watching television, a thin slice to reading—scholars think of media as interwoven with one another and within the context of living our lives.

In this section we first look at traditional media, i.e., before the Internet era began in about the mid-1990s. These media are still around and indeed occupy the bulk of most people's media use. Downloading music is popular, in other words, but most people have the radio on. We then look at the emerging picture of how the Internet is affecting reading.

The Gallup Organization asked people how much time they had spent "yester-day" using different types of media (Gallup Org. 1990). Such a question in the past would have been seen as pieces of a pie: e.g., people spend more time listening to the radio than they do reading newspapers. But of course thinking about practice reminds us that people listen to the radio while they read the newspaper, so to compare media uses this way is misleading. Instead, we look for patterns.

The first thing to notice is that some media are omnipresent, woven into the fabric of everyday life, while others are not (Figure 2, see color insert). Most people spend at least some time every day listening to the radio, watching television, and reading a newspaper. On the other hand, most people spend no time at all reading magazines or books. So we can think of media in two clusters, one that people cannot or do not avoid and one that they can and do avoid. Reading is the latter: Most people most days do not read anything but the paper.

If we look at media users only, as Figure 3 (see color insert) shows, we see that people spend a little time with newspapers and a lot of time with television. Few people spend more than an hour with newspapers and magazines, and few people spend less than an hour with television and radio. Books occupy less time overall, and unlike television and newspapers, there is a fairly wide range of time spent reading; about the same percentage of people (5%–10%) spend a half hour, an hour, or two hours with books. It is also notable that reading for work/school and reading for pleasure occupy about the same amount of time: up to two hours. In the higher time categories they diverge; some people (e.g., students) spend four hours or more reading books for work, but almost no one spends that kind of time in leisure reading.

The same survey tried to explain why people use media. The survey identified relaxation as one reason, and respondents find books and television equally relaxing. A second reason is to do their jobs; more than 60% of employed respondents see reading speed or comprehension as being very important to their work, so the routine practice of reading is essential to many people who are not readers in the sense of being deeply engaged with books. A third reason people use media is to learn. For this purpose, people see a big difference between reading and watching television: 60% of people think books are the better way to learn, whereas 30% think television is better. Interestingly, people also report that reading books is "more rewarding" than watching television by a similar 2:1 ratio. Again we see the high esteem that people accord to books regardless of whether they actually read them.

The inverse relationship between reading and television has been a constant finding since the 1950s. For example, the General Social Survey on media use found that older kids (11–14 and 15–18) who live in households where the television is constantly on or who have televisions in their bedrooms spend significantly less time reading, especially reading books, than others (Roberts & Foehr 2004). This effect of constantly available television remains true even controlling for parents' education (Roberts & Foehr 2004). It seems beyond question that television watching has a negative impact on reading. But what about new media?

At the dawn of the Internet age, Birkerts (1994), among others, sounded the death knell of reading:

> Over the past few decades, in the blink of the eye of history, our culture has begun to go through what promises to be a total metamorphosis. The influx of electronic communications and information processing technologies, abetted by the steady improvement of the microprocessor, has rapidly brought on a condition of critical mass. Suddenly it feels like everything is poised for change; the slower world that many of us grew up with dwindles in the rearview

mirror. The stable hierarchies of the printed page—one of the defining norms of that world—are being superseded by the rush of impulses through freshly minted circuits. The displacement of the page by the screen is not yet total. . .— it may never be total—but the large-scale tendency in that direction has to be obvious to anyone who looks (Birkerts 1994, p. 3).

Obvious or not, the picture is less clear than Birkerts expected. In the first place, technology and books have always been mutually supportive, and this symbiosis goes well beyond the revolutionary impact of printing (Eisenstein 1979). Reading surged when middle-class people became able to afford windows in the eighteenth century (Watt 1957). It surged again in the nineteenth century when railroads gave people periods of idle time (Altick 1957). The late twentieth century held high hopes, yet unrealized, for e-books. Twenty-first century entrepreneurs seek patents for Super Slurper, a compound that can dry books caught up in floods more quickly than previous methods (Knapp 2003).

More specifically, unlike the case of television, the Internet does not seem to be displacing reading. A poll in 2001 shows that Internet users spent exactly the same amount of time reading as people who never used computers at all (NEA 2004, p. 14). A review of the available research suggests that the relationship between reading and going online is not zero-sum but more-more. Holding education constant (both reading and Internet use are strongly associated with education), it appears that the heaviest Internet users are also the heaviest readers (Griswold & Wright 2004). Similar findings appear in the articles collected in *IT & Society* (Robinson 2002): Whereas one article in this collection (Nie) finds that Internet use depresses reading, the others find either no effect (Robinson, Kestnbaum, Neustadtl & Alvarez) or a positive effect (Fu, Wang & Qiu; De Haan & Huysmans).

There are at least two reasons why this might be the case. One is the direct effect: The Internet supports reading and vice versa. Amazon.com, which was first and foremost a bookseller, was the first e-business that many consumers encountered and remains a giant in the book trade, as does its online rival barnesandnoble.com. People tell each other about books in their email. They participate in the Internet book groups that Hartley (2001) found to be proliferating, and they chat in groups devoted to particular authors and genres. And of course people read online constantly, although usually they do not count this as reading. Meanwhile, books and magazines like *Wired* that are devoted to the Internet multiply.

The second reason for the enhancing effect of the Internet on reading is that, as is true for virtually all forms of cultural participation, some people simply do more things than other people do. Those whom Richard Peterson has called "cultural omnivores" do more of everything—attend live performances, listen to music, attend or participate in sports, visit museums—except watch television (Peterson & Kern 1996). Cultural omnivores, who tend to be educated and middle-class, maintain a diverse portfolio of cultural capital (Erickson 1996). They eagerly add the Internet to their other pursuits. The NEA study shows the same: "Literary readers" attend museums and arts performances more than other people of the same education level and social class (NEA 2004).

Other media support reading to a considerable extent. The impact of Oprah Winfrey is the best example, but books and authors appear on talk shows, on cable channels, on radio interviews, and in other print media—consider the multiplying effect of something like the *Times Literary Supplement* or *New York Review of Books*. So the imagery of dividing up a pie does not correspond to people's actual practices.

And yet, even cultural omnivores have limits to their time and energy. Although the evidence is mixed, surveys like that of the NEA suggest a decline in at least some of the time people spend reading in the late twentieth century. The new media, including not just the Internet but also various electronic forms of entertainment, are plausible competitors for time and attention. The NEA study, although it did not directly ask if people substituted Internet surfing for reading, notes that the major drop in literary reading occurred in the 1990s, the same time when large numbers of people were discovering the Internet.

One can reconcile the evidence that Internet use does not depress reading with the evidence that reading is declining overall. Perhaps an elite segment of the general population—highly educated, affluent, metropolitan—has produced both heavy readers and early adopters of the Internet. As Internet use moves into less-advantaged segments of the population, the picture may change. For these groups, it may be that leisure time is more limited, the reading habit is less firmly established, and the competition between going online and reading is more intense.

THE READING CLASS

Reading has always been associated with education and more generally with urban social elites. Although contemporary commentators deplore the decline of "the reading habit" or "literary reading," historically the era of mass reading, which lasted from the mid-nineteenth through the mid-twentieth century in northwestern Europe and North America, was the anomaly. We are now seeing such reading return to its former social base: a self-perpetuating minority that we shall call the reading class.

Whereas nineteenth- and twentieth-century stratification involved what people read (e.g., the classical canon versus working-class newspapers or confession magazines), the new century may resemble earlier eras when a fundamental difference was between who read and who did not. Unlike in the past, most people in the developed world will be capable of reading, and will in fact read as part of their jobs, online activities, and the daily business of living. Only a minority, however, will read books on a regular basis; as Figure 2 shows, books are less omnipresent in people's lives than are other media. An open question for sociologists is whether book readers—the reading class—have both power and prestige associated with an increasingly rare form of cultural capital, or whether the reading class will be just another taste culture pursuing an increasingly arcane hobby.

Discussions of the future of reading formerly revolved around either the education system or the competition from other forms of entertainment. The newer emphasis on reading as it is actually practiced, which has been the primary focus of the present essay, has contributed insights along several dimensions.

One is the sheer prestige of reading. Among the Lancaster residents they studied, Barton & Hamilton (1998) found that the idea of being a reader was imbued with values. Reading was seen as a good thing, and people equated reading with being bright. Earlier British working-class attitudes that had judged readers to be lazy or antisocial had faded. Being a reader meant reading books; just reading magazines or newspapers did not count (Barton & Hamilton 1998, p. 158).

Such prestige has been subject to radical critique: Literacy is strongly associated with social inequality. Indeed, Stuckey (1991) argues that books and the teaching of literacy commit "social violence." In the classic Marxian view, class results from an unfair system of ownership.

> It is possible that a system of ownership built on the ownership of literacy is more violent than past systems, however. Though it seems difficult to surpass the violence of systems of indenture, slavery, industrialism, and the exploitation of immigrant or migrant labor, literacy provides a unique bottleneck. Unlike a gun . . . literacy legitimates itself (Stuckey 1991, p. 18).

Such critiques have had virtually no impact on the social honor accorded to reading and to "being a reader."

The second sociological emphasis is on reading as a product of social organization. An immense infrastructure supports the reading habit. Although education is the most obvious, as are the media tie-ins mentioned above, there exist more specific institutional and corporate forms that encourage and sustain reading. Consider the reading group phenomenon. The United States has the most, with groups going back to nineteenth century women's clubs (Hartley 2001, Long 2003). In the United States (and to a much lesser extent in other book club countries like the United Kingdom, Australia, and New Zealand), there are paid group leaders, book-club consultants, coordinators, books on how to organize a book club, reading group questions in the back of paperback editions—a considerable "book club service industry" (Hartley 2001, p. 118). We might call this the pile-on effect: Reading practices, once they reach some critical mass, generate their own support structure.

The third insight, a product of the first two, is the division between reading as a matter-of-fact practice of just about everyone and the reading of literature, serious nonfiction, and the quality press as an esteemed, cultivated, supported practice of an educated elite. The gap between these two literacies seems likely to widen. The reading class will flourish even if overall reading by the general public declines. An open question for sociologists is whether there exists a relationship between this emerging divide on the one hand and other forms of stratification and inequality on the other.

The *Annual Review of Sociology* is online at http://soc.annualreviews.org

LITERATURE CITED

Altick RD. 1957. *The English Common Reader: A Social History of the Mass Reading Public, 1800–1900*. Chicago: Univ. Chicago Press

Amtower L. 2000. *Engaging Words: The Culture of Reading in the Later Middle Ages*. New York: Palgrave/St. Martin's Press

Andersen J, Sauer E, eds. 2002. *Books and Readers in Early Modern England: Material Studies*. With an afterword by Stephen Orgel. Philadelphia: Univ. Penn. Press

Anghelescu HGB, Poulain M, eds. 2001. *Books, Libraries, Reading, and Publishing in the Cold War*. Washington, DC: Libr. Congr., Cent. Book

Barton D, Hamilton M. 1998. *Local Literacies: Reading and Writing in One Community*. London/New York: Routledge

Becker HS. 1982. *Art Worlds*. Berkeley: Univ. Calif. Press

Birkerts S. 1994. *The Gutenberg Elegies: The Fate of Reading in an Electronic Age*. Boston/London: Faber & Faber

Book Mark. Ltd. 2000. *Reading the Situation: Book Reading, Buying and Borrowing Habits in Britain*. London: Book Mark./Read. Partnersh.

Brandt D. 2001. *Literacy in American Lives*. Cambridge/New York: Cambridge Univ. Press

Brockmeier J, Wang M, Olson DR. 2002. *Literacy, Narrative, and Culture*. Richmond, UK: Curzon

Brooks J. 1985. *When Russia Learned to Read: Literacy and Popular Literature, 1861–1917*. Princeton, NJ: Princeton Univ. Press

Cavallo G, Chartier R, eds. 1999. *A History of Reading in the West*. Transl. Lydia G. Cochrane. Amherst: Univ. Mass. Press. Orig. publ. as *Histoire de le lecture dans le monde occidental*. 1995. Paris: Éd. Leuil. 1997. Rome-Bari: Giuseppe Laterza & Figli Spa

Cherland MR. 1994. *Private Practices: Girls Reading Fiction and Constructing Identity*. London: Taylor & Francis

Children's Lit. Res. Cent., Roehampton Inst., London. 1996. *Young People's Reading at the End of the Century*. London: Book Trust

Coleman J. 1996. *Public Reading and the Reading Public in Late Medieval England and France*. New York: Cambridge Univ. Press

Currie DH. 1999. *Girl Talk: Adolescent Magazines and Their Readers*. Toronto: Univ. Toronto Press

Cushman G, Veal AJ, Zuzanek J. 1996. *World Leisure Participation: Free Time in the Global Village*. Wallingford, UK: CAP Int.

DiMaggio P, Ostrower F. 1992. Race, ethnicity, and participation in the arts: patterns of participation by Hispanics, whites, and African-Americans in selected activities from the 1982 and 1985 Surveys of Public Participation in the Arts. *Res. Div. Rep. #25, Natl. Endow. Arts*. Washington, DC: Seven Locks Press

Eisenstein EL. 1979. *The Printing Press as an Agent of Change: Communications and Cultural Transformations in Early-Modern Europe*. Cambridge, UK: Cambridge Univ. Press

Erickson BH. 1996. Culture, class, and connections. *Am. J. Sociol.* 102:217–51

Fernandez R. 2001. *Imagining Literacy: Rhizomes of Knowledge in American Culture and Literature*. Austin: Univ. Texas Press

Furet F, Ozouf J. 1982. *Reading and Writing: Literacy in France from Calvin to Jules Ferry*. Cambridge, UK: Cambridge Univ. Press

Gallop Org. 1990. *December Wave 2, Field Date 12/13/1990–12/16/1990*. http://institu tion.gallup.com/documents/questionnaire.as px?STUDY=GNS922024. Accessed Feb. 25, 2005

Gen. Soc. Surv. 1998. *Codebook Variable: READFICT*. http://webapp.icpsr.umich.edu/ GSS/rnd1998/merged/cdbk/readfict.htm

Graff HJ. 1987. *The Legacies of Literacy: Continuities and Contradictions in Western Culture and Society*. Bloomington/Indianapolis: Indiana Univ. Press

Griswold W. 2000. *Bearing Witness: Readers, Writers, and the Novel in Nigeria*. Princeton, NJ: Princeton Univ. Press

Griswold W, Wright N. 2004. Wired and well read. In *Society Online: The Internet in Context*, ed. PN Howard, S Jones, pp. 203–22. Thousand Oaks, CA: Sage

Hall C, Coles M. 1999. *Children's Reading Choices*. London/New York: Routledge

Hartley J. 2001. *Reading Groups. A Survey Conducted in Association with Sara Turvey*. Oxford/New York: Oxford Univ. Press

Knapp L. 2003. It sucks, but that's a good thing. *Wired News*. http://www.wired.com/news/technology/0,1282,60614,00.htm. Accessed Sept. 30, 2003

Knulst W, Kraaykamp G. 1997. The decline of reading: leisure reading trends in the Netherlands (1955–1995). *Neth. J. Soc. Sci.* 33:130–50

Knulst W, Kraaykamp G. 1998. Trends in leisure reading: forty years of research on reading in the Netherlands. *Poetics* 26(1):21–41

Lee FR. 2004. Chick-lit king imagines his way into women's heads. *NY Times*, July 29. http://www.ericjeromedickey.com/media/ny times.htm

Link P. 1981. *Mandarin Ducks and Butterflies: Popular Fiction in Early Twentieth Century Chinese Cities*. Berkeley: Univ. Calif. Press

Long E. 2003. *Book Clubs: Women and the Uses of Reading in Everyday Life*. Chicago: Univ. Chicago Press

McHenry E. 2002. *Forgotten Readers: Recovering the Lost History of African American Literary Societies*. Durham, NC/London: Duke Univ. Press

Natl. Endow. Arts. 2004. Reading at risk: a survey of literary reading in America. *Res. Div. Rep. #46*. Washington, DC: Natl. Endow. Arts

Newell S. 2002. *Literary Culture in Colonial Ghana: "How to Play the Game of Life."* Bloomington: Indiana Univ. Press

OECD Stat. Can. 2000. *Literacy in the Information Age: Final Report of the International Adult Literacy Survey*. Paris/Ottawa: OECD Stat. Can.

Olson DR, Torrance N, eds. 2001. *The Making of Literate Societies*. Malden, MA/Oxford: Blackwell

Parush I. 2004. *Reading Jewish Women: Marginality and Modernization in Nineteenth-Century Eastern European Jewish Society*. Trans. S Sternberg. Waltham, MA: Brandeis Univ. Press

People's Daily Online. 2004. *Chinese people read less*, Survey. Aug. 18. http://english.people.com.cn/200408/18/eng20040818_15 3593.html

Peterson RA, Kern RM. 1996. Changing highbrow taste: from snob to omnivore. *Am. Sociol. Rev.* 61:900–7

Roberts DF, Foehr UG. 2004. *Kids and Media in America*. Cambridge/ New York: Cambridge Univ. Press

Robinson JP, Spec. ed. 2002. IT, mass media, and other daily activity. *IT Soc.* Vol. 1, Issue 2. http://www.stanford.edu/group/siqss/itandsociety/v01i02.html

Sharpe K. 2000. *Reading Revolutions: The Politics of Reading in Early Modern Europe*. New Haven, CT: Yale Univ. Press

Stuckey JE. 1991. *The Violence of Literacy*. Portsmouth, NH: Boynton/Cook (Heinemann Educational)

Wagemaker H, ed. 1996. *Are Girls Better Readers? Gender Differences in Reading Literacy in 32 Countries*. Amsterdam: Int. Assoc. Eval. Educ. Achiev.

Wagner DA, Venezky RL, Street BV. 1999. *Literacy: An International Handbook*. Boulder, CO: Westview

Watt I. 1957. *The Rise of the Novel: Studies in Defoe, Richardson, and Fielding*. Berkeley: Univ. Calif. Press

Zill N, Winglee M. 1990. *Who Reads Literature: The Future of the United States as a Nation of Readers*. Cabin John, MD: Seven Locks Press

Annu. Rev. Sociol. 2005. 31:143–62
doi: 10.1146/annurev.soc.31.041304.122249
Copyright © 2005 by Annual Reviews. All rights reserved
First published online as a Review in Advance on March 11, 2005

NEW DIRECTIONS IN CORPORATE GOVERNANCE

Gerald F. Davis

University of Michigan Business School, Ann Arbor, Michigan 48109-1234;
email: gfdavis@umich.edu

Key Words   financial markets, institutional analysis, organization theory, agency
theory

■ **Abstract**   Corporate governance describes the structures, processes, and institutions within and around organizations that allocate power and resource control among participants. Law and economics scholars have developed a view of the public corporation as a nexus-of-contracts whose structure is driven by the requirements of financial markets, and thus features of the corporation and its surrounding institutions are theorized in terms of their function in directing corporations toward share price as a criterion of value. Working from this base, more recent research has studied historical and cross-national variation in governance institutions, producing highly varied interpretations of their sources and function. Sociological work, particularly within organization theory, has critiqued this functionalist view and provided alternative interpretations based on networks, power, and culture. The most promising contemporary work seeks to analyze governance in terms of the dynamics of institutions—where they originate, how they operate, how they change, and how they spread beyond their original purposes.

INTRODUCTION

Investors in corporations require assurance that their contributions—financial capital, human capital, social capital—will generate a return. Corporate governance concerns the institutions that make these investments possible, from boards of directors, to legal frameworks and financial markets, to broader cultural understandings about the place of the corporation in society. Thus, corporate governance consists of "the whole set of legal, cultural, and institutional arrangements that determine what publicly traded corporations can do, who controls them, how that control is exercised, and how the risks and returns from the activities they undertake are allocated" (Blair 1995, p. 3). When public corporations are among the most dominant actors transnationally, examining corporate governance is essential to understanding global structures of power. More broadly, corporate governance describes the institutional matrix that channels financial flows. In a world where foreign exchange trading tops $1.5 trillion per day, it is an essential component of the contemporary world economy.

This article reviews recent research on corporate governance in sociology and law and economics. I focus in particular on the debates that have arisen in the past decade on the financial aspects of corporate governance. [Excellent summaries of work prior to that can be found in Mizruchi's (1996) review of interlocking boards of directors, Keister's (2002) review of financial markets and banking, and Kang & Sorenson's (1999) analysis of the ownership and control of corporations.] I begin with a discussion of managerialism and the contractarian approach to the corporation in finance and law that arose during the 1970s and 1980s. This approach views the corporation and its surrounding institutions as solutions to the problem of accountability and control created by dispersed ownership in large enterprises, and theorizes a set of markets and mechanisms that orient corporate managers toward the criterion of shareholder value. Because of the policy dominance of the contractarian approach, and because it is less familiar to sociologists than other views of the corporation, the review revolves primarily around this framework and its critics. I then discuss sociological approaches to the corporation and their critique of this functionalist approach. More recent work in law and economics responds to the limitations of the earlier functionalist stance by taking history, power, and culture into account in explaining the trajectory of governance institutions around the world, as the next section documents; indeed, financial economists have spawned a sort of para-sociology in attempting to explain cross-national variation in corporate governance over time, and both Marx and Weber have found unexpected admirers. I close by describing especially promising domains of future research as financial markets become ever more central parts of economy and society. The institutional structure of capitalism is increasingly oriented toward the signals generated by financial markets, and there is much sociological work to do on corporate governance in the contemporary economy.

THE CORPORATION AS A NEXUS OF CONTRACTS

Since Berle & Means published their famous book *The Modern Corporation and Private Property* in 1932, the folklore of the American corporate form has become a widely shared myth. The standard story runs as follows: Railroads and other American firms grew to enormous size during the nineteenth and early twentieth centuries in order to serve continent-wide markets economically. The capital needs of such enormous private companies—in contrast to their European counterparts— were too great to be met by wealthy families, and the United States had little precedent for state ownership, leading to dispersed ownership among thousands of shareholders in the largest firms. As Berle & Means (1932) put it, ownership was centrifugal, whereas management control was centripetal. The outcome of this process was the separation of ownership and control, as dispersed shareholders in large corporations became effectively powerless over the professional managers who ran the firms—a situation that came to be called managerialism. Berle & Means argued that managerialist firms were subject to several pathologies that led them to deviate from what profit-maximizing firms did. Freed from the constraints of actively engaged owners, managements of such firms would seek only profits "sufficient to keep the security holders satisfied" (p. 342) and would instead pursue "prestige, power, or the gratification of professional zeal" (Berle & Means 1932, p. 122). By the 1950s, managerialism was regarded as a settled fact: The trends outlined by Berle & Means had allegedly overtaken most substantial enterprises, at least in the United States (Dahrendorf 1959; cf. Zeitlin 1974). So-called managerialist economists (e.g., Marris 1964) built on this characterization of the modern corporation to model the consequences for the economy when firms pursued growth first and profits second, and organization theorists followed suit, assuming ownership to be largely irrelevant (Davis & Stout 1992, Kang & Sorenson 1999).

Yet by the 1970s, theorists in law and economics began to question the plausibility of this account (as did some sociologists—see Zeitlin 1974). Why would sensible people invest in companies whose managers were going to squander their funds? If dispersed ownership was a sign of imminent mismanagement, then surely investors would shun such firms in favor of, say, family-run businesses where the people that ran the company had a stake in doing it well. And if investors shunned these companies, then their share price would suffer, and sooner or later someone would buy the company, fire the laggards in charge, and renovate it for quick profit (Manne 1965). But if corporate managers knew this, they would have an incentive to keep the share price up to avoid unemployment. They might do this in a number of ways: appointing tough-minded outsiders to the board of directors to show that their decision making was subject to thoughtful scrutiny; hiring rigorous auditors to signal the quality of their accounting; incorporating in a state with high-quality investor protection; listing on a stock market with stringent requirements; demanding payment in stock rather than cash to demonstrate that their interests were aligned with those of shareholders; and so on (see Jensen & Meckling 1976 for an influential initial statement).

This insight into the institutional pressures facing managerialist firms was behind the nexus-of contracts (or contractarian) theory of the corporation: financial markets render continuous judgments on corporate performance, and management has good reason to care about these judgments and to demonstrate convincingly that they are guided by the stock market. During the 1970s and 1980s, this solution to the puzzle of managerialism became perhaps the dominant theory of the public corporation, as well as a normative guide for the shareholder value approach to management. To survive, public corporations must demonstrate their fitness to financial markets by showing that they are oriented toward shareholder value. The institutions of corporate governance could thus be seen as a sort of financial global positioning system, a set of devices that mesh to guide corporate executives toward the North Star of shareholder value. Moreover, unlike product markets, whose selection processes may take years to weed out inefficient firms, financial markets are swift in their judgments. The features of public corporations and their surrounding institutions that survive can thus be assumed to serve a function in promoting shareholder value.

Working backwards from this premise, theorists explained the functions of a number of features of public corporations that were previously seen by managerialists as ineffective or even pathological. First, Berle & Means (1932) got it wrong when they claimed that dispersed ownership allowed managers discretion to pursue ends other than profit. Whether ownership was dispersed or concentrated depended on the monitoring needs of the firm: Firms with more variable performance came to have more concentrated ownership than those with predictable performance, and thus in equilibrium the degree of ownership concentration has no effect on profitability (Demsetz & Lehn 1985). Managerialists argued that boards of directors are often staffed by insiders (executives of the company) and their cronies, thus allowing management to evade significant oversight. But insiders know the business better than outsiders do, and outside directors who fail in their tasks as overseers suffer soiled reputations and negative labor market consequences (Fama & Jensen 1983). By the same token, top executives are extravagantly compensated because a well-articulated managerial labor market operates to reward them according to their contribution to shareholder value over the long term, not because they select their own overseers on the board of directors (Fama 1980). And while managerialists saw the proxy system of annual corporate elections as a sham democracy, in which unopposed candidates for director were offered along with policy proposals supported by information from the managers who mailed out the ballots, contractarians see this as a positive feature. Shareholders follow a policy of "rational ignorance": The expected financial benefit of voting wisely is not worth the expense to become informed, and in any case shareholders' specialty in the corporate division of labor is bearing risks through their ownership, not managing (Easterbrook & Fischel 1991).

This functionalist approach to economic structures spread from the features of firms to their surrounding institutions. Scholars of law and economics applied the same economic principles that had worked to explain organizational structures to understanding corporate law and self-regulating stock markets. Thus, corporate law could be seen as a framework for constructing value-maximizing corporate structures, providing off-the-rack contractual solutions for firms that their managers can then customize to their own situation (Easterbrook & Fischel 1991). Law arrives at this situation through competition among providers: Firms can incorporate in any state, whether they have any operations there or not, and thus state legislatures implicitly compete for incorporation fees through the legal "product" they provide, with Delaware (the incorporation state of choice for most large firms) generating nearly 20% of its state budget through corporate fees (Romano 1993). Similarly, firms choose which stock market to list their shares on among competing vendors with different listing standards (Rao et al. 2000). Managers choose among vendors of laws and other governance devices with an eye toward shareholder value: "The corporation and its securities are products in financial markets to as great an extent as the sewing machines or other things the firm makes. Just as the founders of a firm have incentives to make the kinds of sewing machines people want to buy, they have incentives to create the kind of firm, governance structure, and securities the customers in capital markets want" (Easterbrook & Fischel 1991, pp. 4–5). And "If the managers make the 'wrong' decision—that is, choose the inferior term from the investors' point of view—they must pay for their mistake" (p. 17). For instance, investors in Pennsylvania corporations lost approximately $4 billion because of share price declines after the state adopted a strict antitakeover law in 1990.

Corporate structures, state corporate law, and securities markets have all evolved to serve the function of enhancing shareholder value, according to this approach. Also, a number of "reputational intermediaries" serve to enforce shareholder value. Public corporations must have their books certified by an outside auditor, and accounting firms have incentives to maintain their reputation for doing rigorous, high-quality audits because the value of their certification is only as good as their auditing quality. Investment banks do repeat business with the same large investors over and over again, and they accordingly have compelling reasons to underwrite only the securities of firms they have carefully vetted. And financial analysts working at brokerage houses are like private detectives, uncovering all the relevant information about the companies they evaluate and making judicious recommendations to their firms' clients. In each case, incentives to maintain sterling reputations for quality work ensure that accountants, investment bankers, and analysts uphold high standards of corporate governance.

The causal imagery in this approach to corporate governance is of intersecting markets acting to orient the corporation toward shareholder value. Markets for underwriters, accountants, state laws, corporate managers and directors, and the takeover market ("market for corporate control") all combine into an institutional matrix to guide corporate decision making. Underlying all these markets is the stock market. Indeed, share price is the ultimate criterion of value in these accounts, the measure by which all other markets are calibrated. But why? The answer is the efficient market hypothesis (EMH), the claim that financial markets are "informationally efficient"—that is, that they value capital assets (such as shares of stock) according to all available public information about their expected future ability to generate value. Faith in EMH is the bedrock of the contractarian approach: According to Jensen (1988, p. 26), "no proposition in any of the sciences is better documented" than the EMH. Because financial markets are future oriented—they value expected income rather than current or past performance—they are a useful augur of the consequences of present-day actions. Stock market reactions thus provide indications of the wisdom of corporate strategies and structures much more quickly than product market reactions (which may have long lags and, in any case, are well predicted by financial market reactions), and "a firm whose managers feel the necessity to respond to capital market signals will move quicker and will adapt more rapidly to a changing competitive environment" (Gordon 1997, p. 1486). And their future orientation and informational efficiency imply that financial markets can, for a price, provide capital for highly uncertain investments with payoffs expected far in the future, such as with biotech firms, which would have difficulty raising sufficient capital from banks or founders.

The evident success of stock and bond markets has led to an enormous expansion of the uses of similar institutions to fund other income-producing entities, from home mortgages, to credit card receivables, to future payouts of insurance and lawsuit settlements. And to the extent that corporate governance concerns the institutional structures that allow corporations and other entities to trade on financial markets, the domain of its study expands accordingly. Shiller (2003) argues that many social problems are essentially financial market failures. For example, poverty could be greatly reduced if the poor were able to capitalize on expected improvements in future income from education and training by in effect issuing bonds. As the cost of information and communication technologies goes down and their power goes up, the range of things that can be traded on financial markets expands tremendously, making it feasible to solve mere technical problems (such as the lack of a market for "human capital bonds"). It is already possible to speculate in quasi-markets for Hollywood film openings and elections on the Internet, and to buy bonds whose payoffs are tied to natural disasters. The Pentagon briefly (and surreally) contemplated creating an online "market for terror" in which traders could speculate on various classes of tragedy, the better to gather information about possible attacks. (The presumption was that traders had incentives to invest in gathering relevant information and that price changes would reflect the appearance of new data relevant to possible attacks. Critics pointed out that the market created a potential investment opportunity for terrorists to cash in on future attacks.) If the EMH were right, then creating financial markets not only provides better potential matches between investors and those needing capital, but the epistemological side benefit of informative prices (see Wolfers & Zitzewitz 2004 for a general discussion of prediction markets).

Although the plausibility of the EMH is not essential to the study of corporate governance, it is useful to dispel some of the stock critiques that do not hold up to thoughtful scrutiny (see Malkiel 1996, Zuckerman 2004). Some argue that financial markets are myopic and only reward short-term profits, but of course if this were true neither the biotech industry nor any of the many briefly well-funded Internet businesses would have existed. Moreover, some stock market investors (such as public pension funds) have effectively infinite time horizons. The fact that prices change rapidly in response to new information, such as corporate earnings that were lower than expected, is hardly a sign of myopia, although it may be interpreted that way by those who suffer from the price decline. Others argue that the stock market is a giant casino driven by fads and mob psychology. Presumably such individuals are sensible enough to avoid vesting their retirement in CREF or, alternatively, use their superior knowledge of mob psychology to beat the market. [McCloskey (1998) calls this the American question: "If you're so smart, why aren't you rich?"] Moreover, according to law and economics scholars, EMH does not have to be literally true to be useful as the best available option (e.g., compared to investment decisions guided by bank vice-presidents): "[I]t does not matter if markets are not perfectly efficient, unless some other social institution does better at evaluating the likely effect of corporate governance devices" (Easterbrook &

Fischel 1991, p. 19). The wiser proponents of the shareholder value system are pragmatists in the Oliver Wendell Holmes sense. William Allen (1992), for years the most influential jurist in Delaware, asserted that the contractarian/shareholder value approach "is not premised on the conclusion that shareholders do 'own' the corporation in any ultimate sense, only on the view that it can be better for all of us if we act as if they do." And the question of why firms should be run for the benefit of shareholders receives an equally pragmatic response: "[I]f the statute did not provide for shareholders, we would have to invent them" because share price is such a useful criterion of value (Gilson 1981). Shareholders are simply placeholders in this account; the stock market value is what is essential.

There is a fascinating sociological literature on the origins and operations of financial markets that gives insight into the mechanics of where prices come from (see Keister 2002 for a review). Carruthers (1996) finds the origins of many contemporary financial market practices in the financial revolution in England around the turn of the eighteenth century, when a set of reforms implemented to allow the state to finance war via sovereign debt created an apparatus useful for raising finance for other large-scale ventures, such as joint-stock companies. Baker's (1984) famous study of an options exchange shows how networks among traders dampened the volatility of prices, and others have followed with examinations of the origins and impacts of the social structures of financial markets (e.g., Knorr-Cetina & Bruegger 2002). MacKenzie & Millo (2003) interviewed a number of the principals who created the Chicago Board Options Exchange to show how the Black-Scholes options pricing model, initially a relatively poor empirical description of options prices, became true over time as traders implemented the theory. This work makes an essential contribution to understanding market institutions, but from the perspective of law and economics scholars, the critical question is whether there is a plausible alternative, as Easterbrook & Fischel (1991) note above.

CONTEMPORARY SOCIOLOGICAL CRITIQUES OF CORPORATE GOVERNANCE

The contractarian approach to the corporation rapidly established itself as the dominant framework in the 1980s, and it had a substantial influence on public policy and managerial discourse (see Davis & Stout 1992). The notion that corporations should be run to create shareholder value became managerial orthodoxy, taken for granted by investors, executives, and policymakers alike. Yet a number of sociological studies questioned the empirical and theoretical underpinnings of this approach. The general theme of these studies followed from Granovetter's (1985) critique of economic functionalism and atomism: While the contractarian approach contemplates a world relatively free of the friction of social structure and politics, systematic empirical work found pervasive influences of both on the operations of corporate governance mechanisms. Moreover, the approach of working backwards from contemporary institutional structures to infer the function they must serve has a rather notorious history in sociology.

Two important books retell the history of the large U.S. corporation from a nonfunctionalist perspective. Roy's *Socializing Capital* (1997) recovers the origins of the modern corporation by examining the corporate revolution around the turn of the twentieth century. Fewer than ten manufacturers had shares traded on major exchanges in 1890, with a minimal net worth, yet by 1903 the aggregate value of the sector's stocks and bonds was over $7 billion. Incorporation, and selling stock on exchanges, was transformed from a rare and relatively insignificant phenomenon to the essential characteristic of the American corporate system during this period. Roy traces the political, legal, and class roots of this genesis, creating a stark contrast to the traditional law and economics approach: "Compared with efficiency theory, power theory thus proposes a very different agenda for research: Who made the decisions that created large industrial corporations? What were the alternative choices they faced? To what extent did rationality, social influence, or other decision-making logics shape their decisions?" (Roy 1997, p. 14).

Fligstein's (1990) *The Transformation of Corporate Control* traces the history of the large American corporation in the years following the corporate revolution up through the 1980s. The book builds on several themes in organization theory—that corporations have strategies and structures used for achieving characteristic aims (growth and survival) and that those strategies and structures reflect and shape power struggles within organizations; that corporations are embedded in a field of other organizations, including buyers, suppliers, competitors, regulatory agencies, and others, with their own strategies and structures reflecting their own internal power struggles; and that the state defines the rules of the game for their interaction, generating conditions either for turbulence or order. Those running corporations monitor others in their field for hints as to appropriate strategies and structures, and fields may tend toward relatively stable configurations. But configurations that are desirable from the perspective of those running corporations—say, a monopoly or oligopoly—are often undesirable from the perspective of other constituencies, such as their consumers. Thus, the state has intervened at several critical junctures in ways that destabilized the field of the largest corporations, primarily through antitrust legislation: the Sherman Act of 1890, which limited the viability of trusts and cartels; the Clayton Act of 1914, aimed at collusion; and the Celler-Kefauver Act of 1950, limiting vertical and horizontal mergers. Fligstein (1990) thus provides a four-part periodization of the history of the large American corporation. He argues that as fields achieved a form of stability through the use of common strategies and structures, state intervention changed the ground rules of competition and thus generated a search for new strategies and structures adapted to the new ground rules. As these were adopted and spread among large firms, fields achieved a new stability, which was again disturbed by the next round of state regulatory change.

The links between state regulation and organizational action are conceptions of control—"totalizing world views that cause actors to interpret every situation from a given perspective. They are forms of analysis used by actors to find solutions to the current problems of the organization" and are "collectively held and reflected in their organizational fields" (Fligstein 1990, pp. 10, 12). Direct control, the first conception of control, used predatory competition, cartels, and the creation of monopolies to control competition, and it predominated in the late nineteenth century. The manufacturing conception of control sought oligopoly through horizontal mergers (acquiring competitors) and vertical integration (buying suppliers and distributors). When these tactics became problematic, the sales and marketing conception of control took off in the 1920s, focusing on product differentiation and line extension, advertising, and related diversification. Finally, the finance conception of control was encouraged by the Celler-Kefauver Act and promoted the rapid spread of the diversified conglomerate and a variety of "financial ploys to increase the stock price...and the use of financial controls to make decisions about the internal allocation of capital" (Fligstein 1990, p. 15). In each instance, as old conceptions of control were ruled out by state action, firms experimented with new approaches that, once proven successful at promoting growth, spread widely throughout the field of the largest corporations, enhancing the careers of those with the functional expertise that the conception advantaged (manufacturing, sales and marketing, finance) and changing the "functional demography" of those at the top of the largest corporations. Thus, by 1980, the median large American firm operated in three wholly unrelated industries (Davis et al. 1994), and finance was the modal background of their CEOs.

Roy (1997) and Fligstein (1990) both provide sociological critiques of the functionalism inherent in the contractarian approach. Rather than accepting contemporary structures as self-evidently appropriate and inferring an "efficient history" that got us here, they document the critical historical junctures that shaped the developmental trajectory of the corporation. More recent work has also examined the operations of specific current corporate governance mechanisms, such as boards of directors, managerial labor markets, financial analysts, and so on, and uncovered stark divergences from the law and economics view. Boards of directors in practice look little like the antiseptic monitoring devices contemplated by theorists, and are indeed very much social institutions (see MacAvoy & Millstein 2003 for an accessible account). Many sociological governance studies in the past ten years have concerned the impact of interlocking boards of directors, in which individual directors serve on two or more boards at once (see Mizruchi 1996 for research prior to that). The cumulative findings of this literature provide a compelling critique of the shareholder value approach, in which directors are dutiful agents of their shareholder principals disciplined by the operations of a market for corporate directors. Boards with relatively powerful CEOs are more prone to choosing new directors from relatively weak outside boards, while boards that are relatively more powerful than their CEO evidently do the opposite (Zajac & Westphal 1996). Corporate boards are more likely to share members to the extent that they are geographically proximate and located in cities with institutions such as elite social clubs (Kono et al. 1998), but this effect is contingent on the historical economic development of the company's headquarters city (Marquis 2003). And while banks have historically held central positions in city networks, staffing their boards with the CEOs of important local businesses, this practice declined during the 1980s and 1990s as corporations increasingly turned away from banks and toward markets for their debt financing and banks moved into more profitable lines of business than corporate lending (Davis & Mizruchi 1999).

Several studies document what difference board interlocks make, concluding that they act as conduits for information flow from board to board. For instance, companies were more likely to adopt poison pill takeover defenses to the extent that they shared directors with similar companies that had previously done so (Davis & Greve 1997). Directors that had adopted a pill on one of their boards appeared to act as infectious agents, spreading the pill to other boards they served on—despite the fact that institutional investors were almost universally opposed to the pill. Similarly, firms took on more debt when they had bankers on their board (Mizruchi & Stearns 1994), were more prone to making contributions to local nonprofits when their leaders had network ties to nonprofit leaders (Galaskiewicz 1997), and relied less on shared directorships for information about acquisitions when their CEO had access to other relevant sources of high-level intelligence (Haunschild & Beckman 1998). Corporations, in short, were embedded in a network of information flows via the pervasive practice of sharing directors. Board ties can also act as devices for promoting cohesion among elites, a theme going back to C. Wright Mills's *The Power Elite* (1956). For instance, corporations with well-connected boards were less likely to receive an unwanted takeover bid in the 1960s (Palmer et al. 1995), but not during the 1980s (Davis & Stout 1992). And states with densely connected local corporate elites were quicker to adopt antitakeover laws during the 1980s than states with sparse local elite networks (Vogus & Davis 2005).

A related line of work examines board dynamics and compensation practices, including power relations within boardrooms (Gulati & Westphal 1999, Westphal & Poonam 2003), practices for replacing CEOs (Ocasio 1999, Thornton & Ocasio 1999), and the origins of innovations in pay (Westphal & Zajac 1994). Gulati & Westphal (1999), for example, find that firms are less likely to form alliances when they have "independent" boards, implying that such independence generates mistrust. Thornton & Ocasio (1999) document that the process of changing CEOs in college publishers changed over time as publishing was transformed from a gentlemen's game to a commodity business. And Westphal & Zajac (1994) argue that poor-performing firms, and firms with powerful CEOs, adopt incentive compensation programs as a cynical measure to fend off potential outside criticism from shareholders and others, decoupling the rhetoric of shareholder value from actual practice. In each case, the researchers document the influence of both behavioral and structural factors (such as the content of relationships between CEOs and members of their board) and broader cultural factors (such as how changes in the prevailing rhetoric around corporate governance were filtered through discrete corporate practices).

A third line of research examines ownership and changes in control, documenting how different categories of owners—families, banks, or other financial institutions—pursue different agendas through their influence on corporate strategy (cf. Davis & Stout 1992; Palmer & Barber 2001; see Kang & Sorenson 1999 for a review). Palmer & Barber (2001) find that the conglomerateurs of the 1960s, who built the diversified firms of the late 1960s and 1970s, tended to be well-connected social climbers who were unconstrained by family owners. On the other hand, Davis & Stout (1992) find that family owners helped ward off hostile takeover efforts in the 1980s, but that other types of major shareholders (such as banks or other institutional investors) provided no such protection. Thus, ownership—taken as a relatively "asocial" category of explanation in law and economics—turns out to have different meaning depending on who is doing the owning.

Although these studies provide useful insights into the concrete operations of some of the institutions of corporate governance (particularly boards of directors and the market for corporate control), they have not yet generated a robust sociological and institutional alternative to the law and economics approach reviewed above. There are hints at such an approach, however, in some of the recent work on how corporate managers configure themselves to conform, either earnestly or ritualistically, to the perceived demands of their evaluators in capital markets. Following Michael Useem's (1996) book, *Investor Capitalism: How Money Managers Are Changing the Face of Corporate America*, several studies have documented more or less strategic efforts at conformity. Changes in compensation practices came to receive more positive reactions in the stock market when they were rationalized in terms of alignment with shareholder interests rather than with traditional human resource explanations, so naturally companies adopted the sanctioned rationales, even if this had little impact on the practices themselves (Westphal & Zajac 1998). Companies received lower market valuations when the portfolio of industries they operated in differed from the format preferred by financial analysts (Zuckerman 1999), and thus firms tended to divest the ill-fitting components to match the model held by market evaluators, even if those components were quite profitable (Zuckerman 2000). Biotechnology firms received better valuations upon going public (that is, first issuing shares on a stock market) to the extent that they had prominent investors (e.g., those with many alliances) and were underwritten by a prestigious investment bank (Stuart et al. 1999). Reputation ratings of established firms go up when they appoint well-connected directors to their boards, even though this has no discernible impact on corporate performance (Davis & Robbins 2004). And firms announce stock repurchase plans that they never implement, nonetheless receiving upticks in share price (Westphal & Zajac 2001). In combination, these studies suggest a useful new direction for sociological studies of governance, organized around performance and rhetoric in the context of financial markets. I take up this topic in the final section of this review.

RECENT TRENDS IN LAW AND ECONOMICS

Although most sociological work on corporate governance has focused on the operations of discrete institutions in the corporate governance matrix—boards of directors, the takeover market, and so on—there is relatively less work on the institutional matrix itself, with the notable exceptions of the work of Fligstein (1990) and Roy (1997) on the United States and Guillen (2001) on Argentina, Spain, and South Korea. In law and economics, in contrast, a para-sociology has arisen to explain the dynamics of governance institutions and their cross-national diversity. This focus partly reflects economic globalization and the spread of cross-border investment, but much of the research interest stems from practical problems that arose in postsocialist economies in the 1990s. Former Soviet and Eastern Bloc nations made abrupt transitions from state ownership to systems of public corporations, often under the guidance of U.S.-trained economists drawing on the American experience with financial markets, with wildly divergent results (see, e.g., Kogut & Spicer 2002). As events unfolded, and the varying results of postsocialist transitions became apparent, the central question for both policy and research became, "What are the necessary institutional conditions for public corporations to work?"

A flurry of research beginning in the mid-1990s sought to understand the etiology and functioning of corporate governance institutions, sometimes drawing explicitly on sociological theory, and generally taking the American system of corporate governance as the base case. Mark Roe's *Strong Managers, Weak Owners* (1994) highlighted the idiosyncrasy of the American system of corporate governance which, with its weak financial intermediaries and dispersed patterns of ownership, contrasted sharply with Japan and Germany, where large banks held large and influential ownership positions. The central characteristics of the American system, Roe argued, evolved out of a history of financial regulation borne of populist mistrust toward concentrated economic power. With the easy path of monitoring and control by large banks blocked, over time the United States developed a series of second-best institutions to serve these functions. Others argued that the reverse was true: Because American firms such as railroads had capital needs that outstripped the capacities of indigenous investors, their backers created credible institutions to reassure overseas capitalists that their investments in the United States would be safe, setting the stage for the American system to evolve (Coffee 2001). Modigliani & Perrotti (2000) argued that market-based governance institutions of the sort seen in the United States represent a triumph of meritocracy over the particularistic ties seen in bank-centered systems. Societies that could sustain systems of arms-length financing did so, with benefits for economic growth, whereas those that could not were forced to rely on embedded social ties (crony capitalism) to channel capital and monitor investment. Indeed, the dispersion of ownership in the United States is not pathological, but rather a sign of institutional success: The fact that so much capital is invested by so many savvy investors in firms with dispersed ownership is prima facie evidence of the quality of the surrounding institutions.

An influential series of papers by La Porta, Lopez-de-Silanes, Shleifer, and Vishny (now collectively known in law and economics as "LLSV") sought to uncover the conditions that led to this institutional trade-off between bank-centered and market-centered governance, finding that the type of legal code—French civil law and its cognates or English common law—was a primary determinant of the level of investor protection observed in national systems, and thus the vibrancy of financial markets in those nations. Common law countries, including former British colonies such as the United States, provided strong protections for minority investors (those owning noncontrolling blocks of stock), which enabled both the growth of financial markets and the relative dispersion of shareholdings within companies (La Porta et al. 1998). LLSV also argued for a role for Protestantism, with a nod to Weber (e.g., La Porta et al. 1999): Nonhierarchical religions create favorable conditions for the type of horizontal ties that enable trust and thus financial market contracting, and Catholic nations accordingly have relatively smaller financial markets.

The results of legal differences, LLSV argued, were realized in the economic trajectory of former British and French colonies, yet Acemoglu et al. (2001) find that the ultimate cause of different institutions among former colonies was the mortality rate of European colonizers. Low mortality rates encouraged settlement and the development of legal and other institutions that laid the groundwork for later economic growth, even after independence, whereas high mortality rates encouraged extractive approaches to colonization and weak institution building, realized in sustained lower economic growth. Comparisons of the twentieth century history of wealthy economies also cast doubt on the primacy of legal origin for financial system development: Rajan & Zingales (2003) point out that nations in continental Europe had very large equity markets relative to the United States and United Kingdom on the verge of World War I, but they argue that when internal political processes closed economies off to foreign trade and investment, this stunted subsequent financial development. Carlin & Mayer (2003) find a contingency in the relationship between the stage of economic growth and the use of banks or markets to finance industrial activity, suggesting that stock markets are effective at financing newer, risky activities dependent on research and development, which characterizes advanced economies, whereas banks are more effective for funding routine activities and tangible investments of the sort needed by developing economies. Finally, Roe (2003) agrees with Rajan & Zingales (2003) that politics, not legal systems per se, determines the shape of corporate governance systems. Social democracies generally have smaller financial markets and firms with more concentrated ownership than neoliberal states such as the United States, a fact Roe attributes to the incentives of owners to maintain relatively powerful bargaining positions within firms vis-à-vis labor. (Gourevitch 2003 provides an excellent critique and extension of this political model of corporate governance.)

TOWARD A CONTEMPORARY SOCIOLOGY
OF CORPORATE GOVERNANCE

There is a vibrant intellectual community researching and debating the development of corporate governance systems, but sociologists are largely absent from this community. Indeed, it is a peculiar state of affairs when Jeffrey Sachs (2000) (in an article titled "Notes on a New Sociology of Economic Development") needs to remind us of the relevance of Marx for understanding divergent trajectories of capitalist economies. Yet behind much of the recent work in law and economics is a rather stylized depiction of the American (or Anglo-American) system of corporate governance that is often at odds with how that system operates on the ground, as we have seen. As the corporate scandals of the late 1990s and early 2000s indicate, the American system is hardly an arms-length meritocracy organized around impersonal institutions, as portrayed in the theories. Granovetter's (1985) caution against the functionalist tendencies of economic theories of institutions is still apt. This provides an entry point for a sociology of corporate governance.

The sociologically interesting questions going forward focus on explaining the dynamics of the institutions around financial markets. For these markets to work requires an infrastructure of corporate governance—an institutional matrix to guide the entity being traded. As I stated at the outset, investors need assurance that they will get a return, and those that seek to sell financial instruments—from shares of stock to sovereign national debt—need to provide credible evidence that their investors will get a return. That is, they engage in corporate governance. But the logic behind the institutions of corporate governance is not limited to public corporations; it applies to other things traded on financial markets, an increasingly broad category. The significance of this is that entities that seek to attract investors, from states and corporations to bundles of credit card receivables, need to demonstrate their institutional fitness to distant, often dispersed investors. In a world in which financial flows are the lifeblood of the global economy and in which more and more entities are traded on markets, corporate governance is critical to understanding the contemporary world polity and the dynamics of its institutions. "Geared as it is to electronic money—money that exists only as digits in computers—the current world economy has no parallels in earlier times" (Giddens 2000, p. 27). Thus, the focus of a sociology of corporate governance should be on those institutions— where they originate, how they work, how they influence social actors, and how they change.

The institutions of corporate governance at both the micro level (who serves on a board of directors, which investment bank is chosen) and the macro level (laws governing the corporation, mechanisms for trading securities) are self-evidently human constructions. A sociology of corporate governance can provide an understanding of their origins and trajectories that brackets the assumptions of financial economics and is more self-conscious about the limits of functionalist explanation (cf. Fligstein 1990, Roy 1997). Particularly useful is work that unpacks the interaction of theories about the institutions and their actual enactment. Thus,

MacKenzie & Millo (2003) describe how the Chicago Board Options Exchange came into being despite the questionable legitimacy of options at the time, drawing on Callon's (1998) notion of "performativity"—that is, that "economics, in the broad sense of the term, performs, shapes and formats the economy, rather than observing how it functions" (p. 2). Much the same is true of the American institutions of corporate governance and the discovery of hitherto unnoticed markets. The so-called market for corporate control was of relatively trivial importance when Manne (1965) named it, and it held far more significance in the finance-based theory of the firm than it ever did in reality until the 1980s, when sympathetic scholars gained influential policy positions in the Reagan administration and enacted the theory (Davis & Stout 1992). The market for corporate law became more market-like after it was named by law and economics scholars (although the notion of states competing for incorporation fees appears in practice to apply only to Delaware). In short, economic and legal theorists have had substantial influence in formatting the institutions that grew up around the shareholder value system of corporate governance, and tracing their impact is an apt topic for sociological analysis.

The American system of corporate governance is regarded as the prototype market-oriented system of arms-length transactions organized around impersonal financial markets. Yet as Karl Polanyi (1957) famously put it, "The human economy. . . is *embedded and enmeshed* in institutions, economic and noneconomic," including social relationships among the players, and the corporate governance scandals of the early part of this decade highlight the divergence between the American theory of corporate governance and what happens on the ground. The Panglossian portrayal of investment bankers, accountants, and financial analysts all disciplined by a reputational market proved problematic at best, as each faced well-documented conflicts of interest. Market participants are aware of the theories used by the stock market to evaluate companies and can be quite savvy in playing to them. Thus, investment bankers know that firms get better valuations when they are allied with prominent firms (Stuart et al. 1999) and can facilitate these alliances by allocating valuable IPO shares to decision makers at those prominent firms. The CEO of telecommunications firm WorldCom, for instance, made $11 million from the IPO shares he was allocated in startup firms, many of which would have benefited from announced alliances with WorldCom (before it went bankrupt after revelations of accounting fraud). Meanwhile, WorldCom competitor AT&T fired executives of units that failed to achieve the chimerical profitability of their WorldCom counterparts. Enron famously set up a Potemkin trading floor to impress visiting analysts with the volume of their business, while simultaneously hiding much of their real business in off-shore accounting entities invisible to investors.

The social structures in which governance is embedded are themselves both conduits for the spread of practices and acts of rhetoric in themselves. Podolny (2001) describes networks serving as "pipes" (sources of information and resources) and "prisms" (indicators of status for outside evaluators) and the tension between connections created for access to resource and those created to impress the outside world. This tension is at the center of many of the conflicts of interest in corporate governance and is, notably, part of the folklore of participants in these markets, who are acutely sensitive to the signals conveyed by the prestige of their alliance partners, board members, investors, and accounting and law firms. Demands for greater transparency and accountability in corporate governance, such as those in the Sarbanes-Oxley Act of 2002, are often met with the ritualistic adoption of practices and structures intended to convey compliance, much as firms created Equal Employment Opportunity offices as tokens of their compliance with federal antidiscrimination laws (Edelman 1992). Investors may require credible evidence of accountability and transparency in corporate governance, but what is credible is a matter of rhetoric—that is, what does it take to convince others of the validity of one's assertions (McCloskey 1998).

It would of course be an overstatement to regard corporate governance as an entirely symbolic free-for-all, but it is equally inappropriate to believe the antiseptic portrayal of governance in the law and economics literature. Rather, the best approach is to problematize how corporate governance institutions are shaped to respond to financial markets. The need to attract financing can be a potent lever of institutional change. Consumers may buy clothing or electronic goods with little idea of whether they were made by well-paid union labor or in sweat shops. Investors in securities, in contrast, require evidence of effective corporate governance within the firm to "assure themselves of getting a return on their investment" (Shleifer & Vishny 1997, p. 737), and this can generate significant impetus for change. Yet what counts as credible is inherently social, and the American case suggests that one should be skeptical of the direction this change takes. Compliance with external demands often takes the form of cynical adoption of token structures decoupled from actual practice; moreover, when structures are not decoupled, they can often produce unintended consequences that are worse than the problem being addressed. Tetlock (2002) reviews the now-substantial evidence that increasing the accountability of decision makers—their need to explain the rationale for their judgments and choices—is by no means an insurance of superior decision quality, as decision makers become "intuitive politicians." As institutions of corporate governance are adopted by firms, states, and other investment vehicles around the world to enable commensuration (cf. Carruthers & Stinchcombe 1999), the need for careful sociological study becomes more pressing.

Beyond the level of specific firms and governance markets, the concerns around corporate governance extend to the level of national economic development. Nations vary widely in their constellations of governance institutions, even among the wealthiest economies, as the previous section noted. Both postsocialist and emerging market economies have had quite divergent experiences with public corporations and financial markets, and much work remains to be done in explaining this diversity. In law and economics, financial markets are akin to a power source for national economic development, providing local entrepreneurs who conform to the requirements of corporate governance with access to distant capital. In practice, however, entrepreneurs are often like tourists whose appliances do not fit the local outlets. Mauro Guillen (Guillen 2001, Biggart & Guillen 1999) provides useful historical comparisons of the development of economies in Spain, Argentina, and South Korea, rendering a thoughtful interpretation of how national institutional structures articulate with the evolving global division of labor. Again, further research on the dynamics of institutional transference, both among nations and among financial vehicles, is critical to the development of a sociology of corporate governance.

CONCLUSION

The contractarian approach to corporate governance in law and economics has generated a large and variegated literature on the institutions of corporate governance, from why firms structure their board of directors the way they do, to how national economies' growth rates depend on the legal and market institutions in which firms are embedded. At the center of this approach is the notion that financial markets are informationally efficient, and thus that the prices that prevail on these markets are epistemologically privileged as economic guides. Institutions are explained by their function in orienting decision makers toward signals in financial markets. Once documented, these institutions came to be seen as a transferable blueprint for economic vibrancy for economies around the world (see Davis & Useem 2002 for a critique). Sociological work on corporate governance provides a useful curative to this functionalist approach, finding that corporate governance does not work as advertised even in the United States, the prototype case. The late 1990s bubble and related corporate scandals provide vivid evidence consistent with the sociological critique. Yet sociologists have not developed a compelling alternative account of the institutions of corporate governance in an era of hyperexpansive financial markets. I have suggested several areas of research that should prove promising, along with a brief review of some of the more engaging work on this topic in law and economics. We may hope that in five years there will be a fully developed sociology of corporate governance to provide a theoretical counter-weight to the deficiencies of the contractarian approach.

The *Annual Review of Sociology* is online at http://soc.annualreviews.org

LITERATURE CITED

Acemoglu D, Johnson S, Robinson JA. 2001. The colonial origins of comparative development: an empirical investigation. *Am. Econ. Rev.* 91:1369–401

Allen WT. 1992. Our schizophrenic conception of the business corporation. *Cardozo Law Rev.* 14:261–81

Baker WE. 1984. The social structure of a na-tional securities market. *Am. J. Sociol.* 89: 775–811

Berle A, Means GC. 1932. *The Modern Corporation and Private Property*. New York: MacMillan

Biggart NW, Guillen MF. 1999. Developing difference: social organization and the rise of the auto industries of South Korea, Taiwan,

Spain, and Argentina. *Am. Sociol. Rev.* 64: 722–47

Blair MM. 1995. *Ownership and Control: Re-Thinking Corporate Governance for the Twenty-First Century.* Washington, DC: Brookings Inst.

Callon M. 1998. Introduction: the embeddedness of economic markets in economics. In *The Laws of the Markets*, ed. M Callon, pp. 1–57. Oxford: Blackwell

Carlin W, Mayer C. 2003. Finance, investment, and growth. *J. Fin. Econ.* 69:191–226

Carruthers BG. 1996. *City of Capital: Politics and Markets in the English Financial Revolution.* Princeton NJ: Princeton Univ. Press

Carruthers BG, Stinchcombe AL. 1999. The social structure of liquidity, flexibility, markets, and states. *Theory Soc.* 28:353–82

Coffee JC. 2001. The rise of dispersed ownership: the roles of law and the state in the separation of ownership and control. *Yale Law J.* 111:1–82

Dahrendorf R. 1959. *Class and Class Conflict in Industrial Society.* Stanford, CA: Stanford Univ. Press

Davis GF, Diekmann KA, Tinsley CH. 1994. The decline and fall of the conglomerate firm in the 1980s: the deinstitutionalization of an organizational form. *Am. Sociol. Rev.* 59:547–70

Davis GF, Greve HR. 1997. Corporate elite networks and governance changes in the 1980s. *Am. J. Sociol.* 103:1–37

Davis GF, Mizruchi MS. 1999. The money center cannot hold: commercial banks in the U.S. system of corporate governance. *Admin. Sci. Q.* 44:215–39

Davis GF, Robbins GE. 2004. Nothing but net? Networks and status in corporate governance. In *The Sociology of Financial Markets*, ed. K Knorr-Cetina, A Preda, pp. 290–311. Oxford: Oxford Univ. Press

Davis GF, Stout SK. 1992. Organization theory and the market for corporate control: a dynamic analysis of the characteristics of large takeover targets, 1980–1990. *Admin. Sci. Q.* 37:605–33

Davis GF, Useem M. 2002. Top management,

company directors, and corporate control. In *Handbook of Strategy and Management*, ed. A Pettigrew, H Thomas, R Whittington, pp. 233–59. London: Sage

Demsetz H, Lehn K. 1985. The structure of corporate ownership: causes and consequences. *J. Polit. Econ.* 93:1155–77

Easterbrook FH, Fischel DR. 1991. *The Economic Structure of Corporate Law.* Cambridge, MA: Harvard Univ. Press

Edelman LB. 1992. Legal ambiguity and symbolic structures: organizational mediation of civil rights law. *Am. J. Sociol.* 97:1531–76

Fama E. 1980. Agency problems and the theory of the firm. *J. Polit. Econ.* 88:288–307

Fama E, Jensen MC. 1983. Separation of ownership and control. *J. Law Econ.* 26:301–25

Fligstein N. 1990. *The Transformation of Corporate Control.* Cambridge, MA: Harvard Univ. Press

Galaskiewicz J. 1997. An urban grants economy revisited: corporate charitable contributions in the twin cities, 1979–81, 1987–89. *Admin. Sci. Q.* 42:445–71

Giddens A. 2000. *Runaway World: How Globalization Is Reshaping Our Lives.* New York: Routledge

Gilson RC. 1981. A structural approach to corporations: the case against defensive tactics in tender offers. *Stanford Law Rev.* 33:819–91

Granovetter M. 1985. Economic action and social structure: the problem of embeddedness. *Am. J. Sociol.* 91:481–510

Gordon JN. 1997. The shaping force of corporate law in the new economic order. *Univ. Richmond Law Rev.* 31:1473–99

Gourevitch PA. 2003. The politics of corporate governance regulation. *Yale Law J.* 112:1829–80

Guillen MF. 2001. *The Limits of Convergence: Globalization and Organizational Change in Argentina, South Korea, and Spain.* Princeton NJ: Princeton Univ. Press

Gulati R, Westphal JD. 1999. Cooperative or controlling? The effects of CEO-board relations and the content of interlocks on the formation of joint ventures. *Admin. Sci. Q.* 44:473–506

Haunschild PR, Beckman CM. 1998. When do interlocks matter? Alternate sources of information and interlock influence. *Admin. Sci. Q.* 43:815–44

Jensen MC. 1988. Takeovers: their causes and consequences. *J. Econ. Persp.* 2:21–48

Jensen MC, Meckling WH. 1976. Theory of the firm: managerial behavior, agency cost, and ownership structure. *J. Financ. Econ.* 3:305–60

Kang DL, Sorensen AB. 1999. Ownership organization and firm performance. *Annu. Rev. Soc.* 25:121–44

Keister LA. 2002. Financial markets, money, and banking. *Annu. Rev. Soc.* 28:39–61

Knorr-Cetina K, Bruegger U. 2002. Global microstructures: the virtual societies of financial markets. *Am. J. Sociol.* 107:905–50

Kogut B, Spicer A. 2002. Capital market development and mass privatization are logical contradictions: lessons from Russia and the Czech Republic. *Ind. Corp. Chang.* 11:1–37

Kono C, Palmer DA, Friedland R, Zafonte M. 1998. Lost in space: the geography of corporate interlocking directorates. *Am. J. Sociol.* 103:863–911

La Porta R, Lopez-de-Silanes F, Shleifer A, Vishny RW. 1998. Law and finance. *J. Polit. Econ.* 106:1113–55

La Porta R, Lopez-de-Silanes F, Shleifer A, Vishny RW. 1999. The quality of government. *J. Law Econ. Org.* 14:222–82

MacAvoy PW, Millstein IM. 2003. *The Recurrent Crisis in Corporate Governance.* New York: Palgrave Macmillan

MacKenzie D, Millo Y. 2003. Constructing a market, performing a theory: the historical sociology of a financial derivatives exchange. *Am. J. Sociol.* 109:107–45

Malkiel BG. 1996. *A Random Walk Down Wall Street.* New York: W.W. Norton

Manne HG. 1965. Mergers and the market for corporate control. *J. Polit. Econ.* 73:110–20

Marquis C. 2003. The pressure of the past: network imprinting in intercorporate communities. *Admin. Sci. Q.* 48:655–89

Marris R. 1964. *The Economic Theory of "Managerial" Capitalism.* New York: Free Press

McCloskey DN. 1998. *The Rhetoric of Economics.* Madison, WI: Univ. Wis. Press. 2nd ed.

Mills CW. 1956. *The Power Elite.* New York: Oxford Univ. Press

Mizruchi MS. 1996. What do interlocks do? An analysis, critique, and assessment of research on interlocking directorates. *Annu. Rev. Soc.* 22:271–98

Mizruchi MS, Stearns LB. 1994. A longitudinal study of borrowing by large American corporations. *Admin. Sci. Q.* 39:118–40

Modigliani F, Perotti E. 2000. Security markets versus bank finance: legal enforcement and investor protection. *Intl. Rev. Fin.* 1:81–96

Ocasio W. 1999. Institutionalized action and corporate governance: the reliance on rules of CEO succession. *Admin. Sci. Q.* 44:384–416

Palmer DA, Barber BM. 2001. Challengers, elites, and owning families: a social class theory of corporate acquisitions in the 1960s. *Admin. Sci. Q.* 46:87–120

Palmer DA, Barber BM, Zhou X, Soysal Y. 1995. The friendly and predatory acquisition of large U.S. corporations in the 1960s: the other contested terrain. *Am. Sociol. Rev.* 60:469–99

Podolny JM. 2001. Networks as the pipes and prisms of the market. *Am. J. Sociol.* 107:33–60

Polanyi K. 1957. The economy as instituted process. In *Trade and Market in the Early Empires: Economies in History and Theory,* ed. K Polanyi, CM Arensberg, HW Pearson, pp. 243–70. New York: Free Press

Rajan RG, Zingales L. 2003. The great reversals: the politics of financial development in the 20th century. *J. Fin. Econ.* 69:5–50

Rao H, Davis GF, Ward A. 2000. Embeddedness, social identity and mobility: why firms leave the NASDAQ and join the New York Stock Exchange. *Admin. Sci. Q.* 45:268–92

Roe MJ. 1994. *Strong Managers, Weak Owners: The Political Roots of American Corporate Finance*. Princeton, NJ: Princeton Univ. Press

Roe MJ. 2003. *Political Determinants of Corporate Governance: Political Context, Corporate Impact*. New York: Oxford Univ. Press

Romano R. 1993. *The Genius of American Corporate Law*. Washington, DC: Am. Enterprise Inst. Press

Roy WG. 1997. *Socializing Capital: The Rise of the Large Industrial Corporation in America*. Princeton, NJ: Princeton Univ. Press

Sachs J. 2000. Notes on a new sociology of economic development. In *Culture Matters: How Values Shape Human Progress*, ed. LE Harrison, SP Huntington, pp. 29–43. New York: Basic

Shiller RJ. 2003. *The New Financial Order*. Princeton, NJ: Princeton Univ. Press

Shleifer A, Vishny RW. 1997. A survey of corporate governance. *J. Fin.* 52:737–83

Stuart TE, Hoang H, Hybels RC. 1999. Interorganizational endorsements and the performance of entrepreneurial ventures. *Admin. Sci. Q.* 44:315–49

Tetlock PE. 2002. Social functionalist frameworks for judgment and choice: intuitive politicians, theologians, and prosecutors. *Psych. Rev.* 109:451–71

Thornton PH, Ocasio W. 1999. Institutional logics and the historical contingency of power in organizations: executive succession in the higher education publishing industry, 1958–1990. *Am. J. Sociol.* 105:801–43

Useem M. 1996. *Investor Capitalism: How Money Managers Are Changing the Face of Corporate America*. New York: Basic

Vogus TJ, Davis GF. 2005. Elite mobilizations for antitakeover legislation, 1982–1990. In *Social Movements and Organization Theory*, ed. GF Davis, D MacAdam, WR Scott, MN Zald. New York: Cambridge Univ. Press

Westphal JD, Poonam K. 2003. Keeping directors in line: social distancing as a control mechanism in the corporate elite. *Admin. Sci. Q.* 48:361–98

Westphal JD, Zajac EJ. 1994. Substance and symbolism in CEOs' long-term incentive plans. *Admin. Sci. Q.* 39:367–90

Westphal JD, Zajac EJ. 1998. The symbolic management of stockholders: corporate governance reforms and shareholder reactions. *Admin. Sci. Q.* 43:127–53

Westphal JD, Zajac EJ. 2001. Decoupling policy from practice: the case of stock repurchase programs. *Admin. Sci. Q.* 46:202–28

Wolfers J, Zitzewitz EW. 2004. Prediction markets. *J. Econ. Perspect.* 18(2):107–26

Zajac EJ, Westphal JD. 1995. Accounting for the explanations of CEO compensation: substance and symbolism. *Admin. Sci. Q.* 40:283–308

Zajac EJ, Westphal JD. 1996. Director reputation, CEO-board power, and the dynamics of board interlocks. *Admin. Sci. Q.* 41:507–29

Zeitlin M. 1974. Corporate control and ownership: the large corporation and the capitalist class. *Am. J. Sociol.* 79:1073–119

Zuckerman EW. 1999. The categorical imperative: securities analysts and the illegitimacy discount. *Am. J. Sociol.* 104:1398–438

Zuckerman EW. 2000. Focusing the corporate product: securities analysts and dediversification. *Admin. Sci. Q.* 45:591–619

Zuckerman EW. 2004. Structural incoherence and stock market volatility. *Am. Sociol. Rev.* 69:405–32

Annu. Rev. Sociol. 2005. 31:163–97
doi: 10.1146/annurev.soc.30.012703.110637
Copyright © 2005 by Annual Reviews. All rights reserved
First published online as a Review in Advance on April 15, 2005

EMERGING INEQUALITIES IN CENTRAL AND EASTERN EUROPE

Barbara Heyns

*Department of Sociology, New York University, New York, NY 10003;
email: barbara.heyns@nyu.edu*

Key Words   inequality, income distribution, transition, poverty

■ **Abstract**   Market transitions are thought to inevitably produce spiraling inequality on the road to economic growth. This review provides an overview of research evaluating inequality in income and wages in Central and Eastern Europe since 1989. The empirical studies agree that inequality has increased, but disagree about the amount, pace, source, and explanation of change. Patterns of inequality are unrelated to economic performance, to the pace or timing of reform, or to rates of subsequent growth. Inequality increased the most in the least successful countries and the least in those countries with historic cultural connections to the West. Inequalities by age, education, region of the country, and health status increased; differences by gender appear to have declined. Although data are plentiful and promising, it is not yet possible to conclude that patterns of inequality among postcommunist countries are due to the genesis of capitalism, to social and cultural assimilation to the West, to adaptations of redistributive institutions to deal with poverty and unemployment, or to globalization.

INTRODUCTION

The collapse of state socialism constitutes the most dramatic change in European political economy in the twentieth century. For the minority of relatively successful transitional countries, a new economic order seems to be taking shape. This review is an effort to evaluate how income inequality has changed, as both a cause and an effect of postcommunist transformations. How have markets, privatization, and political changes altered patterns of inequality? The tentative answer is both more and less than one might expect.

Despite aspiring to be comprehensive, this review must necessarily neglect many relevant issues. There is a virtual dearth of empirical studies of wealth, for example. Although a tremendous amount of state property has been divested since 1989, the concentration of private ownership is not known. Considering the importance attached to private property in the creation of a market economy, we know very little about the process of wealth accumulation or the distribution of assets (Ferreira 1999). Several countries privatized large state enterprises by issuing vouchers to employees and citizens, and there is evidence that shareholding has

0360-0572/05/0811-0163$20.00

become more concentrated over time (Błaszczyk et al. 2003, Grosfeld & Hashi 2004). Critics argue that insiders and communist managers were the primary beneficiaries, but systematic information is lacking. Agricultural reforms have decollectivized farms; housing cooperatives have sold individual units; laws have been passed regarding restitution or reprivatization of properties confiscated by previous regimes. The distributional impact of such policies, however, is unknown. Wealth, in short, remains enigmatic in postcommunist countries.

Related issues concern elites, both old and new. A great deal of fascinating research exists on the fate of former leaders and party members, the circulation of elites, the managerial bourgeoisie, and postcommunist class structures in general (Böröcz & Róna-Tas 1995, Eyal 2003, Eyal et al. 1998, Hanley & Treiman 2003, Higley et al. 1998, Slomczynski 1998, Szelényi & Kostello 1996, Szelényi et al. 1995, Titma et al. 2003). Needless to say, the transformation of the *nomenklatura* into a *kleptoklatura* has attracted commentary (Frydman et al. 1996, Staniszkis 1991). Questions concerning elites and stratification patterns in postcommunist countries are certainly crucial for the future of inequality. I hope a future review will do them justice.

Geographically, this review must be limited as well. The most research has been done on the four Visegrad countries—the Czech Republic, Slovakia, Hungary, and Poland. If one adds Slovenia, these are the only postcommunist countries that reported a larger GDP in 2000 than in 1989. Moreover, these five countries plus the three Baltic Republics—Estonia, Latvia, and Lithuania—joined the European Union in 2004; two more transitional countries, Bulgaria and Romania, are in line for accession in 2007. This review is limited to these ten European countries and, for contrast, the Russian Republic. Although the evidence suggests that inequalities have grown enormously throughout the former Soviet Union and in Central Asia, these data are not yet trustworthy. Although China is the largest transitional economy, this review largely ignores non-European societies (Riskin et al. 2001).

The very concept of market transition is dubious, implying a common destination, a shared map, and the expectation of arrival after a brief trip or period of adjustment. Numerous authors (Elster et al. 1998, Gal & Kligman 2000, Stark & Bruszt 1998) have enjoined analysts to speak of economic transformation, rather than transition, but changing the terminology does not solve, or even call attention to, the problems of diverse and diverging outcomes, decentered and decentralized authority, or cultural demoralization. Perhaps the largest and least understood changes observed in the last decade are the internal splintering and fragmentation of a system becoming far more differentiated and unequal than before.

In 1989, the world seemed far more simple and straightforward. Western societies were prosperous and confident. Economic policies had generated growth, inspired innovation, and tamed markets. The Washington consensus (Williamson 1997) provided a viable blueprint for growth and development; neither poverty nor inequality were thought to be problematic if economic growth could be achieved. COMECON countries were stagnant, rigid, and seemingly unable to grow. Moreover, certain socialist countries, like China and Hungary, had achieved accelerated growth through experimenting with market mechanisms. Instead of rattling sabers, the USSR was struggling with openness and embryonic forms of democratic discourse. For state socialist countries, especially those bordering Europe, the time was ripe for movement to the West. Eastern Europeans embraced the idea of capitalism, the prospect of becoming independent nations, and any and all institutional arrangements that promised convergence with the West. Market reforms would probably have occurred in 1989 even if every citizen in the Eastern bloc had understood fully the havoc that unemployment, uncertainty, and spiraling inequality could create.

In the textbook versions of liberal economic theory, inequality is viewed as a by-product of economic growth; well-established trade-offs are assumed between efficiency and equality. Without incentives, entrepreneurial activity and risk-taking might cease, capital markets would dry up, and economic growth would grind to a halt. Although excessive inequality was regrettable, it could be remedied in the long run by expanding education or through redistribution. Market economies meant economic growth; with growth, increases in income would eventually trickle— or hopefully flow—to all productive members of a society. The most convincing evidence for such a process was the historical experience of Western countries.

Inequality, however, is linked to economic behavior in more complicated ways than those envisioned by reformers. Equality was a major tenet of socialism and the primary source of communist legitimation; as a normative assumption, it had shaped institutions and attitudes for a generation or more (Austen 2002, Gijsberts 2002). As an ideal, the concept remains embedded in the culture and the economy in ways that are difficult to change or ignore. Bell (2001) compared responses to the question, "Is life in general better or worse now than under communism?" in 1992 and in 1999 in six Eastern European countries. A clear majority in every country believed life was better under communism. Only one country, Poland, was more positive in 1999 than in 1992; Hungary was virtually unchanged. In Bulgaria, the Czech Republic, Romania, and Slovakia, optimism had declined by 10% or more. Slightly different wording produces similar results (Mason & Kluegel 2000). The most important lesson from the first decade seems clear: Markets cannot be installed like a piece of software. They require a legitimate and enforceable legal framework, cultural supports, and a great deal of social learning.

THEORIZING MARKETS AND INEQUALITY

One logical—or sociological—outcome of market transitions has been to raise once again central issues in our field. What are the causes and consequences of social inequality? What are the costs and benefits of redistribution? Do democratic procedures depend on a level playing field and political equality? Do unequal resources generate dissent and polarize communities? Does inequality promote a productive economy by creating incentives and encouraging competition? Needless to say, for most of these questions, the jury is still out. But the transformations under way afford analysts the unique opportunity to observe planned experiments unfold, as countries endeavor to create and implement a market economy.

The most widely debated theory of market transition was developed by Victor Nee, who extended the ideas proposed by Ivan Szelényi. Before the market transition was even a twinkle, Szelényi (1978) suggested that if market inequalities could be corrected by redistribution, then perhaps socialist inequalities required markets for remedy. Nee (1989, 1991) subsequently provided evidence on the patterns of income inequality in rural China as market reforms were put in place. In the province he studied, private activities enhanced earnings for many poor households, while total income inequality barely changed. The influence of cadres declined. Nee's primary contribution was to link political relations to patterns of economic production and distribution. His model asserts that a society embracing market coordination transforms political relations, with economic transactions displacing and mediating political power to a greater extent than before. Markets were viewed as consisting of bilateral relations of exchange; horizontal exchange transactions would supplant hierarchic relations of appropriation. Such a transformation, it was argued, would enhance equality and increase opportunities and channels of mobility for the least advantaged.

In a very simple world, if the poorest groups produced a larger per capita surplus, equality would be enhanced. Industrial socialism is far more complex and multifaceted. Nee's recent contributions (Cao & Nee 2000, Nee & Cao 2002, Nee & Matthews 1996) to the market transition debate acknowledge that urban China is more complex than the rural communities he originally studied, that the state can influence the institutional development of markets, and that outcomes depend on previous developments. Nee argues that the continuity he finds in patterns of elite recruitment may stem from technocratic or meritocratic features common to both old and new regimes, as suggested by Róna-Tas (1994); he also admits that in Eastern Europe large-scale privatization may allow cadres to convert political power into economic benefits, generating "political capitalism" (Staniszkis 1991), although he doubts such conversion would seriously contradict market transition theory. Nee & Cao (2002) conclude that market transition theory does not predict radical change but rather cumulative discontinuities on the margin of the pre-existing system of stratification.

In my view, the chief flaw in Nee's theory is that it remains embedded in a dichotomous conception of economic institutions. Markets and central planning represent two competing, antithetical systems with fundamentally different ways of allocating or distributing economic goods. In untransformed societies, political power rests on redistribution dictated by a centralized plan and a state monopoly of goods and services. Markets are inherently assumed to be unregulated, invisible, and located outside of the state. During transformation, market activities expand by developing private resources, either by appropriating state wealth or by additional production. If private resources grow through greater efficiency and effort, we assume they are coordinated by free markets, even if state policy proposed and promoted them. If the private sector grows by cannibalizing public sector assets or by sabotaging all reforms that aim to restrict privileged forms of rent-seeking, then we fear that distortions from socialism have blocked markets from developing. In practice, both processes expand private resources, but positive outcomes are those attributed to markets.

The traditional rationale for state ownership and control of production and distribution in both the East and the West is to curb inequalities. The traditional reasons for preferring markets to bureaucratic coordination rest on efficiency and the increased productivity of labor when incentives are in place. Free markets provide signals that can help to optimize production, resulting in greater gains but not necessarily greater equality. Indeed, most analysts concede that greater income inequality usually accompanies market deregulation, both because legal control is relaxed and because individual opportunities and incentives are intensified.

Market coordination changes the process of socioeconomic attainment in a number of ways. Nee's hypotheses can be briefly summarized. Markets favor direct producers over redistributors; hence, significant economic transactions occur outside the purview of redistributive power. The expansion of opportunities and incentives allowed through markets enable entrepreneurs to accumulate resources and compete for positions and power held by cadres or socialist elites. Cadres have little net advantage when entering private entrepreneurship; hence markets increase the value of human capital, while returns to political capital dwindle. Markets also enhance the value of cultural capital and urban proximity. Although Nee (1992, 1996) and his associates (Cao & Nee 2000, Nee & Cao 2002, Nee & Matthews 1996) have maintained that these are unexceptional propositions, they have attracted extraordinary controversy and dispute. Szelényi and others attempted a synthesis of the disagreements (Szelényi & Kostello 1996), but their contributions did not settle matters. In China, income inequality has spiraled with increasing marketization, most noticeably in urban and coastal regions of rapid economic growth (Bian & Logan 1996; Bian & Zhang 2002; Riskin et al. 2001; Walder 1996, 2002; Wu 2002; Xie & Hannum 1996; Zhou 2000, Zhou et al. 1996). Although many transitional societies experienced a modest fall in inequality at the outset of market reforms, this was probably due to the transformational recession, and not evidence that markets reduced income inequality (Kornai 1994, Róna-Tas 1994, Szelényi & Kostello 1996).

In China, the state has promoted income equalization in resistance to the market. In recent years, however, incomes in the state sector and to party members have increased at least as fast as among the peasantry, suggesting that the influence of redistributors does not decline with marketization. Finally, the arguments about human capital appear suspect. Wu & Xie (2003) present data showing that the returns to education in China are smaller in the market sector; other factors, such as region and time of entry have a larger impact (Xie & Hannum 1996, Zhou 2000). Xie & Hannum (1996) argue that economic growth depressed returns to education and experience in China between 1985 and 1988. They find no evidence that the socialist elite lost power. State socialist societies had highly developed links between education and work in both industry and political administration, and wages were based on training and experience to a larger extent than is true in capitalist societies. Although communist educational systems may have been based on different conceptions of merit than in the West, schooling was even more critical for attainment; in the Soviet Union, education largely determined social mobility (Titma et al. 2003). Educational returns have increased in Eastern Europe, as one would expect with increasing inequality (Heyns 2004). In 2002, the Eurobarometer found a stronger relationship between education and income in the eight accession candidates than in the European Union as a whole (Alber & Fahey 2004).

Questions of market transition are properly applied to institutional change. At present, the research has focused on winners and losers, rather than on structural alterations in economic and social patterns. The elite of the old regime, variously defined as communist party members, cadres or redistributive elites, have lost elections but not economic status. The new elite, whether defined as entrepreneurs, the self-employed, private sector managers and professionals, or a new bourgeoisie, are still a minority of the population; although incomes have increased, these groups have not assumed power. The distribution of income has hollowed out with increasing inequality (Milanovic 1999), suggesting a decline of the middle classes (McFaul 1996). These changes do not suggest that a consolidation of class position has occurred or that the rules of the game have fundamentally shifted. Recent evidence suggests that liberal policies have had similar effects in the United States (Levy & Murnane 1992, Massey 1996, Massey & Hirst 1998).

SOCIALIST ALLOCATION PATTERNS

Before 1989, economic transactions throughout East Central Europe and the Soviet Union were frequently based on informal trade, barter, or other nonmonetary considerations, often in addition to prices fixed by the state. Special forms of currency or coupons existed that allowed limited purchases of items that were rationed, scarce, or highly subsidized. Although not legal tender, Western currencies were widely accepted, even in state shops. Official exchange rates were a fiction, or served as a state tax on tourists; dollars were generally worth much more on the black market than at the bank. Special stores sold imported goods, but only to designated people, typically elite members of the Communist party. High officials typically had unique access to the best housing, hospitals, facilities, and amenities. Salaries were set by fiat, according to an elaborate wage grid based on qualifications and positions; there were supplements, bonuses, and other extras as well, but often these were not paid in cash. Given these factors, establishing a basis for comparing income or standards of living with monetized market economies is difficult at the very least (Bergson 1984, Centano & Rands 1996, Kende & Strmiska 1987, Kennedy & Białecki 1989).

Social welfare under socialism was premised on the assumption that everyone worked and that poverty was nil. Benefits were allocated largely through the workplace. Although virtually universal, benefits under socialism were not entitlements. They were rewards given in addition to ordinary compensation, and they depended on relations with supervisors and staff as well as on personal needs. Their value correlated with income, increasing rather than reducing inequalities. Income was largely the wages from one's main job plus whatever bonuses or benefits one received. With few exceptions, income-producing property was owned by the state. Banks paid virtually no interest and did not make private loans. Benefits were sometimes paid in cash but more often in kind; medical services, child care, housing, grants, and stipends for education and family vacations were typically arranged through the workplace for nominal fees. Other sources of income—gifts, remittances from abroad, or informal sales—were typically small. Under late-socialist regimes, such extra earnings were not illegal. At the same time, if they were substantial, one suspects they were not reported (Wedel 1986).

The very diversity of informal, quasi-legal transactions suggests the difficulties in assessing inequalities in consumption. Contrary to the received wisdom, however, accurate data on household income and expenditures were collected. Household budget surveys included detailed information about expenditures and consumption, as well as earnings and income by source; moreover, these reports were routinely checked for accuracy with employers. The people's republics may well have collected better data than that available after 1990; certainly response rates were higher. Comparability with recent surveys, however, is problematic. Without the magisterial study of income inequality completed by Atkinson & Micklewright (1992) at the close of the socialist era, the task would verge on the impossible.

Monitoring market transitions has provided analysts with more economic data than ever before. Moreover, the single most-studied variable in postcommunist countries is income inequality (Duke & Grime 1997). At the same time, debates about globalization and economic growth have generated sustained scrutiny of measures and questions regarding their reliability. This review limits attention to research on or with income and earnings data based on national samples, with comparable data for two or more points in time. As is discussed below, interpreting even these measures involves entering contested terrain. Because most comparative studies have relied on Gini coefficients drawn from secondary data sets, these are listed in the Appendix.

The next section provides background and context for the study of income inequality. Although developmental economists have pioneered in developing the models, recent data sets have opened up an enormously fruitful field for empirical work.

INEQUALITY AND GROWTH: THE PUZZLES

Two of the most influential papers on income distributions were both presidential addresses. In 1954, Simon Kuznets (1955) addressed the American Economic Association, and in 1996, Anthony B. Atkinson (1997) delivered his speech to the

Royal Economic Society. These two papers can serve both to summarize a half century of research and to bracket the changes in thinking.

Kuznets (1955) wrote in a time when the meaning and relevance of income distributions were taken for granted; finding accurate data and proper measures was problematic. Atkinson, in contrast, was quite confident about what we can say empirically, but much more tentative concerning questions of equity or social justice. Kuznets presented a theory—or at least a hypothesis with a compelling graph—of the relationship between economic growth and the distribution of income over time. With long-term economic growth, he expected inequality to increase initially, then to stabilize and finally begin to fall, tracing an inverted U-curve over time. Historical data for Germany, Great Britain, and the United States generally confirmed these patterns of change. For most of the nineteenth century, income inequality increased, largely because of sectoral shifts in employment between agriculture and manufacturing. When jobs in manufacturing were saturated, inequality peaked and then began to descend. During the twentieth century, inequality declined. Plotting these changes yields the well-known inverted U-curve between economic growth and inequality.

These conjectures—or stylized facts—proved enormously fruitful, inspiring a steady stream of research ever since. Scholars documented similar trends with better data, with different measures, and in numerous other countries. Robinson (1976) concluded that the Kuznets' curve had acquired the status of an economic law, although under certain circumstances it should be viewed as historical necessity. Development economists estimated growth models with quadratic terms using cross-sectional data (Ahluwalia 1976); the World Bank, in turn, used these models to project growth and inequality far into the future (Anand & Kanbur 1993).

Historical studies tended to show patterns that were roughly consistent with an inverted U-curve in Prussia, Saxony, Sweden, the Netherlands, Finland, and France (Morrisson 2000). British data revealed an ambiguous U-shaped distribution for both earnings and wealth (Williamson 1997). For many countries, it is difficult to demonstrate an initial increase in inequality, nor does a turning point appear at similar points on the growth curve. Wage differentials in Sweden grew from 1870 to World War I, and then decreased (Soderberg 1991). In other parts of Scandinavia, the evidence suggests long-term declines in inequality, irrespective of industrial development. Soltow (1965) found steady declines of inequality from 1840 through 1960 in seven out of eight Norwegian cities that had the requisite data. In Denmark and the Netherlands, the initial rise in inequality might have been related to war, not economic growth. Short-term inequality tended to spike during international conflicts and then fall afterwards. Brenner et al. (1991) conclude that the upswing of initial inequality remains controversial, whereas the downswing is well documented. As Morrisson (2000) notes, the mechanisms suggesting increasing inequality were similar throughout Europe: dualism in labor markets with increasing salaries and productivity in industry. The mechanisms that reduced inequality in the twentieth century are more diverse but better documented: educational expansion, progressive taxation, unionization, and improving agricultural productivity, as well as strong growth in the welfare state.

Interpretations of these historical patterns—and especially the alleged or implied causal factors—vary. Skeptics note that demographic phenomena—urbanization, migration, and population growth—are confounded with economic aspects of industrialization. Van Zanden (1995) argued that Dutch inequalities in income and wealth were a function of the size of urban areas, with large and prosperous towns having higher levels of inequality at virtually all stages of development. Few analysts dispute the enormous inequalities of wealth found in early modern Europe, particularly within cities; most also acknowledge the role played by social transfers and the growth of the welfare state in reducing inequality in modern societies. But the presumption that patterns observed over several centuries in Europe could be used to model economic growth in contemporary developing countries remains controversial.

Industrialization was a lengthy and protracted process; in Europe, it did not happen in a burst of technical innovation or as a sudden takeoff. The image of a depressed agrarian economy that stagnates until entrepreneurship and capital accumulation reach a critical level is clearly wrong. Proto-industrialization set the stage for economic growth in agricultural areas (Adelman & Robinson 1989, Morrisson 2000) and possibly operates in the Third World as well. Industrialization in the Second World was surely state-driven. The temporal processes, however, are far more complex than positing a universal law linking growth and inequality.

Historical data and contemporary surveys of income distributions have proliferated. At present, the problem is not availability or access to data but comparability, consistency, and sometimes credibility. As more and better data have accumulated, the relationship between inequality and economic growth over time has been estimated with consecutive panels and longitudinal national surveys. Increasingly sophisticated models with numerous additional variables and an ever-larger number of countries and time points have not, however, resolved questions of causality or functional form. Sociologists were concerned to test dependency theories, dualism, democratization, and aspects of development or modernization. Models included education and skill differentials, mobility, trade patterns, and a host of democratic process variables regressed on inequality (Alderson & Nielsen 1999; Barro 2000; Bollen & Jackman 1985; Chase-Dunn 1975; Crenshaw 1992, 1993; Cutright 1967; Gustafsson & Johansson 1999; Hewitt 1977; Moller et al. 2003; Muller 1988; Nielsen 1994; Simpson 1990). Economists tested alternative specifications, but typically found some support for Kuznets' curve (Acemoglu & Robinson 2002, Ahluwalia 1976, Anand & Kanbur 1993, Bowman 1997, Deininger & Squire 1998, Fields 2001, Jha 1996, Kanbur 2000, List & Gallet 1999, Papanek & Kyn 1986, Perotti 1993, Ram 1988, Robinson 1976). Kuznets conceptualized inequality as a consequence of growth—or sectoral mobility resulting from industrialization. Inequality was then considered an indicator of economic growth, or as a lagged predictor (Forbes 2000). With endogenous growth theory, inequality became an impediment to growth, either because of imperfect credit markets or political opposition (Aghion et al. 1999, Alesina & Rodrik 1994, Perotti 1993, Persson & Tabellini 1994); recently, models conceptualize inequality as a nonlinear interaction, stalling progress in poor countries while fueling growth in rich ones (Barro 2000). Dollar & Kraay (2002) argue that economic growth is good for the poor even if benefits are unequally distributed, whereas Banerjee & Duflo (2003) conclude that either an increase or a decrease in Gini coefficients produces less growth. Efforts to sort out this conceptual muddle have not been very helpful to date.

Globalization and economic transitions have brought a whole new platter of timely topics to the table. Statistical *glasnost* and a rapid accumulation of cross-national panel data have profoundly augmented data sources, and research has proliferated. Cross-national studies have fared less well than case studies at linking growth and inequality, largely because of problematic assumptions about data comparability and because many of the explanatory variables were highly interrelated. Coherent reviews and thoughtful critiques of this literature are plentiful (Acemoglu & Robinson 2002; Adelman & Robinson 1989; Atkinson & Brandolini 2001, 2003; Gagliani 1987; Lindert & Williamson 2003; Zafirovski 2002).

Income distributions represent a paradigmatic example of science addressing questions of social justice, at least implicitly. Analysts endorsed models that included equity with growth, but most models posit an underlying incompatibility or tension between them. Kuznets' curve provided a reassuring view of the future for developing countries, and one congruent with neo-liberal policies. Economic growth entails inequality, at least initially; but if one persevered, inequality would decline. Industrialization combined with laissez-faire policies toward distribution could produce growth.

The experience of the past 30 years challenges these views. In several affluent countries, income inequality began to increase after decades of relative stability, especially in Britain and the United States. Harrison & Bluestone (1988) dubbed this reversal the "great U-turn"; recently, the trend has spread to many other countries. There is no consensus among economists regarding the significance or likely duration of this shift, or whether one should assume it falsifies the Kuznets' curve. Glomm (1997) thought perhaps it was the first sign of an "N-curve" linking growth and inequality. Tribble (1996) estimated a cubic equation for the U.S. economy, which would imply dramatic increases in income inequality yet to come. Ram (1988) used time-series data for the United States to produce an uninverted U-curve between 1947 and 1988, with a turning point at about 1965. Questioning the validity of the Kuznets' curve is clearly a growth industry (Bound & Johnson 1992, Bowman 1997, Fosu 1993, Glomm 1997, Zafirovski 2002).

Analysts have re-examined the cross-national data used to specify the connection between economic growth and inequality. Combining Asian and Latin American countries in a single cross-cultural model, for example, is clearly problematic. As a group, Asia includes some very poor countries and some fast-growing tigers. Asian countries have traditionally had far more equal income distributions than is true for any Latin American country, with the possible exception of Cuba.

Latin America has tended to grow in a middling way—faster than Bangladesh or Ethiopia, but more slowly than South Korea, China, or Taiwan. Until recently, European countries have usually become both richer and more egalitarian over time. Plotting economic development and income inequality across this broad range of countries yields a near-perfect inverted U-curve that has been remarkably persistent until recently. A consistent relationship, however, does not prove a causal law. Since Kuznets developed the inverted-U hypothesis, there has been a sea change in how income inequality is viewed. At present, the conventional wisdom seems to be that inequality within countries is relatively stable, while the dispersion between them is enormous. In most countries, income distributions change at a glacial pace. Atkinson (1997) has remarked that one should think of episodes of inequality, rather than trends. Periods of growth and episodes of inequality, however, need not be related. Economic growth seems to be compatible with increasing, decreasing, or stable inequality. Moreover, if income distributions reflect stable structural factors within countries, poverty cannot be reduced without redistribution. The more egalitarian the income distribution, the more likely that growth in national income will benefit the poor (Deininger & Squire 1996, 1998; Li et al. 1998; World Bank 2001a).

With respect to Eastern Europe, cataclysmic political and economic changes have fundamentally altered the economic landscape. The obvious reasons to expect inequality to increase are twofold. State subsidies that distributed rewards and benefits and restrained inequality have been curtailed, and a largely unregulated private labor market has emerged. Because informal economic processes increase inequality, it seems logical that legalizing all informal economic activities would unleash greater inequality. Even with indexation, wage controls, and progressive taxation, relaxing price controls creates opportunities for marketing and creative retailing that can at times resemble extortion. Inflation and unemployment have mushroomed, and social benefits are lower than before. Customary methods for creating comparable "baskets of goods" for cross-national comparisons of living standards may no longer suffice (Smeeding & Rainwater 2002). These problems are fundamental to comparing either countries or time periods. As the next section elaborates, data unreliability is an endemic feature.

RELIABILITY OF THE DATA

Analysts who question the validity or consistency of data on income distributions are in good company. Although few dispute the fact that inequality has increased since the outset of market transition, it is not possible to isolate either the causes or the consequences convincingly. Table 1 presents data from the largest Eastern European database, the TRANSMONEE project for all of the formerly communist countries. Table 2 presents the Gini coefficients from the Luxembourg Income Study (LIS), from the World Bank, and from the UNICEF TRANSMONEE project for comparison for those countries with the most reliable data.

TABLE 1   Gini coefficients for transitional countries, selected dates, 1989–2002

	Date		
Per capita household income	**1989–1990**	**1994–1995**	**2001–2002**
Central Europe			
Czech Republic	19.8	21.6	23.4
Hungary	22.5	24.2	26.7
Poland	27.5	32.1	35.3
Slovak Republic	—	23.7	26.7
Slovenia	26.5	26.4	24.4
Baltic countries			
Estonia	28.0	39.8	39.3
Latvia	26.0	—	35.8
Lithuania	26.3	34.7	35.7
Southeast Europe			
Albania	—	—	28.2
Bulgaria	23.3	38.4	37.0
Croatia	36.0	—	—
FYR Macedonia	—	29.5	33.2
Romania	23.7	30.6	35.3
Serbia and Montenegro	—	—	37.8
Former Soviet Union			
Armenia	25.1	42.0	—
Azerbaijan	30.8	—	37.3
Belarus	22.9	25.3	24.5
Georgia	30.1	—	45.8
Kazakhstan	28.1	33.0	—
Kyrgyzstan	27.0	—	37.7
Moldova	25.1	36.0	43.5
Russian Federation	26.5	38.1	45.6
Tajikistan	28.1	—	47.0
Turkmenistan	27.9	—	—
Ukraine	22.8	47.0	36.4
Uzbekistan	28.0	—	26.8

Sources: UNICEF 2004, table 10.12, p. 97; Milanovic (1999), table 4.1, p. 41; World Bank (2003).

One might expect discrepancies by year or by country; however, the data source explains a large part of the variance in Table 2.[1] If one compares published studies that use household budget surveys or raw data published by the national statistical offices, discrepancies multiply. Four Hungarian sociologists criticized international estimates (Andorka et al. 1997), which claimed Hungary was "the most

---

[1]The correlation between the LIS surveys and the TRANSMONEE data is 0.803 (15 data points); between the World Bank data and the TRANSMONEE data it is 0.841 (16 data points). Although higher than those reported by Atkinson & Brandolini (2001) for a sample of OECD countries, these data sources overlap substantially. Without Russia (3 data points), neither correlation would be significantly greater than 0.

TABLE 2   Gini coefficients based on LIS surveys of per capita household income compared with reports by the World Bank and the TRANSMONEE project

Country/Year	LIS	World Bank	MONEE data
Czech Republic			
1992	20.7	—	21.5
1996	25.9	25.4	23.0
2001	—	25.8	23.7
Hungary			
1991	28.3	—	20.9
1994	32.3	30.8	23.4
1996	—	—	24.6
1999	29.5	24.4	25.3
Poland			
1986	27.1	—	—
1992	27.4	—	27.4
1995	31.8	—	32.1
1999	29.3	31.6	33.4
Slovakia			
1992	18.9	25.8	—
1996	24.1	—	23.7
Estonia			
2000	36.1	37.2	38.9
Latvia			
1997	—	33.8	33.0
1998	—	32.4	33.0
1999	—	33.6	32.7
Lithuania			
1999	—	32.2	34.3
2000	—	31.9	35.5
Romania			
1997	27.7	30.3	30.5
1999	—		29.9
Slovenia			
1999	24.9	28.4	24.8
Russia			
1990	—	23.8	26.5
1992	39.3	—	28.9
1995	44.7	—	43.9
1998	—	48.7	37.4
2000	43.4	45.6	43.2

Sources: LIS, Income Inequality Table, http://www.lisproject.org/keyfigures/ineqtable.htm; Smeeding (2004); World Bank (2001b, 2003, 2004).

equal" transitional country. Within Hungary, Gini coefficients for 1987, 1989, 1991, 1993, and 1996 were reported as 0.207, 0.207, 0.195, 0.234, and 0.242, respectively (Kattuman & Redmond 2001). Éltetö & Havasi (1999), in contrast, report an increase from 0.231 to 0.292 between 1987 and 1995, whereas Spéder (1998) argues that the Gini increased after 1992, when it reached 0.295. For Poland, annual Gini coefficients based on the household budget surveys varied between 0.24 and 0.31 between 1985 and 1997, with virtually no consistent increase until after 1995 (Caselli & Battini 1997, Keane & Prasad 2002). For the Czech Republic, Garner & Terrell (1998) estimate the 1989 Gini as 0.176 and that of 1993 as 0.185 based on the microcensus. Using these same data, Večerník (1991, 1995, 1996, 1997) estimated Gini coefficients of 0.19 and 0.27 for 1988 and 1993 respectively. Although it is tempting to conclude that the fault lies with the disparate methods and definitions used, or with the competence of the various agencies that collect and process Eastern European data, this does not seem to be the case. Problems of consistency and comparability exist among the best data sets and the most statistically sophisticated analysts and agencies, as is discussed below. At least one analyst has concluded that panel data on income inequality are "a can of worms" (Parker 2000).

Three data sets are particularly important for the study of income inequality. The LIS began in 1983 with an explicit mandate to assemble and document national databases from different countries that could be made comparable. Although the technical documentation can be somewhat formidable, LIS data represent the gold standard for measuring income distributions. LIS files constitute an important component of most other data sets and are the best documented. The most extensive and frequently used database was assembled by Deininger & Squire (1996) at the World Bank. These data include Gini coefficients and quintile rankings for 135 countries for selected years and have been frequently updated. A third source of secondary data on income distributions was created at the United Nations University/World Institute for Development Economics Research (UNU/WIDER) in Helsinki. This data set includes an even larger array of time periods and 149 countries, including 28 postcommunist countries. The World Income Inequality Database (WIID) overlaps with both sources. Gini coefficients and country data are both published and available online, making the task of data collection almost as easy as downloading a file.

Atkinson & Brandolini (2001, 2003) have carefully reviewed the quality of data available for 16 OECD countries. Although acknowledging that these databases are potentially an outstanding resource, they emphasize the problems and pitfalls of using cross-national panel data on inequality. Comparing the Gini coefficients estimated by Deininger & Squire with those on the LIS website, the authors estimate the correlation between the two scores as 0.48. Considering that seven of the data points are based on the same source, this correlation is far lower than what one customarily expects for reliability, especially for highly aggregated data. Atkinson & Brandolini (2001) admonish researchers intent on studying income inequality not to use existing data sets mechanically or without "some knowledge of the underlying sources."

In a companion article, Atkinson & Brandolini (2003) review 29 studies in economics, political science, and sociology that have relied on cross-national panel data. They reanalyze the data set used by Alderson & Nielsen (2002), estimating similar equations, and demonstrate quite convincingly that regressions based on the World Bank data set incorporate many errors and therefore do not yield stable or consistent effects. The clarity of their procedures and the fact that they replicate Alderson & Nielsen (2002), described as "an exemplar of state of the art research in the field" (Atkinson & Brandolini 2003), make this a learning exercise, not a hatchet job. As we have seen, the data available for Eastern Europe are more consistent than those given for the OECD countries; yet considering the observed disparities and the small number of reliable postcommunist observations, caution is undoubtedly warranted.

In a much-cited paper, Li et al. (1998) argue that income inequality is relatively stable within countries, although it varies quite significantly between countries. Using an unbalanced panel design with Gini coefficients for 49 countries between 1949 and 1994, they show that over 90% of the variance was between countries and not due to temporal changes in the within-country variance. In the random effects model, linear time trends were too small to reach significance in 32 countries, suggesting no change in the level of inequality. Only 17 of the original 49 countries displayed a significant trend in Gini coefficient over time in either a positive or a negative direction, and in 10 of these, the observed change was less than 1% per year. Among the 6 transition countries included in the sample, only Bulgaria, Poland, and China had large and significant increases in inequality during the period studied; inequality increased slightly in Hungary, Croatia, and Yugoslavia, but these trends were insignificant. The authors conclude that inequality differs across countries but is relatively stable within countries over time. If this hypothesis is true, quantitative studies of comparative inequality seem futile.

Cornia et al. (2004) argue that Li et al. (1998) are wrong about the temporal stability of inequality. Their conclusion is largely based on the omission of transitional economies and recent data following liberalization. Using an augmented data set consisting of 73 countries with Gini coefficients calculated from data extending through the mid-1990s, they conclude that inequality increased significantly in 45 out of 73 countries and declined in 16, based on fitting linear time trends. For the remaining countries, a quadratic or hyperbolic trend line fits best, suggesting trend reversals with either accelerating or decelerating inequality in recent years. The UNU/WIDER data set included 28 additional countries, primarily from Eastern Europe and the former Soviet Union, and data points drawn from 1939–1998. Cornia et al. (2004) estimate that 40% of the difference between their model and that of Li et al. is due to functional form, about 25% is due to increasing country coverage, and 30% is due to increasing the time coverage. In the Cornia et al. study, the data base increased from 597 to 804 observations. The authors report that results were quite similar whether regressions were weighted by population or by GDP-PPP.

CONVERGENCE

Closing the income gap with the West was undoubtedly the primary objective of transition, and one pursued by every postsocialist economy. Thus far, this goal has failed. Only five countries—the Visegrad four plus Slovenia—have surpassed the level of income reported in 1989, and only Poland and Slovenia managed to do this is in less than a full decade. Virtually all of the transition countries have shown some positive growth in recent years, however; the most successful countries now resemble Spain or Greece in per capita income and Scandinavia in terms of inequality.

In May 2004, eight formerly communist nations became members of the European Union. At this time, the European Union increased from 15 to 25 countries and from 380 to 455 million people.[2] The land mass grew by one fourth and the total GDP by 5%; average unemployment increased from 8% to 9%. Data published by the European Foundation for the Improvement of Living and Working Conditions (Alber & Fahey 2004, Russell & Whelan 2004) provide statistics on the accession candidates at the time of entry compared with the 15 original countries. Because the new additions average about half the per capita GDP and twice the debt, the average wealth of Europeans declined. Because the growth rate of a number of these new countries are higher, however, one might expect an enlarged Europe to grow faster than before.

Inequality decreased in the European Union as a whole, while poverty increased. As Table 3 indicates, basic subsistence requires a larger share of household expenditures in the postcommunist countries, but the variation compared with the 15 original members is less than one might predict. Food is a larger proportional expense for Eastern Europeans, but housing is much less costly. Inequality in the Baltic countries is larger than that reported for Europe, but much less than that observed in the rest of the former Soviet Union. Although convergence is surely many years away, the range of economic conditions in "new Europe" is less than one might have expected.

POVERTY: MEANING AND MEASUREMENT

Throughout Eastern Europe, newly elected governments struggled with controlling or containing the initial consequences of transition: recessions, unemployment, hyperinflation, destabilized economies, and mushrooming poverty. Informed estimates put the number of new poor at close to 65 million (Braithwaite et al. 2000, Milanovic 1996, Paniccià 2000). Problems of this magnitude were unprecedented, and newly elected governments were often stymied; it seems that the larger the crisis, the lower the probability that the system could respond effectively. In countries

---

[2]In addition to the eight postcommunist countries (see Table 3), Malta and Cyprus were admitted. Bulgaria and Romania are scheduled to join in 2007.

TABLE 3   Comparisons among European Union member states, 2002

Country	Expenditures		Perceived		Quintile ratio	
	% Food	% Housing	% Poor	Poverty	Gini	80/20
Czech Republic	23.2	17.5	8	8.5	25	3.4
Slovakia	29.8	15.8	21	5.4	31	5.4
Hungary	25.0	20.0	10	12.3	23	3.4
Poland	32.3	19.1	15	18.7	30	4.5
Slovenia	24.0	10.7	11	3.6	22	3.2
Estonia	34.0	18.0	18	18.9	35	6.1
Latvia	39.1	17.7	17	15.4	34	5.5
Lithuania	45.7	12.9	16	21.6	32	4.9
Bulgaria[a]	48.2	13.8	16	39.1	26	3.8
Romania[a]	51.9	13.0	17	22.1	30	4.6
EU—Initial 15 countries	10–19	20–31	15	3.4	28	4.4

Source: Eurostat, Monetary poverty in new member states and candidate countries (Dennis & Guio 2003, Russell & Whelan 2004, Alber & Fahey 2004).

[a] Scheduled to become members in January 2007.

with overwhelming problems, such as Russia, systems providing social security were simply overwhelmed (Ackrill et al. 2002, Braithwaite et al. 2000, Commander et al. 1999, Emigh & Szelényi 2001, Förster & Tóth 1997, Hutton & Redmond 2000, Milanovic 1998, Spéder 1998, Szalai 1999, Terrell 2000, Torrey et al. 1998, 1999, World Bank 1996).

Estimates of poverty in Central and Eastern Europe vary enormously by year, country, region, and demographic category (Van de Walle 1996). A highly compressed income structure means that a large share of the population is at risk of poverty when income suddenly declines and prices increase. Equally problematic, socialist workplaces were designed to provide services and support to employees, not to the unemployed. An entirely new set of administrative offices were required to administer aid and establish a social safety net. In many towns, a single large state enterprise was the sole source of employment. For postcommunist workers with specialized skills honed to outdated methods of production, employment opportunities were, and still are, quite bleak. Among the Visegrad countries, unemployment in 2001 ranged from 8.7% in the Czech Republic to over 18% in Slovakia; in Slovenia, unemployment soared between 1993 and 1999, and then began to drop (Stanovnik & Stropnik 2000). The three Baltic states were doing somewhat better, with only Lithuania maintaining double digit figures (Titma et al. 1998, Tuma et al. 2002). In the former Soviet Union, most people were still working, although salaries and benefits could be as much as six months in arrears (Desai & Idson 2000, Gerber 2004). Throughout the region, registered unemployment exceeded that estimated from labor surveys by a considerable amount (Heyns 1998).

In Central Europe, unemployment was often disguised as early retirement, self-employment, or casual work (Hanley 2000, Heyns 1998, Róbert & Bukodi 2004). Only the Czech Republic managed to contain unemployment and inequality during the initial years of the market transition; a common presumption was that they had not really begun the process (Ham et al. 1998, 1999; Matějů 1993, 2000).

The group most economically devastated by the transition was the unemployed, followed by farmers. We must remember, however, that most of the poor were working. World Bank studies suggested that 60% of the poor in Poland and two thirds of the Russian poor were working full-time in 1993 (Milanovic 1999). As a group, the self-employed are the most heterogeneous throughout the region, some earning next to nothing and others reporting sizeable incomes (Hanley 2000, Róbert & Bukodi 2004). Pensioners, surprisingly, were less likely to be poor than average, in part because pensions were indexed to costs of living and in part because many retired persons were moonlighting. In Poland, the majority of households in Poland received more than two thirds of their income from the state until well into the transition (Domański & Heyns 1995).

As the transformational recession subsided, poverty and unemployment also declined, at least in the most western countries. State expenditures on education and other public services have also stabilized. Vulnerable groups and patterns of employment began to resemble those found in market economies. The next sections review issues of inequality by gender, age, and region of residence.

GENDER AND INEQUALITY

In socialist ideology, gender equality was to be realized through productive labor. For both men and women, work was an ethical obligation, a debt owed to the state. During the socialist period, labor force participation grew for both sexes, but especially for women, exceeding that reported in capitalist countries by a fair margin. Educational attainment also grew and early on became equally accessible to men and women. In the Soviet Union and Eastern Europe, the proportion of women enrolled in postsecondary education exceeded that of men a generation or more before it happened in Western Europe. The reasons probably had less to do with gender equity than with industrial policies promoting technical and vocational education for men (Heyns & Białecki 1993), but the consequences were much the same. In 1989, women were better educated than men throughout the region; they were also overrepresented in professions that in the West were highly paid and dominated by men, such as medicine, dentistry, management, law, education, and administration. Of course, these jobs were not paid salaries equivalent to their value in market economies, nor did they permit much self-direction or professional autonomy. Under socialism, manual labor, especially in heavy industry, was highly rewarded—and almost exclusively male. But the educational credentials, foreign languages, and work experience women acquired under socialism turned out to be valuable in a market economy (Białecki & Heyns 1993).

In 1989, women were assumed to be one of the groups most vulnerable to the impending inequities of an unregulated market (Einhorn 1993, Hauser et al. 1993, Wolchik 1999). Contrary to predictions, however, the evidence suggests that women did not fare badly, at least in the early years of the transition (Brainerd 1998, Fodor 2002, Giddings 2002, Ham et al. 1999, Ingham et al. 2001, Newell & Reilly 1996, Paci 2002, Rueschemeyer & Szelényi 1995, Van der Lippe & Fodor 1998). Although in every Central and Eastern European country except Hungary, women's unemployment exceeds that of males (Boeri 2000, Van der Lippe & Fodor 1998), the differences are quite small, typically less than 3% (Fodor 2002). In Eastern Europe, the first layoffs occurred among part-time and seasonal workers, jobs that tended to be held by small-scale agricultural producers or the disabled. Unlike the West, part-time work was not common among Eastern European women (Drobnič 1997).

Women's education has paid off very well in postcommunist countries (Heyns 2004). Using LIS data for Poles aged 30–39, Aro (2004) reports that the returns to higher education increased more for women than for men. In 1987, 29% of all higher-educated women were among the top earnings quartile, compared with 68% of men; in 1992 and again in 1995, more than half of the top salary quartile were women with higher education, compared with 65% of men.

Women are more likely than males to hold and keep jobs in the services and in the public sector, and they are less likely to enter the private sector or become entrepreneurs. Self-employment is largely a male option and frequently a consequence of—or an alternative to—unemployment (Gerber 2004, Hanley 2000, Róbert & Bukodi 2004).

Employment has declined throughout Central and Eastern Europe. Although the private sector has grown, so have unemployment and retirement. Labor force participation rates have declined for both men and women. Men seem more eager to move into private sector employment. Stories are legion about overworked female physicians who remain in state clinics, while male doctors quickly hang out their shingle. Women dominated many of the service professions under socialism, and the demand for health and educational services has meant rising salaries. Women enter business schools in greater numbers than men—a legacy of socialist education—but are much less likely to aspire to owning their own business (Heyns 1996).

Wage rates favored men before the transition. They still do, but the evidence suggests a slight narrowing, at least during the early transition. Brainerd (2000) analyzed changes in wage rates by sex for the four Visegrad countries, Bulgaria, Russia, and the Ukraine; Domański (1997) reported wage gaps for six countries; Orazem & Vodopivec (2000) studied Estonia and Slovenia; Rosenfeld & Trappe (2002), Sorensen & Trappe (1995), Krueger & Pischke (1995), Hauser & Becker (1997), and Frick et al. (1995) studied German changes and provided data on gender. The wage gap in Bulgaria declined between 1987 and 1996, although in 1995 it stood at 26% (Giddings 2002, Jolliffe 2002). These studies are based on cross-sectional data comparing wage rates before and after 1989, but the results are consistent. The gender wage gap among those with jobs declined in every country except Russia and the Ukraine. Although women were more likely to leave the labor force, relative wage rates for those who stayed improved. In the former East Germany, the wage gap between men and women fell by 10% (Hunt 2002); the explanation, however, seems to be that many women with low-paying jobs dropped out of the labor force. Close to 40% of the improvement in the gender gap could be explained by the decline in the number of women employed.

Well-educated women were able to capitalize on their educational attainment because returns to education increased (Giddings 2002, Heyns 2004). Falaris (2004) found that although wage differences were larger in the private sector, the returns to education were higher for Bulgarian women in the public sector.

In the former Soviet Union, sex segregation by sector, occupation, and industry accounts for a large share of the gender gap in earnings (Ogloblin 1999). Gender inequalities worsened during the first five years of transition (Gerber & Hout 1998). Wage inequality between men and women was and still is more extreme in Russia and the Ukraine than in Eastern European countries, which accounts for part of the deteriorating wage gap (Aage 1996, Brainerd 2000, Reilly 1999). Differences in unemployment and labor force participation across countries have varied with the timing and phasing of economic reform. To an unknown extent, such patterns may explain changes in the gender gap.

In Eastern Europe women are more likely to work in the public than the private sector, a pattern common to most industrial societies. In Russia, less than half of all men were employed in the public sector in 1997, compared with over 60% of the women (Brainard 1998). Gerber & Hout (1998) found no evidence for higher returns to education between 1991 and 1995, except for women with higher education. Wages and returns to education were higher in the private sector for both men and women in Moscow, but the gender gap was larger in the private sector (Jovanovic & Lokshin 2004). In Poland in 1996, 73% of full-time employed women were in the public sector, compared with 61% of the men; the returns to education were larger for women, particularly in the public sector (Adamchik & Bedi 2000).

In the Czech Republic and in Slovakia, the public sector employed three times as many women as men (Jurajda 2003). A wage gap exists in both sectors, but gender differentials are larger in the private sector; women make less than 75% of the average male wages. In the public sector in the Czech Republic and in Slovakia, two thirds of the original gender gap can be explained by personal characteristics such as age, education, and experience, or by characteristics of the firm such as the size, occupational segregation, and industry, with one third of the gap unexplained. In the private sector, in contrast, two thirds of the variance remains unexplained. Jurajda (2003) concludes that potential violations of equal pay provisions are much more likely in the private sector of either country.

Women in East Germany were overrepresented in the public sector, and increasingly so since unification (Rosenfeld & Trappe 2002, Sorensen & Trappe 1995). Perhaps public sector employment serves as a "shelter against the devaluation" of socialist human capital and experience, as Rosenfeld & Trappe (2002) maintain. The percentage of men employed in the public sector is about 15% in both parts of Germany; among women, one third are employed in the public sector in West Germany, compared with 43% in the former GDR (Franz & Steiner 2000).

Questions of how gender inequality will evolve in Eastern Europe are still unresolved. The most recent evidence suggests, however, that wage gaps may have increased. On the basis of representative samples in six countries, Domański (2002) concluded that the ratio of female to male earnings in 2000 was between 49% and 63%. Data collected in 1993 gave proportions between 61% and 78%, with the same ordering of countries: Russia, with the lowest ratio, followed by Romania, Poland, Hungary, Bulgaria, and finally Slovakia.

AGE AND INEQUALITY

Poverty rates in Eastern Europe tend to reflect the distribution of income and the demography of households, rather than levels of growth. Age levels predict household income better than gender in most of the countries of Eastern Europe and the Soviet Union (Braithwaite et al. 2000, Förster & Tóth 2001). Among children and the elderly, one expects higher levels of poverty than with working adults. Since the beginning 1990, however, virtually all of the Central and Eastern European countries have increased both the value of pensions and the number of pensioners (Fox 1998, Milanovic 1999, Müller 2000). In fact, aggregate inequality increased in Slovenia, Hungary, and Poland in part because of more generous pensions. In Russia, in contrast, pensions were somewhat equalizing, although all other social transfers appear to be highly regressive (Milanovic 1999).

Most Eastern European countries have reformed their pension systems, both because of spiraling costs and because of pressure from international organizations, such as the World Bank. Early retirements and relatively generous disability pensions threaten to destabilize social security programs throughout the region. Privatizing all or part of the contributions and cutting the benefits was considered the answer. As Zsuzsa Ferge has remarked, it is ironic that the European Union has encouraged accession countries to privatize pension systems and health care, pushing them in the direction of American rather than European welfare policy (Deacon 2000). Poland and Slovenia spent 14% of GDP on pensions in 1996, compared with 12% in all of Western Europe (Müller 2002). Poland, Hungary, and Slovenia have restructured their pension systems, increasing mandatory contributions to private accounts, whereas the Czech Republic retains a state-funded pay-as-you-go system (Cangiano et al. 1998, Gomulka 2001, Müller 2000, Novak 2004).

Poverty among children is both larger and more worrisome than care for the elderly (Bradbury et al. 2001, Förster & Tóth 2001, Galasi & Nagy 2001, MONEE Project 1997). Throughout the region, social transfers and benefits that supported children have been cut back or dismantled. Child care programs, family support, and parental leave policies have been reduced, with funds redirected to cover unemployment; eligibility rules have been tightened and periods of coverage shortened; family benefits are now means-tested and of limited duration. Moreover, in part because reforms and reformers vacillate and because new policies are confusing, social welfare has become erratic and unpredictable over time. The system is thought to have become even more bureaucratized than under socialism and more difficult to navigate for both clients and staff (Haney 2002). Public spending on health care, medicine, and educational materials have declined, with a larger share of the costs being passed on to parents (Micklewright 1999). Enrollment rates in preschool and kindergarten have fallen as well. In contrast, postsecondary schooling has expanded dramatically, suggesting that future inequalities in educational attainment will grow.

As with gender, the poverty headcount depends on both family composition and living arrangements; in Eastern Europe, the average size of households is larger than in other European countries, and fewer people live alone. Birth rates fell sharply after 1989, as did marriage and even divorce rates. But families with many children are still more common than in Western Europe, and they are more likely to be poor. In Russia, Mroz & Popkin (1995) reported that children were suffering from malnutrition, while adults managed somewhat better.

Inequality can influence the rate of child poverty rather dramatically, especially in Eastern Europe. When the income distribution is relatively compressed, the mean and the median tend to be close together. Ranking countries by the proportion of children in households with half the median income yields a rank order that is quite similar to the percentage in poverty as a whole. Russia, Italy, the United Kingdom, and the United States top the list, while the Czech Republic and Slovakia are at the bottom, below Sweden, Norway, and Finland, with barely 2% deprived. If one calculates the poverty rate as the proportion of children who live in households with less disposable income than that implied by the official U.S. poverty line, Eastern European countries soar to the top of the list. In 1992, between 85% and 90% of Eastern European children lived in households below this absolute threshold (Bradshaw 2000).

REGIONAL INEQUALITY

Throughout Eastern Europe, urban-rural and regional inequalities have increased. Capital cities often resemble boom towns, whereas little has changed in the countryside. Urban-rural differences have been exacerbated, increasing political tensions and polarization. Under communism, economic inequality was suppressed for ideological reasons, but regional and sectoral disparities were also minimized. Although the results were never entirely successful, socialist states endeavored to equalize levels of regional development (Bahry & Nechemias 1981). With liberalization, such efforts have been abandoned (Fedorov 2002).

Förster et al. (2005) report that the coefficient of variation of per capita GDP across regions rose between 1995 and 1997 in the Czech Republic (from 31 to 33), in Hungary (from 31 to 36), and in Poland (from 19 to 24). In Hungary especially, territorial disparities widened significantly, with the capital region near Budapest being the only area able to withstand a decline of real GDP. Poland was divided between richer western areas and the poorer eastern parts, with Warsaw in the middle. Regional disparities were greater in Russia and Hungary than in either the Czech Republic or Poland, but both intra- and interregional inequality grew in all four countries during the 1990s. Inequality was higher in the capital cities of Warsaw, Budapest, and Prague than within these countries. In contrast, Moscow was more equal than the Russian Federation as a whole (Förster et al. 2005, Sibley & Walsh 2002).

Fidrmuc (2004) studied the four Visegrad countries between 1992 and 1998. Regional inequalities, particularly urban-rural differences, increased dramatically during this period, while internal migration declined. Although unemployment was positively correlated with emigration from small towns—and the population and wages of the largest urban centers grew—neither jobs nor the prospect of higher wages seems to induce much mobility. The most depressed regions have the shallowest migration streams. For the Czech Republic and Slovakia, the relationship between unemployment and migration was small and barely significant between 1992 and 1998. If regional labor markets were functioning properly, wage levels should be negatively correlated with emigration, but this relationship was insignificant in the countries studied. Over time, unemployment soared while rates of migration fell. Although labor mobility might serve as a mechanism for equalizing regional earnings and unemployment, it has thus far played a limited role. Apparently, Eastern Europeans do not readily respond to economic incentives by moving to more prosperous areas when confronted with unemployment or reduced earnings.

INEQUALITIES IN MORTALITY AND MORBIDITY

The health status of Eastern Europe is lower than that of the West, and has been so since the mid-1960s. The region had relatively high mortality in 1989, which barely changed during the subsequent four years, but then fell by as much as half among the most western countries. The Czech Republic and Slovenia stand out in this regard, but death rates for infants, children, and young adults have dropped since 1995 in the peaceful countries of the region. Life expectancy has fallen, however, at least among males (Watson 1995). Several authors have noted that the initial phase of the market transition was accompanied by severe demographic crises (Cornia & Paniccià 2000).

Few studies of malnutrition or diseases linked to economic deprivation have been conducted since 1989. Poor health in general, however, has been more common in Central and Eastern Europe than in Western Europe (Bobak & Marmot 1996, Carlson 1998, Cornia 1994). Illness and numerous medical complaints are correlated with reports of material deprivation; the ecology of ill health tends to follow regional and national poverty patterns (Bobak et al. 2000). Medical care and drugs are in short supply and perceived as exorbitantly priced.

Morbidity and mortality trends in Western and Eastern Europe diverged considerably during the past three decades. The most striking feature was a decline in average life expectancy and the deterioration of age-specific mortality for the middle-aged, especially men. The former socialist governments took no effective action. Because of the denial of social and environmental problems, social, health, and environmental policy were underdeveloped and deformed. Partly inherited from previous historical traditions, wishful thinking, victimization, and patronizing attitudes were primary ways that the socialist governments dealt with problems. In these circumstances even the few specially supported health education campaigns were doomed to fail. People depended in vain on the omnipotent central state to solve their problems so that health promotion based on the community and self-empowerment did not develop. During the early 1990s, in Eastern and Central Europe no central political strategies were initiated or launched to combat the mortality and morbidity tendencies.

The economic and social prerequisites of a long-term, gradual improvement in the health status are missing in Central and Eastern Europe. A declining standard of living due to recession, growing deprivation, poverty, unemployment, and migration are unfavorable to improvements in health.

Research has confirmed very large differences in mortality and morbidity between East and West, which have not declined markedly with economic change. Differences in standards of living, nutrition, alcohol abuse, smoking, and general stress have all been cited as potential explanations (Watson 1995). Cardiovascular mortality is particularly high and has the characteristic distribution by age, sex, and education: Middle-aged males, particularly those working as unskilled laborers, are the most affected. At the same time, epidemiological explanations cannot account for the magnitude of the East-West divide (Bobak & Marmot 1996). Social factors, such as the continuing deterioration of the environment, interpersonal conflicts, and political repression have also been mentioned. But as Makara (1991) has observed, it is difficult to trace the direct causal connection between Stalinism and high cholesterol.

State-run health care was subsidized but notoriously inadequate under socialism, with the best medical services reserved for the *nomenklatura*. Investments in expensive health services, however, were never a socialist priority. For many years, socialist leaders were ideologically committed to the view that health and medical services were much superior to those found in the West, despite all evidence to the contrary. Hence, educational and preventive programs were never launched (Makara 1994).

Suicides have also increased in the region, according to data compiled by the World Health Organization. Mäkinen (2000) reports suicide rates for every transition country during the periods 1984–1989 and 1989–1994. In the initial period, rates declined for every country except Slovakia. In the five years following 1989, the suicide rate rose dramatically in Eastern European countries, although they declined in most of Central Asia. In Russia and the Baltic countries, rates increased by between 58% and 70%; in Belarus, Ukraine, and Poland, rates increased by 25% to 39%. A common story about the economic transformation and death has been told: During the last years of the communist regime, suicides, homicides, and accidental death rates declined because people were excited and hopeful about change—or perhaps just distracted from their personal problems. After the collapse of communism, these rates rose once again. It is difficult to know, however, whether this increase should be attributed to disappointment in the transition or to deaths that had been postponed temporarily from communist times.

A number of studies have sought to demonstrate the relationship between income inequality and ill health (Asafu-Adjaye 2004, Kawachi & Kennedy 1997, Wilkinson 1996) or to examine the association critically (Burtless & Jencks 2003, Lynch et al. 2004). The data suggest that in all countries, the poorest people have the highest rates of illness and mortality. In wealthy, unequal countries, there are more poor people with reduced chances of remaining well. But the impact of inequality per se is smaller and more difficult to prove. Cross-sectional studies have typically excluded Eastern European countries because of data quality. But these countries provide evidence against the claims that more equal incomes produce better health or health care. Since 1989, health conditions for infants, young children, and women have improved slightly, whereas the mortality of adult males remains very high. Given the longstanding patterns, however, higher death rates do not seem to be transitional or to reflect recent spikes in income inequality.

CONCLUSION

This review has traced theories of economic inequality, growth, and income distributions from the second half of the twentieth century through the present, as background to the issue of how inequality has changed with the demise of communism. Much of this review has involved competing theories or contradictory empirical evidence. At present, all the models of market transition lack convincing quantitative support. Aggregate inequality has increased throughout the region, but whether this is unique to the birth of capitalism or part of global trends is hard to say. Whether the country undertook shock therapy or gradual reform, inequality has increased. Inequalities by gender, age, region, and labor force status follow a predictable path. However, as Blau & Kahn (1996) have shown, comparing inequality between groups within countries can produce misleading trends across countries.

Increasing inequality in transitional countries would not necessarily challenge the Washington consensus, at least as long as it was linked to economic growth rather than recession or stagnation (Rosser & Rosser 2001). However, the evidence here is quite mixed. Without exception, all the countries experienced dramatic declines in output, economic production, and jobs. In every country, fewer people are working now than were working in 1989. Even in the five countries that now have a GDP greater than they had reported in 1989, there are fewer jobs, many more people unemployed, higher rates of poverty, and substantial increases in economic inequality. And in the most obvious failures, such as the former Soviet Union, the transformation has been devastating and may yet become worse.

The World Development Report for 2000/2001, entitled *Attacking Poverty*, provided a new economic understanding of economic inequality. High levels of inequality were not conducive to growth. Economic growth and efficiency were not necessarily incompatible with redistribution. In fact, "inequality can undermine poverty reduction by lowering overall economic growth" (World Bank 2001a, p. 56). Inequality was not construed as an inevitable by-product of growth and prosperity; rather, reducing inequality was a positive goal in its own right and could promote growth while alleviating poverty.

Social and economic transitions have no final chapter. The postcommunist saga is just beginning. The eight countries that joined the European Union in 2004 and the five that have achieved growth with equity are surely in a far better state than the former Soviet Union. The bulk of the evidence indicates that economic development and poverty reduction depend on collective policy choices, and not invisible hands.

APPENDIX: DATA SITES AND RESOURCES FOR INCOME INEQUALITY DATA

- One of the first and most extensive data sets was developed by Klaus Deininger and Lynn Squire of the World Bank. These data can be found at http://www.worldbank.org/research/growth/dddeisqu.htm.

- The most comprehensive data bank for transitional economies is maintained by the UNU/WIDER in Helsinki. The most recent database, WIID2, was released on December 3, 2004, with revisions due in June 2005: http://www.wider.unu.edu/wiid/wiid.htm.

- The LIS archives, documents, and updates income, labor force, and household survey data for 29 industrial countries. Reports and information on data are available at http://www.lisproject.org.

- UNICEF—The TRANSMONEE Project at the Innocenti Research Center in Florence maintains several research units with publications relevant to economic transitions and standards of living for 27 transitional countries in the region: http://www.unicef-icdc.org/research/ESP/MC1.html. Their database can be downloaded at http://www.unicef-icdc.org/research/ESP/tmdatabase.html.

The *Annual Review of Sociology* is online at http://soc.annualreviews.org

LITERATURE CITED

Aage H. 1996. Russian occupational wages in transition. *Comp. Econ. Stud.* 32:35–52

Acemoglu D, Robinson JA. 2002. The political economy of the Kuznets curve. *Rev. Dev. Econ.* 6:183–203

Ackrill R, Dobrinsky R, Markov N, Pudney S. 2002. Social security, poverty and economic transition: an analysis for Bulgaria 1992–96. *Econ. Plan.* 35:19–46

Adamchik VA, Bedi AS. 2000. Wage differentials between the public and private sectors: Evidence from an economy in transition. *Labour Econ.* 7:203–24

Adelman I, Robinson S. 1989. Income distribution and development. In *Handbook of Development Economics*, Vol. 2, ed. H Chenery, TN Srinivasan, pp. 949–1003. Amsterdam: North-Holland

Aghion P, Caroli E, García-Peñalosa C. 1999. Inequality and growth: the perspective of the new growth theories. *J. Econ. Lit.* 37:1615–60

Ahluwalia MS. 1976. Income distribution and development: some stylized facts. *Am. Econ. Rev.* 66:128–35

Alber J, Fahey T. 2004. *Perceptions of Living Conditions in an Enlarged Europe.* Luxembourg: Off. Off. Publ. Eur. Communities. 63 pp.

Alderson AS, Nielsen F. 1999. Income inequality, development, and dependence: a reconsideration. *Am. Sociol. Rev.* 64:606–31

Alderson AS, Nielsen F. 2002. Globalization and the great U-turn: income inequality trends in 16 OECD countries. *Am. J. Sociol.* 107:1244–99

Alesina A, Rodrik D. 1994. Distributive politics and economic growth. *Q. J. Econ.* 104:465–90

Anand S, Kanbur R. 1993. Inequality and development: a critique. *J. Dev. Econ.* 41:19–43

Andorka R, Ferge Z, Tóth IG. 1997. Is Hungary really the least unequal? *Russ. East Eur. Finance Trade* 33:67–95

Aro M. 2004. *Brave new world? Value of education in post-socialist Poland.* LIS Work. Pap. No. 374. http://www.lisproject.org/publications/liswps/374.pdf

Arum R, Müller W, eds. 2004. *The Reemergence of Self-Employment: A Comparative Study of Self-Employment Dynamics and Social Inequality.* Princeton, NJ: Princeton Univ. Press. 466 pp.

Asafu-Adjaye J. 2004. Income inequality and health: a multi-country analysis. *Int. J. Soc. Econ.* 31:195–207

Atkinson AB. 1997. Bringing income distribution in from the cold. *Econ. J.* 107:297–321

Atkinson AB, Bourguignon F, eds. 2000. *Handbook of Income Distribution*, Vol. 1. Amsterdam: Elsevier Sci. 958 pp.

Atkinson AB, Brandolini A. 2001. Promise and pitfalls in the use of "secondary" datasets: income inequality in OECD countries. *J. Econ. Lit.* 39:771–99

Atkinson AB, Brandolini A. 2003. *The panel-of-countries approach to explaining income inequality: an interdisciplinary research agenda.* http://www.nuff.ox.ac.uk/users/atkinson/Mannheim.pdf

Atkinson AB, Micklewright J. 1992. *Economic Transformation in Eastern Europe and the Distribution of Income.* London: Cambridge Univ. Press. 448 pp.

Austen S. 2002. An international comparison of attitudes to inequality. *Int. J. Soc. Econ.* 29:218–37

Bahry D, Nechemias C. 1981. Half full or half empty? The debate over Soviet regional equality. *Slavic Rev.* 40:366–83

Banerjee AV, Duflo E. 2003. Inequality and growth: What can the data say? *J. Econ. Growth* 8:267–99

Barro RJ. 2000. Inequality and growth in a panel of countries. *J. Econ. Growth* 5:5–32

Bell J. 2001. *The Political Economy of Reform in Post-Communist Poland.* Northampton, MA: Elgar. 243 pp.

Bergson A. 1984. Income inequality under Soviet socialism. *J. Econ. Lit.* 22:1052–99

Białecki I, Heyns B. 1993. Educational attainment, the status of women and the private school movement in Poland. In *Democratic Reform and the Position of Women in Transitional Economies*, ed. VM Moghadam, pp. 110–34. New York: Oxford Univ. Press/Clarendon

Bian Y, Logan JR. 1996. Market transition and the persistence of power: the changing stratification system in urban China. *Am. Sociol. Rev.* 61:739–58

Bian Y, Zhang Z. 2002. Marketization and income distribution in urban China, 1988 and 1995. See Leicht 2002, pp. 377–415

Birdsall N, Graham C, eds. 2000. *New Markets, New Opportunities? Economic Mobility in a*

Changing World. Washington, DC: Brookings Inst. Press. 331 pp.

Błaszczyk B, Hoshi I, Woodward R, eds. 2003. *Secondary Privatisation in Transition Economies: The Evolution of Enterprise Ownership in the Czech Republic, Poland and Slovenia.* New York: Macmillan. 268 pp.

Blau FD, Kahn LM. 1996. Wage structure and gender earnings differentials: An international comparison. *Economica* 63:S29–62

Bobak M, Marmot M. 1996. East-West mortality divide and its potential explanations: proposed research agenda. *Br. Med. J.* 312:421–25

Bobak M, Pikhart H, Rose R, Hertzman C, Marmot M. 2000. Socioeconomic factors, material inequalities and perceived control in self-rated health: cross-sectional data from seven post-communist countries. *Soc. Sci. Med.* 51:1343–50

Boeri T. 2000. *Structural Change, Welfare Systems, and Labour Reallocation: Lessons from the Transition of Formerly Planned Economies.* New York: Oxford Univ. Press. 240 pp.

Bollen KA, Jackman RW. 1985. Political democracy and the size distribution of income. *Am. Sociol. Rev.* 50:438–57

Böröcz J, Róna-Tas Á. 1995. Small leap forward: the emergence of economic elites. *Theory Soc.* 24:751–81

Bound J, Johnson G. 1992. Changes in the structure of wages in the 1980s: an evaluation of alternative explanations. *Am. Econ. Rev.* 82:371–92

Bowman KS. 1997. Should the Kuznets effect be relied on to induce equalizing growth: evidence from post-1950 development. *World Dev.* 25:127–43

Bradbury B, Jenkins SP, Micklewright J, eds. 2001. *The Dynamics of Child Poverty in Industrialised Countries.* London: Cambridge Univ. Press

Bradshaw J. 2000. Child poverty: comparison of industrial and transition economies. See Hutton & Redmond 2000, pp. 191–207

Brainerd E. 1998. Winners and losers in Russia's economic transition. *Am. Econ. Rev.* 88:1094–116

Brainered E. 2000. Women in transition: changes in gender wage differentials in Eastern Europe and the former Soviet Union. *Ind. Labor Relat. Rev.* 54:138–62

Braithwaite J, Grootaert C, Milanovic B. 2000. *Poverty and Social Assistance in Transition Countries.* New York: St. Martin's

Brenner YS, Kaelble H, Thomas M, eds. 1991. *Income Distribution in Historical Perspective.* New York: Cambridge Univ. Press

Burtless G, Jencks C. 2003. American inequality and its consequences. In *Agenda for the Nation*, ed. HJ Aaron, JM Lindsay, PS Nivola, pp. 61–108. Washington, DC: Brookings Inst. Press. 432 pp.

Cangiano M, Cottarelli C, Cubeddu L. 1998. *Pension developments and reforms in transition economies.* IMF Work. Pap. http://www.imf.org/external/pubs/ft/wp/wp98151.pdf

Cao Y, Nee VG. 2000. Comment: controversies and evidence in the market transition debate. *Am. J. Sociol.* 105:1175–89

Carlson P. 1998. Self-perceived health in East and West Europe: another European health divide. *Soc. Sci. Med.* 46:1355–66

Caselli GP, Battini M. 1997. Following the tracks of Atkinson and Micklewright: the changing distribution of income and earnings in Poland from 1989 to 1995. *MOCT-MOST* 7:1–19

Centano MA, Rands T. 1996. The world they have lost: an assessment of change in Eastern Europe. *Soc. Res.* 63:369–402

Chase-Dunn C. 1975. The effects of international economic dependence on development and inequality. *Am. Sociol. Rev.* 40:720–39

Commander S, Tolstopiatenko A, Yemtsov R. 1999. Channels of redistribution: inequality and poverty in the Russian transition. *Econ. Transit.* 7:411–47

Cornia GA. 1994. Poverty, food consumption and nutrition during the transition in Eastern Europe. *Am. Econ. Rev.* 84:297–302

Cornia GA, Addison T, Kiiski S. 2004. Income distribution changes and their impact in the post–Second World War period. In

Inequality, Growth, and Poverty in an Era of Liberalization and Globalization, ed. GA Cornia, pp. 26–54. New York: Oxford Univ. Press. 438 pp.

Cornia GA, Paniccià R, eds. 2000. *The Mortality Crisis in Transitional Economies*. New York: Oxford Univ. Press. 456 pp.

Crenshaw EM. 1992. Cross-national determinants of income inequality: a replication and extension using ecological-evolutionary theory. *Soc. Forces* 71:339–63

Crenshaw EM. 1993. Polity, economy and technoecology: alternative explanations for inequality. *Soc. Forces* 71:803–16

Cutright P. 1967. Inequality: a cross-national analysis. *Am. Sociol. Rev.* 32:562–78

Deacon B. 2000. Eastern European welfare states: the impact of the politics of globalization. *J. Eur. Soc. Policy* 10:146–61

Deininger K, Squire L. 1996. A new data set measuring income inequality. *World Bank Econ. Rev.* 10:565–91

Deininger K, Squire L. 1998. New ways of looking at old issues. *J. Dev. Econ.* 57:259–87

Dennis I, Guio A. 2003. Monetary poverty in EU acceding and candidate countries. In *Statistics in Focus: Population and Social Conditions*, Theme 3, 21/2003. Luxembourg: Eurostat

Desai P, Idson T. 2000. *Work Without Wages: Russia's Nonpayment Crisis*. Cambridge, MA: MIT Press. 258 pp.

Dollar D, Kraay A. 2002. Growth is good for the poor. *J. Econ. Growth* 7:195–225

Domański H. 1997. Distribution of incomes in Eastern Europe. *Int. J. Comp. Sociol.* 38: 249–70

Domański H. 2002. Is the East European "underclass" feminized? *Communist Post-Communist Stud.* 35:383–94

Domański H, Heyns B. 1995. Toward a theory of the role of the state in market transition: from bargaining to markets in postcommunism. *Eur. J. Sociol.* 36:317–51

Drobnič S. 1997. Part-time work in Central and Eastern European Countries. In *Between Equalization and Marginalization: Women Working Part-Time in Europe and the United States of America*, ed. H-P Blossfeld, C Hakim, pp. 71–89. New York: Oxford Univ. Press

Duke V, Grime K. 1997. Inequality in postcommunism. *Reg. Stud.* 31:883–90

Einhorn B. 1993. *Cinderella Goes to Market: Citizenship, Gender, and Women's Movements in East Central Europe*. London: Verso

Elster J, Offe C, Preuss UK, Boenker F, Goetting U, Rueb FW. 1998. *Institutional Design in Post-Communist Societies—Rebuilding the Ship at Sea*. New York: Cambridge Univ. Press

Éltetö Ö, Havasi E. 1999. Income inequality and poverty in Hungary in the mid-1990s. *Hung. Stat. Rev.* 77:49–70

Emigh RJ, Szelényi I, eds. 2001. *Poverty, Ethnicity, and Gender in Eastern Europe During the Market Transition*. Westport, CT: Praeger. 210 pp.

Eyal G. 2003. *The Origins of Post-Communist Elites: From Prague Spring to the Breakup of Czechoslovakia*. Minneapolis: Univ. Minn. Press. 238 pp.

Eyal G, Szelényi I, Townsley E. 1998. *Making Capitalism Without Capitalists: Class Formation and Elite Struggles in Post-Communist Central Europe*. New York/London: Verso. 210 pp.

Falaris EM. 2004. Private and public sector wages in Bulgaria. *J. Comp. Econ.* 32:56–72

Fedorov L. 2002. Regional inequality and regional polarization in Russia, 1990–1999. *World Dev.* 30:443–56

Ferreira FHG. 1999. Economic transition and the distributions of income and wealth. *Econ. Transit.* 7:377–410

Fidrmuc J. 2004. Migration and regional adjustment to asymmetric shocks in transition countries. *J. Comp. Econ.* 32:230–47

Fields GS. 2001. *Distribution and Development: A New Look at the Developing World*. Cambridge, MA: MIT Press. 272 pp.

Fodor É. 2002. Gender and the experience of poverty in Eastern Europe and Russia after 1989. *Communist Post-Communist Stud.* 35:369–490

Forbes KJ. 2000. A reassessment of the relationship between inequality and growth. *Am. Econ. Rev.* 90:869–87

Förster MF, Jesuit D, Smeeding T. 2005. Regional poverty and income inequality in Central and Eastern Europe: evidence from the Luxembourg income study. In *Spatial Inequality and Development*, ed. R Kanbur, AJ Venables, Chapter 13. New York: Oxford Univ. Press, 400 pp.

Förster MF, Tóth IG. 1997. Poverty, inequalities and social policies in the Visegrad countries. *Econ. Transit.* 5:505–10

Förster MF, Tóth IG. 2001. Child poverty and family cash transfers in the Czech Republic, Hungary and Poland. *J. Eur. Soc. Policy* 11:324–41

Fosu AK. 1993. Kuznets's inverted-U hypothesis: a comment. *South. Econ. J.* 59:523–32

Fox L. 1998. Pension reform in post-communist transition countries. See Nelson et al. 1998, pp. 370–84

Franz W, Steiner V. 2000. Wages in the East German transition process: facts and explanations. *Ger. Econ. Rev.* 1:241–69

Frick JR, Hauser R, Muller K, Wagner GG. 1995. Income distribution in East Germany in the first five years after the fall of the wall. *MOCT-MOST* 5:79–108

Frydman R, Murphy K, Rapaczynski A. 1996. Capitalism with a comrade's face. *Transition* 2:5–11

Gagliani G. 1987. Income inequality and economic development. *Annu. Rev. Sociol.* 13:313–34

Gal S, Kligman G. 2000. *The Politics of Gender After Socialism: A Comparative-Historical Essay.* Princeton, NJ: Princeton Univ. Press. 169 pp.

Galasi P, Nagy G. 2001. Are children being left behind in the transition in Hungary? See Bradbury et al. 2001, pp. 236–53

Garner T, Terrell K. 1998. A Gini decomposition analysis of inequality in the Czech and Slovak Republics during the transition. *Econ. Transit.* 6:23–46

Gerber TP. 2004. Three forms of emergent self-employment in post-Soviet Russia: entry and exit patterns by gender. See Arum & Müller 2004, pp. 277–309

Gerber TP, Hout M. 1998. More shock than therapy: market transition, employment and income in Russia, 1991–1995. *Am. J. Sociol.* 104:1–50

Giddings LA. 2002. Changes in gender wage differentials in Bulgaria's transition from plan to mixed market. *East. Econ. J.* 28:481–98

Gijsberts M. 2002. Legitimation of income inequality in state-socialist and market societies. *Acta Sociol.* 45:269–85

Glomm G. 1997. Whatever happened to the Kuznets curve? Is it really upside down? *J. Income Distrib.* 7:63–87

Gomulka S. 2001. A great leap forward? Pension reform in the Czech Republic, Hungary, Poland and Romania. In *The Eastern Enlargement of the EU*, ed. M Dąbrowski, J Rostowski, pp. 109–27. Boston: Kluwer. 237 pp.

Grosfeld I, Hashi I. 2004. *The emergence of large shareholders in mass privatized firms: evidence from Poland and the Czech Republic.* FEEM Work. Pap. No. 126.04. http://papers.ssrn.com/sol3/papers.cfm?abstract_id=588906

Gustafsson B, Johansson M. 1999. In search of smoking guns: What makes income inequality vary over time in different countries? *Am. Sociol. Rev.* 64:585–605

Ham JC, Svejnar J, Terrell K. 1998. Unemployment and the social safety net during the transition to a market economy: evidence from Czech and Slovak men. *Am. Econ. Rev.* 88:1117–42

Ham JC, Svejnar J, Terrell K. 1999. Women's unemployment during transition: evidence from Czech and Slovak micro-data. *Econ. Transit.* 7:47–78

Haney L. 2002. *Inventing the Needy: Gender and the Politics of Welfare in Hungary.* Berkeley: Univ. Calif. Press

Hanley E. 2000. Self-employment in post-communist Eastern Europe: a refuge from poverty or road to riches? *Communist Post-Communist Stud.* 33:379–402

Hanley E, Treiman DJ. 2003. *Recruitment into the Eastern European communist elite: dual career paths.* Work. Pap. CCPR-008-03, Calif. Cent. Popul. Res. http://reposito ries.cdlib.org/ccpr/olwp/ccpr-008-03

Harrison B, Bluestone B. 1988. *The Great U-Turn: Corporate Restructuring and the Polarizing of America.* New York: Basic Books

Hauser E, Heyns B, Mansbridge J. 1993. Feminism in the interstices of politics and culture: Poland in transition. In *Gender Politics and Post-Communism: Reflections from Eastern Europe and the Former Soviet Union,* ed. N Funk, M Mueller, pp. 257–73. New York: Routledge

Hauser R, Becker I. 1997. The development of income distribution in the Federal Republic of Germany during the 1970s and 1980s. In *Changing Patterns in the Distribution of Economic Welfare: An International Perspective,* ed. P Gottschalk, B Gustafsson, E Palmer, pp. 184–219. New York: Cambridge Univ. Press

Hewitt C. 1977. The effect of political democracy and social democracy on equality in industrial societies: a cross-national comparison. *Am. Sociol. Rev.* 42:450–64

Heyns B. 1996. Creating capitalists: the social origins of entrepreneurship in post-communist Poland. In *Generating Social Stratification: Toward a New Generation of Research,* ed. A Kerckhoff, pp. 257–89. Boulder, CO: Westview

Heyns B. 1998. Meaning and measurement for the post-communist labor force: employment and unemployment in Poland, 1992–1996. *J. Soc. Sci.* 2:143–57

Heyns B. 2004. *Rates of return to education in post-communist countries.* Presented at ISA-EPG Conf., Prague, Czech Repub.

Heyns B, Białecki I. 1993. Educational inequality in Poland. See Shavit & Blossfeld 1993, pp. 303–35

Higley J, Pakulski J, Wesolowski W, eds. 1998. *Post-Communist Elites and Democracy in Eastern Europe.* London: Macmillan. 301 pp.

Hunt J. 2002. The transition in East Germany: When is a ten percent fall in the gender pay gap bad news? *J. Labor Econ.* 20:148–69

Hutton S, Redmond G, eds. 2000. *Poverty in Transition Economies.* New York: Routledge. 295 pp.

Ingham M, Ingham H, Dománski H, eds. 2001. *Women on the Polish Labor Market.* Budapest: Central Eur. Univ. Press. 333 pp.

Jha SK. 1996. The Kuznets curve: a reassessment. *World Dev.* 24:773–80

Jolliffe D. 2002. The gender wage gap in Bulgaria: a semi-parametric estimation of discrimination. *J. Comp. Econ.* 30:276–95

Jovanovic B, Lokshin MM. 2004. Wage differentials between the state and the private sector in Moscow. *Rev. Income Wealth* 50:107–23

Jurajda Š 2003. Gender wage gap and segregation in enterprises and the public sector in late transition countries *J. Comp. Econ.* 31:199–222

Kanbur R. 2000. Income distribution and development. See Atkinson & Bourguignon 2000, pp. 791–841

Kattuman P, Redmond G. 2001. Income inequality in early transition: the case of Hungary 1987–1996. *J. Comp. Econ.* 29:40–65

Kawachi I, Kennedy BP. 1997. The relationship of income inequality to mortality: Does the choice of indicator matter? *Soc. Sci. Med.* 45:1121–27

Keane MP, Prasad ES. 2002. Inequality, transfers, and growth: new evidence from the economic transition in Poland. *Rev. Econ. Stat.* 84:324–41

Kende P, Strmiska Z. 1987. *Equality and Inequality in Eastern Europe.* New York: St. Martin's

Kennedy MD, Białecki I. 1989. Power and the logic of distribution in Poland. *East. Eur. Polit. Soc.* 3:300–28

Kornai J. 1994. Transformational recession: the main causes. *J. Comp. Econ.* 19:39–63

Krueger AB, Pischke JS. 1995. A comparative analysis of East and West German labor markets: before and after unification. In *Differences and Changes in Wage Structure,* ed.

RB Freeman, LF Katz, pp. 405–45. Chicago: Univ. Chicago Press

Kuznets S. 1955. Economic growth and income inequality. *Am. Econ. Rev.* 45:1–28

Leicht KT, ed. 2002. *Research in Social Stratification and Mobility: The Future of Market Transition*, Vol. 19. New York: Elsevier

Levy F, Murnane RJ. 1992. U.S. earnings levels and earnings inequality: a review of recent trends and proposed explanations. *J. Econ. Lit.* 30:1333–81

Li H, Squire L, Zou H. 1998. Explaining international and intertemporal variations in income inequality. *Econ. J.* 108:26–43

Lindert PH, Williamson JG. 2003. Does globalization make the world more unequal? In *Globalization in Historical Perspective*, ed. MD Bordo, AM Taylor, JG Williamson, pp. 227–71. Chicago: Univ. Chicago Press

List JA, Gallet CA. 1999. The Kuznets curve: what happens after the inverted-U? *Rev. Dev. Econ.* 3:200–6

Lynch J, Smith GD, Harper S, Hillemeier M, Ross, et al. N 2004. Is income inequality a determinant of population health? Part 1. A systematic review. *Milbank Q.* 82:5–99

Makara P. 1991. Dilemmas of health promotion and political changes in eastern Europe. *Health Promot. Int.* 1:41–47

Makara P. 1994. Policy implications of differential health status in East and West Europe: the case of Hungary. *Soc. Sci. Med.* 39:1295–302

Mäkinen IH. 2000. Eastern European transition and suicide mortality. *Soc. Sci. Med.* 51:1405–20

Mason DS, Kluegel JR. 2000. *Marketing Democracy: Changing Opinion About Inequality and Politics in East Central Europe*. Lanham, MD: Rowman & Littlefield. 292 pp.

Massey DS. 1996. The age of extremes: concentrated affluence and poverty in the twenty-first century. *Demography* 33:395–412

Massey DS, Hirst DS. 1998. From escalator to hourglass: changes in the US occupational wage structure, 1949–1989. *Soc. Sci. Res.* 27:51–71

Matějů P. 1993. Who won and who lost in a so-

cialist redistribution in Czechoslovakia? See Shavit & Blossfeld 1993, pp. 251–71

Matějů P. 2000. Mobility and perceived change in life chances in postcommunist countries. See Birdsall & Graham 2000, pp. 291–323

McFaul M. 1996. The vanishing center. *J. Democr.* 7:90–104

Micklewright J. 1999. Education, inequality, and transition. *Econ. Transit.* 7:343–76

Milanovic B. 1996. Income inequality and poverty during the transition: a survey of the evidence. *MOCT-MOST* 6:131–47

Milanovic B. 1998. *Income, Inequality, and Poverty During the Transition from Planned to Market Economy*. Washington, DC: World Bank. 237 pp.

Milanovic B. 1999. Explaining the increase in inequality during transition. *Econ. Transit.* 7: 299–341

Moller S, Bradley D, Huber E, Nielsen F, Stephens JD. 2003. Determinants of relative poverty in advanced capitalist democracies. *Am. Sociol. Rev.* 68:22–51

MONEE Project. 1997. Children at risk in Central and Eastern Europe: perils and promises. *Reg. Monit. Rep. No. 4.* UNICEF ICDC, Florence. http://www.unicef-icdc.org/cgi-bin/unicef/main.sql?menu=/publications/menu.html&testo=Lunga.sql?ProductID=48

Morrisson C. 2000. Historical perspectives on income distribution: the case of Europe. See Atkinson & Bourguignon 2000, pp. 217–60

Mroz TA, Popkin BM. 1995. Poverty and the economic transition in the Russian Federation. *Econ. Dev. Cult. Change* 44:1–31

Muller EN. 1988. Democracy, economic development, and income inequality. *Am. Sociol. Rev.* 53:50–68

Müller K. 2000. *The Political Economy of Pension Reform in East-Central Europe*. Northampton, MA: Elgar. 222 pp.

Müller K. 2002. Beyond privatization: pension reform in the Czech Republic and Slovenia. *J. Eur. Soc. Policy* 12:293–306

Nee V. 1989. A theory of market transition: from redistribution to markets in state socialism. *Am. Sociol. Rev.* 54:663–81

Nee V. 1991. Social inequalities in reforming

state socialism: between redistribution and markets in China. *Am. Sociol. Rev.* 56:267–82

Nee V. 1992. Organizational dynamics of market transition: hybrid forms, property rights, and mixed economy in China. *Admin. Sci. Q.* 37:1–27

Nee V. 1996. The emergence of a market society: changing mechanisms of stratification in China. *Am. J. Sociol.* 101:906–49

Nee V, Cao Y. 2002. Postsocialist inequalities: the causes of continuity and discontinuity. See Leicht 2002, pp. 3–39

Nee V, Matthews R. 1996. Market transition and societal transformation in reforming state socialism. *Annu. Rev. Sociol.* 22:401–35

Nelson JM, Tilly C, Walker L, eds. 1998. *Transforming Post-Communist Political Economies.* Washington, DC: Natl. Acad. Press

Newell A, Reilly B. 1996. The gender wage gap in Russia: some empirical evidence. *Labour Econ.* 3:337–56

Nielsen F. 1994. Income inequality and development: dualism revisited. *Am. Sociol. Rev.* 59:654–77

Novak A. 2004. Pension system reform in Slovenia. *Eur.-Asia Stud.* 56:279–92

Ogloblin CG. 1999. The gender earnings differential in the Russian transition economy. *Ind. Labor Relat. Rev.* 52:602–27

Orazem PF, Vodopivec M. 2000. Male-female differences in labor market outcomes during the early transition to market: the cases of Estonia and Slovenia. *J. Popul. Econ.* 13:283–303

Paci P. 2002. How do men and women fare in transition countries? A new World Bank Report. *Transit. Newsl.* 13:16–19

Pan0ccià R. 2000. Transition, impoverishment, and mortality: How large an impact? See Cornia & Panccià 2000, pp. 104–26

Papanek G, Kyn O. 1986. The effect on income distribution of development, the growth rate and economic strategy. *J. Dev. Econ.* 23:55–65

Parker SC. 2000. Opening a can of worms: the pitfalls of time-series regression analyses of income inequality. *Appl. Econ.* 32:221–30

Perotti R. 1993. Political equilibrium, income distribution and growth. *Rev. Econ. Stud.* 60:756–75

Persson T, Tabellini G. 1994. Is inequality harmful for growth? *Am. Econ. Rev.* 84:600–21

Ram R. 1988. Economic development and income inequality: further evidence on the U-curve hypothesis. *World Dev.* 16:1371–76

Reilly B. 1999. The gender pay gap in Russia during transition, 1992–1996. *Econ. Transit.* 7:245–64

Riskin C, Zhao R, Li S, eds. 2001. *China's Retreat From Equality: Income Distribution and Economic Transition.* Armonk, NY/London: ME Sharpe. 358 pp.

Róbert P, Bukodi E. 2004. Winners or losers? Entry and exit into self-employment in Hungary 1980s and 1990s. See Arum & Müller 2004, pp. 245–76

Robinson S. 1976. A note on the U-hypothesis relating income inequality and economic development. *Am. Econ. Rev.* 66:437–40

Róna-Tas Á. 1994. The first shall be last? Entrepreneurship and communist cadres in the transition from socialism. *Am. J. Sociol.* 100:40–69

Rosenfeld RA, Trappe H. 2002. Occupational sex segregation in state socialist and market economies: levels, patterns, and change in East and West Germany, 1980s and 1998. See Leicht 2002, pp. 231–67

Rosser JB, Rosser MV. 2001. Another failure of the Washington consensus on transition countries. *Challenge* 44:39–51

Rueschemeyer M, Szelényi S. 1995. Socialist transformation and gender inequality: women in the GDR and in Hungary. In *East Germany in Comparative Perspective*, ed. D Childs, TA Baylis, M Rueschemeyer, pp. 81–109. London: Routledge

Russell H, Whelan CT. 2004. Low income and deprivation in an enlarged Europe. *Quality of Life Ser. Rep. Eur. Found. Improv. Living Work. Cond.* Luxembourg: Off. Off. Publ. Eur. Communities. 54 pp. http://www.

eurofound.ie/publications/files/EF03105EN. pdf

Shavit Y, Blossfeld H-P, eds. 1993. *Persistent Inequality: Changing Educational Attainment in Thirteen Countries.* Boulder, CO: Westview. 396 pp.

Sibley CW, Walsh PP. 2002. *Earnings inequality and transition: a regional analysis of Poland.* IZA Disc. Pap. No. 441. http://papers.ssrn.com/abstract=300661

Simpson M. 1990. Political rights and income inequality: a cross-national test. *Am. Sociol. Rev.* 55:682–93

Słomczynski KM. 1998. Formation of class structure under conditions of radical social change: an East European experience. In *The Kalamari Union: Middle Class in East and West*, ed. M Kivinen, pp. 89–117. Brookfield, VT: Ashgate. 341 pp.

Smeeding TM. 2004. *Public policy and economic inequality: the United States in comparative perspective.* LIS Work. Pap. 367. http://www.lisproject.org/publications/LIS wps/367.pdf

Smeeding TM, Rainwater L. 2002. *Comparing living standards across nations: real incomes at the top, the bottom and the middle.* SPRC Discuss. Pap. 120, Soc. Policy Res. Cent., Univ. New South Wales. http://www. sprc.unsw.edu.au/dp/DP120.pdf

Soderberg J. 1991. Wage differentials in Sweden, 1725–1950. See Brenner et al. 1991, pp. 76–95

Soltow L. 1965. *Towards Income Equality in Norway.* Madison: Univ. Wis. Press

Sorensen A, Trappe H. 1995. Gender inequality in the former East Germany. *Am. Sociol. Rev.* 60:398–407

Spéder Z. 1998. Poverty dynamics in Hungary during the transformation. *Econ. Transit.* 6:1–21

Staniszkis J. 1991. *The Dynamics of the Breakthrough in Eastern Europe: The Polish Experience.* Berkeley: Univ. Calif. Press. 303 pp.

Stanovnik T, Stropnik N. 2000. Income distribution and poverty in Slovenia. See Hutton & Redmond 2000, pp. 154–72

Stark D, Bruszt L. 1998. *Postsocialist Pathways: Transforming Politics and Property in East Central Europe.* New York: Cambridge Univ. Press. 284 pp.

Szalai J. 1999. Recent trends in poverty in Hungary. In *Poverty in Transition and Transition Poverty: Recent Developments in Hungary, Bulgaria, Romania, Georgia, Russia, Mongolia*, ed. Y Atal, pp. 32–76. Paris/New York: UNESCO/Berghahn

Szelényi I. 1978. Social inequalities in state socialist redistributive economies. *Int. J. Comp. Sociol.* 10:63–87

Szelényi I, Kostello E. 1996. The market transition debate: toward a synthesis? *Am. J. Sociol. Symp.* 101:1082–96

Szelényi S, Szelényi I, Kovách I. 1995. The making of the Hungarian postcommunist elite: circulation in politics, reproduction in the economy. *Theory Soc.* 24:697–722

Terrell K. 2000. Worker mobility and transition to a market economy: winners and losers. See Birdsall & Graham 2000, pp. 168–91

Titma M, Tuma NB, Roosma K. 2003. Education as a factor in intergenerational mobility in Soviet society. *Eur. Sociol. Rev.* 19:281–97

Titma M, Tuma NB, Silver BD. 1998. Winners and losers in the postcommunist transition: new evidence from Estonia. *Post-Soviet Aff.* 14:114–36

Torrey BB, Smeeding TM, Bailey D. 1998. Vulnerable populations in central Europe. See Nelson et al. 1998, pp. 351–69

Torrey BB, Smeeding TM, Bailey D. 1999. Income transitions in Central European households. *Econ. Dev. Cult. Change* 47:237–57

Tribble R. 1996. The Kuznets-Lewis process within the context of race and class in the US economy. *Int. Adv. Econ. Res.* 2:151–64

Tuma NB, Titma M, Murakas R. 2002. Transitional economies and income inequality: The case of Estonia. In *Transition to Democracy in Eastern Europe and Russia: Impact on Politics, Economy and Culture*, ed. B Wejnert, pp. 111–40. Westport, CT: Praeger. 384 pp.

UNICEF. 2004. *Innocenti Social Monitor 2004*. Firenze: UNICEF Innocenti Res. Cent.

Van der Lippe T, Fodor É. 1998. Changes in gender inequality in six Eastern European countries. *Acta Sociol.* 41:131–49

Van de Walle D. 1996. Common pitfalls in measuring welfare during transition. *Transition* 7:5–6

Van Zanden JL. 1995. Tracing the beginning of the Kuznets curve: Western Europe during the early modern period. *Econ. Hist. Rev.* 48:643–64

Večerník J. 1991. Earnings distribution in Czechoslovakia: Intertemporal changes and international comparison. *Eur. Sociol. Rev.* 7:237–52

Večerník J. 1995. Changing earnings distribution in the Czech Republic: survey evidence from 1988–1994. *Econ. Transit.* 3:355–71

Večerník J. 1996. Incomes in Central Europe: distributions, patterns and perceptions. *J. Eur. Soc. Policy* 6:101–22

Večerník J. 1997. The emergence of the labour market and earnings distribution: the case of the Czech Republic. In *Changing Patterns in the Distribution of Economic Welfare: An International Perspective*, ed. P Gottschalk, B Gustafsons, E Palmer, pp. 370–88. New York: Cambridge Univ. Press

Walder AG. 1996. Markets and inequality in transitional economies: toward testable theories. *Am. J. Sociol.* 101:1060–73

Walder AG. 2002. Markets, economic growth, and inequality in rural China: political advantage in an expanding economy. *Am. Sociol. Rev.* 67:231–53

Watson P. 1995. Explaining rising mortality among men in Eastern Europe. *Soc. Sci. Med.* 41:923–34

Wedel J. 1986. *The Private Poland*. New York: Facts File. 260 pp.

Wilkinson R. 1996. *Unhealthy Societies: The Afflictions of Inequality*. London: Routledge

Williamson J. 1997. The Washington consensus revisited. In *Economic and Social Development into the XXI Century*, ed. L Emmerij, pp. 48–61. Washington, DC: Inter-Am. Dev. Bank

Wolchik SL. 1999. *Czechoslovakia in Transition: Politics, Economics and Society*. New York: Pinter. 390 pp.

World Bank. 1996. *World Development Report 1996: From Plan to Market*. Washington, DC: World Bank

World Bank. 2001a. *World Development Report 2000/2001: Attacking Poverty*. Washington, DC: World Bank

World Bank. 2001b. *World Development Report 2002: Building Institutions for Markets*. Washington, DC: World Bank

World Bank. 2003. *World Development Report 2004: Making Services Work for Poor People*. Washington, DC: World Bank

World Bank. 2004. *World Development Report 2005: A Better Investment Climate for Everyone*. Washington, DC: World Bank

Wu X. 2002. Work units and income inequality: the effect of market transition in urban China. *Soc. Forces* 80:1069–99

Wu X, Xie Y. 2003. Does the market pay off? Earnings returns to education in urban China. *Am. Sociol. Rev.* 68:425–42

Xie Y, Hannum E. 1996. Regional variation in earnings inequality in reform-era urban China. *Am. J. Sociol.* 101:950–92

Zafirovski M. 2002. Income inequality and social institutions: beyond the Kuznets Curve and economic determinism. *Int. J. Soc. Soc. Policy* 22:89–131

Zhou X. 2000. Economic transformation and income inequality in urban China. *Am. J. Sociol.* 105:1135–74

Zhou X, Tuma NB, Moen P. 1996. Stratification dynamics under state socialism: the case of urban China, 1949–1993. *Soc. Forces* 74:759–96

Annu. Rev. Sociol. 2005. 31:199–222
doi: 10.1146/annurev.soc.31.041304.122258
Copyright © 2005 by Annual Reviews. All rights reserved
First published online as a Review in Advance on April 4, 2005

THE SOCIAL CONSEQUENCES OF STRUCTURAL ADJUSTMENT: Recent Evidence and Current Debates

Sarah Babb

Department of Sociology, Boston College, Chestnut Hill, Massachusetts 02467;
email: babbsa@bc.edu

Key Words   globalization, neoliberalism, dependency, World Bank, International Monetary Fund

■ **Abstract**   Thirty years ago, intellectual debates concerning the relationship between wealthy and poor nations could be summed up under the rubric of modernization versus dependency. However, the events of the 1980s and 1990s completely shifted the terms of this debate. Associated with the structural adjustment lending programs of the World Bank and International Monetary Fund, and neoliberal ideology, a new policy discourse suggested that it was only through liberating market forces that poor countries could grow and catch up to the developed world. With 20 years of structural adjustment behind us, what does the evidence suggest about the social consequences of these policies? This review focuses on three different social transformations: changes in the governance of economies, transformations in class structures, and the rise of transnational networks.

INTRODUCTION

Once upon a time, intellectual debates around the relationship between wealthy and poor nations could be summed up under the rubric of modernization versus dependency. For modernization theorists, all good things went together: Capitalist development, democratization, industrialization, urbanization, rational-legal administration, and increased well-being were assumed to be part of a single process that occurred in roughly the same way in all national contexts. In contrast, dependency theorists argued that the domination of rich over poor countries meant that modernization looked quite different at the periphery. Because of such relations of domination, foreign investment and national industrialization did not propel developing countries along the same trajectory as the wealthy democracies, but rather was compatible with manifold economic, political, and social distortions.

Beginning in the 1980s, however, this debate was rendered obsolete by a very different hegemonic order. Whereas modernization and dependency theorists alike had advocated for strong government involvement in promoting economic development, the new conventional wisdom demanded a dramatic downsizing of many government interventions. Associated with the structural adjustment lending programs of the World Bank and International Monetary Fund (IMF), and neoliberal ideology, the new policy discourse suggested that it was only through thus liberating market forces that poor countries could grow and catch up to the developed world. Whereas modernization and dependency theorists were drawn from a range of social science disciplines, both the new model and its most prominent critics tend to be economists. Much of the recent work on the consequences of structural adjustment, therefore, has focused on its economic consequences. This essay, in contrast, seeks to revisit some of the older themes of modernization and dependency through looking at recent literature addressing the social dimensions of recent trends.

STRUCTURAL ADJUSTMENT IN HISTORICAL PERSPECTIVE

Structural adjustment is a relatively recent phenomenon. In the decades following World War II, economic policy in the industrialized core reflected Keynesian economic ideas that prescribed the taming of markets through macroeconomic interventions (see Ruggie 1983). In poorer countries, much more direct state interventions in the economy were tolerated or even encouraged by the core. Even in nominally capitalist developing countries, state-owned enterprises played a significant role in national output during this period; indeed, they were actually encouraged and financed by the World Bank (Kuczynski 1999). Some other key elements of the postwar regime were controls on capital movements (which were explicitly condoned by the charter of the IMF) and systems of protection of domestic industries from foreign competition.

By the end of the 1970s, however, the seeds of a new regime had been sown. First coined by World Bank President Robert McNamara at the end of the 1970s, structural adjustment referred to a set of lending practices whereby governments would receive loans if they agreed to implement specific economic reforms (Kapur et al. 1997, pp. 505–6). Although it was not clear what this meant at the time, only a few years later, World Bank and IMF lending arrangements had begun to aim at an ambitious agenda in keeping with the ascendant Reagan revolution: to encourage free markets and foreign investment.

The moment was precipitated by the outbreak of the Third World debt crisis in 1982. The indebtedness of LDC (least-developed country) governments can be traced back to the 1970s, when low interest rates, high inflation, and a glut of "petrodollars" led international banks to invest in the developing world. When global interest rates rose dramatically at the end of the 1970s, these debts became unsustainable. The debt crisis made persuading governments to implement policy reforms easier because such reforms could be required as preconditions to bailout funds. Privatization was particularly attractive because it both satisfied multilateral lenders and provided much-needed revenues. But there were also more subtle pressures: Trapped under unwieldy debts and stagnating economies, governments were increasingly courting foreign portfolio investors, who were more likely to be attracted to governments that provided strong guarantees to property rights and did not interfere excessively in markets (Stallings 1992, Fourcade-Gourinchas & Babb 2002, Mosley 2003). Governments also came to rely on the advice of U.S.-trained economists in high government posts, whose presence helped foster investor confidence—and who tended to be fervent believers in the need for market reforms (Markoff & Montecinos 1993, Schneider 1997, Domínguez 1997, Babb 2001). All these factors combined to create the conditions for the policy reforms of the following decades.

As a precise technical term, "structural adjustment" leaves a great deal to be desired: The policies associated with this term have shifted over time, and it is no longer associated with any particular lending program. In this review, therefore, I do not use structural adjustment as a technical term, but rather refer to its more interpretive and historical meaning—a term associated with a cluster of overlapping historical and conceptual associations in the same way as are the terms "modernity" or "democracy."

This review examines literature that reflects on the social characteristics of the era of structural adjustment. It is not designed to reflect on recent literature on economic development as measured by growth in national income and productivity. The relationship between globalization and development is at the center of an enormous, thriving, and complicated debate that would merit its own literature review.[1] In contrast, this essay focuses on literature reflecting on the organizational, institutional, and class structures of national societies.

Even leaving aside issues of economic development, the consequences of structural adjustment are enormous, complex, and globe-spanning. I have therefore made several strategic decisions to pare this topic down to a more manageable size. First, I have opted to focus on the experience of developing countries—even though structural adjustment has contributed to the transformation of developed countries as well. Second, I have deliberately excluded literature on formerly state socialist economies, which have been subjected to most of the same policies but under very different historical circumstances. Third, my review focuses disproportionately on the experience of Latin America and the Caribbean, which is the focus of a great deal of the existing literature. Fortunately, in many respects, Latin America represents a relatively good laboratory for gauging the effects of structural adjustment in that it contains a range of incomes per capita, from the poorest of the poor (Haiti) to relatively well-off (Argentina).

---

[1]Readers wishing to learn more about this debate might begin with Gereffi & Wyman 1990, Gereffi 1994, Evans 1995, Rodrik 1997, Guillén 2001, Chang 2002, Stiglitz 2002, Broad 2002, and Cline 2004. Two think tanks, the Institute for International Economics (http://www.iie.com) and the Center for Economic and Policy Research (http://www.cepr.net), provide useful entries into how economists with opposing viewpoints frame the debate.

What consequences has this shift in economic policy regimes had for underdeveloped societies? To what extent have the trends of the past two decades sharpened the distinctions between core and periphery—and to what extent have they brought them closer together? The following sections seek to answer these questions through examining three different social transformations: changes in the governance of economies, transformations in class structures, and the rise of transnational networks.

THE GOVERNANCE OF ECONOMIES

Modernization theorists saw developed and developing countries coming together in an inevitable process of institutional convergence. As Marion Levy contended in 1967, "As time goes on, they and we will increasingly resemble one another. . . because the patterns of modernization are such that the more highly modernized societies become, the more they resemble one another" (Levy quoted in So 1990, p. 33). Has the era of structural adjustment made the periphery more structurally similar to the core? This section evaluates the extent of convergence in the governance of national economies.

Today, states in developing countries are doing a lot less of certain things. They are less directly involved in production: Between 1988 and 1994, LDC governments transferred more than 3000 entities from public to private hands (Bouton & Sumlinski 1996, p. 5). States are also decreasing their protection of domestic industries from foreign competition (through tariffs, licenses, etc.) (compare Lora 2001). They are putting fewer constraints on financial markets, fewer barriers on free movement of capital across their borders, and fewer regulations on labor markets (Lora 2001, Epstein et al. 2003). They are also operating with much tighter fiscal policy: Even during recessions, they are refraining from using their central banks to finance deficit spending. To demonstrate their commitment to noninflationary monetary policies, many have adopted legislation making their central banks independent (Maxfield 1997).

However, although states in developing countries have withdrawn from certain activities, they have simultaneously increased their involvement in others. To offset the revenues lost through removing tariffs, they have reformed their taxation systems to more effectively extract resources, commonly replacing taxes on income and wealth with more easily administered (but more regressive) value-added taxes (Lora 2001). They have strengthened private property rights and expanded these rights for foreign firms—for example, by removing restrictions on foreign ownership of land and productive assets. They have joined the World Trade Organization (WTO), which promotes safeguards for property, including controversial intellectual property safeguards, in conjunction with trade opening (see Sell et al. 2003, Shadlen et al. 2004). In addition to protecting property rights, LDC governments have recently been encouraged to adopt so-called governance reforms—to construct institutional frameworks to help safeguard against market imperfections, such as bankruptcy legislation and judiciary independence (Kapur & Webb 2000, Kaufmann 2004).

The defining feature of the new regime is an increased role for private investment—particularly foreign private investment, in the economy. This trend represents both a continuation of and a break from the postwar governance regime. Foreign direct investment (e.g., Ford setting up a factory in Sao Paolo) was a staple of the "associated-dependent development" or "dependent development" system so sharply criticized by dependency theorists in the 1970s (compare Cardoso 1973, Evans 1979). Recently, however, foreign direct investment has become much more important to the economies of developing countries than it ever was during the heyday of dependency theory. Furthermore, the rise of private foreign portfolio investment (e.g., American investors buying stock in a Mexican telephone company, or buying Mexican government bonds) marks a qualitative historical break from the past. In 1970, portfolio investment in developing countries was, for all practical purposes, nonexistent; in 2000, there was a net inflow of $47.9 billion (World Bank 2001, p. 246).

These trends raise interesting theoretical issues about how to define the new institutional framework or organizing logic governing developing countries (Biggart & Guillén 1999). In at least some respects, the sort of institutions that are emerging resemble the American model of regulatory capitalism (Campbell & Lindberg 1990). Under this model, the tasks prescribed for states include the enforcement of contracts, the regulation of natural monopolies, the administration of taxes, and the provision of infrastructure. Perhaps what we are witnessing throughout the developing world is a process of "institutional isomorphism," converging on the organizational patterns of the industrialized North in general, and the United States in particular (DiMaggio & Powell 1983). This interpretation, if true, would support the homogenizing predictions of modernization theorists.

Indeed, proponents of the new model unintentionally echo modernization theorists in asserting that opening to free trade and foreign investment will ultimately promote greater institutional convergence. Although opening to foreign competition may put inefficient local firms out of business, foreign investment brings improved technologies and management techniques, from which recipient nations will benefit. Because better management and technology increases productivity, more jobs will be available; over time, wages will rise, workers and citizens will demand more of governments and firms, and industrial, social, and environmental regimes will converge with those of the North (Graham 1996, 2000; Frankel 2003; Cline 2004).

In the remainder of this section, however, I argue that any strong claim that developing economies have been "Americanized" would be inaccurate—or at the very least, premature. On the one hand, it is true that state interventions have been replaced with a more uniform model reminiscent of the institutions of core capitalist powers. On the other hand, structural adjustment also illustrates the limits of convergence and has brought about the construction of institutions that depart, sometimes sharply, from the American model (Guillén 2001). Although there is insufficient space here to treat this issue completely, I focus on three divergent institutional outcomes: institutional mismatch, institutional overshooting, and the erosion of social citizenship.

One reason for divergent outcomes is that markets have been transplanted to alien worlds, governed by different norms and rules, and lacking the supporting institutions that took decades or even centuries to develop organically in their original contexts. As a result, there may be a mismatch between new and old institutions. In Mexico, for example, privatization and financial liberalization were conducted without a corresponding revision of bankruptcy legislation, which created the conditions for a $55 billion bailout of the banking system (Carruthers et al. 2001, p. 114). Privatizations in developing nations have often been tainted by long-standing collusions between big business and government, which led to the consolidation of monopolies rather than the establishment of competitive markets (Ramirez 2001, Schamis 2002). Although the governance reforms being promoted by multilateral lenders today are designed to prevent such undesirable outcomes, they are far more difficult to define and implement than the liberalizing reforms initiated in the 1980s (see Kaufmann 2003, 2004).

In addition to institutional mismatch, there is also evidence of institutional overshooting—going beyond the American model. Such overshooting can often be traced to the extreme dependence of these governments on the resources of foreign investors and international financial institutions. Portfolio investors are known to conduct speculative attacks against these governments. Because of the perceived uncertainties of investing in emerging markets, portfolio investors hold the governments of developing countries to much higher standards of behavior than those of their developed counterparts (Martínez & Santiso 2003, Mosley 2003). Third World governments must behave as unusually upstanding global citizens, or face the consequences of capital flight, destabilizing currency depreciations, and macroeconomic mayhem. Partly as a result of such pressures, many Third World governments have maintained very high interest rates and fiscal surpluses (a policy that stands in stark contrast, for example, to the policies of Federal Reserve Chairman Alan Greenspan since the mid-1990s), with negative consequences for growth (Weisbrot 2006).

Governments may also overshoot because of more direct pressures exerted by multilateral organizations, which condition their loans on policy reforms (Kahler 1990, Stallings 1992, Kapur & Webb 2000, Babb 2003). At least some of the reforms promoted by these multilateral organizations seem to have surpassed the American model considerably in their degree of market friendliness. To return to the previous example, the IMF generally conditions its bailout funds on fiscal and monetary targets that are, by U.S. standards, extraordinarily strict (Barro & Lee 2002, Vreeland 2003). To take another example, the World Bank, IMF, and U.S. Agency for International Development (USAID) have been promoting the replacement of publicly funded social security systems with private, individual accounts; social security systems have been privatized throughout Latin America and the formerly communist world (Baker & Kar 2002; Wade 2004b, p. 178). In the United States, however, the privatization of social security has (as this article goes to press) been too politically controversial to implement, despite the best efforts of the current administration to rally support. The World Bank and the IMF have also promoted the implementation of "user fees" on primary education, thus interfering with the ability of poor families to send their children to school (Naiman 2000). One explanation for such overshooting is that multilateral (and certainly bilateral) organizations do not simply function as neutral transmitters of organizational templates, but are also subject to influence by vested economic, political, and organizational interests that influence which kinds of policies get promoted (see Babb & Buira 2004).

In evaluating the institutions being constructed in the new era, it is useful to distinguish between defining institutions of regulatory capitalism, on the one hand, and the institutions for promoting social welfare, on the other [we can think of these as corresponding very roughly to T.H. Marshall's civil citizenship and social citizenship (Marshall 1949)]. The enforcement of property rights and contracts, the regulation of monopolies, support for a standing army, etc., are examples of institutions without which competitive markets cannot function. It is mostly the American variety of these institutions that are being transferred to developing countries (even if with unexpected consequences).

Even in the market-friendly United States, however, these are not the only recognized functions of government. For example, with the exception of radical libertarians of the sort that populate the Cato Institute, most Americans consider it legitimate for governments to tax citizens to finance social programs and public education, regulate firms to guarantee worker safety, and protect citizens from environmental degradation. Overall, the institutions of social citizenship have been less consistently supported by multilateral organizations than the institutions of civil citizenship. The WTO has been criticized for failing to develop sanctions for governments that allow child labor and other practices considered abusive by the International Labor Organization (Khor 2002). Recently, the World Bank and the IMF have begun to require that their most impoverished borrowers set aside a fixed percentage of their expenditures for "pro-poor" spending. However, because these lenders simultaneously require reductions in government spending, deflationary monetary policy, and the repayment of external debts, the effects of these poverty-reduction strategies may be cancelled out (Babb & Buira 2004, p. 11).

Leaving aside the influence of multilateral organizations, the institutions of social citizenship may be eroded simply because developing countries—unlike the United States—are burdened with external debt denominated in foreign currencies. Heavily indebted states have arguably adopted a role that diverges considerably from that adopted by core states: namely, the extraction of domestic resources and their export abroad. In some respects, this role is reminiscent of the colonial dependence of the nineteenth century (Dos Santos 1971). Resources spent on servicing debt are obviously resources that are not being spent on such recognized, basic functions of liberal capitalist government as the provision of public health, education, and infrastructure (see Sachs 2002). A recent IMF study finds that external debt has a statistically significant negative impact on governments' ability to fund social programs (Loko et al. 2003).

Finally, structural adjustment may erode social citizenship by decreasing the bargaining power of states and citizens vis-à-vis private investors. To the extent that they cut into profits, the construction of social welfare–governing institutions tends to be resisted by firms. The history of the industrialized democracies suggests that they are constructed in spite of resistance from firms, by states responding to the demands of organized social groups (see Weir & Skocpol 1985, Esping-Andersen 1999, Amenta 2003). Because Third World citizens and governments are in a disadvantaged bargaining position with respect to foreign investors, and even more so with respect to multilateral organizations like the IMF, they may be hampered in their ability to construct the institutions of social citizenship that developed countries take for granted. This is the premise underlying the famous "race to the bottom" so often cited by global justice activists: In their view, today governments are competing among themselves to attract foreign investors by providing the lowest taxes and the least stringent labor and environmental regulations (see http://www.aboutglobalization.com). Even standard neoclassical economic models provide some support for this idea (see Rodrik 1997, 1998).

However, there are at least two versions of the "race to the bottom" hypothesis. One version supposes that globalization subjects the workers and states of all regions—developed and developing alike—to such competition; the result should be institutional convergence of core and periphery toward uniformly low wages, standards, and social protections. Empirical analyses suggest that the overall trend toward reduced taxes on capital and declining unionization in OECD economies can be traced at least in part to economic globalization (Western 1995, Rodrik 1997). There is also evidence that the North American Free Trade Agreement (NAFTA) has contributed to job losses among low-skilled workers in the United States (Audley et al. 2003). But although the wages of low-skilled workers and taxes on corporations may be declining in the wealthy North, nobody is yet claiming that social protections and environmental regulations in Germany and the United States are being downsized to resemble their counterparts in Zimbabwe and Bolivia. Most global trade and foreign direct investment occur among wealthy countries, rather than between wealthy and poor nations (see Wade 2004b, pp. 172–73). Wealth and power continue to have their privileges, although there is no doubt that some of these privileges have been eroded for non-elites in developed countries.

What I examine here is the second version of the "race to the bottom," which focuses on competition among developing countries. In this view, structural adjustment puts developing countries in a particularly poor bargaining position. Heavily indebted, capital-poor countries with high levels of unemployment are desperate for foreign investment. However, in courting investors, they are flocking to a crowded market niche of similarly desperate countries, all selling low-wage, low-skilled work on the global marketplace (see Gereffi 1994 on the "flying geese" model of development). To make themselves look more competitive to investors shopping around for the best deal, they may offer lower levels of taxation, regulation, etc. If true, this pattern should lead to a polarization between developed and developing countries, with the latter converging among themselves on uniformly low regulatory standards and levels of social protection.

Anyone who has any experience with the antisweatshop movement on college campuses has seen an array of shocking facts; incredibly low wages, long hours, child labor, employer abuses, and wanton toxic dumping (see http://www.sweat shopwatch.org). However, to prove that there is a race to the bottom, we need evidence that the inhabitants of developing countries are worse than they would have been otherwise. Unfortunately, this presents manifold problems of measurement and controlling for extraneous factors. The removal of trade barriers and the opening to foreign investment occurred as part of a complex amalgam of social changes—external debt, increased pressures from multilateral organizations, privatization, vulnerability to balance-of-payments crises, etc.—that cannot be operationalized into a single variable. There are critical measurement problems with some of the most important elements of structural adjustment; "economic openness" itself is remarkably difficult to measure (Agénor 2002). Even assuming good measures for the independent variable, it is important to disaggregate the data to distinguish the impact on different social groups; but the demographic and labor market data from many developing countries are incomplete at best. Because disentangling and analyzing these different factors is so difficult, empirical evaluations of the race to the bottom hypothesis tend to be both partial and hotly contested.

Has state capacity to provide social welfare benefits declined? One circumstance that appears to support this idea is the rise of export-processing zones (EPZs)—special manufacturing areas where Third World governments offer investors exemption from taxation and regulation. According to the World Bank, whereas only a few such zones existed in 1970, by 1996 there were over 500 zones in 73 countries (World Bank 1996). This suggests that Third World governments are competing for foreign direct investment by lessening potentially welfare-enhancing interventions, such as the extraction of fiscal resources. Nevertheless, more optimistic observers would argue that existing taxes and regulations were too onerous to begin with, and that setting up EPZs is a necessary step in fostering economic development, which will ultimately increase human welfare. For reasons discussed in the following section, however, critics could reply that there is little evidence that such economic development is actually occurring (see Weisbrot et al. 2001).

What impact does structural adjustment have on the environment? There is little controversy over global environmentalists' assertion that external debt contributes to environmental degradation—after all, for a heavily indebted nation, the price of a clean and sustainable environment may be unaffordable (Shah 1998). However, other assertions have been hotly contested. For example, the WTO has been accused by activists of systematically undermining national environmental standards by imposing sanctions on governments that try to enforce environmental standards in trade; other observers say these claims are exaggerated (Wallach 2000, Frankel

2003). Supporters of current policies suggest that liberalizing reforms generate economic development and that, in turn, such development increases respect for the environment: There is a strong correlation between environmental standards and GDP per capita (Graham 2000, pp. 131–48; Frankel 2003). Once again, however, this argument rests on the contestable premise that development is occurring in the first place. It also overlooks the fact that not all indices of pollution decline with economic growth (Audley et al. 2003, p. 66). The recent Carnegie Endowment report on the impact of NAFTA finds that it has not been as damaging to the environment as was originally feared, although there have been negative impacts in certain sectors, particularly in rural areas (Audley et al. 2003).

Has structural adjustment weakened labor unions in developing countries? In contrast to the literature on union decline in OECD nations (compare Western 1995, Lambert 2000), there has been little cross-national comparative research on trends in unions in the developing world. The partial accounts that exist paint an ambiguous picture that neither clearly supports nor refutes a race to the bottom in labor organizing. One national case that supports a pessimistic interpretation is that of Mexico, which lifted trade barriers and invited in foreign investment under the auspices of NAFTA. Since the implementation of NAFTA in 1993, real wages in Mexico have declined significantly, the minimum wage has been held down to foster international competitiveness, and unions have been weakened; in line with the predictions of neoclassical theory, unskilled workers appear to have been hurt the most (Cortez 2001, Audley et al. 2003). But it is not clear that the Mexican case can be generalized to the rest of the developing world. Frundt (2002) finds increased rates of unionization in Central America during the period of structural adjustment, although he suggests that the strength of unions may have declined. In a cross-national study, Mosley & Uno (2004) find that neither foreign direct investment nor trade openness are significant correlates of labor rights violations, although they do correlate with region and level of development. Murillo & Schrank (2005) observe that 13 of the 18 collective labor reforms implemented in Latin America between 1985 and 1998 enhanced rather than limited collective bargaining rights, an outcome they attribute partly to the strategies of traditional labor-backed parties and partly to transnational activism (discussed below).

This section has focused exclusively on the governance of national economies, broadly defined to include social welfare–enhancing institutions. However, it is worth mentioning briefly another set of institutions that have been transformed in the era of structural adjustment: namely the rules of national politics. Existing literature on the topic of democratic transitions focuses on Latin America—arguably the continent in which the transformation has been most dramatic. Weyland (2004) argues that although the rise of market-friendly institutions has made Latin American democracy more sustainable, it has simultaneously limited the quality of this democracy (see also Kurtz 2004). The end of the cold war and the opening of national economies to international markets led to increased pressures for minimal procedural democracy, both from the U.S. government and from foreign investors in search of stable investment climates. It also weakened leftist parties and other proponents of radical reforms, decreasing elite groups' perception that dictatorship was the only solution. The net result has been that social groups and political parties are more likely to agree on the means (democratic elections), even if they disagree with the ends. However, Weyland also points out that the changes associated with structural adjustment have also put severe constraints on the quality of democracy. Economic constraints and the threat of capital flight limit the latitude of possible policies. Such restrictions on policies have led to weakened political parties and depressed participation—eerily echoing the apathy of the U.S. electorate. The accountability of elected leaders to their constituents has also declined (see also O'Donnell 1994, Roberts 2002, Stokes 2003, Martínez & Santiso 2003).

Ultimately, what can we conclude about structural adjustment and institutional convergence? At the risk of sounding excessively conciliatory, I suggest that the available evidence echoes aspects of both modernization and dependency theories. On the one hand, institutions still work quite differently in the global South. States continue to service large and unsustainable debts; their policies must respond to the leverage of multilateral institutions and the need to maintain investor confidence. Now more than ever, dependency matters: There are fundamental differences between the roles of states in developed and developing countries that can be traced to large differences in bargaining power. On the other hand, we must concede that developing countries have adopted a model of governance that resembles, in its most general outlines, the sort of capitalism that is practiced in the United States. Whether this appears to have contributed to the further modernization of national societies is explored in the following section.

THE TRANSFORMATION OF CLASS STRUCTURES

The two most hotly debated issues in the literature on liberalizing reforms are (a) whether they have promoted economic development, and (b) whether they have promoted equality. This section attempts to sort through some of the literature on changing national and global class structures.

Although there is not enough space in this review to address debates about economic development in more than a superficial way, we should briefly review some evidence on this point: Economic growth, after all, has consequences for global social structure. The ostensible reason for implementing free-market reforms was that they would generate growth, development, and a convergence of the incomes of developed and developing countries (Williamson 1994, pp. 27–28). Twenty years later, the evidence in favor of these initial claims has been disappointing. For example, from 1960 to 1980, output per person grew 75% in Latin America and 36% in sub-Saharan Africa; in contrast, between 1980 and 2000, it grew by only 6% in Latin America and actually fell by 15% in sub-Saharan Africa (Weisbrot et al. 2001).

These data, however, do not necessarily lead to the conclusion that market liberalization is bad for economic development. One counterargument is that national incomes have been dragged down by large external debts, which are the fault of governments, not market opening. Another counterargument is that market openings have not been carried far enough—if governments could remove remaining barriers to the functioning of markets, then there would be a more impressive rise in national incomes. A related argument is that development takes time, and that developing countries need to wait for the new model to bear fruit. Finally, the model's supporters point out that some countries have been doing very well: India and China, in particular, have been growing very rapidly (Graham 2000, Cline 2004, Weisbrot 2006).

What do the macroeconomic and demographic data tell us about trends in overall global inequality? First, it is important to distinguish between inequality within countries and inequality between countries. The question of inequalities between countries—whether countries like Mexico and India are catching up to countries like the United States and Japan—is quite controversial. Although some observers argue that inequalities across nations have declined, others have come to the opposite conclusion (e.g., Kentor 2001, Dollar & Kraay 2002, Milanovic 2002, Galbraith 2002, Firebaugh 2003). To make sense of this apparent contradiction, Wade (2004a) shows that the answer depends on how researchers measure and compare national wealth. One method is to compare the raw figures on national GDP converted into U.S. dollar amounts, and compare across nations. According to these numbers, there is a clear pattern of rising inequality: some countries have been getting a lot wealthier, and others have been left behind. However, those claiming a convergence in national incomes use numbers that differ in two respects. First, they use numbers that are weighted by population: Thus, the two largest developing countries (India and China) have an enormous impact on the final figures. Second, they use numbers that have been adjusted for purchasing-power parity (PPP), to control for the fact that a dollar in India, for example, will buy a great deal more than a dollar in the United States. The PPP-adjusted national GDPs, weighted for population, show a pattern of rising equality—but this effect disappears when India and China are subtracted from the calculations.

Thus, claims to rising equality across nations are based on the indisputable fact that India and China have been growing at a tremendous pace over the past two decades. What is extremely disputable, however, is whether this economic growth—and hence income convergence—can be attributed to structural adjustment. Neither India nor China is a particularly good representative of free market orthodoxy. Although it has used trade and foreign investment to its advantage, China continues to have an enormous state-owned sector and an inconvertible national currency. India's growth spurt began a decade before it began to implement liberalizing reforms, and protectionist tariffs actually increased during this first phase of growth (Rodrik & Subramanian 2004). Meanwhile, Latin American economies in which market reforms have been implemented in a more orthodox manner have mostly suffered from stagnant levels of economic growth.

The data on global poverty have also generated a lively controversy. Basing their claims on in-depth knowledge of national case studies, a number of critics of structural adjustment have asserted that it has been pushing citizens of developing countries beneath the poverty line (Chossudovsky 1997, Taylor 2001). But in 2002, World Bank Managing Director James Wolfensohn famously declared that the number of people living on less than $1.00 a day had fallen by 200 million (World Bank 2002). Does this mean that the global war on poverty is being won? Wade (2004a) shows that in addition to a number of more minor problems, there is a fundamental methodological error in this claim: It compares figures from 1980 and 1998 that are not comparable because of a significant change in the World Bank's methodology for calculating the poverty line. An alternative is to look at demographic numbers on poverty, such as life expectancy at birth. Life expectancies at birth have increased among poor countries since the 1980s. However, during the 1980–1998 period, the progress of poor countries in catching up to the life expectancy of wealthy ones slowed considerably compared with the previous 20 years (Weisbrot 2006).

The question of inequality within countries is less controversial than the question of between-country inequality, or the question of poverty; even optimistic observers, such as Firebaugh (2003), concede that within national boundaries, income inequality has been increasing. To illuminate how these trends have played out in developing countries, there is a large and growing body of national case studies focusing on various indicators of social well-being and inequality (see Feliciano 2001, Taylor 2001, Amann & Baer 2002, Carneiro & Arbache 2003). Two particularly useful studies are Portes & Hoffman's (2003) study of changing Latin American class structures and the recent Carnegie Endowment report on the impact of NAFTA on Mexico a decade after its ratification (Audley et al. 2003). Whereas the Portes & Hoffman study has the virtue of considering an entire continent's experience through the lens of a range of indicators of inequality and social welfare, the Carnegie study provides a detailed, in-depth account of the complexities of a single nation's experience with opening its economy to its wealthier and more powerful northern neighbors.

Both studies paint sobering portraits of the impact of structural adjustment on national class structures. During the 1980s and 1990s there was an increase in income inequality in Latin America, with a consistent concentration of wealth in the top decile of the population (Portes & Hoffman 2003). Such income polarization has been particularly notable in Mexico. Meanwhile, the percentage of Mexicans beneath the poverty line is still greater than it was in the late 1970s, and real wages have actually declined (Audley et al. 2003).

Of course, the causes of these phenomena are complex, and we should not be too quick to jump to conclusions: The debt crisis in the 1980s and the peso devaluation in the 1990s played important parts in these trends, and it is not easy to disentangle these factors from market liberalization (Audley et al. 2003, p. 18). Such ambiguities notwithstanding, the Mexican experience under NAFTA helps highlight some important processes that are contributing to qualitative changes in national class structures across the developing world. One such process is the movement of rural populations away from their native towns to urban centers or to places where they take jobs as low-wage agricultural workers (Araghi 1995, p. 338). The mass movement off the land is part of a longer-term trend that predates the structural adjustment era by a many decades. However, structural adjustment has accelerated this trend by making traditional and small-scale agriculture even less viable. Under the new regime, small-scale farmers in the developing world receive fewer subsidies, face higher interest rates, and face competition with heavily subsidized and well-capitalized foreign agribusiness (see Bryceson 2002, Crabtree 2002).[2] Mexican government authorities estimate a loss of 1.3 million jobs in the agricultural sector between 1993 and 2002 (Audley et al. 2003, p. 20).

This process of de-agriculturalization is only one of many simultaneous pressures on labor markets that may arise in the era of structural adjustment. A second source of pressure is the privatization of state-owned firms, which often leads to downsizing worker layoffs (Taylor 2001). Over the past two decades, there has been a significant contraction in formal sector employment in developing countries and a corresponding move toward employment in the informal economy (Schaefer 2002, Portes & Hoffman 2003). In other words, the labor force has come to be characterized less by employees and more by independent agents—from small business owners to ambulant chewing-gum sellers to garment pieceworkers. Although the rise of the informal economy is lauded by some observers as a necessary escape valve from cumbersome taxation and government regulations (Tripp 1997, Schneider 2002), other observers point out that it involves replacing stable, state-regulated jobs with a form of employment that tends to be precarious, poorly paid, and less productive (Iztigsohn 2000, Farrell 2004).

A third source of pressure on labor markets in LDCs is the restrictive monetary policy that has become the norm under the structural adjustment regime. To foster the confidence of foreign investors and continue to receive financing from multilateral organizations (particularly the IMF), governments have prioritized the fight against inflation, often changing central bank legislation to take monetary policy out of the hands of the executive (compare Maxfield 1997, Mosley 2003, Babb & Buira 2004). However, reducing inflation to the levels preferred by the international financial community requires high interest rates—and high interest rates decrease domestic investment and increase unemployment (Weisbrot 2006).

Finally, there is evidence that labor markets are being strained by the bankruptcy of domestic firms that cannot compete with the flood of cheap imports from more open trade (Audley et al. 2003, p. 16; Taylor 2001). Just as this job loss contributes to the informalization of the labor force, so it may be contributing to a restructuring of local bourgeoisies. A study by Silva (1996) on the fate of business during Chile's early experiment with liberalizing reforms under the Chicago Boys[3] suggests that large, export-oriented businesses with access to international capital markets may be the hardiest, and that market concentration may result. Although there is

---

[2] According to one estimate, from 1999 through 2001, U.S. corn was sold in Mexico at prices at least 30% below the cost of production (Audley et al. 2003, p. 17).

[3] The Chicago Boys were a group of Chilean economists, educated in the Department of Economics of the University of Chicago, who ran Chilean economic policy under the dictatorship of Augusto Pinochet in the 1970s and 1980s.

evidence from various countries that smaller and domestic-oriented entrepreneurs may "wither away" in the face of foreign competition (Carmody 1998, Tanski & French 2001, Lewis-Bynoe et al. 2002, Ocampo 2003), there have also been unexpected adaptations to new conditions. Schrank (2005) documents the rise of a new class of indigenous investors in the EPZs in the Dominican Republic who have been able to profit from their combination of local connections and access to foreign capital. However, such firms have also suffered from high rates of bankruptcy, suggesting that we should not be too optimistic in our conclusions.

Although few observers are likely to shed sympathetic tears for the declining fortunes of formerly privileged industrialists, the fate of masses of unemployed workers and displaced peasants is cause for concern. In theory, foreign investment is supposed to compensate for labor shedding in inefficient sectors by creating jobs in more efficient, productive firms. Throughout the developing world, there is strong evidence that foreign-owned firms are indeed more efficient and productive than the domestic firms that they are replacing. But more productive plants have often translated into fewer rather than more jobs (Taylor 2001, pp. 3–4; Audley et al. 2003, p. 12). Meanwhile, jobs created in EPZs may be vulnerable to capital flight to other low-wage regions. From 1994 to 2001, foreign direct investment from the United States to Mexico increased from about $5 billion per year to $16 billion per year. But most of the jobs created under NAFTA in the 1990s were in maquiladoras (EPZs), and about 30% of these jobs subsequently disappeared—many relocated to countries such as China where wages are even lower (Audley et al. 2003, pp. 45, 12). Because foreign investment has not effectively compensated for the jobs lost through structural adjustment, many developing countries continue to be plagued with unemployment and poverty-level wages (Portes & Hoffman 2003).

Although a number of studies suggest that structural adjustment has increased class inequality in many countries, the emerging evidence on gender inequality is more complex and ambiguous. In many places, structural adjustment has undermined traditional gendered divisions of labor, both by providing new opportunities for women to work for wages outside the home (e.g., in EPZs), and by contributing to male unemployment (Braunstein 2002, Ganguly-Scrase 2003). However, whether this has led to a general empowerment of women with respect to men is a much more complicated question. Answering this question requires taking a number of other factors into account, such as the position women in developing countries adopt in the labor market. For example, they may come to rely on precarious and poorly paid work in the informal economy, keeping them dependent on male incomes (Itzigsohn 2000). Gender roles may be slow to adapt to changing conditions (as "second shifters" in the United States know all too well), and multinational firms may actually encourage the reproduction of traditional roles (Gutmann 1996, Salzinger 2002). Furthermore, other circumstances related to structural adjustment, such as external debt and reduced government budgets, may undermine the position of women by eliminating resources such as access to education and healthcare (Buchmann 1996, Braunstein 2002). Thus, the impact of structural adjustment on gender inequalities is an area ripe for further research.

Overall, the consequences of structural adjustment for national and global class structures seem more suggestive of dependency than modernization. Under other circumstances, growing income inequality might be seen as compatible with the "Kuznets curve," in which rapid economic growth benefits upper- more than lower-strata groups; a rising tide may lift all boats, but in the early stages of development it may lift some boats more than others. But for the majority of developing countries in the past two decades, the tide has not risen at all, or only barely. Third World societies have undergone major transformations that are supposed to be the hallmarks of modernizing societies—mass movement off the land, urbanization, and industrialization. And yet, these transformations have not been consistently associated with economic growth and declining inequality across nations. This is precisely the sort of contradiction that interested dependency theorists—the emergence of social structures reminiscent of the core in some respects, but with very different underpinnings and consequences.

THE RISE OF TRANSNATIONAL NETWORKS

Their numerous disagreements notwithstanding, a feature shared by modernization and dependency theorists alike was an emphasis on the nation-state as the unit of analysis. Both types of theorists focused on issues of national development and nation-level social transformations. The era of structural adjustment, however, has cast fundamental doubts on the utility of these postwar conceptual categories by contributing to the rise of social networks that span national borders. This section examines literature documenting transnationalism in three areas: business, labor markets, and policy.

Where business is concerned, it is not immediately apparent why transnationalism represents anything new—after all, during the 1970s, large foreign multinationals set up local branches in developing countries. What is new about current trends, however, is the spread of an organizational form characterized by networks rather than hierarchies (Gereffi 1994, Castells 2000, DiMaggio 2001). Today, global production increasingly relies on subcontractors and sub-subcontractors outside the scope of any single firm or nation. The computer one purchases at Best Buy, for example, contains components made and assembled by the workers of different firms in various different nations.

It is common to attribute this new production system to advances in technology (see Castells 2000). Advances in communications (e.g., the Internet) and transportation make it far easier for firms to subcontract to suppliers in faraway countries and to continually shop around for the suppliers that offer the most attractive prices. But the role of structural adjustment in creating these conditions should not be underestimated. Liberalizing reforms, combined with the setting up of EPZs in which regulations are reduced even further, facilitate global production networks by eliminating the friction of tariffs, taxes, complicated labor laws, and red tape. The global production networks that result are with "just-in-time" production:

Retailers order items from their suppliers (and the suppliers from their suppliers, and so on) as they are needed, rather than keeping large inventories in stock.

Among the virtues of this new system is that it is leaner: It eliminates bureaucratic inefficiencies and puts a premium on getting products to consumers quickly and at the lowest possible price. However, critics of the system point out that it is also meaner. In the garment and other industries, this system has been associated with an increased reliance on offshore sweatshop production (Rosen 2002). Whereas bureaucratic firms can be publicly criticized and sanctioned for unethical practices, holding them accountable for the practices of their suppliers, sub-suppliers, and so on down the food chain is much more difficult. Defenders of economic globalization often point out that the affiliates of foreign firms pay on average one third more than the prevailing national wages (Graham 2000, p. 94). But the pants one buys at Target are not produced by the Docker corporation; the company that puts its label on a particular pair of pants may not provide—or even possess—information concerning the conditions under which it was produced (O'Rourke 2003).

However, firms are not alone in using networks that span national borders. A number of scholars have identified a trend toward "globalization from below" through the establishment of transnational migrant networks (Portes 1998, Kyle 2000, Levitt 2001, Massey et al. 2002). Structural adjustment fosters the development of these communities at multiple levels. Most obviously, for the reasons enumerated above, structural adjustment puts pressure on national labor markets, leading to economic incentives to out-migrate (Massey & Espinosa 1997). Meanwhile, foreign direct investment incorporates traditional segments of the population into the paid labor force and contributes to the Westernization of local cultures, making populations ripe for migration (Sassen 1988). High levels of foreign debt contribute to high interest rates in developing countries, which in turn cause their residents to work abroad to save up capital to invest in homes or small businesses (Massey & Espinosa 1997). Under NAFTA, the illegal immigration of Mexicans to the United States has increased significantly, despite increases in border control (Audley et al. 2003, p. 48). A recent United Nations report finds a 14% increase in the total world stock of migrants between 1990 and 2000 alone (UN Popul. Div. 2002).

Transnational migration theorists suggest that new patterns of immigration differ from older waves in that they are not necessarily characterized by assimilation and permanent settlement. Many immigrants maintain strong social ties back home and travel back and forth between countries on a regular basis; others leave spouses and children behind in the expectation that they will return when enough money has been saved (Portes 1998, Levitt 2001, Parrenas 2001). Most recently, a more privileged class of transmigrant has emerged: well-paid, high-tech workers, often from India, with ties to both their receiving country and their country of origin (Schrank 2003). The experiences of transnational elites, which are obviously very different from those of the typical illegal Mexican factory worker, represent an underexplored and fascinating area of investigation.

One striking new trend linked to the rise of transnational migrant networks is the growing importance of remittances—cash sent home to the country of origin—in the economies of developing countries (Parrenas 2001, Orozco 2002, Portes & Hoffman 2003). According to a recent World Bank report, in 2001 the official total of remittances to developing economies was more than $70 billion, and contributed more than 10% to the GDP of nations that included Jordan, Lesotho, Albania, Nicaragua, El Salvador, Cape Verde, and Jamaica (Ratha 2003). Although the World Bank tends to emphasize the beneficial effects of remittances for economic development, qualitative studies of the transmigrant experience emphasize the high human cost incurred by the people who work far from family and community, for low wages, and often without legal rights or protections (see Parrenas 2001, Levitt 2001).

Finally, structural adjustment has been met with a new kind of resistance that also relies on border-spanning social ties. Peter Evans (2000) identifies three kinds of transnational ties contributing to what he terms "counter-hegemonic globalization." First, there are transnational advocacy networks: Globalization has created political openings that allow cross-border activists to leverage changes in state policies (Keck & Sikkink 1998). For example, the Jubilee movement has drawn world attention to the issue of Third World debt and was arguably an important factor in pushing forward the Heavily Indebted Poor Countries initiative endorsed by the World Bank and IMF (Donnelly 2002). Second, workers have strengthened contacts with their allies across borders to help compensate for the lack of bargaining power of workers faced with highly mobile capital (Kidder 2002). Third, there has been a proliferation of consumer-labor networks designed to help compensate for Third World states' inability or unwillingness to enforce fair labor practices, of the sort exemplified by the campus antisweatshop movement (Gereffi et al. 2001, O'Rourke 2003).

FINAL THOUGHTS

The era of structural adjustment has been associated with a number of fundamental and seemingly irreversible social transformations. Some of these changes, such as the rise of global networks, seem to have made the old modernization-dependency debates irrelevant. Others, such as the adoption of U.S.-style patterns of economic governance around the world and the heightened salience of core pressures for policies in the periphery, echo the debates of the 1970s in ways that are interesting and potentially illuminating.

Over the past half-dozen years or so, there have been some signs that the intellectual and political underpinnings of the current order are being eroded, including a resurgence of Third World nationalist rhetoric, international social forums, and the rise and persistence of protests against multilateral organizations. Perhaps most interestingly, a number of prominent economists have begun to critique some of the fundamental tenets of the reigning model (see Stiglitz 2002).

However, although these trends have created space for debate, they have thus far coalesced into neither a school of thought nor a coherent set of policy alternatives. This seems like a propitious time for sociologists to situate themselves within debates about what has happened, what went wrong, and what is to be done. Sociology lost considerable ground during the era of structural adjustment, which gave economists greater disciplinary dominance over discussions of the problems of poor countries. Consequently, many of the broader sociological, historical, and philosophical questions about the nature of modernity were thrust to the margins, as debates came to revolve around rational actors rather than the forces of history. A return to the big questions might be precisely what is needed to build a paradigmatic challenge, and a new terrain for debate.

ACKNOWLEDGMENTS

Many thanks to Andrew Schrank and Mark Weisbrot for their extremely timely and helpful advice on this manuscript.

The *Annual Review of Sociology* is online at http://soc.annualreviews.org

LITERATURE CITED

Agénor P. 2002. *Does globalization hurt the poor?* Policy Res. Work. Pap. 2922, World Bank, Washington, DC

Amann E, Baer W. 2002. Neoliberalism and its consequences in Brazil. *J. Latin Am. Stud.* 34(4):945–59

Amenta E. 2003. What we know about the development of social policy: comparative and historical research in comparative and historical perspective. In *Comparative Historical Analysis in the Social Sciences*, ed. J Mahoney, D Rueschemeyer, pp. 91–130. New York: Cambridge Univ. Press

Araghi FA. 1995. Global depeasantization, 1945–1990. *Sociol. Q.* 36(2):337–68

Audley JJ, Papadmetriou DG, Polaski S, Vaughan S. 2003. *NAFTA's Promise and Reality: Lessons from Mexico for the Hemisphere.* Rep. Carnegie Endowment Int. Peace

Babb S. 2001. *Managing Mexico: Economists from Nationalism to Neoliberalism.* Princeton, NJ: Princeton Univ. Press

Babb S. 2003. The IMF in sociological perspective: a tale of organizational slippage. *Stud. Comp. Int. Dev.* 38(2):3–27

Babb S, Buira A. 2004. *Mission creep, mission push, and discretion in sociological perspective: the case of IMF conditionality.* Presented at 28th G-24 Tech. Group Meet., Geneva, Switzerland. http://www.g24.org/012gva04.pdf

Baker D, Kar D. 2002. *Defined contributions from workers, guaranteed benefits for bankers: the World Bank's approach to social security reform.* Cent. Econ. Policy Res., Washington, DC. http://www.cepr.net/world_bank_social_security.htm

Barro RJ, Lee J. 2002. *IMF programs: Who is chosen and what are the effects?* Work. Pap. 8951, Natl. Bur. Econ. Res., Cambridge, MA

Biggart N, Guillén M. 1999. Developing difference: social organization and the rise of the auto industries of South Korea, Taiwan, Spain, and Argentina. *Am. Sociol. Rev.* 64: 722–47

Bouton L, Sumlinski MA. 1996. *Trends in Private Investment in Developing Countries: Statistics for 1970–95.* Washington, DC: World Bank

Braunstein E. 2002. *Gender, FDI, and women's autonomy: a research note on empirical analysis.* PERI Work. Pap. No. 49, Polit. Econ. Res. Inst., Amherst, MA

Broad R, ed. 2002. *Global Backlash: Citizen Initiatives for a Just World Economy.* New York: Rowman & Littlefield

Bryceson DF. 2002. The scramble in Africa: reorienting rural livelihoods. *World Dev.* 30(5):725–39

Buchmann C. 1996. The debt crisis, structural adjustment and women's education: implications for status and social development. *Int. J. Comp. Sociol.* 37(1–2):5–31

Campbell JL, Lindberg LN. 1990. Property rights and the organization of economic activity by the state. *Am. Sociol. Rev.* 55(10):634–47

Cardoso FH. 1973. Associated-dependent development: theoretical and practical implications. In *Authoritarian Brazil*, ed. A Stephen, pp. 142–76. New Haven, CT: Yale Univ. Press

Carmody P. 1998. Neoclassical practice and the collapse of industry in Zimbabwe: the cases of textiles, clothing, and footwear. *Econ. Geogr.* 74(4):319–32

Carneiro FG, Arbache JS. 2003. The impacts of trade on the Brazilian labor market: a CGE model approach. *World Dev.* 31(9):1581–96

Carruthers B, Babb S, Halliday T. 2001. Institutionalizing markets, or the market for institutions? Central banks, bankruptcy law, and the globalization of financial markets. In *The Rise of Neoliberalism in Institutional Analysis*, ed. JL Campbell, OK Pedersen, pp. 94–126. Princeton, NJ: Princeton Univ. Press

Castells M. 2000. *The Rise of the Network Society.* New York: Basil Blackwell

Chang H. 2002. *Kicking Away the Ladder.* London, UK: Anthem Press

Chossudovsky M. 1997. *The Globalization of Poverty: Impacts of World Bank and IMF Reforms.* London, UK: Zed Press

Cline W. 2004. *Trade Policy and Global Poverty.* Washington, DC: Inst. Int. Econ.

Cortez WW. 2001. What is behind increasing wage inequality in Mexico? *World Dev.* 29(11):1905

Crabtree J. 2002. The impact of neo-liberal economics on Peruvian peasant agriculture in the 1990s. *J. Peasant Stud.* 29(3/4):131–61

DiMaggio P. 2001. Introduction: Making sense of the contemporary firm and prefiguring its future. In *The Twenty-First-Century Firm: Changing Economic Organization in International Perspective*, ed. P DiMaggio, pp. 3–30. Princeton, NJ: Princeton Univ. Press

DiMaggio P, Powell W. 1983. The iron cage revisited: institutional isomorphism and collective rationality in organizational fields. *Am. Sociol. Rev.* 48(2):147–60

Dollar D, Kraay A. 2001. Spreading the wealth. *Foreign Aff.* 81(1):120–33

Domínguez J, ed. 1997. *Technopols: Freeing Politics and Markets in Latin America.* University Park: Penn. State Press

Donnelly EA. 2002. Proclaiming jubilee: the debt and structural adjustment network. See Khagram et al. 2002, pp. 155–80

Dos Santos T. 1971. The structure of dependence. In *Readings in U.S. Imperialism*, ed. KT Kan, DC Hodges, pp. 225–36. Boston: Extending Horiz.

Epstein G, Grabel I, Jomo KS. 2003. *Capital management techniques in developing countries: an assessment of experiences from the 1990s and lessons for the future.* Presented at 25th G-24 Tech. Group Meet., Port-of-Spain, Trinidad and Tobago

Esping-Andersen G. 1999. *Social Foundations of Postindustrial Economies.* New York: Oxford Univ. Press

Evans P. 1979. *Dependent Development: The Alliance of Multinational, State, and Local Capital in Brazil.* Princeton, NJ: Princeton Univ. Press

Evans P. 1995. *Embedded Autonomy: States and Industrial Transformation.* Princeton, NJ: Princeton Univ. Press

Evans P. 2000. Fighting marginalization with transnational networks: counter-hegemonic globalization. *Contemp. Sociol.* 29(1):230–41

Farrell D. 2004. The hidden dangers of the informal economy. *McKinsey Q.* No. 3. http://www.mckinseyquarterly.com/article_abstract.aspx?ar=1448&L2=7&L3=10

Feliciano ZM. 2001. Workers and trade liberalization: the impact of trade reforms in Mexico on wages and employment. *Ind. Labor Relat. Rev.* 55(1):95–126

Firebaugh G. 2003. *The New Geography of Global Income Inequality.* Cambridge, MA: Harvard Univ. Press

Fourcade-Gourinchas M, Babb S. 2002. The rebirth of the liberal creed: paths to neoliberalism in four countries. *Am. J. Sociol.* 108(3):533–80

Frankel J. 2003. *The environment and globalization.* Work. Pap. 10090, Natl. Bur. Econ. Res., Cambridge, MA

Frundt HJ. 2002. Central American unions in the era of globalization. *Latin Am. Res. Rev.* 37(3):7–55

Galbraith JK. 2002. Is inequality decreasing? Debating the wealth and poverty of nations. *Foreign Aff.* 81(4):178–94

Ganguly-Scrase R. 2003. Paradoxes of globalization, liberalization, and gender equality: the worldviews of the lower middle class in West Bengal, India. *Gender Soc.* 17(4):544–66

Gereffi G. 1994. The international economy and economic development. In *The Handbook of Economic Sociology*, ed. NJ Smelser, R Swedberg, pp. 206–33. Princeton, NJ: Princeton Univ. Press

Gereffi G, Garcia-Johnson R, Sasser E. 2001. The NGO industrial complex. *Foreign Policy* 125:56–64

Gereffi G, Wyman DL, eds. 1990. *Manufacturing Miracles: Paths of Industrialization in Latin America and East Asia.* Princeton, NJ: Princeton Univ. Press

Graham EM. 1996. *Global Corporations and National Governments.* Washington, DC: Inst. Int. Econ.

Graham EM. 2000. *Fighting the Wrong Enemy: Antiglobal Activists and Multinational Enterprises.* Washington, DC: Inst. Int. Econ.

Guillén M. 2001. *The Limits of Convergence.* Princeton, NJ: Princeton Univ. Press

Gutmann M. 1996. *The Meanings of Macho: On Being a Man in Mexico City.* Berkeley: Univ. Calif. Press

Itzigsohn J. 2000. *Developing Poverty: The State, Labor Market Deregulation, and the Informal Economy in Costa Rica and the Dominican Republic.* University Park: Penn. State Univ. Press

Kahler M. 1990. Orthodoxy and its alternatives: explaining approaches to stabilization and adjustment. In *Economic Crisis and Policy Choice: The Politics of Adjustment in the Third World*, ed. JM Nelson, pp. 33–61. Princeton, NJ: Princeton Univ. Press

Kapur D, Lewis JP, Webb R. 1997. *The World Bank: Its First Half Century.* Washington, DC: Brookings Inst. Press

Kapur D, Webb R. 2000. *Governance-related conditionalities of the international financial institutions.* G-24 Discuss. Pap. No. 6, Aug.

Kaufmann D. 2003. *Rethinking governance: empirical lessons challenge orthodoxy.* Washington, DC: World Bank Inst. http://www.worldbank.org/wbi/governance/pubs/rethink_gov.html

Kaufmann D. 2004. *Governance redux: the empirical challenge.* Washington, DC: World Bank Inst. http://www.worldbank.org/wbi/governance/pdf/govredux.pdf

Keck ME, Sikkink K. 1998. *Activists Beyond Borders: Advocacy Networks in International Politics.* Ithaca, NY: Cornell Univ. Press

Kentor J. 2001. The long term effects of globalization on income inequality, population growth, and economic development. *Soc. Probl.* 48(4):435–55

Khagram S, Riker JV, Sikkink K, eds. 2002. *Restructuring World Politics: Transnational Social Movements, Networks, and Norms.* Minneapolis: Univ. Minn. Press

Khor M. 2002 (1999). How the South is getting a raw deal at the WTO. In *Global Backlash*, ed. R Broad, pp. 154–57. New York: Rowman & Littlefield

Kidder TG. 2002. Networks in transnational labor organizing. See Khagram et al. 2002, pp. 269–98

Kuczynski P. 1999. Privatization and the private sector. *World Dev.* 27(1):215–30

Kurtz M. 2004. The dilemmas of democracy in

the open economy: lessons from Latin America. *World Polit.* 56(2):262–302

Kyle D. 2000. *Transnational Peasants: Migrations, Networks, and Ethnicity in Andean Ecuador.* Baltimore, MD: Johns Hopkins Univ. Press

Lambert R. 2000. Globalization and the erosion of class compromise in contemporary Australia. *Polit. Soc.* 28(1):93–103

Levitt P. 2001. *The Transnational Villagers.* Berkeley: Univ. Calif. Press

Lewis-Bynoe D, Griffith J, Moore W. 2002. Trade liberalization and the manufacturing sector: the case of the small developing country. *Contemp. Econ. Policy* 20(3):272–88

Loko B, Mlachila M, Nallari R, Kalonji K. 2003. *The impact of external indebtedness on poverty in low-income countries.* IMF Work. Pap. No. 03/6

Lora E. 2001. *Structural reforms in Latin America: what has been transformed and how to measure it.* Work. Pap. No. 466, Inter-Am. Dev. Bank

Markoff J, Montecinos V. 1993. The ubiquitous rise of economists. *J. Public Policy* 13(1):37–38

Marshall TH. 1949 (1963). Citizenship and social class. In *Class, Citizenship and Social Development,* ed. TH Marshall, pp. 71–134. Garden City, NY: Doubleday

Martínez J, Santiso J. 2003. Financial markets and politics: the confidence game in Latin American emerging economies. *Int. Polit. Sci. Rev.* 24(3):363–95

Massey DS, Durand J, Malone NJ. 2002. *Beyond Smoke and Mirrors: Mexican Immigration in an Era of Economic Integration.* New York: Russell Sage Found.

Massey DS, Espinosa KE. 1997. What's driving Mexico-U.S. migration? A theoretical, empirical, and policy analysis. *Am. J. Sociol.* 102(4):939–99

Maxfield S. 1997. *Gatekeepers of Growth: The International Political Economy of Central Banking in Developing Countries.* Princeton, NJ: Princeton Univ. Press

Milanovic B. 2002. True world income distribution, 1988 and 1993: first calculations based on household surveys alone. *Econ. J.* 476:51–92

Mosley L. 2003. *Global Capital and National Governments.* New York: Cambridge Univ. Press

Mosley L, Uno S. 2004. *Racing to the bottom or climbing to the top? Foreign direct investment and labor rights violations.* http://www.nd.edu/~mmosley/mosleyunomay2004.pdf

Mosley P, Harrigan J, Toye J. 1991. *Aid and Power: The World Bank and Policy-Based Lending.* New York: Routledge

Murillo MV, Schrank A. 2005. With a little help from my friends: partisan politics, transnational alliances, and labor rights in Latin America. *Comp. Polit. Stud.* In press

Naiman R. 2000. *World Bank keeps African kids out of school.* http://www.globalexchange.org/campaigns/wbimf/072300wbimf.html

Ocampo JA. 2003. *Latin America's growth frustrations: the macro and the mesoeconomic links.* Semin. Manag. Volatility, Financ. Lib. Growth Emerg. Econ., ECLAC, Santiago, Chile, April 24–25

O'Donnell G. 1994. Delegative democracy. *J. Democr.* 5(1):54–69

O'Rourke D. 2003. Outsourcing regulation: analyzing nongovernmental systems of labor standards and monitoring. *Policy Stud. J.* 31(1):1–29

Orozco M. 2002. Globalization and migration: the impact of family remittances in Latin America. *Latin Am. Polit. Soc.* 44(2):41–69

Parrenas RS. 2001. *Servants of Globalization: Women, Migration, and Domestic Work.* Stanford, CA: Stanford Univ. Press

Portes A. 1998. *Globalization from below: the rise of Transnational Communities.* ESRC Transnatl. Comm. Work. Pap. Ser. WPTC-98-01, Princeton Univ.

Portes A, Hoffman K. 2003. Latin American class structures: their composition and change during the neoliberal era. *Latin Am. Res. Rev.* 38(1):41–82

Ramirez MD. 2001. The Mexican regulatory experience in the airline, banking and telecommunications sectors. *Q. Rev. Econ. Finance* 41(5):657–82

Ratha D. 2003. Workers' remittances: an important and stable source of external development finance. *Glob. Dev. Finance 2003.* Washington, DC: World Bank

Roberts KM. 2002. Social inequalities without class cleavages in Latin America's neoliberal era. *Stud. Comp. Int. Dev.* 36(4):3–34

Rodrik D. 1997 *Has Globalization Gone Too Far?* Washington, DC: Inst. Int. Econ.

Rodrik D. 1998. *Capital mobility and labor.* Presented at NBER Workshop Trade, Technol., Educ., U.S. Labor Mark., April 30–May 1

Rodrik D, Subramanian A. 2004. *From 'Hindu growth' to productivity surge: the mystery of the Indian growth transition.* IMF Work. Pap. No. 04/77

Rosen EI. 2002. *Making Sweatshops: The Globalization of the U.S. Apparel Industry.* Berkeley: Univ. Calif. Press

Ruggie JG. 1983. International regimes, transactions, and change: embedded liberalism in the postwar economic order. In *International Regimes*, ed. S Krasner, pp. 95–231. Ithaca, NY: Cornell Univ. Press

Sachs J. 2002. Resolving the debt crisis of low-income countries. *Brookings Pap. Econ. Act.* 1:2002. http://www.jubileeusa.org/learn_more/BPEA_Sachs.pdf

Salzinger L. 2003. *Genders in Production: Making Workers in Mexico's Global Factories.* Berkeley: Univ. Calif. Press

Sassen S. 1988. *The Mobility of Labor and Capital: A Study in International Investment and Labor Flow.* Cambridge, UK: Cambridge Univ. Press

Schaefer K. 2002. *Capacity utilization, income distribution, and the urban informal sector: an open economy model.* Polit. Econ. Res. Inst. PERI Work. Pap. No. 35, Amherst, MA

Schamis HE. 2002. *Re-Forming the State: The Politics of Privatization in Latin America and Europe.* Ann Arbor: Univ. Mich. Press

Schneider BR. 1997. The material bases of technocracy: investor confidence and neoliberalism in Latin America. In *The Politics of Expertise in Latin America*, ed. MA Centeno, P Silva, pp. 77–95. New York: St. Martin's Press

Schneider F. 2002. *Global Survey on the Size and Importance of the Informal Economy in 110 Countries Around the World.* Washington, DC: World Bank. http://rru.worldbank.org/Documents/PapersLinks/informal_economy.pdf

Schrank A. 2003. The software industry in North America: human capital, international migration, and foreign trade. In *Industrial Agglomeration: Facts and Lessons for Developing Countries*, ed. M Kagami, M Tsuji, pp. 17–32. Chiba: Inst. Dev. Econ./Japan Extern. Trade Organ.

Schrank A. 2005. Entrepreneurship, export diversification, and economic reform: the birth of a 'developmental community' in the Dominican Republic. *Comp. Polit.* In press

Sell SK, Smith S, Biersteker T, Brown C, Cerny P, et al., eds. 2003. *Private Power, Public Law: The Globalization of International Property Rights.* Cambridge, UK: Cambridge Univ. Press

Shadlen KS, Schrank A, Kurtz M. 2005. The political economy of intellectual property protection: the case of software. *Int. Stud. Q.* 49(1):45–71

Shah A. 1998. Debt and the environment. http://www.globalissues.org/TradeRelated/Debt/Environment.asp

Silva E. 1996. *The State and Capital in Chile: Business Elites, Technocrats, and Market Economics.* Boulder, CO: Westview

So AY. 1990. *Social Change and Development: Modernization, Dependency, and World-System Theories.* London, UK: Sage

Stallings B. 1992. International influence on economic policy: debt, stabilization, and structural reform. In *The Politics of Economic Adjustment: International Conflicts, and the State*, ed. S Haggard, RR Kaufman, pp. 41–88. Princeton, NJ: Princeton Univ. Press

Stiglitz JE. 2002. *Globalization and Its Discontents.* New York: Norton

Stokes SC. 2003. *Mandates and Democracy:*

Neoliberalism by Surprise in Latin America. Cambridge, UK: Cambridge Univ. Press

Tanski JM, French DW. 2001. Capital concentration and market power in Mexico's manufacturing industry: Has trade liberalization made a difference? *J. Econ. Issues* 35(3): 675

Taylor L, ed. 2001. *External Liberalization, Economic Performance, and Social Policy.* New York: Oxford Univ. Press

Tripp A. 1997. *Changing the Rules: The Politics of Liberalization and the Urban Informal Economy in Tanzania.* Berkeley: Univ. Calif. Press

UN Popul. Div. 2002. *International Migration Report 2002.* New York: United Nations

Vreeland JR. 2003. *The IMF and Economic Development.* Cambridge, UK: Cambridge Univ. Press

Wade RH. 2004a. Is globalization reducing poverty and inequality? *World Dev.* 32(4): 567–89

Wade RH. 2004b. On the causes of increasing world poverty and inequality, or why the Matthew effect prevails. *New Polit. Econ.* 9(2):163–88

Wallach L. 2000. *The WTO: Five Years of Reasons to Resist Corporate Globalization.* New York: Seven Stories Press

Weir M, Skocpol T. 1985. State structures and the possibilities for 'Keynesian' responses to the Great Depression in Sweden, Britain, and the United States. In *Bringing the State Back In*, ed. P Evans, D Rueschemeyer, T Skocpol, pp. 107–63. Cambridge, UK: Cambridge Univ. Press

Weisbrot M. 2006. *What the Experts Got Wrong About the Global Economy.* New York: Oxford Univ. Press. In press

Weisbrot M, Baker D, Kraev E, Chen J. 2001. *The scorecard on globalization, 1980–2000: twenty years of diminished progress.* Brief. Pap., Cent. Econ. Policy Res., Washington, DC. http://www.cepr.net/globalization/scorecard_on_globalization.htm

Western B. 1995. A comparative study of working class disorganization: union decline in 18 advanced capitalist countries. *Am. Sociol. Rev.* 60(2):179–202

Weyland K. 2004. Neoliberalism and democracy in Latin America: a mixed record. *Latin Am. Polit. Soc.* 46(1):135–58

Williamson J, ed. 1994. *The Political Economy of Policy Reform.* Washington, DC: Inst. Int. Econ.

World Bank. 1996. Export processing zones. *PremNotes* No. 11. Washington, DC: World Bank

World Bank. 2001. *Global Development Finance.* Washington, DC: World Bank

World Bank. 2002. *Global Economic Prospects and the Developing Countries 2002: Making Trade Work for the World's Poor.* Washington, DC: World Bank

Annu. Rev. Sociol. 2005. 31:223–43
doi: 10.1146/annurev.soc.31.041304.122232
Copyright © 2005 by Annual Reviews. All rights reserved
First published online as a Review in Advance on March 30, 2005

INEQUALITY OF OPPORTUNITY IN COMPARATIVE PERSPECTIVE: Recent Research on Educational Attainment and Social Mobility

Richard Breen[1] and Jan O. Jonsson[2]

[1] *Nuffield College, Oxford University, Oxford OX1 1NF, United Kingdom;
email: Richard.breen@nuffield.oxford.ac.uk*
[2] *Swedish Institute for Social Research (SOFI), Stockholm University, Stockholm 106 91,
Sweden; email: Janne.jonsson@sofi.su.se*

Key Words   educational inequality, comparative studies, intergenerational inheritance, social reproduction

■ **Abstract**   Studies of how characteristics of the family of origin are associated with educational and labor market outcomes indicate the degree of openness of societies and have a long tradition in sociology. We review research published since 1990 into educational stratification and social (occupational or class) mobility, focusing on the importance of parental socioeconomic circumstances, and with particular emphasis on comparative studies. Large-scale data now available from many countries and several time points have led to more and better descriptions of inequality of opportunity across countries and over time. However, partly owing to problems of comparability of measurement, unambiguous conclusions about trends and ranking of countries have proven elusive. In addition, no strong evidence exists that explains intercountry differences. We conclude that the 1990s witnessed a resurgence of microlevel models, mostly of a rational choice type, that signals an increased interest in moving beyond description in stratification research.

INTRODUCTION—DEFINING THE AREA

Research in social stratification is a very lively area within sociology, being so near the heart of the discipline itself. A common distinction within this area is between inequality of opportunity and inequality of condition. The former has its origin in the liberal goal that a person's chances to get ahead (attain an education, get a good job) should be unrelated to ascribed characteristics such as race, sex, or class (or socioeconomic) origin. The latter, inequality of condition, is concerned with the distribution of differential rewards and living conditions, either in the simple form of distributions of scarce goods or in relation to different inputs (such as effort and time) or rights (such as citizenship or employment). Of course, the distinction between inequality of opportunity and of condition is not clear cut, but it is a useful tool for organizing a review of the literature.

In the social sciences, studies of inequality of opportunity typically are about attainments of educational qualifications and social positions (occupations, social class, etc.) and how these attainments are associated with ascribed characteristics. Studies of inequality of condition, in contrast, are concerned with income differences or differential rewards in the labor market or in the larger distributional system, including the welfare state. Our aim here is to review research relating to inequality of opportunity, and we concentrate on studies that focus on the social origin of individuals (most often indicated by parental occupational status or education). The literature on inequality based on gender, family type, and race or ethnicity is voluminous, and even though theories and methods partly overlap, there are also special features of these questions that would make a serious treatment of them exceed the space at our disposal.[1] We also restrict ourselves to studies since 1990 (although we reference some older studies), mostly because there are several reviews covering earlier periods.[2] In addition, we concentrate on studies with a comparative perspective, particularly of European nations, to contrast with those of the United States.

In the empirical study of educational inequality and social mobility—or of the occupational attainment process—there are various theories and practices regarding which concepts and classifications to use. When defining social origins and "destinations" (typically meaning current or mature social position), there are at least three commonly used frameworks: prestige scales, socioeconomic indices (SEI), and social class typologies, and within these categories is a multitude of competing alternatives. All these frameworks tend to use occupational information as their backbone, along with information on employment status (to differentiate employers from the self-employed and employees) and sometimes on sector (e.g., to distinguish farming), authority, or expertise. Most empirical studies that we review use a limited number of these indicators, primarily the class schemas devised by Erikson & Goldthorpe (1992) or Wright (1997), SEI (reviewed by Hauser & Warren 1997), or occupational prestige scales (e.g., Ganzeboom et al. 1992). Although many social mobility studies have come to apply a class perspective (using categorical data analysis), studies of the attainment process often use SEI or prestige scales, implying linear modeling such as path analysis or LISREL

---

[1] We acknowledge that there are other indicators of inequality of opportunity that we are not able to cover. One of the most important is the degree of homogamy in marriage, where the argument is that inequality prevails to the extent that spouses are homogamous in attributes such as social origin, education, or ethnicity (e.g., Blossfeld & Timm 2003, Smits et al. 1998 for comparative studies).

[2] For reviews, see Burton & Grusky (1992), Ganzeboom et al. (1991), Kerckhoff (1995), and Kurz & Müller (1987). Although not a proper review, Erikson & Goldthorpe (1992, chapters 1–2) provide critical comments on previous studies. There are many summaries of status attainment research, e.g., Bielby (1981) and, more recently, the 1992 symposium on Blau & Duncan's *American Occupational Structure* (1967) in *Contemporary Sociology* (Vol. 21, No. 5), where further references can be found.

models. For the purposes of this review—to cover the literature on inequality of opportunity—we are rather agnostic about how to understand and measure social origin and destination; we also feel that most of the tools in use are sufficiently well devised to cover the main stories about the degree of inequality, the change over time, and the differences between countries. (The debate of how best to conceive of the social structure is an industry in itself: Good, critical reviews and constructive suggestions are given in, e.g., Erikson & Goldthorpe 1992, Grusky & Sorensen 1998, Sorensen 2000, and Wright 1997.)

We focus mainly on two areas: (*a*) the link between social origins and educational attainment, and (*b*) the overall association between social origins and occupational destinations. We concentrate on empirical findings that document the extent of inequality of opportunity and how it changes over time and differs between countries, as well as on theories that seek to provide explanations of such results. We limit ourselves to studies that are published or accepted for publication.

INEQUALITY OF EDUCATIONAL ATTAINMENT

Educational Inequality: Change Over Time and Differences Between Countries

By the beginning of the 1990s, researchers agreed that the modeling of inequality of educational attainment could not be confined to the traditional linear regression of years of education on social origin. Although a legitimate enterprise, these studies tend to conflate changes in the marginal distributions (e.g., educational expansion) with changes in the underlying association between origin and educational attainment, normally conceptualized as the best measure of inequality of opportunity; furthermore, they did not conceive of the educational career as actors did, namely as a series of transitions between levels. Therefore, researchers came to prefer logit models of transition propensities at successive levels of the educational system, revealing the "pure" association between origin characteristics and educational attainment.[3] This prompted a large-scale comparative project of empirical analyses directed by Shavit & Blossfeld, and brought together in the book *Persistent Inequality* (1993). It included studies of 13 industrial countries (6 Western European, 3 Eastern European, and 4 non-European, including the United States) by experts in the stratification and school systems of the particular country. Most contributors used similar background variables (fathers' occupation/class, fathers' education) and outcomes (years of education; transitions from primary to lower secondary, from lower to higher secondary, and from there onto degree level), and they used identical methods (OLS-regressions of years of education, binomial logit models for transitions). The country chapters assessed

---

[3]The educational transition model was used by Boalt (1947), shown to be pertinent for microlevel theory by Boudon (1974), and found its statistical rigor and popular form in the influential work of Mare (1981).

change in educational inequality via synthetic cohorts from cross-sectional surveys, a method that is not unproblematic but that is widely assumed to give a fair representation of changes over time. The project design was a huge step toward standardization in research, although several inconsistencies still remained (mostly because of problems of data comparability).

The study addressed several macro-oriented hypotheses. According to the modernization hypothesis, one would expect origin effects to decrease generally, whereas the reproduction hypothesis states that inequalities may decrease at lower transitions because of educational expansion, but that this would be compensated for by increasing effects on later transitions. The socialist transformation hypothesis assumes that there would be an initial reduction in origin effects that would be followed by increased effects as new elites pursued their interests. The most important conclusion from the study was the lack of support for any of these hypotheses, mainly because the prevailing pattern was stability in origin effects on educational transitions. According to the analyses, in only two countries—the Netherlands and Sweden—did equalization occur. However, this conclusion has been contested. Subsequent analyses have clearly shown equalization in the case of Germany (Henz & Maas 1995, Jonsson et al. 1996, Müller & Haun 1994), France (Vallet 2004), Italy (Shavit & Westerbeek 1998), and probably Norway (Lindbekk 1998), while the results for Sweden (Jonsson & Erikson 2000) and the Netherlands (Sieben et al. 2001) have been corroborated. Equalization typically has occurred at lower transition points.

Although it is likely that many countries share in a trend toward a decreasing association between social origin and educational attainment, there are some exceptions. For Ireland, Breen & Whelan (1993) and Whelan & Layte (2002) find constancy in the association, and the same seems to prevail in the United States (Hout et al. 1993, Hout & Dohan 1996, Mare 1993). Gerber & Hout (1995) find a mixed pattern for Soviet Russia, with the origin-education association declining at secondary education but strengthening in access to university. In a later paper, Gerber (2000) finds that in post-Soviet Russia the association has, if anything, increased.

Despite all the virtues of the Shavit and Blossfeld project, differences in classifications of social origin in national data sets prohibited the assessment of country differences in the degree of inequality of opportunity. Although it was possible to relate changes in educational inequality in a specific country to national macroevents (such as educational reform), it was not possible to use the multination approach for addressing the question of between-country variation in the importance of macrovariables for international differences in inequality of educational opportunity. Two other comparative studies sought to remedy this.

First, Müller & Karle (1993) fitted log-linear models to CASMIN (Comparative Analysis of Social Mobility in Industrial Nations) data from nine European countries coded into comparable measures of class origin and educational qualifications. They found that the origin-education association showed national-specific patterns (although these are not easily summarized). The relative position of the unskilled working class was most advantageous in France, Poland, and Sweden and least so in West Germany, Ireland, and Northern Ireland. All in all, West Germany and probably the two Irelands appear to occupy a position close to the "rigid" pole, whereas Poland and probably Hungary and Sweden appear to belong at the other end. Second, Jonsson et al. (1996), using more recent data, found that the associations between class origin and educational attainment declined across cohorts in Sweden and Germany but not in England, and that inequality was clearly greatest in Germany, with Sweden being somewhat more equal than England. Because the former study used data mainly collected in the 1970s and the latter only compared three nations, there is only scattered knowledge about how different contemporary countries "rank" in terms of inequality of educational attainment (but compare footnote 9).[4]

Micro-Level and Institutional Explanations of Educational Inequality

Much research shows that characteristics of the family of origin (such as parental socioeconomic status and education, cultural assets, social networks, and parental motivation) are associated with educational outcomes (e.g., de Graaf et al. 2000, Duncan & Brooks-Gunn 1997, Gamoran 2001). These resource differences have their effects both via socialization and educational choice, and one of the most significant trends in the study of inequalities in educational attainment in the past decade has been the resurgence of rational choice models focusing on educational decision making (Breen & Goldthorpe 1997; Erikson & Jonsson 1996a; Esser 1999; Morgan 1998, 2002; for earlier work of this kind, see Boudon 1974 and Gambetta 1987). In these models the choices pupils and their parents make are determined by expected benefits, costs, and probability of success for different educational alternatives. One difference between rational choice models and the standard model of educational decision making employed by economists (for example, Cameron & Heckman 1998) is that the former allow for uncertainty among students about their likelihood of succeeding at a given educational level, which introduces what might otherwise seem (to an economist) like myopia into the decision making process. A number of papers (Becker 2003, Davies et al. 2002, Need & de Jong 2001) test the model presented by Breen & Goldthorpe (1997), and their results are broadly supportive of it. Hillmert & Jacob (2003) develop and test a closely related rational choice model to explain social inequality in access to higher education in Germany.

In individual-level models of educational choice, institutional factors may affect the parameters of the model so that, for example, the perceived costs of an

---

[4]Note that the educational choices that parents make for their children are shaped by the school-to-work link. Because this link is especially strong in countries with an apprenticeship system (Shavit & Müller 1998), such as Germany, working-class parents in these countries may be primarily concerned that their children get a favorable apprenticeship placement and therefore may be less willing to risk enrolling them in higher education.

education or the probabilities of succeeding at university differ according to the organization of schooling. Erikson & Jonsson (1996b) argue that the family of origin plays a crucial role in shaping an individual's school performance and educational aspirations, and these relationships are likely to be fairly invariant over time and space. Rather, the main sources of change over time and differences between countries are variations in the costs, to the student, of secondary and higher education, and variations in the ages at which crucial educational decisions are taken (because the perceived probability of success is more strongly associated with social origin at early, rather than later, transition points). The fact that social origin is more strongly associated with educational attainment at younger ages (e.g., Breen & Jonsson 2000, Mare 1993, Shavit & Blossfeld 1993) implies that comprehensive school reform in which the earliest decision point is postponed reduces inequality of educational opportunity. There is support for this hypothesis from Sweden (Erikson 1996) and Scotland (McPherson & Willms 1987), while in Germany early selection in education is reflected in substantial inequality of attainment. More thorough tests would, however, need to draw on evidence from more countries. Another related institutional factor of potential importance is the type and extent of ability grouping or tracking: Some studies give support, though not unequivocal, for the hypothesis that the early division of pupils into different ability-related streams amplifies inequality (Gamoran 2004, Kerckhoff 1993). There has been a long discussion in the United States of the role of school resources. The most compelling result is that smaller class sizes favor disadvantaged students (Krueger 1999).[5]

The topic of contextual effects on educational attainment attracted growing attention during the 1990s. One important context is the school: Studies not only focus on characteristics of schools such as efficacy in instruction and resource differences, but also examine endogenous social interaction effects that influence school climate, norms, and educational aspirations (see reviews by Mortimer 1997, Sampson et al. 2002, Small & Newman 2001). Studies support the view that there are additional effects of social context on educational attainment, beyond the school, such as growing up in a poor neighborhood, thus boosting the influence of social origin (Erikson 1994, Garner & Raudenbush 1991, contributions to Brooks-Gunn et al. 1997, Mayer 2002). Studies of contextual effects are plagued with problems of endogeneity, or population sorting: Much of what looks like effects of an individual environment may be due to a selection of people with certain

---

[5]Related issues (that we do not cover here) are those of selective schools, "efficient" schools, and school quality defined according to the composition of the student body (see below on contextual effects). Because students from different social backgrounds have different opportunities of attaining high-quality schools (however defined) and because such schools provide superior chances in the labor market, heterogeneity in school quality contributes to educational inequality. Morgan (2001) gives references and presents a critical view and additional analysis on the longstanding issue of Catholic schools. For an interesting, recent study of selective schools, see Dale & Krueger (2002).

characteristics into certain neighborhoods and schools (e.g., Manski 2000). For example, this would be the case if parents who are very motivated and best able to support their children's schooling also actively choose neighborhoods and schools where the socioeconomic context is more privileged. However, even studies that have attempted to solve the endogeneity problem have concluded that the socioeconomic environment has an impact on children's educational success (Erikson 1994, Hanushek et al. 2003, Harding 2003).[6] But environmental effects are probably of a rather modest magnitude: Between 80% and 90% of the variation in school achievement, for example, appears to be between families within schools or neighborhoods (Entwisle et al. 1997, Erikson 1994, Garner & Raudenbush 1991, Mortimer 1997; compare also Solon et al. (2000) for an equally low estimate comparing neighborhood and sibling resemblance in earnings).

SOCIAL MOBILITY

Social Fluidity in Comparative and Temporal Perspective

The traditional measure of a society's openness is the degree to which the attainment of social position is associated with social origin. For a long time, one crucial issue in mobility research was the need to separate structural effects on mobility—which are forced by changes in the social structure (as when a rapid decline of farmers leads to increased mobility out of that class)—from a more "pure" or "exchange" form of mobility. During the 1980s, the dominating research tradition turned to log-linear analysis to solve this issue, benefiting from work by Goodman (e.g., 1979) and Hauser (1978). The study of social mobility now usually distinguishes between the analysis of absolute rates of mobility as a description of flows between social origins and destinations and the analysis of relative rates (in the form of odds ratios), unraveling the net association between the two. This association, often termed social fluidity, was conceptualized as a measure of inequality of opportunity, in much the same way as the logit model of educational transitions. This interpretation is not unproblematic, given the difficulty of inferring inequality of opportunity from data on inequality of outcomes.

The methodological redirection (from OLS regression, path analysis, and the analysis of various mobility indices) allowed analysis of the social structure in

---

[6]The strategies differ between these studies. Erikson (1994) studied the effect of socioeconomic composition in schools in areas with only one school; Hanushek et al. (2003) applied a number of fixed effects (individual, school, school-by-grade, etc.) and, in practice, compared achievement change of those who had either changed environment by moving or who had had the environment changed by changing peer composition, with "stable" pupils; and Harding (2003) used propensity score matching with sensitivity controls. Although all these methods have their problems, the conclusion that there are environmental effects, even if limited in scope, is likely robust. There are also studies using instrumental variables (such as Duncan et al. 1997), but the difficulty of finding instruments is striking.

class terms, i.e., without imposing a unidimensional hierarchical form. The main proponents of this redirection were Erikson & Goldthorpe who, in their major work *The Constant Flux* (1992), sought to portray both the absolute and relative rates of mobility using data, mainly from the late 1960s and early to mid-1970s, from 12 European countries and the United States, Australia, and Japan. They used cross-sectional data (that is, one mobility table per country), but they set new standards in comparative analysis by the rigorous recoding of occupational information in nationally representative data sets into the so-called EGP (Erikson, Goldthorpe, Portocarero) class schema, and by applying advanced and partly new log-linear modeling techniques. Their strategy was first to define a core model of fluidity, including different dimensions of the reproduction process (of which hierarchy, inheritance, and sector were the most important), as laid out in the mobility table of father's class by son's class. All nations were then compared with the core model, and their deviations from it were interpreted by what might be called historically informed macrosociology, and were also tested in a macromodel in a concluding analysis (which, however, the authors did not much emphasize).

As much as the analyses were elegant and innovative, the results and conclusions were surprising and controversial. Rejecting the liberal hypothesis of a common increase in social fluidity driven by industrialization, Erikson & Goldthorpe (1992) concluded that there were small differences between nations in their pattern and degree of fluidity—deviations that were better explained in terms of national peculiarities than in macrosociological regularities such as industrialization or modernization, and there was no or very little change in fluidity across birth cohorts. Their interpretation was that the unequal distribution of resources and power so permeates the social structure as to lead to a general and unchanging level of inequality of opportunity.

The widespread adoption of the EGP class schema greatly facilitated the most recent large-scale comparative mobility project, the results of which were published as *Social Mobility in Europe* (Breen 2004). Taking *The Constant Flux* as its starting point, the aim of this project was to look at temporal change between 1970 and 2000 and cross-national variation among 11 European countries. The book contains chapters on each of these countries, and there is a further empirical chapter, with an explicitly comparative aim, in which all the data sets were put together to allow formal analyses of differences between countries and changes through time. The data used in the project comprised 117 mobility surveys covering the period 1970 to 2000 (the number of tables per country ranging from 2 to 35). In contrast to Erikson & Goldthorpe (1992), whose temporal comparisons were based on the use of age groups taken from a single survey per country, the contributors to *Social Mobility in Europe* were able to make period comparisons using several surveys from each country.

The main findings of this research, which held true for both sexes, were at odds with those of *The Constant Flux*. First, absolute mobility flows had become more similar among countries so that, by the 1990s, variations in class structures and in rates of overall upward and downward mobility were far less than in the 1970s.

Thus, Lipset & Zetterberg's (1959, p. 13) assertion that "the overall pattern of social mobility appears to be much the same in the industrial societies of various western countries," although strictly wrong, was considerably closer to the truth by the end of the twentieth century than hitherto. Second, the authors claim to have found a general tendency, with one or two exceptions, such as Britain, toward increasing social fluidity. Earlier, Hout (1988) had found increasing social fluidity in the United States between 1972 and 1988. Third, Breen & Luijkx (2004b) report considerable cross-national variation in levels of social fluidity. What is the magnitude of these differences between countries? According to Erikson & Goldthorpe's (1992, p. 381) results, given a common pattern of local odds ratios in all the countries in their sample, an odds ratio that took the value of 3 in Czechoslovakia (the most open of their countries) would be equal to 5.3 in Scotland (the least open). Breen & Luijkx's results (2004b, p. 386) similarly show that an odds ratio of 3 in Israel would be an odds ratio of 7 in Germany. They also report that, in the case of the Netherlands, an odds ratio of 4 in the 1970s would have declined to 2.7 by the 1990s.

One striking development in recent research on social mobility is the use of high-quality data from countries outside Western Europe and North America. Japan and Australia have a fairly long history of collecting mobility data, and in a comparison of the two between 1965 and 1985, Jones et al. (1994) found a slight increase in fluidity in Australia but not in Japan (the latter result was also found by Ishida et al. 1991, Ishida 1993). Similarly, Hungary and Poland have long figured in comparative mobility research (e.g., Mach & Peschar 1990, Simkus et al. 1990), but Marshall and his coauthors extended the study of social mobility to state socialist societies in Eastern and Central Europe (Marshall et al. 1995, Marshall et al. 1997). Unfortunately, the samples were rather small, and so statistical tests had little chance of detecting cross-national variations in social fluidity. Social mobility in the former Soviet Union has been studied by Titma et al. (2003) and Gerber & Hout (2004), who find a decline in fluidity in postcommunist Russia [a result also reported by Robert & Bukodi (2004) for Hungary]. There have also been several studies of social mobility in Asian countries, including China (Cheng & Dai 1995, see also the review by Bian 2002), Taiwan and Korea (Park 2004, Phang & Lee 1996), and Hong Kong (Chan et al. 1995). These studies show both similarities and differences in social mobility compared with other industrialized countries, but no robust results concerning change.

Which Are the Most Rigid and the Most Open Countries?

A fundamental question for understanding macrolevel variation in inequality of opportunity, or societal openness, is which countries should be classified as most open and which most rigid. Many scholars have assumed that persistent egalitarian policies should make for greater openness, for example, but, equally, scholars have long thought that the United States is an exceptional case, showing less rigidity than European countries.

A ranking of countries according to degree of openness must be approached cautiously because of data incomparability, conceptual problems, and measurement error. Furthermore, to the extent that countries differ in their patterns of fluidity, ranking them in any unidimensional way is unrealistic. Nevertheless, some characteristics appear to stand out in the reviewed literature. According to Breen & Luijkx (2004a,b), Germany, France, and Italy tend to represent the rigid pole in such a ranking.[7] The Scandinavian countries (particularly Sweden and Norway) together with Hungary and Poland appear to be consistently among the most open countries, as does Israel, whereas the Netherlands has become considerably more open over the past quarter century. England, on the other hand, has, over the same period, gone from being among one of the more open to one of the less open countries because, as noted above, it does not seem to have shared in the widespread trend toward greater fluidity.

An interesting issue is the ranking of the United States. In an attempt to make a comparison with European societies, Erikson & Goldthorpe (1992) concluded that the United States is fairly similar to them; the somewhat higher degree of fluidity they found was attributed to problems of comparability, stemming from lack of precision in the American occupational codings.[8] In a direct comparison between educational inequality in the United States and Sweden (one of the most equal countries in the existing literature), Hout & Dohan (1996) found the two to be very similar.

It is interesting to contrast these results with those found when inequality of opportunity is measured in terms of income. Studies of father-to-son (and sometimes -daughter) income mobility as well as sibling correlations of income[9] show the

---

[7]Germany's position as one of the least fluid societies had been established by earlier research (Erikson & Goldtorpe 1992, chapter 5). Previous analyses have found low rates of mobility (Checchi et al. 1999) and fluidity (Pisati & Schizzerotto 1999) in Italy.

[8]In another study, Erikson & Goldthorpe (1985) tested this by coding the English data with the same degree of uncertainty. The result was that England and the United States showed very similar social fluidity.

[9]Sibling correlations are a measure of the amount of variation in income that is explained by characteristics that siblings share, such as genetic endowments, parental resources, neighborhood characteristics, and, often, school factors. About one half of the sibling correlation is estimated to be due to genetic factors (Björklund et al. 2005), and only a small portion is likely to be due to neighborhood effects (Solon et al. 2000). Sibling correlations have frequently been used in sociology to study the "true" or "maximum" impact of the family of origin on education or social position (e.g., Hauser & Mossel 1985, Jencks 1979). Sieben et al. (2001) report that sibling correlations in educational attainment for East Germany are about 0.3–0.4, whereas in West Germany and the Netherlands they range between 0.40 and 0.55; this level of correlation is also reported for Scotland (lower bound) and England (upper bound), but as high as 0.7 in Spain (Sieben & de Graaf 2001, 2003). Corresponding correlations for the United States were 0.62–0.70 (corrected for measurement error) for brothers in 1973 (Hauser & Featherman 1976). Differences in samples make it difficult to draw conclusions from these estimates, however.

United States to be noticeably more rigid than the countries with which it has been compared (mostly the Nordic countries). In the United States and England, father-to-son elasticities are about 0.45; they are between 0.13 and 0.28 in Sweden and Finland, and 0.34 in Germany (Solon 2002). Brothers' correlations are about 0.4 in the United States, about 0.25 in Sweden, Denmark, and Finland, and even lower in Norway (Björklund et al. 2002).[10] These results point in a different direction to those concerning educational attainment and social fluidity. The most obvious reason for this is that the correlation between education and/or occupation and income is higher in the United States than in the more equal European countries (disregarding England), so even if Americans live in a fairly open society, the prevailing inequalities are more "costly" for a disadvantaged American and more profitable for someone privileged. (The examples are not just randomly chosen: In Björklund et al. (2002), the high degree of American inequality more or less disappears if the analysis excludes blacks or those with earnings in the top and bottom 5%.)

How Can We Explain Change and Inter-Country Differences in Social Fluidity?

What causes variation in social fluidity? This is an important macrosociological question. Sieben & de Graaf (2001), analyzing brothers' correlations from six countries, find mixed support for the hypotheses that more socialist seats in parliament and modernization are associated with more equality of opportunity. Erikson & Goldthorpe (1992) claim that more equal societies are more fluid, whereas Breen & Luijkx (2004b) could not find any general support for this hypothesis. They observe, however, that social fluidity is relatively high in the formerly state socialist countries of Hungary and Poland and in social-democratic Sweden and Norway (see Western & Wright 1994); but although this suggests that redistributive policies may be one way a society can reach a high level of social fluidity, the fact that fluidity is also high in Israel and the Netherlands, for example, indicates that it may not be the only way.

Several analyses have pointed to the importance of the educational system as the driving force behind changes in social fluidity and differences between countries. Indeed, research in the status attainment tradition often finds that in most countries education largely mediates the association between origins and destination (e.g., Treiman & Yip 1989, Warren et al. 2002), whereas class mobility studies most often find stronger remaining "origin effects" in models incorporating educational attainment (Ishida et al. 1995).[11] However, in their study of class mobility, Breen

---

[10]One should note that sibling correlations are not an unproblematic measure. Apart from the fact that they amalgamate all kinds of effects, they also mix effects of parents with those of siblings and peers; and singletons are not included, of course, which may be a problem if the percentage of children without siblings differs between countries and if the origin effects are different for them.

[11]An essential part of this difference is no doubt due to the greater weight put on inheritance effects among the self-employed in class mobility research.

& Luijkx (2004b) argue that the path from origins to destinations via education is mediating an increasing share of the total origin-destination association in several European countries.[12] The importance of this pathway differs, however; it is strongest in Sweden (which might, therefore, be classed as the most meritocratic of the countries they analyze). Although the position of Sweden is consistent with the view that educational inequality is relatively weak there (Erikson & Jonsson 1996a), this is but one of two ways education might influence social fluidity rates. The other is compositional: If there is an association between origins, education, and destinations such that the origin-destination association is weaker at higher levels of education, and if the share of the population with higher levels of education expands, then this compositional change can be expected to lead to an overall reduction in the gross association between origins and destinations. This three-way interaction may be present when, for example, the job markets in which degree-holders operate are particularly meritocratic. Hout (1988) attributes the increase in fluidity in the United States to this effect, as does Vallet (2004) for France. Equalization and compositional effects may occur together because equalization almost certainly implies educational expansion. But as more people attain higher levels of education, the origin-destination association at these higher levels might strengthen (as shown by Vallet 2004), thus offsetting the compositional effect.

Whereas differences in societal characteristics such as modernization, inequality of condition, or the school system are often discussed as causes of international differences in social fluidity, variations in family structure are not. Nonetheless, Biblarz et al. (1997) find that, for the United States, "the farther alternative family structures take children away from their mothers, the more the intergenerational transmission process [between fathers and sons] breaks down. The result is less intergenerational inheritance and resemblance" (p. 1333, text in brackets added). This suggests that international variation in the share of different family types may play some part in explaining differences in social fluidity. Other structural factors may also be important, such as differences in the proportion of immigrants or ethnic minorities. This may affect overall fluidity insofar as advantages attached to social origin are not so easily transmitted for those who move to another country, leading to weaker inheritance effects (Heath & McMahon 1997, Hout & Rosen 2000).

METHODS AND DATA

Research on inequality of opportunity, particularly social mobility research, has always been notoriously technical, although since 1990 it has largely tended to rely on techniques (especially log-linear and log-multiplicative models) developed in

---

[12]The reason for this is not, as is often assumed, that there is a general "tightening bond" between educational qualifications and social position. Empirical studies on Sweden (Jonsson 1996), the United States (Hauser et al. 2000), Britain (Breen & Goldthorpe 2001), Ireland (Whelan & Layte 2002), Russia (Gerber 2003), and France (Vallet 2004) show more or less stable or even decreasing associations.

the 1970s. New technical developments have been extensions of these techniques, and probably the most important was the "unidiff" or "log-multiplicative layer effect model" (Erikson & Goldthorpe 1992, Xie 1992). It has been widely used in recent mobility research because it allows very parsimonious tests of differences in social fluidity across tables. Extensions of this model have been proposed by Goodman & Hout (1998). Other technical developments include the continued recasting, following Logan (1983), of log-linear models as logit models for individual level data (Breen 1994; for an application see Western 1999), and Logan's work (e.g., 1996, 1998) on his "two sided logit model." Researchers have also proposed models that allow the simultaneous modeling of the marginal and joint distributions of the mobility table (Becker 1994, Lang & Agresti 1994, Lang & Eliason 1997, Sobel et al. 1998). Latent class models of mobility have not proved popular, although Breen & Jonsson (1997) use latent class methods to correct for unreliability in reports of social class. There is a long and ongoing tradition of addressing issues of error in continuous measures used in stratification through structural equation modeling with latent variables (Allison & Hauser 1991).

The Mare (1981) model of educational transitions continues to be the main method of studying the origins-education relationship, although it has been extended by Breen & Jonsson (2000) and Lucas (2001), the latter also rebutting some of the criticisms of the identification of the model made by Cameron & Heckman (1998). Particularly in studies of educational attainment, multilevel models are now widely used. Statistical methods for overcoming the problem of unobserved heterogeneity and making causal interpretation more plausible have been improved during the 1990s, but they are not regularly used within stratification research (see the review by Winship & Morgan 1999). No doubt such methods, in addition to improved data collection (including experimental designs), will be important in future studies of inequality of opportunity.

Our knowledge about the world is never better than the data on which it is based. The 1990s witnessed improvements in access to reliable data, many of which are summarized in the comparative volumes cited above (e.g., Breen 2004). Progress has been made in several areas. There are more data and, unlike earlier studies that were often confined to men, more recent data include women. There are also more data points and better quality data, including coding that enables comparative study.[13] In some countries, large-scale data, either from a long series of surveys or via registers or microcensuses, allow the precise estimation of effects in stratification processes (e.g., Erikson & Jonsson 1998). Longitudinal studies in social stratification increase in value as they follow individuals over a long historical time (e.g., Sewell et al. 2004). Finally, there are data collected

---

[13]Many mobility tables have been collected by Ganzeboom and Treiman, who also provide algorithms for coding occupations into different structural variables (e.g., classes, prestige scales). See Ganzeboom's homepage (http://home.scw.vu.nl/~ganzeboom/index.htm) and Ganzeboom & Treiman (1996).

explicitly for comparative purposes, so that measurement and wording in survey questions are designed to be comparable. However, those comparative surveys that are fielded in a large number of countries (such as ISSP and ESS) tend to have sample sizes that are too small to provide adequate statistical power. There is a potential for students of social stratification to increase their use of existing comparative data sets collected for studies of literacy and educational achievement, such as TIMSS.

DEVELOPMENTS AND CHALLENGES

Developments since 1990 in the study of inequality of opportunity have been characterized by a cumulative growth of knowledge alongside persisting disagreements. Among the most robust findings of stratification research are that origin effects are stronger at earlier than later educational transitions; that education mediates a substantial part of the association between origins and destinations; that women display more social fluidity than men; and that the pattern of social fluidity is overwhelmingly shaped by inheritance, hierarchy, and sector effects (distinguishing, in particular, farm from nonfarm sectors), although the relative importance of each of these has been debated (see the December 1992 issue of the *European Sociological Review*). But there have been conflicting findings concerning the degree of cross-national variation and change in both the origin-education and the origin-destination relationships. In the former, the conclusion of almost no change reached in the Shavit & Blossfeld (1993) study has been contradicted by later analyses, while Breen's edited collection disagrees with Erikson & Goldthorpe's (1992) picture of approximate cross-national constancy in social fluidity. How might these be reconciled? First, studies that find no differences have often been based on smaller samples in which it is difficult to reject the null hypothesis. Second, more recent studies have made use of more powerful tests of change, especially the unidiff model. Third, in some cases the data refer to different time periods: That used in Breen (2004) comes from the last three decades of the twentieth century, whereas Erikson & Goldthorpe's data mainly come from around 1970.

Research on inequality of opportunity has been overwhelmingly oriented toward empirical description, with the consequence that convincing explanations of, for example, cross-national variation in the origin-education or origin-destination associations are lacking. A first step toward explanation is to use our existing knowledge to produce an exhaustive list of the set of family resources and institutional factors that impinge on the opportunities of children, and to measure their relative importance in particular societies. A further step is to develop models of the mechanisms through which these associations are generated. Today, many would agree that any theory accounting for social fluidity patterns should be built up from a model of rational actors operating within an institutional framework. There are several theoretical papers that approximate this ideal, to a greater or lesser extent

(Breen 1997, Goldthorpe 2000, Goux & Maurin 1997, Pisati 1997).[14] Such models offer the possibility of deriving testable micromodels of individual behavior, whose parameters might differ according to institutional or other characteristics of different societies, characteristics that ideally should also include the hiring process, given the centrality of employers' actions to allocation decisions.

The development of explanations might be helped by better research design and analytical strategies. For example, few studies of social mobility compare the experiences of different birth cohorts; yet, there are grounds for supposing that, in the normal course of events, change in fluidity is driven less by period change than by cohort replacement (which is reflected in the importance of educational attainment in the social reproduction process). If this is the case, the fluidity that we observe in period data will be a complex combination of historical processes and thus may prove resistant to explanation. A series of repeated cross-sectional data points will increase the opportunities for disentangling period and cohort effects.

The collaborative projects that we have reviewed have been based on increasingly comparable data, which has allowed them to move from visual examination of the results of similar analyses across countries (Shavit & Blossfeld 1993), to meta-analyses (Shavit & Müller 1998), and to direct modeling of individual-level data from different countries (Breen 2004). However, all these projects have used secondary data. The ideal and natural next step is for a group of researchers from different countries to design a comparative project in which data collection and measurement are standardized across nations.

Researchers widely accept that variations in observed mobility flows owe much more to differences (between countries or time points) in the marginal distributions of origins and destinations than to differences in social fluidity (Breen & Luijkx 2004b, p. 384; Erikson & Goldthorpe 1992, pp. 213–14; Grusky & Hauser 1984, p. 29). The emphasis that has been placed on studying fluidity might thus seem excessive, although if our interest is in inequality of opportunity, fluidity is, in fact, the proper thing on which to focus. This is because fluidity is an inherently comparative measure, assessing the advantages of different groups relative to one another. Nevertheless, it would be useful if researchers, when discussing variations in fluidity, calibrated the impact of such variation on observed mobility flows, given particular origin and destination distributions. We would not be surprised to find that apparently large differences in fluidity entailed rather little difference in observed mobility. Furthermore, the use of log-linear models, under which patterns of association are unaffected by scalar transformations of the margins, may have led mobility researchers to underestimate the degree to which structural change can affect inequality of opportunity in the real world.

---

[14]In addition, many economists have sought to explain the relationship between advantage and disadvantage in successive generations, although their work has often been entirely theoretical with no empirical content (Banerjee & Newman 1991, Galor & Zeira 1993) and is usually oriented toward explaining income or earnings (notably Becker & Tomes 1979, Solon 2004; see also the review by Grawe & Mulligan 2002).

ACKNOWLEDGMENTS

We are grateful for comments on a previous draft by Erik Bihagen, Anders Björklund, Robert Erikson, John Goldthorpe, Peter Hedström, Yossi Shavit, Michael Tåhlin, Louis-André Vallet, Chris Whelan, Doug Massey, and an anonymous reviewer. Jonsson acknowledges financial support from the Swedish Council for Working Life and Social Research (FAS D2001-2893).

The *Annual Review of Sociology* is online at http://soc.annualreviews.org

LITERATURE CITED

Allison PD, Hauser RM. 1991. Reducing bias in estimates of linear models by remeasurement of a random subsample. *Sociol. Methods Res.* 19:466–92

Banerjee AV, Newman AF. 1991. Risk-bearing and the theory of income distribution. *Rev. Econ. Stud.* 58:211–35

Becker GS, Tomes N. 1979. An equilibrium theory of the distribution of income and intergenerational mobility. *J. Polit. Econ.* 87:1153–89

Becker MP. 1994. Analysis of cross-classifications of counts using models for marginal distributions: an application to trends in attitudes on legalized abortion. *Sociol. Methodol.* 24:229–65

Becker R. 2003. Educational expansion and persistent inequalities in Germany. *Eur. Sociol. Rev.* 19:1–24

Bian Y. 2002. Chinese social stratification and social mobility. *Annu. Rev. Sociol.* 28:91–116

Biblarz TJ, Raftery AE, Bucur A. 1997. Family structure and social mobility. *Soc. Forces* 75:1319–41

Bielby WT. 1981. Models of status attainment. *Res. Soc. Strat. Mobil.* 1:3–26

Björklund A, Eriksson T, Jäntti M, Raaum O, Österbacka E. 2002. Brother correlations in earnings in Denmark, Finland, Norway and Sweden compared to the United States. *J. Popul. Econ.* 15:757–72

Björklund A, Jäntti M, Solon G. 2005. Influences of nature and nurture on earnings variation: preliminary results from a study of various sibling types in Sweden. In *Unequal Chances: Family Background and Economic Success*, ed. S Bowles, H Gintis, M Osborne Groves. New York: Russell Sage

Blau PM, Duncan OD. 1967. *The American Occupational Structure.* New York: Wiley

Blossfeld HP, Timm A, eds. 2003. *Who Marries Whom? Educational Systems as Marriage Markets in Modern Societies.* Dordrecht, The Neth.: Kluwer

Boalt G. 1947. *Skolutbildning och skolresultat för barn ur olika samhällsgrupper i Stockholm.* (Educational attainment and school performance of children of different social backgrounds in Stockholm.) Stockholm: P.A. Norstedt & Söner

Boudon R. 1974. *Education, Opportunity & Social Inequality.* New York: Wiley

Breen R. 1994. Individual level models for mobility tables and other cross-classifications. *Sociol. Methods Res.* 23:147–73

Breen R. 1997. Inequality, economic growth and social mobility. *Brit. J. Sociol.* 48:429–49

Breen R, ed. 2004. *Social Mobility in Europe.* Oxford: Oxford Univ. Press

Breen R, Goldthorpe JH. 1997. Explaining educational differentials: towards a formal rational action theory. *Ration. Soc.* 9:275–305

Breen R, Goldthorpe JH. 2001. Class, mobility and merit: the experience of two British birth cohorts. *Eur. Sociol. Rev.* 17:81–101

Breen R, Jonsson JO. 1997. How reliable are studies of social mobility? An investigation into the consequences of unreliability in measures of social class. *Res. Soc. Strat. Mobil.* 15:91–112

Breen R, Jonsson JO. 2000. Analyzing educational careers: a multinomial transition model. *Am. Sociol. Rev.* 65:754–72

Breen R, Luijkx R. 2004a. Social mobility in Europe between 1970 and 2000. See Breen 2004, pp. 37–75

Breen R, Luijkx R. 2004b. Conclusions. See Breen 2004, pp. 383–410

Breen R, Whelan CT. 1993. From ascription to achievement? Origins, education and entry to the labour force in the Republic of Ireland during the twentieth century. *Acta Sociol.* 36:3–18

Brooks-Gunn J, Duncan GJ, Aber JL, eds. 1997. *Neighborhood Poverty.* Volume 1. *Context and Consequences for Children.* New York: Russell Sage

Burton MD, Grusky DB. 1992. A quantitative history of comparative stratification research. *Contemp. Sociol.* 21:623–31

Cameron SV, Heckman JJ. 1998. Life cycle schooling and dynamic selection bias: models and evidence for five cohorts of American males. *J. Polit. Econ.* 106:262–333

Chan TW, Lui TL, Wong TWP. 1995. A comparative analysis of social mobility in Hong Kong. *Eur. Sociol. Rev.* 11:135–55

Checchi D, Ichino A, Rustichini A. 1999. More equal but less mobile? Education financing and intergenerational mobility in Italy and in the US. *J. Public Econ.* 74(3):351–93

Cheng Y, Dai J. 1995. Intergenerational mobility in modern China. *Eur. Sociol. Rev.* 11:17–35

Dale SB, Krueger AB. 2002. Estimating the payoff to attending a more selective college: an application of selection on observables and unobservables. *Q. J. Econ.* 117:1491–527

Davies R, Heinesen E, Holm A. 2002. The relative risk aversion hypothesis of educational choice. *J. Popul. Econ.* 15:683–714

de Graaf ND, de Graaf P, Kraaykamp G. 2000. Parental cultural capital and educational attainment in the Netherlands: a refinement of the cultural capital perspective. *Sociol. Educ.* 73:92–111

Duncan GJ, Brooks-Gunn J. eds. 1997. *Consequences of Growing Up Poor.* New York: Russell Sage

Duncan GJ, Connell JP, Klebanov PK. 1997. Conceptual and methodological issues in estimating causal effects of neighborhoods and family conditions on individual development. In *Neighborhood Poverty*, ed. J Brooks-Gunn, GJ Duncan, JL Aber, 1:219–50. New York: Russell Sage

Entwisle DR, Alexander KL, Olson LS. 1997. *Children, Schools, and Inequality.* Boulder, CO: Westveiw

Erikson R. 1994. Spelar valet av skola någon roll? In *Sorteringen i skolan,* ed. R Erikson, JO Jonsson, pp. 132–71. Stockholm: Carlssons

Erikson R. 1996. Explaining change in educational inequality—economic security and school reforms. See Erikson & Jonsson 1996a, pp. 95–112

Erikson R, Goldthorpe JH. 1985. Are American rates of social mobility exceptionally high? *Eur. Sociol. Rev.* 1:1–22

Erikson R, Goldthorpe JH. 1992. *The Constant Flux: A Study of Class Mobility in Industrial Societies.* Oxford: Clarendon

Erikson R, Jonsson JO, eds. 1996a. *Can Education Be Equalized?* Boulder, CO: Westview

Erikson R, Jonsson JO. 1996b. Introduction: explaining class inequality in education: the Swedish test case. See Erikson & Jonsson 1996a, pp. 1–64

Erikson R, Jonsson JO. 1998. Social origin as an interest-bearing asset: family background and labour market rewards among employees in Sweden. *Acta Sociol.* 41:19–36

Esser H. 1999. *Soziologie: Spezielle Grundlagen, i. Situationlogik und Handeln.* Frankfurt am Main: Campus

Galor O, Zeira J. 1993. Income distribution and macroeconomics. *Rev. Econ. Stud.* 60:35–52

Gambetta D. 1987. *Were They Pushed or Did They Jump? Individual Decision Mechanisms in Education.* Cambridge, UK: Cambridge Univ. Press

Gamoran A. 2001. American schooling and educational inequality: a forecast for the 21st century. *Sociol. Educ.* 74(extra issue):135–53

Gamoran A. 2004. Classroom organization and instructional quality. In *Can Unlike Students Learn Together? Grade Retention, Tracking, and Grouping*, ed. HJ Walberg, AJ Reynolds, MC Wang, pp. 141–55. Greenwich, CT: Information Age

Ganzeboom HBG, de Graaf P, Treiman DJ. 1992. A standard international socioeconomic index of occupational status. *Soc. Sci. Res.* 21:1–56

Ganzeboom HBG, Treiman DJ. 1996. Internationally comparable measures of occupational status for the 1988 International Standard Classification of Occupations. *Soc. Sci. Res.* 25:201–39

Ganzeboom HBG, Treiman DJ, Ultee W. 1991. Comparative intergenerational stratification research: three generations and beyond. *Annu. Rev. Sociol.* 17:277–302

Garner CL, Raudenbush SW. 1991. Neighborhood effects on educational attainment: a multilevel analysis. *Sociol. Educ.* 64:251–62

Gerber TP. 2000. Educational stratification in contemporary Russia: stability and change in the face of economic and institutional crisis. *Sociol. Educ.* 73:219–46

Gerber TP. 2003. Loosening links? School-to-work transitions and institutional change in Russia since 1970. *Soc. Forces* 82:241–76

Gerber TP, Hout M. 1995. Educational stratification in Russia during the Soviet period. *Am. J. Sociol.* 101:611–60

Gerber TP, Hout M. 2004. Tightening up: declining class mobility during Russia's market transition. *Am. Sociol. Rev.* 69:677–703

Goldthorpe JH. 2000. *On Sociology.* Oxford: Oxford Univ. Press

Goodman LA. 1979. Simple models for the analysis of association in cross-classifications having ordered categories. *J. Am. Stat. Assoc.* 74:537–52

Goodman LA, Hout M. 1998. Statistical methods and graphical displays for analyzing how the association between two qualitative variables differs among countries, among groups, or over time: a modified regression-type approach. *Sociol. Methodol.* 28:175–230

Goux D, Maurin E. 1997. Meritocracy and social heredity in France: some aspects and trends. *Eur. Sociol. Rev.* 13:159–77

Grawe ND, Mulligan CB. 2002. Economic interpretations of intergenerational correlations. *J. Econ. Perspect.* 16:45–58

Grusky DB, Hauser RM. 1984. Comparative social mobility revisited: models of convergence and divergence in 16 countries. *Am. Sociol. Rev.* 49:19–38

Grusky DB, Sorensen JB. 1998. Can class analysis be salvaged? *Am. J. Sociol.* 103:1187–234

Hanushek EA, Kain JF, Markman JM, Rivkin SG. 2003. Does peer ability affect student achievement? *J. Appl. Econ.* 18:527–44

Harding DJ. 2003. Counterfactual models of neighborhood effects: the effect of neighborhood poverty on dropping out and teenage pregnancy. *Am. J. Sociol.* 109:676–719

Hauser RM. 1978. A structural model of the mobility table. *Soc. Forces* 56:919–53

Hauser RM, Featherman DL. 1976. Equality of schooling: trends and prospects. *Sociol. Educ.* 49:99–120

Hauser RM, Mossel PA. 1985. Fraternal resemblance in educational attainment and occupational status. *Am. J. Sociol.* 9:650–73

Hauser RM, Warren JR. 1997. Socioeconomic indexes for occupations: a review, update, and critique. *Sociol. Methodol.* 27:177–298

Hauser RM, Warren JR, Huang MH, Carter WY. 2000. Occupational status, education and social mobility in the meritocracy. In *Meritocracy and Economic Inequality*, ed. K Arrow, S Bowles, S Durlauf, pp. 179–229. Princeton, NJ: Univ. Princeton Press

Heath AF, McMahon D. 1997. Education and occupational attainment: the impact of ethnic origins. In *Education: Culture, Economy and Society*, ed. AH Halsey, H Lauder, P Brown, AS Wells, pp. 646–62. Oxford: Oxford Univ. Press

Henz U, Maas I. 1995. Chancengleichheit durch die Bildungsexplansion? *Kölner*

Zeitschrift fur Soziologie und Sozialpsychologie. 47:605–33

Hillmert S, Jacob M. 2003. Social inequality in higher education: Is vocational training a pathway leading to or away from university? *Eur. Sociol. Rev.* 19:319–34

Hout M. 1988. More universalism, less structural mobility: the American occupational structure in the 1980s. *Am. J. Sociol.* 93: 1358–400

Hout M, Dohan DP. 1996. Two paths to educational opportunity: class and educational selection in Sweden and the United States. See Erikson & Jonsson 1996a, pp. 207–32

Hout M, Raftery A, Bell EO. 1993. Making the grade. Educational stratification in the United States, 1925–89. See Shavit & Blossfeld 1993, pp. 25–49

Hout M, Rosen H. 2000. Self-employment, family background, and race. *J. Human Resour.* 35:670–92

Ishida H. 1993. *Social Mobility in Contemporary Japan.* Stanford, CA: Stanford Univ. Press

Ishida H, Goldthorpe JH, Erikson R. 1991. Intergenerational class mobility in postwar Japan. *Am. J. Sociol.* 96:954–75

Ishida H, Müller W, Ridge JM. 1995. Class origin, class destination, and education: a cross-national study of industrial nations. *Am. J. Sociol.* 101:145–93

Jencks C, et al. 1979. *Who Gets Ahead? The Determinants of Economic Success in America.* New York: Basic Books

Jones FL, Kojima H, Marks G. 1994. Comparative social fluidity: trends over time in father-to-son mobility in Japan and Australia, 1965–1985. *Soc. Forces* 72:775–98

Jonsson JO. 1996. Stratification in post-industrial society: Are educational qualifications of growing importance? See Erikson & Jonsson 1996a, pp. 113–44

Jonsson JO, Erikson R. 2000. Understanding educational inequality. The Swedish experience. *L'Année sociologique* 50:345–82

Jonsson JO, Mills C, Müller W. 1996. A half century of increasing educational openness? Social class, gender and educational attainment in Sweden, Germany and Britain. See Erikson & Jonsson 1996a, pp. 183–206

Kerckhoff AC. 1993. *Diverging Pathways. Social Structure and Career Deflections.* Boulder, CO: Westview

Kerckhoff AC. 1995. Institutional arrangements and stratification processes in industrial societies. *Annu. Rev. Sociol.* 21:323–47

Krueger AB. 1999. Experimental estimates of educational production functions. *Q. J. Econ.* 114:497–532

Kurz K, Müller W. 1987. Class mobility in the industrial world. *Annu. Rev. Sociol.* 13:417–42

Lang JB, Agresti SR. 1994. Simultaneously modeling joint and marginal distributions of multivariate categorical responses. *J. Am. Stat. Assoc.* 89:625–32

Lang JB, Eliason SR. 1997. Application of association marginal models to the study of social mobility. *Sociol. Methods Res.* 26: 183–212

Lindbekk T. 1998. The education backlash hypothesis: the Norwegian experience 1960–92. *Acta Sociol.* 41:151–62

Lipset SM, Zetterberg HL. 1959. Social mobility in industrial societies. In *Social Mobility in Industrial Society*, ed. SM Lipset, R Bendix. Berkeley: Univ. Calif. Press

Logan JA. 1983. A multivariate model for mobility tables. *Am. J. Sociol.* 89:324–49

Logan JA. 1996. Opportunity and choice in socially structured labor markets. *Am. J. Sociol.* 102:114–60

Logan JA. 1998. Estimating two-sided logit models. *Sociol. Methodol.* 28:139–73

Lucas SR. 2001. Effectively maintained inequality: education transitions, track mobility, and social background effects. *Am. J. Sociol.* 106:1642–90

Mach BW, Peschar J. 1990. On the changing role of education in social reproduction in different sociopolitical systems; a comparative analysis between the Netherlands and Poland. In *Class Structure in Europe: New Findings from East-West Comparisons of Social Structure and Mobility*, ed. M Haller, pp. 92–120. Armonk, NY: M.E. Sharpe

Manski CF. 2000. Economic analysis of social interactions. *J. Econ. Perspect.* 14:115–36

Mare RD. 1981. Change and stability in educational stratification. *Am. Sociol. Rev.* 46:72–87

Mare RD. 1993. Educational stratification on observed and unobserved components of family background. See Shavit & Blossfeld 1993, pp. 351–76

Marshall G, Swift A, Roberts S. 1997. *Against the Odds? Social Class and Social Justice in Industrial Societies.* Oxford: Clarendon Press

Marshall G, Sydorenko S, Roberts S. 1995. Intergenerational social mobility in communist Russia. *Work Employ. Soc.* 9:1–27

Mayer S. 2002. How economic segregation affects children's educational attainment. *Soc. Forces* 81:153–76

McPherson A, Willms JD. 1987. Equalization and improvement: some effects of comprehensive reorganisation in Scotland. *Sociology* 21:509–39

Morgan SL. 1998. Adolescent educational expectations. Rationalized, fantasized, or both? *Ration. Soc.* 10:131–62

Morgan SL. 2001. Counterfactuals, causal effect heterogeneity, and the Catholic school effect on learning. *Sociol. Educ.* 74:341–74

Morgan SL. 2002. Modeling preparatory commitment and non-repeatable decisions. Information-processing, preference formation and educational attainment. *Ration. Soc.* 14:387–429

Mortimer P. 1997. Can effective schools compensate for society? In *Education: Culture, Economy and Society*, ed. AH Halsey, H Lauder, P Brown, AS Wells, pp. 476–87. Oxford: Oxford Univ. Press

Müller W, Haun D. 1994. Bildungsungleichheit im sozialen Wandel. *Kölner Zeitschrift fur Soziologie und Sozialpsychologie.* 46:1–42

Müller W, Karle W. 1993. Social selection in educational systems in Europe. *Eur. Sociol. Rev.* 9:1–23

Need A, de Jong U. 2001. Educational differentials in the Netherlands: testing rational action theory. *Ration. Soc.* 13:71–98

Park H. 2004. Intergenerational social mobility among Korean men in comparative perspective. *Res. Soc. Strat. Mobil.* 20:227–53

Phang HN, Lee SK. 1996. Structural change and intergenerational class mobility: a comparative study of Korea and Taiwan. *Korean J. Sociol.* 30:575–604

Pisati M. 1997. Mobility regimes and generative mechanisms: a comparative analysis of Italy and the United States. *Eur. Sociol. Rev.* 13:179–98

Pisati M, Schizzerotto A. 1999. Pochi promossi, nessun bocciato. La mobilità di carriera in Italia in prospettiva comparata e longitunale. *Stato e Mercato.* 56:249–79

Robert P, Bukodi E. 2004. Changes in intergenerational class mobility in Hungary, 1973–2000. See Breen 2004, pp. 287–314

Sampson RJ, Morenoff JD, Gannon-Rowley T. 2002. Assessing 'neighborhood effects': social processes and new directions in research. *Annu. Rev. Sociol.* 28:443–78

Sewell WH, Hauser RM, Springer KW, Hauser TS. 2004. As we age: a review of the Wisconsin Longitudinal Study, 1957–2001. *Res. Soc. Strat. Mobil.* 20:3–111

Shavit Y, Blossfeld HP, eds. 1993. *Persistent Inequality. Changing Educational Attainment in Thirteen Countries.* Boulder, CO: Westview

Shavit Y, Müller W, eds. 1998. *From School to Work. A Comparative Study of Educational Qualifications and Occupational Destinations.* Oxford: Clarendon Press

Shavit Y, Westerbeek K. 1998. Educational stratification in Italy: reforms, expansion, and equality of opportunity. *Eur. Sociol. Rev.* 14:33–47

Sieben I, de Graaf PM. 2001. Testing the modernization hypothesis and the socialist ideology hypothesis: a comparative sibling analysis of educational attainment and occupational status. *Br. J. Sociol.* 52:441–67

Sieben I, de Graaf PM. 2003. The total impact of the family on educational attainment. *Eur. Soc.* 5:33–68

Sieben I, Huinink J, de Graaf PM. 2001. Family background and sibling resemblance in education attainment: trends in the former FRG, the former GDR, and the Netherlands. *Eur. Sociol. Rev.* 17:401–30

Simkus A, Andorka R, Jackson J, Kam-Bor Y, Treiman DJ. 1990. Changes in social mobility in two societies in the crux of transition. *Res. Soc. Strat. Mobil.* 9:33–78

Small ML, Newman K. 2001. Urban poverty after 'the truly disadvantaged': the rediscovery of the family, the neighborhood, and culture. *Annu. Rev. Sociol.* 27:23–45

Smits J, Ultee W, Lammers J. 1998. Educational homogamy in 65 countries: an explanation of differences in openness using country-level explanatory variables. *Am. Sociol. Rev.* 63:264–85

Sobel ME, Becker MP, Minick SM. 1998. Origins, destinations, and associations in occupational mobility. *Am. J. Sociol.* 104: 687–721

Solon G. 2002. Cross-country differences in intergenerational earnings mobility. *J. Econ. Perspect.* 16:59–66

Solon G. 2004. A model of intergenerational mobility variation over time and space. In *Generational Income Mobility in North America and Europe*, ed. M Corak, pp. 38–47. Cambridge, UK: Cambridge Univ. Press

Solon G, Page ME, Duncan GJ. 2000. Correlations between neighboring children in their subsequent educational attainment. *Rev. Econ. Stat.* 82:383–92

Sorensen AB. 2000. Towards a sounder base for class analysis. *Am. J. Sociol.* 105:1523–58

Titma M, Tuma NB, Roosma K. 2003. Education as a factor in intergenerational mobility in Soviet society. *Eur. Sociol. Rev.* 19:281–98

Treiman DJ, Yip KB. 1989. Educational and occupational attainment in 21 countries. In *Cross-National Research in Sociology*, ed. ML Kohn, pp. 373–94. Newbury Park, CA: Sage

Vallet LA. 2004. Change in intergenerational class mobility in France from the 1970s to the 1990s and its explanation: an analysis following the CASMIN approach. See Breen 2004, pp. 115–48

Warren JR, Hauser RM, Sheridan JT. 2002. Occupational stratification across the lifecourse: evidence from the Wisconsin Longitudinal Study. *Am. Sociol. Rev.* 67:432–55

Western M. 1999. Class attainment among British men: a multivariate extension of the CASMIN model of intergenerational class mobility. *Eur. Sociol. Rev.* 15:431–54

Western M, Wright EO. 1994. The permeability of class boundaries to intergenerational mobility among men in the United States, Canada, Norway and Sweden. *Am. Sociol. Rev.* 59:606–29

Whelan CT, Layte R. 2002. Late industrialization and the increased merit selection hypothesis: Ireland as a test case. *Eur. Sociol. Rev.* 18:35–50

Winship C, Morgan SL. 1999. The estimation of causal effects from observational data. *Annu. Rev. Sociol.* 18:327–50

Wright EO. 1997. *Class Counts. Comparative Studies in Class Analysis.* Cambridge, UK: Cambridge Univ. Press

Xie Y. 1992. The log-multiplicative layer effect model for comparing mobility tables. *Am. Sociol. Rev.* 57:380–95

Annu. Rev. Sociol. 2005. 31:245–61
doi: 10.1146/annurev.soc.31.041304.122322
Copyright © 2005 by Annual Reviews. All rights reserved
First published online as a Review in Advance on April 7, 2005

WHITE RACIAL AND ETHNIC IDENTITY IN THE UNITED STATES

Monica McDermott and Frank L. Samson

Department of Sociology, Stanford University, Stanford, California 94305;
email: mcderm@stanford.edu, flsamson@stanford.edu

Key Words   race awareness, whiteness, racism

■ **Abstract**   This review examines research on white racial and ethnic identity, paying special attention to developments in whiteness studies during the past decade. Although sociologists have long focused on white ethnic identity, considerations of white racial identity are more recent. White racial identity is commonly portrayed as a default racial category, an invisible yet privileged identity formed by centuries of oppression of nonwhite groups. Whiteness has become synonymous with privilege in much scholarly writing, although recent empirical work strives to consider white racial identity as a complex, situated identity rather than a monolithic one. The study of white racial identity can greatly benefit from moving away from simply naming whiteness as an overlooked, privileged identity and by paying closer attention to empirical studies of racial and ethnic identity by those studying social movements, ethnic identity, and social psychology.

INTRODUCTION

Within the past decade, the study of whiteness has attracted a great deal of attention from scholars of such disciplines as history, cultural studies, and communications. Although the impact of this new intellectual movement has been less considerable among sociologists, there has nonetheless been a resurgence of interest in the study of whites as a racial group. This renewed interest reflects demographic changes in the racial makeup of the U.S. population, with increasing numbers of Asians and Hispanics resulting in a corresponding shrinking of the relative size of the white population, highlighting the existence of whites as a racial category rather than as a default identity. At the same time, sociologists of race and ethnicity have rightfully criticized the almost exclusive focus on nonwhites in studies of racial identity, implying that whites have no racial identity but are instead treated as the base group to which others are compared. It would be difficult to sustain such a critique today, as there has been a recent profusion of articles, monographs, and edited volumes on whiteness produced by sociologists.

In many respects, the relative drought of sociological research on white racial identity, per se, is ironic, as the study of European ethnicity among whites had been a bedrock of sociological research throughout much of the twentieth century, as evidenced by such classics as Thomas & Znaniecki (1927), Whyte (1943), and Gans (1982 [1962]). The publication of *Ethnic Options* (Waters 1990) and *Ethnic Identity* (Alba 1990) heralded the end of this era, as the assimilation of European immigrants into American society was found to be all but complete. Consequently, there has been a gradual shift in focus from the study of white *ethnic* identity to white *racial* identity, reflecting the minimal impact of European ancestral origins on the daily life of most Americans. This is a step closer to the long-standing focus of studies of black racial identity, which have often been concerned with identity formation and group attachments among all black Americans (Burlew & Smith 1991, Helms 1990, Resnicow & Ross-Gaddy 1997).

There is a growing realization that one cannot fully understand the existence of racism and racial inequality without paying close attention to the formation and maintenance of white racial identity. While much of the content of any dominant social identity involves privilege (Doane 1997), rarely are there no variations in the degree of privilege bestowed by membership in a socially dominant group. This is especially true when considering a population as socioeconomically diverse as the white population in the United States, where the boundaries and definitions of whiteness are constantly shifting over both time and space. Both historians and legal scholars have outlined the evolution of popular and official definitions of whiteness (Delgado 1995, Haney-Lopez 1996, Jacobson 1998, Roediger 1991); their work highlights the vagaries of racial definitions, as the inclusion of Arabs as white and Chinese as nonwhite seemingly reflect the idiosyncrasies of judges and the dominant political mood more than any consistent pattern of identification. Although history is filled with examples of ethnic groups struggling to be recognized as white, the post–Civil Rights era has witnessed a shift in this process, as many of the legal barriers that corresponded to being identified as nonwhite have been lifted. A growing multiracial population has further complicated the process of racial identification (Daniel 2002, Harris & Sim 2002), reflected in the U.S. Census Bureau's decision to allow respondents to check more than one race for themselves or family members in the 2000 Census.

The ambiguous racial status of post-1965 immigrants from Asia and Latin America highlights the need to understand what it means to be white in the contemporary United States (Bean et al. 2003). There is a rich body of social scientific research on white ethnic identity, racial attitudes, and social movements that, combined with recent work in whiteness studies, reflects central developments and key research questions in the rapidly growing sociological literature on white racial identity.

The focus of this review is solely on white racial and ethnic identity in the United States, initially putting forward a tentative definition of white along with a discussion of racial terminology. We assess significant developments in the field of whiteness studies and the study of European American ethnic identity and briefly review the research on white identity development models by social psychologists (for a more thorough review of the social psychological research on identity, see

Howard 2000). Examples of the formation and uses of white racial identity by white supremacist groups provide a counterpoint to the studies of whiteness and white identity development, many of which are concerned with developing antiracist strategies, especially on college campuses.

WHITE, CAUCASIAN, ANGLO

Although white is typically used to refer to those with European ancestry (Bonnett 1998), local understandings of just what white means vary, often reflecting the racial ecology of a community or region. Debates about the appropriate labels for whites provide an interesting example of the interplay between self-identity and the social context. The terminology used to describe the white population has varied throughout U.S. history, and there remains no consensus as to the optimal term one should use to describe American descendents of European and Middle Eastern immigrants. The U.S. Census has always used the term white, and this is the term most commonly used today. However, other labels such as Caucasian, European American, and Anglo have been used by whites when identifying their racial group membership. Goldstein (1999) finds significant demographic variation in the preferences for one label over another among whites sampled in the 1996 Current Population Survey. Although white is preferred by over 60% of respondents, strong geographic patterns of preference reveal corresponding differences in the meaning of white. For example, white is strongly preferred in the Deep South, where dichotomous black/white racial divisions have long held sway. In contrast, Anglo is more likely to be preferred in both the Southwest and Upper New England than in the rest of the country (although still only reflecting the preferences of a small minority of respondents), demarcating whites in these areas from Hispanics and French Canadians, respectively (Goldstein 1999, p. 19). Caucasian is often preferred by more educated respondents, despite this term's historical association with scientific racism; Goldstein (1999) suspects that this trend reflects these respondents' desires to disassociate themselves from the associations of whiteness with social dominance, as well as a preference for the scientific sound of the term. The use of Caucasian in place of white has become increasingly common in medical literature since the early 1990s (Aspinall 1998), reflecting the ironic resurrection of an arguably racist term.

WHITENESS STUDIES

The scholarship on whiteness in the United States has highlighted several important characteristics of white racial identity: It is often invisible or taken for granted, it is rooted in social and economic privilege, and its meaning and import are highly situational.

Much of the research on white racial identity during the past ten years has focused on how whiteness, and the privileges associated with whiteness, remain invisible to many whites, especially those with limited interracial contact (Delgado & Stefancic 1997, Lipsitz 1998). Instead, whiteness is normative (Hyde 1995), an unexamined default racial category. Although many nonwhites, especially African Americans, are confronted with their race on a daily basis (Feagin & Sikes 1994), many whites do not think of themselves as really having a race at all. In this respect, white is an unmarked identity, such as heterosexual or middle-aged (Brekhus 1998).

One of the earliest identifications of the issue of invisibility was Frankenburg's (1993) attempt to make sense of the racial difficulties encountered by the feminist movement among ostensible allies. Because white feminists could not see the importance of race and its connection with gender inequality, especially their own privilege as white (largely middle-class) women, many black feminists were turned away from active involvement in women's organizations. College (Jackson & Heckman 2002) and high school (Perry 2002) students are often unable to articulate what it means to be white, instead describing it as nothing or a vacuum, although Gallagher (1995) finds that college students exhibit a high degree of racial consciousness, perhaps given his focus on students in a city with a large black population. Frankenberg (2001) has since rejected her earlier understanding of whiteness as simply invisible privilege. The shrinking size of the white population as well as the increased presence of nonwhites in prominent positions has rendered whiteness more visible rather than as an implicit synonym for American.

Associations of whiteness with privilege are more immune to changes in the demographic makeup of the United States than are associations between whiteness and invisibility; if anything, the link between whiteness and privilege is more likely to be strengthened than weakened with an increase in the nonwhite population. Although the privileges associated with whiteness are often obvious to nonwhites (Roediger 1998), many whites themselves fail to see the connection between their opportunities in life and their racial identity, much as their race is generally invisible to them. In some cases, this failure to recognize the connection is due to nonobvious legacies of structural advantage (Lipsitz 1998); in other cases, it stems from a desire to accentuate individual achievement (DiTomaso et al. 2003, Lowery et al. 2004).

In fact, much of the recent work on whiteness concerns how whites minimize, acknowledge, deny, embrace, or feel guilty about their privileged status (Doane & Bonilla-Silva 2003). The denial of white privilege is the foundation of color-blind racism, an ideological assertion of the fundamental equality of all racial groups—not only in terms of rights, but also in terms of experiences—that asserts that race-based programs and policies only serve to further solidify racial divisions (Andersen 2001). This perspective is a reflection of an understanding of white racial identity that assumes its content is like that of any other racial group—we are only humans, not whites, blacks, or Asians. On their surface, such ideas sound remarkably similar to those articulated by antiracists during the Civil Rights movement in the 1960s, yet they are currently aimed at emptying whiteness of its privileged content rather than at transforming whiteness from an identity of social superiority to one of social responsibility (Bonilla-Silva 2003).

The identification of whiteness with social responsibility is a frequent theme in current work on white racial identity. Because white pride has historically been predicated upon a denigration of nonwhites, the articulation of the duties and requirements of whiteness reflects a desire to correlate a conscious white identity with positive attributes. If whiteness is explicitly associated with racism and discrimination yet otherwise relatively bereft of content, there is a tendency to create distance between oneself and whiteness; what is marked as white is not a rich and varied set of cultural practices but socially destructive practices (Appiah & Gutmann 1996). The cultural emptiness and social culpability of white identity is reflected in the tendency of semiautobiographical narratives on whiteness to catalog the advantages of being white (e.g., McIntosh 1988) rather than to describe specific cultural practices, as is more common in narratives about the formation of other racial or ethnic identities.

Links between white racial identity and privilege and/or racism also stimulate calls by scholars and activists for the abolition of whiteness (Ignatiev & Garvey 1996, Mazie et al. 1993, Roediger 1994) without advocating color blindness, instead urging whites to be traitors to their race and to adopt an antiracist identity (O'Brien 2001). The new abolitionist movement suggests that whiteness be repudiated, and whites should instead embrace all that whiteness is not (Winant 2001). Critics of this approach, in turn, suggest that whiteness should not be abolished but instead should itself be studied as an object (Bonnett 1996), as when white identity is defined and examined by black writers (Roediger 1998). On a related note, Omi (2001) argues that a relentless focus on whiteness and white attitudes, as in the new abolitionist movement, is thought to be less likely to erode white supremacy than a consistent understanding of racial identities as relational (Omi 2001).

In addition to the emphasis on invisibility and privilege, a more promising recent trend in research on white racial identity is a focus on whiteness as a situated identity, not as an identity of uniform privilege but as a complex social identity whose meaning is imparted by the particular context in which white actors are located. Poor (Buck 2001), gay (Berube 2001), or otherwise marginalized whites are likely to have a different experience of their privileged racial identity than are others able to see the direct payoff of white skin privilege (Rasmussen et al. 2001). This trend toward considering whiteness as increasingly complex is reflected in the work of one of the first social scientists to write specifically about whiteness as invisible privilege, Ruth Frankenberg (2001), who urges a shift in thinking about white racial identity as more complex than she or others had previously considered. Specifically, she notes that the current "conditions and practice of whiteness" render "the notion that whiteness might be invisible...bizarre in the extreme" (p. 76). Especially as whites become more rather than less likely to have interracial contact, the conditions of whiteness are increasingly explicit. Given the close association between whiteness and socioeconomic privilege, poor and working-class whites are especially likely to be aware of their whiteness as well as to have a complex understanding of what it means to be white in the United States today. For example, Hartigan (1999) finds that poor whites living among blacks in Detroit are more likely to be aware of racial identity as well as to have alternating experiences of shame and pride. While the affluent white gentrifiers Hartigan studies resemble the whites described by the literature on whiteness as privilege, the poverty of the Hillbilly whites across town renders a one-to-one correspondence between whiteness and privilege virtually impossible. In contrast, Royster (2003) details the direct yet unseen benefits of whiteness among working-class men, who receive advantages in employment specifically because of the social networks to which their whiteness gives them privileged access.

The complex and situated character of whiteness is also highlighted among the multiracial population, where switching between white and nonwhite identities is not uncommon (Rockquemore & Brunsma 2002). Storrs (1999) finds that young biracial women in the Northwest are actually more likely to distance themselves from whiteness, instead opting for the more meaningful nonwhite identity. However, identifying as white can grant a psychological sense of superiority to those who are nonblack (Warren & Twine 1997).

SOCIAL PSYCHOLOGICAL THEORIES

Social psychologists have long been concerned with conceptualizing and measuring identity, with white racial identity no exception. Social identity theorists treat white racial identity much like any other dominant group identity; it forms in relation to the other actors in an environment and is constantly subject to change (Ellemers et al. 2002). The differentiation of an in-group from an out-group implies a need to maintain the superiority of one's group over the out-group (Tajfel & Turner 1985); this is clearly evident in the history of discrimination against blacks practiced by whites (Sidanius & Pratto 1999).

Helms (1990) has developed and tested several scales measuring white racial identity development. Much like Cross's (1991) theory of black identity development, Helms proposes a theory of stages that whites pass through on their way to internalizing a racial identity, although for whites the final stage includes accepting a "nonracist core" (Helms 1990, p. 52). Although the particulars of her scale have been subject to debate (Rowe & Atkinson 1995), Helms's identification of a measurement instrument for white racial identity remains one of the standard scales in use today (Hardiman 2001). Along with the diverse white identity scales that preceded hers (see Helms 1990 for a review), the final, ideal stage of white identity development is a rejection of racism.

Despite their differences, each of these social psychological theories of identity development relies primarily on laboratory experiments, typically with college students (Frable 1997). It is unclear how the experience of being white might differ among different populations in more complex social settings.

WHITES AS EUROPEAN AMERICANS

Because many of those who are today considered white were once white ethnics, research on the ethnic identity of whites has touched upon the meanings and construction of white racial identity. European immigrants flooded into the large cities of the Northeast and Midwest during the late nineteenth and early twentieth centuries, and their incorporation into the American racial system has not been without struggle and uncertainty. However, when compared with African Americans, the experiences and hardships of European immigrants were much less difficult, by any measure (Lieberson 1980). Throughout the twentieth century, white ethnic distinctions gradually blurred into a more diffuse European American identity (Alba 1990), especially by the third and fourth generations (Alba & Nee 1997), although most white Americans still claim an ethnic ancestry when responding to the U.S. Census (Lieberson & Waters 1993). In the contemporary United States, white ethnic identity has ranged from a symbolic identity (Gans 1979) to a strategic means of countering African American demands for equality (Formisano 1991, Patterson 1977, Steinberg 1981). Among middle-class whites, ethnic identity is more representative of affinities for certain cultural practices than an important part of whites' self-concept; unlike racial identity, ethnic identity has become optional (Waters 1990). For Barkan (1995), the conscious yet materially tangential ethnic identity represents the fifth stage of a six-stage assimilation process, whereby some nominal cultural ties are maintained with countries of origin yet primary identity rests with the core society.

Historians have traced the many paths by which Irish, Italians, Jews, etc., have become whites. Despite a relatively uncomplicated embrace of whiteness by the descendents of European immigrants (Durr 2003, Sugrue 1996), their ancestors faced a radically different set of attitudes and assumptions about who was to be considered white. At the turn of the century, Irish, Jewish, and Italian immigrants were considered neither white nor black (Allen 1994, Brodkin 1998, Ignatiev 1995, Jacobson 1998). Union organizing that focused on the dignity and privilege of ethnic workers played a critical role in forging a white identity for European immigrants (Roediger 1991). Anti-black activism on the part of immigrant groups also played a crucial role in securing the privileges of whiteness for European immigrants (Olzak & Shanahan 2003), as did the existence of white youth gangs that engaged in racist violence with the tacit approval of adults in their communities (Adamson 2000). The historical and continued importance of white racial and ethnic identity in defended urban neighborhoods is evident in a wide range of locations, including Chicago (Kefalas 2003, Suttles 1972), Detroit (Sugrue 1996), New Jersey (Lamont 2000), Baltimore (Durr 2003), Boston (Formisano 1991), Philadelphia (Kazal 2004b), and New York (Rieder 1985).

As the nation's borders expanded westward, the correlation between white and European American became stronger, with religious and ethnic differences among European immigrants in California fading in the service of a united white front used to marginalize Indians, Asians, and Mexicans (Almaguer 1994). The relative importance of white racial privilege is evident when assessing the socioeconomic attainment of twentieth century European immigrants, as substantial ethnic group differences in human capital at the turn of the century did not manifest themselves in differential outcomes three generations later (Alba et al. 2001).

The ethnic community has been a primary source of identity maintenance for these immigrants and their descendents, and the dispersion of European ethnic groups to suburban neighborhoods is likely a major reason for the declining importance of white ethnic identity (Alba et al. 1997). Among Italian Americans in the New York City region, "the overall population shift can be described as taking people from the most ethnic neighborhoods and placing them in the least" (Alba et al. 1997, p. 908). In other cases, such as among German Americans living in Philadelphia, external shocks such as the nativism stoked by World War II provided an additional push in the direction of assimilation (Kazal 2004a).

Although the main story to tell about white ethnic identity during the past 30 years has been its declining distinctiveness and importance, there are nonetheless some counter-examples, primarily from small, relatively isolated communities of recent European and Middle Eastern immigrants to the United States. Arab Americans are an especially interesting example, as they are officially considered white by the U.S. Census yet often have stronger identification with their countries of origin than with a white racial identity. In Dearborn, Michigan, Lebanese American adolescents categorize each other along a continuum ranging from boater, or one who exhibits immigrant culture, to white (Ajrouch 2000, p. 458). To these teenagers, white embodies both the positive attributes of education and wealth as well as the negative attributes of irresponsibility and a lost sense of familial and community obligation (Ajrouch 2000).

WHITE IDENTITY AND WHITE SUPREMACIST MOVEMENTS

The study of social movements and collective action provides other vantage points from which to analyze the construction and reproduction of white racial and ethnic identity. The sociological literature is replete with explorations of the relationship between ethnic identities and collective action (Green & Seher 2003, Williams 1994). Some studies seek to determine the conditions that lead to ethnic conflict and the specific mechanisms that trigger such phenomena, whereas others explore cases of collective action that may not explicitly rely or focus on white ethnic or racial identities. However, while struggling and mobilizing to protect or acquire particular resources, groups may invoke white ethnic and racial identities in defining constituents, allies, and threats (Formisano 1991, Rieder 1985). In many of these studies, white racial and ethnic identity acts as a by-product or instrumental category masking other conflicts such as competition over material resources, loss of status, etc. (Olzak 1992). However, white racial identity also constitutes the raison d'être for a number of social movements that, despite their small size, are given a comparatively large role in publicly defining white racial identity.

In recent work, sociologists have delved further into understanding the relationship between social movements and whiteness by exploring perhaps the quintessential convergence of white identity and collective action: white supremacist movements. Contemporary white supremacist formations include the Ku Klux Klan, neo-Nazis (and racist skinheads), and militia movements (Dees & Corcoran 1996, Ezekiel 1995, Gallaher 2003, George & Wilcox 1996, Langer 2003, Levitas 2002, Ridgeway 1990). Across these various formations, Christian Identity Church doctrine provides a religiously based justification for white supremacist movements (Burlein 2002, Bushart et al. 1998, Sharpe 2000). This religious doctrine posits a seedline genealogy of the human species with the white racial descendents of Adam (God's creation) pitted against the demonic and mongrel Jewish descendants of Cain (the offspring of Satan and Eve) and his nonwhite consort who hails from the pre-Adamic mud people that gave rise to nonwhite racial stocks (Barkun 1994, Dobratz 2001, Ferber 1998).

Drawing upon the analytical tools of deconstruction most popularly associated with the humanities, Ferber (1998) analyzes white supremacist periodicals and websites to explicate the ways in which white supremacist organizations engage in the production (and elevation) of what is essentially a white, patriarchal, heterosexual masculinity. Building upon Omi & Winant's (1986) racial formation theory and introducing Judith Butler's (1990) work on the construction of gendered identity and subjectivity, Ferber reveals how white supremacist organizations engage in the process of delineating white racial identity primarily through constructing boundaries and framing difference as absolute.

In white supremacist discourse, white racial identity is simply the essential expression of genetically distinct races resulting from the natural evolution of the human species. The case for racial difference is made by constant references to religion (Christian Identity Church doctrine) and science (mobilizing evidentiary claims of physiological and anatomical difference to signify essential racial differences). Arguing for natural gender distinctions is part and parcel of the white supremacist *Weltanschauung*, which argues, for instance, that disparities in math proficiency are simply expressions of genetically encoded, biological differences between males and females. Racial and gender hierarchy is pitched as the consequence of the age-old, natural, evolutionary progress of the human species.

Within this ideological framework, policies such as affirmative action, school desegregation, and residential integration are framed as conspiracies that threaten the natural order by promoting black male–white female intercourse that leads to white racial genocide. Orchestrated by an invented group of mixed-race Jews, the objective is to eradicate the genetically superior white racial stock by introducing biological deficiencies via black male–white female contact and ensuing interracial sexuality, in the end mongrelizing the white race. Even the feminist movement becomes a knowing accomplice to this plot, because threatening the natural, complementary hierarchy (in white supremacist discourse) between males and females throws into question the other natural hierarchy (as the narrative goes) between blacks and whites.

These arguments concern the construction of a patriarchal form of white identity, as white supremacist movements perceive white men as under siege and literally emasculated. The rupture in patriarchal gender roles that removes white women from the protection of white males creates a crisis in which white women, naturally seeking a strong masculine protector and provider, must seek bestial and dominating masculinity through interracial intercourse with black males. The obsession with interracial sexuality is ubiquitous throughout white supremacist discourse. The reiteration and propagation of these narratives, Ferber argues, embodies the gendered construction of a particular racial identity, the white supremacist male (see also Ferber 2004).

Focusing on the contours and characteristics of white supremacist propaganda and mobilizing frames does not sufficiently explain why individuals participate in these movements. Recognizing that these messages may be received and interpreted differently by both constituents and potential recruits, Blee (2002) seeks to understand the microprocesses and mechanisms that recruit and retain active participants in organized white supremacist movements. Contrary to media portrayals of white supremacists as irrational or extremists with pathological dispositions or dysfunctional upbringings, many active participants come from normal backgrounds and lead mainstream lives. Rather than assuming a priori conditions or static interests that predispose individuals to join organized racist groups, Blee argues that recruitment and membership in these organizations for women activists entail the social construction of individual interest. Social interactions with acquaintances, peers, friends, and family members involved in white supremacist organizations may shape, structure, and perhaps define a potential recruit's interests to align with the goals of the organization and its espoused ideologies. Within collective action research, this phenomenon describes the conversion process and highlights the importance of social interaction within movements. In the context of white supremacist organizations, the conversion often involves an incremental change in self-identity (from white to white supremacist) and self-interest (from apathy to advocacy) that takes place during one's involvement in racist activities, and is facilitated by the narrative frame of the organization. Conversion to white supremacist identity is learned, often through retrospective reflection on life events via the lenses provided by white supremacist organizational narratives, rather than revealed as an instantaneous epiphany that brings an individual immediately into the white supremacist fold.

The roles that women play in white supremacist movements sometimes facilitate the reproduction of racist white identities. Given the maintenance of patriarchal gender hierarchies within white supremacist organizations, women most often find themselves in mothering roles, tasked with birthing and childrearing the next generation of white supremacists. Women send children to Aryan schools and help forge the social networks that children grow up within, including Aryan play groups. Some women promote white racial identity through family consumption patterns and through time devoted to making and selling arts and crafts that adhere to white supremacist symbols and themes.

White supremacist movements also provide concrete organizational and institutional settings within which collective white supremacist identities are formed. Organizations and movements furnish the space within which a sense of belonging to a larger white community can be imagined, while providing concrete activities (recruiting, celebrating, protesting, committing violent acts, studying, etc.) that bring individuals together to reaffirm individual and collective white supremacist identity. Movements and organizations also provide a vehicle for the dissemination of a set of cultural markers that often signify white supremacist commitments. These may include clothing, tattoos (e.g., Swastikas), accessories (e.g., Klan crosses), hairstyles, and for many younger adherents, white power music. The relative popularity of such cultural products has even given rise to white power recording and publishing companies (Burghart 1999). Memorizing musical lyrics and reading magazine articles allow supporters to reiterate, rehearse, and reinforce their racist beliefs.

Collective identities are also affirmed while working toward white supremacist organizational goals. The ultimate expression and celebration of white supremacist beliefs is to shoulder the responsibility imparted by one's racial heritage and become a white supremacist activist. Movement organizations provide the infrastructure, networks, resources, and training through which the belief in white racial supremacy can be proven through the exemplary commitment demonstrated by white racist activists. However, white supremacist activities are not solely the purview of organizational cadres. In fact, Blee and other researchers and analysts (Blee 2002, Durham 2002, Whine 1999) have observed the decentralization of white supremacist organizations in light of the law enforcement crackdown following the Oklahoma City bombing in 1995. Going underground or working in small and secret cells, white supremacist activists, although harder to detect, are using technologies such as the Internet to continue to communicate across distances while maintaining some measure of anonymity (Gerstenfeld et al. 2003, Levin 2002, Whine 1999). Evolving information technologies thus provide another vehicle for the reproduction and diffusion of white supremacist racial identity (Burris et al. 2000, Swain 2002).

POINTS OF AGREEMENT AND DEPARTURE

One common theme links these disparate lines of research on white racial identity: The context in which whites are enmeshed influences their perceptions and experiences of being white. Virtually all theorists agree that, whether it is placed in historical context (Allen 1994, Brodkin 1998, Jacobson 1998), class context (Giroux 1997, Hartigan 1999), racial context (Stoddart 2002), or the situational environment (Hartigan 1997), whiteness is not a static, unchangeable, easily definable identity. That is, white racial identity is more of a process than a descriptive;

it reflects the ever-shifting boundaries between different racial groups (Lamont & Molnar 2002, Nagel 1994).

However, attempts at specifying concrete ways in which the process of white racial identity formation varies or experiences of whiteness differ have been considerably lacking; instead, studies show a mix of "pride, denial, and ambivalence" in being white (Jaret & Reitzes 1999). Consequently, we have no standard way of classifying how whiteness, or any other dominant group identity, is experienced. There is agreement that white racial identity is not the same for all groups at all times, but just how this identity differs remains unclear.

The study of white racial identity in the United States can greatly benefit from moving away from simply naming whiteness as an overlooked, privileged identity and by paying closer attention to empirical studies of racial and ethnic identity in the areas of social movements, ethnic identity, and social psychology. In particular, the adherence to standards of evidence—regardless of the methodological approach—is of vital importance to the study of white racial identity. Theoretical reflections on whiteness have far outpaced empirical investigations of the construction, experiences, and meanings of white racial identity in the United States today. Although there are notable exceptions (especially Hartigan 1999), including a spate of recent work on how children and adolescents learn about race in general and whiteness in particular (Bettie 2003, Lewis 2003, Perry 2002, Van Ausdale & Feagin 2001), much of what has been written about white racial identity is rooted in autobiographical reflection. A tendency to generalize from a few individuals or archival fragments to the entire white population has further hampered the process of specifying white identity (Arnesen 2001), although increasingly frequent calls for more empirically grounded studies (i.e., Barrett 2001) should begin to yield progress. Part of the difficulty lies in the fact that while white racial identity is very much in flux, it nonetheless simultaneously encompasses the enduring structural privilege of European Americans (Duster 2001, Lewis 2004). Navigating between the long-term staying power of white privilege and the multifarious manifestations of the experience of whiteness remains the task of the next era of research on white racial and ethnic identity.

The *Annual Review of Sociology* is online at http://soc.annualreviews.org

LITERATURE CITED

Adamson C. 2000. Defensive localism in white and black: a comparative history of European-American and African-American youth gangs. *Ethn. Racial Stud.* 23:272–98

Ajrouch KJ. 2000. Place, age, and culture—community living and ethnic identity among Lebanese American adolescents. *Small Group Res.* 31:447–69

Alba RD. 1990. *Ethnic Identity: The Transformation of White America.* New Haven, CT: Yale Univ. Press

Alba RD, Logan JR, Crowder K. 1997. White ethnic neighborhoods and assimilation: the greater New York region, 1980–1990. *Soc. Forces* 75:883–912

Alba R, Lutz A, Vesselinov E. 2001. How enduring were the inequalities among

European immigrant groups in the United States? *Demography* 38:349–56

Alba R, Nee V. 1997. Rethinking assimilation theory for a new era of immigration. *Int. Migr. Rev.* 31:826–74

Allen TW. 1994. *The Invention of the White Race*. London: Verso

Almaguer T. 1994. *Racial Fault Lines: The Historical Origins of White Supremacy in California*. Berkeley: Univ. Calif. Press

Andersen ML. 2001. Restructuring for whom? Race, class, gender, and the ideology of invisibility. *Soc. Forum* 16(2):181–201

Appiah KA, Gutmann A. 1996. *Color Conscious: The Political Morality of Race*. Princeton, NJ: Princeton Univ. Press

Arnesen EA. 2001. Whiteness and the historians' imagination. *Int. Labor Work.-Class Hist.* 60:3–32

Aspinall PJ. 1998. Describing the "white" ethnic group and its composition in medical research. *Soc. Sci. Med.* 47:1797–808

Barkan ER. 1995. Race, religion, and nationality in American society—a model of ethnicity—from contact to assimilation. *J. Am. Ethn. Hist.* 14:38–75

Barkun M. 1994. *Religion and the Racist Right: The Origins of the Christian Identity Movement*. Chapel Hill: Univ. N. C. Press

Barrett JR. 2001. Whiteness studies: anything here for historians of the working class? *Int. Labor Work.-Class Hist.* 60:33–42

Bean FD, Stevens G, Lee J. 2003. Immigration and race-ethnicity in the United States. In *America's Newcomers and the Dynamics of Diversity*, ed. FD Bean, G Stevens, pp. 224–29. New York: Russell Sage Found.

Berube A. 2001. How gay stays white and what kind of white it stays. See Rasmussen et al. 2001, pp. 234–65

Bettie J. 2003. *Women Without Class: Girls, Race, and Identity*. Berkeley: Univ. Calif. Press. 248 pp.

Blee KM. 2002. *Inside Organized Racism: Women in the Hate Movement*. Berkeley: Univ. Calif. Press

Bonilla-Silva E. 2003. "New racism," colorblind racism and the future of whiteness in America. See Doane & Bonilla-Silva 2003, pp. 271–84

Bonnett A. 1996. White studies: the problems and projects of a new research agenda. *Theory Cult. Soc.* 13(2):145–55

Bonnett A. 1998. Who was white? The disappearance of non-European white identities and the formation of European racial whiteness. *Ethn. Racial Stud.* 21:1029–55

Brekhus W. 1998. Sociology of the unmarked: redirecting our focus. *Soc. Theory* 16:34–51

Brodkin K. 1998. *How Jews Became White Folks and What That Says about Race in America*. New Brunswick, NJ: Rutgers Univ. Press

Buck PD. 2001. *Worked to the Bone: Race, Class, Power, and Privilege in Kentucky*. New York: Monthly Rev.

Burghart D. 1999. *Soundtracks to the White Revolution: White Supremacist Assaults on Youth Music Subcultures*. Chicago: Cent. New Community

Burlein A. 2002. *Lift High the Cross: Where White Supremacy and the Christian Right Converge*. Durham, NC: Duke Univ. Press

Burlew AK, Smith LR. 1991. Measures of racial identity: an overview and a proposed framework *J. Black Psychol.* 17:53–71

Burris V, Smith E, Strahm A. 2000. White supremacist networks on the Internet. *Soc. Focus* 33:215–35

Bushart HL, Craig JR, Barnes ME. 1998. *Soldiers of God: White Supremacists and Their Holy War for America*. New York: Kensington

Butler JP. 1990. *Gender Trouble: Feminism and the Subversion of Identity*. New York: Routledge

Cross WE. 1991. *Shades of Black*. Philadelphia, PA: Temple Univ. Press

Daniel GR. 2002. *More than Black? Multiracial Identity and the New Racial Order*. Philadelphia, PA: Temple Univ. Press

Dees M, Corcoran J. 1996. *Gathering Storm: America's Militia Threat*. New York: Harper-Collins

Delgado R. 1995. *Critical Race Theory: The*

Cutting Edge. Philadelphia, PA: Temple Univ. Press

Delgado R, Stefancic J. 1997. *Critical White Studies: Looking Behind the Mirror*. Philadelphia, PA: Temple Univ. Press

DiTomaso N, Parks-Yancy R, Post C. 2003. White views of civil rights: color blindness and equal opportunity. See Doane & Bonilla-Silva 2003, pp. 189–98

Doane AW. 1997. Dominant group ethnic identity in the United States: the role of "hidden" ethnicity in intergroup relations. *Sociol. Q.* 38:375–97

Doane AW, Bonilla-Silva E. 2003. *White Out: The Continuing Significance of Racism*. New York: Routledge. 328 pp.

Dobratz BA. 2001. The role of religion in the collective identity of the white racialist movement. *J. Sci. Study Relig.* 40:287–301

Durham M. 2002. From imperium to Internet: the National Alliance and the American extreme right. *Patterns Prejud.* 36(3):50–61

Durr KD. 2003. *Behind the Backlash: White Working-Class Politics in Baltimore, 1940–1980*. Chapel Hill: Univ. N. C. Press

Duster T. 2001. The "morphing" properties of whiteness. See Rasmussen et al. 2001, pp. 113–37

Ellemers N, Spears R, Doosje B. 2002. Self and social identity. *Annu. Rev. Psychol.* 53:161–86

Ezekiel RS. 1995. *The Racist Mind: Portraits of Neo-Nazis and Klansmen*. New York: Viking

Feagin JR, Sikes MP. 1994. *Living with Racism: The Black Middle-Class Experience*. Boston: Beacon

Ferber AL. 1998. *White Man Falling: Race, Gender and White Supremacy*. Lanham, MD: Rowman & Littlefield

Ferber AL. 2004. *Home-Grown Hate: Gender and Organized Racism, Perspectives on Gender*. New York: Routledge

Formisano RP. 1991. *Boston Against Busing: Race, Class, and Ethnicity in the 1960s and 1970s*. Chapel Hill: Univ. N. C. Press

Frable DES. 1997. Gender, racial, ethnic, sexual, and class identities. *Annu. Rev. Psychol.* 48:139–62

Frankenberg R. 1993. *White Women, Race Matters: The Social Construction of Whiteness*. Minneapolis: Univ. Minn. Press

Frankenberg R. 2001. Mirage of an unmarked whiteness. See Rasmussen et al. 2001, pp. 72–96

Gallagher CA. 1995. White reconstruction in the university. *Socialist Rev.* 24:165–87

Gallaher C. 2003. *On the Fault Line: Race, Class and the American Patriot Movement*. Lanham, MD: Rowman & Littlefield

Gans H. 1979. Symbolic ethnicity: the future of ethnic groups and cultures in America. *Ethn. Racial Stud.* 2:1–20

Gans H. 1982 (1962). *The Urban Villagers: Group and Class in the Life of Italian-Americans*. New York: Free Press

George J, Wilcox LM. 1996. *American Extremists: Militias, Supremacists, Klansmen, Communists & Others*. Amherst, NY: Prometheus Books

Gerstenfeld PB, Grant DR, Chiang C. 2003. Hate online: a content analysis of extremist Internet sites. *Anal. Soc. Issues Public Policy* 3(1):29–44

Giroux HA. 1997. White squall: resistance and the pedagogy of whiteness. *Cult. Stud.* 11:376–89

Goldstein JR. 1999. *Why Caucasian? A geo-demography of racial labels in the United States*. Work. Pap., Off. Popul. Res., Princeton Univ.

Green DP, Saher RL. 2003. What role does prejudice play in ethnic conflict? *Annu. Rev. Polit. Sci.* 6:509–31

Haney-López I. 1996. *White by Law: The Legal Construction of Race*. New York: NY Univ. Press

Hardiman R. 2001. Reflections on white identity development theory. In *New Perspectives on Racial Identity Development*, ed. CL Wijeyesinghe, BW Jackson III, pp. 108–28. New York: NY Univ. Press

Harris DR, Sim JJ. 2002. Who is multiracial? Assessing the complexity of lived race. *Am. Sociol. Rev.* 67:614–27

Hartigan J. 1997. Green ghettos and the white underclass. *Soc. Res.* 64:339–65

Hartigan J. 1999. *Racial Situations: Class Predicaments of Whiteness in Detroit.* Princeton, NJ: Princeton Univ. Press.

Helms J. 1990. A model of white racial identity development. In *Black and White Racial Identity: Theory, Research and Practice*, ed. J Helms, pp. 49–66. Westport, CT: Greenwood

Howard JA. 2000. Social psychology of identities. *Annu. Rev. Sociol.* 26:367–93

Hyde C. 1995. The meanings of whiteness. *Qual. Sociol.* 18:87–95

Ignatiev N. 1995. *How the Irish Became White.* New York: Routledge

Ignatiev N, Garvey J. 1996. *Race Traitor.* New York: Routledge

Jackson RL, Heckman SM. 2002. Perceptions of white identity and white liability: an analysis of white student responses to a college campus racial hate crime. *J. Commun.* 52:434–50

Jacobson MF. 1998. *Whiteness of a Different Color: European Immigrants and the Alchemy of Race.* Cambridge, MA: Harvard Univ. Press

Jaret C, Reitzes DC. 1999. The importance of racial-ethnic identity and social setting for blacks, whites, and multiracials. *Sociol. Perspect.* 42:711–37

Kazal RA. 2004a. *Becoming Old Stock: The Paradox of German-American Identity.* Princeton, NJ: Princeton Univ. Press. 383 pp.

Kazal RA. 2004b. The interwar origins of the white ethnic: race, residence and German Philadelphia, 1917–1939. *J. Am. Ethn. Hist.* 23:78–132

Kefalas M. 2003. *Working-Class Heroes: Protecting Home, Community, and Nation in a Chicago Neighborhood.* Berkeley: Univ. Calif. Press

Lamont M. 2000. *The Dignity of Working Men: Morality and the Boundaries of Race, Class and Immigration.* New York/Cambridge, MA: Russell Sage Found./Harvard Univ. Press

Lamont M, Molnar V. 2002. The study of boundaries in the social sciences. *Annu. Rev. Sociol.* 28:167–95

Langer E. 2003. *A Hundred Little Hitlers: The Death of a Black Man, the Trial of a White Racist, and the Rise of the Neo-Nazi Movement in America.* New York: Metropolitan

Levin B. 2002. Cyberhate: a legal and historical analysis of extremists' use of computer networks in America. *Am. Behav. Sci.* 45(6):958–88

Levitas D. 2002. *The Terrorist Next Door: The Militia Movement and the Radical Right.* New York: Thomas Dunne/St. Martin's

Lewis AE. 2003. *Race in the Schoolyard: Negotiating the Color Line in Classrooms and Communities.* New Brunswick, NJ: Rutgers Univ. Press. 243 pp.

Lewis AE. 2004. "What group?" Studying whites and whiteness in an era of "color blindness." *Soc. Theory* 22:623–46

Lieberson S. 1980. *A Piece of the Pie: Blacks and White Immigrants since 1880.* Berkeley: Univ. Calif. Press

Lieberson S, Waters MC. 1993. The ethnic responses of whites—what causes their instability, simplification, and inconsistency. *Soc. Forces* 72:421–50

Lipsitz G. 1998. *The Possessive Investment in Whiteness: How White People Benefit from Identity Politics.* Philadelphia, PA: Temple Univ. Press

Lowery BS, Knowles ED, Unzueta MM. 2004. *Framing inequity safely: the motivated denial of white privilege.* Work. Pap., Bus. Sch., Stanford Univ.

Mazie M, Palmer P, Pimentel M, Rogers S, Ruderfer S, Sokolowski M. 1993. To deconstruct race, deconstruct whiteness. *Am. Q.* 45:281–94

McIntosh P. 1988. White privilege: unpacking the invisible knapsack. In *White Privilege: Essential Readings on the Other Side of Racism*, ed. PS Rothenberg, pp. 97–101. New York: Worth

Nagel J. 1994. Constructing ethnicity: creating and recreating ethnic identity and culture. *Soc. Probl.* 41:152–76

O'Brien E. 2001. *Whites Confront Racism: Antiracists and Their Paths to Action.* Lanham, MD: Rowman & Littlefield

Olzak S. 1992. *The Dynamics of Ethnic Competition and Conflict.* Stanford, CA: Stanford Univ. Press

Olzak S, Shanahan S. 2003. Racial policy and racial conflict in the urban United States, 1869–1924. *Soc. Forces* 82:481–517

Omi M. 2001. (E)racism: emerging practices of antiracist organizations. See Rasmussen et al. 2001, pp. 266–93

Omi M, Winant H. 1986. *Racial Formation in the United States: From the 1960s to the 1980s.* New York: Routledge & Kegan Paul

Patterson O. 1977. *Ethnic Chauvinism: The Reactionary Impulse.* New York: Stein & Day

Perry P. 2002. *Shades of White: White Kids and Racial Identities in High School.* Durham, NC: Duke Univ. Press

Rasmussen BB, Klinenberg E, Nexica IJ, Wray M, eds. 2001. *The Making and Unmaking of Whiteness.* Durham, NC: Duke Univ. Press

Resnicow K, Ross-Gaddy D. 1997. Development of a racial identity scale for low-income African Americans. *J. Black Stud.* 28:239–54

Ridgeway J. 1990. *Blood in the Face: The Ku Klux Klan, Aryan Nations, Nazi Skinheads, and the Rise of a New White Culture.* New York: Thunder's Mouth

Rieder J. 1985. *Canarsie: The Jews and Italians of Brooklyn Against Liberalism.* Cambridge, MA: Harvard Univ. Press

Rockquemore KA, Brunsma DL. 2002. *Beyond Black: Biracial Identity in America.* Thousand Oaks, CA: Sage

Roediger DR. 1991. *The Wages of Whiteness: Race and the Making of the American Working Class.* London: Verso

Roediger DR. 1994. *Towards the Abolition of Whiteness: Essays on Race, Politics, and Working Class History.* London/New York: Verso. 201 pp.

Roediger DR, ed. 1998. *Black on White: Black Writers on What It Means to Be White.* New York: Schocken

Rowe W, Atkinson DR. 1995. Misrepresentation and interpretation: critical evaluation of white racial identity development models. *Couns. Psychol.* 23:364–67

Royster DA. 2003. *Race and the Invisible Hand: How White Networks Exclude Black Men from Blue-Collar Jobs.* Berkeley: Univ. Calif. Press

Sharpe TT. 2000. The Christian identity movement: ideology of domestic terrorism. *J. Black Stud.* 30(4):604–23

Sidanius J, Pratto F. 1999. *Social Dominance: An Intergroup Theory of Social Hierarchy and Oppression.* Cambridge, UK: Cambridge Univ. Press

Steinberg S. 1981. *The Ethnic Myth: Race, Ethnicity, and Class in America.* New York: Atheneum

Stoddart K. 2002. Researching white racial identity: a methodological story. *Am. Behav. Sci.* 45:1254–64

Storrs D. 1999. Whiteness as stigma: essentialist identity work by mixed-race women. *Symb. Interact.* 22:187–212

Sugrue TJ. 1996. *The Origins of the Urban Crisis: Race and Inequality in Postwar Detroit.* Princeton, NJ: Princeton Univ. Press

Suttles GD. 1972. *The Social Construction of Communities.* Chicago: Univ. Chicago Press. 278 pp.

Swain CM. 2002. *The New White Nationalism in America: Its Challenge to Integration.* Cambridge, UK/New York: Cambridge Univ. Press

Tajfel H, Turner JC. 1985. The social identity theory of intergroup behavior. In *Psychology of Intergroup Relations,* ed. S Worchel, WG Austin, pp. 7–24. Chicago: Nelson-Hall

Thomas WI, Znaniecki F. 1927. *The Polish Peasant in Europe and America.* New York: Knopf

Van Ausdale D, Feagin JR. 2001. *The First R: How Children Learn Race and Racism.* Lanham, MD: Rowman & Littlefield. 231 pp.

Warren JW, Twine FW. 1997. White Americans, the new minority? Non-blacks and the ever-expanding boundaries of whiteness. *J. Black Stud.* 28:200–18

Waters MC. 1990. *Ethnic Options: Choosing Identities in America.* Berkeley: Univ. Calif. Press

Whine M. 1999. Cyberspace—a new medium

for communication, command, and control by extremists. *Stud. Confl. Terror.* 22(3): 231–45

Whyte WF. 1943. *Street Corner Society: The Social Structure of an Italian Slum.* Chicago: Univ. Chicago Press

Williams RM. 1994. The sociology of ethnic conflicts: comparative international perspectives. *Annu. Rev. Sociol.* 20:49–79

Winant H. 2001. White racial projects. See Rasmussen et al. 2001, pp. 97–112

Annu. Rev. Sociol. 2005. 31:263–84
doi: 10.1146/annurev.soc.31.041304.122159
Copyright © 2005 by Annual Reviews. All rights reserved
First published online as a Review in Advance on February 11, 2005

AGENCY THEORY

Susan P. Shapiro

American Bar Foundation, Chicago, Illinois 60611; email: sshapiro@abfn.org

Key Words   fiduciary, social control, professional, embeddedness, conflict of interest

■ **Abstract**   In an agency relationship, one party acts on behalf of another. It is curious that a concept that could not be more profoundly sociological does not have a niche in the sociological literature. This essay begins with the economics paradigm of agency theory, which casts a very long shadow over the social sciences, and then traces how these ideas diffuse to and are transformed (if at all) in the scholarship produced in business schools, political science, law, and sociology. I cut a swathe through the social fabric where agency relationships are especially prevalent and examine some of the institutions, roles, forms of social organization, deviance, and strategies of social control that deliver agency and respond to its vulnerabilities, and I consider their impact. Finally, I suggest how sociology might make better use of and contribute to agency theory.

INTRODUCTION

Let me introduce myself. I am an agent. The editors of the *Annual Review of Sociology* delegated to me the task of writing an essay on agency theory. They are the principals and together we are bound in a principal-agent relationship. They have a principal-agent relationship with you (the readers) as well. They are your agents, and so am I, although not every agency theorist would agree with my loose conceptualization of your role in this, and few would be interested in you at all (although I am).

I am not sure how or why my principals selected me for this task. Perhaps they "Googled" me. I do use the words "agent," "principal," and "agency relationship" a lot. But I doubt that they used a more sophisticated search engine. If they had, they would have realized that I have never used the words "agency" and "theory" side by side (although I guess it's possible that they did and wanted someone who is not so identified with this peculiar way of understanding social reality or is not solidly in one camp or another in a rather contentious literature).

In any event, in selecting me and all the other authors in this volume, they faced a classic agency problem of asymmetric information. We know far more about ourselves—our abilities, expertise, honesty, etc.—than they do, and we sometimes make matters worse by exaggerating our talents. I know how much

0360-0572/05/0811-0263$20.00

of the agency literature I have bothered to read and how much of it I understand. I know whether I skip the paragraphs in the economics articles that begin, "let gamma be. . ." and then go on to use mathematical fonts I can't even find on my computer. I know better how good a sociologist I am and how analytical and original I am or am capable of being. I know better how many other projects I have on my plate right now and how responsible, conscientious, and diligent I am. Actually I know who would have been a better choice to write this essay. But my editors/principals don't. They never do, and therefore every assignment in this volume is tainted by adverse selection (in the insurance vernacular) or what Arrow (1985) calls "hidden information": they "will attract a disproportionate number of low-quality applicants" (Moe 1984, p. 755). The principals probably could have found someone better but just didn't know enough to identify them or didn't provide incentives compelling enough to attract them. So they got us.

Of course, that is not their only agency problem. Information asymmetries not only mean that principals don't know the true "type" (to borrow from the agency theory jargon) of the varied candidates in the pool of potential agents, but they also don't know what we are doing once they select us. They don't know what I am reading, if anything, or whether I am scouring literature reviews or plodding through the actual primary sources. They don't know whether I have been thorough or fair. They don't know if I got someone else to write this for me or if I plagiarized it. Agency theorists are mostly worried that I might be shirking—not working hard enough, if at all. Many theorists also assume that I am "opportunistic" [pursuing self-interest with "guile" (Williamson 1975)] and will take advantage of the "perquisites" of this appointment for my own benefit. But sadly, my agency-savvy principals didn't give me any perquisites. (I have tried to use my inside information to trade on *Annual Review* futures, but I can't find this product on any of the commodities exchanges.) My principals, then, are also threatened by the version of informational asymmetry known in insurance as moral hazard, or what Arrow (1985) labels "hidden action."

The one thing they can be sure of is that our goals are incompatible. My principals want the "highest-quality scientific literature reviews in the world" that "defin[e] the current state of scientific knowledge," and they want them on time and in the correct format (Annual Reviews 2003, pp. 2, 18). I want the glory with none of the work and desperately need the deadline to be extended. And I will exploit all the information asymmetries I can contrive to insure that I maximize my own interests at their expense.

So what do the poor principals do? Agency theory dictates that my principals will try to bridge the informational asymmetries by installing information systems and monitoring me. My manuscript will be peer reviewed, for example. And because my reputation is tied up in the quality of my work, they can count on some self-regulation on my part. They also offer me incentives in an effort to align my interests with theirs. They tell me that the earlier my manuscript arrives, the closer it will be placed toward the front of the volume. [So the position of this chapter tells you something about my character, that is, if my principals are of the trustworthy type—something the sociologists (Perrow 1986), but apparently not the economists, are worried about.]

As part of this incentive alignment, my principals compensate me, not for my agreement to do this work for them or for the amount of time I spent on the project—consistent with a "behavior-oriented contract"—but for what I actually deliver, an "outcome-oriented contract." They tell me that if the manuscript arrives late, they will not guarantee that they will publish it at all, ever (and you know how difficult it will be to recycle this sort of review essay into another journal). That, of course, shifts the risk to me, because events outside of my control (like the fact that a lightening strike or virus fried my hard drive) or other environmental uncertainties may affect my ability to deliver on our agreement. Agency theory reminds us that, although principals are risk neutral (they have diversified and have plenty of other manuscripts to use), agents are risk averse, because they have placed all their eggs in this one basket. That is another reason our interests conflict, by the way; shrouded behind my information asymmetries, I will do perverse things contrary to my principal's welfare to protect myself from risk. All these efforts undertaken by my principals, coupled with the fact that I still didn't give them exactly what they wanted, constitute agency costs. The trick, in structuring a principal-agent relationship, is to minimize them.

This introduction more or less represents a cartoon version of the classic economics account of agency theory. I begin here because, as in many things, the economics formulation of agency theory is the dominant one and casts a very long shadow over the other social sciences. Because it gets all the attention and there are already excellent reviews of this literature (e.g., Moe 1984; Eisenhardt 1989; Mitnick 1992, 1998), this essay briefly traces some of the alternative disciplinary approaches—especially in law, management, and political science. Then I turn to sociology, where the literature on agency theory is especially sparse, and ask how it could be that a relationship—acting on behalf of another—that could not be more profoundly sociological does not seem to have a niche. Finally, I suggest what that niche might look like.

ECONOMICS AND BEYOND

The main thing missing from my cartoon version of the economics of agency (unfortunately, from this agent's perspective) is any money changing hands. Consequently, a few of the traditional options for aligning my incentives with my principals (commissions, bonuses, piece rates, equity ownership, stock options, profit sharing, sharecropping, deductibles, etc.) are missing, as are some of the governance mechanisms or devices principals contrive to monitor their agents (e.g., boards of directors, auditors, supervisors, structural arrangements, and so forth). Also missing are a few of the things I might have done to reassure my principals or keep their monitors at bay: I could have bonded myself or perhaps posted a hostage who or which wouldn't be released until I turned over the manuscript. All these devices also figure into the accounting of agency costs.

Nonetheless, my case study actually accords better with classic agency theory in economics than the scenarios economists usually model. Ours is a dyadic relationship between individuals; economists study firms and typically focus on the relationship between owners and managers or employers and employees. The assumption of methodological individualism makes this transformation seamless. In the classic articulation of agency theory in economics, Jensen & Meckling (1976) assert that "most organizations are simply legal fictions which serve as a nexus for a set of contracting relationships among individuals" (p. 310). In this paradigm, agency relationships are contracts, and the incentives, monitoring devices, bonding, and other forms of social control undertaken to minimize agency costs constitute the elements of the contract.

Economists make problematic the nature of these contracts. Those with a mathematical bent (in what is known as principal-agent theory) model the "structure of the preferences of the parties," "the nature of uncertainty," and "the informational structure" on contracting practices. A more descriptive and empirical trajectory (known as positive agency theory) examines "the effects of additional aspects of the contracting environment and the technology of monitoring and bonding on the form of the contracts and the organizations that survive" (Jensen 1983, p. 334; see also Eisenhardt 1989).

The assumption that complex organizational structures and networks can be reduced to dyads of individuals is one of many assumptions—regarding efficiency and equilibrium, that individuals are rational and self-interested utility maximizers prone to opportunism, etc.—that are off-putting to other social sciences. To be tractable, however, mathematical modeling requires such simplistic assumptions, as even a very flattering review of that literature concedes:

> [S]uch a framework sometimes encourages highly complex mathematical treatment of trivial problems; form tends to triumph over substance, and analytical concerns tend to take on lives of their own that have little to do with the explanation of empirical phenomena. . ... [M]uch of the current literature focuses on matters of little substantive interest (Moe 1984, p. 757).

One of the economists most identified with agency theory admits that "authors are led to assume the problem away or to define sterile 'toy' problems that are mathematically tractable" (Jensen 1983, p. 333).

Much of the scholarship on agency outside of economics begins by relaxing or jettisoning the unrealistic assumptions of the economics paradigm and transforming the rigid dichotomies into more complex variables. The first assumption to go, of course, is that of a dyadic relationship between individuals. As Kiser (1999) observes, classic agency theory "is an organizational theory without organizations" (p. 150). Scholarship across many disciplines brings organizations of all sorts back in and looks far beyond the economists' favorite poster children of shareholder/manager and employer/employee as they investigate when and how agency relationships are established and regulated. Looking beyond the abstract, cloistered dyad also reveals that actors are not just principals or agents, but often both at the same time—even in the same transaction or hierarchical structure. I may be an agent to the editors of the *Annual Review*, but I am also the would-be principal to the scores of research assistants who I wish existed to assist me on this project. The CEO may be an agent of the stockholders and the board, but he or she is simultaneously the principal in a long chain of principal-agent relationships both inside and outside the corporation. What occurs at some node in that network of agents acting on behalf of the CEO figures significantly in the agency contract between the CEO and the shareholders. Just ask Kenneth Lay at Enron.

Moreover, the assumption of a solitary principal and agent is invariably extended to include multiple principals and agents. This is not just a matter of verisimilitude. Theories become much more complex (and interesting) when they allow for the possibility that collections or teams of principals (or agents) disagree or compete over interests and goals—a feature of agency relationships Adams (1996) dubs the "Hydra factor." How do agents understand and reconcile the duties delegated to them when they are receiving mixed messages and conflicting instructions—and incentives—from multiple principals? How do they do so when the contract is exceptionally vague by design, to paper over the irreconcilable differences among principals with conflicting interests—say, controversial legislation that requires implementation? When do these cleavages among and collective action problems faced by principals give agents opportunities to play one principal off against another?

Multiple agents who have been delegated to undertake a task collectively add other wrinkles to the economists' models. Agents, too, have competing interests; indeed the interests of some agents may be more congruent with those of their principals than with the other agents. Some agents are more risk averse than others; incentives work differently on different agents. Some agents may be free riders. And the existence of multiple principals and multiple agents sometimes increases the informational asymmetries and the difficulties of monitoring. These asymmetries are among the reasons organizational crimes can flourish undiscovered for long periods of time buried in complex structures of action. At other times, multiple parties help to right the imbalance of information, such as when competitive agents leak information to principals in an effort to get an upper hand over other agents (Waterman & Meier 1998).

The assumption that principals are in the driver's seat—specifying preferences, creating incentives, and making contracts that agents must follow—is also problematic (Heimer & Staffen 1998, Sharma 1997). When principals seek out agents for their expert knowledge, when principals are one-shotters and agents repeat players, when principals are unexpectedly foisted into a new role with no time or life experience to formulate preferences, let alone a contract or monitoring strategy [e.g., the new parents of a critically ill newborn (Heimer & Staffen 1998)], the asymmetry of power shifts from the principal to the agent.

Other scholars remove the economists' blinders that cause them to focus only on the self-interest and opportunism of agents and the difficulties of regulating them. Perrow (1986), for example, accuses the economics paradigm of being incapable of keeping its eye on both sides of the principal-agent relationship and of recognizing that agency problems on the agent side of the relationship are often mirrored on the principal side. He observes that the theory is indifferent to principal type that may lead to adverse selection by agents who may be unwittingly drawn to principals who shirk, cheat, and opportunistically seize perquisites for their own use; who deceive (e.g., about hazardous working conditions, opportunities for advancement, etc.); and who exploit their agents. Blind to the asymmetries of power that course through these relationships, classic agency theory, Perrow argues, is profoundly conservative, even dangerous.

Perrow (1986) also rejects the assumption that parties are invariably work averse, self-interested utility maximizers. He observes that in some settings or organizational structures, human beings are other-regarding, even altruistic, and he faults classical agency theory for its inattention to the cooperative aspects of social life. This critique is continued in what has become known in the management literature as stewardship theory, which views agents as good stewards and team players and replaces assumptions of opportunism and conflict of interest with those of cooperation and coordination (Donaldson 1990).

As other disciplines wander away from the market as the site of theoretical and empirical work on agency, the irrelevance or variability of the classic assumptions and solutions to the agency problem becomes even more apparent (Banfield 1975). Work in political science particularly confronts the limitations of a theory of markets. As Moe (1984) observes,

> the more general principal-agent models of hierarchical control have shown that, under a range of conditions, the principal's optimal incentive structure for the agent is one in which the latter receives some share of the residual in payment for his efforts, thus giving him a direct stake in the outcome. . . . For public bureaucracy, however, there is no residual in the ordinary sense of the term (p. 763).

There is no profit that can be distributed to members of public agencies for exemplary behavior. Scholarship on agency relationships, such as between the legislative or executive branch and administrative agencies, may continue to employ economic metaphors: Politicians need to maximize their votes; bureaucrats need to maximize their budgets. But the metaphor fails to capture the range of incentives at play in the political arena, many of which revolve around policy rather than profit (Waterman & Meier 1998). Indeed, the salience of policy commitments undermines our expectation of goal conflict between principals and agents, who may sometimes share policy goals (or, more accurately, some among the collections of multiple principles and agents might do so). The extent, sources, and strategies of compensating for information asymmetries also vary considerably as one moves away from market settings (Waterman & Meier 1998, Worsham et al. 1997, Sharma 1997, Banfield 1975).

Finally, scholars from varied disciplines outside of economics also abandon the assumption of an acontextual, ahistorical, and static relationship between principals and agents (Mitnick 1992). Agency relationships are enacted in a broader social context and buffeted by outside forces—other agency relationships, competitors, interest groups, regulators, legal rules, and the like—that sometimes right informational imbalances, offer or constrain incentives, exacerbate the risk of adverse selection or moral hazard, provide cover or opportunity for opportunism, and so forth. Relationships endure over time, affording principals and agents occasions to gather data about one another. Principals learn better which incentives are likely to work. Agents learn more about the preferences of the principals they serve. They develop reputations. Relationships become embedded as parties develop histories and personal relationships and become entangled in social networks (Granovetter 1985). Over time, agents acquire constituencies other than their principals that buffer them from the contracting, recontracting, and sanctioning of their principals. And as agents (government bureaucrats, corporate managers) outlast their principals (legislators, CEOs), the balance of power between principal and agent may shift.

Management

The agency theory paradigm, first formulated in the academic economics literature in the early 1970s (Ross 1973, Jensen & Meckling 1976) had diffused into the business schools, the management literature, specialized academic and applied practitioner journals, the business press, even corporate proxy statements by the early 1990s, representing a new zeitgeist and becoming the dominant institutional logic of corporate governance (Zajac & Westphal 2004). Corporations announced the adoption of new policies, explicitly invoking agency theory buzzwords about aligning incentives, discouraging self-interested behavior by managers, and reducing agency costs. Indeed, some adopted new policies that embraced an agency rationale without bothering to implement them, simply jumping on the bandwagon of a socially constructed institutional logic that bestowed increased market value on symbolic declarations alone (Zajac & Westphal 2004).

Despite the fascinating case study in social movements (Davis & Thompson 1994), the diffusion of innovations, and the sociology of knowledge that these developments offer, they also had a significant impact on the intellectual agenda of the academy, spawning a massive empirical literature in management and organizational behavior. Agency theory has become a cottage industry that explores every permutation and combination of agency experience in the corporate form. Because the work is largely empirical, it by necessity relaxes some of the assumptions of classic agency theory in economics; it turns dichotomies into continuous variables, breathes life into abstract categories, and situates inquiry in at least some limited context. Still, it is closely wedded to the questions raised in economics and the settings invoked by economic models.

The most popular stream of literature focuses on incentive alignment, particularly compensation policies. Empirical studies consider the types and correlates of and trade-offs between behavior-oriented (salary) and outcome-oriented (piece rates, commissions, bonuses, equity ownership and other devices that link compensation to shareholder wealth) compensation (Eisenhardt 1989). A second stream examines corporate governance and control, such as

- the monitoring role of the board of directors and trade-offs between recruiting inside or outside directors or between separating the roles of board chair and CEO versus filling them with one individual;
- monitoring strategies within the firm [e.g., trade-offs between horizontal (peer-to-peer) and vertical (agent-to-principal) control];
- bonding mechanisms; and
- the agency implications of different forms of capitalization (e.g., paying out dividends and thereby limiting discretionary funds available to managers while also activating the monitoring role of the financial markets when managers must solicit additional funding).

The literature also includes studies of the process and costs of searching for agents, especially in light of the tensions posed by adverse selection.

Another major body of scholarship considers the agency problems, agency costs, efficacy, and trade-offs of different control mechanisms as they intersect and vary by

- length of principal-agent relationship;
- organizational structure and form (e.g., headquarters and subsidiary, outsourcing);
- characteristics of industries, organizations, and employees (e.g., technologies, product demand, diversification, venture capitalist-entrepreneur relationships, family firms, cultural distance between sites, employee education, skill levels, amount of specialized knowledge, autonomy, etc.);
- "programmability" of the task, or how well the required behaviors can be precisely defined (Eisenhardt 1989); and
- organizational environments (e.g., turbulence).

Also coursing through this literature is a debate, sketched earlier, between those who adopt the skeptical, even paranoid, assumptions of agency theory and the costly control mechanisms it propounds and those who have a more hopeful view of human capacities for other-regarding behavior and altruism and argue that agency costs can be mitigated by organizational structures that foster reciprocity, cooperation, embeddedness, and trust (Donaldson 1990, Wright & Mukherji 1999).

Political Science

In exploring the delegation of power and authority in political and government institutions and international organizations, political scientists take agency theory outside of the economic marketplace and the constricting web of assumptions that shroud the economic theory of agency. The political system can, of course, be understood as a complex network of principal-agent relationships composed of citizens, nation states, elected officials, lawmakers, members of the executive branch, administrative agencies, courts, international organizations, ambassadors, bureaucrats, soldiers, police officers, supervisory officials, civil servants, patronage appointees, and even those who monitor other agency relationships inside political institutions and in the market. These actors concurrently play principal and agent roles within and across political organizations.

A general theory of agency emerged in political science (Mitnick 1973) at the same time that it did in economics (Ross 1973), apparently independently. As we have seen, the latter took off spectacularly, becoming quickly institutionalized in an academic literature, specialty journals, and corporate ideologies and practices. The former languished (Moe 1984), developing belatedly as rational choice theory made inroads into political science. As a result, agency theory in political science borrows heavily from the economics paradigm rather than the more sociological conception offered by Mitnick (1973) or even classic works, such as Weber on bureaucracy (Kiser 1999).

The vague outlines of the agency paradigm in political science are the same as those in the classic version: Principals delegate to agents the authority to carry out their political preferences. However, the goals of principals and agents may conflict and, because of asymmetries of information, principals cannot be sure that agents are carrying out their will. Political principals also face problems of adverse selection, moral hazard, and agent opportunism. So principals contrive incentives to align agent interests with their own and undertake monitoring of agent behavior, activities that create agency costs.

The details are quite different, however, for many of the reasons considered earlier. Political scientists assume multiple agents and principals; heterogeneous preferences or goal conflict and competition among principals and among agents as well as between them; problems of collective action; a more complicated palate of interests and therefore different incentives mobilized to control them; varying sources of and mechanisms to mitigate informational asymmetries; an active role for third parties (interest groups, regulated parties, etc.); and a dynamic playing field on which relationships unfold and are transformed.

Political scientists also consider a more diverse set of scenarios for delegating power beyond those inherited from the economics paradigm. Principals may delegate to another to enhance the credibility of their commitments, for self-binding (to ensure their long-term resolve in the face of immediate temptations), or to avoid blame for unpopular policies. These scenarios call for a very different agency contract. Instead of providing incentives and sanctions to align the interests of agents with their own, principals seeking credibility from their agents select agents operating at arm's length, with very different policy preferences, and confer considerable discretion and autonomy to them. These agency contracts grant independence while still seeking to insure accountability (Majone 2001).

Early literature in political science on the iron law of oligarchy, the iron triangle (between Congress, regulatory agencies, and regulated interests), regulatory capture, and bureaucratic drift all give voice to some of the intrinsic difficulties of principal control in political institutions. More recent work employing an agency theory perspective ranges from appellate review of lower court decisions to political corruption and presidential decisions to use force. The largest literatures examine state policy implementation, the relationship between elective institutions and administrative agencies (especially legislators and bureaucrats), and government regulation. Principal-agent perspectives are also commonplace in examinations of international organizations (e.g., central banks, international courts, the European Union) in the literature on comparative politics and international relations.

Political scientists devote far more attention than economists to the details of how principals control agents. There is some work on the selection and recruitment of agents, the role of patronage, political appointments, and the impact of civil service requirements on adverse selection and more on how principals specify their preferences. A body of work considers statutory control (i.e., detailed legislation) and how lawmakers craft legislation to restrict the discretion of those charged with its implementation, specifying administrative structures and procedures to constrain the decision-making process (McCubbins et al. 1989). There are literatures on political oversight and monitoring, including ways in which principals opt for reactive over proactive oversight, relying on third-party monitoring by affected interest groups or the targets of their legislation to detect and report on noncompliance (so-called fire alarms or decibel meters).

There is more attention in political science than in economics to the role of sanctions—budget cuts, vetoing rules or agency actions, reversing court decisions, firing officials or voting them out of office, requiring agency reauthorization or threatening recontracting, etc.—perhaps because, as noted earlier, it is far less easy to align incentives without the financial inducements that flow through economic organizations. The literature also considers the matter of agency costs; when they are too high, principals may decide not to squander resources on them (Mitnick 1998, Banfield 1975). Because politicians may not directly feel the consequences of self-interested, opportunistic agents shirking or undermining their interests (what political scientists call slack, slippage, or bureaucratic drift), the costs of which are generally passed along to the public, monitoring activities may be more lax in political arenas (Waterman & Meier 1998).

Law

Long before there was a theory of agency, there was a law of agency. Indeed, it was not until the twenty-first century that the *Restatement of the Law, Agency* (American Law Institute 2001) replaced "master/servant" with "employer/employee." The law of agency

> encompasses the legal consequences of consensual relationships in which one person (the 'principal') manifests assent that another person (the 'agent') shall, subject to the principal's right of control, have power to affect the principal's legal relations through the agent's acts and on the principal's behalf (American Law Institute 2001, p. 1).

In other words, the central focus of the law of agency is on "the legal consequences of choosing to act through another person in lieu of oneself" (DeMott
1998, p. 1039). Agency doctrine defines the legal obligations that principals have
with third parties for actions that agents took on their behalf. The principal, for
example, may be "bound to contracts and transactions made by the agent and may
be vicariously liable for some instances of the agent's misconduct" (DeMott 1998,
p. 1038). Because principals will be held responsible for the actions of their agents,
the law also attends to the sources of agent authority, clearly demarcating what
constitutes an agency relationship, the rights of principals to control their agents,
and the fiduciary duty and other obligations that agents owe their principals (Clark
1985).

Agency theory borrows jargon from agency law, but adopts neither its definition
nor its central focus. The legal definition of agency is much more narrow even than
that employed in the economics paradigm of agency theory, let alone that found
in the other social sciences.

> [A]gency does not encompass situations in which the 'agent' is not subject
> to a right of control in the person who benefits from or whose interests are
> affected by the agent's acts, who lacks the power to terminate the 'agent's'
> representation, or who has not consented to the representation (American Law
> Institute 2001, p. 2).

> Generally, the alleged agent and principal have met each other face to face,
> or have talked on the telephone, or have otherwise communicated with each
> other in a specific, individualized way. Courts trying to determine the scope
> of their relationship often scrutinize the actual course of dealings between the
> particular parties and try to determine what their actual understanding of their
> particular relationship was (Clark 1985, p. 58).

The relationship between a corporation's shareholders and its directors, for example, does not fall within the legal definition of agency, notwithstanding the
centrality of this relationship in economic agency theory. Principal control is critical in the law of agency because of its focus on third parties and the concern
that when third parties make agreements with agents or are hurt by agents, their
principals will be bound or held responsible. But it is the control itself that the
social sciences make problematic. Therefore, it cannot be defined away by looking
only at the point along a continuum where control is absolute. Moreover, central
questions in the social sciences about the nature of the contract between principal
and agent, the mechanisms by which the former control the latter, and strategies
to contain agency costs are rather peripheral in the law of agency.

Still, when the two paradigms do intersect, the law of agency provides rich
grist for the social scientists' mill—for example, when legal scholars look to the
mechanisms by which principals select their agents; the private norms, instructions,
and messages the principals convey; the nature of the incentives they offer; and the
care they take to monitor the behavior of agents to determine whether corporations
should be held vicariously liable for the criminal conduct of their employees
(DeMott 1997). The law offers normative understandings of agency relationships

and lots of data (if tainted by selection bias), especially when they fail. But it offers little else.

A SOCIOLOGICAL PERSPECTIVE

> Although economists may speak of 'the agency problem,' agency is in fact a solution, a neat kind of social plumbing. The problem is the ancient and ineluctable one of how to attain and maintain control in order to carry out definite, yet varying purposes (White 1985, p. 188).

In his comparative analysis of agency theory applications to state policy implementation in economics, political science, and sociology, Kiser (1999) observes that, compared to the other two disciplines, "the use of agency theory in sociology is in its infancy" and comes from a rather different "intellectual genealogy" (p. 162), largely the work of Weber (1924/1968). [See Kiser (1999) for an illuminating analysis that traces the linkages between abstract components of classic agency theory and Weber's work on the relationship between rulers and their administrative staff.]

Empirical work in sociology that explicitly adopts an agency theory perspective (aside from that described earlier in the organizational behavior and management literatures) can be found in the most unexpected of places—in qualitative comparative historical sociology. In imaginative and richly textured case studies of such things as European colonialism in seventeenth and eighteenth century Asia, Chinese state bureaucratization that occurred two millennia before any of the European states, early modern tax farming, and types of corruption in premodern Asian tax administration, we learn about the tensions between principals and agents, conflicting interests, opportunism, informational asymmetry, agent selection, monitoring, sanctions, incentives, and agency costs (Adams 1996, Kiser 1999, Kiser & Cai 2003). This work links social structure to types of agency relations, and it demonstrates how different combinations of recruitment, monitoring, and sanctioning practices yield different administrative systems. This literature is certainly a far cry from the abstract mathematical models of principal-agent theory in economics.

It is puzzling that agency theory is not invoked elsewhere across the sociological landscape in places one would think would be more hospitable. Perhaps, like me, few sociologists feel comfortable putting the words "agency" and "theory" side by side and find the classic paradigm, its assumptions, and the research questions it inspires off-putting and simplistic. But that has never been our only choice. As long as there has been an economic theory of agency there has been a more sociological alternative. In a series of papers spanning at least 25 years, political scientist Barry Mitnick broke the monopoly on agency theory enjoyed by the economics paradigm and offered an alternative to the assorted baggage that comes with it. Agency, he argued (Mitnick 1998, p. 12) is simply "a general social theory of relationships of 'acting for' or control in complex systems." Agency relationships have two faces, Mitnick observed: "the activities and problems of identifying and providing services of 'acting for' (the agent side), and the activities and problems of guiding and correcting agent actions (the principal side)." Of course, both faces of agency entail costs and at some point it does not pay for principals or agents to perfect their behaviors. So "perfect agency" is rare, and deviant behavior is likely to "persist and be tolerated." Agency theory, then, "becomes a study in the production, the persistence, and the amelioration of failures in service and control" (Mitnick 1998, p. 12), a kind of Murphy's law (Mitnick 1992, p. 76). Mitnick's work repeatedly shows the links between agency theory and sociological literatures from exchange theory to norms, networks, authority, organizations, social control, regulation, trust, social cognition, and so on. Yet it, too, is rarely cited in sociological literature.

The problem may be that "acting for" relationships are too general, embracing too much of what is enacted on our turf. Perhaps sociologists have been studying agency all along and just didn't know it. In the remainder of this essay, I focus on several sites across the social landscape where making agency relationships problematic seems likely to provide the most theoretical purchase.

Agency or "acting for" relationships arise from a number of sources, including

1. the division of labor; we simply do not have time to do everything ourselves (even hunting and gathering), and complex tasks often require more than one actor [Mitnick (1984) calls this practical or structural agency];

2. the acquisition of expertise or access to specialized knowledge [Mitnick (1984) labels this contentful agency];

3. the bridging of physical, social (e.g., brokering or intermediation), or temporal distance [Adams's (1996) study of colonialization provides an example of the challenges of the former; for the latter, see Majone's (2001) discussion of time-inconsistency]; and

4. the impulse to collectivize in order to enjoy economies of scope and scale or protection from risk [Mitnick (1984) calls this systemic or collective agency]; many of these relationships (pensions, insurance, investments, etc.) are what I have called futures transactions that "demand that commitment be conferred far in advance of payoff without any necessary confirmation during the interim that the return on investment will ever be honored" (Shapiro 1987, p. 628).

These varied occasions for agency—especially the last three, in which a formidable physical, social, temporal, or experiential barrier separates principal and agent—pose different agency problems. Several exacerbate problems of asymmetric information; others contribute to adverse selection; some create collective action problems among multiple principals; others provide easy cover for moral hazard and opportunism.

Professions

The sociology of the professions provides a window on agency as expertise, problems of asymmetric information, and one kind of model for delivering agency services. The assumptions of the agency paradigm are stretched where principals seek out agents for their specialized knowledge. Sharma (1997) observes that run-of-the-mill information asymmetry (not knowing what the agent does) is exacerbated in encounters with professionals by knowledge asymmetry as well (not knowing how the agent does a job). Adverse selection is a special problem because principals are unable to evaluate the skills of prospective agents. Principals also have a difficult time specifying an agency contract because they may not know what expert services are required or how much of them, what procedures ought to be followed, or what criteria are appropriate to limit agent discretion. They also have difficulty evaluating the quality of service because "indeterminacy [is] intrinsic in highly specialized tasks" (Sharma 1997, p. 771). Some patients get better despite their physicians; the clients of superb lawyers sometimes lose; and bright, curious, conscientious students may become great sociologists despite incompetent or opportunistic professors.

Professions provide the solution to these agency problems. They boast careful and competitive selection procedures. They offer training and credentialing, licensing, recertification, and mandatory continuing education to solve the principals' problem of adverse selection. They may even establish protocols or specify best practices to limit agent discretion. They create ethics codes to curb the self-interest and opportunism of practitioners. Because principals are unable to determine when they have received exceptional or substandard service, professions self-regulate in varied settings (among peers, within service organizations, within professional associations, and by disciplinary bodies). And professions often offer or promote malpractice insurance to protect principals from the errors or misdeeds of honest and incompetent agents alike. Insurers often provide incentives, stipulate mandatory procedures, and provide loss prevention services to their insureds—adding yet another level of regulation (Heimer 1985, Davis 1996). Professions, then, are social devices to limit agency costs.

Of course, there is a critical literature that provides a rather different frame on the agendas of professions as mechanisms to secure monopoly (e.g., Larson 1977, among many others). But this frame is by no means incompatible with a principal-agent perspective. Indeed offering a credible mechanism to minimize agency costs represents a brilliant marketing strategy and a way to stave off the encroachment of other would-be agents who seek to offer the same services to principals.

Embeddedness

Literatures on embeddedness and trust (Granovetter 1985, Shapiro 1987, Cook 2001) depict a rather different strategy for coping with the agency problem by targeting agent selection, monitoring, and sanctioning. Embedding agency relationships in an ongoing structure of personal relationships solves the problem of adverse selection in the recruitment of agents. Principals frequently know their agent's type because of personal familiarity with potential agents or through members of trusted social networks in which both principal and agent are embedded; agents have track records and reputations. Although neither self-interest nor goal conflict is extinguished by recruiting agents from personal networks, their effects are likely mitigated somewhat. Agents and principals are more likely to share similar interests and values than those found among groups of strangers, and agents are more likely to be other-regarding (altruistic, even) or honest when entrusted with responsibilities for friends, family, neighbors, fellow church or association members, and the like. Monitoring of agent behavior is also usually easier in proximate and continuing relationships in which agents are routinely overseen or surveilled by principals or their associates. And social networks afford a rich array of sanctions for the errant agent (from shaming, ostracizing, or loss of reputation, to more restitutive sanctions).

Despite the celebration of trust as a source of social capital in the literature, embeddedness also has a dark side. Family firms, for example, face unique agency costs. They struggle with adverse selection because nepotism can lead to the selection of less-capable or expert agents. Moreover, because family members are often compensated generously regardless of merit, and their job tenures are relatively secure, principals lack important incentives to constrain agent behavior. Hence, the risk of shirking and free riding by family agents. Because embeddedness is often an excuse to relax vigilant recruitment and monitoring, it provides cover, not only for wayward offspring or relatives, but also for confidence swindlers to feign social intimacy and thereby enjoy unfettered opportunism (Shapiro 1990).

Fiduciaries

In the law of agency, all agents are fiduciaries, but all fiduciaries are not agents (that is because, as you recall, in law agents must be able to control their principals). But these other non-agent fiduciaries are much more interesting—the individuals and organizations acting on behalf of those for whom the asymmetries of information, expertise, access, or power are so great that they cannot pretend to control their agents. We are more interested in the professor who has his pension tied up in TIAA-CREF than the CEO of TIAA-CREF who has delegated some responsibility to an investment analyst working at the company. We are more interested in Terry Schiavo, the comatose Florida woman whose guardian is trying to end life support, than in Jeb Bush, the Florida governor who is maneuvering to continue her persistent vegetative state. Or, more accurately, I propose that sociologists take an interest in the fiduciaries acting on behalf of the former. Organizational and political sociologists have already taken an interest in the agents for the latter.

When agency relationships are at their most asymmetric, the basic logic of classic agency theory breaks down. Preferences are not specified (or at least not heard or satisfied), contracts not formulated, incentives not fashioned, monitoring not mobilized, sanctions not levied—at least not by the principals themselves;

and those who believe that agents are opportunistic might profitably look here for evidence of abuse. Of course, these fiduciaries face a problem as well: Why would anyone ever trust them when their conduct is so unrestrained? Would-be fiduciaries therefore undertake activities to shore up their trustworthiness in an effort to market their wares. The systematic study of the social construction, social organization, and social control of the fiduciary role or impersonal trust is well overdue [Shapiro (1987); see also Majone (2001) for a discussion of trustee or fiduciary relations as an alternative to agency in political science].

Goal Conflict

The classic agency paradigm, with its eye on the principal, perceives goal conflict as the departure of agents from the interests of the principal. Hence, the solution to this agency problem is to come up with incentives that will align the interests of agents with those of the principal. Keep the agent from shirking by paying her a piece rate, perhaps. The agency problem looks quite different from the perspective of the agent, though. Conflicts between the interests of the agents and those of the principal are the least of the agent's problems. The real problem is that the agent is most likely serving many masters, many of them with conflicting interests. Even if the agent is able to silence his or her own interests, there is the matter of how to maneuver through the tangled loyalties he or she owes to many different principals and how to negotiate through their competing interests and sometimes irreconcilable differences. How do you honor the preferences of one when doing so means that you are undermining the interests of another? Can you represent a client suing an insurance company if another lawyer in your firm represents insurance companies? Do you take your patient off antipsychotic drugs because your clinical trial requires subjects begin with a drug washout (possibly followed by a placebo)? Do you audit a company that pays your firm millions of dollars annually for management consulting services? Do you take the kidney of one of your offspring to save another offspring, or perhaps conceive one to use its stem cells or bone marrow for another? Do you read the dissertation or peer review the article? How do agents choose among often incommensurable interests that do not share a common metric along which competing demands can be ranked, costs and benefits weighed, trade-offs evaluated, or rational choices modeled (Espeland & Stevens 1998)?

Only the rare agent has the luxury of aligning her interests with a single principal. Conflict of interest is hardly about shirking or opportunism with guile; it is about wrenching choices among the legitimate interests of multiple principals by agents who cannot extricate themselves from acting for so many. In an economy driven by mergers, diversification, cross-ownership, synergy, interdisciplinary practices offering one-stop shopping, and dizzying job mobility, agents are increasingly buffeted by the conflicting interests of the principals they serve. Classic agency theory misunderstands not only the source of goal conflict but also the social conditions that inflame it. Examining how the social organization of agency relationships gives rise to conflicting interests and how agents (institutional as well as individual) in diverse settings and roles respond is a subject ripe for sociological inquiry (e.g., Shapiro 2003).

Opportunism

Of one thing classic agency theory is sure: There will be agency problems. But it is remarkably vague about the nature of the problems, short of shirking and exploiting perquisites. The term guile does not quite spell out what agents are up to when they act opportunistically either. Sociologists have been studying these agency problems at least since Edwin Sutherland (1940) coined the term white-collar crime in his presidential address to the American Sociological Society. After many years of spirited disagreement, sociologists now agree to disagree about the appropriate definition of white-collar crime. But, aside from those who continue to insist that these are merely the crimes of high-status individuals, many would probably agree that misdeeds committed by individual or organizational agents come fairly close to what they consider to be white-collar crimes. I go further, asserting that we focus on the fiduciary duties of those in positions of trust, and I define white-collar crime as "the violation and manipulation of the norms of trust—of disclosure, disinterestedness, and role competence" (Shapiro 1990, p. 250). But I am not sure that I have convinced other sociologists. Nonetheless, few would contest the characterization of lying (misrepresentation and deception) and stealing (misappropriation, self-dealing, and corruption) by those in positions of trust (i.e., agents) as core elements of what they mean by white-collar crime. Nor would many argue that understanding how the structural properties of agency relationships facilitate misconduct and confound systems of social control is not central to agency theory models regarding policing and sanctioning of agent opportunism.

Although traditional agency theorists write frequently about corruption and probably mean misappropriation or self-dealing when they refer to the exploitation of perquisites, I doubt they would be altogether comfortable with this approach. A whistleblower, for example, would be violating the agency contract as would an employee who silently refused to be complicit in organizational misconduct ordered by his or her principals. Neither of these agency-theory malefactors would be problematic in a sociological conception because, unconstrained by assumptions of methodological individualism, sociologists can juggle many units of analysis and sites and chains of principal/agent relationships simultaneously. Although classic agency theorists seemed surprised when the world learned that their perfect incentives to align the interests of corporate executives and shareholders (giving the former stock options and equity ownership) might result in these executives contriving illicit schemes to inflate stock prices, sociologists, with our eyes on the bigger picture, surely were not. Nor are we convinced that these extraordinarily costly agency failures constitute a refutation of agency theory, as some suggest (Zajac & Westphal 2004); rather, we argue that one needs a more nuanced understanding of principals, agents, and organizations when fashioning complex incentives. (Besides, we have been trained to be mindful of the unanticipated consequences of purposive social action.)

Sociologists have and will continue to make an important contribution to understandings of white-collar and corporate crime (Shapiro 2001). Bringing the insights of agency theory to their inquiry will push the envelope a bit further and sharpen their insights.

Monitoring

There is, of course, an abundance of work in sociology on social control, compliance, organizational governance, policing, and sanctions that will contribute to understanding the agency paradigm. There are also more specialized literatures on the cover up of organizational misconduct and the social control in and of organizations, organizational intelligence, regulation and enforcement, and the sanctioning of white-collar or corporate offenders. These literatures demonstrate that much of what we know about the control of crime in the streets does not work so well when we seek to understand crime in the suites (i.e., agency problems). I cannot possibly review them here or even supply the dozens of citations to the most groundbreaking work in this area.

However, two observations are relevant here. First, because information and knowledge asymmetries ("know what" and "know how") are characteristic of many agency relationships, and because agency relationships are exceptionally opaque [owing to institutions of privacy (Stinchcombe 1963)] and relatively inaccessible to surveillance, self-regulation (drawing on inside information and expertise) plays an important monitoring role. Sociologists have tended to be skeptical of self-regulation—of foxes guarding chicken coops—as an institutionalized conflict of interest. Much good work has proven that stereotype simplistic (e.g., Kagan et al. 2003, Ayres & Braithwaite 1992). But, whatever the efficacy of self-regulation, it requires continued scholarly attention in the policing of agency relationships.

Second, many of the regulatory and self-regulatory arrangements devised to monitor agency relationships are themselves agency relationships. Whether they are internal or external auditors, compliance officers, internal affairs departments, government regulators, insurance companies, investment advisors, or rating agencies (e.g., Standard & Poors or Underwriters Laboratory), the monitors are acting on behalf of some set of principals. And, therefore, they too promise agency problems. They shirk, become coopted, engage in corruption, or perhaps simply monitor the wrong things. In an escalating cycle of agents overseeing agents, we must ask: Who monitors the monitors (Shapiro 1987)?

Insurance and Risk

There is a reason that the basic language of agency theory—adverse selection and moral hazard—comes from insurance. Insurance institutions have been designing contracts and negotiating around the shoals of goal conflict, opportunism, monitoring, and especially incentives long before the social sciences discovered agency. Insurance companies, indeed, know so much about failures of agency that they sell policies (fidelity bonds, for example, or liability policies for breach of fiduciary duty or professional malpractice) to cover such things, putting their money where their mouths are, a risk I doubt few academics would take. As Heimer (1985) demonstrated some time ago, sociologists have a great deal to learn from the social practices of insurance. They still do.

Agency Costs

However hard principals try to minimize them, all agency relationships experience agency costs; about this all the paradigms agree. Agency costs arise from many sources: the costs of recruitment, adverse selection, specifying and discerning preferences, providing incentives, moral hazard, shirking, stealing, self-dealing, corruption, monitoring and policing, self-regulation, bonding and insurance, agents who oversee agents who oversee agents, as well as failures in these costly corrective devices. Because principals cannot observe agent behavior, they "rely on imperfect surrogate measures, which can lead the agent to displace his behavior toward the surrogates in order to appear to be behaving well" (Mitnick 1992, p. 79) (e.g., because student test scores are used to monitor teachers, some teacher/agents coach students on how to take tests rather than teaching them substance or how to think). Agency costs therefore increase because agents are concentrating their efforts on the wrong things.

Costs also increase because organizations are structured to minimize opportunism—checks and balances are created, reporting requirements implemented, redundancies introduced, employees rotated, responsibilities fragmented, layers of supervision added, revolving doors locked, and so on. Costs increase because principals, fearful of abuse, impose procedures, decision rules, protocols, or formularies to limit agent discretion, or their agents do. Ironically, principals who seek out agents because they lack the expertise to make decisions tell their agents how to make decisions on their behalf, or else they tie their hands. Although organizational sociology has demonstrated that agents sometimes bend the rules to better serve their principals, others ritualistically follow the letter rather than the spirit of the law, thereby deepening agency costs. Because we fear that agents might act on their self-interests, we require that they be disinterested; we take agents out of embedded networks where their loyalties and interests are entangled with others, but at the price of losing the social capital, reputation, goodwill, and inside information that they might have used profitably in service of their principals.

In short, because we are fearful that agents will get our preferences wrong, we construct a protective social edifice that insures that they will get them less right. As I wrote in a different context some time ago, these trade-offs between one kind of agency cost over another are akin to the choice between Type I and Type II errors in statistics. Are the constraints set so narrowly that desirable agent behavior is deterred or so flexibly that inappropriate behavior is tolerated (Shapiro 1987)? Either way, you get an error. Mitnick (1998) reminds us that the costs are sometimes just not worth it, and perfect agency is rare indeed.

These reflections about the sources and consequences of agency costs are just that; certainly they warrant more systematic investigation. How do principals make investment decisions about agency costs? For what kinds of agency relationships are costs the highest? Aside from embedding agency service in ongoing social relationships, what strategies do principals employ to minimize agency costs? When do they simply throw up their hands and decide not to delegate at all?

CONCLUSION

Although agency theory may not occupy a niche in sociology, agency relationships are omnipresent, under cover of other aliases—bureaucracy, organizations, professions, roles, markets, labor, government, family, trust, social exchange, and so on—"a neat kind of social plumbing," as White (1985, p. 188) observed. Drawing on agency theory in other disciplines, sociologists have been sensitized not to lose sight of the interaction between agent selection, specification of preferences, designing incentives to align the interests of principal and agent, monitoring, and sanctioning in the "acting for" relationships that unfold on their substantive terrain. But that is just the beginning. Sociology has much more to offer, as I have suggested above, both in examining the sites along the social landscape where agency is especially prominent and, having jettisoned the unrealistic assumptions and abstract models fashioned in the other social sciences, in inquiring in empirical detail about how principals and agents actually choreograph their dance. Are sociologists ready to use "agency" and "theory" side by side? I think not. But that's the good news.

The *Annual Review of Sociology* is online at http://soc.annualreviews.org

LITERATURE CITED

Adams J. 1996. Principals and agents, colonialists and company men: the decay of colonial control in the Dutch East Indies. *Am. Sociol. Rev.* 61:12–28

American Law Institute. 2001. *Restatement of the Law Third, Restatement of the Law, Agency*, Tentative Draft #2 (March 14). Philadelphia: American Law Institute

Annual Reviews. 2003. *Instructions for the preparation of manuscripts.* http://www. AnnualReviews.org

Arrow KJ. 1985. The economics of agency. See Pratt & Zeckhauser 1985, pp. 37–51

Ayres I, Braithwaite J. 1992. *Responsive Regulation: Transcending the Deregulation Debate.* New York: Oxford.

Banfield EC. 1975. Corruption as a feature of governmental organization. *J. Law Econ.* 18:587–605

Clark RC. 1985. Agency costs versus fiduciary duties. See Pratt & Zeckhauser 1985, pp. 55–79

Cook KS, ed. 2001. *Trust in Society.* New York: Russell Sage Found.

Davis AE. 1996. Professional liability insurers as regulators of law practice. *Fordham Law Rev.* 65:209–32

Davis GF, Thompson TA. 1994. A social movement perspective on corporate control. *Admin. Sci. Q.* 39:141–73

DeMott DA. 1997. Organizational incentives to care about the law. *Law Contemp. Probl.* 60:39–66

DeMott DA. 1998. A revised prospectus for a third restatement of agency. *U.C. Davis Law Rev.* 31:1035–63

Donaldson L. 1990. The ethereal hand: organizational economics and management theory. *Acad. Manag. Rev.* 15:369–81

Eisenhardt KM. 1989. Agency theory: an assessment and review. *Acad. Manag. Rev.* 14:57–74

Espeland WN, Stevens ML. 1998. Commensuration as a social process. *Annu. Rev. Sociol.* 24:313–43

Granovetter M. 1985. Economic action and social structure: the problem of embeddedness. *Am. J. Sociol.* 91:481–510

Heimer CA. 1985. *Reactive Risk and Rational Action: Managing Moral Hazard in Insurance Contracts.* Berkeley: Univ. Calif. Press

Heimer CA, Staffen LR. 1998. *For the Sake of the Children: The Social Organization of Responsibility in the Hospital and the Home.* Chicago: Univ. Chicago Press

Jensen MC. 1983. Organization theory and methodology. *Account. Rev.* 58:319–39

Jensen MC, Meckling WH. 1976. Theory of the firm: managerial behavior, agency costs and ownership structure. *J. Financ. Econ.* 3:305–60

Kagan RA, Gunningham N, Thornton D. 2003. Explaining corporate environmental performance: How does regulation matter? *Law Soc. Rev.* 37:51–90

Kiser E. 1999. Comparing varieties of agency theory in economics, political science, and sociology: an illustration from state policy implementation. *Sociol. Theory* 17:146–70

Kiser E, Cai Y. 2003. War and bureaucratization in Qin China: exploring an anomalous case. *Am. Sociol. Rev.* 68:511–39

Larson MS. 1977. *The Rise of Professionalism: A Sociological Analysis.* Berkeley: Univ. Calif. Press

Majone G. 2001. Two logics of delegation: agency and fiduciary relations in EU governance. *Eur. Union Polit.* 2:103–22

McCubbins MD, Noll RG, Weingast BR. 1989. Structure and process, politics and policy: administrative arrangements and the political control of agencies. *Virginia Law Rev.* 75:431–82

Mitnick BM. 1973. *Fiduciary responsibility and public policy: the theory of agency and some consequences.* Presented at Annu. Meet. Am. Polit. Sci. Assoc., 69th, New Orleans

Mitnick BM. 1984. *Agency problems and political institutions.* Presented at Annu. Meet. Am. Polit. Sci. Assoc., 80th, Chicago

Mitnick BM. 1992. The theory of agency and organizational analysis. In *Ethics and Agency Theory*, ed. NE Bowie, RE Freeman, pp. 75–96. New York: Oxford Univ. Press

Mitnick BM. 1998. Agency theory. In *The Blackwell Encyclopedic Dictionary of Business Ethics*, ed. RE Freeman, PH Werhane, pp. 12–15. Malden, MA: Blackwell

Moe TM. 1984. The new economics of organization. *Am. J. Polit. Sci.* 28:739–77

Perrow C. 1986. Economic theories of organization. *Theory Soc.* 15:11–45

Pratt JW, Zeckhauser RH, eds. 1985. *Principals and Agents: The Structure of Business.* Boston: Harvard Bus. Sch. Press

Ross SA. 1973. The economic theory of agency: the principal's problem. *Am. Econ. Rev.* 63:134–39

Shapiro SP. 1987. The social control of impersonal trust. *Am. J. Sociol.* 93:623–58

Shapiro SP. 1990. Collaring the crime, not the criminal: reconsidering the concept of white-collar crime. *Am. Sociol. Rev.* 55:346–65

Shapiro SP. 2001. Crime: white-collar. In *International Encyclopedia of the Social & Behavioral Sciences*, ed. NJ Smelser, PB Baltes, 5:2941–45. Oxford: Elsevier

Shapiro SP. 2003. Bushwhacking the ethical high road: conflict of interest in the practice of law and real life. *Law Soc. Inq.* 28:87–268

Sharma A. 1997. Professional as agent: knowledge asymmetry in agency exchange. *Acad. Manag. Rev.* 22:758–98

Stinchcombe AL. 1963. Institutions of privacy in the determination of police administrative practice. *Am. J. Sociol.* 69:150–60

Sutherland EH. 1940. White-collar criminality. *Am. Sociol. Rev.* 5:1–12

Waterman RW, Meier KJ. 1998. Principal-agent models: an expansion? *J. Public Admin. Res. Theory* 8:173–202

Weber M. 1924/1968. *Economy and Society: An Interpretive Sociology*, ed. G Roth, C Wittich. New York: Bedminister

White HC. 1985. Agency as control. See Pratt & Zeckhauser 1985, pp. 187–212

Williamson OE. 1975. *Markets and Hierarchies: Analysis and Antitrust Implications.* New York/London: Free Press

Worsham J, Eisner MA, Ringquist EJ. 1997. Assessing the assumptions: a critical analysis of agency theory. *Admin. Soc.* 28:419–40

Wright P, Mukherji A. 1999. Inside the firm: socioeconomic versus agency perspectives on firm competitiveness. *J. Socio-Econ.* 28:295–307

Zajac EJ, Westphal JD. 2004. The social construction of market value: institutionalization and learning perspectives on stock market reactions. *Am. Sociol. Rev.* 69:233–57

Annu. Rev. Sociol. 2005. 31:285–304
doi: 10.1146/annurev.soc.31.041304.122246
Copyright © 2005 by Annual Reviews. All rights reserved
First published online as a Review in Advance on February 23, 2005

MULTIETHNIC CITIES IN NORTH AMERICA

Eric Fong and Kumiko Shibuya

*Department of Sociology, University of Toronto, Toronto, Ontario M5S 2J4,
Canada; email: fong@chass.utoronto.ca*

Key Words race, ethnicity, urban

■ **Abstract** The growing Hispanic and Asian populations in most major North American cities have drastically transformed the urban demographic landscape to become racially and ethnically diversified. We review literature on multiethnic cities by focusing on three important aspects of urban structures and processes: racial and ethnic residential patterns, ethnic businesses, and the performance of racial and ethnic groups in the labor market. Although the literature has identified many factors that shape these urban structures and processes, our discussion specifically focuses on the effects of multigroup contexts on urban structures and processes. We focus and compare four major racial and ethnic groups: whites, blacks, Hispanics, and Asians. Specific ethnic subgroups of all four groups are also discussed.

INTRODUCTION

The study of group relations in North America has taken a complex turn. The growing Hispanic and Asian populations in most major North American cities have drastically transformed the urban demographic landscape to become racially and ethnically diversified. In 1900, whites represented more than 88% of the total population of the United States, with blacks dominating the remaining proportion (12%). People of other racial and ethnic groups made up less than 1%. A century later, in 2000, the white population had dropped to 75%, while the black population remained the same at 12%. Other racial and ethnic groups rose to 13% (Hobbs & Stoops 2002). This racial and ethnic diversity has not occurred just in American cities, but also in cities in Canada, another major immigrant receiving country. In Canada, whites overwhelmingly constituted 96% of the total population in 1901. By 2001, visible minority groups (including Asians, blacks, and Hispanics) made up 13% of the Canadian population (Statistics Canada 2004). These numbers vividly show that the present multiethnic context is not uniquely an American experience.

Racial and ethnic diversity is most common in large American cities. In 2000, about two million Asians, six million blacks, and seven million Hispanics were living in the ten largest cities. They represented 7%, 31%, and 25%, respectively, of the total population of these places (Grieco & Cassidy 2001, McKinnon 2001). In Canada, another country with growing racial and ethnic diversity, more than

0360-0572/05/0811-0285$20.00

three million visible minorities (i.e., nonwhite population) were living in the largest 24 metropolitan areas in 2001. They represented 20% of the total population of these areas. In the largest three metropolitan areas, visible minorities made up 29% of the total population.

This new demographic makeup has significant implications for our understanding of today's urban structures and processes. At the very least, most studies today go beyond the black and white dichotomy that dominated the literature in the past (Bobo et al. 2000a, Clark & Blue 2004). As researchers incorporate multiethnic contexts in their studies, the complexity of understanding these contexts is revealed. Most discussions of urban structures and processes in connection to group relations are guided by theories heavily derived from the European integration experiences at the beginning of the twentieth century, when most cities were undergoing industrialization, or by findings based on black-white relations, which were rooted in unique historical and political backgrounds. Today's urban economies are shaped by a different set of economic forces, and the history of Hispanics and Asians in North America differs from the black experience. Thus, theories developed in the past may have only limited application in the study of multigroup relations today.

In this review, we address multiethnic cities by focusing on three important aspects of urban structures and processes: racial and ethnic residential patterns, ethnic businesses, and the performance of racial and ethnic groups in the labor market. Our discussion specifically focuses on the effects of multigroup contexts on urban structures and processes. We focus on and compare four major racial and ethnic groups: whites, blacks, Hispanics, and Asians. In practical terms, we consider the white, black, and Asian populations as being composed of different ethnic groups, whereas we consider Hispanics as an ethnic group with diverse racial backgrounds. In theoretical terms, Asians, blacks, and Hispanics are considered as diverse groups of people who are collectively "racialized" (Cornell & Hartmann 2004, Omi & Winant 1994). We also discuss specific ethnic subgroups of all four groups when it is appropriate.

RESIDENTIAL PATTERNS

Racial and ethnic residential patterns have been a major research area in the study of intergroup relations in cities. Researchers have emphasized that the study of group residential patterns reveals their social relations. Within the voluminous literature on the topic, three fairly distinct yet interrelated areas have drawn considerable attention: residential segregation patterns, racial and ethnic changes in neighborhoods, and suburbanization. Studies of each area have attempted to capture a different but related set of major urban forms.

Residential Segregation in a Multiethnic Context

Over the decades, a significant amount of research has examined racial and ethnic residential segregation (for reviews, see Charles 2003, Clark 1986, Massey 1985).

In the 1960s and 1970s, literature published was largely focused on describing and explaining the trend of black-white residential patterns (Farley 1977, Guest & Weed 1976, Taeuber & Taeuber 1965). As other minority groups have grown, the number of groups included in the analysis has expanded. Studies in the 1970s and early 1980s began to include Hispanics (Massey 1983, 1979; Massey & Mullan 1984). By the mid-1980s, Asians were also incorporated in the analysis to reflect their population growth (Massey & Denton 1987, Massey & Fong 1990, White et al. 1993). At the same time, research extended the scope to study specific Hispanic and Asian ethnic subgroups (Alba et al. 1999; Alba & Logan 1993, 1991; Fong & Shibuya 2000). These results consistently show considerable variations in residential segregation patterns within Hispanic and Asian subgroups.

The dominant approach to understanding residential patterns among various racial and ethnic groups has been to compare the residential patterns of minority groups with those of whites. Recent findings from this line of research, based on American censuses from 1980 to 2000, generally suggest that the residential segregation level of blacks from whites has declined over the decades, while the levels have increased for Asians and Hispanics (Charles 2003, Fischer et al. 2004, Iceland et al. 2002, Johnston et al. 2003, Logan et al. 2004, Wilkes & Iceland 2004). Most studies agree that the obvious decline in segregation levels between blacks and whites is usually found in multiethnic cities or in cities with a small proportion of blacks. Nevertheless, despite the decline over the decades, blacks still experience overall high residential segregation levels (Charles 2003, White et al. 1993). In fact, compared with all other major racial and ethnic groups, including Hispanics, Asians, Pacific Islanders, and Native Americans, blacks remain the most highly segregated group (Iceland 2004). This unique residential pattern of high black residential segregation is found in most major American cities, such as New York (Alba et al. 1995), Detroit (Farley et al. 2000), Boston (Massaagli 2000), Atlanta (Thompson 2000), Los Angeles (Charles 2000), and other major immigrant gateway cities (Clark & Blue 2004).

Studies exploring specific Hispanic and Asian subgroups concomitantly revealed that the residential segregation levels of Hispanic subgroups are related to skin color (Massey 1985, Massey & Bitterman 1985). Using 1970 and 1980 census tract data, Denton & Massey (1989) reported that black Hispanics were highly segregated from non-Hispanic whites and moderately segregated from non-Hispanic blacks. White & Sassler (2000) further asserted that Hispanic "groups with African heritage," such as Puerto Ricans, are less able than non-black Hispanics to translate their education into better neighborhood outcomes. They argued that ethnicity cannot be separated from the racial dichotomy. In addition to comparing residential patterns of Hispanic subgroups on the basis of their skin color, some analyses compared the national origins of Hispanic subgroups. Drawing from both the 1980 census tract level data set [Summary Tape File (STF)] and individual data set [Public Use Microdata Sample (PUMS)], Alba & Logan (1993) estimated that Mexicans have a higher level of proximity with non-Hispanic whites than do Cubans or Puerto Ricans, controlling for other socioeconomic and demographic factors.

A different picture has emerged among Asian ethnic groups. An analysis by White et al. (1993), with data drawn from the 1980 PUMS-F census data file, showed that different Asian ethnic subgroups have similar levels of residential segregation from non-Hispanic whites. The difference in the variation between the most and least segregated Asian ethnic subgroups with non-Hispanic white presence in their neighborhoods was only 8%. Studying these Asian ethnic groups based on data from the subsequent census decade, White et al. (2003) reported that the dissimilarity index among five major Asian ethnic groups (i.e., Chinese, Japanese, Indian, Korean, and Vietnamese) still remains at similar levels, ranging from 0.72 to 0.80.

In Canada, a country also experiencing an increasingly multiethnic representation in its cities, research has documented a similar pattern of residential segregation. Fong (1996) used the 1991 Canadian census to document that Asian ethnic groups and blacks have a lower representation of the charter groups (i.e., British and French) in their neighborhoods when compared with the neighborhoods of other European ethnic groups. Even when controlling for socioeconomic status and nativity, results still showed a clear hierarchy of residential proximity with the charter groups (Fong 1999, Fong & Wilkes 1999). Whereas northern and western Europeans have higher levels of the charter groups in their neighborhoods, blacks, south Asians, east and southeast Asians, and southern Europeans have lower levels. Among Asian groups, as shown in the American data, variations in their segregation levels are moderate (White et al. 2003). However, the Canadian results, different from the American, showed an increase over the decades in residential segregation of most ethnic minority groups, including blacks (Balakrishnan & Hou 1999). The growth of ethnically concentrated neighborhoods has been documented (Hou & Milan 2003, Murdie & Teixeira 2003).

Despite the well-developed literature, few studies have explored residential segregation among minority groups. There is limited information about residential segregation among blacks, various Asian ethnic groups, and Hispanic subgroups. Among those few available studies in the United States, the focus is on levels of residential segregation between blacks and other minority groups (Charles 2003, Fong 1996). These studies show that the levels of segregation between blacks and various Asian ethnic groups are higher than the levels of segregation between blacks and Hispanics. However, seldom do studies document residential segregation between various Asian and Hispanic groups. Given that residential patterns reflect group relations, the failure to explore residential segregation among minority groups can limit the full account of intergroup dynamics, especially among minority groups, in multiethnic contexts.

Another limitation in exploring residential segregation in a multiethnic environment is the existing segregation measurements. These measures have largely been limited to calculating the segregation levels between two groups. The pairwise measure has circumscribed the theoretical development of residential segregation in a multiethnic context (Grannis 2002, Reardon & Firebaugh 2002). It cannot provide a general view of segregation among various racial and ethnic groups.

Although in recent years some indexes have been proposed to capture the segregation levels of more than two groups (Reardon & Firebaugh 2002, Wong 1998), and a few studies have used the entropy index to capture information on more than two groups (Fischer et al. 2004, Iceland 2004), the discussion of segregation based on a multigroup index still requires considerable input.

Effects of Multiethnic Contexts

Various perspectives have been offered to explain patterns of racial and ethnic residential segregation. One perspective views the segregation patterns of various racial and ethnic groups as the result of discrimination, particularly toward blacks (Alba & Logan 1991, Massey & Fong 1990). Another considers group differences in socioeconomic resources and demographic background (Clark 1986). A third perspective has emphasized the urban context, including the local housing market and industrial base (Farley & Frey 1994, Frey & Farley 1996, White et al. 2003). Finally, studies have also argued for consideration of the multiethnic context itself (Farley & Frey 1994, Denton & Massey 1991). Given that a number of reviews (Charles 2003, Clark 1986, Galster 1989) have already evaluated the contribution of the first three hypotheses to the understanding of racial and ethnic residential segregation, and given that this paper focuses on multiethnic cities, the following discussion examines the literature on how a multiethnic context affects residential segregation. However, this is not to suggest that the first three perspectives are not important.

Two dominant lines of research are found in the literature about the effects of a multiethnic context on residential patterns. The first stream of studies focuses on the presence of racial and ethnic groups in the city or neighborhoods. The second explores how the preference of racial and ethnic groups in the neighborhoods affects group distribution in the city and neighborhoods.

EFFECTS OF THE PRESENCE OF RACIAL AND ETHNIC GROUPS   The first line of research literature identifies how the presence of other groups in the city and neighborhoods is related to the residential patterns of a particular group.

Blacks   The results of studies on how the presence of other groups affects blacks' residential patterns with whites are mixed. Although Logan et al. (2004) showed no effect from the proportion of Hispanics or Asians on the residential segregation level of blacks and whites, other studies have different findings. They show that black segregation from whites is lower in cities with higher proportions of other groups (Frey & Farley 1996, Iceland 2004). Various explanations have been suggested for the latter patterns. Frey & Farley (1996) argued that other groups act as a "buffer" to black and white interaction and serve to moderate any antagonistic interaction between the two groups. In a similar vein, Iceland (2004) suggested that the increase in other groups shifts the dominant thinking from the black and white dichotomy to multigroup relations. However, Krivo & Kaufman (1999) argued that black and white segregation is lower only when the presence of other groups is lower as well. They suggested that whites have limited exposure tolerance to other groups. Once a certain level is reached, whites will limit their exposure to all other nonwhite groups, including blacks.

Hispanics   At the metropolitan level, Frey & Farley (1996) found that Hispanic segregation increases when its own group proportion also increases in a metropolitan area. Similarly, focusing at the neighborhood level, Denton & Massey (1991) showed that Hispanic gains in neighborhoods are associated with their growth rates in the city. Decomposing the Theil index into different geographic levels, Fischer et al. (2004) showed a similar pattern, that Hispanic segregation especially grows in a gateway metropolis where Hispanic immigrants have increased considerably. This association has been documented in previous decades as well. Comparing the trends of Hispanic segregation patterns over decades, studies have pointed out that cities that had small Hispanic populations in 1980 have shown a sharp increase in segregation levels in later decades (Iceland 2004). Iceland (2004) suggested that this pattern may reflect the increase in Hispanic population due to immigration to these cities. On the other hand, Logan et al. (2004) argued that the increase in Hispanic segregation in these cities reflects the growth of the Hispanic population from both international migration and differential fertility rate.

Asians   Studies have documented that Asian segregation increases when the overall minority population increases (Iceland 2004, Logan et al. 2004). Denton & Massey (1991) showed that a larger proportion of Hispanic and Asian populations in a metropolitan area is associated with Asian gains in the neighborhoods. However, Logan et al. (2004) specifically emphasized that the growth of the Asian population, largely due to recent immigration, provides a critical mass for Asians to form their own communities. Research also points out that the increase in Asian representation in neighborhoods is related to two unique patterns. First, the increase in Asian immigrants contributes to a higher Asian representation in all neighborhoods, especially in existing multiethnic neighborhoods (Alba et al. 1995). Second, Asians are less likely to gain representation in neighborhoods close to black neighborhoods. It shows some tendency of Asians to avoid black neighborhoods (Denton & Massey 1991).

This brief summary of explanations of how the presence of various racial and ethnic groups affects the residential patterns of other groups reveals that most studies have a strong focus on residential integration with whites or the segregation of the group itself. In addition, most discussions of the city/neighborhood compositions of racial and ethnic groups and their residential patterns are ad hoc in nature. To a lesser extent, the literature has provided a theoretical framework to disentangle how the relations among minority groups themselves are related to their residential patterns. The cumulative facts thus yield an incomplete but potentially complicated picture of multiethnic cities.

EFFECTS OF THE PREFERENCE OF RACIAL AND ETHNIC GROUPS   The second line of research that explores the effect of a multiethnic context on racial and ethnic residential patterns focuses on the preferences of groups in neighborhoods. Although research has provided more understanding about this relationship in recent years, few studies have actual data to document group preference, except Farley et al. (1978, 1983), who used data collected in the Detroit area, or housing audit studies (Yinger 1995). Most studies have been based on indirect implications from analyses of census data.

Spurred in large part by the Multi-City Study of Urban Inequality, a number of studies have been published in recent years on group preference and racial and ethnic residential patterns based on data collected in four major American cities (Charles 2000, Ihlanfeldt & Scafidi 2004). These studies show that whites obviously feel least willing to share neighborhoods with blacks. Ellen (2000) sees these results as indicating that whites stereotype black neighborhoods. There is some suggestion that these patterns are a consequence of a lack of interracial neighborhood contact (Ihlanfeldt & Scafidi 2004). However, findings show that whites feel more comfortable sharing neighborhoods with a considerable proportion of Asians but less comfortable with the same proportion of Hispanics (Charles 2003).

Blacks prefer to reside in integrated neighborhoods rather than in predominantly black or predominantly white neighborhoods. They feel very uncomfortable moving into predominantly white neighborhoods. Hispanics, like blacks, prefer integrated neighborhoods. Although their preference for integrated neighborhoods is similar to blacks, Hispanics prefer most to share neighborhoods with whites but least with blacks (Zubrinsky & Bobo 1996, Farley 1994). To interpret these preferences among blacks and Hispanics, Zubrinsky & Bobo (1996) and Farley et al. (1994) argue that the patterns reflect the reaction of minority groups to prejudice and discrimination. Asians also prefer integrated neighborhoods. Among all groups, whites by far stand out as the group Asians find most desirable to live near (Charles 2000).

Although these studies identify the preference patterns of each group, the preferences are not meant to apply equally for every member in the group. There is evidence that the preferences of groups vary according to the socioeconomic and demographic background of individuals (Bobo & Johnson 2000). Thus, the interpretation of these overall preference patterns of each group must be made cautiously. A dauntingly complex challenge is to propose a general framework for explaining preference priorities among minority groups. Such an understanding would be a critical element for extending the understanding of residential patterns in a multiethnic context.

Neighborhood Changes in Multiethnic Contexts

The study of racial and ethnic composition changes in neighborhoods has a long tradition in sociological literature, beginning with Burgess's (1925) masterpiece on neighborhood changes in Chicago and the presentation of the concentric zone model. It was followed by several major empirical studies over the decades, such as the studies by Duncan & Duncan (1957), Taeuber & Taeuber (1965), and Denton & Massey (1991). Most of these studies focus on the neighborhood transition between blacks and whites.

The study of neighborhood changes began in the 1980s to include other groups in addition to blacks and whites. Massey's (1983) study of the patterns of Hispanic neighborhood change, Clark's (1996) analysis of racial changes in multigroup neighborhoods, the study by Denton & Massey (1991) of racial and ethnic changes in neighborhoods of the 50 largest cities plus 10 cities with large Hispanic populations, and Alba et al.'s (1995) work on the racial and ethnic composition changes in New York neighborhoods all explored neighborhood changes among various racial and ethnic groups. In Canada, there have been a number of such studies in recent years. Fong & Gulia (2000) explored racial and ethnic composition changes in Toronto, Montreal, and Vancouver. Hou & Milan (2003) explored the changes in racial and ethnic composition in black, South Asian, and Chinese neighborhoods. These studies, no matter whether drawn from American or Canadian data, consistently demonstrate that neighborhoods, especially in major cities, have become more integrated than before. Groups are more likely to share neighborhoods. Consequently, mixed neighborhoods are on the rise, and these neighborhoods commonly remain stable over the years.

Most of these studies conclude by questioning the applicability of the traditional unidirectional invasion-succession racial transition hypothesis in understanding neighborhoods in a multiethnic context. They reiterate the diverse paths of neighborhood racial and ethnic composition changes. Denton & Massey (1991) showed that Hispanic neighborhoods are more likely to experience succession than black neighborhoods. Alba et al. (1995) suggested that in New York the evolution to multiethnic neighborhoods is mostly from Hispanic-white neighborhoods with Asians moving in, followed by blacks. Fong & Gulia (2000) showed that there are two paths of change in Canada. The first path is that neighborhoods become more diversified. This change, similar to Alba et al.'s (1995) findings, is mostly found when European groups move into neighborhoods with a majority of charter groups, followed by Asians and blacks. The second path commonly occurs in multiethnic neighborhoods, where there is a reduced presence of Asians and blacks.

Suburbanization in Multiethnic Contexts

Suburbanization has always been considered as an indicator of group integration. Although white ethnic groups, such as German, Irish, and Italians (Alba et al. 1997), experience high levels of suburbanization in their second generation and beyond, blacks maintain a low level of suburbanization despite recent progress. In fact, the description of the "chocolate city" and "vanilla suburbs" (Farley et al. 1978) vividly summarized the suburbanization of racial and ethnic groups after World War II. Blacks still represent a high proportion in the city, while whites have gradually moved to the suburbs (Massey & Denton 1988). Asians, even though recently arrived, have the highest proportion of residents in suburban areas compared with Hispanics and blacks (Alba et al. 1999, Fong & Shibuya 2000). Fong & Shibuya (2000) showed that about 49% of Asians resided in suburbs in 1990. In addition, Fong & Shibuya (2000) showed that there is considerable variation in suburbanization among Asian and Hispanic subgroups, ranging from 57% of Japanese to 15% of Puerto Ricans. Results of other studies show similar patterns (Alba et al. 1999).

Although suburbanization is generally linked to a decline in segregation among minority groups, studies still document considerable variations among them in sharing neighborhoods with whites, even when residing in suburbs (Alba & Logan 1991). The 1980 census data show that all European groups resided in suburban neighborhoods that were almost 90% white (Alba & Logan 1993). At the other end of the continuum, blacks have the lowest level of sharing neighborhoods with whites in suburbs compared with other groups. Among specific Hispanic groups, there is evidence of considerable variations of white presence in their suburban neighborhoods, from only 58% of whites among Cubans to 81% among Mexicans (Alba & Logan 1993). Alba & Logan (1993) argued that this pattern may reflect a voluntary residential clustering among Cubans. At the same time, a growing number of studies have shown that all Asian subgroups, despite their recent arrival, have high percentages, above 80%, of whites in their suburban neighborhoods.

Explanations, guided by the assimilation perspective, suggest that groups are more likely to share neighborhoods when their socioeconomic resources are similar or they have been in the country for a longer period. However, the results show these effects to be varied among groups. They show that blacks' ability to share suburban neighborhoods with whites is related less to socioeconomic resources than to race, whereas Hispanics' ability is related both to their socioeconomic resources and to their duration in the country (Alba & Logan 1993, 1991; Massey & Denton 1988). Results show that Asians' suburbanization is related to their socioeconomic resources only, and not to duration in the country (Alba & Logan 1991, 1993; Logan et al. 1996; Massey & Denton 1987). Some suggest that the Asian patterns reflect their tendency to settle in suburbs soon after their arrival.

Although both Asians and Hispanics have higher percentages of whites in their suburban neighborhoods than do blacks, recent results have also shown that some Asians and Hispanics cluster in suburban neighborhoods. Recent findings by Logan et al. (2002) suggest that more than 20% of almost all minority groups included in their analysis were residing in ethnic neighborhoods in New York and Los Angeles in 1990. Similarly, Fong et al. (2002) found that large proportions of east and southeast Asians, south Asians, and blacks cluster in suburban neighborhoods in Toronto. Logan et al. (2002) further argued that these ethnic neighborhoods reflect two types of communities. One type is the traditional immigrant enclave with less desirable neighborhood characteristics and higher concentrations of immigrants. The second type is the ethnic community with desirable neighborhood characteristics, whose ethnic members have socioeconomic resources. However, there has been limited exploration of the reasons for ethnic clustering in suburban neighborhoods. Among few limited studies, Fong et al. (2002) suggested that ethnic suburban clustering reflects the limited choices of suburban neighborhoods for ethnic households with limited resources who prefer to settle in the suburbs.

Despite research advancing our understanding of the suburbanization patterns of various racial and ethnic groups, there has been heavy emphasis on comparing suburbanization rates among groups or, similar to the study of race and ethnic residential segregation patterns, their levels of sharing neighborhoods with whites. We have little information about sharing suburban neighborhoods with other groups, beyond whites and blacks, or about how the patterns among minority groups reflect the broader race and ethnic relations in the suburbs.

ETHNIC BUSINESSES

Ethnic businesses are not new in North American cities. They have been a source of employment opportunities for members of ethnic groups and have paved a path for the economic mobility of previous generations (Light & Gold 2000, Portes & Bach 1985). Most studies on the topic over the decades have concentrated on structural aspects, such as recruitment (Waldinger 1986, Waldinger & Lichter 2003), participation patterns (Light 1972, Light & Bonacich 1988, Yoon 1997), earnings (Sanders & Nee 1987, Wilson & Portes 1980), or locations of these businesses (Fong et al. 2005; Portes & Jensen 1987). Most discussion has focused on comparing the participation patterns or economic performance of groups, but it has seldom explored intergroup relations in the ethnic business setting.

In recent years, as cities have become increasingly multiethnic, there has been a growing interest in studying intergroup relations in the ethnic business setting. One line of research is to explore the intergroup relations between business owners and customers. These studies have focused on the intergroup interaction patterns of Korean business owners (Lee 2002, Yoon 1997), especially on conflicts in black neighborhoods. Various explanations of this conflict have emphasized the importance of structural factors. Joyce (2003) compared Korean and black conflicts in New York and Los Angeles and found that local political organizations, such as community groups, are important in mobilizing and sustaining the conflicts. Lee (2002) explored the Jewish and Korean business owners in black neighborhoods and suggested that the crucial functions of the businesses themselves, specifically the business niche, created conflict. However, conflict can be reduced for those businesses that require contact with and promote intergroup interaction between business owners and customers. Others argue that the conflict between blacks and Korean business owners reflects the unique middleman status of Korean merchants in the economic structure (Weitzer 1997). Some studies comparing Koreans in black and Hispanic neighborhoods in Los Angeles suggest a more complicated picture of the intersection of race, class, and nativity. Cheng & Espiritu (1989) suggested that racial conflict is strong among Korean business owners in black neighborhoods because of possible class differences. However, less conflict is observed between Korean business owners and local residents in Mexican neighborhoods. These patterns may show that Koreans are considered as legitimate competitors by Mexicans, because both groups have large proportions of immigrants.

Another line of explanation for the intergroup conflict in business settings has documented the importance of group perception and group socioeconomic differences. Yoon (1997) suggested, on the basis of field observations and interviews of Korean business owners in Chicago and Los Angeles, that Korean business owners are more prejudiced against blacks than against Hispanics. He suggested that a negative perception of blacks was developed before their immigration and that their attitudes were reinforced by lack of contact with blacks after immigration. Lee (2002) also argued that class differences, cultural expectations, and sometimes language barriers between new immigrant business owners and local residents may foster conflict between groups.

On a related topic, an increasing number of studies have explored subethnic differentiation within an ethnic group in a business environment. The study by Light et al. (1993) of Iranian businesses showed that ethnic business networks tend to be heavily concentrated within their own subethnic groups, such as Armenian Iranian. In addition, Chiu's (2001) study of Chinese in Toronto documented that Chinese from Hong Kong, Taiwan, and mainland China have their own subethnic business networks and attract customers from their own subethnic groups. However, this set of studies has suffered from the lack of clarity of the concept of subethnicity. The criteria for defining a subethnic group are not well established. Some define subethnic groups by geographic regions, while others associate subethnic groups with differences in place of birth.

LABOR MARKET

An important aspect of understanding a multiethnic city is to explore the labor market performance of racial and ethnic groups. The research literature consistently documents that blacks' income is still lower than whites' despite a gradual improvement over the decades (Neal & Johnson 1996, Smith & Welch 1989). Blacks' income was about 75% of their white counterparts' in 1990 (Smith 2001). At the same time, Hispanics' income was only 67% of whites', with considerable variation among subgroups. Mexicans have the lowest income among Hispanic groups, while the income of Cubans has the smallest gap with whites'. Among Asians, the income of most ethnic subgroups is close to whites' (Nee & Sanders 1988). Some of them, such as Asian Indians and Japanese, even earn more than whites before adjusting for various human capital resources (Holzer 2001).

There is no single explanation for income differences among groups. Instead, a complicated mixture of explanations has been offered. Some explanations focus on the structures and processes of individual metropolitan areas (Bean et al. 1999, Grant & Parcel 1990, Grodsky & Pager 2001, Massey & Denton 1993, Tienda &

Lii 1987). These studies identify societal changes in the city (such as the increasing demand for skills and education or the loss of manufacturing jobs) or structural dimensions of the city economy (such as labor market discrimination, residential locations, or job spatial distribution) (for review, see Darity & Mason 1998, Holzer 2001). This set of literature provides important insights into income differences among groups, especially the poor economic performance of blacks. Another set of explanations focuses on individual differences, such as education level and experience, to explain the different economic performance of groups (Browne et al. 2001).

However, in a multiethnic context, no discussion of racial and ethnic differences in economic performance can advance without addressing the role of the racial and ethnic composition of the city. Overall research suggests that the income of whites is affected by a larger presence of blacks, but not of Hispanics (Tienda & Lii 1987). As for blacks, research has documented two major patterns of black economic performance in relation to the racial and ethnic composition of the city. First, black economic performance is sensitive to the presence of other minority groups, such as Asians and Hispanics. However, some studies differentiate between the favorable effect of the presence of other minorities for blacks with skills and education and the unfavorable effect for those with lower skills (Huffman 2004, Tienda & Lii 1987).

Second, a larger black population can negatively affect blacks' own economic outcomes. To explain this inverse relationship between black economic performance and their population size, researchers have drawn on the group threat hypothesis suggested by Blalock (1956) five decades ago. They argue that blacks' decreased economic performance is related to increased discrimination against them by whites who feel more threatened as the minority population increases (Beggs et al. 1997, McCall 2001, Tomaskovic-Devey & Roscigno 1996). However, this explanation has limited application to multiethnic contexts with various combinations of racial and ethnic minority groups. Lieberson (1980) identified a queuing effect to explain the pattern: Minority groups increasingly cluster in low-paying jobs as their population increases, and the subsequent concentration draws their income down.

Many of these studies of group economic preference have not adequately considered the dynamics of migration of various racial and ethnic groups in and out of the city (Bean et al. 1999). Individuals who have a difficult time finding a job or are unemployed are more likely to move to areas with strong labor markets. Unemployed or discouraged minority group members may move out of the area with a tight labor market to look for better opportunities. Without taking these migration dynamics into consideration, statistical model estimations may confound the potential effects of group size and selective migration of groups (Bean et al. 1999).

With the increase in racial and ethnic diversity in the labor force, another line of research has explored the concentration of groups in various industries and occupations. Most research has attempted to identify industries in which racial and ethnic groups are overrepresented and to analyze the economic consequences for the group members working there (Logan & Alba 1999, Wilson 2003). The formal identification of ethnic concentration in industries—the ethnic economy—was first suggested by Logan et al. (1994). This approach focuses on the overrepresentation of coethnic owners and workers in specific industries. Studies using Logan et al.'s (1994) approach have focused on the relationship between the economic returns and the human capital of ethnic members working in the ethnic economy. Overall, there is evidence that coethnic employees working in the ethnic economy have lower economic returns from their human capital compared with those who work outside the ethnic economy, while coethnic employers have higher economic returns (Zhou & Logan 1989). Further studies highlight that the economic returns of female workers in the ethnic economy are even less favorable (Zhou & Logan 1989). Their economic returns do not relate to their human capital. Some studies go beyond individual human capital and suggest that city contexts also affect the economic returns of those working in the ethnic economy (Fong & Lee 1999). Specifically, residential segregation level, group size, and the local economy all shape the economic returns of those who work in the ethnic economy. However, very few studies have explored how the presence of other racial and ethnic groups and their labor market activities affect the economic returns of those working in the ethnic economy.

In recent years, researchers have differentiated the concept of ethnic niches into industrial and occupational niches. Wilson (2003) has focused on overrepresentation of groups in industry-specific occupational categories, and Rosenfeld & Tienda (1999) have addressed overrepresentation of groups in occupations, and still others have explored the overrepresentation of ethnic business owners in industries (Light & Rosenstein 1995, Logan et al. 1994). Wilson (2003) showed that those industry-specific occupations with high concentrations of blacks, Hispanics, and Asians are low in occupational status and wages. Focusing on ethnic business owners' concentration in industries, Logan & Alba (1999) showed considerable group variations in self-employment rates and levels of ethnic concentration of self-employment in various industries. In addition, the effects of ethnic industrial concentration of self-employment on their economic returns are varied and are not always positive. For example, whereas Korean employers in ethnically concentrated industries earn higher income than others, Chinese do not.

Another line of research on the ethnic market niche focuses on the economic consequences of industrial and occupational succession among groups. Waldinger (1996), using the case of New York, suggests that blacks did not obtain much economic benefit from the industrial and occupational succession in recent decades, whereas Hispanics and Asians with large proportions of immigrants were able to take advantage of it and extend their base. Using census data from 1970 to 1990 on Los Angeles, Chicago, and Atlanta, Rosenfeld & Tienda (1999) suggest that economic gain or loss is inconclusive for group occupational succession. In some occupations, when they were displaced by other ethnic immigrant groups, blacks were pushed up; in other occupations, they were pushed down.

CONCLUSION

The racial and ethnic composition of most North American cities is increasingly diversified. This diversity has brought an array of changes in urban structures and processes. We review findings related to racial and ethnic residential segregation patterns, racial and ethnic composition changes in neighborhoods, suburbanization, intergroup relations in ethnic businesses, and labor market performance of racial and ethnic groups. These topics represent important urban structures and processes that have drawn attention in recent years. The value of these studies is to show the dynamics and complexity of urban structures and processes in a multiethnic context. These studies do not conclude with a single thesis, nor do they portray a clear picture. Neither do they show a disarray of information. Overall, the findings suggest three important themes: First, today's urban structures and processes reflect relations among various racial and ethnic groups in the city; second, these structures and processes are shaped by the presence of various racial and ethnic groups and the groups' preferences; and third, the urban structures and processes, reflecting various minority group relations, in turn shape urban structures and processes involving whites and minority groups.

Despite the overall progress in understanding various urban structures and processes in a multiethnic setting, some fundamental issues remain. First, the literature on multiethnic cities focuses heavily on the comparison of racial and ethnic minority groups with whites, with little attention to comparisons among minority groups. Consequently, we know little about the dynamics among minority groups. Even when studies have attempted to address the issue, their explanations have been ad hoc in nature. This neglect is unfortunate because urban structures and processes can also reflect relations among minority groups. One reason the research may foster this blind spot is that most research is guided by and simultaneously limited by the theoretical perspective. The dominant perspective on the institutional integration of groups in society (Alba & Nee 2003) leads to a focus on comparing groups with whites (Alba & Nee 2003). Thus, the theoretical development of understanding relations among minority groups is limited. In a multiethnic context, we need to extend our understanding of the relations among various minority groups and develop a theoretical framework that incorporates the relationships of these groups and how these relationships in turn shape the urban structures and processes between minority groups and whites.

The multiethnic context also reveals the limitations of the conventional methodology and approaches that only consider two groups in the understanding of urban structures and processes. Most existing indexes for measuring residential segregation levels are pairwise comparisons, and thus have limited ability to capture the dynamics of multigroup segregation. Although some indexes have been proposed to measure multigroup segregation levels, more discussion is badly needed. Similarly, we should be cautious in exploring pairwise intergroup conflicts or in focusing on only two groups in ethnic succession in occupations or industries. When conflicts or ethnic succession occur, there are not necessarily only two groups involved. It is possible for two groups to replace the dominance of one ethnic group in an occupation. Research needs to capture better the multiplicity of groups involved in various situations.

We face major challenges in understanding the dynamics of cities as they become more diversified. Just as previous generations of researchers took up the challenge of analyzing how various European immigrant groups related to one another in North American cities at the beginning of the twentieth century, so, too, today's generation of researchers confronts the challenge of analyzing cities with diverse racial and ethnic groups. These challenges require social scientists to go beyond existing theoretical frameworks and methodology to explore the complexity of the multiethnic group context.

The *Annual Review of Sociology* is online at http://soc.annualreviews.org

LITERATURE CITED

Alba RD, Denton NA, Leung SY, Logan JR. 1995. Neighborhood change under conditions of mass immigration: the New York City region, 1970–1990. *Int. Migr. Rev.* 29: 625–56

Alba RD, Logan JR. 1991. Variations on two themes: racial and ethnic patterns in the attainment of suburban residence. *Demography* 28:431–53

Alba RD, Logan JR. 1992. Analyzing locational attainments: constructing individual-level regression models using aggregate data. *Soc. Methods Res.* 20:367–97

Alba RD, Logan JR. 1993. Minority proximity to whites in suburbs: an individual-level analysis of segregation. *Am. J. Sociol.* 98:1388–427

Alba RD, Logan JR, Crowder K. 1997. White ethnic neighborhoods and assimilation: the greater New York region, 1980–1990. *Soc. Forces* 75:883–912

Alba RD, Logan JR, Stults BJ, Marzan G, Zhang W. 1999. Immigrant groups in the suburbs: a reexamination of suburbanization and spatial assimilation. *Am. Sociol. Rev.* 64:446–60

Alba RD, Nee V. 2003. *Remaking the American Mainstream: Assimilation and Contemporary Immigration.* Cambridge, MA: Harvard Univ. Press

Balakrishnan TR, Hou F. 1999. Residential patterns in cities. In *Immigrant Canada: Demographic, Economic, and Social Challenges*, ed. SS Halli, L Driedger, pp. 116–47. Toronto: Univ. Toronto Press

Barnes JS, Bennett C. 2002. *The Asian population: 2000. Census 2000 brief.* Washington, DC: US Census Bur. http://www.census. gov/prod/2002pubs/c2kbr01-16.pdf

Bean FD, Bell-Rose S, eds. 1999. *Immigration and Opportunity: Race, Ethnicity, and Employment in the United States.* New York: Russell Sage Found.

Bean FD, Van Hook J, Fossett MA. 1999. Immigration, spatial and economic change, and African American employment. See Bean & Bell-Rose 1999, pp. 31–63

Beggs JJ, Villemez WJ, Arnold R. 1997. Black population concentration and black-white inequality: expanding the consideration of place and space effects. *Soc. Forces* 76:65–91

Blalock HM. 1956. Economic discrimination and Negro increase. *Am. Sociol. Rev.* 21:584–88

Bobo LD, Johnson D. 2000. Racial attitudes in the prismatic metropolis: identity, stereotyes, and perceived group competition in Los Angeles. See Bobo et al. 2000b, pp. 83–166

Bobo LD, Oliver ML, Johnson JH Jr, Valenzuela A. 2000a. Analyzing inequality in Los

Angeles. See Bobo et al. 2000b, pp. 3–50

Bobo LD, Oliver ML, Johnson JH Jr, Valenzuela A, eds. 2000b. *Prismatic Metropolis: Inequality in Los Angeles*. New York: Russell Sage Found.

Browne I, Hewitt C, Tigges L, Green G. 2001. Why does job segregation lead to wage inequality among African Americans? Person, place, sector, or skills? *Soc. Sci. Res.* 30473–95

Burgess EW. 1925. The growth of the city: an introduction to a research project. In *The City*, ed. RE Park, EW Burgess, RD McKenzie, pp. 47–62. Chicago: Univ. Chicago Press

Charles CZ. 2000. Residential segregation in Los Angeles. See Bobo et al. 2000b, pp. 167–219

Charles CZ. 2003. The dynamics of racial residential segregation. *Annu. Rev. Sociol.* 29: 167–207

Cheng L, Espiritu Y. 1989. Korean businesses in Black and Hispanic neighborhoods: a study of intergroup relations. *Sociol. Perspect.* 32:521–34

Chiu L. 2001. Subethnicity and identity: sociocultural interpretations of Chinese business titles in Toronto. *Asian Pac. Migr. J.* 10:145–67

Clark WAV. 1986. Residential segregation in American cities: a review and interpretation. *Popul. Res. Policy Rev.* 5:95–127

Clark WAV. 1991. Residential preferences and neighborhood racial segregation: a test of the Schelling segregation model. *Demography* 28:1–19

Clark WAV. 1996. Residential patterns: avoidance, assimilation, and succession. In *Ethnic Los Angeles*, ed. R Waldinger, M Bozorgmehr, pp. 109–38. New York: Russell Sage Found.

Clark WAV, Blue SA. 2004. Race, class and segregation patterns in U.S. immigrant gateway cities. *Urban Aff. Rev.* 39:667–88

Cornell S, Hartmann D. 2004. Conceptual confusions and divides: race, ethnicity, and the study of immigration. In *Not Just Black and White: Historical and Contemporary Perspectives on Immigration, Race, and Ethnicity*, ed. N Foner, GM Fredrickson, pp. 23–41. New York: Russell Sage Found.

Darity WA, Mason PL. 1998. Evidence on discrimination in employment: codes of color, codes of gender. *J. Econ. Perspect.* 12:63–90

Denton NA, Massey DS. 1989. Racial identity among Caribbean Hispanics: the effect of double minority status on residential segregation. *Am. Sociol. Rev.* 54:790–808

Denton NA, Massey DS. 1991. Patterns of neighborhood transition in a multiethnic world: U.S. metropolitan areas, 1970–1980. *Demography* 28:41–63

Duncan OD, Duncan B. 1957. *The Negro Population of Chicago: A Study of Residential Succession*. Chicago: Univ. Chicago Press

Ellen IG. 2000. Race-based neighborhood projection: a proposed framework for understanding new data on racial integration. *Urban Stud.* 37:1513–33

Farley R. 1977. Residential segregation in urbanized areas of United States in 1970: analysis of social class and racial differences. *Demography* 14:497–518

Farley R, Danziger S, Holzer HJ. 2000. *Detroit Divided*. New York: Russell Sage Found.

Farley R, Frey WH. 1994. Changes in the segregation of whites from blacks during the 1980s: small steps toward a more integrated society. *Am. Sociol. Rev.* 59(1):23–45

Farley R, Schuman H, Bianchi S, Colasanto D, Hatchett S. 1978. Chocolate city, vanilla suburbs: Will the trend toward racially separate communities continue? *Soc. Sci. Res.* 7:319–44

Farley R, Steeh C, Jackson T, Krysan M, Reeves K. 1983. Continued racial residential segregation in Detroit: 'chocolate city, vanilla suburbs' revisited. *J. Hous. Res.* 4:1–38

Farley R, Steeh C, Krysan M, Jackson T, Reeves K. 1994. Stereotypes and segregation: neighborhoods in the Detroit area. *Am. J. Sociol.* 100:750–80

Fischer CS, Stockmayer G, Stiles J, Hout M. 2004. Distinguishing the geographic levels and social dimensions of U.S. metropolitan segregation, 1960–2000. *Demography* 41: 37–59

Fong E. 1996. A comparative perspective of racial residential segregation: American and Canadian experiences. *Sociol. Q.* 37:501–28

Fong E, Gulia M. 1999. Differences in neighborhood qualities among major racial/ethnic groups in Canada. *Sociol. Inq.* 69:575–98

Fong E, Gulia M. 2000. Neighborhood change within the Canadian ethnic mosaic, 1986–1991. *Popul. Res. Policy Rev.* 19(2):155–77

Fong E, Lee L. 1999. *Ethnic economy within the city contexts: economic returns of participating in ethnic economy revisited.* Presented at Annu. Meet. Am. Sociol. Assoc., Chicago

Fong E, Luk C, Ooka E. 2005. Spatial distribution of suburban ethnic businesses. *Soc. Sci. Res.* 34(1):215–35

Fong E, Matsuo T, Wilkes R. 2002. *Disentangling the segregation patterns of immigrants in suburbia.* Presented at Annu. Meet. Popul. Assoc. Am., Atlanta

Fong E, Shibuya K. 2000. Suburbanization and homeownership: the spatial assimilation process in U.S. metropolitan areas. *Sociol. Perspect.* 43:137–58

Fong E, Wilkes R. 1999. The spatial assimilation model reexamined: an assessment by Canadian data. *Int. Migr. Rev.* 33:594–620

Frey WH, Farley R. 1996. Latino, Asian, and black segregation in US metropolitan areas: Are multiethnic metros different? *Demography* 33:35–50

Galster G. 1989. Residential segregation in American cities: a further response to Clark. *Popul. Res. Policy Rev.* 8:181–92

Grannis R. 2002. Discussion: segregation indices and their functional inputs. *Sociol. Methodol.* 32:69–84

Grant DS II, Parcel TL. 1990. Revisiting metropolitan racial inequality: the case for a resource approach. *Soc. Forces* 68:1121–42

Grieco EM, Cassidy RC. 2001. *Overview of race and Hispanic origin. 2000 brief.* Washington, DC: US Census Bur. http://www. census.gov/prod/2001pubs/c2kbr01-3.pdf

Grodsky E, Pager D. 2001. The structure of disadvantage: individual and occupational determinants of the black-white wage gap. *Am. Sociol. Rev.* 66:542–67

Guest AM, Weed JA. 1976. Ethnic residential segregation: patterns of change. *Am. J. Sociol.* 81:1088–111

Hobbs F, Stoops N. 2002. *Demographic Trends in the 20th Century, Census 2000 Special Reports, Ser. CENSR-4.* Washington, DC: US Census Bur.

Holzer HJ. 2001. Racial differences in labor market outcomes among men. See Smelser et al. 2001, pp. 98–123

Hou F, Milan A. 2003. Neighbourhood ethnic transition and its socio-economic connections. *Can. J. Sociol.* 28:387–410

Huffman ML. 2004. More pay, more inequality? The influence of average wage levels and the racial composition of jobs on the black-white wage gap. *Soc. Sci. Res.* 33:498–520

Iceland J. 2004. Beyond black and white—metropolitan residential segregation in multiethnic America . *Soc. Sci. Res.* 33:248–71

Iceland J, Weinberg DH, Steinmetz E. 2002. *Racial and ethnic residential segregation in the United States: 1980–2000. Census 2000 Spec. Rep.* Washington, DC: US Gov. Print. Off. http://www.census.gov/hhes/www/res seg.html

Ihlanfeldt KR, Scafidi B. 2004. Whites' neighborhood racial preferences and neighborhood racial composition in the United States: evidence from the multi-city study of urban inequality. *Hous. Stud.* 19:325–59

Johnston R, Poulsen M, Forrest J. 2003. And did the walls come tumbling down? Ethnic residential segregation in four U.S. metropolitan areas 1980–2000. *Urban Geogr.* 24:56–81

Joyce PD. 2003. *No Fire Next Time: Black-Korean Conflicts and the Future of America's Cities.* Ithaca, NY: Cornell Univ. Press

Krivo LJ, Kaufman RL. 1999. How low can it go? Declining black-white segregation in a multiethnic context. *Demography* 36:93–109

Lee J. 2002. *Civility in the City: Blacks, Jews, and Koreans in Urban America.* Cambridge, MA: Harvard Univ. Press

Lieberson S. 1980. *A Piece of the Pie: Blacks*

and White Immigrants Since 1880. Berkeley: Univ. Calif. Press

Light IH. 1972. *Ethnic Enterprise in America: Business and Welfare Among Chinese, Japanese, and Blacks.* Berkeley: Univ. Calif. Press

Light IH, Bonacich E. 1988. *Immigrant Entrepreneurs: Koreans in Los Angeles, 1965–1982.* Berkeley: Univ. Calif. Press

Light IH, Gold SJ. 2000. *Ethnic Economies.* San Diego, CA: Academic

Light IH, Rosenstein C. 1995. *Race, Ethnicity, and Entrepreneurship in Urban America.* New York: Aldine de Gruyter

Light IH, Sabagh G, Bozorgmehr M. 1993. Internal ethnicity in the ethnic economy. *Ethn. Racial Stud.* 16:581–97

Logan JR, Alba RD. 1999. Minority niches and immigrant enclaves in New York and Los Angeles: trends and impacts. See Bean & Bell-Rose 1999, pp. 172–93

Logan JR, Alba RD, Leung SY. 1996. Minority access to white suburbs: a multiregional comparison. *Soc. Forces* 74:851–81

Logan JR, Alba RD, McNulty TL. 1994. Ethnic economies in metropolitan regions: Miami and beyond. *Soc. Forces* 72:691–724

Logan JR, Alba RD, Zhang W. 2002. Immigrant enclaves and ethnic communities in New York and Los Angeles. *Am. Sociol. Rev.* 67:299–322

Logan JR, Stults BJ, Farley R. 2004. Segregation of minorities in the metropolis: two decades of change. *Demography* 41:1–22

Massaagli M. 2000. Residential preference and segregation. In *The Boston Renaissance: Race, Space, and Economic Change in an American Metropolis,* ed. B Bluestone, MH Stevenson, pp. 165–98. New York: Russell Sage Found.

Massey DS. 1979. Effects of socioeconomic factors on the residential segregation of blacks and Spanish Americans in U.S. urbanized areas. *Am. Sociol. Rev.* 44:1015–22

Massey DS. 1983. A research note on residential succession: the Hispanic case. *Soc. Forces* 61:825–33

Massey DS. 1985. Ethnic residential segregation: a theoretical synthesis and empirical review. *Sociol. Soc. Res.* 69:315–50

Massey DS, Bitterman B. 1985. Explaining the paradox of Puerto Rican segregation. *Soc. Forces* 64:306–31

Massey DS, Denton NA. 1987. Trends in the residential segregation of blacks, Hispanics, and Asians. *Am. Sociol. Rev.* 52:802–25

Massey DS, Denton NA. 1988. Suburbanization and segregation in United States metropolitan areas. *Am. J. Sociol.* 94:592–626

Massey DS, Denton NA. 1993. *American Apartheid: Segregation and the Making of the Underclass.* Cambridge, MA: Harvard Univ. Press

Massey DS, Fong E. 1990. Segregation and neighborhood quality: blacks, Hispanics, and Asians in the San Francisco metropolitan areas. *Soc. Forces* 69:15–32

Massey DS, Mullan BP. 1984. Processes of Hispanic and black spatial assimilation. *Am. J. Sociol. Rev.* 89:836–73

Massey DS, White MJ, Phua VC. 1996. The dimensions of segregation revisited. *Sociol. Methods Res.* 25:172–206

McCall L. 2001. Sources of racial wage inequality in metropolitan labor markets: racial, ethnic, and gender differences. *Am. Sociol. Rev.* 66:520–41

McKinnon J. 2001. *The black population: 2000. Census 2000 brief.* Washington, DC: US Census Bur. http://www.census.gov/prod/2001pubs/c2kbr01-5.pdf

Murdie RA, Teixeira C. 2003. Towards a comfortable neighborhood and appropriate housing: immigrant experiences in Toronto. In *The World in a City,* ed. P Anisef, M Lanphier, pp. 132–82. Toronto: Univ. Toronto Press

Neal D, Johnson W. 1996. Black-white differences in wages: the role of pre-market factors. *J. Polit. Econ.* 104:869–95

Nee V, Sanders J. 1988. The road to parity: determinants of the socioeconomic achievements of Asian Americans. In *Ethnicity and Race in the U.S.A.: Toward the Twenty-First Century,* ed. RD Alba, pp. 75–93. New York: Routledge

Omi M, Winant H. 1986. *Racial Formation in the United States: From the 1960s to the 1980s.* New York: Routledge & Kegan Paul

Portes A, Bach RL. 1985. *Latin Journey: Cuban and Mexican Immigrants in the United States.* Berkeley: Univ. Calif. Press

Portes A, Jensen L. 1987. What's an ethnic enclave? The case for conceptual clarity. *Am. Sociol. Rev.* 52:768–71

Portes A, Zhou M. 1999. Entrepreneurship and economic progress in the 1990s: a comparative analysis of immigrants and African Americans. See Bean & Bell-Rose 1999, pp. 143–71

Reardon SF, Firebaugh G. 2002. Measures of multigroup segregation. *Sociol. Methodol.* 32:33–67

Rosenfeld MJ, Tienda M. 1999. Mexican immigration, occupational niches, and labor-market competition: evidence from Los Angeles, Chicago, and Atlanta, 1970–1990. See Bean & Bell-Rose 1999, pp. 64–105

Sanders JM, Nee V. 1987. Limits of ethnic solidarity in the enclave economy. *Am. Sociol. Rev.* 52:745–67

Smelser NJ, Wilson WJ, Mitchell F, eds. 2001. *America Becoming: Racial Trends and their Consequences*, Vol. 2. Washington, DC: Natl. Acad. Press

Smith JP. 2001. Race and ethnicity in the labor market: trends over the short and long term. See Smelser et al. 2001, pp. 52–97

Smith JP, Welch FR. 1989. Black economic progress after Myrdal. *J. Econ. Lit.* 27:519–64

Stat. Can. 2004. *Visible minority groups (15) and sex (3) for population, for Canada, provinces, territories, census metropolitan areas and census agglomerations, 2001 Census—20% sample data.* http://www12.statcan.ca/english/census01/products/standard/themes/ListProducts.cfm?Temporal=2001&APATH=3&Theme=44&FREE=0

Taeuber KE, Taeuber AF. 1965. *Negroes in Cities: Residential Segregation and Neighborhood Change.* Chicago: Aldine

Thompson MA. 2000. Black-white residential segregation in Atlanta. In *The Atlanta Paradox*, ed. DL Sjoquist, pp. 88–115. New York: Russell Sage Found.

Tienda M, Lii DT. 1987. Minority concentration and earnings inequality: blacks, Hispanics, and Asians compared. *Am. J. Sociol.* 93:141–65

Tomaskovic-Devey D, Roscigno V. 1996. Racial economic subordination and white gain in the U.S. south. *Am. Sociol. Rev.* 61:565–89

Waldinger RD. 1986. *Through the Eye of the Needle: Immigrants and Enterprise in New York's Garment Trades.* New York: NY Univ. Press

Waldinger RD. 1996. *Still the Promised City?: African-Americans and New Immigrants in Post-Industrial New York.* Cambridge, MA: Harvard Univ. Press

Waldinger RD, Lichter M. 2003. *How the Other Half Works: Immigration and the Social Organization of Labor.* Berkeley: Univ. Calif. Press

Weitzer R. 1997. Racial prejudice among Korean merchants in African American neighborhoods. *Sociol. Q.* 38:587–606

White MJ, Biddlecom AE, Guo S. 1993. Immigration, naturalization, and residential assimilation among Asian Americans in 1980. *Soc. Forces* 72:93–117

White MJ, Fong E, Cai Q. 2003. The segregation of Asian-origin groups in the United States and Canada. *Soc. Sci. Res.* 32:148–67

White MJ, Sassler S. 2000. Judging not only by color: ethnicity, nativity, and neighborhood attainment. *Soc. Sci. Q.* 81:997–1013

Wilkes R, Iceland J. 2004. Hypersegregation in the twenty-first century. *Demography* 41:23–36

Wilson FD. 2003. Ethnic niching and metropolitan labor markets. *Soc. Sci. Res.* 32:429–66

Wilson K, Portes A. 1980. Immigrant enclaves: an analysis of the labor market experiences of Cubans in Miami. *Am. J. Sociol.* 86:295–319

Wong DWS. 1998. Measuring multiethnic spatial segregation. *Urban Geogr.* 19:77–87

Yinger J. 1995. *Closed Doors, Opportunities Lost: The Continuing Costs of Housing Discrimination.* New York: Russell Sage Found.

Yoon IJ. 1997. *On My Own: Korean Businesses and Race Relations in America.* Chicago: Univ. Chicago Press

Zhou M, Logan JR. 1989. Returns on human capital in ethnic enclaves: New York City's Chinatown. *Am. Sociol. Rev.* 54:809–20

Zubrinsky CL, Bobo L. 1996. Prismatic metropolis: race and residential segregation in the city of the angels. *Soc. Sci. Res.* 25: 335–74

Annu. Rev. Sociol. 2005. 31:305–29
doi: 10.1146/annurev.soc.29.010202.095956
Copyright © 2005 by Annual Reviews. All rights reserved
First published online as a Review in Advance on February 22, 2005

BLACK MIDDLE-CLASS NEIGHBORHOODS

Mary Pattillo

Departments of Sociology and African American Studies, Northwestern University,
Evanston, Illinois 60208; email: m-pattillo@northwestern.edu

Key Words   African Americans, segregation, suburbs, race, class

■ **Abstract**   The black middle class received little scholarly attention from the 1960s through the 1980s, when the emphasis was on studying the black urban poor. Recently, however, there has been an increase in attention to this group and their residential environs. This review covers the topics of racial and class segregation, the comparative well-being of black middle-class neighborhoods, and residential preferences, with some attention to black suburbanization and black gentrification. Research findings clearly show that middle-class blacks in the United States have more favorable residential outcomes than poor blacks but still live in poorer neighborhoods than the majority of whites on all measures. Ethnographic studies explore this marginal position in more depth. I argue that if racial integration is the remedy to various racial disparities, then the more fruitful endeavor may be to study the ideologies, practices, and cultures of white neighborhoods, rather than black ones.

INTRODUCTION

This is the first review in the *Annual Review* of black middle-class neighborhoods. Other reviews have considered racial inequality (Allen & Farley 1986, Pettigrew 1985) and the black poor (Marks 1991, Wilson & Aponte 1985), and Williams (1975) included a section on the residential mobility of blacks, but an explicit focus on nonpoor African Americans has been missing. That the topic of black middle-class neighborhoods now warrants its own review is due in no small part to the growth in the number of black scholars, the younger generation of which is even more likely to come from middle-class backgrounds. I have no conclusive data to make a causal argument, yet considerable circumstantial evidence makes this a reasonable supposition. For example, according to the annual Survey of Earned Doctorates, 56% of African Americans who earned doctorates (in all fields) in 2002 were first-generation college students, compared with 78% who earned the PhD in 1977 (Natl. Opin. Res. Counc. 2002, table 36). Massey et al. (2003) give a portrait of the undergraduate pipeline, reporting that 60% of black freshmen entering selective colleges in 1999 had a father who graduated from college, and 25% of them came from families earning over $100,000 per year.

Given the proportional growth in the black middle class in the post–World War II period, it makes sense that a greater proportion of black college students, hence

0360-0572/05/0811-0305$20.00

black graduate students, and hence black professors will come from the ranks of the middle class. Moreover, the number of black PhDs has grown from 263 doctorates granted to blacks in the social sciences in 1980 to 441 new black social science doctorates in 2000 (Natl. Cent. Educ. Stat. 2002). In sociology, especially, where in 2002 African Americans earned 9% of the doctorates—impressively above the 6% awarded to blacks overall (Natl. Opin. Res. Counc. 2002)—we might expect the exploration of a particularly rich new set of topics.

Although I have argued for the importance of black scholars to the study of black communities, I do not proceed much further on this path. I do not argue that the race and class of a scholar determines his/her topic of study. Despite Lofland & Lofland's (1995) methodological admonition to "start where you are," each person's implementation of this edict is different, pulling on a wide variety of "locations"—class, race, gender, geography, sexuality, ability, health, etc.— if the call is heeded at all. Even more, I do not intend to scrutinize scholars' contributions to the literature on black middle-class neighborhoods as a function of their racial and class identity, or downplay the full participation of white scholars (from poor and nonpoor backgrounds) in the study of middle-class black America. Still, it would be naive and unsociological to completely dismiss this reality. Just as the emergence of a larger contingent of black sociologists in the 1960s sounded the "death of white sociology" (Ladner 1973), the work of middle-class black social scientists entering the academy in the 1980s and 1990s has improved our understanding of the complexities of racial stratification by highlighting the social class diversity of black America (e.g., Dennis 1995, Higginbotham 2001, Landry 1987).

Although the seminal studies of black community life always included a consideration of the enclaves carved out by the small group of middle-class African Americans (Drake & Cayton 1945, DuBois 1996), the spotlight put on the black poor beginning in the 1960s altered that practice. With few exceptions (e.g., Collins 1983, Landry 1987), the focus was on poor blacks in poor neighborhoods, as illustrated by a slew of now-classic "ghetto" ethnographies (e.g., Hannerz 1969, Liebow 1967). But the most influential contribution to the study of black America during this time was the work of William Julius Wilson. In *The Declining Significance of Race* (1978) and *The Truly Disadvantaged* (1987), Wilson galvanized the social science community around the desperate situation and bleak prospects of the black poor. To be sure, middle-class blacks were central to Wilson's theories but only because their successes made the circumstances of the black poor that much more dire. For black residential life, it was the increasing absence of middle-class blacks in black neighborhoods that made them central to Wilson's story.

The passionate debate over the relative importance of class versus race (Willie 1979, 1989) that followed the publication of Wilson's books was a mere sideshow to the research industry that grew up to investigate Wilson's major proposition that low-skilled blacks were being left far behind. Studies of the "underclass," as it was then called, investigated the education, childbearing behavior, marriage patterns, criminal offending, drug and gang involvement, welfare receipt, and social networks of the black, and occasionally Latino, poor (e.g., Jencks & Peterson 1991, Moore & Pinderhughes 1993; see Marks 1991 for a critical review). Much attention was given to the black poor in situ, because Wilson's work emphasized the compounding negative effects of spatially concentrated black poverty. Amid this justifiable scholarly and political frenzy—there were even congressional hearings on the underclass (U.S. Congr. Jt. Econ. Comm. 1989)—the diversity of African Americans and the range of black neighborhoods became a backburner concern.

When middle-class blacks and their residential environs resurfaced as topics of study in the late 1980s and early 1990s, there were four areas of concentration: studies of racial and class residential segregation, the comparative well-being of black and white middle-class neighborhoods, neighborhood racial preferences, and black suburbanization. A fifth and fledgling intervention in this area is an interest in the movement of middle- and upper-class blacks back to poor black neighborhoods. This phenomenon, hesitantly labeled black gentrification, is occurring mostly in cities with large black middle-class populations like New York and Chicago. For this article, I fully review the literature in the first three areas, interspersing the literature on black suburbanization and gentrification throughout. These three subareas are introduced by a section defining terms and concepts employed in studying black middle-class neighborhoods, a section that briefly describes the pre–Civil Rights era residential reality of middle-class blacks, and a section that provides a portrait of the spatial distribution of blacks in the U.S.

CLARIFYING TERMS AND METHODS

For sociologists, none of the words in the phrase "black middle-class neighborhood" is self-evident, each requiring some statement of the author's intent and meaning. In the literature cited here, the terms black or African American most often include black immigrants from the Caribbean, Africa, and elsewhere, but not black Hispanics. The sustained discussion of the differences between American-born and foreign-born blacks is more common in studies of immigration and ethnicity (Foner 2001, Waters 1999), although there is increased attention in urban sociology to black ethnic variation (Adelman et al. 2001, Denton & Massey 1989, Freeman 2002, Logan & Deane 2003).

Whereas defining "black" is challenging, defining "middle class" will never produce full consensus. In the studies reviewed here, this concept is variously operationalized as two to four times the poverty line by family size; the upper ranges of categorical income groupings; the sign and significance of the coefficient on a continuous measure of income; those people who live in a middle-class neighborhood; white-collar workers; and so on. Perhaps most precise would be to title this review "black *nonpoor* neighborhoods" because the income, occupation, and educational range of the middle class is so broad as to include terminal high school graduates as well as those with incomes over $75,000 per year.

"Neighborhood" is perhaps the most straightforward concept, if the least organic. With few exceptions, quantitative studies define the neighborhood as the census tract. This geographic area of 2500 to 8000 residents is widely accepted as approximating a neighborhood when using census data. Qualitative and ethnographic studies of neighborhoods and communities (larger areas that are collections of neighborhoods) derive their objects of study more from indigenous experiences of the social and geographic landscapes.

The social scientific methods of studying black middle-class neighborhoods are as diverse as the answers to who is black, who is middle class, and what is a neighborhood. The two primary approaches are (*a*) to investigate middle-class black individuals as they hold preferences for certain kinds of neighborhoods, make choices about if and/or where to move, and ultimately reside in places that can be compared with the places of other individuals; and (*b*) to study black middle-class neighborhoods as whole contexts that can be compared with other contexts (white neighborhoods, Hispanic neighborhoods), or that can be richly described for the nature of interaction and identity formation therein.

BLACK COMMUNITIES BEFORE KING

Although Dr. Martin Luther King is best known for his crusade to end racial segregation in the South, in 1965–1966 he took the Civil Rights movement north to Chicago, marching through Chicago's white neighborhoods that were as scary as any in Birmingham (Ralph 1993). The northern campaign was focused on ending slums, which were created by the combination of intense racial segregation and gross economic inequalities. Romantic depictions of prewar black communities notwithstanding (see Fainstein & Nesbitt 1996 for a critique of such nostalgia), slums of disproportionate poverty, overcrowded and poor housing, rodent infestation, rampant infectious diseases, and high mortality rates were the reality for most African Americans, even if blacks did not experience their neighborhoods as so overwhelmingly bad. Early residential disparities between blacks and whites (Tolnay et al. 2002) established the patterns that persist into the present and are the framework for understanding both intra- and interracial contemporary neighborhood stratification.

Before the post–World War II economic boom, the black middle class was very small. The percentage of blacks in middle-class occupations did not top 10% until 1960, whereas the white middle class constituted more than 20% of the total white population as early as 1910 (Landry 1987). The small black elite was anchored by professionals and businesspeople who catered to the segregated black community. The fact that the black middle class depended on working-class and poor blacks for their livelihood did not, however, temper the former's disdain for the latter. Drake & Cayton (1993, p. 566) vividly narrate the house call of a black doctor to a poor black family after a domestic dispute turned violent in 1930s Chicago: "For a moment, Dr. Maguire felt sick at his stomach. 'Are these my people?' he thought.

'What in the hell do I have in common with them? This is 'The Race' we're always spouting about being proud of?' " Such derision, which was abundant in both the North and South (Davis 1941, Powdermaker 1939), alternately translated into passionate service to aid the black poor on one hand (Higginbotham 1993) and a determination to move away from them on the other. Even before the onset of the Great Migration, DuBois (1996, p. 305) wrote unabashedly about late nineteenth century black middle-class Philadelphians: "The best classes move to the west and leave the dregs behind." Following this theme of black middle-class flight, Frazier (1932) identified seven zones in Chicago's Black Belt of the 1920s. From the first zone to the seventh zone, the percentage of southern-born heads of households decreased, illiteracy and delinquency rates dropped, the proportion of mulattoes rose, homeownership rates increased exponentially, and the percentage of white-collar male workers rose from 5.8% in zone I to 34.2% in zone VII. The black middle class was small, but they nonetheless attempted to carve out black middle-class residential spaces (also see Kusmer 1976 on Cleveland, and Osofsky 1966 on New York). They were never completely successful, however. The ever-growing demand for housing necessitated that the boundaries of black middle-class areas be imminently permeable to poor blacks because the racial lines that encircled the black community were decidedly not so.

Hence, the term Black Belt, which was used to refer to early black communities in cities across the country, is a telling metaphor. Some invisible but durable strap seemed to geographically confine the black community, and its population bulged as new migrants streamed in from the South. A three-pronged approach hemmed in the black community: (*a*) a legal apparatus of racial restrictive covenants and discriminatory federal appraisal and lending practices (Gotham 2002, Jackson 1985, Sugrue 1996); (*b*) a market strategy of steering black buyers and renters into black neighborhoods or "busting" white blocks to ensure their complete racial transition (Gotham 2002); and (*c*) among some whites, a populist commitment to violence when all else failed to keep blacks out (Gamm 1999, Hirsch 1983). The black middle class was equally subjected to these strictures. Black shopkeepers, clergy, doctors, teachers, dentists, bankers, insurance salespeople, nurses, and social workers lived within the boundaries of the Black Belt and made frequent desperate but futile pushes against the railroad tracks, parks, waterways, and major thoroughfares that were the literal leather of segregation. The situation of the black middle class in the pre–Civil Rights era is most aptly characterized by repeated attempts at class sorting within the constraints of severe racial segregation (Taeuber & Taeuber 1965).

WHERE BLACKS LIVE NOW

Marking a departure from the trends of high and rising racial segregation through the 1960s, the notion of a black neighborhood at all could one day become irrelevant if racial segregation continues to decline as it has since 1970. But given that such movement toward integration is occurring very slowly, this day is not in the near future. In the meantime, the "average" residential environment for African Americans in 2000 was (slightly) majority black and nonpoor. What does this "average" environment mean? Aggregating census data and then characterizing the neighborhoods of African Americans (and whites) can yield findings that may be difficult to interpret. The Lewis Mumford Center for Comparative Urban and Regional Research at the State University of New York at Albany pioneered the analysis and presentation of census data on race, ethnicity, income, and related indicators. Their research characterizes the neighborhoods of the "average" black, white, Hispanic, and Asian person in all 331 U.S. metropolitan areas by, first, figuring the median income in each census tract, which they then assign to each individual residing in that tract, from which they can compute the average of the median tract-level incomes for blacks, whites, Hispanics, and Asians. They do the same calculations for an array of other measures, such as neighborhood poverty, educational level, and housing vacancies, resulting in a comprehensive description of neighborhood characteristics by race and ethnicity.

At the national level, then, the "average" black person lives in a neighborhood with a median income of $35,306, compared with the median income of the average white person's neighborhood, which is $51,459 (Logan 2002, table 2). The average Hispanic person lives in a neighborhood with a slightly higher median income than that of blacks, and the median income in Asians' neighborhoods surpasses that of whites. This disparity in the neighborhood median income persists when comparing affluent blacks and whites with household incomes over $60,000.

The plethora of available census information allows users to paint a picture of the neighborhood environment of the average middle-class African American (household income between $30,000 and $60,000) compared with the average middle-class white person in any metropolitan area. Table 1 gives this portrait for metropolitan Philadelphia (see Anderson 2000 for a narrative description of Philadelphia). I chose Philadelphia because it is the site of the meetings of the American Sociological Association in 2005. Although Philadelphia is a good pick for representing the relatively highly segregated cities of the Northeast and Midwest—the dissimilarity index for both regions is 0.74 (Iceland et al. 2002, table 5-2)—it overstates the extent of black neighborhood disadvantage nationwide because the South and West are more racially integrated, with dissimilarity indexes of 0.58 and 0.56, respectively (Iceland et al. 2002, table 5-2).

Table 1 shows that the average middle-class black person in Philadelphia in 2000 lived in a neighborhood with nearly triple the poverty rate, a smaller proportion of college-educated, professional, employed, and homeowning neighbors, and more vacant houses than the average middle-class white person. The final row of Table 1 gives a partial explanation of these findings. Although the Philadelphia metropolitan region was just over 20% black, the average middle-class black Philadelphian lived in a neighborhood that was over 60% black. Whites were similarly overrepresented in the neighborhoods of middle-class whites. As the more detailed quantitative research reviewed below illustrates, these neighborhood-level inequalities hold up to various statistical controls and specifications.

TABLE 1   Neighborhood social and economic characteristics of the average middle-class black and white person in metropolitan Philadelphia, 2000[a]

Neighborhood indicator	Average middle-class white Philadelphian	Average middle-class black Philadelphian
Neighborhood median income	$53,195	$34,741
Neighborhood poverty rate	7.4%	20.4%
Percent college educated	28.3%	16.5%
Percent professionals	37.4%	28.4%
Neighborhood unemployment rate	4.8%	11.4%
Neighborhood housing vacancy rate	4.6%	10.6%
Homeownership	72.0%	60.5%
Percent "own group"	83.8%	60.9%

[a]Source: Compiled from data reported in *Separate and Unequal: Racial and Ethnic Neighborhoods in the 21st Century.* http://browns4.dyndns.org/cen2000_s4/SepUneq/PublicSeparateUnequal.htm. Accessed Jan. 7, 2005.

The national and Philadelphia snapshots demonstrate that despite the heavy attention given to black poor neighborhoods, the average African American lives in a nonpoor neighborhood with a slight black majority. But what about the distribution of the black population across various neighborhood types? Although the answer is similar to that reached when considering the "average" black person, there are some differences. First, whereas majority black neighborhoods (those with black populations of 50% or greater) made up only 10.7% of all metropolitan neighborhoods in the United States in 2000, just over half (50.4%) of all blacks lived in such neighborhoods. This figure is down from 56.2% in 1990, and 70.3% in 1960, illustrating the clear trend toward desegregation [1990 and 2000 figures come from B. Stults, unpublished data; 1960 figures are from Glaeser & Vigdor (2001), table 2]. Second, in 2000, roughly 30% of blacks lived in neighborhoods that were over 80% black, down from 37% in 1990, again charting trends of desegregation, but also indicating that a nontrivial minority of blacks live in relatively racially homogeneous settings, as do the majority of whites. Third, and finally, of the roughly half of blacks who live in majority black neighborhoods, 36% live in neighborhoods with poverty rates under 20%, the oft-used cutoff for distinguishing poor neighborhoods (Jargowsky 1997). If "nonpoor neighborhood" is defined more liberally, as one where the median family income is above the poverty threshold for a family of four (roughly $20,000), then 87% of blacks who live in majority black neighborhoods live in nonpoor ones. Hence, when viewed in distributional terms, to write about "black middle-class neighborhoods" is to discuss the residential environs of 18% of the total metropolitan black population at the most conservative end, or 44% of the metropolitan black population at the most liberal end.

This descriptive introduction provides a sense of how common black middle-class neighborhoods are, and how likely blacks are to live in them. The strides toward integration are evident, yet inequalities in neighborhood quality linger, with blacks, even middle-class blacks, living in decidedly poorer neighborhoods than comparable whites on every measure.

RESIDENTIAL SEGREGATION

It is almost sociological common knowledge that African Americans have been and remain the most residentially segregated racial/ethnic group in the United States (Iceland et al. 2002, Massey & Denton 1993, Wilkes & Iceland 2004). It is also common practice, although not without controversy, to posit black racial integration with whites as a desired outcome because such segregation has negatively affected myriad life outcomes for blacks, from health to employment (Cutler & Glaeser 1997, Polednak 1997, Williams & Collins 1995), making it a central indicator of racial inequality and/or progress. William Julius Wilson's (1987, p. 7) proposition that "today's black middle-class professionals no longer tend to live in ghetto neighborhoods and have increasingly moved into mainstream occupations outside the black community" raised three related empirical possibilities that researchers endeavored to explore: (*a*) Racial segregation varies by social class for African Americans; (*b*) mobility choices and outcomes for middle-class blacks have come to favor nonblack, nonpoor neighborhoods; and (*c*) as a result, class segregation among African Americans has increased.

A few scholars (Erbe 1975, Simkus 1978) had studied racial segregation by class prior to Wilson's work, but interest grew rapidly after it. This line of research finds that middle-class blacks (variously defined) are slightly less segregated from whites than poor blacks (Farley 1991, Iceland et al. 2005, Massey & Denton 1985, Massey & Fischer 1999); that middle-class blacks, like all blacks, have become less segregated from whites over time (Adelman 2004, Fischer 2003, Iceland et al. 2005); and that blacks who live in suburbs are less segregated from and more exposed to whites than blacks in central cities (Alba & Logan 1993, Massey & Denton 1988, Phelan & Schneider 1996, Stahura 1987, Timberlake 2002; for an exception see Darden & Kamel 2000). Despite generally positive trends in suburbanization, it has not proven to be a palliative to racial segregation (Alba et al. 1994, Cashin 2001, Frey 1994, Galster 1991, Liska et al. 1998, Logan & Alba 1995; see also Wiese 2004 for an historical analysis of black suburbanization), and segregation indexes for middle-class blacks from whites remain high in both cities and suburbs. Iceland et al. (2005) report a national black-white dissimilarity index of 61.5 for those earning $45,000 to $75,000 in 2000. This means that just over 60% of middle-class blacks (or whites) would have to move out of their neighborhoods to replicate the racial composition of the metropolitan area at the neighborhood level. On balance, the black middle class does experience more residential integration than poor blacks, but not full integration in an absolute sense.

To get to these more integrated neighborhoods, middle-class blacks had to leave segregated black neighborhoods in the first place, raising the question: What have been the mobility patterns of nonpoor African Americans? Massey et al. (1994) challenged Wilson on the out-migration hypothesis (see Wilson 1991 and St. John 1995 for rebuttals) using longitudinal data from the Panel Study of Income Dynamics. They found that the probability that a nonpoor black person would leave a poor or very poor black neighborhood actually declined over the two time periods they studied (1970–1973 to 1979–1984). Moreover, wrote Massey et al. (1994), "nonpoor [black] movers from very poor black areas were three times more likely to end up in a poor or very poor black neighborhood than in a nonpoor neighborhood" (p. 434). If anything, this research concluded that middle-class blacks were residentially downwardly mobile, rather than the reverse. This evidence underscored the limited residential options of middle-class blacks, challenging the sanguine portrait painted by Wilson that they were escaping segregation for more integrated, wealthier pastures.

South & Crowder (1998) also took on this question, exploring the mobility choices of blacks and whites by socioeconomic status in the early 1980s. They found a fair amount of heterogeneity in the kinds of moves made by African Americans. Roughly 42% of the moves made by African Americans were from predominately black tracts to other predominately black tracts, and a similar proportion of moves originated and ended in racially mixed neighborhoods (author's tabulation from South & Crowder 1998, table 1). But when blacks made moves between neighborhood types, they were more likely to move to blacker neighborhoods rather than whiter ones. Whites exhibited much less variance in the kinds of moves they made, with 88% of all moves starting from and ending in predominately white tracts. In multivariate analyses, the authors found no significant effects of income or employment on the probability that, conditional on moving, a black person would move to a mixed or white tract. They did, however, find that more educated and married blacks were more likely to move to white tracts, and black homeowners, although less likely to move overall, were more likely to move to white or mixed tracts when they did move, offering some evidence that middle-class blacks are more likely to move to whiter neighborhoods. In a similar study, South & Crowder (1997, table 3) found again that neither income nor employment increased the likelihood that a black person would move, this time to the suburbs (as opposed to moving to the city), but that more highly educated blacks (but not homeowners) were more likely to make suburban moves than their less-educated counterparts. Updating and modifying the research on black mobility and extending the observation period to 1990, Quillian (2002) found an effect of family income on the probability of moving to a white neighborhood, and he replicated the finding of the positive effect of education. Combined, these results show considerable variation in the effects of various measures of class on moving, and thus there is not an overwhelmingly consistent case that being middle class is correlated with moving to whiter or suburban areas for blacks, with the exception of education.

A final line of research spawned by Wilson's out-migration hypothesis focuses on class segregation among blacks. Class segregation, like racial segregation, is often measured at the census tract level, where the index of dissimilarity analyzes the extent to which incomes in census tracts mirror the metropolitan distribution of incomes. Massey & Fischer (2003) update previous studies (Jargowsky 1996, Massey & Eggers 1990) and chart income segregation for blacks and whites at the tract level from 1970 to 2000. Segregation of affluent blacks (defined as those earning four times the poverty line) from poor blacks increased from 0.34 in 1970, to 0.44 in 1980, to 0.52 in 1990, and then declined back to 1980 levels by 2000. Whereas white income segregation followed the same trends, black income segregation was 20%–30% higher across the same periods. Therefore, the 1970s and 1980s were decades of increasing class segregation among African Americans, whereas the 1990s saw a trend toward less class segregation among blacks. These data seem to contradict the findings by Massey et al. (1994) that the probability of a nonpoor black person leaving a poor or very poor black neighborhood declined from the early 1970s to the early 1980s. A possible reconciliation of these findings is that most middle-class blacks left poor black neighborhoods in the 1970s, so that by the early 1980s, the probability of such out-migration had diminished. This reading is consistent with trends in class segregation that show a greater increase in class segregation in the 1970s than in the 1980s. Perhaps a simpler explanation is that the definitions of nonpoor are not comparable across these studies. Massey & Fischer (2003) study the segregation of affluent blacks from poor blacks, and Massey et al. (1994) focus on the mobility of all nonpoor blacks, including working- and middle-class blacks who may have been less successful in segregating themselves from the black poor. Overall, the finding of increased class segregation among blacks is a robust and replicated finding (Jargowsky 1996, Massey & Eggers 1990), lending strong support to Wilson's original hypothesis.

Relatively high levels of black income segregation, however, do not translate into more homogeneously middle-class neighborhoods for African Americans because measures of class segregation are tied to the overall distribution of incomes. Massey & Fischer (2003) report that affluent whites live in neighborhoods where 35% of their neighbors are also affluent, compared with 27% of the neighbors of affluent blacks. Moreover, the fact that blacks of different classes are more likely to live in different census tracts does not take full account of space. The index of dissimilarity does not provide an indication of the proximity of the neighborhoods of middle-class blacks to the neighborhoods of poor blacks. It is "essentially aspatial" (Jargowsky 1996), failing to capture processes of clustering, or "the tendency for black areas to adhere together within one large agglomeration" (Massey & Denton 1993, p. 75). Pattillo-McCoy (2000) illustrates the clustering of Chicago's majority black neighborhoods such that middle-class black neighborhoods are contiguous to areas of concentrated poverty. Beyond Chicago, 16 of the 30 cities studied by Massey & Denton (1993) exhibited significant clustering patterns (also see Iceland et al. 2002). Although the increasing rates of income segregation among blacks from 1970 to 1990 clearly indicate the greater ability of middle-class blacks to separate themselves from poor blacks at the tract level, other relevant statistics, such as persistent racial segregation, the overall distribution of black incomes, and the clustering of black neighborhoods, temper the notion that the black middle class will attain residential parity with whites through out-migration alone.

NEIGHBORHOOD QUALITY

What does the prevalence of racial residential segregation (even with class sorting) mean for the neighborhood experience of middle-class African Americans? In turning to a discussion of the quality of middle-class black neighborhoods and the experience of middle-class blacks in them, I make a corresponding switch to emphasize the qualitative research on the subject. Although quantitative studies (to which I return) offer greater representation and aggregation, the ethnographies of black middle-class neighborhood life give texture.

In Bruce Haynes's *Red Lines, Black Spaces* (2001), William Julius Wilson remains the scholar we all love to debate. Haynes chooses an area that Wilson might have highlighted as exemplary of the destinations of African Americans who out-migrated from black urban enclaves. Runyon Heights, NY, is suburban, middle-income, and homeowning. Still, Haynes shows that physical distance does not allow for social distance from the black poor, and while Runyon Heights's residents may have been able to leave behind poverty, they were not able to escape racial subordination. In Runyon Heights, U.S. blacks and Caribbean blacks, light-skinned and dark-skinned, southerners and Harlemites, from the middle and working classes came together and forged a unified "black" identity in response to their collective exclusion and to threats to their neighborhood's well-being. But it was a decidedly "classed" blackness, one that successfully resisted a redistricting plan to create a second predominately minority voting district because their concerns as middle-class homeowners "would have been overshadowed by the needs of the much larger and poorer [black] west-side community" (Haynes 2001, p. 142). Haynes's study illustrates the vulnerability of black middle-class neighborhoods to the encroachment of black poverty (as well as its growth from within) and the efforts of middle-class black residents to hold the class line (see also Gregory 1998, Owens 1997, Pattillo 2003a, Pattillo-McCoy 1999, and parts of Anderson 1990, Duneier 1992).

Several ethnographies expound on the effects of higher black poverty rates within black middle-class areas for neighborhood social and political cohesion. Valerie Johnson's (2002) study of Prince Georges County, Maryland, the poster suburb for black middle-class America, investigates why, despite their numerical majority, blacks do not control many of the important power levers. She argues that socioeconomic diversity among black Prince Georgians means that blacks have been unable to coalesce around particular interests to advance policy initiatives or elect representatives in large numbers. For example, in the discussion about school busing, affluent blacks were opposed to busing because they lived in the more racially integrated parts of the county, whereas poor blacks who lived primarily "inside the Beltway" supported busing. Ginwright (2002) finds similar ideological disputes between poor and middle-class blacks in an Oakland school setting. The social and human capital of middle-class black school activists overpowered that of the working-class parents in the schools, and the former's visions of an Afro-centric curriculum reigned over the desires of working-class black parents who wanted more college preparatory classes, fairer disciplinary procedures, and physical plant improvements. Research in this vein highlights the particular organizational challenges that confront middle-class blacks and poor blacks in shared residential environments.

John Jackson's book *Harlemworld* (2001) directs attention to the diversity of identities in black Harlem, which he shows is erroneously assumed to be overwhelmingly poor (also see Lacy 2002, 2005; Pattillo 2003b on black identities). Focusing on the construction and fluidity of black identities based on social class, Jackson (2001, p. 89) illustrates this dynamic with a clever story about the "two-party system":

> On a particularly hot and humid summer day, Paul, an African American architect living and working in New York City, celebrated his thirty-first birthday with an extravagant party. In fact, he had two of them: the first with old friends and family members in his mother's Bedford-Stuyvesant apartment that afternoon; the second inside his friend Wilson's plush Harlem brownstone and lasting well into the wee hours of the morning.

Paul's biography—manifested in his two parties with two different guest lists in two different kinds of black neighborhoods (see discussion below about the gentrification of Harlem)—presents an extreme case of the liminality of the black middle-class experience, between humble, racially segregated roots and an upscale, jetsetting future (see also Daniels 2004, Prince 2004, Taylor 2002).

The "inbetweenness" of the black middle-class residential experience is supported by the quantitative literature. Sampson & Wilson (1995) show that African Americans of every socioeconomic status live in qualitatively different kinds of neighborhoods than their white counterparts. Indeed, they report a finding quite common in this literature: "[T]he worst urban contexts in which whites reside are considerably better than the average context of black communities" (p. 42). Alba et al. (1994, p. 427) make an almost identical point about New York suburbs in 1980 when they state that "even the most affluent blacks are not able to escape from crime, for they reside in communities as crime-prone as those housing the poorest whites." Logan & Stults (1999, p. 270) find no evidence to alter this conclusion when studying Cleveland in 1990, parroting, "even affluent blacks live in places with more than double the violent crime rate to which poor whites are exposed." To hammer the point home, Adelman et al. (2001, p. 621) join the chorus. "In fact," they write about their estimates of the poverty rates in the neighborhoods of high-status blacks versus low-status whites, "the residential attainment of these high-SES members of each black group falls below that of even the low-SES non-Hispanic whites" (see also Erbe 1975, DeFrances 1996, Fielding & Taeuber 1991, Massey et al. 1987, Massey & Fong 1990).

Moving from the study of whole neighborhood contexts to the residential out-comes of individual middle-class blacks, Alba et al. (2000) find significant positive effects of household income and education on the proportion of white neigh-bors and the median neighborhood income for blacks in Chicago, Detroit, and Cleveland. Yet their (normatively) promising conclusions—"middle class blacks live with many more white neighbors than poorer blacks do" (Alba et al. 2000, p. 551)—are always tempered by the sobering ones: "[P]ersonal socioeconomic gains by African Americans do not produce a closing of the gap with whites" (p. 554). Moreover, in an interesting twist, the authors find that the whites with whom middle-class blacks live actually have lower incomes than the blacks themselves, calling into question the usefulness of "living with whites" as a straightforward measure of advantage (p. 556). Adelman (2004) directly com-pares middle-class whites and middle-class blacks (rather than inspecting the in-come variable in a regression model) in the 10 metropolitan areas with the largest black populations in 1990, and again found that middle-class blacks lived with more poor neighbors, more single-parent families, and fewer college graduates than did middle-class whites. Strikingly, using a more novel indicator of neighbor-hood quality in each metropolitan area, Adelman (2004) found that middle-class blacks in Houston, for example, lived in neighborhoods where 12.8% of the va-cant units were boarded up, compared with 2.2% for similar whites. This gives a unique sense of the day-to-day visual realities of middle-class blacks that again underscore the resource deficits in their neighborhoods.

NEIGHBORHOOD PREFERENCES

Orlando Patterson (1997) chastises scholars in the social sciences for always seeing the glass half empty. He reads the evidence presented thus far about the lower levels of residential segregation for middle-class blacks compared with poor blacks, and the commensurate upgrading of their residential environs, as proof that conditions have improved dramatically for the black middle class in the post–Civil Rights era. For Patterson, the elusiveness of full parity is still troublesome, but not to the erasure of the clear signs of progress. When reflecting on the factors that un-derlie observed racial segregation and neighborhood quality disparities, Patterson writes:

> Euro-American attitudes now make possible the complete integration of the metropolis *if only Afro-Americans were willing to live in neighborhoods in which they were a quarter of the population.* This is not an unreasonable bargain. Euro-Americans are, after all, over 80% of the population, so there is some give on their part in their willingness to live in neighborhoods with less than their proportion of the population. At the same time, this attitudinal change permits Afro-Americans to live in mixed neighborhoods where the proportion of Afro-Americans is almost twice that found in the general pop-ulation (Patterson 1997, p. 46, emphasis in original; for similar statements,

see Clark 1986, 1991; Clark & Dieleman 1996; Thernstrom & Thernstrom 1997).

The analysis of white and black preferences for varying neighborhood racial compositions is perhaps the most contentious subfield in the study of race and place. The irony of this debate is that both sides are reading the same evidence. It is well established that blacks on the whole prefer neighborhoods that are 50% black and 50% white, and that whites on the whole prefer neighborhoods that are roughly 80% white and 20% black (assuming a bi-racial world). To be sure, both of these scenarios represent some level of racial integration. It is equally clear that these desires cannot be met simultaneously because by the time blacks' compositional preferences are met, the black population has exceeded the tolerance levels (or attraction levels) of most whites, and the neighborhood "tips" (Schelling 1971, 1972). Given these facts, one side must alter their preferences to achieve residential integration. Who should?

This question is obviously a normative, not a scientific, one. Moreover, as many students of segregation and preferences note, the notion that residential segregation is now primarily the result of the individual preferences of whites and blacks overlooks the evidence on the role of institutional discrimination by real estate agents, mortgage lenders, insurers, and appraisers in constraining the choices of African Americans (Galster 1988, Ross & Yinger 2002, Squires & O'Connor 2001, Turner et al. 2002). The debate also assumes that racial residential integration is a goal that trumps (or should trump) other residential desires among blacks and whites, and that if blacks and/or whites just knew that a little more tolerance on their parts could move us to a more residentially integrated country, they would acquiesce. I discuss these considerations of "values" further in the conclusion, returning here to the empirical findings regarding preferences.

Farley et al. (1978) published the first major article on preferences of blacks and whites for neighborhoods of varying racial compositions using data from the Detroit Area Study. They pioneered the "show card" method, in which respondents are shown drawings of a group of houses representing a hypothetical neighborhood. The houses are shaded either black or white to indicate the home of a black or white family, and the cards vary with respect to what proportion of houses are occupied by blacks or whites. Respondents are then asked a series of questions about their preference for, level of comfort in, desire to move into, or likelihood of moving out of such neighborhoods. This method was refined and replicated in the Multi-City Study of Urban Inequality on which a significant amount of this research is based (Adelman 2005, Bobo & Zubrinsky 1996, Charles 2000, Farley et al. 1997, Freeman 2000, Krysan 2002, Krysan & Farley 2002, Timberlake 2000, Zubrinsky & Bobo 1996).

Krysan & Farley (2002, table 1) offer the most straightforward description of the residential preferences of African Americans. Exactly half of the blacks surveyed in Atlanta, Boston, Detroit, and Los Angeles ranked the picture for the hypothetical half black–half white neighborhood as the most attractive, and another 22% ranked this kind of neighborhood the second most attractive (out of five neighborhood choices). Very few blacks (only 2%) found being the only black person in an otherwise all-white neighborhood the most attractive option, while opinions on all-black neighborhoods were split: 27% ranked it the first or second and 48% ranked it the fourth or fifth most attractive alternative. White respondents are often asked a different set of questions and shown different cards, but to provide some perspective on their preferences, roughly 60% of whites across the four metropolitan areas would be uncomfortable in a neighborhood that contained 8 blacks and 6 whites (just over half black) (Farley et al. 1997, figure 4), and only 31% of whites would move into such a neighborhood (Krysan & Farley 2002, p. 960). This degree of willingness of whites to move into majority black neighborhoods shows a significant improvement over time (see Farley et al. 1994). This is the glass-half-full trend that Patterson beseeches scholars to celebrate. Still, the empty half of the glass exposes the point that in some metropolitan areas with especially large black populations (metropolitan New Orleans is 38% black, metropolitan Washington, DC, is 27% black, and many other metropolitan areas are about 20% African American) and in central cities with even higher black concentrations, the aversion of whites to blacks in their neighborhoods makes residential integration very unstable, always bumping up against racial tipping points (see Ellen 2000 for a discussion of stable racial integration).

Beyond describing the neighborhood racial preferences of whites and blacks, this literature goes on to explore why blacks (and whites) hold these preferences. Here, the diversity of indexes and methodological approaches makes comparison difficult, but I present some of the main findings for black preferences here. Krysan & Farley (2002; also see Zubrinsky & Bobo 1996) emphasize the fear that blacks have of white hostility as driving blacks' preferences for half-and-half or slightly majority black neighborhoods, although cases could also be made from their data for the strength of an ideological commitment to integration among blacks who choose the half-and-half neighborhoods, and racial solidarity/affinity among blacks who prefer the all-black neighborhoods. Fear of white hostility is also the major reason behind blacks' unwillingness to move into an all-white neighborhood. (A clear majority of blacks, 89%, are willing to move into a neighborhood that is 75% white).

To understand the particular preferences of middle-class blacks, the authors find that blacks with more education are less likely to want to live in majority black neighborhoods than those with less education, but the effect of income is relatively weak, with only one of the four income categories reaching significance. None of the socioeconomic variables predicted blacks' preferences for a majority white neighborhood over an integrated neighborhood, and neither did they significantly predict blacks' willingness to move into all-white or all-black neighborhoods. Zubrinsky & Bobo (1996) and Freeman (2000) similarly report limited support for a class-based model of residential preferences for blacks. So, again, with the exception of education, middle-class blacks do not seem to hold preferences that are distinct from other blacks with regard to neighborhood racial composition.

Timberlake (2000), using the same data but with different constructs and focusing on Atlanta, stresses in-group affinity among blacks as the major predictor of their preferences and again finds only sparse evidence that class affects blacks' preferences. Bobo & Zubrinsky (1996) find that the "warmer" blacks feel about whites, the more open they are to integration (a different dependent variable). They find no effect of in-group affinity in determining blacks' attitudes toward integration, and they did not study differences by class.

The two studies that investigate how blacks' neighborhood preferences translate into their actual residential environs (Adelman 2005, Freeman 2000) find that blacks who prefer more whites in their neighborhoods are significantly more likely to have more whites in their neighborhoods—indicating that preferences are not completely unattainable—but that the magnitude of the effect is relatively small. For example, Adelman (2005, figure 1) reports that the neighborhoods of blacks who desire to live with proportionally more blacks are 25% white, compared with the neighborhoods of blacks who desire to live with proportionally more whites, which are on average 30% white. This is not a very sizeable return to blacks' preferences for living with whites.

Perhaps the most interesting twist about social class in all these studies is the following: Black homeowners are consistently more likely to prefer integrated neighborhoods over all-black neighborhoods, they prefer fewer black neighbors in general, and they are more willing to move into all-white neighborhoods than renters, yet, despite these preferences, black homeowners consistently live in blacker neighborhoods than renters (Adelman 2005, Alba et al. 2000, Alba & Logan 1993, Freeman 2000, Logan et al. 1996, South & Crowder 1998). That black homeowners' preferences do not match their realities is suggestive evidence that they face discrimination in the housing market, and that entry into predominately homeowning white neighborhoods is more difficult than entry into white neighborhoods with considerable rental housing.

A correlative question regarding the neighborhood racial preferences of blacks and whites is the following: Are the stated preferences actually about race or about some other neighborhood characteristics that may be associated with racial composition? The fact that at least 20% of African Americans express an aversion to all-black neighborhoods (they rate them as least attractive or would not move into them) suggests either a nontrivial amount of self-hate among blacks, or that racial composition is a marker of other neighborhood characteristics that blacks and whites want to avoid. Harris (1999, 2001) has shown, using data from Chicago, that the dissatisfaction of both whites and blacks (a different outcome measure from preferences) in neighborhoods with greater black representation disappears completely for blacks when crime, physical deterioration, schools, and poverty rates are controlled. For whites, those same controls almost erase whites' stated dissatisfaction with black neighborhoods as well. Harris (2001, p. 12) concludes that "Blacks and Whites are not averse to Black neighbors per se, but rather that both prefer high-socioeconomic-status neighborhoods and that these neighborhoods tend to have small Black populations." Leaving aside the possibility that subjective assessments of neighborhood conditions such as crime cannot be disentangled from a neighborhood's racial composition (see Quillian & Pager 2001), Emerson et al. (2001) find evidence contrary to Harris's using data from a national telephone survey. They find a persistent negative association between the percentage of blacks in a hypothetical neighborhood and whites' willingness to buy a house in that neighborhood, controlling for the quality of schools, the crime rate, and housing values. This is an area in which more research is needed to determine if race is simply a proxy for other neighborhood characteristics.

Investigators disagree over the importance of racial neighborhood preferences for creating or perpetuating racial segregation, the roots of these preferences, their relationship to social class for blacks, and their validity in actually measuring racial sensitivities. Nonetheless, there are three important areas of consensus in this subfield. First, as Clark (1991) writes, "the dynamics of change that come from preferences are determined more by whites' decisions than by blacks' or Hispanics' decisions" (p. 17). That is, all students of this issue recognize the greater ability of whites to actualize their preferences through moving into and out of neighborhoods. Second, whites are less tolerant of integration than are other racial/ethnic groups. Zubrinsky & Bobo (1996, p. 367) describe the pathetic irony that "blacks are at once the most open to integration and yet most often seen as the least desirable neighbors." Finally, the actual moving behavior of whites and blacks makes the gulf in tolerance even more clear. Hwang & Murdock (1998) show that 28% of the growth in suburban black populations between 1980 and 1990 happened in suburbs that were 90% or more white, and another 40% of the growth was in suburbs that were 75%–90% white (author's tabulations from Hwang & Murdock 1998, table 1; also see Glaeser & Vigdor 2001, p. 5). These data illustrate that blacks act on their willingness to move into predominately white areas. Studying the actual moving behavior of whites, however, Quillian (2002, p. 212) writes, "Whites move to destinations that are Whiter than their origin [tracts] and are by far most likely to move to the Whitest possible destinations."

CONCLUSION

"After I leave the skyscraper jungle of midtown Manhattan, I head back to my home in (do or die) Bed-Stuy, Brooklyn," writes African American journalist Cora Daniels, corroborating the trend she finds among her black professional interviewees to choose predominately black neighborhoods. She continues, "Sure, I could afford to live in more integrated areas, but I don't want to. I like to come home to a place and be surrounded by folks who would not think of asking me, why?" (Daniels 2004, pp. 178–79). Patterson (1997) would be disappointed with Daniels's choice of neighborhood, as he would with similar declarations made by journalist Sam Fulwood (1996), by Karyn Lacy's (2002, 2005) black suburbanites, by the many black professionals interviewed in Feagin & Sikes's (1995) *Living with*

Racism, and by the upper- and middle-class blacks who have moved back to Harlem and Chicago's South Side to inaugurate an exclusive black cultural renaissance in those areas (Boyd 2000, Pattillo 2003b, Prince 2004, Taylor 2002). Despite the survey data that reveal blacks' clear preference for integration with whites, these are the kinds of statements that instead support arguments that racial segregation results from "neutral ethnocentrism" (Clark 1991) on the part of both whites and blacks, and that the particular segregation of middle-class blacks results from their inability to slough off their racial identities for ones based on class. And who said, after all, that residential integration with whites is still the preeminent goal to which blacks (and whites) should aspire? Legal scholarship on "nonsegregation," as opposed to desegregation or integration (Bell 2001, Calmore 1993, Forman 1971), which emphasizes choice and access and allows for voluntary self-segregation, calls into question the unilateral and in some spheres largely unsuccessful focus on racial integration (of neighborhoods, schools, workforces, etc.). In the housing arena these authors argue that the emphasis on desegregation over the allocation of resources to improve the quality of existing predominately black neighborhoods has retarded any progress in addressing the affordable housing needs of poor African Americans.

Notwithstanding these and other scholarly and political debates about racial segregation and the black neighborhoods it creates, blacks are surely and steadily acting on their stated preferences for integration, and to a much greater extent than are whites. An inspection of contemporary neighborhood-level racial demographics proves that blacks are already being more flexible than their preferences would predict. As already stated, most of the preferences research finds that blacks prefer neighborhoods that are half black and half white; short of this possibility, they prefer slightly more blacks as opposed to slightly more whites. But in 2000, only 20% of African Americans lived in neighborhoods that were 50%–80% black (Glaeser & Vigdor 2001, Table 2). A greater proportion (35.6%) lived in neighborhoods that were 10%–50% black. When informally surveying the racial composition of their metropolitan areas, perhaps blacks do recognize that they are being a bit selfish in wanting to move to half-and-half or slightly blacker neighborhoods, and they prioritize instead the lofty goal of integrated living. Whites, on the other hand, stick to their guns. They say they do not want to live with blacks (they are more willing to live with Hispanics and Asians), and they mean it. They will move out if/when blacks move in (Crowder 2000), and they will almost always choose a white neighborhood over an integrated one (South & Crowder 1998, Quillian 2002). In so doing, they have been able to preserve 56% of all metropolitan neighborhoods as less than 5% black (Glaeser & Vigdor 2001, table 2).

The research to date on black middle-class neighborhoods and their middle-class residents underscores the complexities of this experience. Judging from the weak association between socioeconomic status and racial residential preferences—with the possible exception of education—middle-class blacks are diverse in their feelings about integration, no more or less likely to look for it than their less-well-off racial peers. They profess a taste for integration but a longing for the comfort of segregation. They exhibit simultaneous attraction and aversion to black neighborhoods stemming from their association of black neighborhoods with bad behaviors, but tempered by their belief that blacks are easier to get along with than whites. Among the middle class, there is a growing cadre of romantics who are determined to take back some of the most notoriously disinvested enclaves of black America: Harlem; southeast Washington, DC; Oakland; Chicago's Black Belt. Black preferences overall are no doubt shaped by the daily experience of disadvantage in their current neighborhoods. Although more advantaged than poor blacks, middle-class blacks live with more crime, more poverty, more unemployment, fewer college graduates, more vacant housing, and more single-parent families than similar whites, and indeed than much poorer whites. Moving to the suburbs makes residential life a little more comfortable, but it does not erase the racial disadvantage. These disparities alone underscore the continuing need for race-based affirmative action, for ignoring the importance of race would have college admissions officers, for example, assume that a middle-class black student has it better than a working-class white student.

Finally, middle-class black neighborhoods do not exist in vacuums. They are linked to the preferences and behaviors of whites as individuals and as institutional actors. Whites' growing liberalism on issues of racial integration has contributed to the decrease in racial segregation, the increase in the number of integrated neighborhoods, and the particular neighborhood privileges that middle-class blacks enjoy over poor blacks. But if residential integration is to remain the optimal remedy to the unequal circumstances and outcomes of middle-class blacks, more progress must be made in changing whites' preferences and, particularly, their behaviors. In that vein, perhaps a more fruitful endeavor might be to study the ideologies, practices, and cultures of white neighborhoods, rather than black ones (Kefalas 2003).

ACKNOWLEDGMENTS

I thank Brian Stults for analysis of the 1990 and 2000 censuses to produce the statistics on the distribution of the black population across neighborhood types. Thanks also to John Logan and Douglas Massey for their comments on this paper.

The *Annual Review of Sociology* is online at http://soc.annualreviews.org

LITERATURE CITED

Adelman RM. 2004. Neighborhood opportunities, race, and class: the black middle class and residential segregation. *City Community* 3:43–63

Adelman RM. 2005. The roles of race, class, and residential preferences in the neighborhood racial compositions of middle-class blacks and whites. *Soc. Sci. Q.* 86:209–28

Adelman RM, Hui-shien T, Tolnay S, Crowder KD. 2001. Neighborhood disadvantage among racial and ethnic groups: residential location in 1970 and 1980. *Sociol. Q.* 42: 603–32

Alba RD, Logan JR. 1993. Minority proximity to whites in suburbs: an individual-level analysis of segregation. *Am. J. Sociol.* 98:1388–427

Alba RD, Logan JR, Bellair PE. 1994. Living with crime: the implications of racial/ethnic differences in suburban location. *Soc. Forces* 73:395–434

Alba RD, Logan J, Stults B. 2000. How segregated are middle-class African Americans? *Soc. Probl.* 47:543–58

Allen W, Farley R. 1986. The shifting social and economic tides of black America, 1950–1980. *Annu. Rev. Sociol.* 12:277–306

Anderson E. 1990. *Streetwise: Race, Class and Change in an Urban Community.* Chicago: Univ. Chicago Press

Anderson E. 2000. The emerging Philadelphia African American class structure. *Ann. Am. Acad. Polit. Soc. Sci.* 568:54–77

Bell D. 2001. Bell, J., dissenting. In *What Brown versus Board of Education Should Have Said: The Nation's Top Legal Experts Rewrite America's Landmark Civil Rights Decision,* ed. JM Balkin, pp. 185–200. New York: NY Univ. Press

Bobo L, Zubrinsky CL. 1996. Attitudes on residential integration: perceived status differences, mere in-group preference, or racial prejudice? *Soc. Forces* 74:883–909

Boyd M. 2000. Reconstructing Bronzeville: racial nostalgia and neighborhood redevelopment. *J. Urban Aff.* 22:107–22

Calmore JO. 1993. Spatial equality and the *Kerner Commission Report*: A back-to-the-future essay. *N. C. Law Rev.* 71:1487–518

Cashin S. 2001. Middle-class black suburbs and the state of integration: a post-integrationist vision for metropolitan America. *Cornell Law Rev.* 86:729–76

Charles CZ. 2000. Neighborhood racial-composition preferences: evidence from a multiethnic metropolis. *Soc. Probl.* 47:379–407

Clark WAV. 1986. Residential segregation in American cities: a review and interpretation. *Popul. Res. Policy Rev.* 5:95–127

Clark WAV. 1991. Residential preferences and neighborhood racial segregation: a test of the Schelling segregation model. *Demography* 28:1–19

Clark WAV, Dieleman FM. 1996. *Households and Housing: Choice and Outcomes in the Housing Market.* Rutgers, NJ: Rutgers Univ. Cent. Urban Policy Res.

Collins SM. 1983. The making of the black middle class. *Soc. Probl.* 30:369–82

Crowder K. 2000. The racial context of white mobility: an individual-level assessment of the white flight hypothesis. *Soc. Sci. Res.* 29:223–57

Cutler D, Glaeser E. 1997. Are ghettos good or bad? *Q. J. Econ.* 112:827–72

Daniels C. 2004. *Black Power, Inc.: The New Voice of Success.* Hoboken, NJ: Wiley

Darden JT, Kamel SM. 2000. Black residential segregation in the city and suburbs of Detroit: Does socioeconomic status matter? *J. Urban Aff.* 22:1–13

Davis A. 1941. *Deep South: A Social Anthropological Study of Caste and Class.* Chicago: Univ. Chicago Press

DeFrances CJ. 1996. The effects of racial ecological segregation on quality of life: a comparison of middle-class blacks and middle-class whites. *Urban Aff. Rev.* 31:799–809

Dennis RM. 1995. Introduction: the black middle class as a racial class. *Res. Race Ethnic Relat.* 8:1–17

Denton NA, Massey D. 1989. Racial identity among Caribbean Hispanics: the effect of double minority status on residential segregation. *Am. Sociol. Rev.* 54:790–808

Drake S, Cayton H. 1993. *Black Metropolis: A Study of Negro Life in a Northern City.* Chicago: Univ. Chicago Press

DuBois WEB. 1996 (1899). *The Philadelphia Negro: A Social Study.* Philadelphia: Univ. Penn. Press

Duneier M. 1992. *Slim's Table: Race, Respectability, and Masculinity.* Chicago: Univ. Chicago Press

Ellen IG. 2000. *Sharing America's Neighborhoods: The Prospects for Stable Racial Integration.* Cambridge, MA: Harvard Univ. Press

Emerson MO, Yancey G, Chai KJ. 2001. Does race matter in residential segregation? Exploring the preferences of white Americans. *Am. Sociol. Rev.* 66:922–35

Erbe BM. 1975. Race and socioeconomic segregation. *Am. Sociol. Rev.* 40:801–12

Fainstein N, Nesbitt S. 1996. Did the black ghetto have a golden age? Class structure and class segregation in New York City, 1949–1970, with initial evidence for 1990. *J. Urban Hist.* 23:3–28

Farley R. 1991. Residential segregation of social and economic groups among blacks, 1970–1980. In *The Urban Underclass,* ed. C Jencks, PE Peterson, pp. 274–98. Washington, DC: Brookings Inst.

Farley R, Fielding E, Krysan M. 1997. The residential preferences of blacks and whites: a four-metropolis analysis. *Hous. Policy Debate* 8:763–800

Farley R, Schuman H, Bianchi S, Colasanto D, Hatchett S. 1978. Chocolate city, vanilla suburbs: Will the trend toward racially separate communities continue? *Soc. Sci. Res.* 7:319–44

Farley R, Steeh C, Krysan M, Jackson T, Reeves K. 1994. Stereotypes and segregation: neighborhoods in the Detroit area. *Am. J. Sociol.* 100:750–80

Feagin J, Sikes M. 1995. *Living with Racism: The Black Middle-Class Experience.* Boston: Beacon

Fielding E, Taeuber K. 1992. Spatial isolation of a black underclass: an American case study. *New Community* 19:113–27

Fischer M. 2003. The relative importance of income and race in determining residential outcomes in U.S. urban areas, 1970–2000. *Urban Aff. Rev.* 38:669–96

Foner N, ed. 2001. *Islands in the City: West Indian Migration to New York.* Berkeley: Univ. Calif. Press

Forman RE. 1971. *Black Ghettos, White Ghettos, and Slums.* Englewood Cliffs, NJ: Prentice-Hall

Frazier EF. 1932. *The Negro Family in Chicago.* Chicago: Univ. Chicago Press

Freeman L. 2000. Minority housing segregation: a test of three perspectives. *J. Urban Aff.* 22:15–35

Freeman L. 2002. Does spatial assimilation work for black immigrants in the US? *Urban Stud.* 39:1983–2003

Frey WH. 1994. Minority suburbanization and continued "white flight" in U.S. metropolitan areas: assessing findings from the 1990 census. *Res. Community Sociol.* 4:15–42

Fulwood S. 1996. *Waking from the Dream: My Life in the Black Middle Class.* New York: Anchor Books

Galster GC. 1988. Residential segregation in American cities: a contrary review. *Popul. Res. Policy Rev.* 7:93–112

Galster GC. 1991. Black suburbanization: Has it changed the relative location of races? *Urban Aff. Q.* 26:621–28

Gamm G. 1999. *Urban Exodus: Why the Jews Left Boston and the Catholics Stayed.* Cambridge, MA: Harvard Univ. Press

Ginwright SA. 2002. Classed out: the challenges of social class in black community change. *Soc. Probl.* 49:544–63

Glaeser E, Vigdor J. 2001. Racial segregation in the 2000 census: promising news. *Cent. Urban. Metrop. Policy Rep.* Washington, DC: Brookings Inst. http://www.brookings.edu/es/urban/census/glaeser.pdf. Accessed Aug. 30, 2004

Gotham KF. 2002. *Race, Real Estate, and Uneven Development: The Kansas City Experience, 1900–2000.* Albany: SUNY Press

Gregory S. 1998. *Black Corona: Race and the Politics of Place in an Urban Community.* Princeton, NJ: Princeton Univ. Press

Hannerz U. 1969. *Soulside: Inquiries into Ghetto Culture and Community.* New York: Columbia Univ. Press

Harris DR. 1999. Property values drop when blacks move in, because...: racial and socioeconomic determinants of neighborhood stability. *Am. Sociol. Rev.* 64:461–79

Harris DR. 2001. Why are whites and blacks averse to black neighbors? *Soc. Sci. Res.* 30:100–16

Haynes BD. 2001. *Red Lines, Black Spaces: The Politics of Race and Space in a Black Middle-Class Suburb.* New Haven, CT: Yale Univ. Press

Higginbotham E. 2001. *Too Much to Ask: Black Women in the Era of Integration.* Chapel Hill: Univ. N. C. Press

Higginbotham EB. 1993. *Righteous Discontent: The Women's Movement in the Black Baptist Church.* Cambridge, MA: Harvard Univ. Press

Hirsch A. 1983. *Making the Second Ghetto: Race and Housing in Chicago, 1940–1960.* Chicago: Univ. Chicago Press

Hwang SS, Murdock SH. 1998. Racial attraction or racial avoidance in American suburbs? *Soc. Forces* 77:541–65

Iceland J, Sharpe C, Steinmetz E. 2005. Class differences in African American residential patterns in U.S. metropolitan areas: 1990–2000. *Soc. Sci. Res.* 34:252–66

Iceland J, Weinberg DH, Steinmetz E. 2002. Racial and ethnic residential segregation in the United States: 1980–2000. *Census 2000 Spec. Rep.* Washington, DC: US Census Bur. http://www.census.gov/hhes/www/housing/resseg/pdf/censr-3.pdf. Accessed Aug. 30, 2004

Jackson JL. 2001. *Harlemworld: Doing Race and Class in Contemporary Black America.* Chicago: Univ. Chicago Press

Jackson KT. 1985. *Crabgrass Frontier: The Suburbanization of the United States.* New York: Oxford Univ. Press

Jargowsky PA. 1996. Take the money and run: economic segregation in U.S. metropolitan areas. *Am. Sociol. Rev.* 61:984–98

Jargowsky PA. 1997. *Poverty and Place: Ghettos, Barrios, and the American City.* New York: Russell Sage

Jencks C, Peterson PE, eds. 1991. *The Urban Underclass.* Washington, DC: Brookings Inst.

Johnson VC. 2002. *Black Power in the Suburbs: The Myth or Reality of African American Suburban Political Incorporation.* Albany: SUNY Press

Kefalas M. 2003. *Working-Class Heroes: Protecting Home, Community, and Nation in a Chicago Neighborhood.* Berkeley: Univ. Calif. Press

Krysan M. 2002. Community undesirability in black and white: examining racial residential preferences through community perceptions. *Soc. Probl.* 49:521–43

Krysan M, Farley R. 2002. The residential preferences of blacks: Do they explain persistent segregation? *Soc. Forces* 80:937–80

Kusmer KL. 1976. *The Ghetto Takes Shape: Black Cleveland, 1870–1930.* Urbana: Univ. Ill. Press

Lacy KR. 2005. Black spaces, black places: strategic assimilation and identity construction in middle-class suburbia. *Ethn. Racial Stud.* In press

Lacy KR. 2002. "A part of the neighborhood?": Negotiating race in American suburbs. *Int. J. Sociol. Soc. Policy* 22:39–74

Ladner J. 1973. *The Death of White Sociology.* New York: Random House

Landry B. 1987. *The New Black Middle Class.* Berkeley: Univ. Calif. Press

Liebow E. 1967. *Tally's Corner: A Study of Negro Streetcorner Men.* Boston: Little, Brown

Liska AE, Logan JR, Bellair PE. 1998. Race and violent crime in the suburbs. *Am. Sociol. Rev.* 63:27–38

Lofland J, Lofland LH. 1995. *Analyzing Social Settings: A Guide to Qualitative Observation and Analysis.* Belmont, CA: Wadsworth

Logan JR. 2002. *Separate and Unequal: The Neighborhood Gap for Blacks and Hispanics in Metropolitan America.* Albany, NY: Lewis Mumford Cen. Comp. Urban Reg. Res. http://browns4.dyndns.org/cen2000_s4/SepUneq/SUReport/SURepPage1.htm. Accessed Jan. 7, 2005

Logan JR, Alba RD. 1995. Who lives in affluent suburbs? Racial differences in eleven metropolitan regions. *Sociol. Focus* 28:353–64

Logan JR, Alba RD, Leung SY. 1996. Minority access to white suburbs: a multiregional comparison. *Soc. Forces* 74: 851–81

Logan JR, Deane G. 2003. *Black Diversity in America*. Albany, NY: Lewis Mumford Cen. Comp. Urban Reg. Res. http://browns4. dyndns.org/cen2000_s4/BlackWhite/Black DiversityReport/black-diversity01.htm. Accessed Jan. 7, 2005

Logan JR, Stults BJ. 1999. Racial differences in exposure to crime: the city and suburbs of Cleveland in 1990. *Criminology* 37:251–76

Marks C. 1991. The urban underclass. *Annu. Rev. Sociol.* 17:445–66

Massey D, Charles C, Lundy G, Fischer M. 2003. *The Source of the River: The Social Origins of Freshmen at America's Selective Colleges and Universities*. Princeton, NJ: Princeton Univ. Press

Massey D, Condran GA, Denton NA. 1987. The effect of residential segregation on black social and economic well-being. *Soc. Forces* 66:2–57

Massey D, Denton N. 1985. Spatial assimilation as a socioeconomic outcome. *Am. Sociol. Rev.* 50:94–106

Massey D, Denton N. 1988. Suburbanization and segregation in U.S. metropolitan areas. *Am. J. Sociol.* 94:592–626

Massey D, Denton N. 1993. *American Apartheid: Segregation and the Making of the Underclass*. Cambridge, MA: Harvard Univ. Press

Massey D, Eggers M. 1990. The ecology of inequality: minorities and the concentration of poverty, 1970–1980. *Am. J. Sociol.* 95:1153–88

Massey D, Fischer MJ. 1999. Does rising income bring integration? New results for blacks, Hispanics, and Asians in 1990. *Soc. Sci. Res.* 28:316–26

Massey D, Fong E. 1990. Segregation and neighborhood quality: blacks, Hispanics, and Asians in the San Francisco metropolitan area. *Soc. Forces* 69:15–32

Massey D, Gross A, Shibuya K. 1994. Migration, segregation and the concentration of poverty. *Am. Sociol. Rev.* 59:425–45

Moore J, Pinderhughes R. 1993. *In the Barrios: Latinos and the Underclass Debate*. New York: Russell Sage Found.

Natl. Cent. Educ. Stat. 2002. *Digest of Education Statistics, 2002*. http://nces.ed.gov/programs/digest/d02/tables/PDF/table304.pdf. Accessed Aug. 30, 2004

Natl. Opin. Res. Counc. 2002. *Doctorate recipients from United States universities: summary report, 2002*. http://www.norc.uchicago.edu/issues/sed-2002.pdf. Accessed Aug. 30, 2004

Osofsky G. 1966. *Harlem: The Making of a Ghetto, Negro New York, 1890–1930*. New York: Harper & Row

Owens ML. 1997. Renewal in a working-class black neighborhood. *J. Urban Aff.* 19:83–205

Patterson O. 1997. *The Ordeal of Integration: Progress and Resentment in America's 'Racial' Crisis*. New York: Basic Civitas

Pattillo M. 2003a. Extending the boundaries and definition of the ghetto. *Ethn. Racial Stud.* 26:1046–57

Pattillo M. 2003b. Negotiating blackness, for richer or for poorer. *Ethnography* 4:61–93

Pattillo-McCoy M. 1999. *Black Picket Fences: Privilege and Peril among the Black Middle Class*. Chicago: Univ. Chicago Press

Pattillo-McCoy M. 2000. The limits of out-migration for the black middle class. *J. Urban Aff.* 22:225–42

Pettigrew T. 1985. New black-white patterns: how best to conceptualize them? *Annu. Rev. Sociol.* 11:329–46

Phelan TJ, Schneider M. 1996. Race, ethnicity, and class in American suburbs. *Urban Aff. Rev.* 31:659–80

Polednak AP. 1997. *Segregation, Poverty, and Mortality in Urban African Americans*. New York: Oxford Univ. Press

Powdermaker H. 1939. *After Freedom: A Cultural Study of the Deep South*. New York: Viking

Prince S. 2004. *Constructing Belonging: Class, Race, and Harlem's Professional Workers*. New York: Routledge

Quillian L. 2002. Why is black-white residential segregation so persistent? Evidence on three theories from migration data. *Soc. Sci. Res.* 31:197–29

Quillian L, Pager D. 2001. Black neighbors, higher crime? The role of racial stereotypes in evaluations of neighborhood crime. *Am. J. Sociol.* 107:717–67

Ralph JR. 1993. *Northern Protest: Martin Luther King, Jr., Chicago, and the Civil Rights Movement.* Cambridge, MA: Harvard Univ. Press

Ross SL, Yinger J. 2002. *The Color of Credit: Mortgage Discrimination, Research Methodology, and Fair-Lending Enforcement.* Boston: MIT Press

Sampson RJ, Wilson WJ. 1995. Toward a theory of race, crime and urban inequality. In *Crime and Inequality*, ed. J Hagan, RD Peterson, pp. 37–54. Stanford, CA: Stanford Univ. Press

Schelling TC. 1971. Dynamic models of segregation. *J. Math. Sociol.* 1:143–86

Schelling TC. 1972. A process of residential segregation: neighborhood tipping. In *Racial Discrimination in Economic Life*, ed. AH Pascal, pp. 157–84. Lexington, MA: Lexington Books

Simkus A. 1978. Residential segregation by occupation and race in ten urbanized areas, 1950–1970. *Am. Sociol. Rev.* 43:81–93

South SJ, Crowder KD. 1997. Residential mobility between cities and suburbs: race, suburbanization, and back-to-the-city moves. *Demography* 34:525–38

South SJ, Crowder KD. 1998. Leaving the 'hood: residential mobility between black, white, and integrated neighborhoods. *Am. Sociol. Rev.* 63:17–26

Squires GD, O'Connor S. 2001. *Color and Money: Politics and Prospects for Community Reinvestment in Urban America.* Albany: SUNY Press

Stahura JM. 1987. Characteristics of black suburbs, 1950–1980. *Sociol. Soc. Res.* 71:135–38

St. John C. 1995. Interclass segregation, poverty, and poverty concentration: comment on Massey and Eggers. *Am. J. Sociol.* 100:1325–33

Sugrue TJ. 1996. *The Origins of the Urban Crisis: Race and Inequality in Postwar Detroit.* Princeton, NJ: Princeton Univ. Press

Taeuber KE, Taeuber A. 1965. *Negroes in Cities.* Chicago: Aldine

Taylor DG. 1979. Housing, neighborhoods, and race relations: recent survey evidence. *Ann. Am. Acad. Polit. Soc. Sci.* 441:26–40

Taylor MM. 2002. *Harlem Between Heaven and Hell.* Minneapolis: Univ. Minn. Press

Thernstrom S, Thernstrom A. 1997. *America in Black and White: One Nation, Indivisible.* New York: Simon & Schuster

Timberlake JM. 2000. Still life in black and white: effects of racial and class attitudes on prospects for residential integration in Atlanta. *Sociol. Inq.* 70:420–45

Timberlake JM. 2002. Separate, but how unequal? Ethnic residential stratification, 1980 to 1990. *City Community* 1:251–66

Tolnay SE, Crowder KD, Adelman RM. 2002. Race, regional origin, and residence in northern cities at the beginning of the Great Migration. *Am. Sociol. Rev.* 67:456–75

Turner MA, Ross S, Galster G, Yinger J. 2002. Discrimination in metropolitan housing markets: national results from Phase 1 HDS 2000. *Rep. 410821.* Washington, DC: Urban Inst. http://www.urban.org/url.cfm?ID=410821. Accessed Aug. 30, 2004

U.S. Congr. Jt. Econ. Comm. 1989. *The Underclass: Hearing Jt. Econ. Comm.,* Congr. U.S., 101th Congr., 1st Sess., May 25. Washington, DC: GPO

Waters M. 1999. *Black Identities: West Indian Immigrant Dreams and American Realities.* New York: Russell Sage Found.

Wiese A. 2004. *Places of Their Own: African American Suburbanization in the Twentieth Century.* Chicago: Univ. Chicago Press

Wilkes R, Iceland J. 2004. Hypersegregation in the twenty-first century: an update and analysis. *Demography* 41:23–36

Williams D, Collins C. 1995. US socioeconomic and racial differences in health: patterns and explanations. *Annu. Rev. Sociol.* 21:349–86

Williams RM. 1975. Race and ethnic relations. *Annu. Rev. Sociol.* 1:125–64

Willie CV. 1979. *The Caste and Class Controversy.* Bayside, NY: General Hall

Willie CV. 1989. *The Caste and Class Controversy on Race and Poverty: Round Two of the Willie/Wilson Debate.* Dix Hills, NY: General Hall

Wilson WJ. 1978. *The Declining Significance of Race: Blacks and Changing American Institutions.* Chicago: Univ. Chicago Press

Wilson WJ. 1987. *The Truly Disadvantaged: The Inner City, the Underclass and Public Policy.* Chicago: Univ. Chicago Press

Wilson WJ. 1991. Studying inner-city dislocations: the challenge of public agenda research. *Am. Sociol. Rev.* 56:1–15

Wilson WJ, Aponte R. 1985. Urban poverty. *Annu. Rev. Sociol.* 11:231–58

Zubrinsky CL, Bobo L. 1996. Prismatic metropolis: race and residential segregation in the city of the angels. *Soc. Sci. Res.* 25:335–74

Annu. Rev. Sociol. 2005. 31:331–56
doi: 10.1146/annurev.soc.31.041304.122308
Copyright © 2005 by Annual Reviews. All rights reserved
First published online as a Review in Advance on March 11, 2005

MACROSTRUCTURAL ANALYSES OF RACE, ETHNICITY, AND VIOLENT CRIME: Recent Lessons and New Directions for Research

Ruth D. Peterson and Lauren J. Krivo

Department of Sociology, Ohio State University, Columbus, Ohio 43210;
email: peterson.5@sociology.osu.edu, krivo.1@sociology.osu.edu

Key Words   urban crime, racial/ethnic inequality, structural disadvantage, neighborhood effects, deviance, social control

■ **Abstract**   In 1995, Sampson & Wilson assessed the state of knowledge on race and violence and set forth an approach for future research. We review macrostructural analyses of race, ethnicity, and violent crime since 1995 to evaluate progress in explaining inequality in criminal violence across racial and ethnic groups. Among the important advances are studies that attempt to gain insights from explicit comparisons of racially distinct but structurally similar communities, expansion of work beyond the black-white divide, and incorporation of macrostructural factors into multilevel models of racial/ethnic differences in violence. Yet, progress is limited in all these directions, and additional questions remain. Thus, we offer a perspective and suggestions for future research that will expand knowledge on this important topic.

INTRODUCTION

Periodically, sociologists, policymakers, and others in the United States have called for attention to patterns and explanations of violence, particularly interpersonal criminal violence. During the mid-1990s, these calls resulted in several important efforts, including the National Academy of Sciences' four volumes on *Understanding and Preventing Violence* (Reiss & Roth 1993/1994), the American Sociological Association's workshop and report on the "Social Causes of Violence" (Levine & Rosich 1996), and the National Science Foundation's funding of the National Consortium on Violence Research. Concern with violence is also reflected in daily media accounts of homicide or other violent occurrences. Inevitably, the academic, policy, and media discussions draw attention to the long-recognized link between racial status and interpersonal violence. Media presentations of crime and violence emphasize the racial dimension so strongly that, according to one scholar, crime has become virtually identified with *thecriminalblackman* (Russell 1998).

The racial character of crime reflected in Russell's critique is based on more than media stereotypes. In the United States, blacks are a disproportionate share of those

0360-0572/05/0811-0331$20.00

victimized, arrested, and imprisoned. In 2002, the rate of violent victimization was 34.1 per 1000 for non-Hispanic blacks compared with 26.5 for non-Hispanic whites (Maguire & Pastore 2004). Blacks now represent 38% of persons arrested for violent crimes, but they constitute only 13% of the U.S. population (Federal Bureau of Investigation 2003). In contrast, whites make up 60% of violent arrestees and 75% of the population. The most dramatic differences are for homicide, for which black rates of victimization and offending were 6.2 and 7.6 times those for whites in 2000 (Maguire & Pastore 2004).

Historically, scholars have offered various explanations of the race–violent crime relationship. Some early explanations stressed the purported innate inferiority of nonwhites, especially blacks' presumed childlike qualities and tendencies to "lawless impulse and weak inhibition" (e.g., Brearley 1932, Hawkins 1993). These determinist perspectives gave way to theories emphasizing culture or social structure. Traditional cultural perspectives claim that unique historical experiences of African Americans (slavery, southern upbringing, and devaluation of African culture) led blacks to adopt values, attitudes, and beliefs conducive to the use of violence and the devaluing of the sanctity of life (Curtis 1975, Wolfgang & Ferracuti 1967). These culture-of-violence explanations were widely criticized for being diffuse, nonconcrete, and victim-blaming. Studies also failed to establish empirical support for them (Hawkins 1993, Sampson 1985; compare with Messner 1983a).

In the wake of concerns about cultural explanations, structural perspectives have gained a foothold. Such theories view group differences in crime and violence as stemming from inequality in socioeconomic conditions such as poverty. Merton's (1938) social structure and anomie thesis and Shaw & McKay's (1942) social disorganization perspective are prominent early structural explanations that have set the stage for research on race, ethnicity, and crime.[1] Much of the research that we review here is grounded in contemporary versions of these perspectives. Blau & Blau (1982) set the stage for much of this research in their seminal paper on inequality and violent crime. They drew on Merton's (1938) argument that the disjuncture between cultural goals (economic success) and structural arrangements (socioeconomic resources) inherent in inequality produces feelings of frustration and alienation that are, in turn, reflected in deviant behavior. In democratic societies such as the United States, expressions of frustration in the form of violent crime should be particularly pronounced when socioeconomic inequality is based on ascriptive characteristics like race. In this context, ascriptive inequality is considered inappropriate, reinforcing ethnic and class differences and engendering pervasive conflict, which finds expression in diffuse aggression, including criminal violence. Meritocratic inequality is not expected to lead to frustration and aggression because it is viewed as legitimate. Blau & Blau's (1982) analysis of metropolitan rates of

---

[1]These approaches did not always completely ignore culture. For example, Shaw & McKay (1942) emphasized that conflicting value systems (some of which encourage crime) often characterize lower-class areas and are perpetuated through cultural transmission to whatever groups come to occupy these areas.

violent index crimes showed that interracial socioeconomic inequality has a positive influence on murder, robbery, and assault, confirming their view that criminal violence is the apparent price of racial and economic inequality in this society.

Blau & Blau's (1982) work set off a flurry of studies on socioeconomic inequality and violent crime (e.g., Bailey 1984; Blau & Golden 1986; Huff-Corzine et al. 1986; Land et al. 1990; Loftin & Parker 1985; Messner 1983a,b; Sampson 1986; Williams 1984). Unfortunately, two central problems of this research precluded drawing firm conclusions about the linkage between race and violent crime. General crime rates were examined without accounting for the contribution of different racial groups to the overall rates, and/or explanatory variables were not race-specific. Harer & Steffensmeier (1992) and Messner & Golden (1992) addressed these problems by comparing black and white rates of criminal violence using race-specific predictors (see also LaFree et al. 1992). These racially disaggregated analyses revealed inconsistent results regarding ascriptive inequality. Messner & Golden (1992) found that interracial inequality leads to higher homicide rates for both blacks and whites, whereas Harer & Steffensmeier (1992) found no such effects for the four race-specific violent index offenses.

Others, too, saw the problem inherent in analyses of general rates but incorporated insights from structural approaches rooted in social disorganization. Wilson (1987) provided the most prominent such statement, emphasizing that race differences in crime and other urban social problems are rooted in the different community circumstances of whites and blacks. The most important difference is the extreme concentration of disadvantage that had emerged in the 1970s and 1980s in some black, but few white, inner-city neighborhoods. As Wilson (1987) claimed, these uniquely high concentrations of black poverty created distinctly different social structural milieux characterized by social isolation from mainstream society in which connections to jobs and conventional role models are weak, local stabilizing institutions are compromised, and hence social controls are relatively lacking. This statement echoes those of earlier social disorganization theorists like Shaw & McKay (1942) and Bursik & Webb (1982).

Peterson & Krivo (1993) and Sampson (1987) drew on these themes in investigating the structural context of race-specific patterns of violence. Peterson & Krivo (1993) argued that racial residential segregation is related to heightened black violence because black segregated communities typically suffer from much greater concentrations of the types of community disadvantages associated with violent crime than do white areas. Consistent with the argument, they found that racial residential segregation is a strong predictor of black urban homicide. Sampson (1987) also emphasized the uniquely high levels of economic disadvantage in black neighborhoods, arguing that its most important consequences for crime were through high levels of family disruption. He hypothesized that family disruption undermines the ability of communities to control crime, and, therefore, that black and white crime rates differ because there are higher levels of family disruption in black communities. His analyses of race-specific robbery and homicide arrest rates supported this contention.

Together, contemporary structural approaches to race and violence were pushing work forward in an attempt to consider the meaning of race and racial inequality in society as central to understanding why black levels of street violence exceed by such a large margin levels for whites. However, as we approached the mid-1990s, these efforts had not yet coalesced into either a clear understanding of the sources of the race-crime link or a focused agenda as to how such an understanding could be achieved. Sampson & Wilson (1995) stepped in with an assessment of the state of knowledge on race and violence and set forth their approach regarding how to move forward. In the remainder of this review, we assess the literature that has emerged on race, ethnicity, and violent crime since the publication of their article.

The analysis proceeds in four stages. We begin with a brief review of Sampson & Wilson's paper, and summarize the implications of their approach for future research. Next, we review post-1995 studies regarding how well they address the issues raised in Sampson & Wilson. In the following sections, we assess what additional directions have emerged in post-1995 work and the impact of these on the field. Two stand out: a focus on Latinos and attention to the multiple levels of factors that might be responsible for inequality in crime across groups. Finally, on the basis of our assessment of the current state of knowledge, we offer our own perspective on directions that the field should take to produce a more meaningful understanding of race, ethnicity, and crime. We caution the reader that our review focuses on macrostructural analyses (mainly quantitative) rather than important studies at the individual level. Note, too, that most of this work has focused on race (blacks and whites) rather than on ethnicity, and on between-group rather than within-group patterns.

SAMPSON AND WILSON'S APPROACH

When Sampson & Wilson (1995) appraised the state of extant knowledge on race and criminal violence, they concluded that it was "mired in an unproductive mix of controversy and silence" (p. 37). They saw silence in a near absence of research seeking to explain differential rates of crime across racial and ethnic groups. Indeed, despite the traditions of work noted above, very few studies had yet directly explored race-specific rates of violence.[2] As they claimed, this may have been partly due to a reluctance to give serious attention to the racial context of violent crime for fear of being misunderstood or characterized as racist (Hawkins 1993 and Wilson 1987 also expressed similar sentiments), or to a denial that racial differences were real because of police bias and invalid crime statistics. However, it was also likely rooted in an inability to set such work in motion because appropriate tools were not available, e.g., disaggregated violent crime data, measures

---

[2]In addition to the five studies discussed above, just a few papers used race-specific independent and dependent variables (Corzine & Huff-Corzine 1992, Messner & Sampson 1991, Smith et al. 1992).

of key concepts, and appropriate statistical techniques. Sampson & Wilson (1995) characterized existing research as unproductive because it generally focused on simplistic conceptualizations of racial differences as rooted either in cultures of violence believed to be indigenous to certain populations, particularly African Americans (e.g., Wolfgang & Ferracuti 1967), or in deterministic views of social structure as indicated by relative deprivation (e.g., Blau & Blau 1982). Although scholars had proposed more complex notions that integrated social structure and culture (e.g., Shaw & McKay 1942, Cloward & Ohlin 1960), there was some truth to their claim because much of the work in the 1980s was rooted in Blau & Blau's (1982) structural inequality perspective.

From Sampson & Wilson's point of view, a directed approach was required to improve understanding of the race–violent crime link. They offered a perspective integrating aspects of Wilson's (1987) structural transformation, traditional social disorganization (Kornhauser 1978, Sampson & Groves 1989, Shaw & McKay 1942), and cultural adaptation (Anderson 1978, Hannerz 1969) to guide such efforts. From Wilson (1987), they reiterated that substantial losses of jobs, housing, and population (primarily among the middle class) owing to deindustrialization, together with deliberate policies that concentrated public housing in poor black neighborhoods, disrupted the social and institutional order in ways that threatened social organization (i.e., the ability of the community to realize its common goals). Such structurally induced social disorganization, evidenced largely in inner-city African American communities, should be the proximate determinant of higher crime in black areas. The much lower levels of structural disadvantage among whites, coupled with high levels of segregation from blacks, mean that very high levels of social disorganization would rarely be evident in white communities (see also Massey & Denton 1993). In addition, reminiscent of Shaw & McKay's (1942) original cultural transmission thesis, Bursik & Webb's (1982) modified version of this theme, and Cloward & Ohlin's (1960) delinquency and opportunity theory, Sampson & Wilson (1995) argued that structural barriers and social isolation from mainstream institutions, role models, and patterns of activity give rise to cultural adaptations that "seem to legitimate or at least provide a basis for tolerance of crime and deviance" (p. 50). Because these cultural responses are not autonomous or necessarily enduring, alteration of their social structural underpinnings would reduce or eliminate the tolerance for criminal activity.

In brief, this integrated structural and cultural perspective draws attention to the disparate community contexts of blacks and whites. In fact, the most disadvantaged white neighborhoods have less deprivation than the typical black community. Therefore, white areas are less likely to evidence cultural adaptations that lessen social organization and reduce crime control. In this view, "the sources of . . . crime [are] remarkably invariant across race and rooted instead in the structural differences among communities" (Sampson & Wilson 1995, p. 41).

Sampson & Wilson's perspective was most important for what it suggested about the fundamental features needed to improve research on race, ethnicity, and violence. First, the only way that analysts can evaluate whether the separate conditions of black and white communities are the sources of levels of violence within them is to investigate race-specific crime rates using predictor variables for the relevant populations. Thus, their theoretical focus directed researchers to expand the use of fully race-specific models. They also called for studies that explicitly recognize and test the role of structural differentiation in generating criminal inequality across black and white communities. If structural dissimilarity is at the heart of racial differences in violent crime, then structurally similar black and white communities should have similar levels of violence and demonstrate racially invariant effects of the social conditions. Therefore, research needs to be designed to examine structurally comparable but racially distinct areas. Finally, Sampson & Wilson (1995) highlighted that efforts to examine the mechanisms linking structure to violence were lacking, leaving us with a poor understanding of how race differences in local conditions lead to violence. Their own arguments emphasized the intervening roles of social disorganization and cultural adaptations. But more generally their focus indicates a need to take seriously analyses of what links macrocharacteristics like disadvantage to violent behaviors. In 1995, research incorporating culture, social disorganization, or other potential mediating factors into structural analyses of racial and ethnic differences in violence was lacking.

RESEARCH ON RACE, ETHNICITY, AND VIOLENT CRIME AFTER 1995

There has been a proliferation of research on race, ethnicity, and violent crime since 1995. As the stage had already been set, most studies analyze race-specific outcomes and explanatory variables, and indeed, this approach has become the standard in the field. Researchers have also explored the potential impact of structurally dissimilar contexts, but mainly by assessing racial invariance in effects of predictors of violence. Few studies have directly tackled the importance of inequality in structural circumstances by race. Progress has also been slow in investigating the intervening processes that produce the relationships among race/ethnicity, social structure, and violent crime. In this section, we address these three research areas in turn.

Race-Specific Analyses

The central focus of most post-1995 analyses is whether structural conditions matter for violence when rates are properly disaggregated, and if they matter in the same way for blacks and whites. Generally, race-specific analyses incorporate measures of disadvantage, racial isolation, and/or urban transformation, along with indicators of inequality/strain. Beyond these features, the studies are diverse on several dimensions, making comparisons difficult. A large number examine homicide using Supplementary Homicide Report data, which include race (Krivo & Peterson 2000, Messner & Golden 1992, Parker 2001, Parker & Johns 2002,

Parker & McCall 1999, Parker & Pruitt 2000, Peterson & Krivo 1999, Phillips 1997, Vélez et al. 2003). Others explore additional types of offenses (forcible rape, robbery, aggravated assault, intimate partner violence), relying on FBI aggregate arrest data by race (Harer & Steffensmeier 1992; LaFree & Drass 1996; Lee 2000; Ousey 1999; Shihadeh & Flynn 1996; Shihadeh & Ousey 1996, 1998) or on detailed information from individual police departments (Krivo & Peterson 1996, Kubrin & Wadsworth 2003, McNulty 2001, McNulty & Holloway 2000, Shihadeh & Shrum 2004, Wooldredge & Thistlethwaite 2003). The works also study diverse units: census block groups, census tracts, local neighborhood areas, cities, metropolitan areas, or national time series. And some investigate group rates while others compare rates for local areas that are predominantly of one racial group or another.

One consistent pattern emerges from race-specific studies irrespective of the outcomes, predictors, and units under consideration: Structural disadvantage contributes significantly to violence for both blacks and whites (or nonblacks). This finding is resilient to the exact configuration of factors representing disadvantage, e.g., differing combinations of poverty, income, family disruption, and joblessness/unemployment. Shihadeh & Ousey (1998) also show that the disadvantage-violence relationship is due to the impact of industrial restructuring on white and black disadvantage, supporting Wilson's (1987, 1996) focus on the consequences of deindustrialization.

The Role of Ecological Dissimilarity

Interest in the role of ecologically dissimilar environments across race has been high. However, a variety of problems in research design have precluded the development of sound conclusions. First, a few studies focus on blacks alone (Kubrin & Wadsworth 2003, Phillips 1997, Shihadeh & Flynn 1996). These analyses cannot speak to the influence of the differential social position of groups because the authors make no comparisons.

Second, some research confounds race differences in social conditions with race in measuring central predictors. Sometimes different measures of the apparently equivalent substantive construct are applied in separate black and white models. For example, Parker and colleagues' analyses of homicide include racially distinct disadvantage measures—resource deprivation/segregation for blacks (based on five factors, including segregation and nonemployment), and resource deprivation/affluence for whites (based on three factors, excluding segregation and nonemployment) (Parker 2001, Parker & Johns 2002, Parker & McCall 1999). This strategy produces results that are noncomparable across groups and makes impossible an explicit examination of the role of racial differentiation in circumstances. Others confound race and structural disadvantage by including racial composition itself in the disadvantage index (e.g., Crutchfield et al. 1999, Kubrin 2003, Morenoff et al. 2001). If race is incorporated as part of structural disadvantage, the question of whether apparently racial effects are due to differences in group circumstances cannot be answered.

Third, the largest portion of the research on racial differences in violence is conducted for cities—a relatively high level of aggregation. Regarding racial invariance, most city-level studies demonstrate a mix of similar and dissimilar effects across groups. For example, Shihadeh & Ousey (1998) demonstrated that the link between low-skilled jobs and homicide transcends racial lines, but the percentages of renters and high school dropouts have unique effects for African Americans and whites, respectively. Lee (2000) showed that overall disadvantage and poverty concentration have statistically similar effects for blacks and whites, but age composition, residential density, and region all have significant effects on killings for only one of the racial groups. The main exception to these patterns of inconsistency is Ousey (1999), who found evidence for significant race differences in a wide range of homicide predictors, directly contradicting the racial invariance thesis.

The racial invariance hypothesis—that structural variables predict violent crime in the same way for all racial and ethnic groups—has fared better in neighborhood studies, suggesting that cities are poor units for assessing community-level processes. Analyzing reported rates of violent crime (murder, rape, robbery, and aggravated assault) for census tracts in Columbus, Ohio, Krivo & Peterson (1996) demonstrated that, net of other characteristics, black neighborhoods do not have significantly different levels of violence than their white counterparts in low, high, or extremely disadvantaged areas. McNulty (2001) studied the same outcome for block groups in Atlanta for 1990 and found that disadvantage, residential instability, and all but one control variable have significant effects irrespective of the race that predominates. Morenoff and colleagues' (2001) analyses of homicide rates in black and nonblack Chicago neighborhood clusters showed that economic status and collective efficacy (informal social control) have the same effects on police-reported killings across the two types of areas. However, examining homicide on the basis of vital statistics demonstrated that economic status decreases rates only in nonblack areas, and collective efficacy diminishes murders only in black communities. This result provides the only wrinkle to the pattern of neighborhood racial invariance across the three studies.

Racial invariance is also supported in two studies that examine whether the effect of neighborhood percent black on levels of violence is accounted for by disadvantage and other relevant characteristics. Shihadeh & Shrum (2004) showed that, for Baton Rouge block groups, the effect of percent black on rates of separate violent index offenses is diminished to nonsignificance after controlling for disadvantage and social disorganization. In analyses for Atlanta block groups, McNulty & Holloway (2000) demonstrated that the influence of percent black on rates of five different crimes is substantially reduced (to nonsignificance in two cases) by incorporating disadvantage into models.

Two final neighborhood studies explore racial invariance using race-specific rates for all areas of the city. Almgren et al. (1998) studied age-standardized violent death rates separately for black and nonblack males and females in Chicago Community Areas. They demonstrated that high rates of unemployment are significantly related to levels of homicide for all four race-sex groups. An analysis of white and black male rates of intimate assaults for Hamilton County, Ohio (mainly Cincinnati), showed that five of six predictors have the same influence on the race-specific tract rates (Wooldredge & Thistlethwaite 2003). Overall, then, when neighborhoods rather than cities are considered, racially invariant effects are consistently evident.

Related to invariance, conclusions have also been hampered by researchers' lack of attention to dramatic differences in the structural circumstances of racial and ethnic groups. Addressing this omission requires careful methodological and conceptual consideration of how race impinges on levels of community conditions and violence. Only a few studies have had this consideration specifically in mind. Phillips (2002, p. 350) used regression decomposition to examine gaps in mean homicide rates between non-Latino whites and both non-Latino blacks and Latinos in U.S. metropolitan areas for 1990. This analytic approach allows for quantification of the relative weight of the role of group differences in circumstances versus racial invariance in the effects of these circumstances. Phillips demonstrated that the white-Latino homicide gap would be entirely eliminated if Latinos were as structurally advantaged as non-Latino whites. About half of the black-white homicide gap results from group differences in the structural conditions experienced by the two populations.

Phillips (2002) alerts us to the fruitfulness of Sampson & Wilson's (1995) perspective (i.e., it appears to be entirely appropriate for Latinos) and to the possibility that explanations may be more complex (i.e., the results do not completely explain things for African Americans). Unfortunately, the decomposition results derive from analyses in which virtually no overlap in group characteristics may actually be observed. For example, for the 129 areas in Phillips' study, mean white poverty is 3.6%, and most cases should have white poverty rates below 6.5% (two standard deviations above the mean). In contrast, virtually all localities should have African American poverty rates above 6.5% (the black mean is 17.3%, with rates of 11.3% and 5.3% being one and two standard deviations below this mean). The direction of the pattern is the same when comparing whites and Latinos, but there is somewhat more overlap in the distributions. Regression decomposition models cannot test racial invariance when group circumstances are so widely varying because the group-specific regressions for the gap analysis do not take into account how differences in distributions may influence the effects of predictors.

Krivo & Peterson (1996) attempted to deal with this problem by analyzing a city (Columbus, Ohio) where there is sufficient overlap in the types of neighborhoods in which blacks and whites reside to make appropriate comparisons, i.e., there are both black and white communities with high levels of poverty/disadvantage. Their analyses of crime for 148 predominantly African American and white neighborhoods demonstrated that the effect of disadvantage on violent crime does not differ significantly between black and white communities. Concomitantly, there are no significant differences in criminal violence between neighborhoods of varying racial composition when they are similarly disadvantaged. This is well illustrated

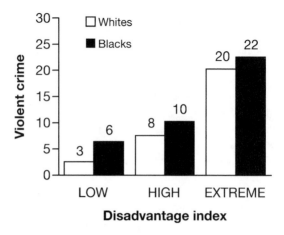

Figure 1   Predicted violent crime rates by disadvantage for black and white communities, Columbus, Ohio, 1990. Source: Krivo & Peterson 1996. Note: The vacancy rate, percent renters, and percent young males are held constant at their mean levels.

in Figure 1, which presents predicted rates of violent crime by racial composition and level of disadvantage for Columbus neighborhoods for 1990. As shown, rates rise notably as one moves across the graph from low, to high, to extreme disadvantage. These increases are very similar for white and black communities, with violent crimes rising by 4 to 5 per 1000 population as the level of disadvantage goes from low to high, and by another 12 when disadvantage increases to an extreme level. Also striking is the dramatic similarity in rates across the racially distinct communities that have the same level of disadvantage. The small differences by race are not significant.

In 2000, Krivo & Peterson provided another example of how research can be conceptualized and designed to address directly the structural similarity claim. Considering homicide rates for U.S. cities, they argued that theoretically important structural factors may have weaker effects on violent crime when disadvantage is particularly widespread because further increases, above already high levels, may not appreciably differentiate communities. For example, going from a 40% to a 50% poverty rate may have much less influence on social organization and, in turn, crime than going from a 10% to a 20% rate. If so, racial differences in the effects of structural conditions may be found because blacks and whites are observed in different portions of the disadvantage distribution. In cities where the two groups are similarly situated relative to disadvantage, comparable effects should prevail.

Their findings, as presented graphically in Figure 2, support this argument. This figure displays predicted rates of black and white homicide at varying levels of disadvantage and, for blacks, homeownership (a measure of residential stability). Predicted values are presented only at levels of white and black disadvantage that are actually observed (between the 10th and 90th race-specific disadvantage percentiles). The results in Figure 2 show that the effects of key social conditions

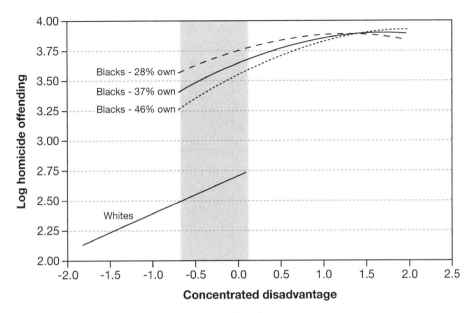

Figure 2 Predicted black and white log homicide offending rates by concentrated disadvantage for U.S. cities in 1990. Source: Krivo & Peterson 2000. Note: Segregation, interracial inequality, young males, percent black, city size, and region are held constant at black mean levels.

are the same for blacks and whites when levels of disadvantage are similarly low. In the shaded portion of the graph, the lines are all relatively parallel, indicating that, as disadvantage increases, homicide rates increase at a comparable rate, whether black or white. Comparing black homicide rates across levels of homeownership also shows that higher rates of black homeownership are associated with lower rates of black homicide; this effect was absent in a general model of black homicide that did not consider comparability in disadvantage.

McNulty (2001) followed up on the perspective and findings of Krivo & Peterson (2000) by replicating their study at the neighborhood level. As Figure 3 shows, his reports of predicted rates of violent crime parallel their findings. Panel A indicates that disadvantage has a curvilinear effect on violent crime across all neighborhoods such that its influence is strong at low levels and then diminishes (even changing direction) when disadvantage is at its highest. However, when race is taken into account (Panel B), white neighborhoods evidence a strong effect of disadvantage on violence because they fall exclusively in the low end of the disadvantage distribution. This factor has a similarly strong effect on violent crime in black neighborhoods in the low range of the distribution that overlaps with observed disadvantage in white areas. The weak effect is only found for black communities because they alone have very high disadvantage levels. McNulty (2001) also demonstrated comparable levels of violent crime in racially distinct but

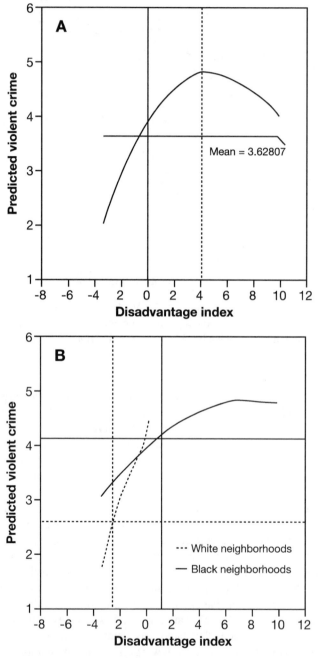

Figure 3   Predicted logged violent crime by levels of disadvantage. (*A*) All neighborhoods. (*B*) Black and white neighborhoods. Source: McNulty 2001.

similarly disadvantaged areas, a finding that is not evident for city-level homicide (see Figure 2 above).

Intervening Processes

The third major concern emanating from Sampson & Wilson (1995) is the need to understand what factors mediate the connection between structural conditions and differential levels of violence. They emphasized social disorganization (informal social control) and cultural adaptations. Over the past 10 years, discussions have paid more attention to these processes as sources of violence. However, there have been few assessments of their mediating influences. Among recent scholars, Anderson (1994, 1999) provides the most in-depth theoretical articulation of the impact of culture on violence on the basis of ethnographic research in predominantly black, inner-city Philadelphia neighborhoods. He argues that, in disadvantaged areas, many residents are socially isolated and have little trust or faith that formal authorities will protect them. In response, a code of the street, a set of informal rules that prescribe and proscribe public behavior, particularly interpersonal violence, has emerged as a defensive mechanism in many inner-city neighborhoods. This code, or oppositional culture, "regulate[s] the use of violence and so suppl[ies] a rationale allowing those who are inclined to aggression to precipitate violent encounters in an approved way" (Anderson 1999, p. 33; see also Anderson 1994, p. 82). A central component of the code of the street is to provide a framework for negotiating respect and responding to the failure to be given "one's proper due." In an analysis of youthful gun violence in two inner-city New York neighborhoods, Fagan & Wilkinson (1998) observe patterns consistent with Anderson's perspective.

If oppositional culture is an adaptive response to adverse social and economic isolation, such a code should not arise in neighborhoods with high levels of social and economic capital (middle-class areas), and the type of violence supported by street codes should depend on neighborhood disadvantage. In particular, where deprivation is high, retaliatory lethal violence, gun assaults, victim resistance to assaults (to maintain respect when challenged), and deference to the power of offenders in robberies should be more common. Two studies evaluated this argument, providing indirect assessments of cultural mediation. Kubrin & Weitzer (2003) demonstrated that cultural retaliatory homicides occur disproportionately in areas of St. Louis characterized by concentrated socioeconomic disadvantage. Baumer and colleagues' (2003) analyses of area-identified National Crime Victimization Survey (NCVS) data also showed that, in disadvantaged areas, assaulters are somewhat more likely to use a gun and have victims who resist, and robbery victims are less likely to nonforcefully resist. Unfortunately, neither study includes an actual measure of a code of the street; they simply infer its existence from the relationship between disadvantage and the nature of crime in areas. This leaves open the question of whether culture, or some other process, is responsible for the observed association.

Sampson and colleagues have attempted to examine the role of both culture and social organization/collective efficacy in the production of violence through the Project on Human Development in Chicago Neighborhoods (PHDCN). These data were collected to allow direct measurement of aspects of social organization (informal social control and cohesion/trust) and subcultural orientations as community properties. In one paper, Sampson & Bartusch (1998) measured aggregate subcultural orientations (tolerance of deviance) to evaluate whether these are produced by racially segregated and structurally disadvantaged circumstances. Their results showed that disadvantaged neighborhoods exhibit more tolerance for crime and deviance but no evidence for a unique black subculture of violence. In fact, African Americans and Latinos are less tolerant of deviance than comparable whites. Yet, "[b]ecause race and neighborhood are confounded, the tendency in the literature has been, incorrectly . . ., to attribute to African Americans a distinct culture of violence" (Sampson & Bartusch 1998, p. 801). Although this research helps identify culture as a structural property situated in place, Sampson & Bartusch (1998) do not evaluate the connection of cultural codes with violence. Their paper also suffers from the problem of including racial composition in the measure of neighborhood disadvantage.

The only other project designed to tap cultural codes of violence was recently conducted in Seattle neighborhoods. Here, Matsueda et al. (2004) measured neighborhood codes by assessing the degree to which residents think that people in their community view violence and defensive posturing as legitimate ways to maintain respect, deal with threats, or get ahead. Early analyses of these data showed that codes of violence are more prevalent in extremely impoverished or affluent areas as well as in African American and, to some extent, Hispanic neighborhoods. Furthermore, mistrust of police mediates a significant proportion of the effects of percents black and Hispanic on codes of violence. This is consistent with Anderson's (1994, 1999) proposition that residents of black impoverished neighborhoods perceive institutions of social control as ineffective and, therefore, must resolve conflicts on their own through violence (Matsueda et al. 2004). Matsueda has conducted additional preliminary analyses that suggest that cultural codes are strong predictors of future rates of violence. And, along with police mistrust, neighborhood codes account for the effects of race on violence (R.L. Matsueda, personal communication).

A few other analyses have explored whether informal social control (or collective efficacy) are intervening mechanisms between structural conditions and violence. In an analysis (not focused on the race-violence connection), Sampson et al. (1997) demonstrated that major portions of the effects of disadvantage, immigrant concentration, and residential stability on various types of violence are mediated through neighborhood collective efficacy. Regarding race, Sampson and colleagues' (2005) analysis of 8- to 24-year-olds in Chicago showed that percent black in the neighborhood is a significant predictor of self-reported violence (net of a host of individual factors). However, the racial composition effect is fully accounted for by the prevalence of immigrants and percentage of employed persons in professional/managerial occupations. Thus, race operates through African Americans' greater exposure to neighborhood risks and lesser exposure to local protective factors. When legal cynicism is included, it serves to increase violence but does not explain the influence of the neighborhood conditions. Interestingly, and in contrast to Sampson et al. (1997) and Morenoff et al. (2001), aspects of informal community control, including collective efficacy, do not have independent effects on neighborhood violence. These findings regarding intervening processes raise fundamental questions: Why does neighborhood structure only sometimes appear to have indirect effects on violence through social organization and, more generally, what are the consistent mediating factors that help to explain the interrelationships among race/ethnicity, structural conditions, and violence?

LATINOS AND IMMIGRATION EFFECTS

Most of the research discussed above derived from observations about the long-standing dramatic division between blacks and whites in the United States. The changing racial and ethnic composition of the U.S. population has, however, begun to push research on violent crime beyond the black-white divide, particularly toward analyses of Latinos. Researchers have generally evaluated whether the structural conditions relevant for black and white violence also apply to Latinos. Acknowledging differences in generational status between Hispanics and blacks, studies have also focused on the impact of immigration on Latino violence. Immigration has been considered a source of crime because (*a*) it purportedly contributes to community social disorganization by impeding communication and cooperation; (*b*) immigrants may turn to crime as a way of compensating for blocked opportunities (i.e., strain); and (*c*) immigrants live in communities where oppositional culture is evident. (See Butcher & Piehl 1998, Lee et al. 2001, Mears 2001, and Tonry 1997 for more detailed discussions of these arguments.)

Martinez and colleagues have been at the forefront of recent macrostructural analyses of Latino violence. They focus on analyzing Latino-specific homicide either alone or in comparison with models for native African Americans and whites, and sometimes immigrant Haitians, Jamaicans, or Latino subpopulations, e.g., Mariel Cubans (Lee & Martinez 2002; Lee et al. 2001; Martinez 1996, 1997, 2000, 2002, 2003; Martinez & Lee 2000). On balance, these studies support the racial/ethnic invariance hypothesis, leading Martinez (2003, p. 40) to conclude that "the basic links among deprivation, disorganization, and homicide are similar for all three ethnic groups [African Americans, Haitians, and Latinos]." Martinez's work also challenges the notion that immigration increases levels of lethal violence; it generally has no effect on homicide. Research examining immigration and violence for a few cities in California and Texas (Alaniz et al. 1998, Hagan & Palloni 1999) and metropolitan areas (Butcher & Piehl 1998) also finds negligible influences of immigration on crime.

These studies support the notion that structural disadvantage matters for violence within a variety of racial and ethnic groups and point to the failure of simple ideas about immigration. However, research on populations other than whites and blacks is slim and mainly limited to homicide. In addition, the studies raise but do not examine an important puzzle: Lethal violence is lower for Latinos and various immigrant groups (e.g., Haitians, Mariel Cubans) than for similarly disadvantaged African Americans. Martinez suggests that Latino barrios may not actually be structurally the same as African American ghettos in terms of social integration through labor market attachment, historical racism and discrimination, and frames of reference used to evaluate their relative deprivation (United States versus abroad). Thus, future research needs to pay closer attention to potential dissimilarities across and within groups of various generations and colors (see also Mears 2001).

MULTILEVEL RESEARCH

The incorporation of macrolevel structural factors into multilevel models of racial/ethnic differences in violence represents an emerging trend. Examples include the studies by Sampson and colleagues noted above (Morenoff et al. 2001; Sampson et al. 1997, 2005). In addition, Crutchfield (1995) examined labor market context effects on self-reported violent offending for white, black, and Latino young adults. He demonstrated that living in an area with a greater prevalence of secondary sector work increases violent criminal involvement among secondary sector workers for all three groups. However, this relationship is stronger for blacks and Latinos than for whites.

Several papers attempt to determine whether individual differences in violence by race and ethnicity are explained by a host of individual and contextual factors. Lauritsen & White's (2001) analysis of nonlethal violence victimization for non-Latino black, non-Latino white, and Latino males and females from area-identified NCVS data demonstrated that, together, community (disadvantage and immigrant concentration) and individual factors explain most of the higher risks for violence among blacks and Latinos compared with whites (see also Lauritsen 2001). Moreover, the influence of neighborhood disadvantage is similar for all the race/ethnic/sex groups. McNulty & Bellair (2003a,b) focused on Asian, black, Hispanic, Native American, and white youths' likelihoods of engaging in serious violence using data from the National Longitudinal Survey of Adolescent Health (McNulty & Bellair 2003a) and the National Educational Longitudinal Study ([NELS], McNulty & Bellair 2003b). They, too, demonstrated that individual characteristics and neighborhood disadvantage explain differential propensities for violence across all groups except Native Americans in the NELS data. However, the most important sources of racial/ethnic inequality vary; the black-white gap is most strongly affected by differences in community disadvantage, whereas the Hispanic-white gap is more strongly influenced by individual factors. Asian youth have similar or lower violent involvement than white adolescents.

WHERE DO WE STAND AND WHERE DO WE GO FROM HERE?

Overall, the studies reviewed above yield one clear conclusion: Structural disadvantage is a major contributor to violence for all racial/ethnic groups studied. Important questions remain: How does structural disadvantage operate to produce violence within and across racial and ethnic groups? Do differences in structures (and intervening processes) explain racial and ethnic differences in violence? Research is only beginning to provide answers to these questions, as is especially evident with respect to how structural disadvantage operates. Cultural codes of the street that support violence do appear to result from structural deprivation, but this conclusion derives from just a few studies (Anderson 1994, 1999; Fagan & Wilkinson 1998; Matsueda et al. 2004; Sampson & Bartusch 1998). In addition, only Matsueda and colleagues' (2004) preliminary research provides direct evidence regarding the connection of these neighborhood codes to violence. Findings are also sparse on the role of social disorganization in group differences in levels of violence. Indeed, only two Chicago studies directly tackle these issues, and they reveal inconsistent (Morenoff et al. 2001) or no (Sampson et al. 2005) effects of collective efficacy on the patterns of violence examined. Other potential mediating mechanisms linking race/ethnicity, social structure, and violence have not yet been identified or examined.

Regarding how well differences in structural disadvantage explain group differences in violence, the most rigorous studies taking into account structural similarity between groups across local communities show that (*a*) the effects of disadvantage and other structural conditions are invariant and (*b*) levels of violence are similar within structurally similar contexts. Unfortunately, there are just two such studies, they address violence only for black and white communities, and they still point to overwhelming differences in the distributions of structural disadvantage by race (Krivo & Peterson 1996, McNulty 2001). Thus, the state of knowledge needs substantial improvement.

How can we move forward to understand better the complex interrelationships among race, ethnicity, and violent crime? We agree that the answer begins with the basic insight that differences in crime and violence are rooted in group differences in the ecological conditions of communities (Sampson & Wilson 1995). However, substantial progress will come only when analysts move beyond this general observation to recognize that race and ethnicity themselves are a part of structure and not just sources of differentiation in community conditions in the United States. Recognizing this fact means not only asking whether levels of violence are the same when blacks, whites, Latinos, and other groups live in the same types of circumstances, but also searching for how race and ethnicity distinguish groups in fundamental ways that serve to reinforce criminal inequality.

Such an approach places primacy on two insights. First, communities that are structurally similar in levels of poverty, employment, and residential stability may be dissimilar in important spatial, political, and other social dynamics that have implications for crime. Pattillo-McCoy (1999) provides evidence of such apparent structural similarity. She assessed how past and current discrimination created a predominantly black middle-class area within Chicago (Groveland) close to areas of higher deprivation. Because neighborhoods have permeable boundaries, Groveland was at risk for the spillover of violence and other problems from these nearby communities. Social relations also crossed the boundaries, particularly through links between young people attending the same high school. These connections fostered a greater likelihood of risky behaviors, including violence. White middle-class communities are rarely in danger of these proximity effects. Predominantly white, heavily impoverished neighborhoods are rare, and most white areas, especially high-income communities, are located far from problems of urban disadvantage.

Martinez (2002) points to apparently comparable conditions related to blacks and Latinos. These groups have similar levels of disadvantage, but he argues that many Latino communities evidence higher levels of labor market attachment (albeit employment in menial jobs) than found in African American areas. Also, historical racism and discrimination toward African Americans have longer and deeper roots than is true for Latinos. And as deprived as conditions may be in U.S. barrios, immigrant Latinos may use their sending countries, with even worse conditions, as frames of reference in evaluating their position relative to others, thus nullifying potential ascriptive inequality effects.

The second insight emanates from the fact that differences across racially and ethnically distinct communities are often so large that they cannot be described as even apparently similar. These inequities are deeply embedded in histories of privilege and oppression and are major sources of the creation and recreation of differential violence that must themselves be directly articulated and explored. As one example, Figures 2 and 3 above provide stark evidence of how disparate urban and community disadvantage levels are between blacks and whites. We must direct attention to both the overlapping (i.e., racially/ethnically distinct but structurally similar) and nonoverlapping (i.e., racially/ethnically distinct and structurally unique) portions of distributions of this type. Significant structural, political, and social factors have created extraordinary freedom from criminogenic conditions for some groups but deep embeddedness in such conditions for others. By articulating and exploring these forces, we will begin to focus attention on how privileged conditions perpetuate the mechanisms by which some communities are able continually to avoid high levels of crime and violence, and why it is so difficult for others to alter the social forces that produce and perpetuate these problems.

Guided by these two insights, researchers should direct attention to important forces that distinguish the apparently similar, and so obviously different, communities of varying colors. Spatial location relative to more or less power-ful and more or less disadvantaged communities is critical to the dynamics that underlie and reproduce violent crime. Several observed patterns are relevant. Dis-advantaged neighborhoods may be near other disadvantaged areas. This has been so true for African Americans that we sometimes find large black belts with high deprivation. In addition, affluent minority neighborhoods may be situated close to areas of high disadvantage. Affluent communities of color in this situation may be subject to some of the same spillover and boundary effects observed among clus-ters of disadvantage. Another distinct spatial pattern is the one so widely observed for middle-class whites: advantaged localities surrounded by similarly advantaged neighborhoods.

Communities of color other than those of African Americans and whites are exposed to various spatial arrangements. For example, some Asian Americans (e.g., of Japanese origin) fit the most common white pattern of advantage sur-rounded by advantage. The same may apply, on a smaller scale, to some immigrant groups (e.g., professional flows from India, Korea, and China) whose geographic settlement patterns are dispersing more into suburban and other nontraditional immigrant-receiving areas. In contrast, owing to social networks between sending and receiving countries, some immigrants may cluster in communities near other poor immigrant and nonimmigrant areas. For example, groups from parts of Africa, Latin America, and the Caribbean (e.g., Somalians, Haitians, and Mexicans) may be clustered near very poor native black populations.

Future research should explore how these varying patterns of spatial isolation add to the ramifications of disadvantage/advantage for violent crime. When dis-advantage surrounds disadvantage, are communities vulnerable to higher levels of offending and victimization because of spillover effects and more expansive prob-lems of social control? Are there greater concentrations of idle persons gathering during times and in places conducive to crime and violence because of unemploy-ment and underemployment? Do clusters of disadvantaged neighborhoods bring local gangs into contact, leading to reciprocal acts of violence across adjacent neighborhoods (Morenoff et al. 2001, Cohen & Tita 1999)? At the other end of the spectrum, are communities ensconced in clusters of affluence likely to have more extensive informal organizational ties to nearby neighborhoods and social networks that span larger geographic areas and facilitate social control? And can middle-class areas protect themselves from the encroachment of criminogenic structural conditions by their distance and isolation from disadvantage and other urban ills? Answering these questions should further explicate the race/ethnicity–violent crime relationship.

Some recent research draws attention to the significance of political resources for violent crime (Bursik & Grasmick 1993, Vélez 2001). Neighborhoods that have strong political and economic connections to city government officials, busi-nesses, developers, and other important local leaders have a greater capacity to maintain or attract residential, commercial, and local institutional entities that pro-vide resources and make investments that contribute to the viability and stability of areas. Such investments may differentiate racial and ethnic communities that are apparently similar in disadvantage, and could be a large part of what separates the most privileged communities (commonly white) from the most disadvantaged areas (commonly nonwhite) (Massey & Denton 1993). Minority and poor areas are less likely to be targeted for investments by financial institutions (Holloway & Wyly 2001, Wallace & Wallace 1998). Conversely, they are more likely to be targeted for disinvestments such as closings of local malls, businesses, or government services (Wallace & Wallace 1998). In contrast, white and more advantaged neighborhoods are likely beneficiaries of investment decisions of political and economic entities. A question for future research is how racial and ethnic inequality in access to resources and investments that result from political and commercial decisions lead to differential levels of violence and crime across groups. Does such inequality affect the willingness and ability of community residents to engage in the monitoring of public space? Does it affect the levels and quality of law enforcement, and as such, how much violence is deterred? To what extent are routine activities that bring individuals together in situational contexts that could lead to violence affected by differential levels of investment?

In addition, scholars should consider the relevance of criminal justice for explaining the race-crime relationship. Indeed, the organization and practices of the criminal justice system have implications for the positioning of groups in U.S. society. First, criminal justice policies regarding which behaviors to criminalize, laws to enforce, and punishments to attach to criminal behaviors may affect racial and ethnic groups differentially. Notably, drug enforcement activities often target minority rather than white areas, distinguishing these groups and setting the stage for more or less violence, as some dangerous individuals will be taken out of communities while other persons will rely on force in their transactions to control markets and avoid detection. Second, neighborhoods of different colors have varying relations with and views of criminal justice organizations (Bobo & Johnson 2004). Criminal justice agencies also have differential experiences with and perceptions of areas with varying racial/ethnic compositions. Because such views may determine residents' willingness to call for formal intervention and agencies' deployment of criminal justice resources to communities, they have implications for the degree to which crime and violence are held in check.

Finally, a growing body of literature points to the differential implications of increasing levels of incarceration for communities of different racial, ethnic, and class compositions (Rose & Clear 1998). High levels of incarceration of residents and release of prisoners (which are considerably more common for black and Hispanic than white areas) have been hypothesized to reduce neighborhood stability and thereby increase rates of crime and violence. However, to the extent that violent career offenders are incarcerated, levels of community crime may decrease. Other consequences may flow from high levels of imprisonment. Felon disenfranchisement of community members affects their ability to elect local decision makers and may, thereby, diminish public social control (e.g., Uggen & Manza 2002). Imprisonment may also result in the importation into areas of gangs formed in prison, increasing potentially violent criminal networks in communities. Conversely, some violent gangs may "die" when key members are incarcerated. As with spatial patterns and political context, understanding how racial and ethnic groups are differentially positioned with respect to criminal justice policy and practice, and in turn how these relate to crime and violence, will shed light on the structural sources of racial and ethnic differences in crime.

The perspective proposed here implies that researchers must find ways to examine the sources of violence while taking into account the racial (and ethnic) structure of society. From our perspective, the key factors for exploration reflect the spatial, political, and criminal justice constructs discussed above. Research should take a variety of forms: quantitative studies examining economically comparable but racially/ethnically diverse neighborhoods across numerous cities; focused city studies in places where some minority neighborhoods are advantaged and some white ones are disadvantaged; and in-depth, qualitative case studies of critical comparisons of neighborhoods (e.g., middle-class black, white, and Cuban areas, or white middle-class communities in outer suburban versus inner-city or suburban locations) like that exemplified in Sullivan (1989).

Our review of prior work leads us to suggest that future explorations of the race-violence link should be broadened in five additional ways. First, as noted, extant research focuses on homicide and to a lesser degree other violent index offenses. Importantly, emphasizing street crimes may reify the stereotype of *thecriminalblackman*. Thus, analyses of violence must be broadened to include exploration of inequality in all types of interpersonal violence that occur at home, work, school, and other public and private settings. Otherwise, Sampson & Wilson's (1995) admonition of silence and unproductive work will indeed be true in the future.

Second, much interpersonal violence, especially when looking beyond street crime, is affected by gender relations and dynamics that have largely been unexplored in structural analyses (Alder & Worrall 2004). Gender should be particularly important for violence involving girls and women as either victims or offenders. However, the effects of gender may be altered in complex ways by individuals' race and class and by the racial and class composition of the areas in which females live. Although not definitive, recent work by Miller & Like (2004) provides evidence that is suggestive on this point. They show how African American girls in heavily impoverished black neighborhoods in St. Louis experience high levels of violent victimization owing to gendered power relations that emerge within these distressed and racially isolated conditions. Here, young women must rely on their own resources to deal with violence. This puts them at risk for both further victimization and engagement in violence as a defense (see also Miller 2001 and Miller & White 2003 for closely related observations). Yet, to determine whether such gendered dynamics of violence are different for other groups in varying contexts, we need comparative information for girls of other races and from more affluent and nonblack settings. Future research should conduct the types of qualitative and quantitative research that will shed light on these complex interactions and how they fit into the type of perspective proposed here.

We also urge that studies of race, ethnicity, and violent crime broaden their focus beyond blacks and whites. Given the increasing diversity of U.S. society, exploding the black-white divide to include comparisons within and across a variety of racial and ethnic groups is critical. Martinez and colleagues have provided a start with their focus on Latinos. Yet, we need to incorporate additional racial/ethnic groups and make comparisons within as well as across these groups. This will produce a richer understanding of race, ethnicity, and violent crime. Related to the changing diversity of the society, greater attention should be given to monitoring and assessing immigration effects, including examining groups from multiple additional countries, e.g., Somalia, Vietnam, Korea. One important issue is whether there is evidence of segmented assimilation whereby violent involvement among the children of disadvantaged (and particularly black) immigrants is greater than among their immigrant parents.

Fourth, we encourage the trend toward multilevel research. Such an approach will facilitate sounder assessment of the structural determinants of aggregate violence patterns because it allows researchers to address concerns about individual selection effects into areas compared with actual structural contextual influences. Finally, analysts should move beyond the contemporary time frame, the central city, and the United States. Examining change over time in the relationships discussed above and making comparisons to other racially and ethnically diverse societies will go a long way toward revealing the patterning and etiological complexity that characterizes racial and ethnic inequality in violent crime.

ACKNOWLEDGMENTS

The authors thank William C. Bailey, Christopher R. Browning, Ross L. Matsueda, and the reviewers for their insightful comments on earlier versions of this paper.

The *Annual Review of Sociology* is online at http://soc.annualreviews.org

LITERATURE CITED

Alaniz ML, Cartmill RS, Parker RN. 1998. Immigrants and violence: the importance of neighborhood context. *Hispanic J. Behav. Sci.* 20:155–74

Alder C, Worrall A, eds. 2004. *Girls' Violence: Myths and Realities*. Albany: SUNY Press

Almgren G, Guest A, Immerwahr G, Spittel M. 1998. Joblessness, family disruption, and violent death in Chicago, 1970–90. *Soc. Forces* 76:1465–93

Anderson E. 1978. *A Place on the Corner*. Chicago: Univ. Chicago Press

Anderson E. 1994. The code of the streets. *Atl. Mon.* 273:80–94

Anderson E. 1999. *Code of the Street: Decency, Violence, and the Moral Life of the Inner City*. New York: Norton

Bailey WC. 1984. Poverty, inequality, and city homicide rates: some not so unexpected findings. *Criminology* 22:531–50

Baumer E, Horney J, Felson R, Lauritsen JL. 2003. Neighborhood disadvantage and the nature of violence. *Criminology* 41:39–72

Blau JR, Blau PM. 1982. The cost of inequality: metropolitan structure and violent crime. *Am. Sociol. Rev.* 47:114–29

Blau PM, Golden RM. 1986. Metropolitan

structure and criminal violence. *Sociol. Q.* 27:15–26

Bobo LD, Johnson D. 2004. A taste for punishment: black and white Americans' views on the death penalty and the war on drugs. *Du Bois Rev.* 1:151–80

Brearley HC. 1932. *Homicide in the United States.* Chapel Hill: Univ. N.C. Press

Bursik RJ, Grasmick HG. 1993. Economic deprivation and neighborhood crime rates. *Law Soc. Rev.* 27:263–83

Bursik RJ, Webb J. 1982. Community change and patterns of delinquency. *Am. J. Sociol.* 88:24–42

Butcher KF, Piehl AM. 1998. Cross-city evidence on the relationship between immigration and crime. *J. Policy Anal. Manag.* 17:457–93

Cloward RA, Ohlin LE. 1960. *Delinquency and Opportunity: A Theory of Delinquent Gangs.* Glencoe, IL: Free Press

Cohen J, Tita G. 1999. Diffusion in homicide: exploring a general method for detecting spatial diffusion processes. *J. Quant. Criminol.* 15:451–93

Corzine J, Huff-Corzine L. 1992. Racial inequality and black homicide: an analysis of felony, nonfelony, and total rates. *J. Contemp. Crim. Just.* 8:150–65

Crutchfield RD. 1995. Ethnicity, labor markets, and crime. In *Ethnicity, Race, and Crime: Perspectives Across Time and Place*, ed. DF Hawkins, pp. 194–211. Albany: SUNY Press

Crutchfield RD, Glusker A, Bridges GS. 1999. A tale of three cities: labor markets and homicide. *Sociol. Focus* 32:65–83

Curtis LA. 1975. *Violence, Race, and Culture.* Lexington, MA: Lexington Books

Fagan J, Wilkinson DL. 1998. Guns, youth violence and social identity in inner cities. In *Crime and Justice: Annual Review of Research*, ed. M Tonry, MH Moore, 24:105–88. Chicago: Univ. Chicago Press

Federal Bureau of Investigation. 2003. *Uniform crime reports.* http://www.fbi.gov/ucr/02cius.htm

Hagan J, Palloni A. 1999. Sociological criminology and the mythology of Hispanic immigration and crime. *Soc. Probl.* 46:617–32

Hannerz U. 1969. *Soulside: Inquiries into Ghetto Culture and Community.* New York: Columbia Univ. Press

Harer MD, Steffensmeier D. 1992. The differing effects of economic inequality on black and white rates of violence. *Soc. Forces* 70:1035–54

Hawkins DF. 1993. Inequality, culture and interpersonal violence. *Health Aff.* 94:1–16

Holloway SR, Wyly EK. 2001. 'The color of money' expanded: geographically contingent mortgage lending in Atlanta. *J. Hous. Res.* 12:55–90

Huff-Corzine L, Corzine J, Moore DC. 1986. Southern exposure: deciphering the South's influence on homicide rates. *Soc. Forces* 64:906–24

Kornhauser RR. 1978. *Social Sources of Delinquency: An Appraisal of Analytic Models.* Chicago: Univ. Chicago Press

Krivo LJ, Peterson RD. 1996. Extremely disadvantaged neighborhoods and urban crime. *Soc. Forces* 75:619–50

Krivo LJ, Peterson RD. 2000. The structural context of homicide: accounting for racial differences in process. *Am. Sociol. Rev.* 65:547–59

Kubrin CE. 2003. Structural covariates of homicide rates: Does type of homicide matter? *J. Res. Crime Delinq.* 40:139–70

Kubrin CE, Wadsworth T. 2003. Identifying the structural correlates of African-American killings: What can we learn from data disaggregation? *Homicide Stud.* 7:3–35

Kubrin CE, Weitzer R. 2003. Retaliatory homicide: concentrated disadvantage and neighborhood culture. *Soc. Probl.* 50:157–80

LaFree G, Drass KA. 1996. The effect of changes in intraracial income inequality and educational attainment on changes in arrest rates for African Americans and whites, 1957 to 1990. *Am. Sociol. Rev.* 61:614–34

LaFree G, Drass KA, O'Day P. 1992. Race and crime in postwar America: determinants of African-American and white rates, 1957–1988. *Criminology* 30:157–88

Land KC, McCall PL, Cohen LE. 1990. Structural covariates of homicide rates: Are there any invariances across time and social space? *Am. J. Sociol.* 95:922–63

Lauritsen JL. 2001. The social ecology of violent victimization: individual and contextual effects in the NCVS. *J. Quant. Criminol.* 17:3–32

Lauritsen JL, White NA. 2001. Putting violence in its place: the influence of race, ethnicity, gender, and place on the risk for violence. *Criminol. Public Policy* 1:37–59

Lee MR. 2000. Concentrated poverty, race, and homicide. *Sociol. Q.* 41:189–206

Lee MT, Martinez R Jr. 2002. Social disorganization revisited: mapping the recent immigration and black homicide relationship in northern Miami. *Sociol. Focus* 35:363–80

Lee MT, Martinez R Jr, Rosenfeld R. 2001. Does immigration increase homicide? Negative evidence from three border cities. *Sociol. Q.* 42:559–80

Levine FJ, Rosich KJ. 1996. *Social Causes of Violence: Crafting a Science Agenda.* Washington, DC: Am. Sociol. Assoc.

Loftin C, Parker RN. 1985. An errors-in-variable model of the effect of poverty on urban homicide rates. *Criminology* 23:269–85

Maguire K, Pastore AL, eds. 2004. *Sourcebook of criminal justice statistics.* http://www.albany.edu/sourcebook

Martinez R Jr. 1996. Latinos and lethal violence: the impact of poverty and inequality. *Soc. Probl.* 43:131–46

Martinez R Jr. 1997. Homicide among the 1980 Mariel refugees in Miami: victims and offenders. *Hispanic J. Behav. Sci.* 19:107–22

Martinez R Jr. 2000. Immigration and urban violence: the link between immigrant Latinos and types of homicide. *Soc. Sci. Q.* 81:363–74

Martinez R Jr. 2002. *Latino Homicide: Immigration, Violence and Community.* New York: Routledge

Martinez R Jr. 2003. Moving beyond black and white violence: African American, Haitian, and Latino homicides in Miami. In *Violent Crime: Assessing Race and Ethnic Differences,* ed. DF Hawkins, pp. 22–43. New York: Cambridge Univ. Press

Martinez R Jr, Lee MT. 2000. Comparing the context of immigrant homicides in Miami: Haitians, Jamaicans, and Mariels. *Int. Migr. Rev.* 34:794–812

Massey DS, Denton NA. 1993. *American Apartheid: Segregation and the Making of the Underclass.* Cambridge, MA: Harvard Univ. Press

Matsueda RL, Drakulich K, Kubrin C. 2004. *Neighborhood codes of violence.* Presented at Workshop to Set a National Agenda for the Study of Race, Ethnicity, Crime and Criminal Justice, Columbus, OH

McNulty TL. 2001. Assessing the race-violence relationship at the macro level: the assumption of racial invariance and the problem of restricted distributions. *Criminology* 39:467–90

McNulty TL, Bellair PE. 2003a. Explaining racial and ethnic differences in adolescent violence: structural disadvantage, family well-being, and social capital. *Justice Q.* 20:201–31

McNulty TL, Bellair PE. 2003b. Explaining racial and ethnic differences in serious adolescent violent behavior. *Criminology* 41:709–48

McNulty T, Holloway SR. 2000. Race, crime, and public housing in Atlanta: testing a conditional effects hypothesis. *Soc. Forces* 79:707–29

Mears DP. 2001. The immigration-crime nexus: toward an analytic framework for assessing and guiding theory, research, and policy. *Sociol. Perspect.* 44:1–19

Merton RK. 1938. Social structure and anomie. *Am. Sociol. Rev.* 3:672–782

Messner SF. 1983a. Regional and racial effects on the urban homicide rate: the subculture of violence revisited. *Am. J. Sociol.* 88:997–1007

Messner SF. 1983b. Regional differences in the economic correlates of the urban homicide rate: some evidence on the importance of the cultural context. *Criminology* 21:477–88

Messner SF, Golden RM. 1992. Racial inequality and racially disaggregated homicide rates: an assessment of alternative theoretical explanations. *Criminology* 30:421–47

Messner SF, Sampson RJ. 1991. The sex ratio, family disruption, and rates of violent crime: the paradox of demographic structure. *Soc. Forces* 69:693–713

Miller J. 2001. *One of the Guys: Girls, Gangs, and Gender*. New York: Oxford Univ. Press

Miller J, Like T. 2004. *Race, inequality and gender violence: a contextual examination.* Presented at the Workshop to Set a National Agenda for the Study of Race, Ethnicity, Crime and Criminal Justice, Columbus, OH

Miller J, White NA. 2003. Gender and adolescent relationship violence: a contextual examination. *Criminology* 41:1207–48

Morenoff JD, Sampson RJ, Raudenbush SW. 2001. Neighborhood inequality, collective efficacy, and the spatial dynamics of urban violence. *Criminology* 39:517–59

Ousey GC. 1999. Homicide, structural factors, and the racial invariance assumption. *Criminology* 37:405–25

Parker KF. 2001. A move toward specificity: examining urban disadvantage and race- and relationship-specific homicide rates. *J. Quant. Criminol.* 17:89–110

Parker KF, Johns T. 2002. Urban disadvantage and types of race-specific homicide: assessing the diversity in family structures in the urban context. *J. Res. Crime Delinq.* 39:277–303

Parker KF, McCall PL. 1999. Structural conditions and racial homicide patterns: a look at the multiple disadvantages in urban areas. *Criminology* 37:447–78

Parker KF, Pruitt MV. 2000. Poverty, poverty concentration, and homicide. *Soc. Sci. Q.* 81:555–70

Pattillo-McCoy ME. 1999. *Black Picket Fences.* Chicago: Univ. Chicago Press

Peterson RD, Krivo LJ. 1993. Racial segregation and urban black homicide. *Soc. Forces* 71:1001–26

Peterson RD, Krivo LJ. 1999. Racial segregation, the concentration of disadvantage, and black and white homicide victimization. *Sociol. Forum* 14:495–523

Phillips JA. 1997. Variation in African-American homicide rates: an assessment of potential explanations. *Criminology* 35:527–59

Phillips JA. 2002. White, black, and Latino homicide rates: why the difference? *Soc. Probl.* 49:349–73

Reiss AJ Jr, Roth JA, eds. 1993/1994. *Understanding and Preventing Violence.* Vols. 1–4. Washington, DC: Natl. Acad. Press

Rose DR, Clear TR. 1998. Incarceration, social capital, and crime: implications for social disorganization theory. *Criminology* 36:441–80

Russell KK. 1998. *The Color of Crime: Racial Hoaxes, White Fear, Black Protectionism, Police Harassment, and Other Macroaggressions.* New York: NY Univ. Press

Sampson RJ. 1985. Race and criminal violence: a demographically disaggregated analysis of urban homicide. *Crime Delinquency* 31:47–82

Sampson RJ. 1986. Effects of inequality, heterogeneity, and urbanization on intergroup victimization. *Soc. Sci. Q.* 67:751–66

Sampson RJ. 1987. Urban black violence: the effect of male joblessness and family disruption. *Am. J. Sociol.* 93:348–82

Sampson RJ, Bartusch DJ. 1998. Legal cynicism and (subcultural?) tolerance of deviance: the neighborhood context of racial differences. *Law Soc. Rev.* 32:777–804

Sampson RJ, Groves WB. 1989. Community structure and crime: testing social-disorganization theory. *Am. J. Sociol.* 94:774–802

Sampson RJ, Morenoff JD, Raudenbush S. 2005. Social anatomy of racial and ethnic disparities in violence. *Am. J. Public Health* 95:225–32

Sampson RJ, Raudenbush SW, Earls F. 1997. Neighborhoods and violent crime: a multilevel study of collective efficacy. *Science* 277:918–24

Sampson RJ, Wilson WJ. 1995. Toward a theory of race, crime, and urban inequality. In

Crime and Inequality, ed. J Hagan, RD Peterson, pp. 37–54. Stanford, CA: Stanford Univ. Press

Shaw C, McKay H. 1942. *Juvenile Delinquency and Urban Areas*. Chicago: Univ. Chicago Press

Shihadeh ES, Flynn N. 1996. Segregation and crime: the effect of black social isolation on the rates of black urban violence. *Soc. Forces* 74:1325–52

Shihadeh ES, Ousey GC. 1996. Metropolitan expansion and black social dislocation: the link between suburbanization and center-city crime. *Soc. Forces* 75:649–66

Shihadeh ES, Ousey GC. 1998. Industrial restructuring and violence: the link between entry-level jobs, economic deprivation, and black and white homicide. *Soc. Forces* 77: 185–206

Shihadeh ES, Shrum W. 2004. Serious crime in urban neighborhoods: Is there a race effect? *Sociol. Spectrum* 24:507–33

Smith MD, Devine JA, Sheley JF. 1992. Crime and unemployment: effects across age and race categories. *Sociol. Perspect.* 35:551–72

Sullivan M. 1989. *Getting Paid: Youth Crime and Work in the Inner City*. New York: Cornell Univ. Press

Tonry M, ed. 1997. *Ethnicity, Crime, and Immigration: Comparative and Cross-National Perspectives*. Chicago: Univ. Chicago Press

Uggen C, Manza J. 2002. Democratic contraction? The political consequences of felon disenfranchisement in the United States. *Am. Sociol. Rev.* 67:777–803

Vélez MB. 2001. The role of public social control in urban neighborhoods: a multilevel analysis of victimization risk. *Criminology* 39:837–64

Vélez MB, Krivo LJ, Peterson RD. 2003. Structural inequality and homicide: an assessment of the black-white gap in killings. *Criminology* 41:645–72

Wallace R, Wallace D. 1998. *A Plague on Your Houses: How New York Was Burned Down and National Public Health Crumbled*. New York: Verso

Williams KR. 1984. Economic sources of homicide: reestimating the effects of poverty and inequality. *Am. Sociol. Rev.* 49:283–89

Wilson WJ. 1987. *The Truly Disadvantaged: The Inner City, the Underclass, and Public Policy*. Chicago: Univ. Chicago Press

Wilson WJ. 1996. *When Work Disappears: The World of the New Urban Poor*. New York: Alfred A. Knopf

Wolfgang MM, Ferracuti F. 1967. *The Subculture of Violence Towards an Integrated Theory in Criminology*. London: Tavistock

Wooldredge J, Thistlethwaite A. 2003. Neighborhood structure and race-specific rates of intimate assault. *Criminology* 41:393–422

Annu. Rev. Sociol. 2005. 31:357–79
doi: 10.1146/annurev.soc.31.041304.122155
Copyright © 2005 by Annual Reviews. All rights reserved
First published online as a Review in Advance on April 8, 2005

AFFIRMATIVE ACTION AT SCHOOL AND ON THE JOB

Shannon Harper and Barbara Reskin

*Department of Sociology, University of Washington, Seattle, Washington 98195;
email: reskin@u.washington.edu*

Key Words   discrimination, race, employment, education, diversity, sex

■ **Abstract**   Affirmative action (AA) addresses individuals' exclusion from opportunities based on group membership by taking into account race, sex, ethnicity, and
other characteristics. This chapter reviews sociological, economic, historical, and legal scholarship on AA. We first consider the emergence of group-based remedies,
how protected groups are defined, and proportional representation as a standard for
inclusion. We then summarize the research on AA in education (including busing) and
in employment. The concluding section reviews societal responses to AA, including
attitudes, challenges, and political responses. As public and judicial support for AA
has waned, employers and educators have increasingly turned toward diversity as a
rationale for including underrepresented groups. Despite this change, many employers
and educators continue to take positive steps to include minorities and women.

INTRODUCTION

In the 1960s and 1970s, policy makers responded to the Civil Rights movement and
the pervasive race discrimination that had produced it by implementing programs
to foster minorities' inclusion in major U.S. institutions. In K-12 schools, these
included court-ordered busing and magnet schools. Selective public and private
colleges and universities voluntarily implemented race-based outreach, explicitly
considering race in admission and funding decisions. Governments at the city,
state, and federal levels set aside a proportion of public contracts for minority- and
female-run firms. Executive orders (EOs) required government contractors and
government agencies to assess and address minorities' and women's underrepresentation. Some employers not covered by these regulations voluntarily undertook
positive steps to make jobs accessible to a wider range of workers. Restrictions on
congressional redistricting sought to end practices that had excluded blacks from
the political process. Although these activities involved different actors operating
in different societal spheres using different tactics and under the auspices of different regulatory bodies, all represented positive actions to promote racial and gender
inclusion. In short, all constitute affirmative actions.

0360-0572/05/0811-0357$20.00

Affirmative action (AA) involves the "remedial consideration of race, ethnicity, or sex as a factor...in decision making..." to integrate institutions (Leiter & Leiter 2002, p. 1). Organizations pursue AA by changing how they distribute scarce opportunities, sometimes directly redistributing those opportunities in part on the basis of membership in an underrepresented group. Observers distinguish between "hard" and "soft" AA. The former directly considers group membership in allocating opportunities; the latter increases inclusion without taking race or sex into account (Malamud 2001). A more useful classification by Oppenheimer (1989) better reflects the range of affirmative activities. At one extreme are strict quotas that make race or sex a deciding factor. At the other are affirmative commitments not to discriminate. Between these are preference systems that give minorities or women some edge over white men; self-examination activities in which organizations review whether and why minorities or women are underrepresented in certain slots, and if they are, how to achieve a more balanced representation; and outreach plans that increase minorities' and women's representation in the pool from which applicants are chosen. AA activities are also classified by whether they were mandated or voluntarily implemented and whether the organization is a public or private entity—distinctions with implications for which practices are permissible.

This chapter reviews sociological, economic, historical, and legal scholarship on AA.[1] We begin by considering the emergence of group-based remedies, and conclude with societal-level responses to AA. In between we summarize research on AA in education and employment, the two largest AA efforts in the United States.

Although AA in both education and employment aims to foster minorities' and women's inclusion in domains that had been closed to them, they differ in fundamental ways. AA in education resulted from the initiative of institutions of higher education whose leaders recognized that AA was a necessary part of their mission, and it relied primarily on race-conscious preferences. In contrast, AA in employment slipped into American life through the back door as the result of a series of politically motivated presidential EOs. Over time it has been shaped by federal statutes, judicial rulings, and administrative decisions and evolved into a variety of activities that rely primarily on race-neutral practices.

PROHIBITED CHARACTERISTICS AND PROTECTED GROUPS

Like antidiscrimination laws, AA aims to end discriminatory exclusion. The logic and implementation of the two approaches differ sharply, however. Legislators passed the 1964 Civil Rights Act (CRA) to end discrimination that "violate[s]

---

[1]Government agencies have also used AA in granting broadcast licenses, selecting juries, legislative redistricting, and other programs. For additional information, see Leiter & Leiter (2002), Skrentny (1996), and Swain (2001, pp. 325–27).

clear and uncontroversial norms of fairness and formal equality" (Sturm 2001). Antidiscrimination law provides a mechanism for recompensing individual victims and changing the behavior of discriminating organizations. It is enforced primarily through complaints by persons who believe they have suffered discrimination based on a prohibited characteristic, usually race, color, national origin, religion, sex, or disability (Reskin 2001, p. 580). Although law makers understood that the law's object was to end discrimination against people of color, the CRA's injunction against discrimination made discrimination against a white person or a black person on the basis of race equally illegal.

Shortly after Congress passed the CRA, President Lyndon Johnson issued an EO to ensure nondiscrimination against minorities by federal contractors. The enforcement agency interpreted Johnson's order as requiring contractors to take active steps to prevent discrimination. The EO obliged contractors to act pre-emptively to identify and eliminate discriminatory barriers (Graham 1992). Thus, whereas antidiscrimination laws offer redress to individuals after they experienced discrimination, AA regulations aim to protect members of groups vulnerable to exclusion, thereby preventing discrimination from occurring.

Creating Protected Groups

Although the primary objective of AA was to protect African Americans, Johnson's EO followed Title VII in creating other "official minorities" (i.e., pro-tected groups). Thus, the CRA and the 1965 and 1967 EOs listed race, color, national origin, creed, and sex. Of course, these characteristics define groups that have been included (e.g., men) as well as excluded (e.g., women). Because the goal of the EO was to require federal contractors to actively protect members of groups that had customarily been excluded, the EO in effect protected Asians, but not whites; Mexican Americans, but not Italian Americans; women, but not men (Leiter & Leiter 2002). Groups' inclusion depended on whether they were "anal-ogous to blacks" (Skrentny 2002, p. 90). This operationalization of the EO has precipitated resentment toward AA. First, AA challenged entitlements of mem-bers of groups that had been automatic (Brown et al. 2003). Second, "presump-tively equat[ing]" membership in certain groups with disadvantage conferred AA benefits on all members of protected groups, regardless of whether they had per-sonally been excluded (LaNoue & Sullivan 2001, p. 72). This presumption of disadvantage gave protected-group status to Hispanic and Asian immigrants who arrived after Congress had theoretically ended discrimination (Graham 2001). Thus, group-based AA among heterogeneous groups produced overly inclusive categories (Leiter & Leiter 2002, p. 3). In addition, some have argued that AA has largely benefited the most advantaged members of protected groups (or members of the most advantaged groups), persons who can succeed without AA (Wilson 1996). For example, Malamud (2001) claimed that selective colleges admit the best-prepared members of protected groups to diversify their student bodies with the minimal impact on academic standards. Few empirical studies have assessed this supposition (but see Leonard 1990; Brown et al. 2003, p. 25). Nonetheless, concern exists that "when all members of minority groups are equally eligible for affirmative action, the best-off among them will prevail—and. . .African Americans will [probably] lose out" (Malamud 2001, p. 321). Certainly the proliferation of protected groups has enabled organizations to diversify while still excluding African Americans, the group for whom AA was designed (Skrentny 2002, chapter 4).

The growing number of protected groups has also contributed to charges of over-inclusiveness (LaNoue & Sullivan 2001). Over time, Johnson's EO was amended to include the disabled and Vietnam veterans (Graham 2001). Scores of educational institutions and small government AA programs chose which groups to protect. For example, the Small Business Administration's (SBA) minority set-aside program included persons whose ethnic ancestry was Asian Indian and Indonesian, but excluded Afghans, Iranians, Jews, women, and disabled veterans. Although decisions reflect "racial and ethnic presumptions of. . .disadvantage" (LaNoue & Sullivan 2001), they are also influenced by bureaucratic convenience, political considerations, and advocacy-group pressure (LaNoue & Sullivan 2001, p. 73; Robinson 2001). Lobbying, however, is not sufficient. Jews, Poles, and Italians, as well as umbrella organizations for white ethnic groups, have actively sought official minority status, but gatekeepers have concluded that they were less disadvantaged than blacks, Hispanics, and women. Given AA's dichotomous framing of the included and the excluded, "national policy racialized ethnics as privileged whites" (Skrentny 2002, p. 314). People who resemble protected groups in their degree of disadvantage but are excluded from AA have been a significant source of opposition to AA (Malamud 2001, p. 320).

Assessing Exclusion

To quantify the extent of exclusion, researchers and administrators compare the proportion of a group included in a position or institution with its share of the eligible population. AA enforcement agencies often monitor the sex, race, and ethnic composition of organizations' members and encourage organizations to use this monitoring practice to assess any imbalance. In the early years of AA, the enforcement agency investigators viewed underrepresentation as indicating exclusionary practices and encouraged contractors to establish informal hiring quotas (Skrentny 2001, p. 89), although the Supreme Court banned the use of race-based quotas except under extraordinary circumstances (see Defining the Boundaries of Affirmative Action, below). However, the courts have upheld the use of disproportional representation as a standard to assess sex-based exclusion because it holds distinctions based on sex to a lower level of scrutiny. Thus, the courts have interpreted Title IX of the 1972 Education Act as permitting proportional representation as a standard for whether universities' athletic programs are free of sex discrimination (Leiter & Leiter 2002, p. 229). Proportional parity is problematic as a standard of exclusion, however, when the entities under examination are small because disparities can result by chance (Malamud 2001).

AFFIRMATIVE ACTION IN EDUCATION

Primary and Secondary Education

AA in education first appeared as busing. The Supreme Court's 1954 decision in *Brown v. Board of Education* struck down government-mandated, race-based school segregation. After years of foot dragging, the high court ruled in 1968 that school districts that had operated segregated schools had an "affirmative duty to take what[ever] steps" were needed to end racial discrimination (*Green v. County School Board*).[2] This decision led to busing children on the basis of their race to integrate schools. [Some districts implemented magnet schools, another form of AA (Leiter & Leiter 2002, p. 111).]

Although many school districts in both the South and the North obeyed desegregation orders by busing black students to predominantly white schools, and sometimes the reverse (Graham 2001, p. 66), busing was not popular. In 1974, the Supreme Court ruled that Detroit could not bus students across district lines to integrate its schools (*Milliken v. Bradley*). Within-district busing survived longer, but by the 1990s the courts ended court-ordered busing (Epps 2002; Orfield & Eaton 1996, p. 19–21) (see, for example, *Riddick v. School Board of City of Norfolk* 1996; *Board of Education of Oklahoma City v. Dowell* 1991; *Freeman v. Pitts* 1992; *Missouri v. Jenkins* 1995), and some courts banned racial preferences in admissions to elite or magnet schools (Freedberg 1997). Busing had reduced black students' concentration in predominantly minority schools (Thernstrom & Thernstrom 1997, pp. 323–28). However, desegregation efforts have now all but disappeared, and school segregation has returned to its pre-AA levels (Farkas 2003, pp. 1128–29; Orfield 2001, p. 32, table 9). Minorities have given up on trying to integrate public schools and now focus on increasing funding for predominantly minority schools (Van Slyke et al. 1994).

Higher Education

Until the 1960s, most college students were white Protestants from middle- or upper-class families (Bowen & Bok 1998, Lemann 1999, Orfield 2001, p. 4). In 1960, only 2% of students in northern colleges and universities were black (Coleman 1966, p. 443), and of the 146,000 African American college students, over half attended all-black colleges (Thernstrom & Thernstrom 1997, p. 389). The more prestigious the school, the fewer blacks on campus (Thernstrom & Thernstrom 1997, p. 390). Twenty-two states legally mandated racially segregated education, and ending segregation at some schools took a decade-long legal struggle.

---

[2]Congress granted federal funds to states to finance public schools contingent on substantial desegregation as measured by the percentage of minority students in majority white schools (Thernstrom & Thernstrom 1997, p. 320).

By the late 1960s and early 1970s, however, many selective schools[3] had undertaken AA, voluntarily recruiting students from underrepresented groups (Astin & Oseguera 2004, p. 322). Accrediting organizations for professional programs such as the American Association of Medical Colleges also encouraged campus AA (Skrentny 2002, pp. 168–69). Skrentny (2002, pp. 165–68, 171) attributed these efforts to university leaders' "fear of violence" given "black discontent" in cities and on campuses.

Race-neutral efforts for racial inclusion were not sufficient for more than token integration, partly because selective colleges and universities had recently begun requiring SAT or ACT tests for admission (Lemann 1999, p. 173). Because white and Asian applicants tended to outscore blacks and Hispanics (Jencks & Phillips 1998), standardized tests reduced blacks' and Hispanics' chances of admission. To prevent this from undermining AA efforts, selective institutions started treating race as a "plus factor" in admissions or reserving some slots for minorities (Bowen & Bok 1998). The University of California (UC), for example, created "special action" admissions with lower cutoffs for minorities (Douglass 2001, Skrentny 2002, p. 166). By the 1970s, racial preferences were the norm in selective schools and existed for nonblack minorities. White women were not included in most of these programs (except for athletics); ending sex discrimination had been sufficient to end women's exclusion (Skrentny 2002, p. 168).

However, race-based preferences by public universities violated the Equal Protection Clause of the 14th Amendment as well as Title VI of the 1964 CRA, which barred educational institutions from discriminating. In 1978, the Supreme Court addressed this issue in *Bakke v. Regents of the University of California*, a challenge to admissions at the UC Davis Medical School by a white man. The Court ruled that a public school could not give categorical preferences on the basis of race except to remedy past discrimination (Davis's Medical School was new). Justice Powell opined that diversity was a "compelling state interest," signaling that states could use AA to foster diversity, as long as they assessed each application individually. *Bakke* told other universities that racial preferences were legal and even provided a legal rationale for them. Thereafter, the use of race preferences increased (Douglass 2001, pp. 123, 127; Welch & Gruhl 1998).

The turning point for AA in higher education came almost 20 years after *Bakke*, in 1995 when the UC regents barred UC from taking into account race, religion, sex, color, ethnicity, or national origin.[4] One year later, Californians passed a referendum abolishing the use of these characteristics in public education or employment. Washington State voters followed suit in 1998, and in 2000 Florida ended AA in higher education. Meanwhile, the Federal Appellate Court for the Fifth District overruled *Bakke* after the University of Texas Law School's

---

[3] Selective colleges and universities are defined as those in the top quintile of selectivity in admissions standards.
[4] By this time, Congress had endorsed AA in education by authorizing scholarships targeted to women and minorities (Stephanopoulus & Edley 1995, section 10.1).

separate admissions standards for whites and minorities were challenged (*Hopwood v. Texas* 1996). Subsequently, the Supreme Court clarified its stance on race-sensitive practices in two cases against the University of Michigan. In a case against Michigan's law school (*Grutter v. Bollinger* 2003), the Court reaffirmed *Bakke*, holding that diversity is a compelling state interest that warrants transgressing from the Equal Protection Clause. However, in *Gratz v. Bollinger* (2003), it struck down the undergraduate school's practice of automatically adding points to minorities' admission scores. Thus, universities may consider race to enhance diversity, but only as part of individualized assessments of each applicant. States barred from using race-sensitive AA have sought ways to maintain minority enrollment. California, Texas, Florida, and Colorado took advantage of high levels of secondary school segregation in implementing plans that guaranteed admission to a fixed percentage of top-ranked graduates from every high school.

Some have proposed using class-based AA to preserve racial and ethnic diversity (Kahlenberg 1996). Class-based AA is legal and in keeping with a tradition of considering class in admissions, either in needs-based financial aid, the consideration of economic disadvantage in recruiting or admissions, or legacy preferences (Carnevale & Rose 2003). Public support for class-based AA depends on how it is structured. Only a minority of Americans support preference for a low-income applicant whose scores are "slightly worse" than those of a high-income applicant (Carnevale & Rose 2003, table 3.8). Although class-based AA would broaden educational opportunity and increase economic diversity, the racial composition of the poor means that it could not maintain the levels of minority representation generated by race-based AA (Kane 1998b; Wilson 1999, pp. 97, 99).

Impact of Affirmative Action in Higher Education

AA has substantially increased the numbers of students of color in selective colleges and universities (Holzer & Neumark 2000a; Leiter & Leiter 2002, p. 140), and whites' share—but not their numbers—of slots has fallen (Kane 1998b, p. 438). Nonetheless, black and Hispanic students remain underrepresented in selective institutions, and whites increasingly outnumber minorities among college graduates (US Bur. Census 2004).

Some observers have suggested that AA puts minority students in competition with better prepared whites, raising minorities' dropout rate (Cole & Barber 2003; Thernstrom & Thernstrom 1997, p. 388). In fact, attending more selective schools raises minorities' graduation rates compared with their counterparts at nonselective schools (Bowen & Bok 1998; Brown et al. 2003, p. 116). Also, schools that implemented stronger forms of AA had higher minority retention rates than schools whose implementation was weaker (Hallinan 1998, p. 749). After graduating, AA beneficiaries get good jobs and serve their communities at similar rates as whites (Bowen & Bok 1998; Kane 1998a, pp. 19, 43; Kane 1998b, p. 445).

One avenue for assessing the impact of AA is to examine the effect of eliminating it. After California and Washington voters ended race and sex preferences in state-run education or employment, applications to UC and the University of Washington fell, apparently because the elimination of AA sent a negative signal to minorities regarding their welcome (Chambers et al. 2005, Wierzbicki & Hirschman 2002). Texas's post-*Hopwood* percentage plan lowered blacks' and Hispanics' share of admitted applicants 11 and 8 percentage points, respectively, despite substantial outreach. In addition, blacks' share and Hispanics' share of University of Texas enrollees fell by one fifth and one seventh, respectively (Tienda et al. 2003).

Two principal strategies have reduced the impact of banning racial preferences: expanding admissions criteria to incorporate applicants' personal challenges and background characteristics (Leiter & Leiter 2002, p. 155) and targeted recruiting. Both strategies are costly (as are individualized assessments of every application that *Gratz* requires). Leiter & Leiter (2002, p. 155) claim that universities have employed a third strategy: "deft fiddling." Sander (2003) hypothesizes that "back-door admission" allowed UC Berkeley to increase its number of minorities the year after California's ban on AA was implemented. Despite universities' back-door or front-door tactics, minority enrollments have fallen at schools that ended AA (Brown et al. 2003, p. 114; Leiter & Leiter 2002, pp. 155; Tienda et al. 2003).

Research on law schools indicates that AA has substantially increased minority representation in legal education and the legal profession (Lempert et al. 2000, Wightman 1997); that bar-exam passage does not differ for minorities admitted through AA and those accepted solely on the basis of their grades and LSAT scores (Leiter & Leiter 2002, p. 140; Alon & Tienda 2003); and that the post-law-school differences between these two groups are minor (Lempert et al. 2000). However, Sander (2004) claims that ending AA would increase the number of African American lawyers. Although fewer blacks would enter law school, he predicts that a higher proportion would pass the bar. Re-analysis of Sander's data led Chambers et al. (2005) to the opposite conclusion: Ending AA at elite law schools would reduce African Americans' representation from 7% to 1%–2% (lower if their application rates declined when they learned that they would be among a tiny minority). Chambers et al. (2005) project that if law schools stopped considering race in admissions, blacks would all but disappear not only from elite law schools but also from law faculty, federal law clerkships, and top law firms.

Affirmative Action in Higher Education and Diversity

In *Bakke* and *Grutter*, the Supreme Court concluded that states had a compelling interest in racial diversity in higher education. Corporate America, the military, and some academic associations submitted amicus briefs indicating their agreement. Of the little research that has examined the effects of diversity on students' educational experiences, some suggests that it benefits all students in their intergroup relations and ability to understand others' perspectives (Gurin 1999, Orfield & Whitla 2001, Whitla et al. 2003). According to a retrospective study of University of Michigan graduates, students who interacted with diverse peers had a greater sense of commonality with members of other ethnic groups, were more likely to have racially or ethnically integrated lives five years after graduating, and more often reported that their undergraduate education had helped prepare them for their current job (Gurin 1999). The strongest evidence for the impact of diversity comes from an experiment in which white students were randomly assigned a white or minority roommate. Assignment to a minority roommate led to more contact and greater comfort with members of other races and more support for AA policies at the year's end (Duncan et al. 2003). These results are consistent with Allport's (1954) contact hypothesis, which holds that sustained, institutionally supported contact among people of different races reduces prejudice when these people are interdependent and of equal status. Diversity does not necessarily increase contact, however. Several observers have commented on racial segregation on campus, and a longitudinal survey of 159 schools indicates that increased minority presence on campus reduces white students' sense of community (Leiter & Leiter 2002, p. 151). In sum, although preliminary evidence suggests that diversity may affect students' attitudes, almost no rigorous evidence supports this conclusion (Holzer & Newmark 2000a).

AFFIRMATIVE ACTION IN EMPLOYMENT

Congress mounted an attack on race discrimination in 1964 when it passed the omnibus CRA. Title VII of the CRA prohibited discrimination on the basis of race, color, creed, or sex in all aspects of employment. The enactment of the CRA was acclaimed by the media as a huge victory for the Civil Rights movement, for Lyndon Johnson, and for African Americans (Graham 1990).

AA was created in a very different way, unheralded, and with few expectations. Since 1941, every president had banned race discrimination by federal (or defense) contractors through an EO, thereby repaying political debts to African Americans without a fight with Congress (Skrentny 1996). Johnson's 1965 EO followed this pattern; in fact, it simply copied a 1961 EO issued by Kennedy. Both orders required federal contractors to refrain from discriminating at every stage of the employment process and to take positive steps—that is, affirmative action—to ensure that they treated workers equally, regardless of their race.[5] Johnson's AA differed from Kennedy's in two important ways. First, in 1967, he amended his EO to include women as a protected group. Second, his administration established an enforcement agency—the Office of Federal Contract Compliance (OFCC, later OFCCP) that could debar contractors who failed to comply with AA requirements (although it rarely took such action).

AA is required of only a subset of employers. In the private sector, only large companies with substantial government contracts must practice AA; these employ about 30 million persons (Off. Fed. Contract Compliance 2002). [In comparison, Title VII applies to all employers with at least 15 employees, which covers an

---

[5]Kennedy also launched "Plans for Progress" to encourage employers to voluntarily pursue AA. The program's primary effect was to demonstrate that voluntary AA did not increase minorities' access to good jobs, at least in the early 1960s (Anderson 2004, pp. 64–65).

estimated 80 million employees (US EEOC 2004).] As is discussed below, many employers voluntarily practice some type of AA.

Since the late 1940s, federal agencies have also been under EOs requiring active steps to ensure nondiscrimination. Federal agencies took AA more seriously only after Congress passed the 1972 Equal Employment Opportunity Act, which required AA (Kellough 1992). In 2000, approximately 3.5 million federal jobs were subject to this law (US Bur. Census 2000). Additionally, state EOs and statutes require many state agencies to practice AA.

Defining the Boundaries of Affirmative Action

Permissible AA practices vary by the type of employer (public or private) and the authority under which AA was enacted. The legality of some AA practices differs across spheres and depends on its basis (race or sex). For example, although the Supreme Court has accepted diversity as a rationale for race-based AA in higher education, it is not clear whether diversity can be used to justify race-based AA in employment (Malamud 2001).[6]

A number of judicial decisions have helped shape the boundaries of AA in employment, and the changing political slant of the federal judiciary has affected which practices are legal (Reskin 1998). For instance, the Court has restricted most uses of hard AA in employment. It has ruled that private employers may voluntarily implement hard AA without violating Title VII, provided that the preferences are temporary and do not interfere excessively with the rights of members of the majority (*United Steel Workers v. Weber* 1979). The Equal Protection Clause subjects similar AA efforts by public employers to a higher level of judicial scrutiny. To justify race-based preferences, the Court requires a compelling state interest and a narrowly tailored remedy. In contrast, it holds remedial sex-based preferences to an intermediate level of scrutiny (see *Johnson v. Santa Clara County Department of Transportation* 1987; Malamud 2001, pp. 314–29). The Supreme Court applied strict scrutiny to AA in federal contracting in *Adarand v. Pena* (1995), overruling the use of race in awarding government contracts.

Judicial enforcement of Title VII has created the most controversial form of AA—court-ordered hiring or promotion quotas to remedy blatant and long-standing discrimination. Although court-ordered quotas are rare (Burstein 1991), they draw considerable attention. The Supreme Court has upheld such quotas as long as they are narrowly tailored, serve a compelling state interest, and take into account the rights of members of the majority (Bruno 1995, p. 13).

The legislative branch has also stepped in periodically to define or limit acceptable AA. During the 1970s, Congress endorsed AA by designating Vietnam

---

[6]An appellate court ruled against a school district that laid off a white rather than a black employee to maintain diversity among staff in one department (*Taxman v. Piscataway* 1997). Piscataway settled the case with the assistance of a civil rights organization rather than risk Supreme Court review (Malamud 2001).

veterans and the handicapped as protected groups. In the latter case, AA goes beyond increased outreach and recruitment to require that employers provide "reasonable accommodations" for the functional limitations of disabled workers (US Dep. Labor, Off. Disabil. Employ. Policy 2003).

Employers' Practices

The extra efforts that AA has required of contractors vary, ranging from conducting utilization analyses, outreach and recruitment, and active monitoring of employment patterns to—for a brief period in the late 1960s—using quotas. Since 1971, the OFCCP has required large nonconstruction contractors to annually produce AA plans based on a utilization analysis of their employment of women and minorities relative to the relevant labor pool. The plans must include goals and timetables for addressing substantial disparities revealed in the analysis (Bruno 1995, p. 8). Companies are not required to meet their goals, but if audited they must be able to show they made a good faith effort to do so.

Apart from what the courts bar and the EO requires of federal contractors, we know little about the practices employers include in any AA efforts (for fuller discussions, see Holzer & Neumark 2000b, Reskin 1998). The OFCCP provides little concrete guidance on what practices employers may use to reach their goals. Moreover, although federal contractors are expected to address groups' underrepresentation through outreach and training, Title VII forbids contractors from discriminating in favor of members of protected groups when making hiring or promotion decisions.

Summarizing employers' practices is further complicated by the fact that many noncontractors have voluntarily implemented a variety of soft AA practices (Edelman & Petterson 1999). Many employers who are not federal contractors advertise openings broadly and have formalized personnel practices (Dobbin et al. 1993, Holzer & Neumark 2000b, Kelly & Dobbin 1998, Konrad & Linnehan 1995). These largely race- and gender-neutral practices address sources of exclusion. Broadly advertising job openings, for instance, can avoid exclusion that stems from network recruitment and hiring (Braddock & McPartland 1997, Lin 2000, Portes & Landolt 1996).

The intensity of employers' AA efforts has varied with the politics of AA. The number of firms with AA or equal employment opportunity (EEO) offices grew in the 1970s and early 1980s (Dobbin et al. 1993). With declining political support for AA and increasing attention to the diversity of the future workforce, many employers replaced voluntary AA programs with "diversity management" (Ryan et al. 2002), and by 1998 three quarters of Fortune 500 companies had diversity programs and 88% tried to "hire for diversity in some way" (Ryan et al. 2002). Although diversity initiatives ostensibly move beyond race and sex, recruitment efforts are most often targeted at blacks, Hispanics, and women, and less at older workers or persons for whom English is a second language (Ryan et al. 2002).

The Impact of Affirmative Action in Employment

The limited knowledge of which employers practice AA and what they are doing in its name hampers assessing the impact of AA in employment. Also, AA's effects may be confounded with those of antidiscrimination laws and with increasing human capital among minorities and women. The bulk of research on the impact of AA has been quantitative and cross-sectional, although a detailed ethnography of AA in the Army showed how one organization created an effective program (Moskos & Butler 1996). Additional ethnographic studies of how AA is practiced in other workplaces would be illuminating.

The impact of AA in employment among federal contractors depends almost entirely on OFCCP's enforcement of the EO requiring AA. OFCCP enforcement has varied over the agency's lifetime, roughly coincident with presidential administrations. The effects of AA have also differed across protected groups. In the years from its birth to 1973, a period of weak enforcement, AA raised black men's— but not women's—employment in unskilled jobs in contractor firms relative to noncontractors (Heckman & Payner 1989, Leonard 1991, Smith & Welch 1984). Enforcement efforts escalated between 1974 and 1980, resulting in a rapid rise in the employment of black women by federal contractors (Welch 1989). Black men continued to be employed at higher rates by contractors than by noncontractors, and this difference showed up in white-collar and skilled craft jobs as well as blue-collar jobs (Leonard 1990, 1991). The wages of both black men and women rose in this period. Blacks' increased representation in white-collar and skilled craft jobs is consistent with AA's reduction in race and perhaps sex segregation. However, some employers have used race- and sex-based job assignments to cater to a minority or female market or clientele, creating occupational ghettos (Collins 1997, Durr & Logan 1997, Malamud 2001). This practice simultaneously opens jobs to the excluded and segregates them, ultimately limiting their opportunities (Frymer & Skrentny 2004, p. 722).

Further establishing that enforcement is necessary for effective AA, compliance reviews, explicit goals, and sanctions have been instrumental in increasing minority employment (Leonard 1990). Some employers have admitted that they would not have implemented programs "to increase fairness" without the risk of sanctions or the possibility of incentives (Hartmann 1996). With conservatives in the White House during the 1980s, enforcement declined, ending the advantage for minorities and women employed by federal contractors over those employed by noncontractors (Leonard 1990, Stephanopoulos & Edley 1995).

Underlying the strong effect of enforcement is the importance of organizational commitment to AA. Researchers have shown that the commitment of top leaders is a key determinant of AA outcomes (Baron et al. 1991). People in charge are positioned to alter organizational practices because they can influence the way things are done and obtain conformity through reward systems (Konrad & Linnehan 1995; N. DiTomaso, unpublished paper). Consider the Army's AA experience. The Army's commitment to racial equality throughout the ranks while maintaining standards meant that it provided training to ensure that the persons it promoted were qualified. The dual commitment to standards and racial equality enabled the Army to achieve both, while winning acceptance of its AA efforts (Moskos & Butler 1996, pp. 71–72). In sum, AA has improved minorities' and women's positions in the labor market. Although the sources and estimated strengths of these effects have varied, they do not appear to have resulted from quotas (Leonard 1990) or come at the cost of lower productivity (Holzer & Neumark 2000a).

In addition to affecting workers' distribution across jobs, AA promoted changes in labor markets and employers' practices. Few employers changed their employment practices or implemented new structures in response to Title VII and AA until 1971, when the OFCCP imposed utilization analyses as a monitoring tool (Kelly & Dobbin 1998). Firms began to change after the OFCCP outlined how it would monitor contractors and the Supreme Court accepted the disparate-impact theory of discrimination in *Griggs v. Duke Power* (1972), which expanded the legal meaning of discrimination to include neutral employment practices with an unjustified and adverse impact on protected groups (Stryker 2001). They scrutinized personnel practices and created EEO and AA structures and practices. These included targeting recruitment and establishing special training programs for women and minorities (Kelly & Dobbin 1998). When government and judicial support for AA waned in the 1980s and 1990s, the structures remained initially because they rationalized employment decisions (Kelly & Dobbin 1998) and later because they served as tools to promote and manage diversity (Kelly & Dobbin 1998, Ryan et al. 2002). Importantly, as AA transformed organizations, it was increasingly "rooted in strategies to maximize the[ir] performance" (Frymer & Skrentny 2004, p. 721).

SOCIETAL RESPONSES TO AFFIRMATIVE ACTION

Attitudes About Affirmative Action

The creation of protected groups collided with the ideologies of equal opportunity and meritocracy (but see Berg 2001). As Patterson (1997, p. 148) puts it, many viewed AA as "collective remediation in a heterogeneous society traditionally accustomed to a highly individualistic ethic." Critics charge that in creating group rights, AA compromises the principle of merit-based allocation, discriminates against innocent persons, fosters inefficiency, harms its intended beneficiaries, and perpetuates racism by making color relevant (Leiter & Leiter 2002, p. 233; Thernstrom & Thernstrom 1997).

Levels of support for AA depend on the specific policy mentioned (Krysan 2000). Within employment, the degree of approval for race-conscious AA (i.e., racial preferences) is far lower than that for race-neutral AA (outreach, mentoring). Surveys that find little support for AA tend to ask about practices that are illegal and rare (Kravitz et al. 1997). For at least two decades, corporations have almost universally supported AA because it protects them from discrimination lawsuits and because they see a need for a diverse workforce (Leiter & Leiter 2002, p. 86).

Because many white males are excluded from AA's benefits, we would expect racial differences in support for AA. Overall, whites are less supportive of AA than blacks. Support for racial preferences in hiring and promotion decisions is significantly higher among blacks than whites, and the race gap is even larger with respect to support for quotas in college admissions (Schuman et al. 1997). However, researchers have cautioned against exaggerating black-white differences in support for AA (Bobo 2001, Swain 2001, Wilson 1999). Disapproval of AA is not simply a matter of opposition to racial equality. The majority of Americans support racial equality, but support drops significantly if government intervention is involved (Schuman et al. 1997). However, Kinder & Sanders (1996) claim that the white-black gap in support for AA has widened. Contributing to the gap is the disparity in whites' and blacks' beliefs about how much blacks remain disadvantaged in American society (Davis & Smith 1996).

Although opponents frame their disapproval of AA in terms of fairness, survey data cast doubt on the claim that whites' opposition to AA stems from their commitment to meritocracy. The more committed whites are to the belief that hard work should be rewarded, the more positive their attitudes toward AA (Bobo 2001).[7] From analyzing social surveys, Bobo concludes that whites' opposition to AA resides in their sense of group-based entitlement. Group identification is consistent with the much greater support among blacks for AA for native-born blacks than for recent immigrants that Swain et al. (2001) observed in focus groups. Swain and colleagues also found that Latinos' level of support for AA was closer to blacks' and that Asian Americans' level was closer to whites'. As Patterson (1997, p. 159) argues, AA invokes the sense of group position for both excluded groups and groups that are already securely in: Both tend to support policies that will advantage them.

Others oppose preferences because they believe they harm beneficiaries (Steele 1991). Whether preferences reduce self-esteem depends on whether recipients of group-based preferences believe they were selected solely on the basis of their group membership. If they do, then beneficiaries' self-evaluations suffer. If beneficiaries believe they were selected on the basis of both personal merit and group membership, their self-esteem does not suffer (Major et al. 1994). Others, of course, may stigmatize individuals whom they believe are beneficiaries of preferences.

Although better information may not dispel the criticisms of many opponents, opposition to AA is based, at least in part, on several misconceptions. Most people are presumably unaware that different legal standards govern AA in higher education, federal contracting, and voluntary AA in employment. Across these spheres, the prevalence of race-conscious AA varies from considerable in higher education to minimal in employment. The visibility of race-conscious AA in higher education has probably led Americans to assume that AA in employment is also race

---

[7]Individuals who strongly supported meritocracy were less opposed to AA when there was evidence of discrimination (Son Hing et al. 2002).

conscious. The media and the public have largely ignored the differences between these various forms of AA (Duster 1998, Patterson 1997, Stryker et al. 1999), sometimes even equating AA and quotas (L. Bobo, personal communication).

The existence of open preferences for minorities has probably led whites to overstate AA's prevalence, to believe that AA limits their own opportunities, and to conclude that AA prioritizes minority group status over qualifications (Davis & Smith 1996, Reskin 1998, Royster 2003). Surveys show that Americans believe that minority preferences in employment are rampant (Davis & Smith 1996). This perception is not supported by either the law or the body of empirical evidence attesting to the persistence of race and sex discrimination in employment (Bertrand & Mullainathan 2004, Kirschenmann & Neckerman 1991, Pager 2003, Turner et al. 1991).

Public opinion can exert an important influence on political action (Burstein 1998). As we discuss below, politicians have manipulated public opinion and public misunderstanding about AA to further their interests.

Challenges to Affirmative Action

Opposition to AA has taken the form of legal activism, voice, and exit. Organized opposition, initiated by a small number of actors, has relied primarily on two tacks: judicial challenges and referenda to eliminate AA. Voter referenda ended AA in public employment and education in California and Washington but at the time of this writing have not succeeded in other states. Opponents have had some success in using the courts to challenge the explicit use of race in decision making by public agencies in apparent violation of the Equal Protection Clause. For example, the appellate court decision in *Hopwood* against the University of Texas and the more recent *Gratz* decision against the University of Michigan have been important precedents, influencing the admissions process at all public universities (Aldave 1999, p. 314). Indeed, in the wake of the *Gratz* decision, the threat of costly lawsuits prompted several public and private universities that had considered race for scholarships or academic enrichment programs to end such programs or open them to all comers (Malveaux 2004).

Organized opposition to AA should vary directly with its visibility and the number of people whom it has adversely affected. Consistent with this expectation, busing drew immediate and strong opposition. Relatively large numbers of people were affected, and opponents could literally see the policy in action. Cities implemented school busing without much protest except for Little Rock (where opposition was directed against integration per se) and Boston, which endured days of anti-busing demonstrations and violent protests (Lukas 1985, p. 259). More often, opponents mobilized, in the South, by transferring their children from public schools to "segregation academies," or, in the North, by moving to all-white suburban school districts. In addition, opponents began filing legal challenges shortly after busing's onset, some of which wended their way to the Supreme Court. Busing's ultimate demise in the 1990s resulted from whites' abandonment of urban schools for predominantly white school districts and from activist conservative judges vacating earlier court-ordered busing, declaring districts unified (i.e., integrated; Orfield & Eaton 1996).

AA in university admissions did not produce many people who publicly identified themselves as having been harmed. Whites who had been rejected for admission faced the same problem that members of traditionally excluded groups encounter: not knowing whether their rejection was because others were better qualified or because of their race. Students apply to "safety schools" as insurance because they recognize that admissions at selective schools are highly competitive. Furthermore, because many majority students are admitted, protesting one's rejection is a public acknowledgment that one was not good enough. Finally, the number of majority group members displaced by AA is not large (Kane 1998b). Presumably for these reasons most legal challenges have been mounted by organizations rather than by individuals. The Center for Individual Rights (CIR), a conservative public interest organization, has filed most of the challenges to AA in academia, finding plaintiffs by advertising in campus newspapers and paying the litigation expenses (Stohr 2004; see also Zemans 1983, p. 700). CIR spokespersons indicate that they will scrutinize universities for deviations from full-file reviews. Given universities' commitment to preserve minority enrollments, further lawsuits seem likely.

Challenges to AA in employment reach the courts (and the media) through a different path. They are initially filed as discrimination complaints under Title VII of the CRA or state antidiscrimination agencies. Even at the complaint stage, just a small minority of race discrimination charges come from whites—between 1991 and 2001, just 6% (Hirsh & Kornrich 2005), and the EEOC rejected the overwhelming majority of reverse-discrimination complaints as unfounded (Blumrosen 1996). The low prevalence of race discrimination complaints by whites is consistent with the small proportion of whites who report having been harmed by AA (Davis & Smith 1996). A few cases that have gone to court have had the support of a union or a men's rights group (Faludi 1991), but organized opposition to AA in employment has emerged primarily in the political sphere.

Politicization of Affirmative Action

AA's basis in group rights can easily be translated into a political tool. The political influence of various ascriptive groups has created opportunities for politicians, and politicians have regularly tried to exploit AA for political gain by supporting or opposing it (Skrentny 2002, p. 86). As noted above, politicians have responded to pressure from various constituencies to be included as protected groups under AA programs.

In several other instances, AA has been used to polarize voters. Political calculations regarding his prospects in the 1964 election contributed to Johnson's commitment to AA (Skrentny 1996). Nixon supported a scheme known as the "Philadelphia Plan" in part because he saw a political benefit in implementing what amounted to hiring quotas for blacks in white-run unions in an attempt to divide the traditional Democratic base (Anderson 2004, p. 138). The ensuing controversy delivered the union vote to Nixon. Reagan ran for office partly on the basis of his opposition to AA. Although he did not end AA for federal contractors, his administration did not enforce AA regulations.

Public opinion can also exert an important influence on political action (Burstein 1998). As discussed above, public attitudes toward AA are based in part on misperceptions about the content of AA policies. Politicians have occasionally contributed to the confusion about what AA actually entails, as when Senator Orrin Hatch (1994) equated AA with quotas:

> I want to emphasize that affirmative action means quotas or it means nothing. It means discrimination on the basis of race or sex. It does not mean remedial education [or] special programs for the disadvantaged.... It has nothing to do with equality of opportunity.... Affirmation action is about equality of results, statistically measured.... All distinctions [between quotas and "goals," "targets," and "timetables"] dissolve in practice.

Quotas figured prominently in the congressional debate over the 1991 Civil Rights Act, with President George H.W. Bush characterizing the legislation as "quota bills" (Stryker et al. 1999). Although the 1991 Act addressed AA indirectly, his characterization may have strengthened the equation of AA and quotas in some people's minds, laying the groundwork for the challenges that AA faced in the following years (Stryker et al. 1999). Despite explicit opposition, politicians have not launched a concerted campaign to eliminate AA. Instead, Reagan and his successors created a federal judiciary that has chipped away at AA, invalidating group-based preferences in public contracting and employment and restricting them in education. A wealth of excellent scholarship has traced the political history of AA (see, e.g., Anderson 2004; Belz 1991; Blumrosen 1993; Graham 1990; Skrentny 2001, 2002; Stryker 2001).

CONCLUSIONS

Substantial disparities remain among whites, Asians, Hispanics, and African Americans in the quality of colleges they attend, the proportions who graduate, their labor force participation and unemployment rates, their distribution across neighborhoods and occupations, and their earnings (Darity & Mason 1998; Jaynes & Williams 1989; Massey & Denton 1993; Reskin 2001, 2002). Social scientists have debated whether group-based AA is the appropriate way to address these disparities. Commentary on both sides is readily available (Bergmann 1996, Crosby 2004, Glazer 1975, Orfield & Kurlaender 2001, Patterson 1997, Sowell 1972, Thernstrom & Thernstrom 1997, Tienda et al. 2003). Most of the supportive commentary emphasizes persistent or even growing disparities. Commentators who oppose AA acknowledge that disparities persist, but they support other remedies (often increasing minorities' human capital) or argue that in overriding meritocratic distribution AA's costs outweigh the benefits.

In the early years of AA, government decision makers and judicial decisions viewed it as temporary. As antidiscrimination regulations eradicated discrimination from U.S. institutions, they expected the need for AA to disappear. As AA integrated organizations, network recruitment would maintain inclusion. Better jobs for minorities would produce more competitive minority college applicants in the next generation. Over time the effects of helping provide initial access into these institutions would multiply.

Research does not support these scenarios. Many AA efforts have succeeded in opening new opportunities to women and minorities in both education and employment. However, these gains have often been contingent on active enforcement and administrative support of AA, neither of which has been consistently present for AA. Public schools became more racially integrated during busing but have now returned to their pre-busing segregation levels. Minority college enrollments increased with hard AA, but fell in states that abolished AA. Federal contracting firms provided better opportunities for women and minorities than noncontractors only as long as the OFCCP enforced the EO. California public agencies whose budgets depended on greater integration became more integrated at the same time that nontargeted agencies became more segregated (Baron et al. 1991).

Meanwhile, the terms of the debate have literally changed. Declining support for AA has led employers and universities to pursue the more innocuous goal of diversity. Although diversity programs may or may not seek to provide access to members of protected groups, like AA they emphasize group membership. In this respect, the debate over AA reflects fundamental tensions about the relationship between underrepresentation and inequality.

The intense attention to AA in the United States has diverted scholars from other countries' efforts to include the formerly excluded.[8] Several nations have implemented some form of AA, although many differ radically from American AA. This diversity both over time and cross-nationally can be seen as an extended natural experiment with substantial variation across spheres, protected groups, implementation, and public and political responses. Despite this wealth of information, Hochschild's (1995) assessment still holds: "[T]he debate over the empirical consequences of affirmative action. . .is striking for its high ratio of claims to evidence" (p. 100). There is every reason to believe that AA will be topical for some time to come. Both social science and public policy stand to gain from additional scholarly analyses.

ACKNOWLEDGMENTS

Our colleague Lynne Taguchi contributed to this chapter in several important ways, especially in bringing cross-national research on AA to our attention. We are grateful to Stephanie Liddle, Doug Massey, E.M. Read, and an anonymous reviewer for their help. All errors are our own.

---

[8]See Darity & Nembhard (2000), Sowell (2004), Teles (2004) for discussions of AA in other nations. Space limits prevent our discussing AA in other societies.

The *Annual Review of Sociology* is online at http://soc.annualreviews.org

LITERATURE CITED

Aldave BB. 1999. Affirmative action and the ideal of "justice for all." *Res. Soc. Strat. Mobil.* 17:303–17

Allport G. 1954. *The Nature of Prejudice.* Cambridge, MA: Addison-Wesley

Alon S, Tienda M. 2003. *Hispanics and the 'misfit' hypothesis: differentials in college graduations rates by institutional selectivity.* Presented at Color Lines Conf., Cambridge, MA

Anderson TH. 2004. *The Pursuit of Fairness.* New York: Oxford Univ. Press

Astin AW, Oseguera L. 2004. The declining "equity" of American higher education. *Rev. High. Educ.* 27:321–41

Baron JN, Mittman BS, Newman AE. 1991. Targets of opportunity: organizational and environmental determinants of gender integration within the California Civil Service, 1979–1985. *Am. J. Sociol.* 96:1362–401

Belz H. 1991. *Equality Transformed.* New Brunswick, NJ: Transactions

Berg I. 2001. Race, stratification, and group-based rights. In *The Problem of the Century*, ed. E Anderson, D Massey, pp. 115–41. New York: Sage

Bergman BR. 1996. *In Defense of Affirmative Action.* New York: Basic

Bertrand M, Mullainathan S. 2004. Are Emily and Greg more employable than Lakisha and Jamal? A field experiment on labor market discrimination. *Am. Econ. Rev.* 94:991–1013

Blumrosen AW. 1993. *Modern Law.* Madison: Univ. Wisc. Press

Blumrosen AW. 1996. *Declaration.* Statement submitted to Supreme Court of California in Response to Proposition to 209, Sept. 26

Bobo L. 2001. Race, interest, and belief about affirmative action. See Skrentny 2001, pp. 191–213

Bowen WG, Bok D. 1998. *The Shape of the River: Long-Term Consequences of Considering Race in College and University Admissions.* Princeton, NJ: Princeton Univ. Press

Braddock JH, McPartland JM. 1987. Social science evidence and affirmative action policies: a reply to commentators. *J. Soc. Issues* 43:133–43

Brown MK, Carnoy M, Currie E, Duster T, Oppenheimer DB, et al. 2003. *Whitewashing Race: The Myth of a Color-Blind Society.* Berkeley: Univ. Calif. Press

Bruno A. 1995. Affirmative action in employment. *Congr. Res. Serv. Rep. 95–165 GOV.* Library of Congress, Washington, DC

Burstein P. 1991. "Reverse discrimination" cases in the federal courts: mobilization by a countermovement. *Sociol. Q.* 32:511–28

Burstein P. 1998. *Discrimination, Jobs, and Politics.* Chicago: Univ. Chicago Press

Carnevale AP, Rose SJ. 2003. Socioeconomic status, race/ethnicity, and selective college admissions. *Res. Rep.* Century Found., New York. http://www.tcf.org/Publications/Education/carnevale_rose.pdf

Chambers DL, Clydesdale T, Kidder WC, Lempert RO. 2005. The real impact of eliminating affirmative action in American law schools. *Stanford Law Rev.* In press

Cole S, Barber E. 2003. *Increasing Faculty Diversity: The Occupational Choices of High Achieving Minority Students.* Cambridge, MA: Harvard Univ. Press

Coleman JS, Campbell EQ, Hobson CJ, McPartland J, Mood AM, et al. 1966. *Equality of Educational Opportunity.* Washington, DC: Dep. Health, Educ. Welf.

Collins SM. 1997. *Black Corporate Executives: The Making and Breaking of a Black Middle Class.* Philadelphia, PA: Temple Univ. Press

Crosby F. 2004. *Affirmative Action Is Dead; Long Live Affirmative Action.* New Haven, CT: Yale Univ. Press

Darity WA, Mason PL. 1998. Evidence on discrimination in employment: codes of color, codes of gender. *J. Econ. Perspect.* 12:63–90

Darity WA, Nembhard JG. 2000. Racial and

ethnic inequality: the international record. *Am. Econ. Rev.* 90:308–11

Davis JA, Smith TW. 1996. *General Social Surveys, 1972–1996.* Chicago: Natl. Opin. Res. Cent.

Dobbin F, Sutton JR, Meyer JW, Scott WR. 1993. Equal opportunity law and the construction of internal labor markets. *Am. J. Sociol.* 99:396–427

Douglass JA. 2001. Anatomy of a conflict: the making and unmaking of affirmative action at the University of California. See Skrentny 2001, pp. 118–44

Duncan GJ, Boisjoly J, Levy DM, Kremer M, Eccles J. 2003. *Empathy or antipathy? The consequences of racially and socially diverse peers on attitudes and behaviors.* Work. Pap., Inst. Policy Res., Northwestern Univ.

Durr M, Logan JR. 1997. Racial submarkets in government employment: African American managers in New York State. *Soc. Forum* 2:353–70

Duster T. 1998. Individual fairness, group preferences, and the California plan. In *Race and Representation: Affirmative Action*, ed. R Post, M Rogin, pp. 111–34. New York: Zone

Edelman LB, Petterson S. 1999. Symbols and substance in organizational response to civil rights law. *Res. Soc. Strat. Mobil.* 17:107–35

Epps E. 2002. Race and school desegregation: contemporary legal and educational issues. *Perspect. Urban Educ.* 1(1):3 http://www.urbanedjournal.org/archive/Issue%201/FeatureArticles/article0003.html

Faludi S. 1991. *Backlash.* New York: Crown

Farkas G. 2003. Cognitive skills and noncognitive traits and behaviors in stratification processes. *Annu. Rev. Sociol.* 29:541–62

Freedberg L. 1997. Affirmative action under attack at venerable, prestigious Boston Latin. *San Francisco Chronicle*, Dec. 11

Frymer P, Skrentny JD. 2004. The rise of instrumental affirmative action: law and the new significance of race in America. *Conn. Law Rev.* 36:677–723

Glazer N. 1975. *Affirmative Discrimination:* *Ethnic Inequality and Public Policy.* New York: Basic

Graham HD. 1990. *The Civil Rights Era: Origins and Development of National Policy.* New York: Oxford Univ. Press

Graham HD. 1992. The origins of affirmative action: civil rights and the regulatory state. *Ann. Am. Acad. Polit. Soc. Sci.* 523:50–62

Graham HD. 2001. Affirmative action for immigrants? The unintended consequences of reform. See Skrentny 2001, pp. 53–70

Gurin P. 1999. The compelling need for diversity in education. *Mich. J. Race Law* 5:363–425

Hallinan MT. 1998. Diversity effects on student outcomes: social science evidence. *Ohio State Law J.* 59:733–54

Hartmann H. 1996. Who has benefited from affirmative action in employment? In *The Affirmative Action Debate*, ed. GE Curry, pp. 77–96. Cambridge, MA: Addison-Wesley

Hatch O. 1994. Loading the economy. In *Equal Employment Opportunity*, ed. P Burstein, pp. 261–67. New York: Aldine de Gruyter

Heckman JJ, Payner BS. 1989. Determining the impact of federal antidiscrimination policy on the economic status of blacks: a study of South Carolina. *Am. Econ. Rev.* 79(1):138–77

Hirsh CE, Kornrich S. 2004. *The context of discrimination: the impact of firm conditions on workplace race and sex discrimination.* Presented at Annu. Meet. Am. Sociol. Assoc., San Francisco, CA

Hochschild J. 1995. *Facing Up to the American Dream.* Princeton, NJ: Princeton Univ. Press

Holzer H, Neumark D. 2000a. Assessing affirmative action. *J. Econ. Lit.* 308:483–568

Holzer H, Neumark D. 2000b. What does affirmative action do? *Ind. Labor Relat. Rev.* 53:240–71

Jaynes GD, Williams RM, eds. 1989. *A Common Destiny.* Washington, DC: Natl. Acad. Press

Jencks C, Phillips M. 1998. *The Black-White Test Score Gap.* Washington, DC: Brookings Inst.

Kahlenberg RD. 1996. *The Remedy: Class, Race, and Affirmative Action.* New York: Basic

Kane T. 1998a. No alternatives: the effects of color-blind admissions in California. In *Chilling Admissions*, ed. G Orfield, E Miller, pp. 33–50. Cambridge, MA: Harvard Educ. Publ. Group

Kane T. 1998b. Racial and ethnic preferences in college admissions. See Jencks & Phillips 1998, pp. 431–56

Kellough JE. 1992. Affirmative action in government employment. *Ann. Am. Acad. Polit. Soc. Sci.* 523:117–30

Kelly E, Dobbin F. 1998. How affirmative action became diversity management: employer response to antidiscrimination law, 1961 to 1996. *Am. Behav. Sci.* 41(7):960–84

Kinder DR, Sanders LM. 1996. *Divided by Color.* Chicago: Univ. Chicago Press

Kirschenmann J, Neckerman KM. 1991. "We'd love to hire them but. . .": the meaning of race for employers. In *The Urban Underclass*, ed. C Jencks, PE Peterson, pp. 203–34. Washington, DC: Brookings Inst.

Konrad AM, Linnehan F. 1995. Formalized HRM structures: coordinating equal employment opportunity or concealing organizational practices? *Acad. Manag. J.* 38:787–820

Kravitz DA, Harrison DA, Turner ME, Levine EL, Chaves W, et al. 1997. *Affirmative Action: A Review of Psychological and Behavioral Research.* Washington, DC: Soc. Ind. Org. Psychol.

Krysan M. 2000. Prejudice, politics, and public opinion. *Annu. Rev. Sociol.* 26:135–68

LaNoue GR, Sullivan JC. 2001. Deconstructing affirmative action categories. See Skrentny 2001, pp. 71–86

Leiter S, Leiter WM. 2002. *Affirmative Action in Antidiscrimination Law and Policy: An Overview and Synthesis.* Albany: SUNY Press

Lemann N. 1999. *The Big Test: The Secret History of American Meritocracy.* New York: Farrar, Straus & Giroux

Lempert RO, Chambers DL, Adams TK. 2000. Michigan's minority graduates in practice. *Law Social Inq.* 25:395–506

Leonard J. 1990. The impact of affirmative action regulation and equal employment law on black employment. *J. Econ. Perspect.* 4:47–63

Leonard J. 1991. The federal anti-bias effort. In *Essays on the Economics of Discrimination*, ed. EP Hoffman, pp. 85–113. Kalamazoo, MI: W.E. Upjohn Inst. Employ. Res.

Lin N. 2000. Inequality in social capital. *Contemp. Soc.* 29:785–95

Lukas JA. 1985. *Common Ground.* New York: Knopf

Major B, Feinstein J, Crocker J. 1994. Attributional ambiguity of affirmative action. *Basic Appl. Soc. Psychol.* 15:113–41

Malamud DC. 2001. Affirmative action and ethnic niches: a legal afterword. See Skrentny 2001, pp. 313–45

Malveaux J. 2004. Know your enemy: the assault on diversity. *Black Issues High. Educ.* 21:32–33

Massey DS, Denton NA. 1993. *American Apartheid.* Cambridge, MA: Harvard Univ. Press

Moskos CC, Butler JS. 1996. *All That We Can Be: Black Leadership and Racial Integration the Army Way.* New York: Basic

Off. Fed. Contract Compliance. 2002. *Facts on Executive Order 11246—affirmative action.* http://www.dol.gov/esa/regs/compliance/ofccp/aa.htm

Oppenheimer D. 1989. Distinguishing five models of affirmative action. *Berkeley Women's Law J.* 4:42–61

Orfield G. 2001. Schools more separate: consequences of a decade of resegregation. Final Rep., Harvard Univ. Civil Rights Proj., Cambridge, MA. http://www.civilrightsproject.harvard.edu/research/deseg/separate_schools01.php

Orfield G, Eaton SE. 1996. *Dismantling Desegregation: The Quiet Reversal of Brown v. Board of Education.* New York: New Press

Orfield G, Kurlaender M, eds. 2001. *Diversity Challenged: Evidence on the Impact of*

Affirmative Action. Cambridge, MA: Harvard Univ. Civil Rights Proj.

Orfield G, Whitla D. 2001. Diversity and legal education: student experiences in leading law schools. See Orfield & Kurlaender 2001, pp. 143–74

Pager D. 2003. The mark of a criminal record. *Am. J. Sociol.* 108:937–75

Patterson O. 1997. *The Ordeal of Integration*. Washington, DC: Civitas

Portes A, Landolt P. 1996. The downside of social capital. *Am. Prospect* 46:18–21, 94. http://epn.org/prospect/26/26-cnt2.html

Reskin BF. 1998. *The Realities of Affirmative Action*. Washington, DC: Am. Sociol. Assoc.

Reskin BF. 2001. Discrimination and its remedies. In *Sourcebook on Labor Market Research: Evolving Structures and Processes*, ed. I Berg, A Kalleberg, pp. 567–600. New York: Plenum

Reskin BF. 2002. Rethinking employment discrimination. In *The New Economic Sociology: Developments in an Emerging Field*, ed. MF Guillen, R Collins, P England, M Meyer, pp. 218–44. New York: Russell Sage

Robinson JO. 2001. *Affirmative Action: A Documentary History*. Westport, CT: Greenwood

Royster DA. 2003. *Race and the Invisible Hand*. Berkeley: Univ. Calif. Press

Ryan J, Hawdon J, Branick A. 2002. The political economy of diversity: diversity programs in Fortune 500 companies. *Sociol. Res. Online* 7(1). http://www.socresonline.org.uk/7/1/ryan.htm

Sander RH. 2003. Colleges will just disguise racial quotas. *LA Times*, June 30

Sander RH. 2004. A systemic analysis of affirmative action in law schools. *Stanford Law Rev.* 57:367–483

Schuman H, Steeh C, Bobo LD, Krysan M. 1997. *Racial Attitudes in America: Trends and Interpretations*. Cambridge, MA: Harvard Univ. Press

Skrentny JD. 1996. *The Ironies of Affirmative Action: Politics, Culture, and Justice in America*. Chicago: Univ. Chicago Press

Skrentny JD, ed. 2001. *Color Lines: Affirmative Action, Immigration, and Civil Rights Options for America*. Chicago: Univ. Chicago Press

Skrentny JD. 2002. *The Minority Rights Revolution*. Cambridge, MA: Harvard Univ. Press

Son Hing LS, Bobocel DR, Zanna MP. 2002. Meritocracy and opposition to affirmative action: making concessions in the face of discrimination. *J. Pers. Soc. Psychol.* 83:493–509

Sowell T. 1972. *Black Education*. New York: David McKay

Sowell T. 2004. *Affirmative Action Around the World: An Empirical Study*. New Haven, CT: Yale Univ. Press

Steele S. 1991. *The Content of Our Character*. New York: Harper Perennial

Stephanopoulos G, Edley C. 1995. *Affirmative Action Review. A Report to the President*. Washington, DC: US Gov. Print. Off.

Stohr G. 2004. *A Black and White Case: How Affirmative Action Survived Its Greatest Legal Challenge*. Princeton, NJ: Bloomberg

Stryker R. 2001. Disparate impact and the quota debates: law, labor market sociology, and equal employment policies. *Sociol. Q.* 42:13–46

Stryker R, Scarpellino M, Holtzman M. 1999. Political culture wars 1990s style: the drum beat of quotas in media framing of the Civil Rights Act of 1991. *Res. Soc. Strat. Mobil.* 17:33–106

Sturm S. 2001. Second generation employment discrimination: a structural approach. *Columbia Law Rev.* 101:458–568

Swain CM. 2001. Affirmative action: legislative history, judicial interpretations, public consensus. In *America Becoming: Racial Trends and Their Consequences*, ed. NJ Smelser, WJ Wilson, F Mitchell, pp. 318–47. Washington, DC: Natl. Acad. Press

Swain CM, Greene KR, Wotipka CM. 2001. Understanding racial polarization on affirmative action: the view from focus groups. See Skrentny 2001, pp. 214–37

Teles SM. 1998. Why is there no affirmative action in Britain? *Am. Behav. Sci.* 41(7):1004–27

Thernstrom S, Thernstrom A. 1997. *America in Black and White*. New York: Simon & Schuster

Tienda M, Leicht KT, Sullivan T, Maltese M, Lloyd K. 2003. *Closing the gap? Admissions and enrollments at the Texas public flagships before and after* affirmative action. Work. Pap. No. 2003-01, Off. Popul. Res., Princeton Univ. http://www.texastop 10.princeton.edu/publications/tienda012103. pdf

Turner MA, Fix M, Struyk RJ. 1991. *Opportunities denied, opportunities diminished: race discrimination in hiring*. Work. Pap., Urban Inst., Washington, DC

US Bur. Census. 2000. *QT-P25. Class of worker by sex, place of work, and veteran status: 2000*. http://factfinder.census.gov

US Bur. Census. 2004. *Statistical Abstract of the United States*. http://www.census.gov/ prod/www/statistical-abstract-04.html

US Dep. Labor, Off. Disabil. Employ. Policy. 2003. *Affirmative action and people with disabilities*. http://www.dol.gov/ odep/pubs/ek98/affirmat.htm

US EEOC. 2004. *Indicators of Equal Employment Opportunity—Status and Trends*. Washington, DC: US Equal Employ. Oppor. Comm.

Van Slyke D, Tan A, Orland M. 1994. *School Finance Litigation: A Review of Key Cases*. Washington, DC: Finance Project

Welch F. 1989. Affirmative action and discrimination. In *The Question of Discrimination: Racial Inequality in the U.S. Labor Market*, ed. S Schulman, W Darity Jr, pp. 153–89. Middletown, CT: Wesleyan Univ. Press

Welch S, Gruhl J. 1998. Affirmative action and minority enrollments in medical and law schools. *Ohio State Law J.* 59:607–732

Whitla DK, Orfield G, Silen W, Teperow C, Howard C, Reede J. 2003. Educational benefits of diversity in medical school: a survey of students. *Acad. Med.* 78:460–66

Wierzbicki S, Hirschman C. 2002. *The end of affirmative action in Washington State and its impact on the transition from high school to college*. Presented at Annu. Meet. Pop. Assoc. Am., Atlanta, GA

Wightman LF. 1997. The threat to diversity in legal education: an empirical analysis of the consequences of abandoning race as a factor in law school admission decisions. *NY Univ. Law Rev.* 72:1–53

Wilson WJ. 1996. *When Work Disappears*. New York: Knopf

Wilson WJ. 1999. *Bridge Over the Racial Divide*. Berkeley: Univ. Calif. Press

Zemans FK. 1983. Legal mobilization: the neglected role of the law in the political system. *Am. Polit. Sci. Rev.* 77:690–703

Annu. Rev. Sociol. 2005. 31:381–99
doi: 10.1146/annurev.soc.31.041304.122317
Copyright © 2005 by Annual Reviews. All rights reserved
First published online as a Review in Advance on April 7, 2005

EMERGING THEORIES OF CARE WORK

Paula England

Department of Sociology, Stanford University, Stanford, California 94305-2047;
email: pengland@stanford.edu

Key Words   gender, motherhood, work, inequality, feminism

■ **Abstract**   Care work is done in the home as well as in markets for pay. Five theoretical frameworks have been developed to conceptualize care work; the frameworks sometimes offer competing answers to the same questions, and other times address distinct questions. The "devaluation" perspective argues that care work is badly rewarded because care is associated with women, and often women of color. The "public good" framework points out that care work provides benefits far beyond those to the direct recipient and suggests that the low pay of care work is a special case of the failure of markets to reward public goods. The "prisoner of love" framework argues that the intrinsic caring motives of care workers allow employers to more easily get away with paying care workers less. Instead of seeing the emotional satisfactions of giving care as its own reward, the "commodification of emotion" framework focuses on emotional harm to workers when they have to sell services that use an intimate part of themselves. The "love *and* money" framework argues against dichotomous views in which markets are seen as antithetical to true care.

INTRODUCTION

Some jobs involve providing care for pay; child care providers, teachers, nurses, doctors, and therapists all provide care. Some care is provided without pay; for example, parents rear their children and adults care for their disabled kin. This review surveys emerging scholarship on paid and unpaid care work. Most of it comes from gender scholars. They take an interest because women do such a high proportion of paid and unpaid care work, so that how well a society rewards care work impacts gender inequality. But gender arrangements also affect how care is provided; increasing women's employment means that more of the care of children and disabled elders is provided by paid workers rather than unpaid female family members.

I review both empirical and theoretical work, but organize my discussion around five conceptual frameworks deployed in the literature. I evaluate their logic as well as how well they fit available empirical evidence. In some cases, these frameworks offer different (competing or complementary) answers to the same questions. In other cases, they address distinct questions. The "devaluation" framework emphasizes that cultural biases limit both wages and state support for care work because

0360-0572/05/0811-0381$20.00   **381** of its association with women. It addresses the question of why care work has low pay relative to its skill demands. The "public good" framework emphasizes the indirect benefits of care work to people other than the direct recipients of care. This answers questions about the benefits of care work, but also speaks to why it is difficult for care workers to be paid commensurate with these public benefits. The "prisoner of love" framework emphasizes altruistic motivations for and intrinsic rewards of care work and that these may lead care workers to accept low pay. Thus, it also offers an explanation for the low pay of care work. The devaluation, public good, and prisoner of love frameworks all suggest that the low rewards of care work may lead to an inadequate supply of care labor. The "commodification of emotion" framework argues that service work done for pay forces workers to alienate themselves from their true feelings, and argues that global capitalist penetration leads to a care gap between the haves and the have nots. Although this framework is not aimed at explaining the low pay of care work relative to other work, it does paint a different picture of the experience of doing care work. The prisoner of love framework focuses on the intrinsic rewards of altruism, whereas the commodification of emotion framework sees care work as even more alienating than other kinds of work. The "love *and* money" framework rejects the dualism that assumes markets are inherently pervaded by narrow selfishness and corrupt altruistic motives, while assuming that families, nonprofit institutions, and informal groups are wellsprings of genuine care. Against the prisoner of love framework, it argues that low pay is not a necessary result of the altruistic rewards of work. Against the commodification of emotion framework, it rejects the idea that work involving care is inherently more alienating than other work.

GENDER BIAS AND THE DEVALUATION OF CARE WORK

The gender gap in pay is the result more of men and women working in different jobs than of the sexes being paid differently in the same work (Petersen & Morgan 1995). Research on comparable worth shows that predominantly female jobs pay less than male jobs, after adjusting for measurable differences in educational requirements, skill levels, and working conditions (England 1992, Kilbourne et al. 1994, Sorensen 1994, Steinberg 2001, Steinberg et al. 1986). These penalties are experienced by both men and women in predominantly female occupations, but because women are disproportionately represented in these occupations, these penalties contribute to the gender gap in pay. Authors documenting these penalties have proposed the devaluation framework as an explanation of the relatively low pay of female occupations, including those involving care. Cultural ideas deprecate women and thus, by cognitive association, devalue work typically done by women. This association leads to cognitive errors in which decision makers underestimate the contribution of female jobs to organizational goals, including profits. It may also lead to normative beliefs that those doing male jobs deserve higher pay. These cultural biases probably have their strongest effect when new jobs are being instituted in the economy. Once relative wage scales are set up, disparities are perpetuated by organizational inertia in jobs' relative wage rates, or the use of market surveys of wages in other firms to set jobs' pay levels.

Extending this devaluation view, some argue that female-dominated jobs involving care are especially devalued because care is the quintessentially female-identified activity (Cancian & Oliker 2000, England & Folbre 1999, England et al. 2002). To test this, researchers examined whether those in care work earn less than other workers after controlling for jobs' requirements for education, skill, and working conditions, and even their sex composition. For example, England (1992, chapter 3) examined the relative pay of a broader category called nurturant work. In addition to including the things called care work, such as child care work, teaching, nursing, and therapy, this category included all jobs involving giving a face-to-face service to clients or customers of the organization for which one works. Thus, it included jobs such as sales workers, ushers, waiters, and receptionists. In retrospect, I think a better term for what England was measuring is Leidner's (1993) term, "interactive service work." Using 1980 Census data, with detailed Census occupational titles, England (1992) found that occupations involving interactive service work had a pay penalty; a 1990 replication found the same results (England et al. 2001). These penalties are net of the sex composition of the occupation. Other research has examined the returns to the kinds of social skills used in care work. In an analysis of the New York State civil service jobs, Steinberg et al. (1986, p. 152) found that jobs involving communication with the public and group facilitation paid less than other jobs, net of skill demands. Kilbourne et al. (1994) developed a scale to measure nurturant skill, largely from measures in the *Dictionary of Occupational Titles*, assessing whether jobs involve dealing with people and communication. They found that, other things being equal, workers in such occupations suffered a wage penalty.

In more recent work, England and colleagues (2002) operationalized care work as those occupations providing a service to people that helps develop their capabilities. The main categories of jobs termed care work were child care, all levels of teaching (from preschool through university professors), and health care workers of all types (nurses aides, nurses, doctors, physical and psychological therapists).[1] Controlling for skill demands, educational requirements, industry, and sex composition, we found a net penalty of 5%–10% for working in an occupation involving care (one exception was nursing, which did not seem to experience the pay penalty of other care work). Thus, overall the evidence suggests that care work pays less than we would expect, given its educational and other requirements. This finding is consistent with the devaluation framework, although there is no direct evidence that the mechanism is the cultural devaluation of jobs because they are filled largely with women and subsequent institutionalization of this devaluation in wage structures.

---

[1]The difference between this measure (in England et al. 2002) and the measure called nuturant work (England 1992) is that the latter includes interactive service work such as retail sales, receptionists, and waitressing.

The devaluation perspective can be applied to race as well as to gender. Although paid care work requiring a college degree is done largely by white women, much care work without such requirements is done by women of color, some of whom are immigrants (Hondagneu-Sotelo 2001, Misra 2003, Romero 1992). The work done by these women is the lowest paid. Is the relative pay of this work influenced by racist assumptions that devalue work associated with people of color? Kmec (2002) has documented that jobs with a higher proportion of minority workers pay less, net of workers' education. However, the study was not able to use the detailed controls for occupational demands used in the gender devaluation literature because of data limitations, so this conclusion is provisional.

But what about unpaid care work, the most time-intensive example of which is parenting? Women do the lion's share of parental work. Recent data show that women spend about twice as much time as men in childrearing in married couple families (Sayer et al. 2004). How are women economically supported while they are raising children and either not employed or employed less fully for pay than they otherwise would be? The traditional answer is that they are supported by their husbands. But what about mothers without husbands or cohabitational partners? This is a growing group in all industrial societies owing to increased divorce and nonmarital births. If these women are not supported by their own earnings or child support voluntarily supplied by the fathers of their children, then they are supported by the state or state-mandated child support.

Scholarship on gender and the welfare state focuses on how much the state provides public support for such women and their children through direct payments, child allowances (received by married couples as well in affluent nations other than the United States), and state-supported child and health care (O'Connor et al. 1999, Orloff 1996, Sainsbury 2001). The conceptual framework of devaluation of activities associated with women is present in this literature as well, although the term devaluation is typically not used. But as gender scholars have pointed out, gendered assumptions are built into welfare states—that men can be relied upon to support their families and thus that the forms of economic insecurity the state needs to address are those that occur to men, such as unemployment because of disability or economic downturns and the need to retire in old age. Benefits are often conditioned on prior employment. They often offer little for the mother without prior employment because she has been caring for her children. Or if she has a claim to retirement benefits, it is based on marriage rather than care. Payments to lone mothers are not only smaller, but they are much more controversial, especially in the United States. Indeed, the Personal Responsibility and Work Opportunity Reconciliation Act of 1996, usually called welfare reform, eliminated a federal entitlement of those meeting the means test to welfare, and allowed states to institute lifetime time limits on welfare receipt. The fact that welfare recipients are disproportionately women of color may further erode public support for welfare. Overall, it seems that what men do is seen as a basis of citizenship rights more than what women do (Glenn 2000). This difference in treatment is consistent with the devaluation perspective, suggesting that the same cultural processes of devaluing activities associated with women and persons of color are reflected in political decisions of the state.

CARE AS PUBLIC GOOD PRODUCTION

All work is of some benefit to someone, or it would not be done. But some scholars have argued that both paid and unpaid care work have more indirect social benefits than other kinds of work. Economists define public goods as those that have benefits from which it is impossible to exclude people who do not pay. Even staunch neoclassical economists recognize that, in the case of public goods, because the social return is greater than the private return, markets will undersupply, and thus there is an argument for state provision. Education is the classic example. Although there are private returns to those receiving the education (e.g., increased earnings), there are much more diffuse spillover effects that encourage economic growth. Coleman (1993) argued that society has an interest in how well parents do the job of parenting, and he suggested that to get the incentives right, the state should offer payments to parents based on whether their children turn into a net benefit or drag on society. Recently, gender scholars have pointed out that all care work, paid and unpaid, may create public goods. Folbre (1994a, 2001) argues that having and rearing children benefit people in society other than the children themselves. England et al. (2002) made an analogous argument about paid care work. This social benefit is at the core of the public good framework.

Care work, whether paid or unpaid, often includes investment in the capabilities of recipients. At issue is not only how care imbues cognitive skills that increase earnings, but more broadly that receiving care also helps recipients develop skills, values, and habits that benefit themselves and others (England & Folbre 2000). Care helps recipients develop capabilities for labor market success as well as for healthy relationships as a parent, friend, or spouse. Care contributes to the intellectual, physical, and emotional capabilities of recipients. These capabilities contribute to recipients' own and others' development and happiness. The benefits that accrue to the direct recipient also benefit indirect recipients. The direct beneficiaries of care are the student who is taught, the patient of the nurse or doctor, the client of the therapist, and the child cared for by a parent or child care worker. But when a direct recipient of care learns cognitive skills, stays or gets healthy, learns how to get along with others, or learns habits of self-control, others also benefit.

The many benefits of care to indirect beneficiaries make it arguably a public good. But how do the benefits of care diffuse to indirect beneficiaries? Education is an obvious example. Schooling makes people more productive, increasing their later productivity in a job, which benefits the owner and customers of the employing organization. As another example, if a client in psychotherapy learns to listen deeply and articulate his wants in a nonblaming way, this is likely to benefit his spouse, children, friends, and coworkers.

In the 1970s, Marxist feminists made a similar but narrower point (Dalla Costa & James 1972). They argued that homemakers were among those exploited by capitalists because their caretaking of their husbands and children made the current and next generation of workers more productive. Thus, in making profits, capitalists extract surplus value from homemakers as well as from paid workers. Those proposing the broader public good framework for care work do not necessarily subscribe to the Marxist labor theory of value. They see the indirect beneficiaries of care to be all of us, not merely capitalist employers. If children given love and taught patience and trustworthiness turn out to be better spouses when they grow up, their spouses benefit. If they are better parents, their children benefit. If they are better neighbors, the social capital of the community increases. If they become good Samaritans rather than predators, safety goes up, and the costs of building and maintaining prisons go down, benefiting their fellow citizens. Benefits to all these indirect recipients accrue because care workers help develop the capabilities of direct beneficiaries, and these beneficiaries spread them through social interaction. The extent to which benefits of caring labor will go beyond the direct beneficiary to others depends, in part, on how altruistic the beneficiary is—which is often a function of the kind of care she or he received.

The claim that care work, more than other kinds of work, produces public goods hinges mainly on the fact that care work involves a higher ratio of investment in capabilities than production of items immediately consumed.[2] For example, the manager of a toy manufacturing plant, as well as the secretaries, janitors, and assembly workers in the firm, and the sales people selling toys contribute to providing something (toys) that consumers enjoy. But it is unclear that providing toys to a child leads him or her to later provide benefits to others. You could substitute those who produce clothes, makeup, furniture, and so forth for those providing toys.[3] By contrast, the care-giving functions of teaching a child discipline and reading and of providing her with healthcare are much surer to lead to benefits for others.

On the central claim of the public good framework for understanding care—that paid or unpaid care work creates diffuse social benefits beyond its immediate beneficiaries—there is no direct confirmatory or disconfirmatory evidence, nor has a relevant research strategy been proposed. The evidence is largely indirect. First, there is some evidence for a public good aspect to fertility (Lee & Miller 1990). That is, the costs of rearing children, especially in the United States, are borne

---

[2]This is not to deny a consumption as well as investment aspect of receiving care. For example, the fun a child has playing with his or her babysitter may make the child happier immediately without increasing his or her long-term capabilities. And care of an elderly person beyond a certain age is no longer an investment in future capabilities but a provision of comfort to increase the quality of his or her life now. Nonetheless, the claim is that the ratio of investment to consumption is higher with care work.

[3]One can imagine some noncare jobs that provide goods that increase recipients' capabilities as much as care work, and thus may create diffuse benefits for indirect recipients as well. For example, those who produce nutritious food, products that increase our health, or educational toys and books arguably contribute to human capabilities and thus lead to the same social interaction multipliers.

mostly privately (except for public education). But, with the pay-as-you-go Social Security system in the United States, as soon as children reach the age to have earnings, they contribute to the retirement of their parents' generation through the Social Security payroll tax (Lee & Miller 1990). Thus, because few of the costs (except school) of childrearing have been collectivized, but one of the major economic benefits of having children (their support for their elders in retirement) has been collectivized, having and rearing children has benefits for the viability of the Social Security system (Folbre 1994b). Second, there is evidence of social benefits of education—benefits to other individuals that go beyond the earning power of those who are educated (Bowen 1977, Wolfe & Wolfe 2003).

The low wages of care work can also be seen as indirect evidence that care produces public goods. In the previous section, research documenting a care penalty was presented as evidence for the devaluation perspective, arguing that care work pays less than we would otherwise expect because of its association with women. Another possible explanation for the wage penalty in care work is the public good aspect of the work. The standard economic argument is that public goods will be underprovided by markets because there is no way to capture and turn into profits (or wages, we might note) the benefits that come through social interaction. How could the school teacher, through market forces, get a return from the future spouse or child of her student, who benefits from the student's enhanced earnings? How can a parent receive payment from all the retirees on Social Security whose checks are financed from her child's wages? (She may collect Social Security herself, but note that she would get the same benefit if she had never had the child.) But if some social process (anomalous to economists) does recruit people into care jobs, we would expect that the wage will not reflect the diffuse social benefits of the work. Those using the public good framework have pointed to the low net wages of care work as evidence that care work creates public benefits not reflected in the wage received (England & Folbre 1999, England et al. 2002).

The public good framework has also been used to interpret policy implications of the wage penalty for motherhood. Several recent studies find a wage penalty for motherhood in the United States (Budig & England 2001; Lundberg & Rose 2000; Neumark & Korenman 1994; Waldfogel 1997, 1998a,b). A motherhood penalty has also been found in the United Kingdom (Harkness & Waldfogel 1999, Joshi & Newell 1989) and Germany (Harkness & Waldfogel 1999). Why do mothers earn less? First, although mothers have very high rates of employment today [for example, over 40% of women with children under one year of age are in the labor force (Klerman & Leibowitz 1999)], many women still lose at least some employment time to childrearing (Cohen & Bianchi 1999, Klerman & Leibowitz 1999). Women have no earnings while they are not employed, reducing their lifetime earnings and affecting their pensions. Intermittent employment also affects women's wage level when they return to work because employers reward experience and seniority. Budig & England (2001) found that about 40% of the motherhood wage penalty results from moms losing experience and seniority. Another portion of the motherhood penalty comes from the minority of moms who work part-time and that part-time work generally pays less per hour (Budig & England 2001, Waldfogel 1997). After experience, seniority, part-time status, and many job characteristics are controlled, there is still a residual penalty for being a mother (Budig & England 2001, Waldfogel 1997). This residual penalty could be an effect of motherhood on productivity. But a recent experimental study provides evidence that some of it is discrimination by employers against mothers. Correll & Benard (2004) asked students to help screen applications for a job. Subjects were told that a company was hiring for a mid-level marketing position in a telecommunications company, that the company wanted feedback from younger adults because they are heavy users of communications technology, and that the company would incorporate their rating when making hiring decisions. They evaluated resumes of fictitious applicants (presented to them as real applicants), indicating whom they would hire and at what salary. Compared with female applicants whose resume mentioned no children, those mentioning small children were less often recommended for hire and, if recommended, were offered lower starting salaries (Correll & Benard 2004).[4]

What does the relative pay of mothers compared with other women have to do with public goods? The research reviewed above clarifies how various labor market processes in our economy—the return to continuous labor market experience, the lower hourly pay of part-time work, and employers' discrimination between mothers and nonmothers—disadvantage mothers. But Budig & England (2001) argue that if the unpaid care work that goes with motherhood is creating a public good, then the inequity is more unjust and the state should intervene to lessen the penalty. For example, the state could prohibit discrimination based on motherhood (Williams & Segal 2003). Another possibility is for the state to mandate that employers hold the jobs of workers who take parental leave after the birth or adoption of a child. Although the Family and Medical Leave Act of 1993 requires this, the mandated leave is unpaid, it is only for six weeks, and small firms are exempted. Gornick & Meyers (2003) argue for public policies that provide state payments for (gender-neutral) parenthood leave for a few months. In their scheme, employers are required to hold jobs (so that previously accrued seniority rights are preserved), and the state provides replacement of a certain proportion of the

---

[4]An interesting question, beyond the scope of Correll & Benard's study, is whether this discrimination is statistical or based on erroneous information about group differences. That is, one possibility is that motherhood does affect productivity on the job (especially given the limited parenting work done by many fathers), and employers know this, so, on the basis of this generalization, they discriminate against all mothers because, although they lose some excellent workers that way, the generalization has enough truth to it that they gain more than it would cost them to measure productivity individually before hire. In this case, it is statistical discrimination. Another possibility is that a cognitive bias exists; employers are incorrect about the group differences in productivity. Something between these two possibilities may be occuring as well. For discussion on the legal status of the motherhood penalty, see Budig & England (2001) and Williams & Segal (2003). Correll & Benard did not find men to suffer a fatherhood penalty, and analyses of survey data show that men's earnings go up after having a child (Lundberg & Rose 2000).

wage. Their proposals are based, in part, on the public good argument, as well as on evidence of how such policies have worked in European nations.

CARING MOTIVES AND PRISONERS OF LOVE

What's love got to do with it? Does genuine care or altruism motivate care work and provide some intrinsic reward for those who do it? Feminist writings on care contain both an insistence that care work really is hard work, as well as a concern for the negative consequences for society if we lose truly caring motivations for care work. Sometimes the word care itself is used to describe a motive or a moral imperative (Noddings 1984, Tronto 1987). Leira (1994) and Waerness (1987) emphasize the ways care work departs from traditional economistic views, which define work as an activity performed despite its intrinsic disutility, simply in order to earn money. According to Abel & Nelson (1990, p. 4), "caregiving is an activity encompassing both instrumental tasks and affective relations. Despite the classic Parsonian distinction between these two modes of behavior, caregivers are expected to provide love as well as labor." Cancian & Oliker (2000, p. 2) define caring as a combination of feelings and actions that "provide responsively for an individual's personal needs or well-being, in a face-to-face relationship." Folbre has defined caring labor as work that provides services based on sustained personal (usually face-to-face) interaction, and is motivated (at least in part) by concern about the recipient's welfare (Folbre 1995, Folbre & Weisskopf 1998). Stone (2000) talks about how professional care workers (e.g., nurses) often want to talk to patients and show them real love but are frustrated by bureaucratic requirements that make this difficult. Implicit in much of this discussion is the idea that the recipients of care will be better off if the person giving care really cares about them than if they are motivated strictly by money.

What is the effect on the care workers' wage of having some altruism as one of the motivations for doing care work? When neoclassical economists confront evidence of the pay penalty in care work, they generally suggest that the correct explanation lies in the theory of compensating differentials (e.g., Filer 1989). (See England 1992, pp. 69–73, and Jacobs & Steinberg 1990 for criticisms of the claim that this theory explains the low pay of most female jobs.) The theory calls attention to differences between jobs in their intrinsic rewards or penalties. Nonpecuniary amenities or disamenities will affect how many people are willing to work in a job at any given wage. Thus, according to the theory, employers will have to pay more to compensate for nonpecuniary disamenities of jobs, and they can hire for less in jobs with nonpecuniary amenities, all else equal. Of course, there is variation in tastes among workers. The theory says that if the marginal worker sees the intrinsic properties of the work as an amenity, this permits a lower wage. If the marginal worker sees the work as onerous compared with other jobs, the employer will have to pay a higher wage to fill the job. In this view, if the marginal worker to caring occupations finds satisfaction in helping people, this will allow employers to fill the jobs with lower pay than in comparable jobs without the helping component.

More simply put, the low pay may be made up for by the intrinsic fulfillment of the jobs. Indeed, this is the common economists' alternative to the claim that care is paid less (relative to skill) because of devaluation. Because neither the tastes of the marginal worker nor employers' processes of devaluation are observed, empirical evidence cannot adjudicate between the two views. In this orthodox neoclassical view, there is no policy problem with the low wages of care work; if women do not find the intrinsic rewards to make up for the low pay, they will enter other jobs. If they cannot find other types of jobs because of hiring discrimination, then economists see that as the problem policy should address, rather than the relative pay of care work.[5]

Folbre (2001) has coined the term prisoner of love for this effect of care workers' caring motives on their pay. But her model differs from the standard economic view of compensating differentials in seeing altruistic preferences as at least in part endogenous to doing the work. Rational choice theorists, including economists, generally assume preferences to be exogenous and unchanging. But paid care workers may become attached to care recipients after they start the job, and this may make it difficult for them to withhold their services in order to demand more remuneration for them (England & Folbre 2003, Himmelweit 1999). Evidence of the impact of jobs on workers comes from the research of Kohn and others, who suggest that individuals in jobs requiring more intellectual skill get smarter (Kohn et al. 1983). Similarly, in jobs requiring care, individuals may become more caring. Although I know of no evidence of this, it makes sense that child care workers become attached to the toddlers they see every day, nurses empathize with their patients, and teachers worry about their students. These emotional bonds put care workers in a vulnerable position, discouraging them from demanding higher wages or changes in working conditions that might have adverse effects on care recipients. A kind of emotional hostage effect occurs.

Owners, employers, and managers are less likely to have direct contact with clients or patients than are care workers. Therefore, they can generally engage in cost-cutting strategies without feeling their consequences. Sometimes they can even be confident that adverse effects of their decisions on clients will be reduced by workers' willingness to make personal sacrifices to maintain high-quality care. For instance, workers may respond to cutbacks in staffing levels by intensifying their effort or agreeing to work overtime. This perspective suggests an equity problem of taking advantage of altruistic motives. It also suggests that if the motives are endogenous to doing the work, and people realize this, women may increasingly forego such work because they know they will become prisoners of love. It is like the decision not to have a child because one knows it is too taxing to be a

---

[5]Economists also point to excess supply as a cause of the low pay in some jobs. However, this is hard to argue for the care sector because there are many exogenous sources of increasing demand. For example, the aging population covered by Medicare increases the need for medical care, and women's increased employment increases the need for child care and other services that substitute for homemakers' production.

good parent. As more women have the option to choose non-care work to avoid becoming prisoners of love, the supply of care work may be jeopardized.

The prisoner of love phenomenon applies not only to paid work, but also to struggles between mothers, fathers, and the state. Although mother love (and father love) may spring partly from nature, they are undoubtedly cultivated by the experience of providing care to one's child. If this is true, then gendered practices that assign child care to mothers mean that mothers will develop greater caring for their children than either their male partners or others. In the case of divorce, one way to understand men's failure to pay child support is that they know they can count on the mother's willingness to care for the child anyhow and share her money with the child—rather than to retaliate by abandoning the child. In matters of welfare reform, we can also see mothers as prisoners of love. If they did not care about their children, they could bargain more successfully with the state for higher welfare payments by threatening to put their children in foster care. The state pays foster parents much more than it pays welfare mothers—precisely because mothers' love and sense of obligation to their children can be counted on even in the absence of pay. Thus, state actors would not see such a threat by mothers as credible; they are prisoners of their love for their children.

THE COMMODIFICATION OF EMOTION

What happens when care is a commodity? The idea that the provision of care through markets may harm those who do the work is identified largely with Hochschild (1983), who coined the term emotional labor in *The Managed Heart*. She emphasized how being recruited by capitalists to sell one's emotion is harmful to workers. *The Managed Heart* was largely a study of the occupation of flight attendants, based on interviews with flight attendants and those who devise their training, and on observation of the training. Hochschild was struck by how flight attendants were taught to display feelings that they did not actually feel—to be cheerful even when sad, deferential to passengers even when furious at their disrespectful behavior. She argued that many jobs in the new service economy require workers to act emotions they do not really feel. Sometimes they even require deep acting, where the actor comes to feel the feelings prescribed. (See Smith-Lovin 1998 and Steinberg & Figart 1999 for reviews of research following the lead of Hochschild.) Whereas the prisoner of love view focuses on how care work is emotionally satisfying—so much so that workers will take a lower wage—Hochschild worried about psychological distress from deep acting. That is, one theory sees nonpecuniary amenities and the other disamenities of care work. Wharton has conducted a number of empirical tests to see if those in jobs requiring emotional labor have lower job satisfaction or worse mental health. In general, she did not find this (Wharton 1993, 1999), and found some evidence that many workers like the social interaction their jobs afford them. Under certain circumstances, however, emotional labor was taxing, as when workers had to combine emotional labor with low control and autonomy (Wharton 1999).

In more recent work, Hochschild (2000; 2003, especially chapter 14) has focused on the global penetration of capitalist market forces, and how they have special consequences for women and their families in poor countries. Her focus is on women who migrate from poor to rich countries to take jobs as nannies (see also Hondagneu-Sotelo 2001, Romero 1992). Some of these women have left their own children at home with kin to come to work in a richer country for a better economic future for their families. It is very poignant that they care for affluent, usually white, American children while their own children are left back home to experience their mother's love only through memory. The situation is similar to that of African American women in earlier periods who cared for white children in white homes, while leaving their own children at home, except that here children are not across town but across the world, only seldom visited. This situation is encouraged by the increased employment of well-educated American women (who then need child care for their children) and the large disparity between the wages available in poor and rich nations (one motivation for migration). One could use Hochschild's earlier work on emotional labor to analyze how taxing it is to have to feign love for someone else's children. But Hochschild finds even more poignant the cases in which nannies come to really love their American charges and feel closer to them than to their own children, given the distance. She describes the First World as extracting love from the Third World, and sees it as analogous to extraction of raw materials by colonial powers. She worries that Third World children pay the price, although she does not provide evidence that the children whose mothers come are worse off than they would be if their mothers stayed—that is, that the trade-off between losing their mothers' time and gaining the money their mothers earned was not worth it.

Just as we can ask of the public good view how we know that other kinds of work do not provide diffuse benefits as much as care, one can ask of Hochschild's view how we know that care work is more alienating than other kinds of work. After all, the vast majority of male immigrant workers and many women immigrants are not nannies, but rather clean houses or work in factories or restaurants. Some of them, too, have left wives or children at home. So what is unique about international migration is not doing care work or leaving children behind. Hochschild's answer, somewhat implicit, is that it is always alienating and exploitative when one has to sell one's labor (in this sense she draws on Marx), but it is not as bad to sell the use of one's hands and head as to sell one's heart, and thus it is worse when employers in one country hire people from another to do care work than when they hire immigrants to do other kinds of work.

REJECTING THE DICHOTOMY BETWEEN LOVE AND MONEY

The love *and* money perspective rejects the idea of an oppositional dichotomy between the realms of love and self-interested economic action. Leading voices promoting this view are Nelson (1999; 2004; J. Nelson, unpublished manuscript) and Zelizer (2002a,b). They contest the deeply ingrained habit of dichotomizing spheres even when the evidence does not support this, a habit apparent in neo-classical economics as well as in Marxism. Nelson sees dichotomizing habits of thought as rooted in tacit assumptions about gender. Because male and female are seen as opposite, and because gender schema organize so much of our thinking, we develop a dualistic view that "women, love, altruism, and the family are, as a group, radically separate and opposite from men, self-interested rationality, work, and market exchange" (Nelson & England 2002). Zelizer (2002a) calls this the "hostile worlds" view.

In this dichotomizing scheme that Nelson and Zelizer are contesting, we cannot pay care workers well and still get people doing the work who bring genuine, felt care to the work. Moreover, profit-making firms or waged labor can only contaminate or erode love. Feminist economist Himmelweit (1999), while acknowledging that care workers sometimes show genuine care, relies on this same dichotomy when she says that genuine care remains if it resists complete commodification. Hochschild's (1983) view of the perils of commodification seems to draw from this oppositional imagery to conclude that workers are harmed when they have to sell a part of themselves, and that this is worse the more intimate the part of the self involved. Held (2002) supports decent pay for care work, but argues that true values of care can only be maintained if such work is not in the private sector, where she believes that the bottom line prevails, but rather is kept in the non-profit or governmental sector (Held 2002). Thus, she, too, assumes the polarity of spheres that Nelson and Zelizer critique, but makes the good pole (for purposes of organizing paid care work) the nonprofit and state sectors.

Zelizer and Nelson argue that the claim that only profits and self-interest rule in the market, while more caring values rule in families, nonprofits, or governments, is an assumption that authors often feel no need to document. Zelizer (2002b) contests this assumption, arguing that culture often rules in such matters, so that norms specify the way that money and sentiment can be combined for particular kinds of ties. Nelson (2004; J. Nelson, unpublished manuscript) rejects the idea that the well-being of workers or care recipients is determined so readily by whether it is in the capitalist market sector or other sectors such as the private family, nonprofit organizations, or the state. After all, gender scholars have shown the patriarchal nature of the family in many social settings, as well as the tendency of the welfare state to devalue women's care work as a basis for citizenship rights. Nelson (2004; J. Nelson, unpublished manuscript) does not want to see the private sector let off the hook, and she thinks there is some cause for optimism. Just as individual workers combine motives involving love and money, she argues that, both neoclassical and Marxist theory notwithstanding, it is possible that private-sector firms can operate with a simultaneous eye to profits and other values—fair pay for workers, quality care services for clients even if they could be duped into less, and avoiding environmental degradation. Nelson (2004; J. Nelson, unpublished manuscript) and Zelizer (2002a,b) are not sanguine that this is a simple matter, but they believe that the dichotomizing hostile worlds view is an assumption rather than an empirically supported description of the world. Nelson (2004; see also Folbre & Nelson 1900, Nelson & England 2002) argues that we need empirical research to search for the mechanisms of specific problems rather than assumptions about oppositional spheres. Consider the question of whether it is possible for people to have access to adequate care by people whose motives are caring, or the question of whether we could change wage structures to get rid of the penalty for doing care work. Analysis should try to ascertain which particular structural or cultural features of behavior in markets, families, or states have which consequences, rather than assuming that solving these problems is impossible as long as care is done as waged work in private-sector firms.

Experimental psychologists and economists have studied the effects of payment on intrinsic motivation—willingness to expend effort on a task without extrinsic reward. Because doing care work for love or out of altruism is one example of intrinsic motivation, this line of research may apply to whether paying (more) for care work increases or decreases the supply of and quality of care. It should be noted, however, that none of the tasks in the experimental literature involved care work. The typical experiment involves children or college students in the laboratory asked to do a task that holds some intrinsic interest for many, with no reward offered at first. The experimentally manipulated variable is whether an extrinsic reward is offered later. The dependent variable of interest is how much subjects continue to undertake the task in a later period when no reward is offered to either experimental or control group. Studies often find that after being offered a reward for something, subjects do less of the task than they did in the earlier period when no reward was forthcoming. On this basis, some have argued that extrinsic rewards crowd out intrinsic motivation (Deci et al. 1999, Eisenberger & Cameron 1996, Frey & Jegen 2001). The underlying theory most psychologists use to understand this is to assume that individuals find autonomy and self-esteem inherently rewarding, and that when subjects have the sense that conditioning rewards on performance is controlling, they may associate the task with more negative affect and hence repeat it less. At first glance, this interpretation suggests that paying care workers might actually lead to less intrinsic care motivation—so that perhaps real care would be drained out of the workers by high pay. However, the ensuing research shows that this effect is conditional on circumstances. Many of the experiments discussed in this literature focus on the effect of crossing the highly charged symbolic divide between things done for no money at all versus those done for money, rather than on the effects of increases in pay. But a nonexperimental study of volunteer work suggests that, although offering any pay may reduce the hours of this work people do, once the zero point is crossed, higher pay increases the hours people do the semivolunteer work (Frey & Goette 1999). This suggests that, for care work that is already paid, raising the pay would have no adverse impact on intrinsic motivation. Furthermore, ensuing experimental research shows that the effects of extrinsic rewards are affected by the form they take (Eisenberger & Cameron 1996, Frey & Jegen 2001). The experiments suggest that extrinsic rewards that are seen as "controlling" reduce intrinsic motivation for a task, whereas those that are seen as "acknowledging" increase intrinsic motivation. Rewards that are seen as controlling are those coupled with close supervision or judgments by supervisors that raise questions about the recipients' competence and threaten their self-esteem. Acknowledging rewards are those that send the message that the recipient is trusted, respected, and appreciated (Frey 1998, Frey & Goette 1999, Frey & Jegen 2001). These results suggest that the more that pay is combined with trust and appreciation, the less it drives out genuine intrinsic motivation—especially important in care work. Furthermore, the experimental research shows that unexpected rewards increase intrinsic motivation more than expected rewards. This line of research exemplifies the love *and* money framework—it looks at specific mechanisms of achieving desireable results in care work, rather than assuming that the world is divided into two opposite systems.

CONCLUSION

Serious research on the care sector is just beginning. Several empirical generalizations have come out of the research: that an increasing amount of care is done by paid workers (rather than at home by women without pay); that women's unpaid care for their families is a more controversial basis for state support than men's employment or military service; that those who do care work for pay often report intrinsic motivations; and that paid care work pays less than would be predicted by its skill level, and even less than other predominantly female jobs at its skill level. There is a fair degree of consensus on these empirical generalizations. More challenging has been conceptualizing care with a theoretical apparatus that explains the source of these empirical regularities. Why do care workers earn less than those in similarly skilled jobs? Why is welfare controversial? Which method of organizing care best combines caring motives, an adequate supply of care, and an erasure of the economic penalty for care? Do love and money drive each other out?

I have organized this review around emergent theories about care work—five frameworks that offer differing perspectives on these questions. The devaluation perspective argues that care work is badly rewarded because the jobs are filled with women, and because care is associated with the quintessentially gendered role of mothering. The public good framework points out that care work provides benefits far beyond those to the direct recipient, and that it is hard to capture some of these benefits in the wage of the worker without state action to do so; in this view, this would be a problem even if care work were done by men. But the devaluation view may help us understand why it is so hard to get political consensus for state support of paid or unpaid carework—because it is done by women, and often women of color. The prisoner of love framework focuses on the genuine care that motivates some care workers, pointing out the cruel irony that these intrinsic motives may make it easier for employers to get away with paying care workers less. One framework sees the commodification of emotion as problematic. It focuses on harm to workers when they have to sell services that use an intimate part of themselves, and harm to children in poor nations when their mothers are under economic pressure to come to richer countries and leave them behind. In contradistinction to the idea that someone is always harmed when care is sold, the love *and* money framework argues against dichotomous views in which markets are seen as antithetical to true care, and against the view that true care can only be found in families, communities, nonprofit organizations, or state action. This framework calls for empirical studies to reveal which mechanisms cause specific problems, such as inadequate care available to those who need it, work rules that do not allow real care to be expressed, and low pay for care workers. This framework suggests that, rather than assuming a hostility between pay or profits and care, we should test the claims of the other conceptual frameworks discussed here, and some of their implications may be found to have merit. Women's employment is here to stay, and although much care will continue to be given by family members, much of the care given to children, the sick, and the elderly will be provided by paid care workers. How this sector is organized is consequential not just for gender, class, and race inequality, but for all of society.

The *Annual Review of Sociology* is online at http://soc.annualreviews.org

LITERATURE CITED

Abel E, Nelson M. 1990. *Circles of Care: Work and Identity in Women's Lives*. Albany: SUNY Press

Bowen HR. 1977. *Investment in Learning: The Individual and Social Value of American Higher Education*. San Francisco: Jossey-Bass

Budig MJ, England P. 2001. The wage penalty for motherhood. *Am. Sociol. Rev.* 66:204–25

Cancian FM, Oliker SJ. 2000. *Caring and Gender*. Thousand Oaks, CA: Pine Forge

Cohen PN, Bianchi SM. 1999. Marriage, children, and women's employment: What do we know? *Mon. Labor Rev.* 122:22–31

Coleman JS. 1993. The rational reconstruction of society. *Am. Sociol. Rev.* 58:1–15

Correll S, Benard S. 2004. *Getting a job: Is there a motherhood penalty?* Work. Pap., Dep. Sociol., Cornell Univ.

Dalla Costa M, James S. 1972. *The Power of Women and the Subversion of the Community*. Bristol, UK: Falling Wall

Deci EL, Koestner R, Ryan RM. 1999. A meta-analytic review of experiments examining the effects of extrinsic rewards on intrinsic motivation. *Psychol. Bull.* 125:627–68

Eisenberger R, Cameron J. 1996. Detrimental effects of reward: Reality or myth? *Am. Psychol.* 51:1153–66

England P. 1992. *Comparable Worth: Theories and Evidence*. New York: Aldine de Gruyter

England P, Budig MJ, Folbre N. 2002. Wages of virtue: the relative pay of care work. *Soc. Probl.* 49:455–73

England P, Folbre N. 1999. The cost of caring. *Ann. Am. Acad. Polit. Soc. Sci.* 561:39–51

England P, Folbre N. 2000. Reconceptualizing human capital. In *The Management of Durable Relations*, ed. W Raub, J Weesie, pp. 126–28. Amsterdam, The Neth.: Thela Thesis

England P, Folbre N. 2002. Care, inequality, and policy. In *Child Care and Inequality: Re-Thinking Carework for Children and Youth*, ed. FM Cancian, D Kurz, S London, R Reviere, M Tuominen, pp. 133–44. New York: Routledge

England P, Folbre N. 2003. Contracting for care. In *Feminist Economics Today*, ed.

J Nelson, M Ferber, pp. 61–80. Chicago: Univ. Chicago Press

England P, Thompson J, Aman C. 2001. The sex gap in pay and comparable worth: an update. In *Sourcebook of Labor Markets: Evolving Structures and Processes*, ed. I Berg, AL Kalleberg, pp. 551–65. New York: Kluwer Academic/Plenum

Filer R. 1989. Occupational segregation, compensating differentials, and comparable worth. In *Pay Equity: Empirical Inquiries*, ed. RT Michael, HI Harmann, B O'Farrell, pp. 153–70. Washington, DC: Natl. Acad. Press

Folbre N. 1994a. Children as public goods. *Am. Econ. Rev.* 84:86–90

Folbre N. 1994b. *Who Pays for the Kids? Gender and the Structures of Constraint.* New York: Routledge

Folbre N. 1995. "Holding hands at midnight": the paradox of caring labor. *Fem. Econ.* 1:73–92

Folbre N. 2001. *The Invisible Heart: Economics and Family Values.* New York: New Press

Folbre N, Nelson J. 2000. For love or money—or both? *J. Econ. Perspect.* 14:123–40

Folbre N, Weisskopf T. 1998. Did father know best? Families, markets and the supply of caring labor. In *Economics, Values and Organization*, ed. A Ben-Ner, L Putterman, pp. 171–205. New York: Cambridge Univ. Press

Frey BS. 1998. Institutions and morale: the crowding-out effect. In *Economics, Values, and Organization*, ed. A Ben-Ner, L Putterman, pp. 437–60. Cambridge, UK: Cambridge Univ. Press

Frey BS, Goette L. 1999. *Does pay motivate volunteers?* Work. Pap. Ser. No. 7, Inst. Empir. Res. Econ., Zurich

Frey BS, Jegen R. 2001. Motivation crowding theory: a survey of empirical evidence. *J. Econ. Surv.* 15:589–611

Glenn EN. 2000. Creating a caring society. *Contemp. Sociol.* 29:84–94

Gornick JC, Meyers MK. 2003. *Families That Work: Policies for Reconciling Parenthood and Employment.* New York: Russell Sage Found.

Harkness S, Waldfogel J. 1999. *The family gap in pay: evidence from seven industrialised countries.* CASE Paper 30, Cent. Anal. Soc. Exclusion, London Sch. Econ., London. http://sticerd.lse.ac.uk/dps/case/cp/CASEpaper30.pdf

Held V. 2002. Care and the extension of the market. *Hypatia* 17:19–33

Himmelweit S. 1999. Caring labor. *Ann. Am. Acad. Polit. Soc. Sci.* 561:27–38

Hochschild AR. 1983. *The Managed Heart: Commercialization of Human Feeling.* Berkeley: Univ. Calif. Press

Hochschild AR. 2000. The nanny chain. *Am. Prospect* 11:32–36

Hochschild AR. 2003. *The Commercialization of Intimate Life: Notes from Home and Work.* Berkeley: Univ. Calif. Press

Hondagneu-Sotelo P. 2001. *Domestica: Immigrant Workers Cleaning and Caring in the Shadows of Affluence.* Berkeley: Univ. Calif. Press

Jacobs JA, Steinberg RJ. 1990. Compensating differentials and the male-female wage gap: evidence from the New York State comparable worth study. *Soc. Forces* 69:439–68

Joshi H, Newell M-L. 1989. *Pay Differentials and Parenthood: Analysis of Men and Women Born in 1946.* Coventry, UK: Univ. Warwick Inst. Employ. Res.

Kilbourne BS, England P, Farkas G, Beron K, Weir D. 1994. Return to skill, compensating differentials, and gender bias: effects of occupational characteristics on the wages of white women and men. *Am. J. Sociol.* 100:689–719

Klerman JA, Leibowitz A. 1999. Job continuity among new mothers. *Demography* 36:145–55

Kmec JA. 2002. *Minority job concentration and wages.* Work. Pap., Dep. Sociol., Washington State Univ.

Kohn ML, Schooler C, Miller J, Miller KA, Schoenbach C, Schoenberg R. 1983. *Work and Personality: An Inquiry into the Impact of Social Stratification.* Norwood, NJ: Ablex

Lee RD, Miller T. 1990. Population policy and

externalities to childbearing. *Ann. Am. Acad. Polit. Soc. Sci.* Spec. Iss. *World Population: Approaching the Year 2000*, ed. SH Preston, 510:17–32

Leidner R. 1993. *Fast Food, Fast Talk: Service Work and the Routinization of Everyday Life.* Berkeley: Univ. Calif. Press

Leira A. 1994. Concepts of caring: loving, thinking, and doing. *Soc. Serv. Rev.* 68:185–201

Lundberg S, Rose E. 2000. Parenthood and the earnings of married men and women. *Labour Econ.* 7:689–710

Misra J. 2003. Caring about care. *Fem. Stud.* 29:387–401

Nelson J. 1999. Of markets and martyrs: Is it OK to pay well for care? *Fem. Econ.* 5:43–59

Nelson J. 2004. *Feminist economists and social theorists: Can we talk?* Work. Pap., Glob. Dev. Environ. Inst., Tufts Univ.

Nelson JA, England P. 2002. Feminist philosophies of love and work. *Hypatia* 17:1–18

Neumark D, Korenman S. 1994. Sources of bias in women's wage equations: results using sibling data. *J. Hum. Resourc.* 29:379–405

Noddings N. 1984. *Caring: A Feminine Approach to Ethics and Moral Education.* Berkeley: Univ. Calif. Press

O'Connor JS, Orloff AS, Shaver S. 1999. *States, Markets, Families: Gender, Liberalism and Social Policy in Australia, Canada, Great Britain, and the United States.* New York: Cambridge Univ. Press

Orloff AS. 1996. Gender in the welfare state. *Annu. Rev. Sociol.* 22:51–78

Petersen T, Morgan LA. 1995. Separate and unequal: occupation-establishment sex segregation and the gender wage gap. *Am. J. Sociol.* 101:329–65

Romero M. 1992. *Maid in the U.S.A.* London: Routledge

Sainsbury D. 2001. Social welfare policies and gender. In *International Encyclopedia of the Social & Behavioral Sciences*, ed. N Smelser, PB Baltes, pp. 14476–81. Amsterdam: Elsevier

Sayer LC, Bianchi SM, Robinson JP. 2004. Are parents investing less in children? Trends in mothers' and fathers' time with children. *Am. J. Sociol.* 110:1–43

Smith-Lovin L. 1998. On Arlie Hochschild, *The Managed Heart*: emotion management as emotional labor. In *Required Reading: Sociology's Most Influential Books*, ed. D Clawson, pp. 113–19. Amherst: Univ. Mass. Press

Sorensen E. 1994. *Comparable Worth: Is It a Worthy Policy?* Princeton, NJ: Princeton Univ. Press

Steinberg RJ. 2001. Comparable worth in gender studies. In *International Encyclopedia of Social & Behavioral Sciences*, ed. NJ Smelser, PB Baltes, pp. 2393–97. Oxford, UK: Oxford Univ. Press

Steinberg RJ, Figart DM. 1999. Emotional labor since *The Managed Heart. Ann. Am. Acad. Polit. Soc. Sci.* 561:8–26

Steinberg RJ, Haignere L, Possin C, Chertos CH, Trieman D. 1986. *The New York State Pay Equity Study: A Research Report.* Albany, NY: Cent. Women Gov., SUNY Press

Stone DA. 2000. Caring by the book. In *Care Work: Gender, Labor and the Welfare State*, ed. MH Meyer, pp. 89–111. London: Routledge

Tronto JC. 1987. Beyond gender differences to a theory of care. *Signs* 12:644–63

Waerness K. 1987. On the rationality of caring. In *Women and the State*, ed. AS Sassoon, pp. 207–34. London: Hutchinson

Waldfogel J. 1997. The effects of children on women's wages. *Am. Sociol. Rev.* 62:209–17

Waldfogel J. 1998a. The family gap for young women in the United States and Britain: Can maternity leave make a difference? *J. Labor Econ.* 16:505–45

Waldfogel J. 1998b. Understanding the family gap in pay for women with children. *J. Econ. Perspect.* 12:137–56

Wharton AS. 1993. The affective consequences of service work: managing emotions on the job. *Work Occup.* 20:205–32

Wharton AS. 1999. The psychological consequences on emotional labor. *Ann. Am. Acad. Polit. Soc. Sci.* 561:158–76

Williams J, Segal N. 2003. Beyond the maternal wall: relief for family caregivers who are discriminated against on the job. *Harvard Women's Law J.* 26:77–162

Wolfe BL, Haveman RH. 2003. Social and nonmarket benefits from education in an advanced economy. In *Education in the 21st Century: Meeting the Challenges of a Changing World*, ed. Y Kodrzychi, pp. 207–34. Boston: Fed. Res. Bank Boston

Zelizer VA. 2002a. How care counts. *Contemp. Sociol.* 31:115–19

Zelizer VA. 2002b. Intimate transactions. In *The New Economic Sociology: Developments in an Emerging Field*, ed. MF Guillen, R Collins, P England, M Meyer, pp. 274–300. New York: Russell Sage Found.

Subject Index

A

Access to care
    improving to reduce
        disparities, 76
Accountability
    of elected leaders to their
        constituents, 208
Acta Sociologica, 17–18
Activism, 47
    in communities, using
        literacy, 133
    strategies of, 59–60
Actors
    corporate, 2
    institutional, whites as, 323
    transnational, public
        corporations being among
        the most dominant, 143
Adarand v. Pena, 370
The Adolescent Society, 4–6
Advantaged social groups, 76
    See also Gender advantage
Affirmative action (AA), 253,
        357–74
    attitudes about, 370–73
    challenges to, 371–72
    in education, 365–69
    in employment, 365–69
    in higher education, impact
        of, 361–65
    in the Army, 368
    prohibited characteristics
        and protected groups,
        358–60
    societal responses to, 362,
        369–73
African American
    defining, 307
African American
    communities
    high disadvantage

levels in, 341–43
    importance of black
        scholars to the study of,
        306
    levels of family disruption
        in, 333
    typical, deprivation rates in
        white neighborhoods vs.,
        335
African American feminists,
        248
African American
    homeowners
    living in blacker
        neighborhoods than
        renters, 320
    preferring integrated
        neighborhoods, 320
African American men
    their having sex with white
        women being promoted,
        253
    See also
        thecriminalblackman
African American middle
        class
    proportional growth
        following World War II,
        305
African American
    middle-class
    neighborhoods, 305–23
    black communities before
        King, 308–9
    clarifying terms and
        methods, 307–8
    neighborhood preferences,
        317–21
    neighborhood quality,
        315–17
    neighborhood social and

economic characteristics,
        311
    residential segregation,
        312–15
    where blacks live now,
        309–12
African American mortality
    rates, 78
African American
    neighborhoods
    attention on declining, 307
    business owners in, 294
    in Philadelphia, 310–11,
        343
    poor, concentrations of
        public housing in, 335
African American poor
    social distance around, 315
African American rates of
    homicide
    victimization and
        offending, 332
African Americans
    authors, 64
    "chick-lit" by, 129
    culture of devalued, 129,
        332
    effects of the presence of
        racial and ethnic groups
        on, 289–90
    health conditions of,
        78–79
    protecting, 363
    romantics determined to
        take back disinvested
        enclaves of, 323
    scholars
        importance to the study
            of black communities,
            306
Age and inequality, 183–84

Agency costs, 281–82
Agency law, 272–73
Agency problems
  becoming coopted, 280
  engaging in corruption,
    280
  monitoring the wrong
    things, 280
  shirking, 280
Agency relationships, 269
  embedding, 276
  monitoring, 277
  omnipresence of, 282
  opportunities to play one
    principal off against
    another, 267
Agency theory, 263–82
  author's self-introduction,
    263–65
  classic, 266, 268, 278
  dangers of, 268
  economics and beyond,
    265–74
  a sociological perspective,
    274–82
AIDS activism, 65
Alba, Richard, 109
Allen, William, 149
Altruism, 389–90
Amazon.com, 137
American (Anglo-American)
    system
  of corporate governance,
    156
American Association of
    Medical Colleges, 366
American Economic
    Association, 169
American occupational
    codings, 232
American society
  multiple identity groups
    undermining common
    cultural fabric of, 50
American Sociological
    Association (ASA), 3,
    310

Section on Rational
  Choice, 19
"Social Causes of
  Violence," 331
American Sociological
  Society, 279
Analyse & Kritik, 17
Angelou, Maya, 64
Anglo-American system
  of corporate governance,
    156
Anglos
  term for white racial and
    ethnic identity in the U.S.,
    247
Anomie thesis
  and social structure, 332
Antidiscrimination laws, 158
Anti-immigrant sentiment
  rise of, 114
Antinuclear movement, 54
Antisweatshop movement,
    207, 216
Antitakeover laws, 147
Anxiety disorders
  generalized, 89
Apprenticeship placement,
    227n
Arab Americans
  officially considered white,
    252
Argentina, 159
ASA
  See American Sociological
    Association
Asian countries
  dissimilarity index among
    ethnic groups from, 288
  social mobility in, 231
Asian Pacific Islanders, 78
Asians
  effects of the presence of
    racial and ethnic groups
    on, 290
  protecting, 363
Assessment of immigrant
  assimilation, 107–11

immigrant replenishment,
    119–21
  new empirical and
    theoretical challenges,
    105–22
  new immigrant gateways,
    111–18
Assimilation, 293
  of immigrants, 107–11
  language, 108
*Assimilation in American
    Life*, 106
The *Asymmetric Society*, 16
Atkinson, Anthony B., 169
Atlanta, 297
  large black middle-class
    population in, 338
Attacking Poverty, 187
Attainment
  See Educational attainment
Attributional styles, 92
Auditors
  as agents, 280
  outside, 147
Authority relations
  Barnardian view of, 16

B
*Bakke v. Regents of the
    University of California*,
    366, 368
Bankruptcy legislation, 204
Banks
  holding ownership
    positions in Japan and
    Germany, 154
Bargaining situations, 35
Barnardian view of authority
    relations, 16
Baseline discrimination, 90
Baseline psychological
    distress, 90
Baton Rouge
  large black middle-class
    population in, 338
"Behavior-oriented"

contracts, 265
Belgium
  sociological practice in,
    10
Binomial logit models
  for transactions, 225
Biotech firms, 147
"Bivalent" collectivities, 53
Black and white log homicide
    offending rates
  predicted by concentrated
    disadvantage for U.S.
    cities, 341
"Black Belt"
  of Chicago, 309, 322
"Black discontent," 366
Blackness
  in neighborhoods, 320
  pride in, 309
Blacks
  See African Americans
Black-Scholes options pricing
    model, 149
Black-white dissimilarity
    index
  national, 312
Block groups, 338
*Board of Education of
  Oklahoma City v.
  Dowell*, 365
Books
  and book clubs, 134–35,
    139
  high hopes for e-books,
    137
  -in-the-broader-context
    approach, 128
"Borderlands," 58
Borjas, George, 108
Boundaries of affirmative
    action
  defining, 370–71
Brown v. Board of Education,
    365
Bulmer, Martin, 106
Burgess, Ernest, 106
Bush, George H.W., 377

C
California
  affirmative action in, 375
  ethnic differences among
    European immigrants in,
    251
  Mexican immigrants in,
    113–14
  voting in, 367
California Proposition 187,
    14
Canada
  Korean immigrants to, 92
  multiethnic cities in, 285,
    288
Capital
  flight of, 204
  required for investment,
    143
Cardiovascular mortality, 186
Care work
  devaluation of, 382–85
  emergency theories of,
    381–96
  improving access to, thus
    reducing disparities, 76
  for pay, 381
  as production of public
    good, 385–89
  unpaid, 384
Carnegie Endowment
  report on environmental
    impact of NAFTA, 208,
    211
CASMIN (Comparative
    Analysis of Social
    Mobility in Industrial
    Nations) data, 226
Catholic schools, 228n
  "functional communities"
    around, 8
Cato Institute, 205
Caucasians
  term for white racial and
    ethnic identity in the U.S.,
    247
"Causal regression," 11

Cautions
  about identity politics,
    66–68
Celler-Kefauver Act of 1950,
    150–51
Center for Advanced Study in
    the Behavioral Sciences,
    3
Center for Economic and
    Policy Research, 201n
Center for Individual Rights
    (CIR), 376
Central and Eastern Europe
  age and inequality, 183–84
  convergence, 178
  emerging inequalities in,
    163–88
  gender and inequality,
    180–83
  inequalities in mortality
    and morbidity, 185–87
  inequality and growth,
    169–73
  poverty, meaning and
    measurement, 178–80
  regional inequality, 184–85
  reliability of the data,
    173–77
  socialist allocation
    patterns, 168–69
  theorizing markets and
    inequality, 165–68
Chicago, 291, 295, 297
  Black Belt of, 309, 322
  Civil Rights movement
    brought north to, 308
  large black middle-class
    population in, 307, 314,
    317, 338
  "One Book, One Chicago,"
    135
Chicago Board Options
    Exchange, 149, 157
Chicago school of sociology,
    106, 109
"Chick-lit"
  African American, 129

Child care
  gendered practices in, 391
  providers of, 381
Child poverty
  inequality influencing the
    rate of, 184
Children
  English, reading habits in,
    130–31
  media use by, 129, 136
Children of Immigrants
    Longitudinal Study,
    108
Chile
  "Chicago boys" in, 212
China, 129
  rapid growth in, 210
  social mobility in, 231
  state bureaucratization in,
    274
  transitional economy in,
    164
Chinese
  in Toronto, 295
Chiswick, Barry, 108
Christian Identity Church, 253
CIR
  See Center for Individual
    Rights
Citizenship
  civil, 205
  civil and social, 205
  movements of, 58
  rights of
    demands for
      group-differentiated, 50
Civil citizenship, 205
Civil law
  French, 155
Civil Rights Act (CRA),
    358–59, 362, 365,
    372–73
Civil Rights movement, 118,
    248, 358, 365
  brought north to Chicago,
    308
  See also Post–Civil Rights

era; Pre–Civil Rights era
Class-based movements, 54
Class inequality
  structural adjustment
    increasing, 213
Class politics, 48
  versus identity politics,
    52–53
Class segregation among
    blacks, 313–14
  trends in, 314
Class structures
  transformation of, 209–14
Clayton Act of 1914, 150
Cleveland
  large black middle-class
    population in, 316–17
Coleman, James S.
  biographical sketch, 2–3
  early career substantive
    studies, 3–4
  education and social policy,
    4–10
  mathematical sociology
    and methods, 10–12
  *Medical Innovation, A
    Diffusion Study*, 4
  pluralism in organizations
    and communities, 3
  purposive action and
    rational choice theory,
    12–19
  sociology of, 1–19
"Coleman Reports," 4, 6
Collectivities
  "bivalent," 53
  people reading in groups,
    132
College admissions
  "back-door," 364
  testing for, 362
Collusions
  between big business and
    government, 204
Columbus, Ohio
  large black middle-class
    population in, 338

rates of violent crime in,
    340
COMECON countries, 164
Commodification
  of emotion, 391–92, 395
  of protest, 64
Common law
  English, 155
Communications
  advances in, 214
  dynamics of, 36
Communism
  collapse of, 187
  legitimizing, 165
  view that life was better
    under, 165
Communities
  activism in using literacy,
    133
  black, levels of family
    disruption in, 333
  black, study of, 306
  of color, 349
  inner-city, in New York
    City, 343
Community Conflict, 3
Comparative perspective
  inequality of opportunity
    in, 223–37
  social fluidity in, 229–31
Compensating differentials
  theory of, 389
Compliance
  Equal Employment
    Opportunity offices
    tokens of, 158
  officers as agents, 280
Concentrations
  of power, 3
  of public housing, in poor
    black neighborhoods, 335
Conflicts
  of interest, 278
  Korean and black, 294
  Korean and Mexican, 295
  social, 26
    highlighting the impact

of the group on justice
assessments and
reactions, 38–40
Conformity pressures, 35
Congressional redistricting
restrictions on, 361
Consolidation of monopolies,
204
The Constant Flux, 230
Constituents
accountability of elected
leaders to, 208
Contemporary sociological
critiques of corporate
governance, 149–53
Contemporary Sociology, 17
Contemporary world
economy, 143
Contractarian/shareholder
value approach, 149
Contractarian theory
of corporate governance,
145, 147, 159
Contracting practices, 266
Contracts
"behavior-oriented," 265
enforcement of, 203, 205
making so agents must
follow, 267
nexus-of, 145
"outcome-oriented," 265
Control
conceptions of, 150
corporate, 270
of crime on the streets, 280
Cooption
a problem in agencies, 280
Coping
religious, in the African
American community, 94
research on, 88
Corporate law
market for, 157
Corporate structures
evolution of, 147
Corporations
actors in, 2

boards of
sharing members, 151
contractarian theory of,
145, 147
each a nexus of contracts,
144–49
embedded in a network of
information flows, 152
fees, 146
governance of, 270
American
(Anglo-American)
system of, 156
contemporary
sociological critiques
of corporate
governance, 149–53
and control, 270
the corporation as a
nexus of contracts,
144–49
discovery of hitherto
unnoticed markets, 157
new directions in,
143–59
recent trends in law and
economics, 154–55
toward a contemporary
sociology of, 156–59
investors in, 143
profits from
contribution of female
jobs to, 382
public, 143, 145, 147
Corruption
a problem in agencies, 280
CRA
See Civil Rights Act
Crime
on the streets, controlling,
280
white-collar, 279
See also
thecriminalblackman;
Violent crime
"Cultural omnivores," 137
Currency depreciations

destabilization from, 204
Czech Republic
See Visegrad countries

D
Daniels, Cora, 321
"Death of white sociology,"
306
Debt crisis
in Mexico, 211
in the Third World, 200
Declaration of Independence,
28
*The Declining Significance of
Race*, 306
Decomposition
of the Theil index, 290
Deininger, Klaus, 188
Delaware
incorporation state of
choice, 146
Denmark
elasticities in, 233
wage dissimilarities in, 170
Dependency theory, 199–200,
209, 214
Depreciations
currency, destabilization
from, 204
Depression
major, 89
See also Great Depression
Deprivation rates
white neighborhoods vs.
typical black
communities, 335
Deserving
by individuals, 27
in justice levels, 29
Destabilization
from currency
depreciations, 204
"Detached" identities, 67
Detroit
large black middle-class
population in, 317
Devaluation

of African culture, 332
of care work, 381–85
of the Mexican peso, 211
Developing countries, 201
    privatizations in, 204
*Dictionary of Occupational
    Titles*, 383
Disadvantage
    effect on violent crime, 339
    high levels of in black
        communities, 341–43
    membership in groups, 34
    structural, 337, 347
Discrimination
    baseline, 90
    chronic expectation of, 91
    chronic experiences of, 89
    ending exclusion from, 362
    and health, 89–90
    self-reported, 89
    See also
        Antidiscrimination laws
Disease-specific morbidity
    and mortality
    indicators of health status,
        77
Disinvested enclaves of black
    America
    romantics determined to
        take back, 323
Dispersed ownership, 145
Disruption
    of families, levels of in
        black communities, 333
Dissimilarity index
    black-white, 312
Distributive justice, 26–27, 38
    research in, 29–30
Diversity
    managed, 371
    needed in the workforce,
        374
    racial and ethnic, 285
    replacing affirmative action
        goals, 378
Divorce rates
    increasing in all industrial

societies, 384
Dominican Republic, 213
Do the Right Thing (film),
    89n
Durkheim, Emile, 3

E

Earnings
    parity in, 107
E-books
    high hopes for, 137
Ecological dissimilarity,
    337–43
    predicted violent crime
        rates by disadvantage,
        340–42
    role of, 337–43
Economic boom
    in the post–World War II
        period, 308
Economic globalization, 55,
    206
Economics and agency
    theory, 265–74
    law, 272–74
    management, 269–70
    political science, 270–72
    See also Recent trends in
        law and economics
Economic sociology, 16
Economists
    experimental, 394
    managerialist, 145
Economy
    embedded and enmeshed in
        institutions, 157
    informal, increasing
        employment in, 212
Education
    affirmative action in,
        365–69
    affirmative action in higher
        education and diversity,
        368–69
    attainment in, 107, 385
        and social mobility,
            recent research

on, 77, 80, 223–37
    inequality in, 225–29
        change over time and
            differences between
            countries, 225–27
        micro-level and
            institutional
            explanations of,
            227–29
        and social mobility, 224
    primary and secondary, 365
    qualifications for, 234n
    and social policy, 4–10
        The Adolescent Society,
            5–6
        *Equality of Educational
            Opportunity*, 6–7
        games and experiential
            learning, 7
        public and private
            schools, families, and
            educational outcomes,
            8–9
        school desegregation
            and "white flight," 7
    for women, 181
Education Act of 1972, 364
Efficient market hypothesis
    (EMH), 147–48
Elected leaders
    accountability to their
        constituents, 208
Electronic money, 156
Emasculation
    of white men, 254
Embeddedness, 276–77
    of agency relationships,
        276
    of identities, 67
Emergency theories of care
    work, 381–96
    care as production of
        public good, 385–89
    caring motives and
        prisoners of love, 389–91
    commodification of
        emotion, 391–92

gender bias and the devaluation of care work, 382–85

rejecting the dichotomy between love and money, 392–95

EMH See Efficient market hypothesis

Emotional hostage effect, 390

Employers' practices regarding affirmative action in employment, 371

"Encapsulated interest" accounts, 14

Endogenous social interaction effects, 228

Enforcement of contracts, 203, 205 of property rights, 205

England literacy practices in, 133

English common law, 155

Enron, 157, 267

Entropy index, 289

Environmental degradation, 207

Environmental impact of structural adjustment, 207

Environmentalists global, 207

Environmental movement, 54

Environmental regulations social protections and, 206

Environmental standards undermining, 207

Epidemiology risk-factor, 81

EPZs See Export-processing zones

Equal Employment Opportunity (EEO) Act, 370 token compliance with, 158, 371

Equality as a major tenet of socialism, 165 See also Inequality

Equality of Educational Opportunity, 6–9

Equal Protection Clause of the 14th Amendment, 366–67, 370, 375

Equity formulations of consensus, 39 problems with altruistic motives, 390

Essentialist identities invoking, 60, 67

Ethnic businesses in multiethnic cities in North America, 294–95

Ethnic diversity, 251, 285

Ethnic Identity, 246

Ethnic Options, 246

Ethnomethodology, 77n

Eurobarometer, 168

European Americans whites as, 251–52

European colonialism, 274

European ethnicity among whites, 245–46

European immigrants, 119–20, 299 in California, ethnic differences among, 251

European Sociological Review, 236

European Union accession for Romania, 65 comparisons of poverty among member states, 179

"Everyday racism," 89

Evolutionary game theory, 14

Exchange/purposive action models, 11–12

Executive orders (EOs) presidential, 361–63

Expectation of discrimination

chronic, 91

Expectations states theory, 77n

Experimental economists, 394

Export-processing zones (EPZs), 207, 213

F

Fair labor practices, 216

Fairness issues, 25, 35, 374 perceptions of, 26

Family disruption in black communities, levels of, 333

Family and Medical Leave Act of 1993, 388

Fathering, 388n

Father love, 391

Fear of being labeled racist, 334

Federal Reserve Bank, 204

Feminists black, 248 contributing to mongrelization of white race, 254 Marxist, 385 standpoint theory of, 60

Ferge, Zsuzsa, 183

Fidelity bonds, 281

Fiduciaries, 277–78

Financial capital, 143

Financial markets, 158

Financial regulation American system of, 154

Finland elasticities in, 233

First World extracting love from the Third World, 392

Fixed-effects regression models, 82

Fluidity See Social fluidity

Ford Motor Company, 203

Foreign-born population

growth in, 111

Foreign direct investment, 203
  Third World governments competing for, 207

Formal sector employment in developing countries, 212

Foundations of Social Theory, 1, 12–19

14th Amendment
  Equal Protection Clause of, 362–63, 366, 371

Frameworks for care
  commodification of emotion, 382
  devaluation, 381–85
  love *and* money, 382
  prisoner of love, 382, 389–91
  public good, 382, 385–89

France
  openness of, 232
  position of unskilled class in, 226
  social fluidity in, 234

Frankenberg, Ruth, 249

Freeman v. Pitts, 361

French civil law, 155

Frey, William, 109

Fulwood, Sam, 321

Functional impairments
  indicator of health status, 77

"Funds of knowledge," 117

G

Gallup Organization, 135

Game playing, 7
  and experiential learning, 7

Game theory
  evolutionary, 14

Gender
  advantage from in reading, 131
  and assumptions built into welfare states, 384

in child care practices, 391
  and the dynamics of violence, 351
  See also African American men; White men; White women

Gender bias and the devaluation of care work, 382–85

Gender inequality, 180–83, 213, 248, 381

Generalized anxiety disorders, 89

General Social Survey, 128, 136

"Generation"
  concept of, 107

German Americans, 119
  in Philadelphia, 252
  suburbanization of, 292

Germany
  banks holding ownership positions in, 154
  elasticities in, 233
  openness of, 232
  position of unskilled class in, 227

Gini coefficients, 172–73, 176–77
  based on LIS surveys of per capita household income, 175
  for transitional countries, 174

Glasnost, 172

Globalization
  economic, 55, 206
  and environmentalists, 207
  facilitating movements around status identities, 65
  governance structures for, 68
  justice in, 206
  and nation states' decline in importance, 68
  poverty and, 210

and the "race to the bottom," 206–7
  relationship to development, 201
  sexuality in, 65

Global South, 209

Goals
  Michelsian displacement of, 16

Governance
  corporate, 143–59, 270
  of economies, 202–9
  global structures for, 68

Government regulators
  as agents, 280

Graff, Harvey, 135

Gratz v. Bollinger, 363, 371

The Great Depression, 107, 119

The Great European Migration, 119–20

Greenspan, Alan, 204

Green v. County School Board, 361

Griggs v. Duke Power, 369

Group-differentiated citizenship rights
  demands for, 50

Group identity
  development of, 33
  influence on justice assessments and reactions, 33–34

The group in justice research, 29–38
  categorization of the roles of, 30
  effects of group structure on determining justice, 31–33
  importance of group context, 37–38
  influence of group identity on justice assessments and reactions, 33–34
  role of group interaction processes on justice

assessments and
reactions, 34–37
use of a group standard to
determine justice, 30–31
Groups
defining, 28, 33
people reading in, 132,
134–35
protected, 373
Group solidarity
Hechter's theory of, 14
Group-specific health
practices, 88
Group-specific stress, 77n
Group standard
use of to determine justice,
30–31
Group structure
effects on determining
justice, 31–33
impact of, 33
Group threat hypothesis, 296
Group-value model
of procedural justice, 34,
36
Growth
inequality and, 169–73
Grutter v. Bollinger, 367–68

H
Harlem, 322–23
Harlemworld, 316
Hatch, Orrin, 376
Hawaiians
native, 78
Haynes, Bruce, 315
Health disparities
based on race/ethnicity and
socioeconomic position,
75–76
defining, 75
patterns of, 77–79
persistence in, 76
research on, 93
social psychology of,
75–95
Heavily Indebted Poor

Countries initiative, 216
Hechter's theory
of group solidarity, 14
"Heightened vigilance," 90,
91n
Heterosexuality
challenging the
immutability of, 62
Higher education, 365–67
affirmative action in, and
diversity, 368–69
Higher Learning (film), 89n
Hillbilly whites, 250
Hispanics
effects of the presence of
racial and ethnic groups
on, 290
neighborhood change
among, 287, 292
Historical materialism
Marxist, 60
Homeowners
black, preferring integrated
neighborhoods, 320
Homicide rates
black, of victimization and
offending, 332
interracial inequality
leading to higher, 333
mean, gaps in, 339
Homophobia
in America, 52
Homosexuality, 57
decriminalizing, 65
efforts to normalize, 57
gender organizing in, 57
Hong Kong
social mobility in, 231
Hopkins Games Project, 7
Hopwood v. Texas, 367–68,
375
Household accounts
using literacy, 133–34
Housing
See Public housing
Houston
women's groups in, 134

Hungary
openness of, 232
position of unskilled class
in, 227
social fluidity in, 233
See also Visegrad countries
Huntington, Samuel, 121
Hurston, Zora Neale, 64
"Hydra factor," 267
Hypervigilance, 91

I
Identities
invoked as if they were
essentialist, 60
unmarked, 248
Identity politics, 47–68
antithesis of, 56
approaches to, 49–58
cautions, 66–68
as cultural politics, 49–51
integrative approaches
contesting the terms of
the debate, 58–66
neo-Marxist approaches to
identity politics, 49–53
new social movements
approach to identity
politics, 53–55
research needed, 66–68
social constructionist,
postmodernist, and
poststructuralist
approaches to identity
politics, 56–58
"Identity talk," 63
IMF
See International Monetary
Fund
Immigrant assimilation,
107–11
intermarriage, 110–11
linguistic patterns, 109–10
residential patterns, 109
socioeconomic status,
108–9
Immigrant groups

European, 299
Immigration, 105
    laws restricting, 105
    in the new gateways,
        115–17
    waves of, 121–22
Immigration Reform and
    Control Act (IRCA),
    113–14
Season Agricultural Work
    Proviso, 114
Income inequality, 82
    closing with the West, 178
    components of
        socioeconomic position,
        81–82
    increasing in Latin
        America, 211
Indebtedness
    of least-developed country
        governments, 200
India
    rapid growth in, 210
Indigenous groups
    demands for political
        sovereignty, 65
"Individualistic positivism,"
    18
    See also "Structural
        individualism"
Individuals
    comparisons across, 29
    congruence of their
        propensities with
        structural constraints, 77
    social origin of, 224
    whites as, 323
Industrialization, 105
    history of democracies
        during, 206
    social fluidity driven by,
        230
    state-driven, 171
Industrial societies
    divorce rates increasing in,
        384
    nonmarital births

increasing in, 384
Inequalities in Central and
    Eastern Europe, 163–88
    and age, 183–84
    convergence, 178
    and growth, 169–73
    in mortality and morbidity,
        185–87
    and poverty, 178–80
    regional, 184–85
    reliability of the data,
        173–77
    socialist allocation
        patterns, 168–69
    theorizing markets and,
        165–68
    within-country stability in,
        173
Inequality
    a by-product of economic
        growth, 165
    educational, and social
        mobility, 224
    influencing the rate of child
        poverty, 184
    interracial, leading to
        higher homicide rates for
        all, 333
    in wages, 182
    See also Gender inequality
Inequality of opportunity
    defining the area, 223–25
    developments and
        challenges, 236–37
    inequality of educational
        attainment, 225–29
    methods and data, 234–36
    recent research on
        educational attainment
        and social mobility,
        223–37
    social mobility, 229–34
Infant mortality rates, 78
Informal economy
    growing employment in,
        212
Inner-city communities

in New York City, 343
Innocenti Research Center,
    173, 188
Institute for International
    Economics, 201n
Institutions
    actors
        whites as, 323
    explanations
        of educational
            inequality, 227–29
    investors, 152
    "isomorphism," 203
    power within
        identity politics and,
            64–66
"Instrumentality" approach,
    14
Insurance companies
    as agents, 280–81
Insurance and risk, 280–81
Integrated neighborhoods
    black homeowners
        preferring, 320
Integrative approaches to
    identity politics, 58–66
    attributing causality to
        identity, 63–64
    experience, identity, and
        strategy, 59–63
    identity politics and
        institutionalized power,
        64–66
"Interactive service work,"
    383
"Intergroup dialogue," 39n
Interlocking boards, 151
Intermarriage
    of immigrants, 106, 108,
        110–11
Internal affairs departments
    as agents, 280
International Labor
    Organization, 205
International Monetary Fund
    (IMF), 199, 204, 212
    structural adjustment

lending programs of, 199
Internet use, 214, 255
   becoming ubiquitous, 131
   dawn of, 136
   not displacing reading,
      137–38
Interracial inequality
   leading to higher homicide
      rates for all, 333
Interracial sexuality, 254
Intersex movement, 62
*Introduction to Mathematical
   Sociology*, 10–11
Investments
   advisors
      as agents, 280
   banks, 147
   opportunities
      for terrorists, 148
      uncertain, 147
*Investor Capitalism: How
   Money Managers Are
   Changing the Face of
   Corporate America*, 153
Investors
   confident, 201
   corporate, 143
   institutional, 152
   portfolio, 204
IRCA
   See Immigration Reform
      and Control Act
Ireland
   position of unskilled class
      in, 227
Irish-Americans, 119
   suburbanization of, 292
Islamism
   political, 55
"Isomorphism"
   institutional, 203
Israel
   openness of, 232
   social fluidity in, 233
ISSP survey, 236
Italian Americans
   in New York City, 252

suburbanization of, 292
Italy
   openness of, 232

J

Jackson, John, 316
Japan
   banks holding ownership
      positions in, 154
Japanese Americans, 78
JE
   See Justice evaluation
      formula
Jews
   business owners
      in black neighborhoods,
         294
   descendants of Cain as
      demonic and mongrel,
         253
   immigrants to New York
      City, 118
Jobs
   intrinsic fulfillment
      provided by, 390
Johns Hopkins University
   Department of Social
      Relations, 3
Johnson, Lyndon, 359, 365,
   372
Johnson, Valerie, 315
*Johnson v. Santa Clara
   County Department of
   Transportation*, 366
Jubilee movement, 216
Justice
   individual deserving, and
      the group, 26–29
   influence of group identity
      on, 33–34
   perceptions of, 31, 41
   use of a group standard to
      determine, 30–31
Justice evaluation (JE)
   formula, 30
Justice in the group, 25–41
   bringing the group

back in, 40–41
   examining the roles of the
      group in justice research,
         25–41
   justice, individual
      deserving, and the group,
         26–29
   roles of the group in justice
      research, 29–38
   social conflict, highlighting
      the impact of the group on
      justice assessments and
      reactions, 38–40
Justice-related research, 38
"Just-in-time" production,
   214

K

Kennedy, John F., 365
King, Martin Luther, 308
   black middle-class
      neighborhoods before,
         308–9
   Civil Rights movement
      brought north to Chicago
      by, 308
Kleptoklatura, 164
*Kölner Zeitschrift für
   Soziologie und
   Sozialpsychologie*, 18
Korean business owners, 297
   in black neighborhoods,
      294
   See also South Korea
Korean immigrants
   to Canada, 92
Ku Klux Klan, 253, 255
Kuznets, Simon, 169
"Kuznets curve," 170–72, 214

L

Labeling
   and the fear of being called
      racist, 334
Labor
   market for
      in multiethnic cities in

North America, 295–97
movements
past, 54
theory of value in
Marxism, 386
Labor force
and complicated labor
laws, 214
increase in racial and
ethnic diversity in, 296
Lacy, Karyn, 321
Language assimilation, 108
three-generation model of,
110
Latin American class
structures, 211
Latinos
health conditions of, 78
and immigration effects,
345–46
Lay, Kenneth, 267
Lazarsfeld, Paul, 2, 5
Least-developed country
(LDC) governments, 202
indebtedness of, 200
restrictive monetary
policies, 212
Lebanese Americans
in Michigan, 252
Legal perspectives
agency theory and, 272–74
See also Agency law; Civil
law; Common law;
Corporate law; Recent
trends in law and
economics; State
corporate law
Legitimization
of communism, 165
Levy, Marion, 201n
Life expectancy at birth
poverty and, 211
Linguistic patterns
of immigrants, 109–10
Lipsit, Seymour Martin, 2
LIS
See Luxembourg

Income Study
LISREL, 224
Literacy
men gaining more quickly
than women, 129
myths about, 127, 135
practices of, 133
Literature
on multiculturalism, 60
of social movement
approaches, 59
See also "Chick-lit"
Living with Racism, 321–22
"LLSV" (papers by La Porta,
Lopez-de-Silanes,
Shleifer, and Vishny),
155
Lobbying, 360
Logan, John, 109
Logit models
binomial, for transactions,
225
two-sided, 235
Log-linear modeling
techniques, 230
"Log-multiplicative layer
effect model," 235
Los Angeles
neighborhood change in,
292, 295, 297
Louis Mumford Center for
Comparative Urban and
Regional Research, 310
Luxembourg Income Study
(LIS), 173, 175–76
archives of, 188
surveys of per capita
household income, Gini
coefficients based on, 175

M
MacArthur Scale of
Subjective Social Status,
82
Macro-macro transitions, 17
Macro-oriented hypotheses,
226

Macrostructural analyses of
race, ethnicity, and
violent crime, 331–52
conclusions and research
needed, 347–52
Latinos and immigration
effects, 345–46
multilevel research, 346–47
research on race, ethnicity,
and violent crime after
1995, 336–45
Sampson and Wilson's
approach, 334–36
Major depression, 89
The Managed Heart, 391
Managerialism, 144
Managerialist economists,
145
Maquiladoras, 213
Marginalization, 50, 389
Marital affinities
for individuals from same
broad racial category, 110
Markets
competitive, 204
discovery of hitherto
unnoticed, 157
financial, 158
national labor, structural
adjustment putting
pressure on, 215
securities, evolution of,
147
transition, 187
Marshall, T.H., 205
Marxism, 144, 392–93
classic view of, 139
and historical materialism,
60
labor theory of value, 386
relevance of, 156
Marxist feminists, 385
Marxist historical
materialism, 60
Mathematical sociology, 2,
10–12
exchange/purposive action

models, 11–12
stochastic process models, 11
structural research methods, 11
The Mathematics of Collective Action, 10–12
McNamara, Robert, 200
"Mechanism" approach to social theory, 13
    "action-formation" mechanism, 13
    "situational" mechanism, 13
    "transformational" mechanism, 13
Medical Innovation, A Diffusion Study, 4
Medicare
    aging population covered by, 390n
Men
    gaining literacy more quickly than women, 129
Meritocracy, 374n
Merton, Robert, 2
Mexican Americans, 109, 119–20
Mexico
    debt crisis in, 211
    rapid growth in, 210
Michelsian goal displacement, 16
Michigan
    Lebanese Americans in, 252
Micro-level explanations of educational inequality, 227–29
Micro-micro transitions, 17
"Middle-class"
    defining, 307
Middle-class black and white persons
    in metropolitan Philadelphia, neighborhood social and

economic characteristics of average, 311
Migration
    See also Out-migration hypothesis
Militia movements, 253
Milliken v. Bradley, 361
Mills, C. Wright, 152
Minority group population increases, 296
Mismanagement, 145
Missouri v. Jenkins, 361
Mixed neighborhoods
    on the rise, 292
MMRI
    See Multidimensional Model of Racial Identity
Mobility
    social, educational inequality and, 224
The Modern Corporation and Private Property, 144
Modernization theorists, 199–203, 209, 214, 226
Monetary policies
    restrictive, of LDCs, 212
Money
    driving out love, 395
    electronic, 156
Monitors
    monitoring the wrong things, 280
Monogamous commitment, 57
Monopolies
    consolidation of, 204
    regulation of natural, 203
Mood disorders, 79
Moral community
    activation of, 40
Morbidity
    inequalities in, 185–87
Mortality
    black rates of, 78
    cardiovascular, 186
    inequalities in, 185–87
Motherhood

wage penalty for, 387
Mother love, 391
Mud people, 253
Multi-City Study of Urban Inequality, 291
Multiculturalism
    literature on, 60
Multidimensional Model of Racial Identity (MMRI), 87
Multiethnic cities in North America, 285–99
    ethnic businesses, 294–95
    labor market, 295–97
    residential patterns, 286–94
Multiethnic contexts, 289–91
    the preference of racial and ethnic groups, 291
    the presence of racial and ethnic groups, 289–90
    and residential patterns, 289–91
Multigroup contexts
    effects on urban structures and processes, 286, 298
Multilateral organizations, 205
Multiple identity groups
    undermining common cultural fabric of American society, 50
Multiracial identities, 88
    growing populations of, 110, 246
Music
    downloading, 135
    promoting white power, 255
Muslim Americans, 25

N
NAFTA
    See North American Free Trade Agreement
Narrative action theory, 18
National Academy of Science, 331

National Consortium on
Violence research, 331
National Crime Victimization
Survey (NCVS), 343,
346
National Educational
Longitudinal Study
(NELS), 346
National Institutes of Health,
79n, 108
Nationalism
research on, 67
Serbian, 55
Nationalist rhetoric
in the Third World, 216
National labor markets
structural adjustment
putting pressure on, 215
National Longitudinal Survey
of Adolescent Health,
346
National Longitudinal Survey
of Immigrants, 108
National Science Foundation
National Consortium on
Violence research, 331
Nation states' decline in
importance
globalization and, 68
Native Americans, 78
Natural monopolies
regulation of, 203
NCVS
See National Crime
Victimization Survey
NEA study, 131, 137–38
Nee, Victor, 166
Negotiation sessions, 35
Neighborhood
defining, 308
Neighborhoods
black, attention on
declining, 307
black homeowners
preferring integrated, 320
black middle-class, 305–23
mixed, on the rise, 292

"nonpoor," 311
See also Public housing
NELS
See National Educational
Longitudinal Study
Neoliberal ideology, 199
structural adjustment
lending programs of, 200
Neo-Marxism, 48–49, 56
approaches to identity
politics, 49–53, 58
class politics versus
identity politics, 52–53
consequences of identity
politics, 51–52
identity politics as cultural
politics, 49–51
Neo-Nazis, 253
The Netherlands, 131
equalization in, 226
openness of, 232
social fluidity in, 233
wage dissimilarities in, 170
Network analysis
history of, 11
Networks
power-balanced, 35
New directions in corporate
governance, 143–59
contemporary sociological
critiques of corporate
governance, 149–53
the corporation as a nexus
of contracts, 144–49
recent trends in law and
economics, 154–55
toward a contemporary
sociology of corporate
governance, 156–59
New immigrant gateways,
111–18
accounting for the
changing geography of
American immigration,
113–15
immigrants in the new
gateways, 115–17

states in which
foreign-born population
doubled between 1990
and 2000 and the top
three sending regions, 112
uniqueness of new
immigrant gateways,
117–18
New Left
failures of, 53
New literacy studies, 128
New Orleans
large black middle-class
population in, 319
New social movements
(NSM) approach to
identity politics, 53–55,
58
theory of, 54–55
New York City
Harlem, 322–23
inner-city communities in,
343
Italian Americans in, 252
Jewish immigrants to, 118
large black middle-class
population in, 307, 309
neighborhood change in,
292, 297
New York Second Generation
study, 109
New York Times Book Review,
134
Nexus-of contracts, 145
Nixon, Richard M., 376
Nomenklatura, 164, 186
Nonhierarchical religions,
155
Protestantism, 155
Nonlethal violence
victimization, 346
Nonmarital births
increasing in all industrial
societies, 384
"Nonpoor neighborhoods,"
311
Nonwhite racial stocks, 253

North American Free Trade
Agreement (NAFTA),
206
Carnegie Endowment
report on environmental
impact of, 208, 211
increasing illegal
immigration from
Mexico, 215
weakening unions, 208
North Carolina
experience with
immigrants, 111, 115–17
Northern Ireland
position of unskilled class
in, 227
Norway
elasticities in, 233
openness of, 232
wage dissimilarities in, 170
"Notes on a New Sociology
of Economic
Development," 156
NSM
See New social movements
approach

O

Occupations
coding
American, 232
prestige of, 77
specialization within, 107
OECD economies, 174n, 177,
206
income inequality in, 81
union decline in, 208
OFCCP
See Office of Federal
Contract Compliance
Offending and victimization
rates of black homicide in,
332
Office of Behavioral and
Social Sciences
Research, 79n
Office of Federal Contract

Compliance (OFCCP),
365, 367–69, 374
Office of Refugee
Resettlement (ORR),
115
Oklahoma City bombing, 255
OLS-regressions, 225
"One Book, One Chicago,"
135
Openness
ranking of countries
according to degree of,
231–33
"Operation Enduring
Freedom," 25
"Operation Infinite Justice,"
25
Opportunity
inequality of, 225
See also Investment
opportunities
Oprah's Book Club, 135
Options pricing model
Black-Scholes, 149
Organizations
and corporate actors, 16–17
theory of, 266
ORR
See Office of Refugee
Resettlement
"Outcome-oriented"
contracts, 265
Out-marriage, 110
Out-migration hypothesis,
313
Ownership
banks holding in Japan and
Germany, 154
dispersed, 145

P

Panel Study of Income
Dynamics, 313
Parenting
closure in, 8
costs of, 386
as unpaid care work, 384

Parity
in earnings, 107
proportional, 360
Park, Robert, 106
Parsons, Talcott, 389
Path analysis, 224
Patriot movement, 66
Patterson, Orlando, 317, 319
Peace movement, 54
Pension systems, 183
People's Daily, 129
Personal Responsibility and
Work Opportunity
Reconciliation Act of
1996, 384
Peso devaluation, 211
Peterson, Richard, 137
Philadelphia, 376
black neighborhoods in,
310–11, 343
German Americans in, 252
Pinochet, Augusto, 212n
Pluralism in organizations
and communities, 3
Pluralistic policy research, 10
Poland
openness of, 232
position of unskilled class
in, 226–27
social fluidity in, 233
See also Visegrad countries
Polanyi, Karl, 157
Policy research
pluralistic, 10
social, 10
*The Polish Peasant in Europe
and America*, 106
"Political capitalism," 166
Political Islamism, 55
Political science
agency theory and, 270–72
Political sovereignty
demands by indigenous
groups for, 65
Politicization of affirmative
action, 376–77
Politics

See Identity politics
Poor black neighborhoods
  concentrations of public
    housing in, 335
Portfolio investors, 204
Positive agency theory, 266
Positivism
  See "Individualistic
    positivism"
"Post-citizenship"
  movements, 58
Post–Civil Rights era, 246,
    317
Postcommunist era, 188
Postmodernism, 55, 58, 60
  as an approach to identity
    politics, 56–58
Poststructuralism
  as an approach to identity
    politics, 56–58
Post–World War II period
  economic boom in, 308
  proportional growth of the
    black middle class in, 305
Poverty
  among blacks, 315
  in Central and Eastern
    Europe, 178–80
  comparisons among
    European Union member
    states, 179
  global, 210
  and life expectancy at
    birth, 211
Power-balanced networks, 35
The Power Elite, 152
*Power and the Structure of
    Society*, 16
Pre–Civil Rights era
  residential reality of
    middle-class blacks in,
    307
Preferences
  in black middle-class
    neighborhoods, 317–21
  of racial and ethnic groups
    effects of, 291

specifying, 267
Presidential executive orders
    (EOs), 357–58
Prestige
  occupational, 77
  of reading, 139
Pricing models
  Black-Scholes options, 149
Primary and secondary
    education, 361
Prince Georges County,
    Maryland
  large black middle-class
    population in, 315
Principal-agency
  relationships, 270
Principal-agent theory, 266
Prisoners of love
  caring motives and, 389–91
Privatizations
  in developing nations, 204
Procedural justice, 36–37
  group-value model of, 34,
    36
Prohibited characteristics and
    protected groups,
    358–60
  assessing exclusion, 360
  creating protected groups,
    359–60
Project on Human
    Development in Chicago
    Neighborhoods
    (PHDCN), 344
Property rights
  enforcement of, 205
"Pro-poor" spending, 205
Proportional parity, 360
Proposition 187 (California),
    114
Protectionist tariffs, 210
Protest
  commodification of, 64
Protestantism
  nonhierarchical, 155
  a role for, 155
Psychological distress, 78

baseline, 90
Psychosocial explanations,
    81n
Psychosocial risk factors, 76
Psychotherapy, 385
Public corporations, 145, 147
  among the most dominant
    actors transnationally,
    143
Public goods
  defining, 385
Public health initiatives
  improving to reduce
    disparities, 76
Public housing
  concentrated in poor black
    neighborhoods, 335
Public and private schools,
    families, and educational
    outcomes, 8–9
Public Use Microdata Sample
    (PUMS), 287
Publishing
  transformation of, 152
PUMS
  See Public Use Microdata
    Sample
PUMS-F
  census data, 288
Purchasing power parity
    (PPP), 210
Purposive action and rational
    choice theory, 2, 12–19
  citations to *Foundations of
    Social Theory*, 18
  norms, 14–15
  organizations and
    corporate actors, 16–17
  social capital, 15–16
  trust, 13–14

Q

"Queer dilemma," 62
Queer Nation, 56
Queer politics, 56–57
Queer theory, 55
Quintile rankings, 176

R

Race
and criminal violence, 334
as a "plus factor" in
admissions, 362
"The Race"
being proud of, 309
Race, discrimination, and
health, 86–93
contingencies in the effects
of discrimination on
health, 92–93
discrimination and health,
89–90
perceiving and reporting
discrimination, 90–92
racial/ethnic identity,
86–88
Race/ethnicity
health disparities based on,
75–76
Race, ethnicity, and violent
crime
intervening processes,
343–45
race-specific analyses,
336–37
recent research on, 336–45
role of ecological
dissimilarity, 337–43
Race-specific studies, 336–37
Race-specific violent index
offenses, 333
"Race to the bottom," 206–7
"Race traitors," 61
Racial and ethnic groups,
86–88
Asians, 290
blacks, 289–90
differences in rates of
criminal violence,
denying, 334
diversity among, 285
effects of the presence of,
289–90
Hispanics, 290
vagaries of defining, 246

Racial and ethnic identity in
the U.S.
promotion of, 254–55
white, 245–56
Racial genocide
white, 253
Racism
in America, 52
Racists
fear of being labeled, 334
skinheads, 253
"Radical multiculturalists,"
50
Rating Agencies
as agents, 280
Rational choice theory, 2, 17,
271
Rationality & Society, 19
Readers, 128–32
the reading class, 138–39
solitary, "ideology" of, 134
Reading
death knell of, 136
the Internet not displacing,
137
most people spending little
time in, 136
prestige of, 139
social infrastructure of, 134
as social practice, 132
by youth, 130–32
Reading in the twenty-first
century, 127–39
in groups, 134–35
how we read, 132–35
practice, 132–34
reading and other media,
135–38
who reads, 128–32
Reagan, Ronald, 157, 376
Rearing children
costs of, 386
Recipient-preferred justice
patterns, 32
Redistricting
congressional, restrictions
on, 357

Red Lines, Black Spaces, 315
Regional inequality, 184–85
Regression models
fixed-effects, 82
Regulation
financial, American system
of, 154
of natural monopolies, 203
Regulatory capitalism
American model of, 203
Relative deprivation theory,
31
Religions
nonhierarchical, 155
Religious coping
in the African American
community, 94
Residential integration, 253
Residential patterns
of immigrants, 109
Residential patterns in
multiethnic cities,
286–94
effects of multiethnic
contexts, 289–91
neighbor changes in
multiethnic contexts,
291–92
residential segregation in a
multiethnic context,
286–89
suburbanization in
multiethnic contexts,
292–94
Residential segregation
in black middle-class
neighborhoods, 312–15
in a multiethnic context,
and residential patterns,
286–89
patterns in, 287
*Restatement of the Law,
Agency*, 270
Restrictive monetary policies
of LDCs, 212
"Reverse affirmations," 61
Revue française de

sociologie, 17
Reward and
   punishment-based
   strategies, 35
*Riddick v. School Board of
   City of Norfolk,* 361
Rights
   group-differentiated
      citizenship, 50
   growth of concept, 13
Risk-factor epidemiology, 81
Roe, Mark, 154
Role theory, 77n
Romania
   European Union accession
      for, 65
Royal Economic Society, 170

S

Sachs, Jeffrey, 156
Same-sex sexualities, 65
Sarbanes-Oxley Act of 2002,
   158
SBA
   See Small Business
      Administration
School desegregation, 253
   and "white flight," 7
"Schultze's Law," 7
Season Agricultural Work
      Proviso, 114
Securities
   evolution of markets for,
      147
   underwriting, 147
Segregation
   class, among blacks, 313
   racial, decreasing, 309–10
"Segregation academies," 375
SEI
   See Socioeconomic indices
Self-blaming attributional
      styles, 92
Self-employment, 181
Self-rated health, 77
Self-reported discrimination,
   89

SEP
   See Socioeconomic
      position
September 11 terrorist attack,
   25
Serbian nationalism, 55
SES
   See Socioeconomic status
Sexism
   in America, 52
Sexualities
   interracial, 254
   same-sex, 65
Shareholder value approach,
   145, 149, 151
   See also
      Contractarian/shareholder
      value approach
Sherman Act of 1890, 150
Skinheads, 253
Slovakia
   See Visegrad countries
Small Business
      Administration (SBA),
      360
SNCC
   See Student Nonviolent
      Coordinating Committee
Social barriers, 110
Social capital, 15–16, 143
"Social Causes of Violence,"
   331
Social citizenship, 205
   structural adjustment
      eroding, 206
Social conflict
   highlighting the impact of
      the group on justice
      assessments and
      reactions, 38–40
Social consequences of
      structural adjustment
   governance of economies,
      202–9
   recent evidence and current
      debates, 199–217
   rise of transnational

networks, 214–16
   structural adjustment in
      historical perspective,
      200–2
   transformation of class
      structures, 209–14
Social constructionism, 55,
   60
   approach to identity
      politics, 56–58
Social disorganization
      theorists, 333
Social fluidity
   cross-national constancy
      in, 236–37
   driven by industrialization,
      230
Social identity theory, 33–34,
   250
Social infrastructure
   of reading, 134
Social interaction effects
   endogenous, 228
Socialism
   equality a major tenet of,
      165
   past movements in, 54
   social welfare under, 168
Socialist allocation patterns,
   168–69
Socialist movements
   past, 54
Socialist transformation
      hypothesis, 226
Socializing Capital, 149
Social mobility, 229–34
   in Asian countries, 231
   educational inequality and,
      224
   explaining variation in
      social fluidity, 233–34
   extending study of to state
      socialist societies, 231
   and inequality of
      opportunity, 229–34
   ranking of countries
      according to degree of

openness, 231–33
social fluidity in
comparative and temporal
perspective, 229–31
Social Mobility in Europe,
230
Social movement approaches,
48
literature of, 59
Social organization
problems in, 2
Social origin
of individuals, 224
Social policies
change in related to status
identities, 68
unintended consequences
of, 7
Social policy research, 10
Social position, 234n
Social practice
reading as, 132
Social protections
and environmental
regulations, 206
Social psychology, 25
concepualizing identity and
discrimination, 93
nonwhite racial and ethnic
identity in the U.S., 250
Social psychology of health
disparities, 75–95
patterns of health
disparities, 77–79
race, discrimination, and
health, 86–93
social structure and
personality as an orienting
framework, 79–80
socioeconomic position
and health, 80–86
Social responsibility
whiteness identified with,
249
*Social Sciences Citation
Index (SSCI)*, 2, 4–5, 8,
11, 17

Social Security system
pay-as-you-go, 387
viability of, 387
Social stratification, 223
longitudinal studies in, 235
Social structure and
personality (SSP)
as an orienting framework,
79–80
Social theory
"mechanism" approach to,
13
Social welfare
under socialism, 168
Socioeconomic composition
in schools, 229n
Socioeconomic indices (SEI),
224
Socioeconomic position
(SEP)
advancing from one
generation to the next, 106
explaining the association
with health, 84–86
health disparities based on,
75–76
subjective components of,
81–84
uncovering and specifying
the subjective, 80–86
Socioeconomic status (SES)
of immigrants, 108–9
Sociological perspective on
agency theory, 274–82
agency costs, 281–82
embeddedness, 276–77
fiduciaries, 277–78
goal conflict, 278–79
insurance and risk, 280–81
monitoring, 280
opportunism, 279–80
professions, 276
Sociological social
psychology, 79
Sociology
Chicago school of, 106,
109

economic, 16
mathematical, 2
South Korea, 159
social mobility in, 231
Sovereignty
demands by indigenous
groups for political, 65
Spain, 159
Squire, Lynn, 188
SSP
See Social structure and
personality
St. Louis
violent victimization in,
351
Standardization in research,
226
Standard survey measures
underestimating
experiences of
discrimination, 90
Standpoint theory
feminist, 60
State corporate law
evolution of, 147
State University of New York
at Albany
Louis Mumford Center for
Comparative Urban and
Regional Research, 310
Status identities, 64
Status-oriented culture, 82
STFs
See Summary Tape Files
Stochastic process models, 11
*Strong Managers, Weak
Owners*, 154
Structural adjustment, 210–14
defining, 201
environmental impact of,
207
eroding social citizenship,
206
in historical perspective,
200–2
increasing class inequality,
213

putting pressure on national labor markets, 215
social consequences of, 199–217
Structural adjustment lending programs, 200
Structural advancement
nonobvious legacies of, 248
Structural constraints
incongruent with individual propensities, 77
Structural disadvantage, 337, 347
Structural equation modeling, 235
"Structural individualism," 13
Structural research methods, 11
Student Nonviolent Coordinating Committee (SNCC), 64–65
Subjective components of socioeconomic position, 81–84
income inequality, 81–82
subjective status, 82–84
Suburbanization in multiethnic contexts and residential patterns, 292–94
Summary Tape Files (STFs), 287
Supplementary Homicide Report data, 336
Supremacist formations
learned, 254
white, 253
Survey of Earned Doctorates, 305
Sweden, 226–28
elasticities in, 233
equalization in, 226
openness of, 232
position of unskilled class in, 226–27

wage dissimilarities in, 170
Szelényi, Ivan, 166

T

Taiwan
social mobility in, 231
Tariffs
protectionist, 210
Taxes
administration of, 203
Teachers
providing care, 381
role of, 7
Temporal perspective
social fluidity in, 229–31
Terrorists
investment opportunities for, 148
thecriminalblackman
stereotype of, 331, 351
Theil index
decomposing, 289
Theorizing markets and inequality, 165–68
Theory and Society, 17
Therapists
providing care, 381
Third World
citizens and governments, 206–7
debt crisis in, 200, 204, 216
the First World extracting love from, 392
nationalist rhetoric in, 216
Thomas, W.I., 106
Toronto
neighborhood change in, 292, 295
Traditional cultural perspectives, 332
Transactions
binomial logit models for, 225
The Transformation of Corporate Control, 150
Transgender organizing, 63
Transitional countries

Gini coefficients for, 174
Transition markets, 187
TRANSMONEE project, 173, 175, 188
The Truly Disadvantaged, 306
"Two-sided logit model," 235
Type A behavior patterns, 84

U

UC Davis Medical School, 362
Understanding and Preventing Violence, 331
Unemployment, 145
UNICEF, 173, 188
Union Democracy, 3, 10
Unions
getting votes from, 376
weakened by NAFTA, 208
United Kingdom
book clubs in, 134–35
reading habits in, 128
United Nations, 215
United Nations University/World Institute for Development Economics Research (UNU/WIDER), 176–77, 188
United Steel Workers v. Weber, 370
University of Michigan, 363–64, 371
University of Texas Law School, 362, 371
Unpaid care work, 384
Unskilled workers
hurt most by NAFTA, 208
Urban structures and processes
effects of multigroup contexts on, 286
U.S. Agency for International Development (USAID), 204

U.S. Army
  affirmative action in, 372
U.S. Census Bureau, 109–10,
  247, 383
U.S. Civil Rights Act of
  1964, 6
U.S. Constitution
  See 14th Amendment
U.S. Department of Health
  and Human Services
  Office of Refugee
  Resettlement, 115
U.S. National Academy of
  Sciences, 3
U.S. Supreme Court, 360–71
USAID
  See U.S. Agency for
  International
  Development
Useem, Michael, 153

V

Victimization
  nonlethal violence, 346
  rates of black homicide in,
  332
  violent, in St. Louis, 351
Vigilance
  "heightened," 90
  See also Hypervigilance
Violence
  denying racial differences
  in rates of, 334
  gendered dynamics of, 351
  nonlethal victimization,
  346
  race and, 334
Violent crime
  denying racial differences
  in rates of, 334
  effect of disadvantage on,
  339
  index offenses
  race-specific, 333
  logged, as predicted by
  levels of disadvantage,
  342

race and, 334
and race and ethnicity,
  recent research on,
  336–45
rates by disadvantage for
  black and white
  communities in
  Columbus, Ohio,
  predicted, 340
victimization from in St.
  Louis, 351
Visegrad countries, 164–65,
  179–85
Voting
  allowed to white men, 28
  unions getting out the vote,
  376

W

Wage inequality, 182
Wage penalty
  for motherhood, 387–88
Washington
  affirmative action in, 371
  voting in, 363
Washington, D.C.
  consensus in, 164
  large black middle-class
  population in, 319
Weber, Max, 144, 155
Welfare
  controversy over, 395
  reforming, 384
Welfare state
  gendered assumptions built
  into, 384
  growth of, 171
West Germany
  position of unskilled class
  in, 227
Whistleblowers, 279
White-collar crime, 279
White men
  allowed to vote, 28
  as under siege and
  emasculated, 254
White neighborhoods

deprivation rates, vs.
  typical black
  communities, 335
Whiteness, 247–50
  burgeoning interest in, 245
  calls for the abolition of,
  249
  emptying of its privilege
  content, 248
  identifying with social
  responsibility, 249
  identity issues
  social culpability of, 249
  and white supremacist
  movements, 252–55
  as normative, 248
  See also "Death of white
  sociology"
White race
  feminists contributing to
  the mongrelization of, 254
White racial and ethnic
  identity in the U.S.,
  245–56
  currently in flux, 256
  point of agreement and
  departure, 255–56
  social psychological
  theories, 250
  white, Caucasian, Anglo,
  247
  white identity and white
  supremacist movements,
  252–55
  whiteness studies, 247–50
  whites as European
  Americans, 251–52
Whites
  European ethnicity among,
  245–46
  failing to protect, 359
  Hillbilly, 250
  income of, 296
  as individuals and as
  institutional actors, 323
  as the racial descendants of
  Adam, 253

racial genocide by, 253
racial identity
delineating, 253
term for white racial and
ethnic identity in the U.S.,
247
working-class, 250
See also Nonwhite racial
stocks
White supremacist
Weltanschauung, 253
White women
seeking bestial and
dominating masculinity,
254
WIID
See World Income
Inequality Database
Wilkinson, Richard, 81–82
Wilson, William Julius,
306–7, 313
Winfrey, Oprah, 134–35
impact of, 138
Wired magazine, 137

Wolfensohn, James, 211
Women
men gaining literacy more
quickly than, 129
roles played in white
supremacist movements,
254
See also White women
Women's education, 181
Workers
hurt most by NAFTA, 208
marginal, 389
Working-class whites, 250
World Bank, 170, 173, 176,
180, 188, 199, 204–5,
207, 211, 216
structural adjustment
lending programs of,
200
WorldCom, 157
World Development Report,
187
World economy
contemporary, 143

World Health Organization,
186
World Income Inequality
Database (WIID), 176
World Trade Organization
(WTO), 202, 205, 207
World War II
See Post-World War II
period
WTO
See World Trade
Organization

Y

"Young Turks," 3
Youth
reading, 130–32
Youth movement, 54

Z

*Zeitschrift für die gesamte
Staatswissenschaft*, 19
Zeitschrift für Soziologie, 18
Znaniecki, Florian, 106

Cumulative Indexes

CONTRIBUTING AUTHORS, VOLUMES 22–31

A

Abell P, 30:287–310
Allan E, 22:459–87
Anand N, 30:311–34
Andrews KT, 30:479–506
Ariovich L, 30:23–46
Arum R, 26:395–418
Auerhahn K, 24:291–311

B

Babb S, 31:199–222
Bawah A, 29:465–86
Beamish TD, 29:443–64
Bean FD, 30:221–42
Benford RD, 26:611–39
Berezin M, 23:361–83
Bergesen AJ,
    30:395–408
Bernstein M, 31:47–74
Bian Y, 28:91–116
Bianchi SM, 25:307–33
Biggart NW, 29:443–64
Bollen KA, 27:153–85
Bonacich P, 27:213–34
Borg MJ, 26:43–61
Boudon R, 29:1–21
Breen R, 31:223–43
Brewster KL, 26:271–96
Browne I, 29:487–513
Brubaker R, 24:423–52
Buchmann C, 27:77–102
Burawoy M, 26:693–95
Burris BH, 24:141–57

C

Calavita K, 23:19–38
Callero PL, 29:115–33
Camic C, 24:453–76
Campbell JL, 28:21–38

Caren N, 27:213–34
Carruthers BG,
    30:23–46
Carter S, 28:243–69
Centeno MA, 29:363–90
Cerulo KA, 23:385–409
Chafetz JS, 23:97–120
Charles CZ, 29:167-207
Chaves M, 27:261–81
Clawson D, 25:95–119
Clawson MA, 25:95–119
Clay K, 26:525–46
Clemens ES, 25:441–66
Cook JM, 25:441–66;
    27:415–44
Cook KS, 27:387–413
Corcoran M, 26:241–69
Coughlin BC, 29:41–64

D

Danziger SK, 26:241–69
Davis GF, 31:143–62
Davis MS, 25:245–69
Dellinger K, 25:73–93
Deskins DR Jr, 27:445–77
DeVault ML, 22:29–50
DiMaggio P, 23:263–87;
    27:307–36
Dimitrova D, 22:213–38
Dohan D, 24:477–98

E

Earl J, 30:65–80
Edelman LB,
    23:479–515
Edling CR, 28:197–220
Edwards B, 30:479–506
Ellison CG, 25:363–94
England P, 31:381–99

Espeland WN, 24:313–43
Estes SB, 23:289–313

F

Farkas G, 29:541–62
Felson RB, 22:103–28
Fennell ML, 23:215–31
Fernandez RM,
    30:545–69
Ferrell J, 25:395–418
Fine GA, 27:387–413
Firebaugh G, 26:323–39
Fisher AP, 29:335–61
Fong E, 31:285–304
Foschi M, 26:21–42
Franzosi R, 24:517–54
Freese J, 29:233–56
Friedkin NE, 30:409–25
Friedland R, 27:125–52
Fuller L, 26:585–609
Fung A, 29:515–39
Furstenberg FF Jr,
    29:23–39

G

Galtz N, 22:437–58
Gamson J, 30:47–64
Gannon-Rowley T,
    28:443–78
Garton L, 22:213–38
Gieryn TF, 26:463–95
Gille Z, 28:271–95
Giordano PC, 29:257–81
Giuffre PA, 25:73–93
Giugni MG, 24:371–93
Glanville JL, 27:153–85
Glass JL, 23:289–313
Goldman M, 26:563–84
Gornick JC, 30:103–24

Gorski PS, 27:261–81
Gortmaker SL, 23:147–70
Green DP, 27:479–504
Griswold W, 31:127–41
Grob DB, 22:377–99
Gross N, 24:453–76
Guillén MF, 27:235–60
Gulia M, 22:213–38
Guo G, 26:441–62

H
Haddad CJ, 25:575–96
Hage JT, 25:597–622
Halaby CN, 30:507–44
Handel MJ, 29:135–65
Haney LA, 26:641–66
Hannum E, 27:77–102
Hargittai E, 27:307–36
Harper S, 31:357–79
Haythornthwaite C,
    22:213–38
Hechter M, 23:191–214;
    26:697–98
Hegtvedt KA, 31:25–45
Heimer CA, 27:47–76
Heinz JP, 27:337–62
Heyns B, 31:163–97
Hitlin S, 30:359–93
Hoffman K, 29:363–90
Howard JA, 26:367–93

I
Ingram P, 26:525–46

J
Jackman MR, 28:387–415
Jacobs JA, 22:153–85
Jasper JM, 27:283–305
Jayakody R, 28:117–41
Jenness V, 30:147–71
Jiménez TR, 31:105–25
John D, 22:299–322
Jonsson JO, 31:223–43

K
Kalil A, 26:241–69
Kalleberg AL, 26:341–65

Kalmijn M, 24:395–421
Kanazawa S, 23:191–214
Kane EW, 26:419–39
Kang DL, 25:121–44
Kao G, 29:417–42
Karen D, 27:187–212
Karlin J, 25:575–96
Kaufman J, 30:335–57
Keister LA, 26:63–81;
    28:39–61
Kennedy MD, 22:437–58
Kmec JA, 25:335–61
Kollock P, 24:183–214
Korpi W, 29:589–609
Korteweg AC, 25:47–71
Krivo LJ, 31:331–56
Krysan M, 26:135–68
Kurzman C, 28:63–90

L
LaFree G, 25:145–68
Laitin DD, 24:423–52
Lamont M, 28:167–95
Laumann EO, 27:337–62
Lawler EJ, 25:217–44
Lee J, 30:221–42
Leicht KT, 23:215–31
Li J-CA, 29:233–56
Lichter DT, 23:121–45;
    28:117–41
Lie J, 23:341–60
Lieberson S, 28:1–19
Liker JK, 25:575–96
Lin N, 25:467–88
Link BG, 27:363–85
Lipset SM, 22:1–27
Liska AE, 23:39–61
Lobao L, 27:103–24
Lye DN, 22:79–102
Lynn FB, 28:1–19

M
Macmillan R, 27:1–22
Macy MW, 28:143–66
Mahoney J, 30:81–101
Manza J, 26:297–322
Marsden PV, 31:1–24

Martin A, 30:65–80
Massey DS, 26:699–701
Matthews R, 22:401–35
Mayer KU, 23:233–61
McBrier DB, 25:335–61
McCarthy B, 28:417–42
McCarthy JD, 30:65–80
McDermott M, 31:245–61
McDonnell T, 31:127–41
McFalls LH, 27:479–504
McLanahan S, 26:703–5
McLeod JD, 31:75–103
McPherson M, 27:415–44
Mechanic D, 22:239–70
Menger P-M, 25:541–74
Messner SF, 26:83–106
Meyer DS, 30:125–45
Meyer K, 27:103–24
Misra J, 29:487–513
Mizruchi MS, 22:271–98
Moaddel M, 28:359–86
Mohr JW, 24:345–70
Moller S, 26:63–81
Molnár V, 28:167–95
Moon D, 30:47–64
Morenoff JD, 28:443–78
Morgan DL, 22:129–52
Morgan SL, 25:659–706
Morgan SP, 22:351–75
Morrill C, 29:391–415
Morris AD, 25:517–39
Morris M, 25:623–57
Munger F, 22:187–212

N
Nagel J, 26:107–33
Nakao K, 24:499–516
Nee V, 22:401–36
Nelson RL, 27:337–62
Nelson TJ, 30:427–51
Neuman WR, 27:307–36
Newman K, 27:23–45
Noumbissi A, 29:465–86

O
O'Connor A, 26:547–62
Olick JK, 24:105–40

Oppenheimer VK,
  23:431–53
O'Rand AM, 30:453–77
Orbuch TL, 23:455–78
Ó Riain S, 26:187–213;
  28:271–95
Orloff A, 22:51–78
Owens L, 28:63–90

P

Page KL, 24:57–76
Parker RN, 24:291–311
Pattillo M, 31:305–29
Peterson RA, 30:311–34
Peterson RD, 31:331–56
Pettigrew TF, 24:77–103
Phelan JC, 27:363–85
Pichardo NA, 23:411–30
Piliavin JA, 30:359–93
Podolny J, 24:57–76
Polletta F, 27:283–305
Pontell HN, 23:19–38
Portes A, 24:1–24
Powell B, 28:243–69
Powell WW, 30:199–220
Presser S, 29:65–88

R

Radelet ML, 26:43–61
Rao H, 29:391–415
Ray R, 25:47–71
Reskin B, 31:357–79
Reskin BF, 25:335–61;
  26:707–9
Ridgeway CL,
  25:191–216
Rindfuss RR, 26:271–96
Robbins J, 24:105–40
Robert SA, 25:489–516
Robinson JP, 27:307–36
Rochefort DA, 22:239–70
Rosenfeld RA, 30:103–24

S

Salaff J, 22:213–38
Sampson RJ, 26:711–14;
  28:443–78

Samson FL, 31:245–61
Sánchez-Jankowski M,
  24:477–98
Sanders JM, 28:327–57
Schaeffer NC, 29:65–88
Schegloff E, 26:715–20
Schnittker J, 31:75–103
Schooler C, 22:323–49
Schurman RA, 26:563–84
Schwartzman KC,
  24:159–81
Schwarz N, 24:239–64
Scott WR, 30:1–21
Seefeldt KS, 26:241–69
Seidman G, 25:419–40
Seron C, 22:187–212
Settersten RA, 23:233–61
Shanahan MJ, 26:667–92
Shapiro SP, 31:263–84
Shelton BA, 22:299–322
Sherkat DE, 25:363–94
Shibuya K, 31:285–304
Shuey KM, 30:453–77
Sibanda A, 29:465–86
Sloane D, 22:351–75
Small ML, 27:23–45
Smelser NJ, 25:1–18
Smith CS, 24:25–56
Smith JK, 27:479–504
Smith RA, 28:509–42
Smith V, 23:315–39
Smith-Lovin L, 25:191–216;
  27:415–44
Smith Maguire J, 30:173–97
Smock PJ, 26:1–20
Snellman K, 30:199–220
Sniderman PM,
  22:377–99
Snipp CM, 29:563–88
Snow DA, 26:611–39
Sørensen AB, 25:121–44
Soule SA, 24:265–89;
  30:65–80
South SJ, 26:83–106
Spilerman S, 26:497–524
Stecklov G, 27:153–85
Steelman LC, 28:243–69

Steffensmeier D,
  22:459–87
Stevens ML, 24:313–43
Stinchcombe AL,
  23:1–18
Stolte JF, 27:387–413
Strang D, 24:265–89
Su C, 30:545–69
Suchman MC,
  23:479–515
Swedberg R, 29:283–306

T

Thompson JS,
  29:417–42
Thornton PH, 25:19–46
Thye SR, 25:217–44
Tillman R, 23:19–38
Tilly C, 26:721–23
Tolnay SE, 29:209–32
Trappe H, 30:103–24
Travis J, 29:89–113
Turk AT, 30:271–86

U

Udehn L, 28:479–507
Useem B, 24:215–38

V

Valenzuela A Jr,
  29:307–33
van der Lippe T,
  28:221–41
van Dijk L, 28:221–41
Vaughan D, 25:271–305
Venkatesh SA, 29:41–64
Visher CA, 29:89–113

W

Wade LD, 29:233–56
Washington RE,
  27:187–212
Waters MC, 31:105–25
Watts DJ, 30:243–70
Wejnert B, 28:297–326
Wellman B, 22:213–38
Welsh S, 25:169–90

Werum R, 28:243–69
Western B, 25:623–57
Willer R, 28:143–66
Williams CL, 25:73–93
Wilson J, 26:215–40
Winant H, 26:169–85
Winship C, 25:659–706

Wise PH, 23:147–70
Woodberry RD,
   24:25–56
Wright N, 31:127–41

Y

Young AA Jr, 27:445–77

Z

Zald MN, 29:391–415
Zhao H, 26:441–62
Zhou M, 23:63–95
Zuberi T, 29:465–86
Zukin S, 30:173–97
Zussman R, 23:171–89

CHAPTER TITLES, VOLUMES 22–31

Prefatory

Steady Work: An Academic Memoir	SM Lipset	22:1–27
On the Virtues of the Old Institutionalism	AL Stinchcombe	23:1–18
Social Capital: Its Origins and Applications in Modern Sociology	A Portes	24:1–24
Preface—Looking Back at 25 Years of Sociology and the *Annual Review of Sociology*	NJ Smelser	25:1–18
Barking Up the Wrong Branch: Scientific Alternatives to the Current Model of Sociological Science	S Lieberson, FB Lynn	28:1–19
Beyond Rational Choice Theory	R Boudon	29:1–21
Teenage Childbearing as a Public Issue and Private Concern	FF Furstenberg Jr.	29:23–39
Reflections on a Half-Century of Organizational Sociology	WR Scott	30:1–21
The Sociology of James S. Coleman	PV Marsden	31:1–24

Theory and Methods

Talking Back to Sociology: Distinctive Contributions of Feminist Methodology	ML DeVault	22:29–50
Focus Groups	DL Morgan	22:129–52
An Introduction to Categorical Data Analysis	D Sloane, SP Morgan	22:351–75
Innovations in Experimental Design in Attitude Surveys	PM Sniderman, DB Grob	22:377–99
Feminist Theory and Sociology: Underutilized Contributions for Mainstream Theory	JS Chafetz	23:97–120
Sociological Rational Choice Theory	M Hechter, S Kanazawa	23:191–214
People's Accounts Count: The Sociology of Accounts	TL Orbuch	23:455–78
Diffusion in Organizations and Social Movements: From Hybrid Corn to Poison Pills	D Strang, SA Soule	24:265–89
Commensuration as a Social Process	WN Espeland, ML Stevens	24:313–43
Measuring Meaning Structures	JW Mohr	24:345–70

Contemporary Developments in
Sociological Theory: Current Projects
and Conditions of Possibility   C Camic, N Gross   24:453–76
Using Computers To Analyze
Ethnographic Field Data: Theoretical
and Practical Considerations   D Dohan,   24:477–98
                                     M Sánchez-Jankowski

Narrative Analysis–or Why (and How)
Sociologists Should be Interested in
Narrative   R Franzosi   24:517–54
Sexuality in the Workplace: Organizational
Control, Sexual Harassment, and the
Pursuit of Pleasure   CL Williams,   25:73–93
                                     PA Giuffre,
                                     K Dellinger

Gender and Sexual Harassment   S Welsh   25:169–90
The Gender System and Interaction   CL Ridgeway,   25:191–216
                                     L Smith-Lovin

Bringing Emotions into Social Exchange
Theory   EJ Lawler, SR Thye   25:217–44
The Estimation of Causal Effects From
Observational Data   C Winship,   25:659–706
                                     SL Morgan

Race and Race Theory   H Winant   26:169–85
Multilevel Modeling for Binary Data G Guo, H Zhao   26:441–62
Closing the "Great Divide": New Social
Theory on Society and Nature   M Goldman,   26:563–84
                                     RA Schurman

Feminist State Theory: Applications to
Jurisprudence, Criminology, and the
Welfare State   LA Haney   26:641–66
Sociological Miniaturism: Seeing the Big
through the Small in Social Psychology   JF Stolte, GA Fine,   27:387–413
                                     KS Cook

From Factors to Actors: Computational
Sociology and Agent-Based Modeling   MW Macy, R Willer   28:143–66
Mathemetics in Sociology   CR Edling   28:197–220
Global Ethnography   Z Gille, S Ó Riain   28:271–95
Integrating Models of Diffusion of
Innovations: A Conceptual Framework B Wejnert   28:297–326
Assessing "Neighborhood Effects": Social
Processes and New Directions in
Research   RJ Sampson,   28:443–78
                                     JD Morenoff,
                                     T Gannon-Rowley

The Changing Faces of Methodological
Individualism   L Udehn   28:479–507

The Science of Asking Questions   NC Schaeffer,   29:65–88
    S Presser

The Changing Picture of Max Weber's
    Sociology   R Swedberg   29:283–306
Narrative Explanation: An Alternative to
    Variable-Centered Explanation?   P Abell   30:287–310
Values: Reviving a Dormant Concept   S Hitlin, JA Piliavin   30:359–93
Durkheim's Theory of Mental Categories:
    A Review of the Evidence   AJ Bergeson   30:395–408
Panel Models in Sociological Research:
    Theory into Practice   CN Halaby   30:507–44

Social Processes

The Division of Household Labor   BA Shelton, D John   22:299–322
Modeling the Relationships Between
    Macro Forms of Social Control   AE Liska   23:39–61
New Forms of Work Organization   V Smith   23:315–39
New Social Movements: A Critical Review   NA Pichardo   23:411–30
Breakdown Theories of Collective Action   B Useem   24:215–38
Warmer and More Social: Recent
    Developments in Cognitive Social
    Psychology   N Schwarz   24:239–64
Was It Worth the Effort? The Outcomes
    and Consequences of Social Movements   MG Giugni   24:371–93
Women's Movements in the Third World:
    Identity, Mobilization, and Autonomy   R Ray, AC Korteweg   25:47–71
A Retrospective on the Civil Rights
    Movement: Political and Intellectual
    Landmarks   AD Morris   25:517–39
Nonstandard Employment Relations:
    Part-time, Temporary, and Contract
    Work   AL Kalleberg   26:341–65
Schools and Communities: Ecological and
    Institutional Dimensions   R Arum   26:395–418
Framing Processes and Social Movements:
    An Overview and Assessment   RD Benford,   26:611–39
    DA Snow

Violence and the Life Course: The
    Consequences of Victimization for
    Personal and Social Development   R Macmillan   27:1–22
Cases and Biographies: An Essay on
    Routinization and the Nature of
    Comparison   CA Heimer   27:47–76
Collective Identity and Social Movements   F Polletta, JM Jasper   27:283–305
Violence in Social Life   MR Jackman   28:387–415
The Sociology of the Self   PL Callero   29:115–33

The "New" Science of Networks | DJ Watts | 30:243–70
Social Cohesion | NE Friedkin | 30:409–25
Doing Justice to the Group: Examining the
    Roles of the Group in Justice Research | KA Hegtvedt | 31:25–45
Identity Politics | M Bernstein | 31:47–74
The Social Psychology of Health
    Disparities | J Schnittker, | 31:75–103
    | JD McLeod |

Assessing Immigrant Assimilation: New
    Empirical and Theoretical Challenges | MC Waters, | 31:105–25
    | TR Jiménez |

Institutions and Culture

Comparative Medical Systems | D Mechanic, | 22:239–70
    | DA Rochefort |
Cultural and Social-Structural
    Explanations of Cross-National
    Psychological Differences | C Schooler | 22:323–49
Culture and Cognition | P DiMaggio | 23:263–87
The Family Responsive Workplace | JL Glass, SB Estes | 23:289–313
Fundamentalism Et Al: Conservative
    Protestants in America | RD Woodberry, | 24:25–56
    | CS Smith |

Aphorisms and Clichés: The Generation
    and Dissipation of Conceptual Charisma | MS Davis | 25:245–69
Recent Developments and Current
    Controversies in the Sociology of
    Religion | DE Sherkat, | 25:363–94
    | CG Ellison |

Cultural Criminology | J Ferrell | 25:395–418
Artistic Labor Markets and Careers | P-M Menger | 25:541–74
Volunteering | J Wilson | 26:215–40
How Welfare Reform is Affecting
    Women's Work | M Corcoran, | 26:241–69
    | SK Danzinger, |
    | A Kalil, KS Seefeldt |

The Choice-Within-Constraints New
    Institutionalism and Implications for
    Sociology | P Ingram, K Clay | 26:525–46
Religious Nationalism and the Problem of
    Collective Representation | R Friedland | 27:125–52
Sport and Society | RE Washington, | 27:187–212
    | D Karen |
Social Implications of the Internet | P DiMaggio, | 27:307–36
    | E Hargittai, |
    | WR Neuman, |
    | JP Robinson |

The Scale of Justice: Observations on the
Transformation of Urban Law Practice — JP Heinz, RL Nelson, — 27:337–62
EO Laumann

Welfare Reform: How Do We Measure
Success? — DT Lichter, — 28:117–41
R Jayakody

The Study of Islamic Culture and Politics:
An Overview and Assessment — M Moaddel — 28:359–86
Relationships in Adolescence — PC Giordano — 29:257–81
Still "Not Quite as Good as Having Your
Own"? Toward a Sociology of Adoption — AP Fisher — 29:335–61
The Economic Sociology of Conventions:
Habit, Custom, Practice, and Routine in
Market Order — NW Biggart, — 29:443–64
TD Beamish

The Use of Newspaper Data in the Study of
Collective Action — J Earl, A Martin, — 30:65–80
JD McCarthy,
SA Soule

Consumers and Consumption — S Zukin, — 30:173–97
J Smith Maguire
The Production of Culture Perspective — RA Peterson, — 30:311–34
N Anand

Endogenous Explanation in the Sociology
of Culture — J Kaufman — 30:335–57
Reading and the Reading Class in the
Twenty-First Century — W Griswold, — 31:127–41
T McDonnell,
N Wright

Formal Organizations

Computer Networks as Social Networks:
Collaborative Work, Telework, and
Virtual Community — B Wellman, J Salaff, — 22:213–38
D Dimitrova,
L Garton, M Gulia,
C Haythornthwaite

What Do Interlocks Do? An Analysis,
Critique, and Assessment of Research
on Interlocking Directorates — MS Mizruchi — 22:271–98
The Changing Organizational Context of
Professional Work — KT Leicht, — 23:215–31
ML Fennell

Sociology of Markets — J Lie — 23:341–60
The Legal Environments of Organizations — LB Edelman, — 23:479–515
MC Suchman
Network Forms of Organizations — J Podolny, KL Page — 24:57–76

What Has Happened to the US Labor Movement? Union Decline and Renewal	D Clawson, MA Clawson	25:95–119
The Dark Side of Organizations: Mistake, Misconduct, and Disaster	D Vaughan	25:271–305
Politics and Institutionalism: Explaining Durability and Change	ES Clemens, JM Cook	25:441–66
Perspectives on Technology and Work Organization	JK Liker, CJ Haddad, J Karlin	25:575–96
Organizational Innovation and Organizational Change	JT Hage	25:597–622
Birds of a Feather: Homophily in Social Networks	M McPherson, L Smith-Lovin, JM Cook	27:415–44
Covert Political Conflict in Organizations: Challenges from Below	C Morrill, MN Zald, H Rao	29:391–415
New Directions in Corporate Governance	GF Davis	31:143–62

Political and Economic Sociology

Gender in the Welfare State	A Orloff	22:51–78
Market Transition and Societal Transformation in Reforming State Socialism	V Nee, R Matthews	22:401–35
From Marxism to Postcommunism: Socialist Desires and East European Rejections	MD Kennedy, N Galtz	22:437–58
Politics and Culture: A Less Fissured Terrain	M Berezin	23:361–83
Computerization of the Workplace	BH Burris	24:141–57
Globalization and Democracy	KC Schwartzman	24:159–81
The Sociology of Entrepreneurship	PH Thornton	25:19–46
Ownership Organization and Firm Performance	DL Kang, AB Sørensen	25:121–44
States and Markets in an Era of Globalization	S Ó Riain	26:187–213
Political Sociological Models of the U.S. New Deal	J Manza	26:297–322
The Trend in Between-Nation Income Inequality	G Firebaugh	26:323–39
Wealth and Stratification Processes	S Spilerman	26:497–524

Socialism and the Transition in East and
Central Europe: The Homogeneity
Paradigm, Class, and Economic
Inefficiency   L Fuller   26:585–609
Is Globalization Civilizing, Destructive, or
Feeble? A Critique of Five Key Debates
in the Social Science Literature   MF Guillén   27:235–60
Financial Markets, Money, and Banking   LA Keister   28:39–61
Comparative Research on Women's
Employment   T van der Lippe,   28:221–41
    L van Dijk
Skills Mismatch in the Labor Market   MJ Handel   29:135–65
Day Labor Work   A Valenzuela Jr.   29:307–33
The Lopsided Continent: Inequality in
Latin America   K Hoffman,   29:363–90
    MA Centeno
Associations and Democracy: Between
Theories, Hopes, and Realities   A Fung   29:515–39
The Sociology of Property Rights   BG Carruthers,   30:23–46
    L Ariovich
Protest and Political Opportunities   DS Meyer   30:125–45
The Knowledge Economy   WW Powell,   30:199–220
    K Snellman
New Risks for Workers: Pensions, Labor
Markets, and Gender   KM Shuey,   30:453–77
    AM O'Rand
Advocacy Organizations in the U.S.
Political Process   KT Andrews,   30:479–506
    B Edwards
Space in the Study of Labor Markets   RM Fernandez,   30:545–69
    C Su
Emerging Inequalities in Central and
Eastern Europe   B Heyns   31:163–97
The Social Consequences of Structural
Adjustment: Recent Evidence and
Current Debates   S Babb   31:199–222

Differentiation and Stratification

Gender Inequality and Higher Education   JA Jacobs   22:153–85
Law and Inequality: Race, Gender... and,
of Course, Class   C Seron, F Munger   22:187–212
Intermarriage and Homogamy: Causes,
Patterns, and Trends   M Kalmijn   24:395–421
Declining Violent Crime Rates in the
1990s: Predicting Crime Booms and
Busts   G LaFree   25:145–68

Feminization and Juvenilization of
Poverty: Trends, Relative Risks, Causes,
and Consequences | SM Bianchi | 25:307–33
The Determinants and Consequences of
Workplace Sex and Race Composition | BF Reskin,
DB McBrier,
JA Kmec | 25:335–61

Social Networks and Status Attainment | N Lin | 25:467–88
Inequality in Earnings at the Close of the
Twentieth Century | M Morris, B Western | 25:623–57
Wealth Inequality in the United States | LA Keister, S Moller | 26:63–81
Chinese Social Stratification and Social
Mobility | Y Bian | 28:91–116
The Study of Boundaries in the Social
Sciences | M Lamont, V Molnár | 28:167–95
Race, Gender, and Authority in the
Workplace: Theory and Research | RA Smith | 28:509–42
The Dynamics of Racial Residential
Segregation | CZ Charles | 29:167–207
Racial and Ethnic Stratification in
Educational Achievement and
Attainment | G Kao, JS Thompson | 29:417–42
The Intersection of Gender and Race in the
Labor Market | I Browne, J Misra | 29:487–513
Cognitive Skills and Noncognitive Traits
and Behaviors in Stratification Processes | G Farkas | 29:541–62
Gender and Work in Germany: Before and
After Reunification | RA Rosenfeld,
H Trappe,
JC Gornick | 30:103–24

Inequality of Opportunity in Comparative
Perspective: Recent Research on
Educational Attainment and Social
Mobility | R Breen, JO Jonsson | 31:223–43
White Racial and Ethnic Identity in the
United States | M McDermott,
FL Samson | 31:245–61

Individual and Society

Adult Child-Parent Relationships | DN Lye | 22:79–102
Mass Media Effects on Violent Behavior | RB Felson | 22:103–28
The Measurement of Age, Age Structuring,
and the Life Course | RA Settersten Jr,
KU Mayer | 23:233–61

Identity Construction: New Issues, New
Directions | KA Cerulo | 23:385–409

Reactions Toward the New Minorities of
    Western Europe   TF Pettigrew   24:77–103
Social Memory Studies: From "Collective
    Memory" to the Historical Sociology of
    Mnemonic Practices   JK Olick, J Robbins   24:105–40
Social Dilemmas: The Anatomy of
    Cooperation   P Kollock   24:183–214
Alcohol, Drugs, and Violence   RN Parker,   24:291–311
        K Auerhahn
Ethnic and Nationalist Violence   R Brubaker,   24:423–52
        DD Laitin
Double Standards for Competence: Theory
    and Research   M Foschi   26:21–42
Ethnicity and Sexuality   J Nagel   26:107–33
Prejudice, Politics, and Public Opinion:
    Understanding the Sources of Racial
    Policy Attitudes   M Krysan   26:135–68
Social Psychology of Identities   JA Howard   26:367–93
Racial and Ethnic Variations in
    Gender-Related Attitudes   EW Kane   26:419–39
A Space for Place in Sociology   TF Gieryn   26:463–96
Pathways to Adulthood in Changing
    Societies: Variability and Mechanisms
    in Life Course Perspective   MJ Shanahan   26:667–92
Education and Stratification in Developing
    Countries: A View of Theories and
    Research   C Buchmann,   27:77–102
        E Hannum
Religious Pluralism and Religious
    Participation   M Chaves,   27:261–81
        PS Gorski
Conceptualizing Stigma   BG Link, JC Phelan   27:363–85
Reconsidering the Effects of Sibling
    Configuration: Recent Advances and
    Challenges   LC Steelman,   28:243–69
        B Powell,
        R Werum, S Carter
Ethnic Boundaries and Identity in Plural
    Societies   JM Sanders   28:327–57
The African American "Great Migration"
    and Beyond   SE Tolnay   29:209–32
The Potential Relevances of Biology to
    Social Inquiry   J Freese, J-CA Li,   29:233–56
        LD Wade
Racial Measurement in the American
    Census: Past Practices and Implications
    for the Future   CM Snipp   29:563–88

The Sociology of Sexualities: Queer and
  Beyond   J Gamson, D Moon   30:47–64
Agency Theory   SP Shapiro   31:263–84

Demography

Gender and Crime: Toward a Gendered
  Theory of Female Offending   D Steffensmeier,   22:459–87
                                                    E Allan

The First Injustice: Socioeconomic
  Disparities, Health Services Technology,
  and Infant Mortality   SL Gortmaker,   23:147–70
                                                    PH Wise

Women's Employment and the Gain to
  Marriage: The Specialization and
  Trading Model   VK Oppenheimer   23:431–53
Cohabitation in the United States: An
  Appraisal of Research Themes,
  Findings, and Implications   PJ Smock   26:1–20
Crime and Demography: Multiple
  Linkages, Reciprocal Relations   SJ South,   26:83–106
                                                    SF Messner

Fertility and Women's Employment in
  Industrialized Nations   KL Brewster,   26:271–96
                                                    RR Rindfuss

Socioeconomic Status and Class in Studies
  of Fertility and Health in Developing
  Countries   KA Bollen,   27:153–85
                                                    JL Glanville,
                                                    G Stecklov

Population and African Society   T Zuberi,   29:465–86
                                                    A Sibanda,
                                                    A Bawah,
                                                    A Noumbissi

America's Changing Color Lines:
  Immigration, Race/Ethnicity, and
  Multiracial Identification   J Lee, FD Bean   30:221–42
Multiethnic Cities in North America   E Fong,   31:285–304
                                                    K Shibuya

Urban and Rural Community Sociology

Growing Up American: The Challenge
  Confronting Immigrant Children and
  Children of Immigrants   M Zhou   23:63–95
Socioeconomic Position and Health: The
  Independent Contribution of
  Community Socioeconomic Context   SA Robert   25:489–516

Urban Poverty After *The Truly Disadvantaged*: The Rediscovery of the Family, the Neighborhood, and Culture — ML Small, K Newman — 27:23–45

The Great Agricultural Transition: Crisis, Change, and Social Consequences of Twentieth Century US Farming — L Lobao, K Meyer — 27:103–24

The Urban Street Gang After 1970 — BC Coughlin, SA Venkatesh — 29:41–64

Transitions from Prison to Community: Understanding Individual Pathways — CA Visher, J Travis — 29:89–113

Low-Income Fathers — TJ Nelson — 30:427–51

Black Middle-Class Neighborhoods — M Pattillo — 31:305–29

Macrostructural Analyses of Race, Ethnicity, and Violent Crime: Recent Lessons and New Directions for Research — RD Peterson, LJ Krivo — 31:331–56

Policy

The Savings and Loan Debacle, Financial Crime, and the State — K Calavita, R Tillman, HN Pontell — 23:19–38

Poverty and Inequality Among Children — DT Lichter — 23:121–45

Sociological Perspectives on Medical Ethics and Decision-Making — R Zussman — 23:171–89

The Changing Nature of Death Penalty Debates — ML Radelet, MJ Borg — 26:43–61

Poverty Research and Policy for the Post-Welfare Era — A O'Connor — 26:547–62

Hate Crime: An Emergent Research Agenda — DP Green, LH McFalls, JK Smith — 27:479–504

Ideas, Politics, and Public Policy — JL Campbell — 28:21–38

New Economics of Sociological Criminology — B McCarthy — 28:417–42

Welfare-State Regress in Western Europe: Politics, Institutions, Globalization, and Europeanization — W Korpi — 29:589–609

Explaining Criminalization: From Demography and Status Politics to Globalization and Modernization — V Jenness — 30:147–71

Sociology of Terrorism — AT Turk — 30:271–86

Affirmative Action at School and on the Job — S Harper, B Reskin — 31:357–79

Emerging Theories of Care Work — P England — 31:381–99

Historical Sociology

US Social Policy in Comparative and Historical Perspective: Concepts, Images Arguments, and Research Strategies	E Amenta, C Bonastia, N Caren	27:213–34
Early Traditions of African-American Sociological Thought	AA Young Jr, DR Deskins Jr.	27:445–77
The Sociology of Intellectuals	C Kurzman, L Owens	28:63–90
Comparative-Historical Methodology	J Mahoney	30:81–101

Sociology of World Regions

Sociological Work in Japan	K Nakao	24:499–516
Is South Africa Different? Sociological Comparisons and Theoretical Contributions from the Land of Apartheid	G Seidman	25:419–40

Special Supplement: Reflections on Sociology in the 21st Century

A Sociology for the Second Great Transformation	M Burawoy	26:693–95
Agenda for Sociology at the Start of the Twenty-First Century	M Hechter	26:697–98
What I Don't Know About My Field But Wish I Did	DS Massey	26:699–701
Family, State, and Child Well-Being	S McLanahan	26:703–6
Getting It Right: Sex and Race Inequality in the Work Organizations	BF Reskin	26:707–9
Whither the Sociological Study of Crime	RJ Sampson	26:711–14
On Granularity	E Schegloff	26:715–20
How Do Relations Store Histories?	C Tilly	26:721–23

ANNUAL REVIEWS
Intelligent Synthesis of the Scientific Literature

Annual Reviews – Your Starting Point for Research Online
http://arjournals.annualreviews.org

- Over 900 Annual Reviews volumes—more than 25,000 critical, authoritative review articles in 32 disciplines spanning the Biomedical, Physical, and Social sciences— available online, including all Annual Reviews back volumes, dating to 1932

- Current individual subscriptions include seamless online access to full-text articles, PDFs, Reviews in Advance (as much as 6 months ahead of print publication), bibliographies, and other supplementary material in the current volume and the prior 4 years' volumes

- All articles are fully supplemented, searchable, and downloadable— see http://soc.annualreviews.org

- Access links to the reviewed references (when available online)

- Site features include customized alerting services, citation tracking, and saved searches

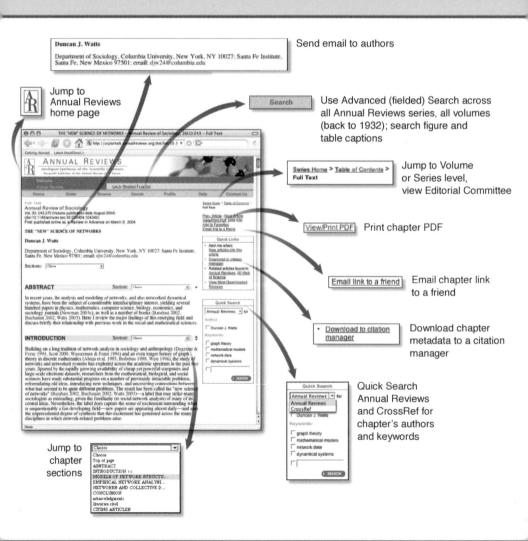